Assessing the
Mentally Retarded

Assessing the Mentally Retarded

Edited by

Johnny L. Matson, Ph.D.

*Director, Office of Research
and Associate Professor
Department of Learning, Development, and Special Education
Northern Illinois University
DeKalb, Illinois*

Stephen E. Breuning, Ph.D.

*John Merck Program for Multiply Disabled Children
Department of Psychiatry
Western Psychiatric Institute and Clinic
University of Pittsburgh School of Medicine
Pittsburgh, Pennsylvania*

Grune & Stratton
A Subsidiary of Harcourt Brace Jovanovich, Publishers

New York	London		
Paris	San Diego	San Francisco	São Paulo
Sydney	Tokyo	Toronto	

Library of Congress Cataloging in Publication Data

Main entry under title:

Assessing the mentally retarded.

Includes bibliographies and index.
1. Mentally handicapped—Testing—Addresses, essays,
lectures.   I. Matson, Johnny L.   II. Breuning,
Stephen E.   [DNLM: 1. Mental retardation—Diagnosis.
2. Disability evaluation.   3. Psychological tests.
WM 304 A846]
RC570.A755   1983   616.85'8807'5   83-13011
ISBN 0-8089-1607-6

Grune & Stratton, Inc.
111 Fifth Avenue
New York, New York 10003

Distributed in the United Kingdom by
Grune & Stratton, Inc. (London) Ltd.
24/28 Oval Road, London NW 1

Library of Congress Catalog Number 83-13011
International Standard Book Number 0-8089-1607-6
Printed in the United States of America

Contents

Preface   vii

Contributors   ix

Part 1   Basic Concepts

1. Overview of Methods   3
   Steven Beck

2. Behavioral Assessment   27
   Paul E. Bates and Harold B. Hanson

3. Empirical Strategies   65
   Alan D. Poling and Carol Parker

4. Assessing Intelligence   87
   Rowland P. Barrett and Stephen E. Breuning

Part 2   Psychiatric Problems

5. Psychopathology   115
   Johnny L. Matson and Cynthia Frame

6. Medication Effects   143
   Lori A. Sisson and Stephen E. Breuning

7. Social Skills   181
   Karen Christoff and Jeffrey Kelly

Part 3   Community Adaptation

8. Self-care Skills   209
   Jan Wallander, Nancy Hubert, and Carolyn Schroeder

9. Vocational Training   247
   Bruce Menchetti, Frank R. Rusch, and Sister Diane Owens

10. Language   285
    Mark L. Sundberg

11. Ecological Patterns   311
    Michael L. Jones, Todd R. Risley, and James E. Favell

12. Academic Skills   335
     Paul Weisberg, Edward V. Sims, Jr., and Bruce A. Weinheimer

Part 4 Medical Concerns

13. Neurological Disorders   399
     Edward Page-El and Bruce P. Hermann

Part 5 Litigation

14. Legal Concerns   437
     Robert G. Griffith

     Index   455

Preface

The field of mental retardation and developmental disabilities has seen much growth in recent years, particularly since the Kennedy administration and the major impetus for funding research centers and other programmatic research. Such funding and the financial support at all levels of government for services to the mentally retarded have created an information explosion that has revolutionized thinking in the areas of identification, prevention, and treatment of the existing conditions that make up the complex and multifaceted problems that fall under the general rubric of mental retardation.

One of the areas that has seen the most rapid growth is assessment research. Given the multidisciplinary nature of research within the broad field of mental retardation, the amount and diversity of the developments are staggering. This research seems to be expanding at an ever increasing rate to the point where even the most diligent researcher in the field cannot keep up with new assessment methods and technology. Given this backdrop the authors felt obliged to make an effort to pull existing information together in one source. Such was the genesis for this book.

This volume is based on empirical data rather than on past practice alone or opinion as to what constitutes the best methods of assessment. As a result, the reader may find areas of omission with respect to particular assessment methods. We have not deluded ourselves that the present text is all-inclusive. Thus, for example, many traditional methods of assessment employed by the physician may not be emphasized due to the sheer number of such methods, and a number of excellent books are available on the topic. We have, however, obtained what we believe to be an excellent chapter on neurological disorders that should prove to be of value to many involved with medical assessment. Other topics covered include assessing self-help and social skills, language and academic training, and many other behaviors that are often very problematic among the mentally retarded, as well as intelligence testing.

As the editors of this volume, we are most proud of the persons who agreed to prepare chapters. We believe that they are well respected researchers in their disciplines who have presented material that is at the cutting edge of advances in assessment of the mentally retarded.

The book is written primarily for the practitioner, advanced graduate student, or researcher who may wish to become more acquainted with the views of those in his or her area of expertise or who wishes to become more knowledgeable about advances being made in related areas. As noted, the material presented is empirical and, as a result, should provide information about other materials on the topic while giving some idea of what we know and what we need to research. What we have presented is not the last word, but rather a statement on an area that still requires additional development.

Johnny L. Matson, Ph.D.
Stephen E. Breuning, Ph.D.

Contributors

Rowland P. Barrett, Ph.D.
John Merck Program for Multiply Disabled Children, Department of Psychiatry, Western Psychiatric Institute and Clinic, University of Pittsburgh School of Medicine, Pittsburgh, Pennsylvania

Paul E. Bates, Ph.D.
Department of Special Education, Southern Illinois University at Carbondale, Carbondale, Illinois

Steven Beck, Ph.D.
Department of Psychology, Ohio State University, Columbus, Ohio

Stephen E. Breuning, Ph.D.
John Merck Program for Multiply Disabled Children, Department of Psychiatry, Western Psychiatric Institute and Clinic, University of Pittsburgh School of Medicine, Pittsburgh, Pennsylvania

Karen A. Christoff, Ph.D.
Department of Psychology and Human Development, University of Mississippi Medical School, Jackson, Mississippi

James E. Favell, Ph.D.
Department of Psychology, Western Carolina Center, Morganton, North Carolina

Cynthia Frame, Ph.D.
Department of Psychology, University of Georgia, Athens, Georgia

Robert G. Griffith, Ed.D.
Department of Special Education, Temple University, Woodhaven Program, Philadelphia, Pennsylvania

Harold B. Hanson, M.A.
Behavioral Analysis and Therapy Department, Southern Illinois University of Carbondale, Carbondale, Illinois

Bruce P. Hermann, Ph.D.
Department of Neurology, University of Illinois Medical Center, Chicago, Illinois

Nancy C. Hubert, Ph.D.
Department of Psychiatry, UCLA Medical School, Harbor Medical Center, Los Angeles, California

Michael L. Jones, M.A.
Department of Human Development, The University of Kansas, Lawrence, Kansas

Jeffrey A. Kelley, Ph.D.
Department of Psychiatry and Human Behavior, University of Mississippi Medical School, Jackson, Mississippi

Johnny L. Matson, Ph.D.
Department of Learning, Development, and Special Education, Northern Illinois University, DeKalb, Illinois

Bruce M. Menchetti, Ph.D.
Career Education for the Handicapped, Furman University, Greenville, South Carolina

Sister Diane M. Owens, M.Ed.
University of Illinois at Urbana-Champaign, Champaign, Illinois

Edward Page-El, M.D.
Diagnostic and Assessment Program, Illinois Institute for Developmental Disabilities; Department of Neurology and Pediatrics, University of Illinois Medical Center and Rush Presbyterian St. Lukes Medical Center, Chicago, Illinois

Carol Parker, Ed.S.
Schoolcraft Community Schools, Schoolcraft, Michigan

Alan D. Poling, Ph.D.
Department of Psychology, Western Michigan University, Kalamazoo, Michigan

Todd R. Risley, Ph.D.
Department of Human Development, The University of Kansas, Lawrence, Kansas

Frank R. Rusch, Ph.D.
Department of Special Education, University of Illinois at Urbana-Champaign, Champaign, Illinois

Carolyn S. Schroeder, Ph.D.
Departments of Pediatrics and Psychiatry, University of North Carolina Medical School, Chapel Hill, North Carolina

Edward V. Sims, Jr., M.A.
Early Childhood Day Care Center, Department of Psychology, The University of Alabama, University, Alabama

Lori A. Sisson, M.S.
John Merck Program for Multiply Disabled Children, Western Psychiatric Institute and Clinic, University of Pittsburgh School of Medicine, Pittsburgh, Pennsylvania

Mark L. Sundberg, Ph.D.
Regional Center of East Bay, Oakland, California

Jan L. Wallander, Ph.D.
Department of Psychology, University of Southern California, Los Angeles, California

Bruce A. Weinheimer, M.S.
Department of Psychology, The University of Alabama, University, Alabama

Paul Weisberg, Ph.D.
Early Childhood Day Care Center, Department of Psychology, The University of Alabama, University, Alabama

PART 1

Basic Concepts

Steven Beck

1
Overview of Methods

Twenty-five years ago the assessment of mental retardation was relatively simple. Psychometrically sound standardized intelligence tests were administered to derive an individual's IQ, which was then compared to the theoretical normal distribution of scores found in the test manual. If the intelligence quotient score fell one standard deviation below the mean, the individual was typically labeled "mentally retarded." The determination of mental retardation and its defining characteristics have evolved over the years, however, to include other dimensions in addition to intellectual functioning. For example, the American Association on Mental Deficiency (AAMD), in revised editions (Grossman, 1973, 1977), using terminology from a classification espoused earlier by Heber (1959), now defines mental retardation as "significantly subaverage general intellectual functioning existing concurrently with deficits in adaptive behavior manifested during the developmental period" (before the age of 18). Two or more standard deviations below the mean on standardized intelligence tests is the criteria for subaverage intellectual functioning, such as a score of 68 on the Stanford-Binet (Terman & Merrill, 1973), or a score of 69 on the Revised Wechsler Intelligence Scale for Children (Wechsler, 1974). The inclusion of adaptive behavior in the AAMD definition was a crucial development for the assessment of mental retardation; assessing adaptive behavior is now comparable to determining IQ in establishing levels of mental retardation. The third criteria of the definition, that retardation must be evident by age 18, differentiates mental retardation from traumatic or deteriorative disorders occurring in adulthood. As a result of this three-dimensional definition, the assessment of mental retardation has become more complex, requiring more than one assessment device.

   The majority of psychologists and educators endorse the assessment procedures and criteria currently employed in classifying the mentally retarded (Erickson,

1982), although others (Ross, 1980; Thorne, 1970) have criticized specific assessment methods (e.g., what is measured by intelligence tests) and the potentially serious implications of arbitrarily classifying individuals as mentally subnormal based upon theoretical, statistical constructs of intelligence. Further, in the wake of behaviorally-based treatment programs that have strengthened and increased the behavioral repertoires of the mentally retarded, investigators (Kazdin & Straw, 1976; Ross, 1980; Shapiro & Barrett, 1981) now agree that the primary purpose of assessment is not to determine if an individual fits a diagnostic category, but to identify client behaviors that require modification and determine if the effects of treatment are sufficient.

In this chapter, a brief introduction to the concept of intelligence and adaptive behaviors, as well as information about prevalence rates, classification systems, and etiological factors associated with mental retardation, will be followed by a discussion of assessment methods commonly used with the mentally retarded. Although this overview may be familiar to the student of mental retardation, it provides necessary background for understanding issues in assessing the condition.

DEFINING INTELLIGENCE

The search for a definition of intelligence has had a checkered history in the annals of psychology. Many definitions have been proposed and strongly debated (Cronbach, 1975) and a uniformly accepted definition is still far from fruition. Most early definitions were global and included as common elements the ability to learn, the amount of acquired knowledge, and the ability to adapt to the environment. More contemporary approaches have involved more complex explanations for defining intelligence. The introduction of statistical procedures, such as factor analysis, have allowed for the possible identification of relatively independent components that could, supposedly, determine if intelligence is comprised of several specific factors or a more pervasive general factor. Theorists such as Cattell (1964), Guilford (1968), Jensen (1969), Piaget (1952), Spearman (1904), and Terman and Merrill (1937) have each produced extensive bodies of work underlying similar, and occasionally very divergent aspects of the construct "intelligence." Perhaps the most current influential theorist regarding intelligence is David Wechsler, because of the prominence his instrument has achieved in the present testing movement. Wechsler's notions of intelligence involves multiple dimensions. Besides more pure notions of intelligence, such as the ability to think abstractly or the ability to possess perceptual organization or visual-motor coordination, intelligence also consists of variables such as motivation, alertness, anxiety, and impulsivity. In other words, instead of purely cognition of intellective skills representing intelligence, Wechsler also believes that non-cognitive factors which affect intellectual performance are also worthy of assessment (Wechsler, 1950).

DEFINING ADAPTIVE BEHAVIOR

Adaptive behavior refers primarily to the manner in which an individual meets the standards of personal independence and social responsibility expected of his or her age and cultural group. Since these expectations vary for different age groups, deficits in adaptive behavior vary at different ages. Consequently, the measurement of adaptive behavior can present greater problems in assessment because of the variability due to maturational and cultural factors and mercurial changes that can accompany the developing child. Generally speaking, during preschool years, sensory-motor development, including tasks such as grasping objects, sitting alone, crawling, standing, walking, feeding one's self, or toileting skills is of greatest importance. These skills are conceptualized as ordinarily developing in a sequential pattern, building upon previous skills that have been mastered. During childhood, the emergence of mastery of academic, socialization, and self-control skills best represent adaptation. During adolescence and adulthood, vocational skills and the ability to behave within community standards without supervision illustrate adaptive behaviors.

Investigators have also looked at behaviors measured by the existing scales designed to assess adaptation. Leland, Shellhaas, Nihira, and Foster (1967) analyzed several rating scales and identified 12 major areas of adaptive behavior: self-help skills, communication, socialization of interpersonal skills, locomotion, self-direction, occupational skills, economic activity, neuromotor development, personal responsibility, social responsibility, emotional adjustment, and health. As noted by Robinson and Robinson (1976) the first eight dimensions correspond with independent functioning, while both personal and social responsibility, supposedly important components of adaptive behaviors, are relatively ignored by most scales.

INCIDENT RATES AND CLASSIFICATION OF THE MENTALLY RETARDED

While figures vary due to differences in criteria for the diagnosis of mental retardation, estimates of the incidence of this condition range from 1 percent (APA, 1980) to 3–5 percent of the population (Birnbrauer, 1976) to as high as 6–9 percent of children requiring special education because of impaired intellectual functioning (Kolb, 1973). Despite this rather wide range, it is generally accepted that approximately 3 percent of the population fit the criteria of mental retardation using the definition provided by the American Association on Mental Deficiency (Office of Mental Retardation Coordination, 1972).

A potential problem with classifying any smaller sample as "different" from the general larger population is to assume the smaller sample encompasses a homogeneous class of individuals that are somehow qualitatively different from persons in the representative "normal" sample. For example, most laymen and professionals agree there are individual differences in people with normal or upper levels of intelligence due to an interaction of genetic and environmental factors; however, a similar interplay of etiological factors that produce individual differences in the mentally retarded may not be assumed to occur because the mentally retarded are often viewed as a homogenous group.

Zigler (1967) addressed the fact that mentally retarded individuals are indeed a heterogeneous group. His theory is based upon a polygenic model of intelligence which assumes that intelligence is a result of a number of discrete genetic units, with IQ distributions falling between 50 and 150. Zigler proposes that since an IQ of approximately 50 appears to be the lower limit of intelligence, the etiology of this form of low intelligence reflects the same factors that determine normal intelligence. In other words, an individual with an IQ of 50 represents the lower end of the normal distribution of intelligence that is nontheless a normal manifestation of the available genetic pool. Individuals with an IQ of 50 are as integral a part of the distribution curve as are the 3 percent of the population whose IQs are viewed as superior. However, Zigler realizes there are exceptions to the theoretical distribution. Specifically, there are individuals whose IQ scores are below 50, and as such, they comprise the second group of mentally retarded; namely individuals who have identified genetic or organic defects. A more appropriate representation of the empirical distribution of intelligence involves the two curves seen in Figure 1. The curve indicating the normal bell-shaped curve represents the polygenic distribution of intelligence; the second curve represents all those individuals whose intellectual functioning reflects factors other than the normal polygenic elements. The superimposed curve also represents a somewhat normal distribution having a mean of approximately 35, and are ranged from 0 to 70. Zigler's model underscores the notion that the mentally retarded are a heterogeneous group of individuals, that perhaps can be conceptualized as representing two rather broad, yet distinct groups; normal individuals who are of low intelligence due to probably cultural and familial factors and defective individuals who have identifiable physiological defects.

Another common method used to classify the mentally retarded is by degree. Within the group of mentally retarded persons, four levels of classification are typically recognized. These individuals and their corresponding IQ scores are seen in Table 1.

This classification focuses on measured intelligence and has some predictive value as to the maximum educational attainment of a child. Children who are mildly mentally retarded are expected to learn basic academic skills of reading, writing, and computation, anywhere from third to sixth grade levels, while the moderately mentally retarded child may learn to distinguish some written signs and do simple computation of numbers. Severe and profoundly mentally retarded children are not expected to benefit from any academic training.

While this classification may give indications of a child's academic poten-

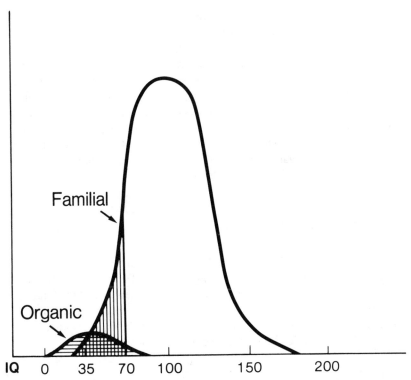

Fig. 1-1. Distribution of intelligence according to Zigler's two-group approach [From Ross, A. O. *Psychological disorders of children: A behavioral approach to theory, research, and therapy.* New York: McGraw-Hill, 1980. With permission.]

tial or capacity, it is important to realize the discretionary nature of these categories. For example, as Ross (1980) points out, it seems foolish to label a child with an IQ of 54 "moderately retarded," while with a score of 55 this same child would be called "mildly retarded." Furthermore this classification system is heavily based on measured intelligence and until recently has not taken into account degree of impairment and adaptive functioning. Although the child with higher intellectual

Table 1-1
Classification of the Mentally Retarded

Levels of Retardation	IQ Scores Stanford-Binet/Wechsler		Educable Terms	Mental Age Range
Mild	67–52	69–55	Educable	8 yrs, 6 mos–10 yrs, 10 mos.
Moderate	51–36	54–40	Trainable	6 yrs, 1 mo.–8 yrs, 5 mos.
Severe	35–20	39–25		3 yrs, 9 mos.–6 yrs, 0 mos.
Profound	19 & below	24 or below extrapolated		Below 3 yrs, 9 mos.

functioning may be expected to acquire more adaptive skills, the relationship between IQ and degree of adaptive impairment is not linear. Another potential problem
with this accepted labeling procedure is that statements such as educable or trainable have inferential implications that may, unfortunately, obviate further assessment. Again as noted by Ross (1980), a concern with an arbitrary, yet potentially
predictive IQ test score is the self-fulfilling prophesy notion that a child who receives low scores will be excluded from specific academic subject matters and
the end result will be that such an individual will not learn to read or write, just as
his "test" scores had "predicted." The predictive validity of this classification
system will be raised again later in this chapter when discussing underlying assumptions of standardized intelligence tests.

ETIOLOGICAL FACTORS

If one adopts Zigler's (1967) two-group model of mental retardation, the
distinction between cultural-familial and physiogically defective mentally retarded
individuals is critical for understanding mental subnormality and for future prevention of factors resulting in these conditions. This section will present a brief
discussion of cultural-familial mental retardation and the most common genetic
and birth-related complications associated with mental subnormality.

Cultural-Familial Mental Retardation

This loose category accounts for the majority of children diagnosed as mentally retarded. Approximately 70 to 80 percent of mentally retarded individuals
have mild to moderate retardation with no known genetic or physiological impairment. As stated before, many researchers propose that mild mental retardation
simply represents the lower end of the normal IQ distribution and is not reflective
of pathological conditions. The fact that mentally retarded persons are not over-
represented in the population is cited to support such a view. There are four criteria by which the child is judged to exhibit retardation in this category (Grossman,
1973). The most obvious is that the child must function at a retarded intellectual
and adaptive level. Second, there must be evidence of retarded intellectual functioning in the immediate or larger family. Third, there must be no clear indication of a cerebral pathologic condition. Finally, the child's background will usually
be impoverished, with substandard education, housing, and medical care. There
may also be, but not necessarily, a history of prematurity, frequent infections,
diseases, and accidents, but none serious enough to account alone for the child's
slow intellectual and adaptive development. Thus, a diagnosis of retardation due
to psychosocial disadvantage rests chiefly on the absence of neurologic symptoms and primarily on family background (Robinson & Robinson, 1976).

Although theorists have posited that children who fit the above criteria may still have some biological defect that underlies the cognitive and adaptive deficit (Zigler & Balla, 1971), these qualitative biological differences, if they do exist, are usually impossible to ferret out from the cumulative effects of an impoverished family background and upbringing. What does seem clear, however, is the strong connection between poverty and cultural-familial retardation. For example, Voght (1973) found that children of families with incomes under $6,000 per year have illiteracy rates two to three times above the country's average. Inadequate nutrition, exposure to toxic substances such as lead, and bacterial and viral infections are frequently found among the poor. Not only are poor children exposed to greater health risks, their health rate is grossly inferior to that of children of sounder economic backgrounds. Poor children also have little exposure to materials that are used in school, and begin school already lacking in resources that prepare them for school demands. Robinson and Robinson (1976) note that living conditions of the poor have a number of other consequences on child-rearing, such as raising children in disorganized, chaotic, and crowded conditions, all of which have the effect of preventing optimal socialization and development. Children of poverty typically view home as a place to escape, and consequently adolescents leave home early unprepared and uneducated for employment and the multitude of problems that confront someone trying to make it on their own. The consequence of all this is that the adolescent starts a family and the cycle of poverty and poor intellectual and adaptive development is perpetuated again.

While there is a clear link between poverty and poor intellectual performance and poor adaptive behaviors, the implication that conditions of poverty predispose one towards mental retardation has been criticized on the basis that middle class norms should not be used to evaluate children's behaviors or academic performance (Baratz & Baratz, 1970), and that such labeling continually keeps the lower class individuals mired in the same situation generation after generation (Ryan, 1971). It is unfair to blame individuals for a multiplicity of factors that leads one to be labeled "mentally retarded." Nonetheless, Robinson and Robinson (1976) addressing this issue state:

It is a fact that most schools do reflect the dominant, middle-class orientation of the society and, furthermore, that a very large part of one's success both at school and out of it, during childhood and during adulthood, depend precisely upon one's ability to cope in terms of these dominant norms . . . children whose families function within a distinct subcultural group have a double burden, and for them they must learn to function in at least two worlds . . . (p. 178).

Genetic Factors Associated With Mental Retardation

Genetic factors can play a causal factor in mental retardation. This section will be divided into three categories, syndromes due to chromosomal abnormalities, abnormalities due to inheritance or inborn differences, and factors due to birth complications. The more common form of these syndromes will be briefly discussed.

Chromosomal Abnormalities

Anomolies in chromosomes can involve sex or the somatic chromosomes. Turner's Syndrome and Klinefelter's Syndrome are well-documented conditions that result from the absence of the Y chromosome (Turner's Syndrome) or an additional X chromosome (Klinefelter's Syndrome). Since such aberrations in sex chromosomes are relatively uncommon and low intellectual functioning is not always a feature of the disorders, somatic chromosomes, which are more frequently associated with these disorders, will be presented.

The most prevalent chromosomal cause of moderate to severe mental retardation is Down's Syndrome. Down's Syndrome is caused by a genetic imbalance, the presence of an extra set of genes of the number 21 chromosome. The incidence of this disorder is relatively high, one in every 700 births, with maternal eggs being a contributing factor. Mothers giving birth after age 35 increase the likelihood of giving birth to a child with Down's Syndrome, for mothers age 45 or older, the risk is approximately one in every 40 births.

Down's Syndrome affects many aspects of physical development. Certain physical and affective features of these children, such as slanted eyes, epicanthal folds, saddle-like low bridge noses, and protruding tongues, as well as being affectionate and friendly children are a few of the striking similarities found in the majority of these children. However, with Down's Syndrome children, there appears to be no relationship between physical appearance and IQ (Domino & Newman, 1965). There are other serious complications associated with this condition. For example, in perhaps 40 percent of these children there is a defect in the development of the heart. Retarded intellectual and adaptive development becomes more apparent as the Down's Syndrome infant grows older. As with any other mentally retarded individual, Down's Syndrome children show remarkable variability, with intelligence estimates from profound to mild retardation and in some cases normal levels, and considerable differences in developmental milestones and adaptive behaviors.

Dominant and Recessive Gene Disorders

In this heterogeneous group of disorders, the absence or malfunction of a necessary enzyme results in abnormal metabolism and subsequent retardation in growth and intellectual deficiency. A dominant genetic condition is usually one in which a parent has the condition. Dominant gene syndromes associated with mental retardation are relatively infrequent since retarded individuals bear children at reduced rates and therefore do not pass on as many defective genes. For a recessive gene to be inherited a homozygous state is necessary which requires that the affected child inherits the defective gene from both parents. Under these relatively rare circumstances, the risk of such a combination is one of every four pregnancies.

The most common recessive condition is phenylketonuria (PKU). This condition has been found to occur in one out of every 17,000 births. This condition is related to a high incidence of mental retardation, a byproduct caused by the absence of the enzyme phenylalanine hydroxylase which is responsible for transformation of phenylalanine into tyrosine. PKU manifests high rates of behavior disorders, such as hyperactivity and severe temper tantrums. Because of pyrosine deficiency, these children usually have blond hair and blue eyes. This condition must be suspected and a diagnostic workup undertaken with any mentally retarded child with such features. Inexpensive screening methods for PKU have been developed. Laboratory tests include presence of abnormal metabolites in the urine and elevated blood level of phenylalanine. Mass screening for newborn infants has been made mandatory in some states. Early diagnosis and dietary treatment prevents mental retardation if the condition is recognized during the first few weeks of life. On the other hand, children who are diagnosed after six years of age do not seem to show any improvement in IQ, regardless of dietary treatment instituted (Hassibi & Chess, 1980).

Many disorders due to specific recessive or dominant genes have been identified although descriptions of these disorders are beyond the scope of this chapter. It is important to note, for assessment purposes, that carrier parents of many of these disorders (e.g., Myotonic Dystrophy, a dominant gene condition [Schrott, Karp, & Omenn, 1973] and Galactosemea, a recessive condition involving a disorder of carbohydrate metabolism) can be identified and preventive means are available.

Prenatal, Perinatal, and Postnatal Physical Factors

While most studies are correlational or retrospective, making such studies tentative due to validity concerns, prenatal, perinatal and postnatal factors have been implicated as causes of mental retardation. For example, severe malnutrition, maternal alcoholic intake, and chronic viral and bacterial infection in pregnant women are known to increase the risk of mental retardation in infants. Anoxia, low birth weight, and prematurity in newborns has also been linked with higher rates of mental retardation. However, to suggest that exposure of such factors as alcohol, infections, or low birth rate are causal in some cases of mental retardation may be too simplistic an explanation. For example, Abel (1980) states that although the most serious affects of uterine exposure to excessive alcohol is mental retardation, the physical characteristics associated with this condition secondary to the alcoholic intake (e.g., altered nutrition) cannot be ruled out as etiological factors in the impairment of functioning.

ASSESSMENT STRATEGIES

As mentioned earlier, in the evaluation of an individual, the label or categorization of ''mentally retarded'' is the least important task for the assessor. While this diagnostic classification may be necessary for administrative purposes, this categorization does not necessarily specify the most important task of assessment, namely, the behavioral capabilities and limitations of a given individual. Demonstrations that mentally retarded persons can improve on many practical, adaptive skills (e.g., self-care, classroom behavior, verbal responsiveness) when trained in a systematic fashion using learning-based techniques emphasize the fact that several assessment methods are required to identify target behaviors and evaluate training programs for individuals who have low intelligence.

The need for assessment and treatment programs are increasing given the deinstitutionalization movement and current trend towards greater reliance on community based facilities. Additionally, Reiss, Levitan, and McNally (1982) contend that mentally retarded individuals experience psychological disturbances (e.g., phobias, anxiety-related problems, depression, social withdrawal, schizophrenia) at a greater rate compared to the nonretarded population. Consequently, if retarded individuals are to be trained and assessed for adaptive community living as well as treated for emotional disturbances, the range of behaviors requiring treatment is so broad that no single test or scale can fully assess the extensive behaviors required to demonstrate appropriate and adaptive functioning. The purpose of this book is devoted to the task of properly assessing the broad range of behaviors requiring modification for the mentally retarded. This chapter will introduce four general assessment strategies that typically are commonly employed to assess lowfunctioning persons. Topics covered include advantages and limitations of interviewing, intelligence and achievement tests, behavioral checklists and rating scales, and behavioral observations. Finally, consideration will be given to identifying relevant behaviors for the selection of further assessment and subsequent treatment.

Interviews

The interview is seen as an indispensable part of any psychological assessment. Due to its unstandardized nature and flexibility, this format is usually viewed as the first assessment method used to begin to collect diagnostic information. In fact, the interview has been used as the primary assessment device, although this practice has been criticized because of the over-reliance on self-report data and the fact that the majority of information collected from interviews is viewed as unnecessary (Peterson, 1968). Nonetheless, interviews will continue to be a popular method for gathering information because of the several advantages this method has to offer compared to other assessment strategies (Linehan, 1977). Besides being convenient, interviews allow for flexibility in obtaining information that otherwise might be overlooked in more structured, limited assessment approaches. The interview is typically seen as allowing for the assessment of more "clinical information." Emotional disturbances such as depression, anxiety, and interpersonal problems can be more amenable to discussion and evaluation in an interview format. Indeed, depending upon the skill of the interviewer and the interviewee's verbal skills, fund of knowledge, and willingness to discuss relevant topics, significant information can be covered in an interview that otherwise would not appear in more structured assessment methods.

Another advantage of the interview format that has been emphasized in the assessment literature is that this vehicle allows for the assessor to form an interpersonal relationship with the client. This relationship should convey a feeling of concern, warmth, and interest that purportedly facilitates the ability to obtain considerable information, some of which would not be elicited under a normal dyadic exchange. Although it has not been empirically demonstrated that these interviewer characteristics provide for more accurate assessment (Morganstern, 1976), the underlined assumption of a good interviewer-client relationship is that it will allow the client to be more comfortable and trustworthy of the interviewer so that information relevant for making proper assessment decisions will be more readily discussed.

Finally, the decided advantage of interviewing compared to other assessment strategies is that when assessing special populations, such as the mentally retarded, this format allows the interviewer to collect information from persons who may be limited in their ability to provide information by other means, most notably by standardized or paper and pencil measures. Persons who have impaired thought processes or who are illiterate may simply be unwilling to provide information in other ways or without first establishing a relationship with the assessor. Along similar lines, Shapiro and Barrett (1981) view interviewing the mentally retarded individual as closely resembling an interview with a child, requiring the interviewer to be flexible, patient, and able to express him or herself clearly.

A major function of a diagnostic interview for the mentally retarded is to obtain a developmental history and to assess the current functioning of a client. Depending upon the client's receptive and expressive communication skills the amount of information collected from interviews may not be very helpful. For this reason it is advisable to interview the client's parents or significant others who can provide additional or supplemental information. Furthermore, each parent may be more knowledgeable about his or her own background and thus contribute to a more accurate picture of the client's genetic heritage. Other information, particularly parents' age at the time of pregnancy and number of pregnancies and births before and after the client's birth, as well as the academic and vocational success of siblings, may give important clues as to the nature of the causative factors. If possible, more verifiable information from hospital's or physician's files, such as the weight of the client at birth and his or her apgar score, illnesses, traumas, as well as developmental milestones may allow the assessor to make inferences as to the relevant contribution of organic and environmental factors in the etiology and current functioning of the client's behavior.

Limitations

Besides the obvious fact that some retarded individuals have verbal deficits, there are additional factors when interviewing the mentally retarded and their significant others that are problematic. As already mentioned, the primary source of assessment information is usually collected from parents, caretakers, or significant others who have had extensive contact with the client. However, it is well docmented that information obtained from parents may not be very accurate (valid) nor are facts collected from one parent to another consistent (reliable) (Evans & Nelson, 1977). While parents of nonhandicapped children tend to be more accurate when describing factual events (e.g., medical information and developmental landmarks) compared to more emotionally charged material (Yarrow, Campbell, & Burton, 1970), there is no data that shows that parents with developmentally delayed children demonstrate the same objectivity when chronicling their children's development. Since parents of developmentally delayed children appear to experience significantly more emotional upheaval than do parents of nonhandicapped children (Friedrich & Friedrich, 1981) it seems plausible that parents with handicapped children may be more likely to present inaccuracies that place the parents and the child in a more positive light. Ideally, when collecting information the assessor should have concurrent validation from other sources, otherwise the accuracy of such information should not be accepted on its face validity.

Moreover, recent studies by Sigelman and her colleagues (Sigelman, Budd, Spanhel, & Schroenrock, 1981; Sigelman, Schroenrock, Spanhel, Thomas, Winere, Budd, & Martin, 1981) question the validity of self-report data collected when interviewing the mentally retarded person. Their findings show that mentally retarded individuals, and particularly those with severe and profound mental retardation, tend to acquiesce to specific questions. In other words, they respond affirmatively to questions regardless of its content. Consequently when mentally retarded individuals are asked yes or no questions, their answers are likely to be invalid. Questions that require a forced choice or an either/or answer, therefore, should be avoided when interviewing individuals with severe and profound mental retardation.

In summary, for the purpose of collecting diagnostic information, the interview appears to have several advantages, most notably its convenience, flexibility, and the fact that the unstructured format lends itself as a means to form a working relationship with the client. Unfortunately, limitations of the interview format are considerable due to suspect validity and reliability of self-report data collected from the mentally retarded and from significant others. Consequently, this assessment method may not be a particularly valid strategy and should always be used in conjunction with other assessment methods.

Standardized Intelligence Tests and Achievement Tests

The use of standardized intelligence tests is an obvious choice for assessing the mentally retarded individual. Emphasis is given to the "standardized" nature of these instruments. This term indicates that uniform procedures should prevail when testing an individual to better compare the individual's performance against established norms that have been derived under similar conditions. Standardized tests of intelligence also denote that intelligence is constructed on the assumption of a normal distribution of "intelligence." The most common individual intelligence tests are the Stanford-Binet Intelligence scale (Terman & Merrill, 1973), the Revised Wechsler Intelligence Scale for Children (WISC-R) (Wechsler, 1974), the Wechsler Preschool and Primary Scale of Intelligence (WPPSI) (Wechsler, 1967), and the Wechsler Adult Intelligence Scale (WAIS) (Wechsler, 1981). These tests have abandoned the simple rational of IQ, which is obtained by dividing an individual's mental age by his chronological age and multiplying by 100, in favor of the deviation IQ. The deviation IQ is a form of a standard score in which the obtained distribution of IQs is converted to a normal distribution with a mean of 100 and a standard deviation. The standard deviation for the Stanford-Binet is 16; for the Wechsler scales the standard deviation is 15.

The Stanford-Binet is probably the most widely recommended intelligence test because it assesses children as young as 2 years old and derives relatively low levels of ability. The format is also appealing to children with lower mental functioning. According to Sattler (1982) the subtest of the Stanford-Binet can be classified within seven broadly defined categories: language, memory, conceptual thinking, reasoning, numerical reasoning, visual-motor, and social intelligence. Individuals complete various tasks that sample abilities in each of the above areas, and from this a global estimate of intellectual ability is obtained.

The Wechsler scales are presently the most popular and researched intelligence tests. In particular, the WISC-R, which covers the age range 6 to 18, is widely used for the diagnosis of mental retardation since it is generally accepted that the diagnosis should be made prior to the age of 18. The instrument is, however, limited since it is not normed for children under six and does not accurately reflect IQ scores for children scoring below the mild level of mental retardation. The Wechsler scales contain 12 subtests that correspond to a number of broadly defined categories that reflect intelligence. Such abilities as verbal comprehension, short and long term memory, acquired knowledge, abstract thinking, verbal expression, freedom from distractibility, perceptual and visual organization, visual memory, and understanding of cause-effect relationships are the more conspicuous skills that are assessed. The 12 subtests of the Wechsler scales are divided into verbal and performance scores each of which yields an IQ score and a full scale (global) IQ that is representative of the combined performances.

Due to the extensive research produced on the WISC-R this instrument appears to give the fairest assessment for those children who are labeled mentally retarded due to cultural-familial factors (Kaufman, 1979). To give an example of the type of information available from the WISC-R, it has been shown that one way to begin to identify the mentally retarded children who present with nonorganic etiologies is by noting that such children often score higher on spatial subtests that are at least dependent on educational or cultural opportunities (i.e., Picture Completion, Block Design, and Object Assembly) while they score lower on acquired knowledge that assesses verbal-scholastic skills (i.e., Information, Arithmetic, and Vocabulary) (Lutey, 1977).

While the WISC-R and Stanford-Binet, used in conjunction with other assessment methods, provide sufficient information about a mentally retarded individual's cognitive strengths and weaknesses, the assessment of infant behavior is more difficult. The two most popular standardized tests, WPPSI (Wechsler, 1967) and the Bayley scales of infant development (Bayley, 1969), indicate that low scores, in contrast with normal or high scores, during infancy are much more reliable predictors of future behavior (Erickson, 1968; Knolboch & Pasamanick, 1967; Smith, Flick, Ferris, & Sellman, 1972; VanderVeer & Schweid, 1974). Nonetheless, caution should be exercised when attempting to predict an infant's future course of development based upon a singular test score with low or at best moderate validity and reliability, regardless of the child's initial scores. For example, several studies have shown that children judged as definitely mentally retarded at age 2 or 3 may not be judged so later on (Holden, 1972; Koch, 1963).

The achievement tests, such as the Peabody Individual Achievement Test (PIAT) (Dunn & Markwardt, 1970) and the Wide Range Achievement Test (WRAT) (Jastak & Jastak, 1965) are routinely used as additional measures for children in the mild range of mental retardation. These achievement tests assess abilities related to academic performance, such as spelling, reading, and mathematics. Used in combination with intelligence tests, these tests can begin to identify diagnostic information or indicate further evaluation, particularly when there are discrepancies between cognitive ability and academic performance.

Limitations

Intelligence tests have been severely criticized primarily because of the singular reliance given to intelligent quotient scores. In the past, IQ scores have been perceived as immutable reflections of the construct of intelligence. Subsequently, the ramifications of low scores greatly influenced educational placement of the mentally retarded. These scores are still typically viewed as predictors of school and vocational performance. Undoubtedly, the relationship between an IQ and the ability to learn in school or in some job training seems indisputable, however, in reality the test score only reflects the present performance; it does not perfectly predict, or at times even closely predict future potential (Ross, 1980). Additionally, a score derived from an intelligence test does not necessarily provide information about the level of competence an individual can achieve as a function of concentrated or thorough systematic training.

A related concern with scores derived from intelligence tests is the fact that they are constructed on a statistical premise, specifically the assumption of a normal distribution of intelligence based upon the standardization of the instrument. The validity of the underlying assumption that scores are predetermined and generally distributed along the bell-shaped curve is rarely questioned. A by-product of this theoretical notion is that those individuals whose scores fall two or three deviations below the mean are assigned labels, such as ''moderately'' or ''severely'' mentally retarded. These labels can too often become reified, allowing one to draw unsubstantiated inferences about an individual's present and future behavior. For instance, an individual whose IQ is 50 is supposedly functioning at the moderate level of mental retardation and is ''trainable,'' suggesting that he or she can learn rudimentary academic skills (e.g., counting) and has a low ceiling of adaptive behaviors in his or her repertoire. When in fact, further assessment may very well show that the child is functioning adequately in several adaptive skills that would have gone undetected without additional assessment. In summary, intelligence testing, in the hands of a knowledgeable assessor, is but one of several measures necessary for a competent evaluation of mental retardation. It is critical to understand that the purpose of the intelligence test is not diagnose or to pin a label to someone, but to better understand the individual by assessing their cognitive strengths and weaknesses (Kaufman, 1979).

Behavior Checklist and Rating Scales

As the reader is already aware, the classification of mental retardation rests, by definition, on three criteria: onset of condition, the assessment of intellectual functioning, and adaptive behaviors. Consequently, the use of behavior checklist and rating scales for measuring functioning skills are commonplace. The popularity of these inventories stems from the practical advantages of the instruments for identifying current observable behaviors and for assessing the impact of treatment interventions upon functional skills. In addition, these instruments are quick and efficient to use, yield easily quantifiable data, and usually do not require professional training. These checklists rely on informal observations, typically provided by families, teachers, or ward attendants who are knowledgeable about clients' competencies. Numerous behavior problem checklists and rating scales are available to measure adaptive behavior/social competence, however, in this section the scales that are predominantly used with the mentally retarded will be discussed.

In a study designed to survey state policies regarding the measurement of adaptive behaviors, Morrow and Coulter (1978) requested that agencies list the specific measures of adaptive behaviors with which they were familiar. The four most frequently mentioned measures were the American Association of Mental Deficiencies (AAMD) Adaptive Behavior Scale-Public School Version (Lambert, Windmiller, Cole, & Figueroa, 1974), the Vineland Social Maturity Scale (Doll, 1965), the System of Multicultural Pluralistic Assessment (SOMPA) (Mercer & Lewis, 1977), and the AAMD Adaptive Behavior Scale-1975 revision (Nihira, Foster, Shellhaas, & Leland, 1975).

Presently, the most widely used method of assessing adaptive behavior, chiefly because of its comprehensiveness and large standardization sample, is the revised AAMD Adaptive Behavior Scale (ABS) (Nihira et al., 1975). Part I is developmentally organized and designed to assess an individual's progress in 10 areas of functioning (independent functioning, physical development, economic activity, language development, number and time, domestic activity, vocational activity, self-direction, responsibility, and socialization). Part II is designed to assess maladaptive behaviors composed of 14 domains (violent and destructive behavior, antisocial behavior, rebellious behavior, untrustworthy behavior, withdrawal, stereotype behavior and odd mannerisms, inappropriate interpersonal manners, unacceptable vocal habits, unacceptable or eccentric habits, self-abusive behavior, hyperactive tendencies, sexually abherant behavior, psychological disturbances, use of medication), and indirectly, the individual's ability to meet social norms. These domains are not organized around the developmental format. Scoring is computed by first computing subdomain totals and finally domain totals. The raw domain score for each behavior is then compared against normative data for mentally retarded individuals ranging in age from 3 to 69 years residing in U.S. institutions. One weakness of the scale is that it does not provide an overall rating of adaptive behavior.

The newest of the rating scales can be found in the Multifactored System of Multicultural Pluralistic Assessment (SOMPA) (Mercer & Lewis, 1977). Congruent with the emphasis upon pluralistic measurement, this total system of assessment consists of nine sets of measures used within three separate assessment models: medical, social-system, and pluralistic. One of the several measures with the social-system assessment is the Adaptive Behavior Inventory for Children (ABIC), for children ages 5 through 11. The ABIC was not designed to be used outside of the total SOMPA package and while discussing this scale independent of the total package is against the spirit intended by Mercer and Lewis, it will be presented because it is viewed as a promising measure of adaptive behavior and will probably be used in the future (Shapiro & Barrett, 1981).

The ABIC requires a knowledgeable informant to evaluate client expectencies as mastered, emerged, or latent in relation to several classes of behaviors called role performances (family, community, peer, non-academic, earner/consumer, self-maintenance). Items are placed in chronological order from simplest to most difficult organzed around a developmental-hierarchical format. Scaled scores based on normative data are obtained and these scores identify the client's level of adaptive behavior within each role.

The oldest measure, and for many years, the best available measure of adaptive behavior (Heber, 1961) was the Vineland Social Maturity Scale (Doll, 1965). The format of the Vineland is similar to that of the ABIC. The rater assesses clients' competencies as mastered, emergent, or latent within several classes of behavior (self-help, self-direction, occupation, communication, locomotion, and socialization) based on a structure discussion with a knowledgeable informant. As with many other scales, the Vineland is organized on the basis of developmental competencies, from age 0 to 30, and uses a hierarchical format to assess formal age which can also be converted to an IQ score. Finally, there are many other behavior checklists and rating scale instruments that can be used with the mentally retarded. However, the discussion of each instrument would be exhaustive and the above instruments were chosen based on the fact that they are, at present, widely used measures of adaptive behavior.

Limitations

There appear to be few disadvantages or troublesome interpretive problems with ratings and/or behavior checklists assuming, of course, that raters objectively assess the individual. One may want to use more than one informant to evaluate a given individual, although the three scales described above have acceptable reliability and validity. While checklists and rating scales are not precise enough to be used independent of other assessment strategies, they do begin to help the professional identify the client's behavioral strengths and classes of behavior requiring intervention and as such are an important part of any assessment package. The criticism of these instruments, however, is that they are usually normed solely on institutionalized mentally retarded populations, hence, these scales cannot be used to discriminate between normal and retarded individuals. Similarly, a lack of normative data on a nonretarded population prevents assessors from identifying and/or comparing the success of intervention programs on target behaviors for the mentally retarded to that of a normal population.

Another limitation of most measures of adaptive behavior is that they have been developed based on needs of staff working with the mentally retarded, primarily in institutional settings. With the current emphasis on deinstitutionalization, mainstreaming, and maintaining persons in halfway houses in the community, instruments aimed at specific social and community competencies are also necessary (Kazdin & Matson, 1981). Examples of such instruments are the California Preschool Social Competency Scale (Levine, Elzey, & Lewis, 1969), the Fairview Social Skills Scale (Ross & Gianpiccoli, 1972) and the Social and Prevocational Information Battery (Halpen, Raffeld, Irvin, & Link, 1975). Similar to the more traditional adaptive behavior measures and checklist, these more specialized scales are based on a developmental continuum but the classes of behaviors involve more adaptive community skills such as shopping and cooking skills, making correct change, and so forth.

Finally, according to Shapiro and Barrett (1981), of the three scales presented the AAMD-Revised Adaptive Behavior Scale is the best for assessing adaptive behavior because of its ability to evaluate the strengths and weaknesses of broad behavior classes. In comparison, according to these authors, the ABIC is normed on nonretarded children and can only validly be employed when given with the entire SOMPA package, while the Vineland is out-dated, lacks breadth, and does not facilitate strategies for intervention.

Behavioral Observation

Of all the assessment methods, behavioral observation is the most direct and precise. Intuitively, a critical feature of any assessment package should include observing overt responses under natural conditions. Due to the emphasis given to this assessment strategy in the behavioral literature this method has become widely used. From a behavioral perspective, retardation is viewed solely from the stand-point of behavior rather than from the perspective of inferential psychological or intellectual functioning. In this way, behavior can be categorized in such areas as deficits, excessive, or problems in environmental stimulus control (Ferster, 1965; Gardner, 1971; Kanfer & Grimm, 1977). Examples of behaviors exhibited by the mentally retarded vary, of course, from individual to individual just as with any other population. One may suppose that an individual labeled mentally retarded would primarily exhibit behaviors classified as deficits. Yet mentally retarded individuals are as likely to display responses categorized as behavioral excesses, such as stereotyped behaviors that could prevent the individual from living opti-mally in his or her environment. An example of a response labeled stimulus control problem would be an individual who would have difficulty following in-structions, a behavior that is likely to be exhibited by mentally retarded individuals.

Directly observing behaviors can accomplish several goals. First, it can fa-cilitate the identification or selection of a client's target responses. Similar to classes or domains of behaviors that were discussed under behavior checklist and rating scales, these broad behavioral categories provide a way to focus on targeting more specific responses for intervention. Behavioral observations can also reveal the extent to which the target response is actually performed prior to any intervention and under what stimulus conditions. Behavioral assessment then focuses upon the frequency or duration of the target behaviors and the antecedents and conse-quences that maintain the behavior's occurrence. Finally, direct observation can determine if the duration of the behavior after treatment is significantly different from the response prior to treatment.

There are well-known methods of assessing and recording behavior using the direct observation strategy of assessment. Shapiro and Barrett (1981) identi-fied event sampling and time sampling as the two strategies most commonly ap-plied in behavioral assessment. Event sampling involves either recording the frequency or duration of the specified behavior for a defined time period. A fre-quency measure is when the observer merely tallies the number of responses that occur. This measure is usually employed when the target response is discrete, is emitted at a relatively constant duration, and has a clearly observable beginning and end (e.g., hitting an individual). Duration measures, on the other hand, are used for a target response that is more continuous. For this measure the observer records, usually with a stop watch, the time a response begins and ends (e.g., crying). Response durations are usually collected when responses are intense and when a feasible goal is to increase or decrease the length of time a response lasts (Kazdin & Straw, 1976).

While event sampling is employed when a specific behavior is discrete, time sampling often provides the assessor with more meaningful information (e.g., social skills). Time sampling can occur in a single or continuous interval (e.g., 30 min), or a block of time can be broken into shorter intervals (e.g., each observed interval is equal to 10 sec). In the latter noncontinuous observation method the target response is scored as occurring or not occurring. The only difference between continuous and noncontinuous time sampling is that in noncontinuous sampling the observer is allowed to stop at specified times to record data.

Depending upon the target response being observed, the assessor must decide which observation method will allow the target responses to be observed most accurately. Frequency and duration measures usually do not require as much observer training, whereas time sampling can allow for multiple target behaviors to be observed simultaneously and often allows for more complex and relevant target responses, such as types of interactions between an individual and his or her peers.

Finally, if the data are to be valid, it is vital that there be agreement between independent observers when the response occurs or does not occur. Low agreement between observers can signify that either one of the independent observers misjudged if a response occurred or not, or more likely, the behavior under study does not have the three characteristics necessary for accurate measurement, namely, objectivity, clarity, and completeness (Hawkins & Dobbs, 1975; Kazdin & Straw, 1976). Objectivity refers to the behavior being observable without referring to inner states of the individual; clarity means the definition of the response is unambiguous, and completeness refers to the fact that the response has a beginning and an end and can be delineated from all other responses. Depending upon the observation strategy employed, there are methods for calculating agreement between raters. The interested reader is referred to the spring issue (1977) of the *Journal of Applied Behavior Analysis* for extended discussion of different reliability calculations associated with each method.

Limitations

As with all assessment methods, there are problems associated with behavioral observations. One obvious disadvantage is that the presence of an observer may alter the individual's behavior to the extent that it is no longer representative of his or her actions. Observations can occur in an analogue setting or other contrived situations that may elicit the problem behavior, but it is often difficult to replicate the relevant antecedent and consequent conditions that maintain the behavior in the client's natural environment. Additionally, low frequency or highly variable behaviors that are worthy of an intervention attempt (e.g., physical, violent, or destructive behaviors) may not occur under observation periods, requiring additional observations and manpower. Along similar lines, perhaps the biggest disadvantage associated with behavioral observations is the manpower, equipment (e.g., tape recorders, ear jacks, coding sheets), training, and time required to insure the accuracy of target responses. Training and time is more pronounced with interval recording because responses that are observed in this method are usually more complicated compared to more specific circumscribed responses that lend themselves to frequency counts of duration measures.

IDENTIFYING RELEVANT TARGET RESPONSES FOR ASSESSMENT

An obvious problem confronting the assessor is choosing what target behavior to identify. As previously discussed, through informal observation and information accrued from other assessment strategies, target responses can be narrowed from broader categories. It is not uncommon, however, that this approach may identify more than one general category or domain of behaviors in addition to several specific responses that require treatment. For example, data collected from interviews, standardized testing, and behavior rating scales may indicate that an individual displays behavior deficits labeled lack of communication skills. More direct behavioral observation pinpoints several responses that comprise the behavioral deficit, such as lack of eye contact, giving inappropriate responses to questions, and poor articulation. Similarly, the same client may also display behaviors that can be identified through the various assessment methods as excessive motility. Further observation identifies the individual's excessive motility as represented by constantly walking rapidly from one end of the room to another with his head down and his hands in his pockets. In such a situation how does one decide which behavior should be further assessed and treated? Knowledge from the client's past treatment history, that can influence which target behaviors to modify first, may suggest that one response class may be more amenable to a specific intervention. Other factors that may dictate which behaviors to tackle first are, which problem behaviors are most bothersome to staff members or which behaviors have been successfully modified by staff in other clients. More often, however, such information is not available.

Two methods have been developed for identifying the appropriate foci for treatment and rehabilitative programs (Kazdin, 1977). The first method, called social comparison, requires the observation of the behaviors of "normals" as a means of establishing acceptable levels of functioning. The second method, called subjective evaluation, involves the pooling of the opinion of persons who are in a position to evaluate the importance of various behaviors.

A good example of social comparison in the establishment of treatment goals is found in a study conducted by Nutter and Reid (1978). These authors were interested in training institutionalized mentally retarded women to dress themselves and to select their own clothing in such a way as to coincide with current fashion. These authors observed the style of dress of over 600 women in the community where the institutionalized residents would eventually be residing. Color combinations and specific garments worn by the community residents were recorded. Based on this information, the institutionalized women were trained to choose popular color combinations in appropriate clothes so they would blend more easily with community standards.

Clements, Bost, DuBois, and Turpin (1980) employed a subjective evaluation method to determine the severity of the behaviors contained in part of the

Revised Adaptive Behavior Scale (Nihira et al., 1975). Thirty-three psychologists with experience in mental retardation rated on an 11-point scale what behaviors were viewed as maladaptive. These experts identified self-abusive, violent, and destructive behaviors as the most serious behaviors requiring immediate attention. In short, these two methods provide the means to identify and evaluate areas of treatment. The chapter on Behavioral Assessment in this book provides further information about social validation and the selection of behaviors for treatment.

CONCLUSION

A theme underlying the chapters in this book is that the task of assessment is to use various assessment methods to identify target behaviors for implementing and evaluating treatment. The emphasis should not be merely on the number of assessment methods employed, but instead on having sufficient knowledge to match the appropriate assessment method with the nature of the target behavior, the characteristics of the client, the setting in which the assessment takes place, and the purpose of the assessment (Mash & Terdal, 1981). It should be evident that no one assessment method is inherently more valid or useful than another, and each approach has unique advantages and disadvantages. This fact would seem to suggest that multimethod assessments may be the trend of the future. The state of the art in assessing the mentally retarded, as with other populations, while perhaps beyond the infancy stage, demands further development and refinement.

REFERENCES

Abel, EL. Fetal alcohol syndrome: Behavioral teratology. *Psychological Bulletin*, 1980, *87*, 39–50

American Psychiatric Association. *Diagnostic and statistical manual of mental disorders* (3rd ed.). Washington, DC: American Psychiatric Association, 1980

Baratz, SB, & Baratz, JC. Early childhood intervention: The social science base of institutional racism. *Harvard Educational Review*, 1970, *40*, 29–50.

Bayley, N. *Manual for the Bayley scales of infant development*. New York: Psychological Corporation, 1969

Birnbrauer, JS. Mental retardation. In H Leitenberg (Ed.), *Handbook of behavior modification and behavior therapy*. Englewood Cliffs, NJ: Prentice Hall, 1976

Cattell, RB. *Personality and social psychology*. San Diego: Robert R. Knapp, 1964

Clements, PR, Bost, LW, DuBois, YG, & Turpin, WB. Adaptive behavior scale part two: Relative severity of maladaptive behavior. *American Journal of Mental Deficiency*, 1980, *84*, 465–469

Cronbach, LJ. Five decades of public controversy over mental testing. *American Psychologist*, 1975, *30*, 1–14

Doll, EA. *Vineland social maturity scale*. Circle Pines, MN: American Guidance Service, 1965

Domino, G, & Newman, D. Relationship of physical stigmata to intellectual subnormality in mongoloids. *American Journal of Mental Deficiency*, 1965, *69*, 541–547

Dunn, LM, & Markwardt, FC. *Peabody Individual Achievement Test*. Circle Pines, MN: American Guidance Service, 1970

Erickson, MT. *Child psychology* (2nd ed.). Englewood Cliffs, NJ: Prentice Hall, 1982

Erickson, MT. The predictive validity of the Cattell infant intelligence scale for young mentally retarded children. *American Journal of Mental Deficiency*, 1968, *72*, 728–731

Evans, IM, & Nelson, RO. Assessment of child behavior problems. In AR Ciminero, KS Calhoun, & HE Adams (Eds.). *Handbook of behavioral assessment*. New York: Wiley, 1977

Ferster, CB. Classification of behavioral pathology. In L Krasner, & LP Ullman (Eds.), *Research in behavior modification*. New York: Holt, Rinehart, & Winston, 1965

Friedrich, WN, & Friedrich, WL. Psychosocial aspects of parents of handicapped and nonhandicapped children. *American Journal of Mental Deficiency*, 1981, *85*, 551–553

Gardner, WI. *Behavior modification in mental retardation*. Chicago: Aldine, 1971

Grossman, HJ (Ed.). *Manual on terminology and classification in mental retardation, 1973 revision*. Washington, DC: American Association of Mental Deficiency, 1973

Grossman, HJ (Ed.). *Manual on terminology and classification in mental retardation, 1977 revision*. Washington, DC: American Association on Mental Deficiency, 1977

Guilford, JP. Intelligence has three facets. *Science*, 1968, *160*, 615–620

Halpern, A, Raffeld, P, Irvin, LK, & Link, R. *Examiners manual for the social and prevocational information battery*. Monterey, CA: CTB/McGraw Hill, 1975

Hassibi, M, & Chess, S. Mental retardation. In JR Bemporad (Ed.), *Child development in normality and psychopathology*. New York: Brunner/Mazel, 1980

Hawkins, RP, & Dobbs, W. Behavioral definitions in applied behavior analysis: Explicit or implicit. In BC Etzel, JM LeBlanc, & DM Baer (Eds.), *New developments in behavioral research: Theory, methods, and applications*. In honor of Sidney W. Bijou. Hillsdale: Lawrence Erlbaum Assoc., 1975

Heber, RF. A manual on terminology and classification in mental retardation (Rev. ed.). *American Journal of Mental Deficiency*, 1959, *64* (Monograph Suppl.), 1961

Holden, RH. Prediction of mental retardation in infancy. *Mental Retardation*, 1972, *10*, 28–30

Jastak, JF, & Jastak, CR. *The wide range achievement test*. Wilmington, DE: Guidance Associates of Delaware, 1965

Jensen, AR. Intelligence, learning ability, and socioeconomic status. *Journal of Special Education*, 1969, *3*, 23–35

Kanfer, KH, & Grimm, LG. Behavioral analysis: Selecting target behaviors in the interview. *Behavior Modification*, 1977, *1*, 7–28

Kaufman, AS. *Intelligent testing with the WISC-R*. New York: Wiley, 1979

Kazdin, AE. Assessing the clinical or applied significance of behavior change through social validation. *Behavior Modification*, 1977, *1*, 427–452

Kazdin, AE, & Matson, JL. Social validation in mental retardation. *Applied Research in Mental Retardation*, 1981, *2*, 39–53

Kazdin, AE, & Straw, MK. Assessment of behavior of the mentally retarded. In M Hersen, & AS Bellack (Eds.), *Behavioral assessment: A practical handbook*. New York: Pergamon, 1976

Knolboch, H, & Pasamanic, B. Prediction from the assessment of neuromotor and intellectual status in infancy. In J Zubin, & GA Jervis (Eds.), *Psychopathology of mental development*. New York: Grune & Stratton, 1967

Koch, RA. A longitudinal study of 143 mentally retarded children (1955–1961). *The Training School Bulletin*, 1963, *1*, 4–11

Kolb, LC. *Modern clinical psychiatry* (8th ed). Philadelphia: W. B. Saunders, 1973

Lambert, NM, Windmiller, M Cole, L, & Figueroa, R. *AAMD adaptive behavior scale-public school version*. Washington, DC: American Association of Mental Deficiency, 1974

Leland, H, Shellhaas, M, Nihira, K, & Foster, R. Adaptive behavior: A new dimension in the classification of the mentally retarded. *Mental Retardation Abstracts*, 1967, *4*, 359–387

Levine, S, Elzey, FF, & Lewis, M. *Manual for the California preschool and social competency scale*. Palo Alto, CA: Consulting Psychologist Press, 1969

Linehan, MM. Issues in behavioral interviewing. In JD Cone, & RP Hawkins (Eds.), *Behavioral assessment: New directions in clinical psychology*. New York: Bruner/Mazel, 1977

Lutey, C. *Individual intelligence testing: A manual and sourcebook* (2nd ed.). Greeley, CO: Carol L. Lutey Publ., 1977

Mash, EJ, & Terdal, LG. Behavioral assessment of childhood disturbance. In EJ Mash & LG Terdal (Eds.), *Behavioral assessment of childhood disorders*. New York: Guilford Press, 1981

Mercer, JR, & Lewis, JE. *System of multicultural pluralistic assessment* SOMPA. New York: Psychological Corporation, 1977

Morganstern, KP. Behavioral interviewing: The initial stages of assessment. In M Hersen, & AS Bellack (Eds.), *Behavioral assessment: A practical handbook*. New York: Pergamon, 1976

Morrow, HW, & Coulter, WA. A survey of state policies regarding adaptive behavior. In WA Coulter, & HW Morrow (Eds.), *Adaptive behavior: Concepts and measurements*. New York: Grune & Stratton, 1978

Nihira, K, Foster, R, Shellhaas, M, & Leland H. *American association on mental deficiency, 1975 revision*. Washington, DC: American Association on Mental Deficiency, 1975

Nutter, D, & Reid, DH. Teaching retarded women a clothing selection skill using community norms. *Journal of Applied Behavior Analysis*, 1978, *11*, 475–487

Office of Mental Retardation Coordination. Mental retardation source book (DHEW Publication No. 05 73–81). Washington, DC: Department of Health Education and Welfare, 1972

Peterson, DR. *The clinical study of social behavior*. New York: Appleton-Century-Crofts, 1968

Piaget, J. *The origins of intelligence in children* (2nd ed.). New York: International Universities Press, 1952

Reiss, S, Levitan, GW, & McNally, RJ. Emotionally disturbed mentally retarded people: An underserved population. *American Psychologist*, 1982, *37*, 361–367

Robinson, HB, & Robinson, NM. *The mentally retarded child: A psychological approach* (2nd ed.). New York: McGraw-Hill, 1976

Ross, AO. *Psychological disorders of children: A behavioral approach to theory, research, and therapy*. New York: McGraw-Hill, 1980

Ross, RT, & Gianpiccolo, JS. *Fairview social skills scale*. Costa Mesa, CA: Fairview State Hospital, 1972

Ryan, W. *Blaming the victim*. New York: Random House, 1971

Sattler, JM. *Assessment of children's intelligence* (2nd ed.). Philadelphia: Saunders, 1982

Schrott, HG, Karp, L, & Omenn, GS. Prenatal prediction in myotonic dystrophy: Guidelines for genetic counseling. *Clinical Genetics*, 1973, *1*, 152–168

Shapiro, ES, & Barrett, RP. Behavioral assessment of the mentally retarded. In JL Matson, & F. Andrasik (Eds.), *Treatment issues and innovations in mental retardation*. New York: Plenum, 1981

Sigelman, CK, Budd, EC, Spanhel, CL, & Schroenrock, CJ. When in doubt, say yes: Acquiescence in interviews with mentally retarded persons. *Mental Retardation*, 1981, *2*, 53–58

Sigelman, CK, Schroenrock, CJ, Spanhel, CL, Thomas, SG, Winer, JL, Budd, EC, & Martin, PW. Surveying mentally retarded persons: Responsiveness and response validity in three samples. *American Journal of Mental Deficiency*, 1981, *84*, 479–486

Smith, AC, Flick, GL, Ferriss, GS, & Sellman, AH. Prediction of developmental outcome at seven years from prenatal, perinatal, and postnatal events. *Child Development*, 1972, *43*, 495–507

Spearman, C. General intelligence objectively measured and determined *American Journal of Psychology*, 1904, *15*, 201–293

Terman, LM, & Merrill, MA. *Measuring intelligence*. Boston: Houghton Mifflin, 1937

Terman, LM, & Merrill, MA. *The Stanford-Binet intelligence scale*, (3rd ed.). Boston: Houghton Mifflin, 1973

Thorne, JM. A radical behaviorist approach to diagnosis in mental retardation. *Mental Retardation*, 1970, *8*, 2–5

Wechsler, D. Cognitive, conative, and non-intellective intelligence. *American Psychologist*, 1950, *5*, 78–83

Wechsler, D. *Manual for the Wechsler preschool and primary scale of intelligence*. New York: Psychological Corporation, 1967

Wechsler, D. *Manual for the Wechsler intelligence scale for children—revised*. New York: Psychological Corporation, 1974

Wechsler, D. *Wechsler adult intelligence scale—revised*. New York: Psychological Corporation, 1981

VanderVeer, B, & Schweid, E. Infant assessment: Stability of mental functioning in young retarded children. *American Journal of Mental Deficiency*, 1974, *79*, 1–4

Voght, DK. *Literacy among youths 12–17 years*. US DHEW Publication No. (HRA) 74–1613. Washington, DC: US Government Printing Office, 1973

Yarrow, MR, Campbell, JD, & Burton, RV. Recollections of childhood: A study of the retrospective method. *Monographs of the Society for the Research in Child Development*, 1970, *34* (Serial No. 138), 5

Zigler, E. Familial mental retardation: A continuing dilemma. *Science*, 1967, *155*, 292–298

Zigler, E, & Balla, DA. Luria's verbal deficiency theory of mental retardation and performance of sameness, symmetry, and opposition tasks: A critique. *American Journal of Mental Deficiency*, 1971, *75*, 400–413

Paul E. Bates
Harold Hanson

2

Behavioral Assessment

Mentally retarded persons are frequently characterized by the presence of inappropriate behaviors such as aggression, disruption, and stereotyped movement (Forehand & Baumeister, 1976). This characterization stems primarily from observations made in institutional settings. For example, Berkson and Davenport (1962) documented an inverse relationship between the occurrence of high rates of stereotypical behavior and level of intelligence. Self-injurious behavior (SIB) has also been observed to frequently occur in institutionalized populations (Ross, 1972). Although inappropriate behavior patterns have been associated with mentally retarded persons, it is inappropriate to attribute these patterns to mental retardation itself. Alternative explanations for the high incidence of inappropriate behavior include: history of institutionalization, segregated schooling, inadequate curriculum sequences, failure to learn socially appropriate alternatives, limited exposure to non-handicapped models, and minimal community experiences. Given these contributing factors, statements regarding the association of mental retardation and inappropriate behavior must be closely guarded.

How one views the origin of behavior will influence the choice of assessment and treatment techniques. If behavior is considered to be the result of relatively unchanging intraorganismic variables, assessment will be directed toward intrapsychic processes and personality traits that are assumed to be stable across situations. These approaches to assessment neglect the powerful influence of environmental variables and do not address what a person might do under more habilitative circumstances.

High rates of inappropriate behavior are less related to mental retardation and other intrapsychic processes than they are to many of the environmental influences previously listed. Since these environmental influences are highly variable and subject to unique interaction effects of person and setting, standardized assessments are inadequate and inappropriate. As a result, a more precise approach to assessment of inappropriate behavior is required. Behavioral assessment provides such an alternative. According to Mash (1979):

Behavioral assessment is characterized at a conceptual level by a view of human behavior as predominantly under the control of contemporaneous environmental variables rather than determined by underlying intrapsychic mechanisms or inferred personality traits. (p. 24)

In contrast to other assessment methods, behavioral assessment is far more sensitive to the peculiarities of specific situations and resulting performance differences because it is a thorough assessment utilizing several observation methods for direct observation of multiple behaviors in multiple settings. Applied behavior analysis, with its emphasis on direct assessment of socially significant behavior in natural settings, is the methodology that is best suited for these assessment purposes. Various aspects of this methodology are developed and discussed throughout this chapter.

Unique goals of behavioral assessment include the identification of behaviors in need of change and the variables that control the occurrence of those behaviors (Nelson & Hayes, 1979). To accomplish these goals, a broad and multidimensional approach to assessment is required. In Figure 2-1, a hierarchy of assessment activities is presented. This hierarchy proceeds from an initial determination of the need to more formally assess particular behaviors to an assessment of these behavior(s) under generalization conditions. By viewing assessment in such a multidimensional and interrelated manner, the programmatic usefulness of the evaluation information may be increased. From such an assessment, it is more likely that effective program decisions will be made and that the interpersonal competence of mentally retarded persons will be enhanced. In this chapter, the components of this assessment model are described in detail and several examples are provided as illustrations of its applicability.

ESTABLISH SOCIALLY SIGNIFICANT PROGRAM OBJECTIVES

The identification of behaviors as inappropriate and possibly in need of change is a subjective decision. Categories of behavior that are commonly considered to be inappropriate are non-compliance, stereotypic, self-injurious, aggressive/disruptive, and chronic vomiting and pica. Specific behaviors within these categories are judged inappropriate, abnormal, or aberrant on the basis of response topography, frequency, intensity, or environment in which they occur (Gaylord-Ross, 1980). For example, whether non-compliance is judged a problem will depend on the situational nature of the directive as well as the frequency of occurrence. In some cases non-compliance is an appropriate behavior (e.g., refusing a ride from a stranger, refusing to indiscriminately lend money); while in other cases non-compliance is only judged a problem if it occurs at a high rate.

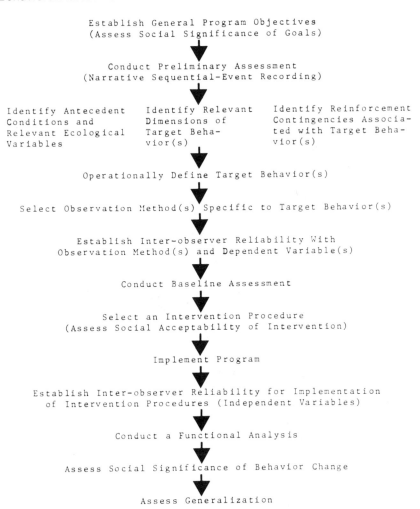

Fig. 2-1. Multidimensional hierarchy of assessment procedures

If a behavior is judged a problem on the basis of informal observations of its excessive, deficit, or situational characteristics, a decision must be made regarding whether to invest time and energy into conducting a more formal assessment. This decision undoubtedly will involve an investigation of program priorities. Sulzer-Azaroff and Mayer (1977) provide several guidelines relevant to this investigation. According to these authors, the formal assessment process should proceed if answers to the following questions are affirmative:

1. Have several people concurred that a problem exists?
2. Have direct or informal solutions been documented?

3. Does the decision to proceed with assessment and possibly intervention have priority and support from significant persons?

In addition to the above criteria, aspects of the inappropriate behavior will influence the decision to pursue more formal assessment procedures. Specifically, these include behaviors that are dangerous to oneself or others and behaviors that are excessive to the point of disrupting acquisition of alternative skills and/or the learning process of other persons.

As is obvious from the above decision rules, a great deal of subjectivity is involved. One assessment method that more objectively approaches this subjective process is social validation. Social validation assessment refers to a three-part process for determining the social significance of program goals, acceptability of intervention procedures, and clinical value of program results (Kazdin, 1977b; Wolf, 1978). Kazdin (1977b) operationalized the social validation process by identifying two methods that have been used to validate various intervention efforts. These methods are social comparison and subjective evaluation. In this section, these methods are discussed as they relate to the identification of program objectives. Subsequently, social validation assessment is further discussed in regard to the acceptability of treatment programs and the significance of program results.

Social comparison has been used to identify specific behaviors that differentiate a person from a particular reference group. For example, a selected peer group can be directly observed to ascertain the level of behavior(s) that typically is expected. According to Kazdin (1977b), the social comparison approach requires observations of the client's peers who are similar in subject and demographic characteristics, but who differ in performance on the target behavior(s). One might conclude that mentally retarded persons of similar age constitute such a peer group. With respect to inappropriate behavior patterns, however, observations of this peer group might provide justification for levels of behavior that are acceptable for the mentally retarded, but not for non-handicapped persons. The social rejection in integrated settings that might result from this goal setting process would be unacceptable. An alternative approach would be to view the performance of non-handicapped persons as the ultimate program goal and to establish short-term client objectives toward this end. O'Brien and Azrin (1972) used the performance of non-handicapped restaurant patrons to establish standards of performance for eating behaviors. By comparing the performance of non-handicapped persons to a group of institutionalized mentally retarded individuals, a performance discrepancy was noted and treatment goals established.

Subjective evaluation is the other social validation assessment method for determining target behaviors. This method consists of obtaining the opinion of persons who are knowledgeable about the behavior patterns of mentally retarded persons and/or who have a special relationship with the client (Kazdin & Matson, 1981). Specific examples of this technique are found in surveys of sheltered workshop personnel (Mithaug & Hagmeier, 1978) and competitive employers (Rusch,

Schutz, & Agran, in press) for the purpose of identifying requisite behaviors for success in these settings. In the Rusch et al. survey of competitive employers in the service industry, the following social survival skills were identified as important by 90 percent or more of the respondents: immediate compliance to instructions, less than 1–2 major disruptive episodes per month, and less than 3–5 inappropriate contacts per day with strangers.

Social comparison and subjective evaluation procedures are presently used informally to identify priority target behaviors. For increased accountability and sophistication in treatment programs, more precise social validation assessment is warranted. These social validation attempts should result in the identification of competencies that are incompatible with the presence of inappropriate behaviors. Inappropriate behaviors in most cases can be reduced by teaching these socially appropriate alternatives rather than specifically administering contingencies for problem behaviors.

PRELIMINARY ASSESSMENT

Once the social significance of a behavior or set of behaviors has been established, structured narrative observations are recommended as preliminary assessment activities. These activities may unveil contributing antecedent and consequence conditions as well as elucidate the relevant dimensions of the target behavior(s). Sequential event recording is an assessment method that has been used to obtain structured narrative observations. This procedure involves direct observation and narrative recording of the events that occur before (antecedents) and after (consequences) a specific behavior or class of behaviors. A three-column data sheet with space provided for describing antecedents (A), behavior (B), and consequences (C) is usually used for sequential event recording. An example of this assessment method, commonly called ABC recording, is presented in Figure 2-2.

Sequential event recording should result in greater sensitivity to the interrelationship between behavior and environment. A concern for these interrelationships and interdependencies has been called an ecological perspective (Willems, 1974). This perspective has stimulated the development of an ecobehavioral approach to assessment. The ecobehavioral approach requires detailed analysis of the person within the physical and cultural milieu (Rogers-Warren & Warren, 1977). Many aspects of the behavior-ecology interdependency can be identified through a comprehensive ABC analysis. Each aspect of the ABC assessment is discussed as it relates to an ecobehavioral approach.

Antecedents

Antecedent variables include all stimulus conditions that are present prior to the emission of a behavior. In behavioral assessment, most emphasis has been placed on antecedent conditions that immediately precede target behaviors. These

Client: _____

General Behaviors to be Recorded:

O: _____

Date: _____

TIME	ANTECEDENTS	BEHAVIOR	CONSEQUENCES
5:30 PM	1. At bank work area, client is alone after being assigned cleaning duties by the supervisor.	1. Client skips steps in assigned job sequence using his own methods for doing the tasks. He looks at himself in the mirror, arranges his clothes repeatedly, and mumbles to himself. Stretches, yawns, and moves slowly.	1. Inadequate amount of work completed at a low level of quality.
5:55 PM	2. Supervisor checks on client.	2. Client stops dusting shelves and starts to move trashcans when he sees the supervisor coming.	2. Supervisor checks the completed work and reprimands client for doing little. Prompts client to do the job as taught and to work faster. Tells client to "shape up" and that dusting is not a contract job.
6:30 PM	3. Supervisor returns to check on client.	3. Client is looking in window and straightening his clothes. Does not see supervisor coming.	3. Supervisor reprimands client for not working. Tells client he can be laid off for poor performance.
6:50 PM	4. Supervisor returns and sees poorly done work. Few tasks have been started. Reprimands worker and threatens him with a lay-off.	4. Client responds loudly "I do my work but I'm tired! You don't care!"	4. Supervisor tells client to sit in the van until he cools down.

Fig. 2-2. ABC recording form

General Behaviors to be Recorded: Off-Task, Verbal Aggression, Incorrect Job Performance

32

Table 2-1
Antecedent Stimulus Conditions of Relevance to Behavior
Management of the Mentally Retarded

Interpersonal Variables (Teacher Related)
    Ratio
    Proximity
    Instructions
    Reprimands
    Reinforcers

Interpersonal Variables (Peer Related)
    Number
    Proximity
    Functioning Level (Handicapped vs. Non-Handicapped)
    Age
    Modeling
    Instructions
    Reprimands
    Reinforcers

Setting Variables
    Segregated Residential (Institution) vs. Integrated Residential (Natural Home or Small Group Home)
    Segregated School (No Non-Handicapped) vs. Integrated School (Age Appropriate Non-Handicapped Peers Present)
    Presence of Objects to Manipulate
    Type of Objects Available
    Presence of Furniture
    Arrangement of Furniture
    Noise Level
    Temperature
    Lighting

Structure Variables
    Schedule of Activities
    Curriculum of Socially Appropriate Alternatives

conditions include interpersonal, setting, and structural variables. Antecedent variables from these categories are listed in Table 2-1. Combinations of these variables cumulatively constitute the ecology or context for all behavior, appropriate and inappropriate.

The powerful influence of antecedent variables has been documented by several independent sources. Wolfensberger (1972) suggested that the presence of inappropriate behavior in severely handicapped persons may be largely attributed to common ecological conditions of large institutions, i.e., crowding and absence of ojects. In an empirical study of environmental enrichment (adding people and objects to the institutional environment), Baumeister and Forehand (1973) found an inverse relationship between the degree of enrichment and the frequency of stereotypical behavior. Further, crowded conditions (common in congregate residential living arrangements involving the mentally retarded) have been shown to be correlated with increases in aggressive behavior (Rago, Parker, & Cleland, 1978). Finally, excessive noise, heat, cold, and insufficient lighting have all been shown to negatively influence learning.

Although antecedent conditions exert powerful control over the presence of particular behavior patterns, relatively little attention has been directed toward assessing or manipulating these variables. With ABC recording as an initial assessment strategy, it may be possible to identify antecedent conditions that are associated with particular behavior patterns. From such an assessment, the ecology or context of behavior is better understood, and hence, more successful program decisions may be made.

Behavior

According to Foster and Cone (1980), a behavioral assessment system is ecologically valid when the right dimension of the right behavior is observed in the right setting. These authors further point out that "right" should not connote a singular approach. In fact, they suggest that hybrid observation systems involving the measurement of multiple dimensions of different behaviors are more useful and will be used more frequently in the future.

ABC recording is well suited for clarifying the dimensions of various motoric behaviors emitted by mentally retarded persons. From these observations, it is possible to identify all relevant target behaviors and to determine whether frequency, duration, magnitude, or a combination of these dimensions is most appropriate for further assessment. For example, the narrative descriptions of behavior in Figure 2-2 provide the basis for more refined assessment of on-off task, verbal aggression, and correct job performance.

Consequences

Consequences are those environmental changes or events that follow a behavior. These environmental changes can have a reinforcing, punishing, or neutral effect on the behaviors that they follow. Reinforcing consequences result in strengthening the behaviors that they follow, whereas punishing consequences suppress the behaviors that precede them. By conducting an ABC analysis, naturally occurring reinforcement or punishment contingencies may be identified. In some cases, simple manipulation of these consequence events may alter the occurrence of particular behaviors to the point where they are no longer problematic.

Consequences may serve the dual role of influencing the rate of occurrence of the behaviors that precede them and also operate as discriminative stimuli for subsequent behaviors. A verbal reprimand, for example, (e.g., "You're working too slow.'') may result in a decrease in off-task behavior, but also operate as a stimulus for verbal aggression (e.g., ''Leave me alone!'').

Through an ABC analysis, the interrelationship between antecedents, behavior(s), and consequences can be closely examined. By collecting ABC data across several days, the dependent variable(s) can be more precisely defined, the relationship of antecedent and consequence conditions more clearly identified, and the situational appropriateness of behavior more empirically evaluated. This information should contribute to the efficiency and effectiveness of subsequent assessment and intervention practices.

OPERATIONAL DEFINITIONS OF TARGET BEHAVIORS

After socially valid behaviors have been identified and preliminary assessment procedures have revealed the relevant dimensions of these behaviors, operational definitions need to be developed to ensure accurate and reliable observation. According to Sulzer-Azaroff and Mayer (1977), an operational definition is ''The product of breaking down a broad concept, such as 'aggressive' into its observable and measurable component behaviors (frequency of hitting or biting others, duration of scream, and so on)'' (p. 520). Poorly defined behaviors will result in invalid and unreliable assessment data, thus jeopardizing any conclusions about the target behavior(s) and the effectiveness of various intervention procedures. Conversely, a well constructed definition reduces sources of variability and allows for a clearer understanding of the role of specific intervention efforts (Hersen & Barlow, 1976; Sidman, 1960). Precise definitions of target behaviors also facilitate communication in the field to other professionals who may encounter similar behavior problems, promote communication and consistency among persons in direct contact with the target person, and focus attention on specific target behaviors that are inappropriate and in need of improvement.

Several example definitions from the literature for which interobserver agreement (reliability) has already been established are presented in Table 2-2. The quality of an operational definition is ultimately judged by the degree of interobserver reliability that can be demonstrated and the value of program decisions that emanate from using a particular behavioral description. According to Lindsley (1964), ''the prosthesis can be no more accurate than the descriptions of the target deficit and behavioral goal'' (p. 67).

OBSERVATIONAL ASSESSMENT METHODS

When the target behaviors have been defined and relevant dimensions of these behaviors identified, observational assessment methods must be selected. Every effort must be made to select the observation method that most accurately

Table 2-2

Example Definitions of Inappropriate Behaviors Exhibited by
Mentally Retarded Persons

Stereotypical Behaviors

Hyperventilation

"Heavy breathing, occurring in conjunction with hand waving near the face, side-to side head movements, and head bobbing" (Nunes, Murphy & Hutchings-Ruprecht, 1977, p. 240).

Hand Gestures

"Flicking of either hand at the wrist, usu-ally directed outward from the body as if to pick lint from his clothing. This appeared spontaneously without identifiable stimuli. Subsidiary, but not necessarily collateral, activities included rocking and bounding in a chair" (Weisberg, Passman, & Russell, 1973, p. 488).

Self-Injurious Behavior

Head Banging

"Any contact between any part of the head and any part of the hand or of a solid object (including the floor and chairs) is to be counted. Each contact will be counted as one response. If the subject breaks contact with one part of her hand while maintaining such with another part of the same hand, no new responses will be counted regardless of how many more times the subject hits herself. However, if the subject maintains contact with one hand while hitting herself with the other hand or with a solid object, a new response is to be counted. If the subject hits herself with both hands at the same time, two responses will be counted unless both hands are clasped together" (Corte, Wolf, & Locke, 1971, p. 703).

Face Slaps

"Rapidly bringing one or both hands to the subject's face with the palm in apparent contact with the face" (Tanner & Ziegler, 1975, p. 55).

Rumination/Pica

Vomiting

"Vomiting food into the oral cavity or from the oral cavity. When force feed thrusting of the abdomen resulted in a 'full-cheeked' appearance, as well as instances when the vomitus was actually visible, the target behavior was scored" (Simpson & Sasso, 1978, p. 146–147).

Scavenging

"The gathering and eating of any non-nutritive substances, e.g., trash or feces. A scavenging episode was defined as the presence of trash or feces around or in the mouth or on the hands" (Foxx & Martin, 1975, p. 155).

Aggressive/Disruptive

Choke

"A choke was recorded when the subject held an aide or resident by the neck and squeezed (complete choke) or when the sub-ject's hand reached the neck of an aide or resident but was knocked away before the subject could squeeze (attempted or partial choke)" (Vukelich & Hake, 1971, p. 217).

and efficiently measures behavioral dimensions of interest. Naturalistic observation of free behavior (Cone, 1978) is the category of assessment that most appropriately applies to measurement of aberrant behavior. This method of assessment usually requires independent observers who covertly or overtly record various dimensions of the target behaviors. Dimensions of target behaviors that are commonly of interest are frequency, duration, and latency. For these behavioral dimensions, observational procedures and recording methods are subsequently described with illustrations of their applicability to commonly encountered behavior problems. Special equipment and instrumentation have been used in many cases to augment direct observation. Several references and descriptions of these aids are presented in table form. Finally, several issues related to direct observation procedures are briefly discussed.

Frequency Recording

Many behaviors are defined as inappropriate on the basis of frequency of occurrence. Frequency is defined as the number of times a behavior occurs in an observation period that is standard in length and time of day. Some behaviors are judged as inappropriate because they occur too infrequently (e.g., number of instructions followed correctly) whereas other behaviors are targeted because they occur too often (e.g., number of handshakes).

For accurate and reliable assessment of response frequency, behaviors must be discrete (i.e., have a clear start and stop) and be uniform in length of occurrence (Bailey & Bostow, 1979). Frequency measures have been used for behaviors that leave relatively permanent evidence of their occurrence (e.g., number of windows broken, number of chairs turned over, etc.) and for behaviors that are more transient in nature (e.g., number of hits to face).

Frequency recording is usually conducted by observers who position themselves in such a way that they can easily see the emission of the targeted behaviors. These observers use a data recording form such as that presented in Figure 2-3. Important information that needs to be on this form includes client's name, observer's name, target behaviors, and date and time of observation. Ample space needs to be provided to tally the target behaviors each time they occur. Data sheets are usually attached to clipboards to facilitate ease of recording. Although it is recommended that observation periods be standard, minor deviations are common in most applied settings. For this reason, the conversion of frequency measures to rate per minute is a common practice. Examples of the conversion are provided in Figure 2-3.

The frequency of multiple behaviors can be assessed concurrently as long as the frequency of occurrence of one or more of the behaviors is not extremely high. For example, observers have been able to simultaneously record as many as six categories (Hardiman, Goetz, Reuter, & LeBlanc, 1975; Porterfield, Herbert-Jackson, & Risley, 1976); however, if the rate of a single behavior is exception-

Frequency Data Recording

Consumer's Name Tom H.

Observer's Name Jason A.

Date	Begin Time	End Time	Behavior of Interest	Frequency Tally	Total Frequency	Total Minutes	Rate Per Minute
6/16	10:00	11:00	Swearing	ʇʜʟ ʇʜʟ ı	11	60	.183
6/16	10:15	11:00	Swearing	ʇʜʟ ʇʜʟ	10	45	.222

Fig. 2-3. Frequency data form

Table 2-3

Behavior Problem by Direct Observation Method Matrix of
66 Studies Involving Moderately and Severely Handicapped Persons

| | Observation Method | | |
Behavior Problem	Frequency	Duration	Interval Time Sampling
Aggressive/Disruptive	15	2	9
Stereotypic	9	3	17
SIB	19	2	0
Vomiting/Pica	8	0	4

ally high (e.g., 50 or more a minute), it may be difficult to accurately record even one behavior over lengthy observation sessions. For recording response frequency, many mechanical aids are available that make it easier to record high rate behaviors and/or multiple variables.

As mentioned previously, accuracy and efficiency were important criteria by which an observation procedure was to be judged. With high rate and/or multiple dependent measures, accuracy of frequency data may be jeopardized. The efficiency of this method may also be questionable since continuous observer attention is required during the observation period. Despite some of these concerns, frequency recording is the most commonly used assessment method for measuring inappropriate behaviors emitted by mentally retarded persons. Renzaglia and Bates (1983) analyzed 66 studies involving behavior reduction programs with developmentally disabled individuals. Using these representative studies, a behavior problem by observation method matrix was constructed (see Table 2-3). As is evident from this table, frequency measurement has been used in the majority of studies involving aggressive/disruptive, self-injurious, and vomiting/pica behaviors.

Duration Recording

In some cases, the most salient dimension of an inappropriate behavior is duration (the length of time during which an event occurs). Some behaviors are judged problematic because they occur for too short of a time period (e.g., length of time on-task) and others because they occur too long (e.g., length of a work break).

To appropriately use duration recording, reliable observations of the onset and offset of the behavior must be made. Further, a timing device (e.g., stopwatch) is required for accurate recording. In practice, duration observations should be conducted over a standard length observation period (e.g., one hour) and common time of the day. Preferably a timing device should be used that can easily be started and stopped as well as maintain cumulative duration for at least one hour. Many stopwatches, calculators, and digital watches have this capability. An example duration data form is presented in Figure 2-4. If total length of the observa-

Duration Data Recording

Consumer's Name ___Ed T___

Observer's Name ___Cindy M___

Behavior(s): Out of Seat (refer to definition)

Measurement: Duration Recording (use of stop watch required)

Date	Data Collection Time		Total Time	Duration of Time Out of Seat	Total Percentage Duration of Ob. Period
	Start	Stop			
6/2	9:00 AM	10:00 AM	60 M	20 M	33$\frac{1}{3}$%
6/3	9:05 AM	10:00 AM	55 M	19 M	36$\frac{1}{3}$%
6/4	9:10 AM	10:00 AM	50 M	15 M	30%

Fig. 2-4. Duration data form

40

tion period is recorded, it is possible to convert the cumulative duration of a behavior to a percentage of total time observed. In the example, "time in seat" is converted to a percentage of total time observed. This measure may have more practical significance to the clinician than the total duration figure.

Duration recording yields a very precise measurement of a behavior's length of occurrence. This method is particularly well suited for behaviors with easily determined starts and stops. Since continuous observer attention and a timing device are required for accurate assessment, it may be difficult to simultaneously observe more than one subject and behavior at a time. The appropriateness of duration recording is also questionable in situations involving high rate behaviors of short duration.

Duration has not been a dimension of inappropriate behavior that has been investigated very often with the mentally retarded (see Table 2-3). With infrequently occurring behaviors of long and varying duration, however, this recording procedure is probably the most appropriate. With the assistance of specialized recording equipment, many of the logistical problems associated with duration recording may be minimized.

Latency Recording

Latency recording is a time-related measure that refers to the length of time that elapses between the onset of a stimulus and the occurrence of a specific behavior. Examples include length of time it takes for a person to comply to an instruction and length of time between successive scoops of food.

It is common to think of shorter response latencies as being more appropriate (e.g., following instructions immediately), however, in some cases, longer response latencies are desired (e.g., increasing time between bites to prevent food stuffing). Latency recording requires very precise identification of the onset of a task demand and accurate measurement of time elapsed prior to occurrence of a behavior or set of behaviors. As with duration recording, continuous observer attention is required and a timing device must be used. Given the observation demands of latency recording, its use is usually restricted to specific behaviors of one or two subjects. In the literature, latency recording is commonly reported as a version of duration recording, with duration referring to the interval of time between the presentation of a stimulus and a response.

Interval Time Sample Recording

Interval time sample recording refers to several different observation techniques that may be appropriate when behaviors of interest are not clearly discrete and/or continuous observation is impractical. With interval time sampling, a standard observation period is divided into a series of equal length intervals, usually ranging from 5 seconds to 10 minutes. The observer then records the occurrence

(+) or non-occurrence (–) of a behavior or set of behaviors for each time interval. In some cases, the observation intervals are continuous for an established time period whereas in others, the intervals are interspersed with recording time periods. Multiple variations of interval time sample recording have been reported, including whole-interval time sampling, partial-interval time sampling, and momentary time sampling. Each of these options is described and example data sheets are provided.

Whole-interval time sampling

With whole-interval time sampling, continuous observation is required for the length of each interval. An occurrence (+) of the target behavior is scored if the behavior occurs throughout the entire interval. This procedure is best suited for behaviors that are expected to occur for long periods of time without interruption and provides an approximation of response duration. Since this method of interval recording underestimates the duration of a response, it provides a conservative approximation of total duration.

The length of observation intervals for this method is usually less than 30 seconds, with 10-second intervals being the most common. In a 30-minute observation session with 10-second intervals, a total of 180 observations (+) or (–) would be made. These data, as with partial-interval and momentary time sampling, are typically reported as the percentage of intervals in which the target behavior occurred.

The observational demands of whole-interval time sampling are such that is difficult to use for multiple subjects and multiple dependent variables. Also, this method is inappropriate for measuring fleeting behaviors (e.g., stereotypical behaviors, non-compliance, etc.). In these instances, partial-interval recording and momentary time sample recording are possible alternatives.

Partial-Interval Time Sampling

With this measurement procedure, a response is recorded as an occurrence when a single instance of the behavior is observed in the interval. This method is often used to record frequently occurring behaviors of short duration whose onset and offset are unclear. For example, stereotypical behaviors of head weaving, body rocking, and finger flapping may be appropriate for this observation technique. Since only a single instance of the behavior is sufficient to constitute an entire interval as an occurrence, this procedure tends to overestimate the occurrence of the behavior. For behaviors that are targeted for reduction, this observation method provides a relatively conservative evaluation of program success. A possible advantage of this technique is that as soon as one instance of the behavior occurs, the observer does not have to maintain observation for the remainder of the interval. If the behavior is of low frequency and/or the intervals are short (10–20 seconds), however, continuous attention by the observer is usually required.

Partial-interval time sampling is particularly useful for observing multiple

	1	2	3	4	5	6	7	8	9	10
Student: A										
Staff: Reinforcement	5									
Demand	3									
Physical Contact	6									
Verbal Contact	2									
Reprimand	—									
Student: Stereotypic	1									
Self-Injurious	—									
Noisemaking	—									
Aggression	—									
Appropriate Manipulation of Objects	4									
Appropriate Communication	—									
Student B										
Staff: Reinforcement	—									
Demand	—									
Physical Contact	—									
Verbal Contact	—									
Reprimand	4									
Student: Stereotypic	1									
Self-Injurious	2									
Noisemaking	3									
Aggression	—									
Appropriate Manipulation of Objects	—									
Appropriate Communication	—									

Fig. 2-5. Sample data sheet used to record staff and student behaviors

behaviors and/or multiple individuals. Within the same interval, several behaviors could be observed in a single individual or several persons could be observed in regard to a few behaviors. In Figure 2-5, an example data sheet is presented in which multiple staff and student behaviors were recorded for 30-second intervals, alternating observations from one student to the next. Included in this example is another variation of partial-interval recording, i.e., the recording of order of occurrence. Rather than simply recording (+) or (–), the sequential ordering of the responses as they occur may provide additional information that reveals behavior sequences (chains) that commonly occur. If a series of problem behaviors appear interrelated in a consistent manner, the focus of intervention might be more specifically directed.

Momentary Time Sampling

This method of assessment requires that the behavior occurs at the moment an interval ends for that behavior to be scored as an occurrence. Momentary time sampling may be most appropriate for behaviors that persist for long periods of time and/or occur quite frequently. Also, this method of assessment may be selected when it is not feasible to continuously observe a subject for extended periods of time. Examples of behaviors commonly observed by this method are attending to task, stereotypic behaviors of high frequency, and in-seat behavior. The major advantage of this procedure is that the observer need not continuously watch the subject. Since observation is only necessary at specific moments, the observer is free to do other things during the interval. With fairly long intervals (e.g., one to 10 minutes), it is possible for the observer to maintain consistent measurement with minimal disruption in his or her other activities. Figure 2-6 provides the reader with a blank data sheet that could be used for whole-interval, partial-interval, and momentary-interval recording.

Observation Equipment Instrumentation

In addition to the standard observation equipment (e.g., clipboard, data sheet, and pencil), other equipment and instrumentation have been used to assess human behavior. Based primarily on a review of technical notes and brief communications appearing in the *Journal of Applied Behavior Analysis,* a table of observation equipment/instrumentation was developed (see Table 2-4). In this table, the reader is provided with references and a brief description of equipment/instrumentation that has been used for frequency, duration, and latency assessment. Also, one-way observation devices and permanent product records are presented.

Issues in Observational Assessment

The selection of the appropriate observation system for a particular behavior is a key element in behavioral assessment. If possible, it is advisable to compare two or more observational procedures in an attempt to more empirically arrive at a choice of assessment methods. For example, Powell and associates have compared the accuracy and efficiency of whole, partial, and momentary recording techniques (Powell, Martindale, & Kulp, 1975; Powell, Martindale, Kulp, Martindale, & Bauman, 1977). Generally the results of these investigations suggest that momentary time sampling provides the best estimate of a behavior's duration.

Regardless of the direct observation system(s) selected, observer bias, observer expectancy, code complexity, and reactivity are possible sources of variance that apply across all assessment methods. Failure to control for these influences may increase inaccuracy in data collection and reduce the effectiveness of program decision making. As a control for bias and expectancy, observers should be naive regarding the target person's history and unaware of the program goals. If these conditions are not possible, frequent reliability checks are warranted (see subsequent section). The complexity of the observation code needs to be empirically evaluated to determine how much information at what frequency of occurrence can be reliably recorded. Since multiple behavior assessment is likely to

Interval Time Sampling

Consumer's Name: _____

Observer's Name: _____

Time Sample Method: _____

Interval Length: _____

Scoring Code: Occurrence (+), Nonoccurrence (-)

Behavior Code: 1. _____
2. _____
3. _____
4. _____
5. _____
6. _____

Date	Behavior Code	Start Time	Intervals	Stop Time	Total Occurrence	Percent Occurrence

Fig. 2-6. Interval time sample data form

45

Table 2-4

Equipment/Instrumentation for Behavioral Assessment

Reference	Equipment
	Frequency Assessment
Aitchison (1972)	A point book for recording points in a token economy.
Boer (1968)	A stenograph machine that allows for recording the frequency of coded behaviors.
Coleman and Toth (1970)	A digital counter in a box that is controlled by a hand-held counter. The digital counter will click and light up when a reinforcer is earned.
Colman and Boren (1969)	A point-recording matrix for subject behavior in a token economy program.
Guitar and Andrews (1977)	A mini-calculator used as a cumulative counter for rapidly occurring events.
Katz (1973)	A golf score counter in conjunction with a wristwatch that is worn on the wrist.
Lindsley (1968)	A two-digit wrist counter.
Mattos (1968)	A hand-held digital counter with five keys each registering three digits.
Milby, Willcutt, and Hawk (1973)	A master data matrix and individual card system for recording individualized as well as standard behavioral measures in a token economy.
Schroeder (1972)	Transducers mounted onto tools to measure work behavior (tool usage), which is recorded on totalizing counters. Interresponse lines can also be recorded on numeric printers.
Tate (1968)	A system composed of a work station and a console unit consisting of a running time meter for recording session length, counter for tasks completed, and a status indicator to sign what schedule or reinforcement is in effect, etc.
Wood, Callahan, and Alevizos (1977)	A behaviorally based log book that provides for the recording of low-frequency unusual behavior and aggressive behaviors.
	Duration Assessment
Baker and Whitehead (1972)	A portable recording apparatus the basic unit of which is an eight-channel Rustrak, Model 292-8 event recorder. Allows for a choice of either continuous or interval rating with time-sampling procedures.

Fitzsimmons (1978)	An electronic timer (a calculator with a stopwatch built in). It will compute rate given the frequency and ends itself to limited holds.
Foxx and Martin (1971)	A small, portable timer with an alarm function that can fit in a pocket.
Frankel and Weber (1978)	Multi-channel timing apparatus for the collection of observational duration data based on calculator circuits mounted on a common circuit board placed on the back of a legal-sized clipboard.
	A scoring sheet, placed on the clipboard allows simultaneous collection of frequency data and the transcription of the contents of the digital displays.
Katz (1973)	A wristwatch in conjunction with a golf score counter that is worn on the wrist.
Kubany and Sloggett	An observing and coding procedure for estimating the percent of time students in a classroom engage in appropriate and inappropriate behavior.
Quilitch (1972)	A cassette tape recorder with intervals mounted on the tape for use as a portable programmed, audible timer.
Strang and George (1975)	A time-lapse clock turned on and off at a predetermined noise threshold affords a measure of noise duration. While noise is below the threshold a series of button lights on a wooden clown figure were lighted one at a time every 20 seconds to provide feedback to students in a classroom.
Worthy (1968)	A miniature, portable timer and audible signaling device that can provide a time base for an interval observational system.

Latency Assessment

Greenwald (1977)	A simple switching mechanism that operates two tape recorders one of which is in the play mode and the other in the record mode.

One-Way Observation Devices

Brechner, Linder, Meyerson, and Hays (1974)	A shade screen that interrupts light transmission in one direction only using Kaiser Aluminum shade screen. This allows for making film or videotape recordings and can accommodate time-lapse photography.
Hanson, Tyler, and Hedge (1976)	Existing glass or plastic glass substitute can be converted easily to a one-way mirror by using an aluminum vapor-coated, polyester film.
Knapp (1978)	A portable, one-way screen.

(continued)

Table 2-4 (continued)

Reference	Equipment
	Permanent Product Record
Bernal, Gibson, Williams, and Pesses (1971)	A timer-activated cassette recorder to record at various times of the day.
Boer (1968)	A stenograph machine that allows for recording the frequency of coded behaviors.
Carroll (1977)	Charts covered by a plastic sheet which can be written with pens. The assembly can be bolted to a wall.
Edleson (1978)	Portable electronic calculator with paper printout.
Lehrer (1970)	A credit card system for collecting data at point transactions in a token economy.
Logan (1970)	A ''paper money'' system with simulated bills on which the behavior can be recorded that was reinforced with the ''paper money.''
Nordquist (1971)	A microphone secured by the mouth of the subject with a videotape recorder was used for studying children's verbal behavior.
Sanders, Hopkins, and Walker (1969)	A time-lapse camera for recording simple and complex behaviors.

increase, more attention to this possible source of error is needed. Finally, the issue of reactivity (change in performance as a result of being aware that one is being observed) has been extensively discussed and investigated by several researchers. In some cases involving mentally retarded clients, reactive effects have been demonstrated while in others, no reactivity has been evinced. As early as 1943, Arrington provided the following suggestions for decreasing this possible source of error: observe during informal activities, observe in settings where visitors are common, and shift attention from one individual to another. Other suggestions have included familiarizing the target subjects with the presence of observers and the use of hidden observers.

Although the accuracy or quality of data is of primary importance, the quantity of data collection is an issue of great concern in applied settings. As a general rule, no more data should be collected than realistically can be used for making program decisions. Daily data collection is recommended, however, the amount of information recorded per day may vary considerably. Every effort should be made to identify the most efficient observation schedule that still yields programmatically useful information.

In addition to direct observation methods, self-observation is an assessment method that is worthy of increased attention. In self-observation, the individual immediately records his or her own behavior in much the same way as an independent observer. Since many behaviors occur at times and in places where external observers are not present, self-recorded observations provide a source of data that has primarily been unavailable. To improve the accuracy of self-observation data, providing training in self-recording, conducting accuracy checks, and reinforcing accuracy are recommended practices.

In this section, several issues that may influence the accuracy and ultimate value of observational data have been briefly discussed. More extensive discussion of these issues is available elsewhere (Foster & Cone, 1980; Kazdin, 1977b; Kent & Foster, 1977; Nelson, Lipinski, & Boykin, 1978). As multiple observation methods are applied across behaviors, analysis and interpretation of these data will depend on careful attention to the issues mentioned above.

INTEROBSERVER RELIABILITY

The effectiveness of data based decision making is dependent on reliability of measurement. In behavioral assessment, reliability usually refers to the degree of agreement obtained by two or more individuals who use an identical observation method to record the same behavior(s). The calculation of interobserver agreement (reliability) can be done in several different ways. With frequency recording, the reliability coefficient can be obtained by determining agreement on frequency of behaviors observed in a given time period. For example, if observer 1 recorded 10 instances of hitting behavior and observer 2 recorded 9 instances, reliability is determined by dividing the smaller obtained frequency by the larger, i.e., $9 \div 10$ = 90 percent. With duration and latency data, reliability is calculated by dividing the smaller total time obtained by the larger time recorded. For example, if observer 1 recorded 30 minutes of tantrum behavior in an hour and observer 2 recorded 45 minutes of tantruming in the same period, interobserver agreement for the duration measurement would be 75 percent (i.e., $30 \div 45$). Conventionally, 90 percent or better is considered adequate reliability. With more complex behaviors that may be extremely difficult to observe, however, agreement coefficients of 80 percent or better may be acceptable.

With interval data, there are several different ways to determine interobserver agreement. Two methods frequently reported are interval by interval and occurrence agreement. For the following set of data obtained by two persons observing the on-task behavior of a mentally retarded adult, these methods are briefly explained.

Intervals (15 sec.): Momentary Recording

	1	2	3	4	5	6	7	8	9	10	11	12	13	14	15	16	17	18	19	20
Observer #1	–	–	+	–	–	–	–	+	+	–	–	–	–	+	+	+	+	–	+	–	–
Observer #2	–	–	+	–	–	–	–	+	+	–	–	–	+	–	+	–	–	–	–	–

For interval by interval reliability, an agreement is counted in each interval in which both observers recorded either a (+) or a (–). In the preceding example intervals 1–13, 15, 17, 19, and 20 would be scored as agreements and intervals 14, 16, and 18 would be scored as disagreements. The formula for determining reliability would be as follows:

$$\frac{\text{Agreements (17)}}{\text{Agreements (17) + Disagreements (3)}} \times 100 = 85$$

Occurrence reliability is a method for determining interobserver agreement that only includes intervals in which one or both observers recorded the occurrence of a behavior, i.e., on-task. In the above, example, intervals 3, 8, 9, 13, and 15 would be scored as agreements and intervals 14, 16, and 18 would be scored as disagreements. The formula for determining reliability would be as follows:

$$\frac{\text{Agreements (5)}}{\text{Agreements (5) + Disagreements (3)}} \times 100 = 62.5$$

By each of the above methods for determining interobserver agreement, the resulting coefficients of 85 and 62.5 may lead to different conclusions about accuracy of the data. In the first case, the reliability coefficient is marginally acceptable, whereas in the second, this coefficient is far below conventional standards.

The consensus of professional opinion is that occurrence reliability is a more stringent test of interobserver agreement. Regardless of the interobserver agreement method used, however, it is recommended that reliability be demonstrated prior to program implementation and evaluated periodically across all phases of a behavior reduction program. Training of observers and various types of feedback have been suggested as effective strategies to establish acceptable reliability and maintain consistency of observation. If acceptable levels of reliability cannot be established with increased observer training, the operational definitions must be revised or the observational system(s) changed until satisfactory interobserver agreement is demonstrated (Hersen & Barlow, 1976).

BASELINE ASSESSMENT

Before selecting and implementing an intervention procedure, baseline assessment data should be collected in all settings in which the target behaviors are of importance. These settings may include home, school, work, and community. Baseline assessment conditions should be as similar to the anticipated posttreatment conditions as possible. In most cases, baseline data should be collected until the performance level of the behavior is stable or a trend in the data is evident in a countertherapeutic direction (e.g., swearing at peers is steadily increasing). The detection of "stability" or "trend" in assessment data is aided by graphic displays. Graphic displays of data should result in the presentation of information

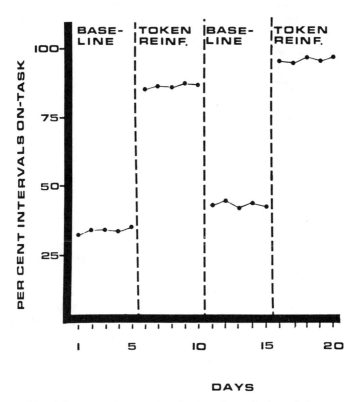

Fig. 2-7.   Attending to task during baseline and token reinforcement

in a manner that promotes ease of understanding. If data are made understandable, it is probable that this information will be used more effectively for decision making. For example, inspection of the sample graph presented in Figure 2-7 indicates a clear relationship between token reinforcement and on-task behavior.

Although approximately 5 days of baseline data usually will be sufficient, the severity of certain behaviors (e.g., extreme SIB, physical aggression) may mitigate the appropriateness of lengthy baseline assessments. In these cases, there may be social pressure to intervene immediately without the collection of any baseline data. Although these authors acknowledge the validity of such concerns, it is still advisable to collect some initial assessment data, even if the amount of data may be extremely limited. Without this data, there is little objective basis on which to evaluate the effectiveness of specific intervention efforts.

SOCIAL ACCEPTABILITY OF PROCEDURES

Since intervention with aberrant behaviors may necessitate the use of procedures that are relatively intrusive (e.g., punishment techniques), the social acceptability of these procedures should be examined. Unfortunately, this examination rarely occurs and little has been written about this aspect of social validation. Avoiding this issue by neglecting to subject various intervention procedures to public scrutiny, however, only promotes misunderstanding and may ultimately undo the effectiveness of such efforts.

According to Wolf (1978), the likelihood that the program will be adopted and supported by others will play a key role in overall program success. If the target person (consumer), teacher, or significant other are opposed to specific intervention procedures, treatment success could be sabotaged. At the very minimum, the consumer or guardian, or both, should be involved in treatment selection.

Some data have been generated relevant to this aspect of social validity. Foxx and Azrin (1972) reported that care-givers found restitution overcorrection procedures more acceptable than time-out or response contingent shock. In a discussion article, Homer and Peterson (1980) suggest that differential reinforcement procedures provide a more preferred response suppression approach than other reductive techniques. Kazdin (1980, 1981) has recently completed two laboratory studies in which college students were provided information and given the opportunity to view videotape sequences of different intervention techniques. In Kazdin's 1980 study, reinforcement of incompatible behavior and non-exclusionary time-out were preferred over an isolation procedure. When isolation was established as part of a contingency contract, however, the acceptability of this procedure increased substantially.

Kazdin (1981) furthered this line of research by presenting slightly different problem situations (aggressive behavior and non-compliant behavior), providing different treatment options, and suggesting the presence of differing side effects (weak or strong). For both problem situations, the order of treatment acceptability (most acceptable to least) was : (1) reinforcement, (2) positive practice, (3) time-out, and (4) medication. The presence of negative side effects resulted in suppressing the rated acceptability of all treatments, but did not result in significant interaction effects.

As applied behavior analysis interventions are extended into more natural community settings, detailed assessment of treatment acceptability should be programmatically valuable. In this vein, Menchetti, Rusch, and Lamson (in press) have provided us with an excellent example of extending this aspect of social validation to food service employers. A few of their results pertinent to decreasing inappropriate behaviors of the mentally retarded are: no employers would allow yelling as an error correction, 64 percent would not allow an error to be ignored,

93 percent would not allow inappropriate behavior to be ignored, and 65 percent would not allow token reinforcement systems to be used.

Several important considerations must be made when selecting behavior management procedures for specifically defined behaviors. With specific behavior problems, several different procedures that have been used effectively should be identified. These procedures may include differential reinforcement, extinction, response cost, time-out, overcorrection, and presentations of aversive consequences. The selection of a specific procedure will depend on multiple factors, including evidence of effectiveness, degree of intrusiveness, social acceptability, and the competencies of the training staff. If the training staff is unfamiliar with a particular procedure, either this procedure cannot be used or the staff must be provided adequate training. When aversive procedures are suggested, the following program steps must be taken: (1) obtain informed consent, (2) conduct a human rights review, (3) have adequate professional supervision, and (4) include positive reinforcement for alternative behaviors.

In summary, the reductive procedure that is selected for a behavior problem should be the least intrusive, albeit effective procedure available. This procedure must have the support of the consumer, training staff, and supervisory personnel. Behavior contracting is a method that is often used to formalize this support by specifying the mutual responsibilities and cooperative working relationships of all persons participating in a behavior management program. Once a procedure has been selected, assessment concerns shift to an evaluation of program effectiveness. Central to this evaluation is the issue of procedural reliability.

PROCEDURAL RELIABILITY

Procedural reliability is a measure of consistency by which an intervention is implemented in the prescribed manner. To determine procedural reliability, independent observers record the specific components of an intervention. Reliability is calculated by comparing these independent observations. For example, Martin, Pallotta-Cornick, Johnstone, and Goyos (1980) collected procedural reliability on a supervisory strategy in a sheltered workshop involving staff delivered general work prompts, corrective feedback, and number of interactions with clients. An independent observer's assessment of staff behavior was compared to a supervisor's record of the staff's adherence to the specified program.

Although the importance of reliability has been emphasized in regard to assessment of the target behaviors (dependent variables), procedural reliability has been largely ignored in applied behavior analysis research (Bailey & Bostow, 1979; Billingsley, White, & Munson, 1980). Considering the effort put into the training of staff and the specification of intervention procedures, it is surprising that little has been reported concerning the reliability of adherence to intervention procedures (Billingsley et al., 1980). Assessment of procedural reliability is important as it cannot be automatically assumed that procedures are implemented properly and continuously or even implemented at all (Kazdin, 1978).

Since consistent implementation of the intended treatment procedure is absolutely essential for a valid assessment of program effectiveness, evaluation of procedural reliability is necessary. This aspect of program assessment is certain to become an integral component of applied behavior analysis research in the future. In behavior reduction programs, where controversial procedures may be prescribed, documentation of procedural reliability is essential.

FUNCTIONAL ANALYSIS

A functional analysis refers to the investigation of relationships between independent and dependent variables. Independent variables are those antecedent and consequence conditions that can be manipulated, while dependent variables are measured behaviors. With a functional analysis, we are attempting to show that the strength of a behavior is dependent on the presence or absence of specific antecedent or consequence conditions (independent variables).

As discussed previously, baseline assessment of the dependent variable(s) should precede the manipulation of antecedent or consequence variables. This initial assessment information provides a comparison base from which the effectiveness of specific independent variables can be evaluated. The existence of a functional relationship can be documented by demonstrating that the manipulation of an independent variable results in a change in the performance level and/or trend of the dependent variables.

Several single subject research designs have been successfully used for the purpose of investigating and confirming the existence of functional relationships. In a review of 56 studies involving behavior management interventions with mentally retarded persons, Bates and Wehman (1977) found that the reversal design was used to evaluate treatment effectiveness in 43 percent of the studies. Figure 2-7 provides the reader with an example of the reversal design. Inspection of this figure reveals that increases in the target behavior were dependent on the presence of the independent variable. Although this design has been the most frequently used procedure, it has come into increasing disfavor because it requires a reversal of treatment gains in order to demonstrate a functional relationship between variables. In the past few years, the multiple baseline and multielement design have emerged as alternative evaluation procedures that do not require the premature termination of a treatment procedure. It is beyond the scope of this chapter to present the subtleties of those research designs and other alternative means for conducting a functional analysis. For more in-depth understanding of those procedures, Hersen and Barlow (1976) have written an excellent text.

One of the primary goals of behavioral assessment is to identify the variables that control the occurrence of specific behaviors. Accurate measurement of all relevant behaviors and behavioral dimensions, plus the systematic manipulation of antecedent and consequence conditions, make such a functional analysis possible. By conducting these analyses, our understanding of environmental conditions that promote prosocial behvior and suppress inappropriate behavior is increased.

SOCIAL SIGNIFICANCE OF BEHAVIOR CHANGE

A functional analysis identifies the existence of a relationship between independent variables (e.g., treatment components) and dependent variables (e.g., target behaviors). The documentation of such a relationship has little meaning unless we can demonstrate the social value or clinical significance of the behavior change. According to Wolf (1978), "If we aspire to social importance, we must develop systems that allow our consumers to feedback about how our applications relate to their values, to their reinforcers" (p. 213). Social validation outcome assessment provides the practitioner with a system for involving consumers and others in the process of evaluating program results. As discussed previously, social comparison and subjective evaluation are two specific methodologies that have been used for social validation purposes.

In the O'Brien and Azrin (1972) study, the posttreatment eating behaviors of institutionalized mentally retarded persons actually exceeded their social comparison group, i.e., customers at a local restaurant. Matson, Kazdin, and Esveldt-Dawson (1980) used a sample of four non-handicapped children to establish "comparative" levels of performance on a social skills assessment. As an outcome evaluation of social skills training with two moderately mentally retarded children, the scores of the mentally retarded children were compared to the "normal" comparison group. Scores of the retarded children equalled or surpassed those attained by children of normal intelligence. By demonstrating that the training program resulted in performance increases that made mentally retarded individuals indistinguishable from the non-handicapped comparison group, the significance of behavior change assumes social value.

Subjective evaluation is another technique for assessing the social value of behavior change. In an attempt to verify the apparent success of a program to reduce the number of conversational topics repeated by a mentally retarded man in a vocational setting, Rusch, Weithers, Menchetti, and Schutz (1980) surveyed co-workers regarding their opinion on program effectiveness. Surprisingly, the co-workers rated the client as unimproved. Evidently, the behavior change was insufficient to influence co-worker ratings and/or the observation system was too narrowly focused to identify all clinically significant aspects of the target behavior.

Recently, Davis, Bates, and Cuvo (in press) validated the effectiveness of a program that resulted in competitive work production levels by a moderately mentally retarded worker in a food service setting. Co-worker ratings of the worker's performance before and after a training program confirmed the success of the program.

Social validation assessment needs to be an integral part of all habilitation efforts involving mentally retarded persons. By selecting significant goals, selecting acceptable treatments, and producing socially valuable outcomes, the goals of normalization are more attainable (Kazdin & Matson, 1981).

GENERALIZATION ASSESSMENT

The social value of program outcomes is strongly influenced by the degree of generalization that is demonstrated. Stokes and Baer (1977) define generalization as,

The occurrence of relevant behavior under different, non-training conditions (i.e., across subjects, settings, people, behavior, and/or time) without the scheduling of the same events in those conditions as had been scheduled in the training conditions. (p. 350)

Unfortunately, extensive assessment of generalized program effects has not been common practice. According to Kazdin (1977a), assessment results may be specific to the restricted set of conditions under which they were recorded. Since the success of an intervention program is ultimately judged by the degree to which behavior changes are evidenced in a variety of different contexts, assessment activities must be multifaceted. Drabman, Hammer, and Rosenbaum (1979) proposed a conceptual framework (i.e., Generalization Map) for conducting such a multifaceted assessment. In Figure 2-8, generalization assessment activities associated with this conceptual framework are presented. These assessment activities highlight the importance of analyzing multiple behaviors [target behavior(s) and non-target behavior(s)] emitted by multiple subjects (target and non-target subjects), in multiple settings (treatment and non-treatment), at different times (during treatment and after treatment). Although such a complete generalization assessment is not always necessary, the fact that we need to be more comprehensive in our assessment practices cannot be disputed.

· Much of the concern for a more broad-based assessment of generalized program effects can be traced to an increased ecological perspective in behavioral assessment. According to Willems (1974), research is needed that investigates unanticipated outcomes of behavior change programs. Voeltz and Evans recently (1982) emphasized that treatment outcome cannot be determined unless intended and unintended dependent variables are measured.

The assessment of inappropriate behavior must include an extensive investigation of generalization. From such an analysis, the effectiveness of specific intervention procedures can be judged more accurately and responsibly. The examples provided in Figure 2-8 are suggestive of the multiple assessment options that could be pursued.

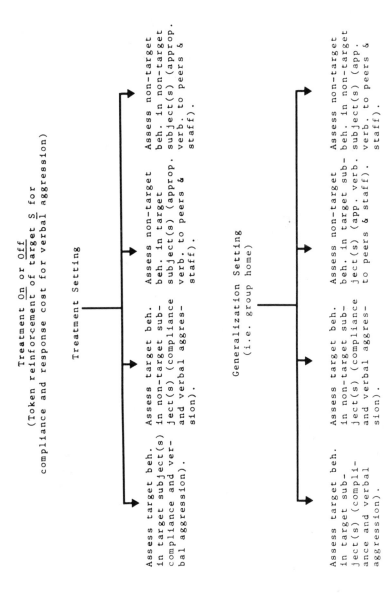

Treatment <u>On</u> or <u>Off</u>
(Token reinforcement of target $\underline{S}$ for
compliance and response cost for verbal aggression)

Treatment Setting

Assess target beh. in target subject(s) compliance and verbal aggression).

Assess target beh. in non-target subject(s) (compliance and verbal aggression).

Assess non-target beh. in target subject(s) (approp. verb. to peers & staff).

Assess non-target beh. in non-target subject(s) (approp. subject(s) verb. to peers & staff).

Generalization Setting
(i.e. group home)

Assess target beh. in target subject(s) (compliance and verbal aggression).

Assess target beh. in non-target subject(s) (compliance and verbal aggression).

Assess non-target beh. in target subject(s) (app. verb. verb. to peers & staff).

Assess non-target beh. in non-target subject(s) (app. verb. to peers & staff).

Fig. 2-8. Generalization assessment across behaviors, subjects, settings, and time

57

CONCLUSION

In this chapter several components of a comprehensive behavioral assessment were described. These components were integrated into a multidimensional model of assessment procedures. Common to all dimensions of this model is an applied behavior analysis orientation and methodology. A brief overview of the assessment procedures associated with this model is subsequently presented.

Initially a decision must be made regarding whether to invest time and energy into more formal assessment and possible intervention with particular behaviors. A key component of this decision will be the social significance of the behavior(s) of interest. With inappropriate behavior patterns, social significance is often defined in terms of the excessive, deficit, or situational characteristics of the behavior. An emerging methodology for determining social significance is social validation assessment. Two methods of social validation assessment are social comparison and subjective evaluation. Social comparison relies on observations of a peer group for the purpose of identifying target behaviors, while subjective evaluation requires the behavior ratings of significant others to establish program priorities.

When social significance has been established, structured narrative observations of antecedent conditions, behavior(s) of interest, and consequence events are recommended. Through these observations, the interrelationships and interdependencies of behavior and environmental variables can be more fully analyzed. This analysis is consistent with the ecobehavioral approach and results in a more thorough understanding of the target behavior(s).

From these narrative assessments, definitions of target behaviors are developed to ensure valid and reliable observation. A well-written definition is stated in terms of the operations used in its measurement. The resulting ''operational definitions'' assist the practitioner in selecting the assessment method that most efficiently and accurately measures relevant behavioral dimensions. Frequency, duration, latency, and interval time sampling are direct observation procedures that are useful for assessing inappropriate behaviors in a variety of different settings. The unique characteristics of particular behaviors and availability of assessment resources (e.g., personnel, time, equipment, etc.) will influence the selection of specific observation procedures. In many instances it is advisable to use multiple assessment methods to measure different dimensions of the same behavior. With whatever observation method selected, the assurance of interobserver agreement (reliability) in measuring the target behavior is a necessity. Several alternative procedures are available for calculating reliability with different observation methods. Minimal standards in this area include periodic reliability checks throughout all phases of a program and interobserver agreement coefficients of 80 percent or better.

Prior to the implementation of a behavior change program, observational assessment data should be collected in all settings in which the target behavior is of importance. These observations constitute the baseline from which the effectiveness of specific intervention programs is evaluated. After baseline data have been collected, an intervention procedure must be selected and implemented. In behavior reduction programs involving relatively intrusive procedures, social acceptability of the intervention is extremely important. A social validation process is recommended as one method for documenting the acceptability and support for a program. This process generally involves the presentation of program alternatives and the rating of acceptability by significant persons (e.g., consumers, program personnel, relatives, etc.).

Consistent adherence to the intended procedures is essential when a program is implemented. The assessment of procedural reliability (degree of agreement between written procedures and actual procedures) has recently been proposed as one method for assuring consistent program implementation. If a program is implemented consistently and behaviors are measured reliably, an evaluation of the relationship between independent and dependent variables becomes possible. This evaluation is referred to as a functional analysis. Several single-subject research designs are particularly useful for conducting a functional analysis and for investigating the effectiveness of specific intervention efforts. Another aspect of program evaluation is the social significance of behavior change. The social comparison and subjective evaluation methods of social validation assessment are helpful in this determination. By showing that programs have resulted in performance that makes participants more like non-handicapped persons and/or more acceptable to others, the social significance of behavior change is established.

Finally, a comprehensive assessment is not complete until the target behaviors are observed under generalization conditions. At a minimum this requires observation of behavior(s) in different settings and at different times (during and after program). Other aspects of a generalization assessment include observations of multiple behaviors (target and non-target) in program participants and non-participants. From these generalization assessments, information is accumulated from which program effectiveness can be more thoroughly evaluated.

Each dimension of the model described above contributes to the overall value of the assessment process. By systematically incorporating multiple procedures in behavioral assessment, our understanding of behavior-environment interrelationships is broadened and our ability to assist mentally retarded persons in acquiring socially competent behavior is advanced.

As the assessment process becomes more sophisticated, attention must expand from the evaluation of single inappropriate behaviors to an analysis of multiple dependent behaviors in multiple settings with multiple assessment methods. Further, social validation should prove extremely useful for the purposes of identifying socially significant program goals, selecting socially acceptable treatment procedures, and evaluating the social value of program results.

Future research is needed to assist us in better selecting unique assessment methods for unique presenting problems. As more complex behavioral observation systems are designed for multiple assessment purposes, interpretation of these data will pose new problems. Researchers need to develop more sophisticated procedures for analyzing relationships and interrelationships between variables.

The value of assessment data is ultimately dependent on the quality of program decisions that emanate from use of the information. According to Agras, Kazdin, and Wilson (1979), a complete behavioral assessment reveals the current causes that determine the presenting problem. By using the multidimensional assessment model presented in this chapter, it is more likely that contributing variables will be isolated, effective program decisions will be made, and treatment effectiveness will be comprehensively evaluated.

REFERENCES

Agras, WS, Kazdin, AE, & Wilson, GT. *Behavior therapy: Toward an applied clinical science*. San Francisco: Freeman, 1979

Aitchison, RA. A low-cost, rapid delivery point system with "automatic" recording. *Journal of Applied Behavior Analysis*, 1972, *5*, 527–528

Arrington, RE. Time sampling in studies of social behavior: A critical review of techniques and results with research suggestions. *Psychological Bulletin*, 1943, *40*, 81–124

Bailey, JS, & Bostow, DE. *Research methods in applied behavior analysis*, 1979

Baker, JG, & Whitehead, G. A portable recording apparatus for rating behavior in free-operant situations. *Journal of Applied Behavior Analysis*, 1972, *5*, 191–192

Bates, P, & Wehman, P. Behavior management with the mentally retarded: An empirical analysis of the research. *Mental Retardation*, 1977, *15*, 9–12

Baumeister, AA, & Forehand, R. Stereotyped acts. In NR Ellis (Ed.), *International review of research in mental retardation* (Vol. 7). New York: Academic Press, 1973

Berkson, G, & Davenport, RK. Stereotyped movements in mental defectives: I. Initial survey. *American Journal of Mental Deficiency*, 1962, *66*, 849–852

Bernal, ME, Gibson, DM, Williams, DE, & Pesses, DI. A device for automatic audio tape recording. *Journal of Applied Behavior Analysis*, 1971, *4*, 151–156

Billingsley, F, White, OR, & Munson, R. Procedural reliability: A rationale and an example. *Behavioral Assessment*, 1980, *2*, 229–241

Boer, AP. Application of a simple recording system to the analysis of freeplay behavior in autistic children. *Journal of Applied Behavior Analysis*, 1968, *1*, 335–340

Brechner, KC, Linder, DE, Meyerson, L, & Hays, VL. A brief report on a device for unobtrusive visual recording. *Journal of Applied Behavior Analysis*, 1974, *7*, 499–500

Carroll, PJ. A durable recording and feedback system. *Journal of Applied Behavior Analysis*, 1977, *10*, 339–340

Coleman, R, & Toth, E. The adaptations of commercially available radio control equipment to behavior therapy. *Journal of Applied Behavior Analysis*, 1970, *3*, 221–222

Colman, AD, & Borens, JJ. An information system for measuring patient behavior and its use by staff. *Journal of Applied Behavior Analysis*, 1969, *2*, 207–214

Cone, JD. The behavioral assessment grid (BAG): A conceptual framework and taxonomy. *Behavior Therapy*, 1978, *9*, 882–888

Corte, HE, Wolf, MM, & Locker, BJ. A comparison of procedures for eliminating self-injurious behavior of retarded adolescents. *Journal of Applied Behavior Analysis*, 1971, *4*, 201–213

Davis, P, Bates, P, & Cuvo, A. Training a mentally retarded female to work competitively: Effect of graphic feedback and a changing criterion design. In *Education and Training of the Mentally Retarded* (in press).

Drabman, R, Hammer, D, & Rosenbaum, MS. Assessing generalization in behavior modification with children: The generalization map. *Behavioral Assessment*, 1979, *1*, 203–219

Edleson, JL. An inexpensive instrument for rapid recording of "in vivo" observations. *Journal of Applied Behavior Analysis*, 1978, *4*, 502

Fitzsimmons, JR. A behavioral tachometer. *Journal of Applied Behavior Analysis*, 1978, *11*, 438

Forehand, R, & Baumeister, AA. Deceleration of aberrant behavior among retarded individuals. In M Hersen, RM Eisler, & PM Miller (Eds.), *Progress in behavior modification* (Vol. 2). New York: Academic Press, 1976

Foster, J, & Cone, J. Current issues in direct observation. *Behavioral Assessment*, 1980, *2*, 313–338

Foxx, RM, & Azrin, NH. Restitution: A method of eliminating aggressive-disruptive behavior of retarded and brain damaged patients. *Behavior Research and Therapy*, 1972, *10*, 15–27

Foxx, RM, & Martin, ED. Treatment of scavenging behavior (coprophagy and pica) by overcorrection. *Behavior Research and Therapy*, 1975, *13*, 153–162

Foxx, RM, & Martin, PL. A useful portable timer. *Journal of Applied Behavior Analysis*, 1971, *4*, 60

Frankel, F, & Weber, D. A portable low-cost multi-channel timing apparatus for collection of observational duration data. *Journal of Applied Behavior Analysis*, 1978, *11*, 522

Gaylord-Ross, R. A decision model for the treatment of aberrant behavior in applied settings. In W Sailor, B Wilcox, & L Brown (Eds.), *Methods of instruction for severely handicapped students*. Baltimore: Paul H. Brookes, 1980

Greenwald, M. Audiotaping social-skills responses. *Journal of Applied Behavior Analysis*, 1977, *310*, 254

Guitar, B, & Andrews, G. An inexpensive counter. *Journal of Applied Behavior Analysis*, 1977, *10*, 530

Hanson, RH, Tyler, RM, & Hedge, BA. An inexpensive one-way mirror. *Journal of Applied Behavior Analysis*, 1976, *9*, 212

Hardiman, SA, Goetz, EM, Reuter, KE, & LeBlanc, JM. Primes, contingent attention, and training: Effects on a child's motor behavior. *Journal of Applied Behavior Analysis*, 1975, *8*, 399–410

Hersen, M, & Barlow, DH. *Single case experimental designs*. New York: Pergamon Press, 1976

Homer, AL, & Peterson, L. Differential reinforcement of other's behavior: A preferred response elimination procedure. *Behavior Therapy*, 1980, *11*, 449–471

Katz, RC. A procedure for concurrently measuring elapsed time and response frequency. *Journal of Applied Behavior Analysis*, 1973, *6*, 719–720

Kazdin, AE. Artifact, bias, and complexity of assessment: The ABC's of reliability. *Journal of Applied Behavior Analysis*, 1977, *10*, 141–150 (a)

Kazdin, AE. Assessing the clinical or applied importance of behavior change through social validation. *Behavior Modification*, 1977, *1*, 427–451 (b)

Kazdin, AE. Acceptability of alternative treatments for deviant child behavior. *Journal of Applied Behavior Analysis*, 1980, *13*, 259–273

Kazdin, AE. Acceptability of child treatment techniques: The influence of treatment efficacy and adverse side effects. *Behavior Therapy*, 1981, *12*, 493–506

Kazdin, AE, & Matson JL. Social validation in mental retardation. *Applied Research in Mental Retardation*, 1981, *2*, 39–53

Kent, R, & Foster, S. Direct observational procedures: Methodological issues in naturalistic settings. In A Ciminero, K Calhoun, & HE Adams (Eds.), *Handbook of behavioral assessment*. New York: Wiley, 1977

Knapp, CW. A portable, one-way observation screen. *Journal of Applied Behavior Analysis*, 1978, *11*, 284

Kubany, ES, & Sloggett, BB. Coding procedure for teachers. *Journal of Applied Behavior Analysis*, 1973, *6*, 338–344

Lehrer, P, Schif, L, & Kris, A. The use of a credit card in a token economy. *Journal of Applied Behavior Analysis*, 1970, *3*, 289–291

Lindsley, OR. Direct measurement and prosthesis of retarded behavior. *Journal of Education*, 1964, *147*, 62–81

Lindsley, OR. A reliable wrist counter for recording behavior rates. *Journal of Applied Behavior Analysis*, 1968, *1*, 77

Logan, DL. A "paper money" token system as a recording aid in institutional settings. *Journal of Applied Behavior Analysis*, 1970, *3*, 183–184

Martin, G, Pallotta-Cornick, A, Johnstone, G, & Goyos, AC. A supervisory strategy to improve work performance for lower-functioning clients in a sheltered work shop. *Journal of Applied Behavior Analysis*, 1980, *13*, 183–190

Mash, EJ. What is behavioral assessment? *Behavioral Assessment*, 1979, *1*, 23–29

Matson, J, Kazdin, A, & Esveldt-Dawson, K. Training interpersonal skills among mentally retarded and socially dysfunctional children. *Behaviour Research and Therapy*, 1980, *18*, 419–429

Mattos, RL. A manual counter for recording multiple behavior. *Journal of Applied Behavior Analysis*, 1968, *1*, 130

Menchetti, BM, Rusch, FR, & Lamson, DS. *Social validation of behavioral training techniques: Assessing the normalizing qualities of competitive employment*, (in press)

Milby, JB, Willcutt, HC, & Hawk, JW. A system for recording individualized behavioral data in a token program. *Journal of Applied Behavior Analysis*, 1973, *6*, 333–338

Mithaug, DE, & Hagmeier, LD. The development of procedures to assess prevocational competencies of severely handicapped young adults. *AAESPH Review*, 1978, *3*, 94–115

Nelson, R, Lipinski, D, & Boykin, R. The effects of self recorders' training and the obtrusiveness of the self recording device on the accuracy and reactivity of self monitoring. *Behavior Therapy*, 1978, *9*, 200–208

Nelson, RO, & Hayes, SC. Some current dimensions of behavioral assessment. *Behavioral Assessment*, 1979, *1*, 1–16

Nordquist, VM. A method for recording verbal behavior in free-play settings. *Journal of Applied Behavior Analysis*, 1971, *4*, 327–331

Nunes, DL, Murphy, RJ, & Hutchings-Ruprecht, ML. Reducing self-injurious behavior of severely retarded individuals through withdrawal of reinforcement procedures. *Behavior Modification*, 1977, *1*, 499–515

O'Brien, F, & Azrin, NH. Developing proper mealtime behaviors of the institutionalized retarded. *Journal of Applied Behavior Analysis*, 1972, *5*, 389–399

Porterfield, JK, Herbert-Jackson, E, & Risley, TR. Contingent observation: An effective and acceptable procedure for reducing disruptive behavior of young children in a group setting. *Journal of Applied Behavior Analysis*, 1976, *9*, 55–64

Powell, J, Martindale, A, & Kulp, S. An evaluation of time sample measures of behavior. *Journal of Applied Behavior Analysis*, 1975, *8*, 463–469

Powell, J, Martindale, B, Kulp, S, Martindale, A, & Bauman, R. Taking a closer look: Time sampling and measurement error. *Journal of Applied Behavior Analysis*, 1977, *10*, 325–332

Quilitch, HR. A portable programmed, audible timer. *Journal of Applied Behavior Analysis*, 1972, *5*, 18

Rago, WV Jr, Parker, RM, & Cleland, C. Effect of increased space on the social behavior of institutionalized profoundly retarded male adults. *American Journal of Mental Deficiency*, 1978, *82*, 554–558

Renzaglia, A, & Bates, P. Teaching socially appropriate behavior. In M Snell (Ed.), *Systematic instruction of the moderately and severely handicapped* (2nd ed.). Columbus: Merrill, 1983

Rogers-Warren, A, & Warren, S (Eds.). *Ecological perspectives in behavior analysis*. Baltimore: University Park Press, 1977

Ross, RT. Behavioral correlates of levels of intelligence. *American Journal of Mental Deficiency*, 1972, *76*, 515–519

Rusch, FR, Schutz, RP, & Agran, M. *Validating entry-level survival skills for service occupations: Implications for curriculum development* (in press)

Rusch, FR, Weithers, Menchetti, JA, & Schutz, RP. Social validation of a program to reduce topic repetition in a non-sheltered setting. *Education and Training of the Mentally Retarded*, 1980, *15*, 208–215

Sanders, RM, Hopkins, BL, & Walker, MB. An inexpensive method for making data records of complex behaviors. *Journal of Applied Behavior Analysis*, 1969, *2*, 221–222

Schroeder, SR. Automated transduction of sheltered workshop behaviors. *Journal of Applied Behavior Analysis*, 1972, *5*, 523–525

Sidman, M. *Tactics in scientific research*. New York: Basic Books, 1960

Simpson, R, & Sasso, G. The modification of rumination in a severely emotionally disturbed child through overcorrection procedures. *AAESPH Review*, 1978, *3*, 145–150

Stokes, TF, & Baer, DM. An implicit technology of generalization. *Journal of Applied Behavior Analysis*, 1977, *10*, 349–367

Strang, HR, & George, JR III. Clowning around to stop clowning around: A brief report on an automated approach to monitor, record, and control classroom noise. *Journal of Applied Behavior Analysis*, 1975, *8*, 471–474

Sulzer-Azaroff, B, & Mayer, GR. *Applying behavior analysis procedures with children and youth*. New York: Holt, Rinehart and Winston, 1977, pp. 11–25

Tanner, BA, & Zeiler, M. Punishment of self-injurious behavor using aromatic ammonia as the aversive stimulus. *Journal of Applied Behavior Analysis*, 1975, *8*, 53–58

Tate, BG. An automated system for reinforcing and recording retarded work behavior. *Journal of Applied Behavior Analysis*, 1968, *1*, 347–348

Voeltz, L, & Evans, I. The assessment of behavioral interrelationships in child behavior therapy. *Behavioral Assessment*, 1982, *4*, 131–165

Vukelich, R, & Hake, DF. Reduction of dangerously aggressive behavior in a severely retarded resident through a combination of positive reinforcement procedures. *Journal of Applied Behavior Analysis*, 1971, *4*, 215–225

Weisberg, P, Passman, RH, & Russell, JE. Development of verbal control over bizarre gestures of retardates through imitative and nonimitative reinforcement procedures. *Journal of Applied Behavior Analysis*, 1973, *6*, 487–495

Willems, EP. Behavioral technology and behavior ecology. *Journal of Applied Behavior Analysis*, 1974, *7*, 151–165

Wolf, MM. Social validity: The case for subjective measurement or how applied behavior analysis is finding its heart. *Journal of Applied Behavior Analysis*, 1978, *11*, 203–214

Wolfensberger, W. *The principle of normalization in human services*. Toronto: National Institute of Mental Retardation, 1972

Wood, DD, Callahan, EJ, Alevizos, PN, & Teigen, JR. A behaviorally based log book. *Journal of Applied Behavior Analysis*, 1977, *10*, 706

Worthy, RC. A miniature, portable timer and audible signaling device. *Journal of Applied Behavior Analysis*, 1968, *1*, 159–160

Alan Poling
Carol Parker

3

Empirical Strategies

Assessment simply involves collecting information about an individual. One major purpose of assessment is to identify individuals with certain characteristics. For example, the mentally retarded exhibit significantly subaverage intellectual functioning existing concurrently with defecits in adaptive behavior, both manifested during the developmental period (Grossman, 1977). A second purpose of assessment is to guide caregivers in determining an individual's needs, and developing interventions to meet these needs. Ascertaining whether the selected treatments are successful is the final end served by assessment.

This chapter summarizes general strategies of treatment evaluation. Special emphasis is placed on procedures apt to be useful to caregivers in their daily attempts to meet the needs of the mentally retarded, and the problems likely to be encountered when these procedures are employed.

GENERAL CONSIDERATIONS IN
TREATMENT EVALUATION

The sole objective of treatment evaluation is to determine whether one variable, the intervention of interest, produces a desired change in a second variable, often some aspect of a client's behavior. This is best done by employing the experimental methods of science. There is no mystery to experimentation. One determines whether an independent variable (treatment) affects a dependent variable (measure of behavior) by comparing levels of the dependent variable when the independent variable is and is not operative (or is operative at different values). Factors other than the independent variable are held as constant as possible across conditions, thus if levels of the dependent variable differ when treatment is and is not present (or is present at different values), it is logical to assume that behavior changes as a function of treatment, which is therefore deemed active.

Two tactics can be adopted in treatment evaluation. In one, treatment levels are varied and comparisons made between individuals. In the other, treatment levels are varied and comparisons made within individuals. Regardless of whether within-subject or between-subjects comparisons are arranged, the behavior of interest must be adequately quantified. In general, an assessment device can be evaluated along the dimensions of validity (i.e., does it actually measure the phenomenon of interest?), reliability (i.e., does it provide an unvarying measure across time and situations if the phenomenon of interest does not change?), and sensitivity (i.e., is it capable of changing as a result of intervention?). The various assessment devices that can be used with the mentally retarded are discussed elsewhere in this volume. We simply want to emphasize that performance can be indexed in many ways, which do not necessarily yield comparable results. This can be seen in Figure 3-1, which shows how a hypothetical behavior would be scored if different strategies of direct observation were employed.

In direct observation, another person actually watches the client and records his or her behavior. To facilitate recording and quantification, time-sampling and intermittent time-sampling* procedures are commonly used. In time-sampling, an observational period is divided into discrete intervals and the observer records whether or not the behavior appeared in each interval, whereas in intermittent time-sampling observation occurs in only a few intervals, typically selected at random. With either observational system, partial interval or whole interval recording may be used. In partial interval recording, an observer scores (i.e., indicates that the target behavior occurred in) any interval in which the response definition was met, regardless of the duration of occurrence of the behavior. In whole interval recording, an interval is scored only if the response definition was met without interruption throughout the interval.

Figure 3-1 depicts how a hypothetical response would be scored during baseline (no treatment) and treatment sessions under partial interval time-sampling, whole interval time-sampling, partial interval intermittent time-sampling, and whole interval intermittent time-sampling procedures. Also presented in this figure are the values that would be obtained if the response were quantified according to frequency or duration of occurrence. Depending on mode of assessment, the data presented in the figure indicate that treatment increased, decreased, or had no effect on the target behavior. The treatment evaluator cannot afford to be cavalier with regard to specific aspects of direct observation—they do make a difference.

In selecting an observation system, be sure that the system adopted maxi-

---

*Several diverse terms have been used to describe the methods of data collection we discuss (see Repp et al., 1976), and inconsistencies are occasionally apparent in the way a particular term is used by different writers. Thus one must pay close attention to how behavior actually was scored in an investigation, irrespective of the name assigned to the method of data collection.

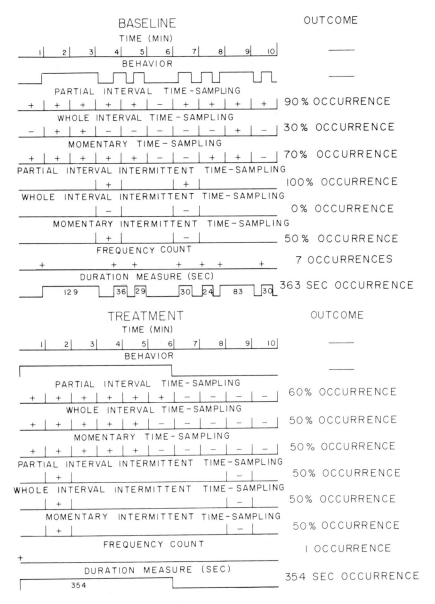

Fig. 3-1. Results obtained if a hypothetical behavior were scored using various strategies of direct observation

mally reflects the aspects of behavior that are changeworthy. Beyond this, systems that arrange frequent observation are to be preferred to those that fail to do so, for the more frequently behavior is sampled (i.e., observation is arranged), the greater the likelihood that obtained data will actually reflect the level of occurrence of the behavior. Finally, when treatments that may produce negative side effects are under consideration, an acceptable observational system must make provision for their detection. The importance of evaluating possible negative side effects is especially great when pharmacotherapies are considered, since neuroleptics, the drug class most frequently prescribed to alter the behavior of mentally retarded individuals, are known to produce severe and lasting side effects, including tardive dyskinesia (Breuning, Davis, & Poling, 1982; Breuning & Poling, 1982; Ferguson & Breuning, 1982).

Assessing side effects, like desirable outcomes of treatment, require careful definition of the condition of concern. A good response definition is objective, clear, and complete (Hawkins & Dobes, 1977; Kazdin, 1982). A definition is objective to the extent that it specifies observable events, clear to the extent that it unambiguously describes the physical form of these events, and complete insofar as it delineates the boundaries for inclusion and noninclusion.

Even if the behaviors of interest are well defined and the conditions of observation carefully chosen, data garnered through direct observation may lead to erroneous conclusions. As Poling, Cleary, and Monaghan (1980) indicate:

As transducers, humans are invariably suspect. Folklore suggests that lay observations are an imperfect reflection of actual happenings, and a large and growing body of data indicates that allegedly scientific observations sometimes provide an inaccurate index of the variables being considered (Bailey, 1977; Johnson & Bolstad, 1973; Johnston & Pennypacker, 1980). Among the factors demonstrated to influence reported observations are the observer's motivation and expectations (e.g., Rosenthal, 1966), the specifics of the observational situation (e.g., Johnson & Bolstad, 1973), the observational and data recording techniques that are used (e.g., Repp, Roberts, Slack, Repp, & Beckler, 1976), and the characteristics of the behavior being monitored (e.g., Johnston & Pennypacker, 1980). (p. 243)

To partially control for the fallibility of human observers, we recommend that "blind" observers, unaware of experimental conditions, be employed wherever possible. If this is not done, evaluation of clients' behavior, and even the clients' behavior itself, may be affected by the observer's expectations concerning the effects of treatment (for an intentional demonstration of such effects see Breuning, Ferguson, & Cullari, 1980). Unfortunately, some treatments allow observers to easily detect their presence or absence. In these cases, a truly blind experiment cannot be arranged. This, however, certainly does not justify informing observers as to conditions and expected outcomes.

Beyond utilizing blind observers, the treatment evaluator probably ought to occasionally arrange to have two observers independently and simultaneously monitor performance so that a measure of interobserver agreement can be calculated (for methods of calculation see Hawkins & Dotson, 1975; Kazdin, 1982). Despite arguments to the contrary, a high degree of interobserver agreement does not definitively prove that either observer is accurately rating a client's behavior, nor that the observational procedure is valid or reliable as these terms are traditionally used (for a discussion of why this is so see Hawkins & Dotson, 1975). As Kazdin (1982) indicates, calculation of interobserver agreement is nonetheless worthwhile, for at least three reasons. First, a high degree of interobserver agreement suggests that the target behavior is adequately defined. Second, using multiple observers and repeatedly checking interobserver agreement over time provides a partial check on the consistency with which response definitions are applied. Third, when multiple observers are used in the course of a treatment evaluation, it is necessary that their ratings of behavior be consistent. If not, behavior will appear variable across time as a function of the different observers who are scoring it. Such imposed viability may obscure treatment effects. Requiring high levels of interobserver agreement decreases the likelihood that the idiosyncrasies of individual observers will confound treatment evaluation.

In closing our brief overview of quantifying behavior through direct observation, we should mention that this assessment technique often can be profitably combined with other techniques, such as self-reports, behavioral checklists, permanent product measures, or automated recording of responding. In addition to other chapters in this volume, several sources provide adequate coverage of these techniques (Ciminero, Calhoun, & Adams, 1977; Cone & Hawkins, 1977; Hayes, 1978; Hersen & Bellack, 1981) and should be consulted by treatment evaluators who are unsure of their dependent measure. Though we cannot even begin to address the many and complex considerations involved in selecting a good assessment device, the importance of doing so cannot be overemphasized. This is widely acknowledged by scientists in many areas. For example, applied behavior analysts almost always provide careful descriptions of the manner in which behavior is quantified (Kelly, 1977), and have written literally thousands of pages addressing the topic.

Demonstrating that the behavior of interest is adequately quantified is fundamental to any meaningful treatment evaluation. Of equal importance is ensuring that the treatment being considered is actually implemented in the manner intended. A treatment can be effective only insofar as it is employed, and employed correctly: Insulin not taken at all, or insulin eaten, will hardly reduce a diabetic's hyperglycemia. Yet, when injected subcutaneously in appropriate doses, the drug's value in managing diabetes is unquestioned. The importance of following the prescribed medication regimen would in this case be obvious to patient and physician alike. However, as Barber (1976) emphasizes, when behavioral research with humans is considered, it is not uncommon to find that the way clients are treated bears little resemblance to the intended treatment protocol.

Consider a situation in which a mentally retarded student is regularly interrupting classroom activities by inappropriately verbalizing. The teacher consults

with a psychologist concerning the problem, who after a moment's hesitation inti-
mates that a differential-reinforcement-of-other behavior (DRO) reinforcement
schedule just might be an appropriate treatment. The psychologist goes on to describe how this treatment is to be implemented, saying that the student should
receive a dime each time an interval of 30 seconds elapses without an inappropriate verbalization; inappropriate verbalizations, which are carefully defined, will
reset this interval. The teacher says she understands this schedule and will try it.

    In actuality, it is impossible for the teacher to consistently implement this
treatment while attending to other required tasks. Thus, the DRO 30-second schedule is inconsistently implemented for a few days, during which time inappropriate verbalizations continue at the pretreatment level. The teacher reports this to
the psychologist; they conclude that the treatment is ineffective and adopt another strategy. In point of fact, the treatment was ineffective as implemented, but
this says nothing concerning the efficacy of the DRO 30-second schedule that the
psychologist advocated. In this case, treatment evaluation is rendered meaningless by what Barber (1976) terms an "experimenter failure to follow the procedure effect." Here, the procedure is clearly and adequately described by the person
who designed it, but it is not implemented as described. A similar error can occur
when the steps involved in treatment are not specified in detail. Barber (1976)
concisely describes the problem associated with this "investigator loose procedure effect" as follows:

Of course, it is difficult to draw conclusions from experiments based on such loose proto-
cols because the procedures can vary with the moment-to-moment predilections of the
experimenter. A study based on such imprecise procedures is unscientific in that science is
based on the premise that procedures of an experiment are specified in sufficient detail so
that they can be replicated in other laboratories. If the procedures are imprecise, other
laboratories cannot proceed to replicate them and to cross validate the results. (p. 16)

    Relatively little has been written concerning techniques for ensuring that treat-
ments are implemented as intended and reported. Surely it is important that those
who design treatments and those who implement them communicate openly and
extensively. Practical considerations must always be included in selecting a
treatment, and care taken to ensure that those responsible for an intervention know
precisely what is required of them. In this regard, when the designer of a treatment differs from its implementor, it is advisable for the former to role play as a
client who actually is undergoing treatment. In this way, he or she can determine
whether treatment is performed as desired. In addition, weaknesses in the treatment protocol may become apparent during role playing sessions, and be corrected before the treatment is used in earnest.

    However, knowing that the treatment is consistently and appropriately im-
plemented in contrived role play sessions does not necessarily mean that the same
will hold true in the real treatment milieu. This can only be demonstrated by monitoring the behavior of the caregiver, as well as the client. This is rarely done in

applied behavior analysis (see Peterson, Homer, & Wonderlich, in press), but treatment evaluation certainly presupposes that both the independent variable (treatment) and dependent variable (behavior of interest) be carefully quantified, and that the description of these variables be full and accurate. If these conventions are not met, the results of an experiment are at best meaningless and at worst misleading. Thus, the treatment evaluator must demonstrate to his or her own satisfaction, and to that of the audience concerned with the outcome of the evaluation, that the dependent variable is accurately indexed and the independent variable implemented in the manner intended. Finally, he or she must sequence conditions such that observed changes in the dependent variable can be logically attributed to the actions of the independent variable. The manner in which conditions are sequenced determines the design of an experiment. Basic experimental configurations are the primary topic of the remainder of this chapter.

EXPERIMENTAL STRATEGIES

The manner in which an experiment is conducted depends on several factors. One is the experimenter's training and experience. A traditional clinician well-versed in statistical analysis is unlikely to favor the same designs as an applied behavior analyst for whom statistics are anathema. A second is the research question that the study is attempting to answer. An investigator concerned with whether methylphenidate (Ritalin, CIBA) interacts with a response cost procedure in managing off-task behavior is obliged to use a different, and probably more complex, design than the researcher who is asking whether a particular timeout procedure is effective in reducing head-banging in one child. As discussed subsequently, all research designs are limited with regard to the kinds of information they can provide, thus matching research design to research question is of no small consequence. A third factor that influences experimental design is the availability of resources such as personnel, time, money, equipment, and subjects (clients). Of necessity, pragmatism is the guiding philosophy of the treatment evaluator.

Experiments can be considered along a number of dimensions; three of particular significance are depicted in Figure 3-2. This figure, which is quite similar to one previously developed by Huitema (1976), emphasizes that experiments can differ with respect to whether: (1) demonstration of a treatment effect depends primarily upon a comparison of the behavior of the same subject(s) under different conditions or the behavior of different subjects under different conditions, (2) a subject's behavior is observed a single time or repeatedly, and (3) data are analyzed through inferential statistics or visually.

Discussions of experimental design frequently do not clearly differentiate these three dimensions. Instead, within-subject and between-subjects designs are contrasted. Between-subjects designs are presented as involving single observations of each subject's performance and statistical data analysis, while repeated

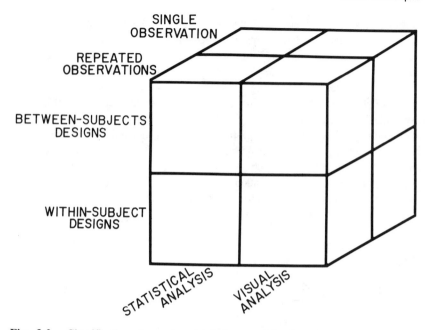

Fig. 3-2. Classification of experimental designs resulting from the division of designs along three dimensions

observations and visual data analysis are represented as features of within-subject designs. If one reads the psychological literature, there is some justification for this conception. For example, most studies published in the *Journal of Applied Behavior Analysis* involve a within-subject analysis, repeated observations of behavior across conditions, and visual analysis of data. Such studies are represented by the lower right front cell in Figure 3-2, and are often compared to the kinds of studies represented by the upper left rear cell in that figure (e.g., Poling & Cleary, in press; Wysocki & Fuqua, 1982). This comparison helps to isolate issues of experimental design, and is of unquestionable heuristic value. However, each of the cells in Figure 3-2 represents an experiment that actually could be conducted. Nothing prevents one from statistically analyzing data from single-subject designs, utilizing repeated measures in between-subjects designs, or combining within-subject and between-subjects comparisons in the same study. The manner in which subjects are exposed to the various conditions and data are collected and analyzed should be determined by the kind of information the researcher desires. No one approach to research is infallible, or suitable for all applications. In the following pages, we discuss the strengths and weaknesses of several experimental configurations. Within-subject and between-subjects designs are considered separately. Our level of analysis is intended to be meaningful for readers with little prior knowledge of treatment evaluation. Where appropriate, readers are referred to additional sources for further coverage.

WITHIN-SUBJECT DESIGNS

Whether a treatment improves, worsens, or has no effect on behavior can only be determined by comparing the client's performance when treatment is and is not operative, that is, through the use of a within-subject design. At its simplest, the comparison involves initially recording behavior during a no treatment, or baseline, condition, then implementing treatment and continuing to record behavior during this phase. In the shorthand used to describe experimental design, the letter A typically is used to denote a baseline phase and the letter B to designate an initial treatment. Other letters, beginning with ''C,'' are used to designate subsequent treatments. In this notation, the configuration described above is an A-B design.

The primary advantage of an A-B design is the ease with which it can be arranged. In medicine, education, and clinical psychology alike, it is common practice to first assess a client's problem, then implement a treatment to alleviate it. Assessment continues while treatment is in effect, and a comparison of measures taken before and during treatment declares the worth of treatment. This is much like what a person with a headache does when he or she takes a single 5 grain aspirin tablet and attempts to determine whether it alleviates pain. The strategy is compelling enough to convince most of us whether aspirin is or is not effective in dealing with headaches. Of course, the more conservative might wish to test the drug a number of times before reaching a firm conclusion. In addition, if one wanted to describe aspirin's effects to a friend, it would be useful to somehow quantify the magnitude of the perceived pain at various times before and after the aspirin was taken. Even if this were done, and the headache's magnitude decreased progressively from the time the tablet was swallowed, a skeptic might argue that this does not prove anything about the drug's action: Pain might simply have begun to diminish at the time the drug was taken, regardless of whether or not aspirin was ingested. Thus, the skeptic has no faith in aspirin's analgesic powers, though the individual who had the headache remains an advocate of the drug.

This example, though hardly standard textbook fare, makes a number of points about experimental design. First, a treatment evaluation that convinces one person may not convince another. Treatment evaluation can be very conservative, adhering to the many conventions of scientific analysis, or more liberal, even haphazard. What constitutes an adequate treatment evaluation depends upon the consequences of an erroneous judgment, and the audience who is going to use the data collected. Second, as noted earlier, a treatment cannot be adequately evaluated unless the condition of interest is appropriately measured. Third, when an observed relation between a treatment and outcome can be repeated, faith that the relation is real grows. Fourth, some experimental designs are such that observed changes in the dependent variable cannot be attributed with confidence to treatment. The A-B design falls in this category.

This is the design's primary weakness: due to its logical structure, the A-B design can provide only weak and equivocal confirmation of a treatment's effects. When this design is used, one can never be sure that a change in behavior that occurs coincidentally with intervention is not the result of other, unknown factors (extraneous variables) that fortuitously become operative when treatment is implemented. Consider a situation in which a mentally retarded student's low level of on-task behavior is the condition treatment, perhaps a behavior modification program, is intended to alleviate. On-task behavior is assessed via a whole interval time-sampling procedure. During the seven days of baseline, on-task behavior occurs on average during 32 percent of the observational intervals, with a range across days of 17 to 48 percent. Over the 10 days the behavior modification program is in effect, on-task behavior occurs on average during 68 percent of the observational intervals, with a range over days of 47 to 82 percent.

Given these data, it can be safely said that the student spent more time on-task during treatment. However, it is by no means obvious that the behavior modification was responsible for the observed, and quite real, improvement.

Assume that at the start of the assessment period the student was receiving a medication that interfered with on-task performance. Unknown to the educators, the medication regimen was permanently terminated at the time the behavior modification program started. This change in medication, rather than the intervention of interest, may have produced the observed improvement.

Certainly this specific scenario is unlikely, but many factors beyond changes in medication can produce effects like those desired of treatment (Campbell & Stanley, 1966). The A-B design does not adequately control any of these extraneous variables, and for that reason is not favored by researchers. It is nonetheless a useful design in clinical practice, since it does provide for meaningful demonstration of behavior change.

Because the A-B design is weak in its ability to demonstrate a functional relation between an independent and dependent variable, other designs are preferable in those situations where it is important to show not only that behavior improved, but that this improvement can be attributed to a specifiable intervention as well. Withdrawal designs allow this to be done. Adding a final baseline phase to an A-B configuration makes of it a withdrawal design (also, but probably misleadingly, termed a reversal design [Hersen & Barlow, 1976]), specifically an A-B-A. In this and all other withdrawal designs (e.g., A-B-A-B, B-A-B-A-C-A-C), conditions alternate sequentially between baseline and treatment. If behavior changes from the initial baseline level when treatment is implemented, and returns to the baseline level when treatment is terminated, there is good reason to believe that the intervention actually is responsible for the observed behavior change.

It is, of course, always possible that some extraneous variable became active and inactive coincident with treatment, and actually produced the behavior change. This problem cannot be absolutely obviated with any design; the stronger designs simply reduce its likelihood. Recall our example of a change in medication confounding the effects of treatment under an A-B design. If an A-B-A design had been used, for treatment effects to have been confounded medication should have been removed at the onset of the B condition and reinstated at the start of the second A phase. Only given this unlikely double coincidence would behavior systematically differ from treatment to the two baseline phases. In our example, this would not have occurred, thus no erroneous conclusions would have been reached had an A-B-A design been employed. Thus, as is usually true, the withdrawal design is preferable to the A-B design. As Hersen and Barlow (1976) discuss, withdrawal designs also are more likely to yield sound conclusions than B designs, which consist only of a treatment phase, or case-study designs, which involve a description (preferably augmented by data; see Hersen & Barlow, 1976) of the events that transpire during treatment, and their apparent outcome. These designs, like the A-B, can offer hunches as to the efficacy of treatment, but cannot conclusively demonstrate a relation between an independent and dependent variable.

Though withdrawal designs can do so, they are not without shortcomings. One is that they are inappropriate for evaluating interventions that produce irreversible effects, since the logic of withdrawal designs demands that performance returns to or near the initial baseline level when treatment ends. If not, any observed behavior change during treatment cannot be attributed to the intervention. A second limitation of withdrawal designs involves the ethics of terminating a treatment associated with beneficial behavior change only to show that behavior returns to its initial, undesirable level. Because of these limitations, alternatives to withdrawal designs are required. Two other within-subject designs that allow for meaningful treatment evaluation are the multiple baseline and the multielement baseline.

The multiple-baseline design involves a sequence of A-B manipulations staggered in time. In this design, a number of dependent measures, typically three or four (Kazdin & Kopel, 1975), are taken. These dependent measures can represent different behaviors of a single individual, the same or different behaviors of two or more individuals, or the same behavior of a single individual under different circumstances. Each dependent measure must require change in the same direction, and all dependent measures should be independent (i.e., changing one ought not affect the others).

The multiple-baseline typically begins with all dependent measures being taken during baseline (treatment absent) conditions. When performance stabilizes (i.e., shows no upward or downward trend, and relatively little variability over time), treatment is implemented for one dependent measure. Thus, if the aggressive behavior of three separate individuals constitute the dependent measures, one person is exposed to treatment, while the other dependent measures (i.e., the behavior of the other two individuals) continue to be recorded under baseline conditions. When the behavior first treated stabilizes in the presence of the intervention, treatment is begun for a second behavior. This process continues until all behaviors are treated.

With the multiple-baseline design, a treatment's efficacy is evident when each dependent measure changes when and only when treatment is implemented for that behavior. If two or more behaviors are apparently affected when treatment is implemented for one of them, the design's logic dictates that this effect cannot unambiguously be attributed to treatment. This is because such data might simply reflect a non-independence of the behaviors, but could also involve the action of some extraneous variable coincidentally activated at the onset of treatment. These two possibilities can be evaluated by terminating treatment and checking whether both behaviors return to pre-treatment levels. If so, it is reasonable to conclude that treatment is effective and the two behaviors non-independent. If not, the action of an extraneous variable cannot be ruled out, and the intervention's efficacy remains moot.

The multiple-baseline design is not limited by the two shortcomings of withdrawal designs. It can deal with treatments that produce irreversible effects (so long as the dependent measures are independent) and does not require countertherapeutic behavior change to show the efficacy of treatment. For these reasons, the design's popularity has increased in recent years (Kelly, 1977). Kazdin and Kopel (1975) provide detailed coverage of this design, and offer a number of practical recommendations for its appropriate use.

Another within-subject design of some value is the multielement baseline design (Ulman & Sulzer-Azaroff, 1975). In this design, a given individual is exposed to different conditions in a rapidly alternating sequence. Each condition is associated with readily discriminable stimuli (environmental features), and the absolute efficacy of treatment is determined by comparing performance during treatment with performance during a baseline condition, while the relative efficacy of two or more interventions is assayed by contrasting performance in each. As an example of this design, the head-banging of a mentally retarded student who moves from classroom to classroom at hourly intervals during the school day might be treated by verbal reprimands during hour one, a timeout procedure during hour two, a response cost procedure during hour three, and not treated at all during hour four. The best treatment should in principle become evident by comparing rates of head-banging over the four hours.

The multielement baseline design can deal with treatments that produce irreversible effects, does not require countertherapeutic behavior change, and yields a wealth of information in a short time. For the design to yield sound conclusions, however, there must be no carryover effects from one condition to another, and behavior must be equally modifiable in all conditions. Ulman and Sulzer-Azaroff (1975) provide detailed coverage of this design. Similar experimental configurations that provide for the rapid alternation of conditions are termed the "alternating treatment design" by Barlow and Hayes (1979), and the "simultaneous treatment design" by Kazdin and Hartmann (1978), and are discussed by these authors.

Several other within-subject designs have been developed and are occasionally useful in research in clinical practice, though they cannot be addressed here.

Four recent books (Hersen & Barlow, 1976; Johnston & Pennypacker, 1980; Kazdin, 1982; Kratochwill, 1978) fully cover the many ways that within-subject comparisons can be arranged.

Before leaving within-subject designs, we should reiterate that data from such designs commonly are analyzed visually, although inferential statistics can certainly be applied to them (Kratochwill, 1978). In visual analysis, data are simply graphed across conditions and the graph perused by the treatment evaluator, who makes a judgment as to whether treatment was beneficial. Several aspects of the data are considered in making this judgment, including mean performance, trends, variability, and overlap of data from different phases. There are no generally established standards for visual data analysis, although Kazdin (1982) and others have made worthwhile suggestions for facilitating the process. In general, those who visually analyze data are conservative, in that they tend not to accept a treatment as effective unless its effects are large and clear. In fact, it may be justifiable to consider as trifling even a treatment that clearly improves behavior relative to baseline unless the change demonstrably improves the client's lot in a real way. This is the issue of the clinical, as opposed to experimental or statistical, significance.

Clinical significance can be determined in three ways: (1) By comparing obtained levels of behavior during treatment with criterion levels set before treatment. These criterion levels (treatment objectives) define solution of the behavioral problem which treatment is hoped to ameliorate. (2) By comparing the performance of the individual undergoing treatment with that of similar individuals who do not manifest the behavioral problem for which treatment was applied. (3) By having those who defined the problem evaluate the success of its treatment. These strategies and their attendant strengths and weaknesses are fully described by Wolf (1978) and Van Houten (1979).

If a treatment is shown to produce clinically significant effects in one client, the researcher (but not necessarily the clinician) will be concerned with the generality of the findings—with what other clients and under what other conditions will the treatment prove valuable? Ultimately, this can only be answered by empirical test. One learns the range of applicability of a treatment by testing it with an ever widening range of clients, problem behaviors, and environmental circumstances. This notwithstanding, it is generally assumed that the results of a properly conducted within-subject experiment will generalize at minimum to individuals and conditions substantially like those employed in the reported study.

This belief is held most strongly when a treatment is shown to produce similar results in more than one individual. Within-subject experiments surely can be conducted with a single person, and this is why they are so valuable in the clinic. However, researchers typically study more than one participant, though it is common for them to be relatively homogeneous with respect to problem behavior, presence of mental retardation, and other factors likely to affect the success of intervention. When treatment similarly affects two or more such homogeneous clients, there is good reason to believe that the treatment will be of value in other individuals with similar characteristics. When results differ across clients, however, the generality of treatment becomes questionable.

Ideally, in such circumstances, the researcher will experimentally isolate the factors responsible for the differential sensitivity of the various individuals (Sidman, 1960). This, however, has rarely been done in clinical practice (Poling & Cleary, in press). It seems that the usual practice is for researchers to only report interventions that are extremely powerful, in that they produce like effects across all individuals tested, or to simply present a treatment as being effective in some proportion of tested clients. Azrin (1977) advocates this latter strategy, although he recommends that the next step in a research project is to ascertain how the treatment must be modified to meet the needs of those who failed to benefit from the initial intervention. When one begins asking actuarial questions, such as ''What proportion of subjects are benefitted by treatment A, as opposed to treatment B?'', the experimental design of necessity involves between-subjects comparisons. The next section introduces this research tactic.

BETWEEN-SUBJECTS DESIGNS

A design is considered between-subjects if groups of participants are exposed to different conditions (e.g., one group receives treatment, a second does not), and the effects of treatment are determined by comparing group performances. The information gleaned from such an analysis is unlike that obtained from within-subject designs. Rather than precisely delineating a treatment's effects on one participant's behavior, the researcher who utilizes between-subjects designs ascertains the average effect of treatment on the behavior of an entire group of participants. Thus, the magnitude and even the direction of a treatment effect revealed through a between-subjects design may vary from individual to individual.

Beyond differing in the kind of information they provide, within-subject and between-subjects designs differ along several other dimensions as well. Obviously, the number of participants required differs between the two approaches. While only one participant may be needed for many within-subject designs, several to hundreds may be needed for between-subjects evaluations. This number varies according to the specific design chosen and is of course limited by the number of potential participants available.

The manner in which individuals are selected and assigned to experimental conditions is an important aspect of between-subjects comparisons, though not a factor in within-subject designs. Ideally, subjects are randomly selected from the entire population for whom statements of treatment efficacy are to be made. If this is not possible, the experimental design is not necessarily flawed; however, one is limited to generalizing treatment effects to individuals similar to those who participated in the study. Unfortunately, when participants are not randomly selected it is often difficult to specify the relevant characteristics of the population they represent, and therefore to specify the extent to which findings may be generalized to other groups.

More important to the logic of between-subjects comparisons than the random selection of participants is the random assignment of individuals to the various experimental conditions. Random assignment requires that all participants have an equal and independent opportunity for assignment to any particular condition, and assures that all groups will be probabilistically equivalent on all characteristics. If this is in fact true, no systematic bias will confound the treatment effects for any group, thus groups can be compared without concern that observed differences in performance reflect nontreatment variables. In fairness, it should be noted that nonequivalent groups can be compared, although this is rarely advisable. Huitema (1980) offers a thorough, though technical, analysis of the problems of data analysis associated with nonequivalent groups.

The manner in which data are usually collected is another major difference between the two designs. Measurements on the dependent variable for each participant are taken only once or twice during the course of most between-subjects evaluations. Though some designs may dictate that more measures be taken, the emphasis is almost never on continuous and repeated measures as is common in within-subject designs. Thus, as traditionally used, between-subjects designs provide little or no information about how a client's behavior changes over the course of treatment. This information is, of course, of great clinical value.

The data analysis procedures used with the two approaches also typically differ. As described previously, treatment effects are most often evaluated through a visual inspection of the data collected under a within-subject design. Between-subjects designs, on the other hand, are almost exclusively analyzed using statistical procedures (Hopkins & Glass, 1978; Kirk, 1968, provide the details of such procedures). It suffices here to note that statistical analyses begin with the hypothesis that the difference between groups is zero in the absence of treatment effects (assuming random assignment of participants to groups). Mathematical formulas are used to determine the probability of obtaining the observed differences in dependent variable group means (or some other measure of central tendency) if there truly is no difference between the groups. This obtained probability value is compared to a maximum probability value (alpha level) specified before the onset of the investigation. The alpha level is usually .05 (Cowles & Davis, 1982), and less frequently .01. If the obtained probability level is less than the selected alpha level, it is concluded that the difference between groups did not occur by chance and is therefore a result of treatment. Inferential statistics are well developed, and can provide a parsimonious summary of the results of logically complex evaluations. It is obligatory, however, that statistical tests be used appropriately. That is, they must be suitable for the data being analyzed, and their assumptions must not be violated. If not, the outcome of a test may be erroneous. Thus those who use inferential statistics in treatment evaluation must take great care to use them appropriately.

Although several differences between within-subject and between-subjects designs as usually employed have been outlined, experimental configurations are best viewed as falling somewhere along a continuum with pure between-subjects designs at one end and pure within-subject designs at the other. This is apparent in considering two common and useful experimental configurations, the randomized groups and the repeated measures designs.

The randomized groups design can be thought of as a true between-subjects design. The experimenter begins with some population of interest, for example, all mildly mentally retarded students in a particular school's remedial reading program. Given the defined population, the experimenter either randomly selects a sample for inclusion in the study or includes all members (if this is feasible). In either case, participants are assigned at random to the various conditions of interest. Perhaps a teacher is interested in evaluating the relative efficacy of phonics and sight-word approaches to teaching reading to the population described above, which consists of 40 students. She would randomly assign each student to either the phonics program or the sight-word program until there were twenty students in each group, then proceed to teach the students according to assigned treatment conditions. After some specified length of instruction, the teacher would obtain a dependent variable measure for each student, perhaps a score on a standardized reading achievement test. The average score for each group would then be compared through statistical techniques. Results would hold for the population of interest, but not necessarily for any other students. Further testing with other participants would, however, extend the generality of the results.

The repeated measures design is one example of a group design bearing characteristics of both within-subject and between-subjects designs. Relatively few subjects are required for this design as compared to most other group designs. As with the randomized groups design, the experimenter either randomly selects subjects for participation in the study or includes all members of the population of interest. However, rather than randomly assigning each subject to one treatment, each subject undergoes all treatments, the order of which is randomized. For example, a supervisor may be interested in choosing an optimal reinforcement schedule for a group of mentally retarded adults who perform an assembly task in a sheltered workshop. Perhaps he wishes to compare the number of units assembled when the workers are given a token for each unit completed with the number of units assembled when every fifth and every tenth unit completed is followed by a token. The supervisor would randomly select, for example, ten workers for participation. Each of the ten would, at some time, be exposed to all three reinforcement conditions for a period of time, perhaps one week. However, the supervisor would randomly assign the order in which the workers were exposed to the conditions. For example, worker 1 might receive a token for every fifth unit completed during the first week, for every unit completed during the second week, and for every tenth unit completed during the third week. Worker 2 might receive a token for every unit assembled during the first week, after every tenth unit assembled during the second week, and after every fifth unit assembled during the final week. During the course of the study, the supervisor would monitor the number of units assembled per worker on a weekly basis. At the end of the third week, the average number of units assembled per week for each condition would be compared for differences. A within-subject comparison could also be made to examine differences for individual subjects under each reinforcement condition. This is an important and often ignored point: there is no reason why data cannot be analyzed so as to disclose how each participant is affected by treatment, as well as how participants taken as a group are affected. This would require repeated measures, but would yield maximal information.

Between-subjects comparisons can be arranged in innumerable ways; our examples demonstrate the logic of such designs, but by no means exhaust the possibilities. Any traditional textbook of experimental design (Kirk, 1968) presents several specific experimental configurations involving between-subjects comparisons.

These designs, taken as a whole, have been soundly criticized by behavior analysts (Hersen & Barlow, 1976; Johnston & Pennypacker, 1980) for several reasons. Very often it is simply not practical to implement group designs. These designs require large numbers of participants with similar characteristics and therapeutic needs. It is very difficult in most cases to locate and gain access to such groups of individuals.

The organization of most settings where large numbers of individuals are found can also render a between-subjects evaluation unfeasible. For example, classroom assignments or daily activity schedules of institutions may prohibit the formation of groups or random assignment of participants. Although such a problem does not preclude a group study, it does make for difficult interpretation of results (Huitema, 1980).

The cost of conducting a group study can also be prohibitive. An experimenter must consider the cost of implementing a treatment with a large number of individuals, monitoring their performance, and analyzing the results.

There are ethical issues to be considered in designing a between-subjects evaluation of treatment effects as well. Parents, teachers, or administrators often object to randomly assigning individuals to a control (no treatment) or a potentially less efficacious treatment condition. It is difficult to justify to such concerned persons the withholding of treatment in the name of science or evaluation.

The data analysis procedures typically employed with group designs have also been criticized. Usually results for entire groups are averaged and then compared for differences. Such mathematical manipulations often mask variability between subjects within a group. Perhaps a treatment is extremely helpful to one segment of the group, rather harmful to another segment, and of no benefit or detriment to a third segment. A statistical analysis may reveal a very weak or nonsignificant treatment effect for the group, when in fact large differences in effectiveness actually exist from individual to individual. Selecting from a homogeneous pool of individuals or controlling statistically for systematic differences which may bias results may safeguard against this difficulty, but neither procedure guarantees a decrease in variability or the clinical meaningfulness of averaged results. It should be noted, however, that a between-subjects design does not mandate a statistical analysis. Nothing prevents an experimenter from visually inspecting the data to determine the differential effects of the treatment on a group of individuals.

Another difficulty related to data analysis of between-subjects designs is the distinction between clinical and statistical significance. Let us say, for example, that students exposed to a behavior modification procedure score on average lower on an aggressiveness checklist than do untreated controls. This difference is significant at the .01 level. The difference in aggressiveness between the two groups, however, is not recognizable by the aides who must control the wards where the students reside. Thus, a statistically significant effect apparently is not clinically significant. Any report of the statistical significance of a treatment effect should be accompanied by an evaluation of the practical importance of such an effect, which can be accomplished through the strategies discussed in the context of within-subject designs.

It was mentioned previously that between-subjects and within-subject designs can differ along several dimensions, the most important of which is the kind of information provided through each analysis. This difference is not trivial; one kind of design is particularly well suited for answering a limited range of research questions. Only within-subject comparisons provide a good answer to the question, "Did this person benefit from treatment?" Since this is precisely the issue in the evaluation of clinical treatment, these designs are of particular value to the audience for whom this chapter is written. Nonetheless, between-subjects comparisons are occasionally appropriate for day-to-day clinical treatment evaluations, and for research applications (Hersen & Barlow, 1976; Kazdin, 1982; Poling & Cleary in press).

Combined within-subject and between-subjects analyses are required to answer actuarial questions. For example, one could determine what percentage of institutionalized mentally retarded persons acquired adequate toileting skills within a month of exposure to a training procedure only by exposing a sizable number of residents to this procedure, then determining (by comparison to pretested performance) which of these persons acquired appropriate skills. This would obviously involve a within-subject analysis. However, in the final step, data would be pooled across individuals, and expressed in a summary value, e.g., 16 of 20 participants exhibited appropriate performance. This value expresses a between-subjects comparison.

A between-subjects design would also be appropriate for situations where one is concerned with the average gain across individuals that can be expected when a particular treatment is implemented. Such data might, for example, help an educator to decide whether to adopt a particular reading program. Although the value of that program with specific students could only be determined through a within-subject analysis, information concerning average expected gains would help to make the initial decision.

Data concerning the average effect of two or more reading programs would be even more useful, and one major application of between-subjects designs is in comparative research at a molar level. Though comparative research certainly can be conducted via within-subject designs, between-subjects comparisons are well suited for such applications. For example, suppose two toilet training programs have been developed, and one is interested in knowing whether the length of training required by either of the programs is shorter than the other. Such a question, again concerning average effect, can only be answered through a between-subjects approach. Such an approach can also provide valuable information about the interactions of two or more treatments, and the manner in which client characteristics influence the outcome of intervention.

The use of between-subjects designs is also necessary when the aim is to modify group behavior or when the behavior of individuals cannot be isolated or manipulated. For instance, a teacher may be interested in decreasing the overall noise level in the classroom. Since all members of the class contribute to the noise level, any attempt to decrease it necessitates a group design. Or, a shopkeeper may desire to determine whether signs decrease shoplifting. Since there is no control over who enters the store when signs are and are not present, her conclusions almost invariably would rest upon between-subjects comparisons.

CONCLUSIONS

This chapter provides no more than the barest introduction to treatment evaluation. Of necessity, several important general issues were ignored. These include the problems involved in conducting comparative research, the need for parametric evaluations of many interventions, and the significance of assessing transfer and maintenance of treatment gains. In addition, no mention was made of the strategies best suited for evaluating particular interventions, for instance pharmacotherapies. Many sources thoroughly address general issues of treatment evaluation (Hersen & Barlow, 1976; Johnston & Pennypacker, 1980; Kazdin, 1982), while others analyze the evaluation of particular interventions.

However, despite the potential complexities of treatment evaluation and the many writings devoted to it, the essential features of a sound evaluation can be simply stated: (1) The behavior to be changed (depenent variable) must be adequately defined and measured. (2) The treatment (independent variable) must be consistently administered according to the selected protocol. (3) The sequencing of conditions (experimental design) and method of data analysis must allow observed changes in the dependent variable to be attributed with confidence to treatment. If these three conditions are met, the evaluation is, in principle, sound.

Throughout the chapter, we have consistently referred to clinical treatment evaluations as experiments, for they are just that—attempts to ascertain through application of the scientific method whether one thing affects another. Though the experimental method provides the only reasonable means of determining the outcome of intervention, it must be emphasized that any one evaluation can lead to an erroneous conclusion: a treatment may appear effective when in fact it is not, or an intervention that is actually beneficial may seem without worth. Because of this, undue emphasis should not be placed on the outcome of any one experiment. While careful documentation of performance over time will certainly show whether a client's behavior improved in the course of intervention, even the strongest experimental configurations cannot demonstrate conclusively that intervention was uniquely responsible for the observed change. Though this minor uncertainty does not reduce the client's improvement, it certainly should ensure caution on the part of investigators, especially when they begin speculating about the generality of their findings and the worth of their interventions.

Acknowledgment

Preparation of this chapter was supported by a Faculty Research Fellowship awarded to Alan Poling by Western Michigan University.

REFERENCES

Azrin, NH. A strategy for applied research: Learning based but outcome oriented. *American Psychologist*, 1977, *32*, 140–149

Bailey, JA. *Handbook of research methods in applied behavior analysis.* New York: Plenum, 1977

Barber, TX. *Pitfalls in human research.* New York: Pergamon, 1976

Barlow, GH, & Hayes, SC. Alternating treatments design: One strategy for comparing the effects of two treatments in a single subject. *Journal of Applied Behavior Analysis*, 1979, *12*, 199–210

Breuning, SE, Davis, V, & Poling, A. Pharmacotherapy with the mentally retarded: Implications for clinical Psychologists. *Clinical Psychology Review*, 1982, *2*, 79–114

Breuning, SE, Ferguson, DG, & Cullari, S. Analysis of single-double blind procedures, maintenance of placebo effects, and drug induced dyskinesia with mentally retarded persons. *Applied Research in Mental Retardation*, 1980, *1*, 175–182

Breuning, SE, & Poling, A. Pharmacotherapy with the mentally retarded. In J Matson & R Barrett (Eds.), *Psychopathology of the mentally retarded.* New York: Grune & Stratton, 1982

Campbell, DT, & Stanley, JC. *Experimental and quasi-experimental designs for research.* Chicago: Rand McNally, 1966

Ciminero, AR, Calhoun, KS, & Adams, HE. *Handbook of behavioral assessment.* New York: John Wiley & Sons, 1977

Cone, JD, & Hawkins, RP (Eds.). *Behavioral assessment: New directions in clinical psychology.* New York: Bruner-Mazel, 1977

Cowles, M, & Davis, C. On the origins of the .05 level of statistical significance. *American Psychologist,* 1982, *37*, 553–558

Ferguson, DG, & Breuning, SE. In SE Breuning & A Poling (Eds.), *Drugs and Mental Retardation.* Springfield, IL: Charles C. Thomas, 1982

Grossman, HJ (Ed.). *Manual on terminology and classification in mental retardation.* Washington, DC: American Association on Mental Deficiency, 1977

Hawkins, RP, & Dobes, RW. Behavioral definitions in applied behavior analysis: Explicit or implicit. In BC Etzel, JM LeBlanc, & DM Baer (Eds.), *New developments in behavioral research: Theory, methods, and applications*. In honor of Sidney W. Bijou. Hillsdale, NJ: Lawrence Erlbaum, 1977

Hawkins, RP, & Dotson, VA. Reliability scores that delude: An Alice in Wonderland trip through misleading characteristics of interobserver agreement scores in interval recording. In E Ramp & G Semb (Eds.), *Behavior analysis areas of research and application*. Englewood Cliffs, NJ: Prentice-Hall, 1975

Hayes, SN. *Principles of behavioral assessment*. New York: Gardner, 1978

Hersen, M, & Barlow, DH. *Single case experimental designs: Strategies for studying behavior change*. New York: Pergamon, 1976

Hersen, M, & Bellack, AS. *Behavioral assessment*. New York: Pergamon, 1981

Hopkins, KD, & Glass, GV. *Basic statistics for the behavioral sciences*. Englewood Cliffs, NJ: Prentice-Hall, 1978

Huitema, BE. *The misuse of statistics in behavior modification research*. A paper presented at the second annual convention of the Midwestern Association of Behavior Analysis, Chicago, 1976

Huitema, BE. *The analysis of covariance and alternatives*. New York: John Wiley & Sons, 1980

Johnson, SM, & Bolstad, OD. Methodological issues in naturalistic observation: Some problems and solutions for field research. In LA Hammerlynck, LD Handy, & EJ Mash (Eds.), *Behavior changes: Methodology, concepts, and practice*. Champaign, IL: Research Press, 1973

Johnston, JM, & Pennypacker, HS. *Strategies and tactics of human behavioral research*. Hillsdale, NJ: Lawrence Erlbaum, 1980

Kazdin, AE. *Single-case research designs*. New York: Oxford University Press, 1982

Kazdin, AE, & Hartmann, DP. The simultaneous treatment design. *Behavior Therapy*, 1978, *9*, 912–922

Kazdin, AE, & Kopel, SA. On resolving ambiguities of the multiple-baseline design: Problems and recommendations. *Behavior Therapy*, 1975, *6*, 601–608

Kelly, MB. A review of observational data-collection and reliability procedures reported in the Journal of Applied Behavior Analysis. *Journal of Applied Behavior Analysis*, 1977, *10*, 97–101

Kirk, RE. *Experimental design: Procedures for the behavioral sciences*. Belmont, CA: Brooks/Cole, 1968

Kratochwill, TR (Ed.). *Single-subject research: Strategies for evaluating change*. New York: Academic Press, 1978

Peterson, L, Homer, AL, & Wonderlich, SA. The integrity of independent variables in behavior analysis. *Journal of Applied Behavior Analysis*, (in press)

Poling, A, & Cleary, J. Single subject designs. In SE Breuning, J Matson, & A Poling (Eds.), *Applied psychopharmacology: Assessment of medication effects*. New York: Grune & Stratton (in press)

Poling, A, Cleary, J, & Monaghan, M. The use of human observers in psychopharmacological research. *Pharmocology Biochemistry & Behavior*, 1980, *13*, 243–246

Repp, AC, Roberts, DM, Slack, DJ, Repp, CF, & Beckler, MS. A comparison of frequency, interval, and time-sampling methods of data collection. *Journal of Applied Behavior Analysis*, 1976, *9*, 501–508

Rosenthal, R. *Experimenter effects in behavioral research*. New York: Appleton-Century-Crofts, 1966

Sidman, M. *Tactics of scientific research*. New York: Basic Books, 1960

Ulman, JD, & Sulzer-Azaroff, B. Multielement baseline design in educational research. In E Ramp & G Semb (Eds.), *Behavior analysis: Areas of research and application*. Englewood Cliffs, NJ: Prentice-Hall, 1975

Van Houten, R. Social validation: The evolution of standards of competency for target behaviors. *Journal of Applied Behavior Analysis*, 1979, *12*, 581–591

Wolf, MM. Social validity: The case for subjective measurement or how behavior analysis is finding its heart. *Journal of Applied Behavior Analysis*, 1978, *11*, 203–214

Wysocki, T, & Fuqua, RW. Methodological issues in the evaluation of drug effects. In SE Breuning & A Poling (Eds.), *Drugs and mental retardation*. Springfield, IL: Charles C. Thomas, 1982

Rowland P. Barrett
Stephen E. Breuning

4

Assessment of Intelligence

This chapter is concerned with the assessment of intelligence. Over the years there have been many attempts to define this concept. Each definition, in one form or another, has emphasized (1) the individual's capacity to learn, (2) the amount of information and knowledge the individual has acquired, and (3) the individual's skill in adapting to the environment and to environmental change. Variations in definitions have tended to emphasize what a given definer believes to be of main importance. Definitions have further varied in terms of why an individual has strengths or weaknesses along one or more of the three dimensions listed above and how these strengths and weaknesses are related statistically. These have included (1) developmental analyses (Brunner, 1964; Piaget, 1950), (2) learning analyses (Bijou, 1966), (3) neurological-biological analyses (Cattell, 1971; Halstead, 1947; Hebb, 1949), and (4) psychometric analyses (Guilford, 1968; Spearman, 1904; Thurstone, 1938). At present, there is no data based reason to wholly select or reject any existing definition of intelligence. And, however one chooses to define intelligence, it is clear that consideration of developmental environmental, and neurological-biological variables is essential. (The interested reader is referred to Maloney & Ward [1979] and Robinson & Robinson [1976], for thorough discussions of the concept of intelligence.)

Given the problems and frustrations inherent in attempting to define the concept of intelligence, one rightly may ask "if we do not know what intelligence is, how do we know we can measure it?" The answer, quite simply, is "we cannot." We can, however, abandon the notion of intelligence and discuss what a so-called "Intelligence Test" can yield in terms of functional information.

In general, the intellectual test may be viewed as a multiple-probe or sampling procedure designed to assist in the assessment of a complex behavioral repertoire. Each of the available tests (discussed below) samples individual differ-

ences along various dimensions of behavior, and provides one method of quantifying these differences. The value of these tests is debatable. They have been
lauded as one of psychology's greatest accomplishments (Herrstein, 1973), and
lamented as one of its most opprobrious (Kamin, 1974). Clearly, both positions
are extremes. It is our contention that how a test is utilized and how the findings
are interpreted are typically what psychology should be shameful of; not the tests
themselves.

Early Developments

The initial intent of the formal intellectual assessment was to aid mentally
retarded children. In 1904, Alfred Binet, a French physician, was contracted by
the French Minister of Public Instruction to develop a testing procedure which
would screen for children whose academic aptitudes were so low as to require
placement in special programs. The intent was to identify these children prior to
their failure in regular programs. The first such test was published by Binet and
Simon in 1905. This measure was a 30-item test arranged in order of increasing
difficulty. In 1908 the test was revised. Items were still arranged in terms of increasing difficulty with chronological age being the criterion of difficulty. This
marked the origination of the concept "mental age." A final revision of this test
occurred in 1911, just before Binet's death.

In developing and using the Binet-Simon Scale, Binet was adamant that the
test was a practical diagnostic device and not designed to "make a distinction
between acquired and congenital feeblemindedness" (Binet & Simon, 1905). Binet was more adamant in his arguments against the notion that intelligence was a
fixed quantity that could not be augmented by environmental factors (Binet, 1913).

The Binet-Simon Scale was brought to America and translated into English
by Henry Goddard in 1908. Goddard was the director of the Vineland Training
School for the Mentally Retarded in Vineland, New Jersey. It was through
Goddard's work and research that the intent and use of the Binet-Simon Scale
dramatically changed. Unlike his French predecessors of the 1800s, Esquirol,
Itard, and Sequin, Goddard was unsuccessful in educating and training the mentally retarded. Goddard began to actively preach the doctrine of fixed intelligence
and inheritability.

In the course of arguing the notion of inheritable fixed ability, Goddard became active in the eugenics movement. This movement was founded by Galton
in 1883 as a science of improving inherent racial qualifities. In conjunction with
his involvement in the eugenics movement, Goddard "provided evidence" that
not only were the mentally retarded of fixed ability, but also were dangerous to
society. Goddard was interested in genealogical tracings and in 1912 reported the
case of Martin Kallikak. Kallikak, a word derived by Goddard from the Grecian
words "good" and "evil", was a Revolutionary War soldier who fathered an
illegitimate son by a mentally retarded girl. Through his genealogical tracing,

Goddard identified 480 descendants from this single sexual interaction with the girl. Of these 480 descendants, 143 were identified as mentally retarded. Goddard (1912) further reported that there was a high incidence of alcoholism, criminality, illegitimacy, and promiscuity among these 143 descendants. It was further noted that Kallikak went on to marry a woman of normal intelligence and none of these problems arose.

In 1916, Terman and his associates at Stanford University revised the Binet-Simon Scale and published the Stanford-Binet Intelligence Scale. Terman was active in the eugenics movement and like Goddard believed very strongly that the mentally retarded were dangers to society. Terman's views and intended use of the Stanford-Binet were elucidated in the opening chapter of the test booklet:

Intelligence tests will bring tens of thousands of these highgrade defectives under the surveillance and protection of society. This will ultimately result in curtailing the reproduction of feeblemindedness and in the elimination of an enormous amount of crime, pauperism, and industrial inefficiency. (Terman, 1916, p. 6–7)

In a later writing (Terman, 1917) entitled "The Menace of Feeble-Mindedness," Terman stated that:

Only recently have we begun to recognize how serious a menace it is . . . the feeble-minded continue to multiply . . . we must prevent, as far as possible, the propagation of mental degenerates . . . curtailing the increasing spawn of degeneracy. (p. 165)

By the 1930s the eugenics movement, aided by a 1929 report by A.D. Tredgold of the British Royal Commiddion stating that 90 percent of mental retardation was inherited, and the growing shift to custodial care in institutions due to overcrowded conditions and lack of financial support, sufficiently scared society into believing that the mentally retarded were a menace to society, incapable of learning, and spreaders of idiocy, degeneracy, crime, and disease. Institutions were moved or created away from large urban areas and no longer held an educative and habilitative purpose. Society was no longer sending individuals to institutions for training but rather to segregate its undesirable elements. This included many minor offenders who were identified as being mentally retarded and institutionalized. In addition to the wrongful institutionalization of massive numbers of individuals, sterilization laws flourished and it was not uncommon to find sterilization a prerequisite for discharge from an institution (Goldstein, 1964). By 1972, upwards of 50 percent of the states had statutes permitting involuntary sterilization (Krischell, 1972). Since 1972, this percentage has decreased dramatically (Robinson & Robinson, 1976).

Recent Developments

Until the 1950s the development of new psychological tests and test batteries flourished. These included the Army Alpha and Army Beta group screening tests of World War I, the Rorschach Inkblots first described in 1921, the first of the Wechsler scales in 1939, and the Leiter International Performance Scale in 1948. While test use and development continued, there was little additional impact on the plight of the mentally retarded.

During the 1950s several important events occurred, which brought the problems of the mentally retarded to national attention. In 1950 a group of parents of mentally retarded children in Minneapolis, Minnesota met for the first time. By the end of that year, over 20 such groups joined together and formed the National Association of Parents and Friends of Retarded Children. In 1952 this group expanded and was renamed the National Association for Retarded Children. This group was the forerunner of today's National Association for Retarded Citizens which has over 250,000 members (this latest renaming occurred in 1973). During World War II over 715,000 men were rejected from the armed services on the grounds of mental deficiency, which called attention to the ubiquity of mild mental retardation. In 1958, Masland, Sarason, and Gladwin published their book *Mental Subnormality* which emphasized the social, psychological, and cultural determinants of mental retardation. Also, in 1958, Public Law 85-926 appeared and provided for the training of professionals in special education. This act was the first Federal legislation specific to the mentally retarded.

Optimism continued in the 1960s as the Federal government increased its interest in and support for the study of mental retardation. In this decade, important advances were made in understanding etiological factors (e.g., PKU, maternal rubella), and effective behavior management procedures were used for the first time. Data collected during the 1970s gave reason for continued, if less than exuberant, optimism. Beyond continuing the scientific study of mental retardation, the 1970s were characterized by a growing concern for the rights of the mentally retarded. *Wyatt v. Stickney* (1972) resulted in the landmark "Minimum Constitutional Standards for Adequate Habilitation of the Mentally Retarded" which emphasized "the right to habilitation including medical treatment, education, and care, suited to their needs, regardless of age, degree of retardation or handicapped condition . . . right to the least restrictive conditions necessary to achieve the purposes of habilitation;" (p. 396). Several subsequent rulings were similar (*New York State ARC v. Rockefeller*, 1975; *Welsch v. Likens*, 1977). Maloney and Ward (1979), Robinson and Robinson (1976), and Sprague (1982) provide good coverage of the rights of mentally retarded individuals (also see Griffity, later in this book).

Also in the 1950s and 1960s, psychological assessment reached its peak and a strong antitesting sentiment arose. There were a number of reasons that contributed such as: (1) concerns about invasion of privacy and confidentiality, (2) tests being viewed as secret and mystical (believed necessary for content validity), (3) outright misuse and charlatanism, (4) professional concern over predictive validity, (5) cultural bias, (6) concern that psychological assessment is contrary to humanism, (7) the onset of behaviorism which called for observational analysis of behavior, and (8) concern that many psychologists are not adequately trained to administer tests and interpret test results. Maloney and Ward (1979) discuss these issues in detail.

IQ and the Definition and Classification of Mental Retardation

Early definitions of mental retardation were vague, imprecise, and based solely on an intelligence test score (IQ), or in terms of adult behavior (for a review see Blanton, 1975, or Robinson & Robinson, 1976). In the past decade, attempts have been made to "objectify" definitions of mental retardation as well as make them applicable to children, adolescents, and adults (Grossman, 1977; Hobbs, 1975).

While there are several contemporary definitions of mental retardation, such as Bijou's (1966) definition emphasizing the individual having a limited behavior repertoire due to inadequate experimental history, and Mercer's (1973) definition emphasizing socially defined status and roles, the definitions of the American Association of Mental Deficiency (AAMD; Grossman, 1977) and the American Psychiatric Association (in Diagnostic and Statistical Manual-III, DSM-III), are the two most widely used.

Both the AAMD and DSM-III definitions follow guidelines proposed by Heber (1961) and define mental retardation in terms of subaverage general intellectual functioning, concurrent deficits in adaptive behavior, and onset during the developmental period. Within these definitions, subaverage intellectual functioning refers to an IQ two or more standard deviations below the men, deficits in adaptive behavior refer to a lack of behaviors necessary to meet the standards of personal independence and social responsibility expected for a given chronological age, and developmental period refers to the period of time between birth and the 18th birthday.

These two definitions differ from previous definitions in a number of important ways. First, adaptive behavior is analyzed on an individual basis in terms of maturation, learning, and social adjustment appropriate for the chronological age. For example, the development of sensorimotor skills (e.g., walking, talking) are emphasized during infancy and preschool years, academic skills are emphasized during adolescence, and economic, vocational, and socialization skills are emphasized during adulthood. Second, present behaviors are emphasized. Clinicians do not have to rely on historical notes, and predictions of future functioning are minimized. This acknowledges that an individual may be mentally retarded in one setting, but not in another, and that it is possible for an individual to acquire the skills necessary to become non-retarded. The notions of "incurability," "inheritability," and "permanence" are minimized. And third, all three of the components in the definition of mental retardation must be met for an individual to be considered mentally retarded. For example, an individual having an IQ of 60 but living and working independently would not be considered mentally retarded.

Likewise, an individual with an IQ of 85 who displayed severe deficits in adaptive behaviors would not be considered mentally retarded. This is not to say, however, that this individual is not developmentally disabled (see Diagnosis of Mental Retardation later in this chapter). The primary distinction between the AAMD and DSM-III definitions is that the AAMD definition avoids differentiation of mental retardation from other childhood disorders such as attention deficit disorder, autism, childhood schizophrenia, or hyperactivity, while the DSM-III definition does not. The relative merits of a differential diagnosis are debatable because of the difficulty in obtaining agreement on the dimensions which distinguish mental retardation from other childhood disorders (Matson & Barrett, 1982).

Mental retardation is typically classified according to severity, or degree, although other modes of classification (e.g., clinical symptoms, etiology) are sometimes used. The most widely used classification system is the one suggested by the AAMD (Grossman, 1977). This system classifies mental retardation as mild, moderate, severe, or profound based on an individual's score on an intelligence test in conjunction with present level of adaptive functioning. The DSM-III system uses the same four classifications, but differs from the AAMD system in that assignment to a classification is based solely on IQ. Thus there is some inconsistency in the DSM-III system as two criteria (IQ and level of adaptive functioning) must be met for a determination of mental retardation, but only one criterion must be met (IQ) in the determination of degree of mental retardation.

Quoting from the AAMD manual (Grossman, 1977), the four degrees of mental retardation are defined as follows:

1. *Mild mental retardation,* a term used to describe the degree of mental retardation present when intelligence testing scores range more than 2 and up to 3 standard deviations below the norm (52 to 67 on the Stanford-Binet and 55 to 60 on the Wechsler Scales): many educable retarded individuals function at this level; such children usually can master basic academic skills while adults at this level may maintain themselves independently or semi-independently in the community.

2. *Moderate mental retardation,* a term used to describe the degree of mental retardation when intelligence testing scores range more than 3 and up to 4 standard deviations below the norm (36 to 51 on the Stanford-Binet and 40 to 54 on the Wechsler Scales): many trainable individuals function at this level; such persons usually can learn self-help, communication, social and simple occupational skills but only limited academic or vocational skills.

3. *Severe mental retardation,* a term used to describe the degree of mental retardation when intelligence testing scores range more than 4 and up to 5 standard deviations below the norm [20 to 35 on the Stanford-Binet and 25 to 39 on the Wechsler Scales (extrapolated)]: such persons re-

quire continuing and close supervision but may perform self-help and simple work tasks under supervision, sometimes called dependent retarded.

4. *Profound mental retardation,* a term used to describe the degree of mental retardation present when intelligence testing scores are more than 5 standard deviations below the norm [19 and below on the Wechsler Scales (extrapolated)]: such persons require continuing and close supervision but some persons may be able to perform simple self-help tasks: profoundly retarded persons often have other handicaps and may require total life support systems for maintenance. (p. 149)

A slightly different classification system is used in educational settings. Three classifications based on severity, learning ability, and IQ are used. The first classification is for the educable mentally retarded/impaired (EMR or EMI), the second classification is for the trainable mentally retarded/impaired (TMR or TMI), and the third classification is for the severely and profoundly mentally retarded/impaired (SMI or PMI). The EMI group consists of individuals with IQs in the 50/55–70/75 range (varies with schools) and school emphasis is on developing basic academic (e.g., reading, spelling, writing) skills and independent to semi-independent community living skills. The TMI group consists of individuals with IQs in the 25/35–50/55 range and school emphasis is on developing self-care, prevocational, and socialization skills. The SMI group consists of individuals with IQs below 25/35 and school emphasis is on developing basic self-care.

IQ and the Prevalence and Distribution of Mental Retardation

Prevalence of mental retardation refers to the number of mentally retarded individuals in a population at a given point in time (Heber, 1970). There are disagreements as to the prevalence of mental retardation in the United States with estimates ranging from .05 percent to 13 percent of the population. However, about 3 percent is generally accepted as the rule-of-thumb. This 3 percent estimate correlates highly with the number of individuals having IQs two or more standard deviations below the mean (below 68 on the Stanford-Binet and below 70 on the Wechsler scales). Using calculations similar to the ones presented by Dingman and Tarjan (1960) with adjustments based on a 1980 general population of 222 million people, it is estimated that there are 7,247,940 mentally retarded individuals in the United States. The prevalence and distribution of mental retardation in the United States is presented per degree of mental retardation in Table 4-1.

Of the 7,247,940 mentally retarded individuals in the United States, approximately 190,000 (2.6 percent) reside in public institutions for the mentally retarded, 33,000 (0.5 percent) reside in private institutions, and 32,000 (0.4 percent) reside in public psychiatric institutions (Robinson & Robinson, 1976). The remain-

Table 4-1
Prevalence and Distribution of Mental Retardation in the United States

Classification	Standard Deviation Range	IQ Range		Number of Individuals	Percentage of MR Population
		Stanford-Binet	Wechsler		
Mild	−2.01 to −3.00	52–67	55–69	6,450,667	89.0
Moderate	−3.01 to −4.00	36–51	40–54	434,876	6.0
Severe	−4.01 to −5.00	20–35	25–39	253,678	3.5
Profound	Below −5.00	<20	<25	108,719	1.5
				Total = 7,247,940	100

Reprinted from Poling, AD & Breuning, SE. Overview of mental retardation. In SE Breuning & AD Poling (Eds.), *Drugs and Mental Retardation*. Springfield, IL: Charles C. Thomas, 1982. With permission.

ing 96.5 percent are not institutionalized. Even though mildly mentally retarded individuals account for 89 percent of the mentally retarded individuals in the United States, they account for only 9.5 percent of the institutionalized mentally retarded population. Conversely, severely and profoundly mentally retarded individuals account for only 5 percent of the mentally retarded individuals in the United States, but for 73.5 percent of the institutionalized mentally retarded population (Hobbs, 1975; Poling & Breuning, 1982).

There are several factors that affect the prevalence and distribution of mental retardation. Three of the most important are age, geographic region, and racial-ethnic background. Surveys show that during the school years and particularly adolescence there is a sharp peak in prevalence while there is a drop in adulthood. This appears to be due to the fact that most of the mildly mentally retarded individuals are recognized as such only during the school years. The school environment is more structured and demanding and lends itself to the identification of academic, behavioral, and social deficits. Only the more extreme individuals (e.g., severe and profound) are identified in the preschool years. Institutional admissions of mildly mentally retarded individuals primarily occur between the ages of 12–19 (40 percent) and are related to behavior problems. Individuals from more impoverished geographic regions and minority group members are more likely to be classified as mentally retarded (mostly mild). These individuals are more likely to have less formal education, be illiterate, and have deflated IQs.

IQ and the Diagnosis of Mental Retardation

The prevalence estimation of 3 percent and the corresponding values in Table 4-1 must be viewed with caution because they may be greatly altered by the method of assessment used in making the diagnosis of mental retardation. Despite the widespread use of the AAMD and DSM-III definitions and their specification of three criteria to be met in making a diagnosis of mental retardation, it is not uncommon to find diagnosis being one-dimensional. These one-dimensional diagnoses are typically based on IQ alone with a ceiling cutoff score of 70. That is, all individuals with IQs below 70 are mentally retarded. When this is done, prevalence is close to 3 percent. However, if a two-dimensional diagnosis is used (IQ plus adaptive behavior deficits) the prevalence may fall closer to 1 percent (Mercer, 1973). In this latter case, the incidence of mental retardation (number of new cases within specified period—usually one year) remains about 3 percent.

Intelligence Tests

In the following pages we will review several intelligence tests frequently used with the mentally retarded. By no means are we exhausting all possibilities. For a more thorough review of available tests, the reader is referred to Anastasi (1976), Salvia and Ysseldyke (1981), and Sattler (1974).

Stanford-Binet Intelligence Scale

Among the most widely used of the psychological assessment devices for measuring intelligence is the Stanford-Binet Intelligence Scale, Form L-M (Terman & Merrill, 1973). Currently in its third revision of the original 1916 edition (others being 1937, 1960), its use with the mentally retarded is particularly frequent because it extends to relatively low levels of ability (age 2) and presents an appealing format that allows numerous opportunities for successful performance (Robinson & Robinson, 1976). The subtests of the Stanford-Binet (L-M) can be classified within seven broadly defined categories: language, memory, conceptual thinking, reasoning, numerical reasoning, visual-motor, and social intelligence (Sattler, 1974). Essentially, individuals are asked to complete tasks purported to sample abilities in each of these areas. Through ". . . the sinking of shafts at (these) critical points" (Terman & Merrill, 1937, p. 4), a global estimate of intellectual ability is obtained. A resultant mental age score is then matched against normative data for chronological age and a corresponding deviation IQ ($\bar{x} = 100$, SD $= 16$) score is obtained.

Despite the routine use of the Stanford-Binet (L-M) and its popular acknowledgement among clinical psychologists as the "test of choice" when assessing pre-school children between the ages of two and 4 ½ years, the test has not been without criticism, particularly in regards to its most recent revision.

Although the standardization sample of the 1972 Stanford-Binet (L-M) included a suitable number of subjects (N = 2100 in seven communities), the test manual included no data concerning the demographic characteristics of the sample. Salvia, Ysseldyke, and Lee (1975) indicated that, with the 1972 renorming, although the norms of the test changed, placement of items at appropriate age levels did not. Thus, an "average" child must now perform above grade level to earn an average IQ.

In addition, neither reliability nor validity data were included in the test manual regarding the 1972 edition. The authors reported data obtained on earlier versions of the test (i.e., 1960 revision), assuming these data applied to the current revision.

Given the inadequate description of the normative sample, the bias introduced with the renorming, and the absence of adequate reliability and validity data, the 1972 Stanford-Binet (L-M) has questionable merit for use in making major educational, treatment, or placement decisions.

The Wechsler Scales

A second set of instruments for the measurement of intelligence are the Wechsler Scales: Wechsler Preschool and Primary Scale of Intelligence (Wechsler, 1967), Wechsler Intelligence Scale for Children—Revised (Wechsler, 1974), and the Wechsler Adult Intelligence Scale (Wechsler, 1955). Commonly known as the WPPSI, WISC-R and WAIS, respectively, these tests are the chief rivals of the Stanford-Binet. They are commonly employed with older children, adolescents, and adults functioning within the moderate and mild ranges of mental retardation, but are limited with younger children to those functioning only in the mild range of mental retardation because of the inability of the WISC-R and WPPSI to accurately reflect IQ levels below 60 (see Discussion for elaboration).

Similar to the Stanford-Binet (L-M), the Wechsler scales contain subtests that correspond to a number of broadly defined categories which, theoretically, reflect critical areas of intellectual ability (e.g., general knowledge, social judgment, numerical reasoning, verbal conceptual thinking, language, auditory memory, nonverbal reasoning, perceptual organization. visual memory, visual-motor, and motor speed). The subtests of the Wechsler scales are grouped into Verbal and Performance subscales which yield deviation IQs for both in addition to a Full Scale IQ ($\bar{x} = 100$, SD $= 15$) representative of collective performance and global intelligence.

The WAIS was standardized on 1700 subjects, the WISC-R on 2200, and the WPPSI on 1200. All samples were stratified based on age, sex, geographic region, urban-rural residence, race, edication, and occupation (or occupation of head-of-household), with the proportion of individuals included in each sample commensurate with the findings of the 1950 United States census.

Unlike the test manual for the Stanford-Binet (L-M), technical manuals accompanying the WPPSI, WISC-R, and WAIS, present extensive reliability data. Split-half reliability estimates for Verbal IQs range from .91 to .96, while Performance IQs range from .89 to .95 (with only one estimate below .90), and the Full-Scale IQ from .95 to .97.

Various studies (Salvia & Ysseldyke, 1981) have established the concurrent validity of the Wechsler Scales by correlating scores with other intelligence test scores. Correlations range from .82 to .95 for Full-Scale IQs.

Generally speaking, the reliability data provided by the Wechsler test manuals suggest that it is sufficiently high for use in making educational, treatment, and placement decisions. Limited validity data suggest the same. The tests have the additional advantage of providing subtest scores, which aid greatly in the identification of the tested individuals' relative strengths and weaknesses, as well as subscale (Verbal, Performance) and Full-Scale IQs which facilitate diagnostic clarity.

Slosson Intelligence Test

The Slosson Intelligence Test (Slosson, 1971) is a short test patterned after the Stanford-Binet (L-M), containing many highly similar items, and thus sampling a similar range of behaviors. The items range in difficulty from the 0.5 month through the adult level (18 + years). The test provides an age score which is in turn transformed into a ratio IQ. The variability of the mean and standard deviation of the test scores across age levels should also be noted. The means for the IQs range from 91.7 at age 15 to 114.6 at age 4. Similarly, the standard deviations range from 16.7 at age 17 to 31.2 at age 18 or older.

The normative sample for the Slosson was composed of various groups of individuals, inadequately described in the test manual, from New York State. No data concerning the proportion of individuals making up the classes included in the sample are provided.

The only reliability data provided consists of a test-retest reliability coefficient obtained on 139 persons ranging in age from 4 to 50 years. The sampling procedure does not prevent the confounding of true-score variance and chronological age variance, possibly resulting in a spuriously high coefficient (Salvia & Ysseldyke, 1981).

Correlations between the Slosson and the Stanford-Binet (L-M) constitute the validity data. The values range from .90 to .98; however, it should be remembered that the items on these two particular tests are highly similar.

Although the Slosson was designed as a screening device, care should be taken in its use and interpretation due to variable mean and standard deviation values and limited reliability and validity. In essense, it is not recommended for use in major educational, placement, and treatment decision-making.

McCarthy Scales of Children's Abilities

The McCarthy Scales of Children's Abilities (MSCA; McCarthy, 1972) consist of 18 subtests, for use with 2½ to 8½ year-olds, that sample block building, puzzle solving, pictoral memory, word knowledge, number questions, tapping sequence, verbal memory, right-left orientation, leg coordination, arm coordination, imitative action, draw-a-design, draw-a-child, numerical memory, verbal fluency, counting and sorting, opposite analogies, and conceptual grouping. These 18 tests make up the Verbal, Perceptual-Performance, Quantitative, Memory, Motor, and General Cognitive Scales. The test yields a scaled score ($\bar{x} = 100$, SD = 16) for the General Cognitive Scale, as well as separate scores ($\bar{x} = 50$, SD = 10) for the five remaining scales.

The MSCA was standardized on 100 children at each age level, stratified on the basis of sex, age, race, geographic region, father's occupation, and urban-rural residence, with proportions reflecting the 1970 U.S. census data.

The reliability coefficients reported were all calculated using the split-half method, with the exception of those for three subtests, which were calculated using the test-retest method. The coefficients range in value from .79 to .93 for the six major scales.

The test manual presents limited predictive and concurrent validity data based on studies correlating MSCA scores with various other intelligence test scores. Although the studies provide some support for the concurrent validity of the device, the samples in these studies were small, thus they provide limited information.

In summary, the standardization of the MSCA appears to be very good, the reliability better than average. The validity, however, has not been conclusively shown. As Salvia and Ysseldyke (1981) point out, no exceptional children were included in the sample, thus invalidating the use of this test with those populations.

Test of Receptive Skills or Non-verbal Tests

Each of the above mentioned tests provide information concerning both verbal and performance skills. However, with many individuals, particularly those with limited ability to emit vocal or gestural (i.e., sign language, symbol system) responses, the use of scales designed for special populations may be warranted. These tests primarily assess receptive language skills and should not be considered as comprehensive tests of so called intelligence. Only a very small sample of behavior is examined and these tests are of limited utility in assessment when used alone. Nonetheless, these tests are widely used with the mentally retarded and often provide the only applicable method of norm-referenced assessment.

Two of the more frequently used tests with the mentally retarded are the *Pictorial Test of Intelligence* (French, 1964) and the *Leiter International Performance Scale* (adapted by Arthur, 1950). The French Pictorial views six domains: picture vocabulary; form discrimination; information/comprehension; similarities; size/number; and immediate recall. This test is appropriate for individuals between the ages of three and eight years, has a mean of 100 and SD of 16, is adequately normed, has acceptable measures of reliability and validity, and scoring is fairly simple.

The Arthur Adaptation of the Leiter assesses analogies, discrimination, generalization, pattern completion, and sequencing. This test is reported appropriate for individuals between the ages of 2 and 18 years and has a mean of 95 and SD of 16. Because of the mean of 95 the scoring instructions require that five free points be added to the score. Results from the Leiter must be viewed cautiously as there are no normative data, reliability is unknown, and validity is low to non-existent. Administration and scoring are awkward as many of the test items require color discriminations while the scoring manual is illustrated in black and white.

General Considerations in Intelligence Testing

Regardless of which test an examiner selects, there are several general issues which must be considered. These issues have implications for how a test is administered as well as how the results are interpreted.

Use of Cutoff Scores

An IQ of 70 has become the conventional cutoff for mental retardation. Despite what the stated criterion are, persons scoring 70 or below are very often labeled mentally retarded. As stated earlier, the AAMD and DSM-III definitions of mental retardation require an IQ to be two or more standard deviations below the mean. This is not necessarily equivalent to a cutoff score of 70. As shown in Table 4-1, the Wechsler cutoff score for mental retardation is equivalent to a cutoff of 70 because its standard deviation is 15. But the Stanford-Binet cutoff is 67 because its standard deviation is 16. Thus, a person with a Stanford-Binet score of 68 is not two or more standard deviations below the mean. While the Stanford-Binet and Wechsler tests are the most commonly used, numerous other intelligence tests may appear as part of a diagnosis. The standard deviations of these tests must be utilized in making the diagnostic decision. For example, the Slosson Intelligence Test has a SD of approximately 24 and to be considered mentally retarded an individual would have to score 51 or lower. Other tests, as discussed above, have different SDs.

IQs as Fixed Values

Obtained IQs should not be considered as absolute fixed numbers. These scores, because of measurement error, only represent approximations of a "true" score. The obtained score is only one of a number of possible scores that may be achieved with a different sample of questions or with the same questions at different times. Each test has a standard error of measurement (SEM) that, simply put, reflects how much variation from the true score there may be. This variation increases as one estimates the true score at higher confidence intervals. For example, the Stanford-Binet has a SEM of 5.1. This means that with a 68 percent confidence interval an obtained score is within 5.1 points (+ or −) of the true score 68 percent of the time. However, using a 95 percent confidence interval the SEM doubles (two deviations) to 10.2 and indicates that the obtained score is within 10.2 points of the true score 95 percent of the time (Nunnally, 1967). Thus, a score of 66 on the Stanford-Binet indicates that 68 percent of the time the person's true score will be somewhere between 61 and 71, and 95 percent of the time the true score will be between 56 and 76. To actually estimate a true score, one would subtract the test mean (usually 100) from the obtained score, multiply this by the test's reliability coefficient, then add this product to the test mean (Salvia & Ysseldyke, 1981). With a Stanford-Binet score of 66 and a reliability coefficient of .80, the estimated true score would be 73 [(66 − 100) (.80) + 100]. When an obtained score is below the test mean and the reliability coefficient is less than 1.00, the estimated true score is always higher than the obtained score (Salvia & Ysseldyke, 1981). In this case, using the obtained score of 66 as an absolute may represent a misdiagnosis of mental retardation (i.e., Stanford-Binet cutoff of 67).

Cultural Bias

Much has been written concerning the inherent biases against minorities with most standardized tests. The mentally retarded are clearly a minority group and very few assessment devices have been designed with the mentally retarded in mind. Few tests have been standardized on a population of mentally retarded individuals. Nevertheless, the available tests are being used with the mentally retarded and can yield useful information if used judiciously.

Changes Over Time

It is a serious error to assume that a mentally retarded person's "score" is constant. There may be great fluctuation in scores across time for obvious reasons such as fatigue and illness, but also for a more subtle reason—lack of motivation. Numerous studies (Ayllon & Kelly, 1973; Breuning, 1982a; 1982b; Breuning & Davidson, 1981; Breuning & Davis, 1981; Breuning, Ferguson, Davidson, & Poling, in press; Breuning & Zella, 1978; Clingman & Fowler, 1976; Young, Bradley-Johnson, & Johnson, 1982; Willis & Shibata, 1978) have convincingly shown that the IQs of individuals having pretest IQs below the "norm" can be increased by approximately 20 points if reinforcement is delivered contingent upon correct responding to test items. However, such effects are minimal to non-existent as initial (pretest) scores reach 100 and above (Breuning & Zella, 1978; Clingman & Fowler, 1976).

With this data in mind, one may ask which score should be used in making a diagnosis of mental retardation and treatment planning—one obtained under standard conditions or under reinforcement conditions? For example, individuals are often assessed and then their IQ is relied upon heavily in the decision making process. For example, as reported by Breuning and Davis (1981), the position of the Department of Mental Health in Michigan is that centers for the mentally retarded/developmentally disabled are not to typically service individuals with IQs above 70. The 70 cutoff is irrespective of the score being two or more standard deviations below the norm. Often independent of adaptive skills, an individual with an IQ below 70 is easily admitted to many institutions for the mentally retarded/developmentally disabled. If a score is above 70, admission is much more difficult.

There are other clinical implications as well. For example, depending on how a person is tested, there may be classification changes. Breuning and Davis (1981) found that if scores obtained under standard conditions were used, four of five clients in one group would be labeled moderately mentally retarded and the fifth would be labeled profoundly mentally retarded. However, if scores obtained under a reinforcement condition were used, three clients would not be labeled mentally retarded and two would be labeled mildly mentally retarded.

An additional clinical concern relates to predictive validity. Willis and Shibata (1978) justifiably express concern that scores obtained under reinforcement conditions may only be predictors of success in reinforcement based educational and habilitative programs and scores obtained under standard conditions may only be predictors of performance in more traditional educational and habilitative programs. The findings of Breuning and Davis (1981) suggest that this is not always so. Concomitant with increases and decreases in IQs, they found increases and decreases in the availability of habilitative programs. Eleven of the participants in the study received new ancillary programs following increases in their scores. The performance of nine of these 11 participants was sufficient for them to continue in their new programs. On the other hand, six participants were reported to be dropped from programs following decreases in their scores despite acceptable performances within their programs. These findings suggest that in many cases "IQs are not an accurate predictor of performance in educational and habilitative programs, but rather an accurate predictor of the availability of educational and habilitative programs" (Breuning & Davis, 1981, p. 319).

There are no clear guidelines as to when, or why, examiners would choose to use reinforcement versus standard conditions. However, examiners must decide whether they are attempting to determine which test items the mentally retarded client can correctly respond to, or which test items the client will respond to. Concern over the possible violation of standard procedures is irrelevant here because administration procedures of these tests were never standardized with a mentally retarded population. The issues are complex and "examiners must carefully weigh the possible influence of IQs and whether or not their client would best be served by being tested under standard or reinforcement conditions" (Breuning & Davis, 1981, p. 320).

Medication Effects

Recent surveys have shown that as many as 50 percent of the mentally retarded residing in institutions or community foster homes/group homes are receiving a psychoactive medication (Breuning & Poling, 1982a, 1982b). Most of these medications can seriously impair adaptive and cognitive function and therefore, have implications for psychoeducational assessment. This is particularly true if reinforcement conditions are utilized as part of the intellectual assessment process. The results of two recent studies (Breuning & Davidson, 1981; Breuning, Ferguson, Davidson, & Poling, in press) have shown that mentally retarded individuals obtained improved IQs under reinforcement conditions only when the individuals were not receiving drugs such as Haldol (McNeil Pharmaceutical), Mellaril (Sardoz), or Thorazine (Smith, Kline & French). A recent study by Breuning (1982b) suggests that hyperactive mentally retarded children may show improved IQs when tested under both standard and reinforcement conditions while receiving an optimal dose of Ritalin (CIBA). This is tentative data at this time. The interested reader is referred to a recent article which addresses medication/intellectual assessment issues in detail (Breuning, Davis, & Poling, 1982) and to the chapter by Sisson and Breuning in this book.

Psychoeducational Tests

It is well accepted, even in the most conservative of testing circles, that a singular reliance on the results of intelligence tests (e.g., mental age, IQ) provides insufficient data for the comprehensive assessment of an individual's cognitive abilities. This applies equally to the intellectually average and gifted as well as the mentally retarded. As such, additional measures are employed as supplements to intelligence testing.

The achievement test is one such additional measure commonly used with mentally retarded populations as an adjunct to intelligence tests. Again, as with intelligence tests, the principal intent of the achievement test is diagnostic through the assignment of grade and age equivalents based on normative data. Results of achievement tests are typically used to identify relative strengths and weaknesses in skill areas related to school performance and the underlying potential to bene-fit from academic instruction.

Although achievement tests using a group format are more routinely used with nonretarded school-age children, individually administered achievement tests such as the *Peabody Individual Achievement Test* (PIAT) (Dunn & Markwardt, 1970) and the *Wide Range Achievement Test* (WRAT) (Jastak & Jastak, 1978) have widespread use with children in the mild range of mental retardation.

The PIAT is comprised of subtests designed to measure abilities in several areas related to education performance (e.g., general knowledge, spelling, reading recognition, reading comprehension, mathematics). The standardization sample for the PIAT included 2899 public school students from 29 participating school districts. At least 200 students were sampled within each of the 13 grade levels for which normative data are presented. According to Salvia and Ysseldyke (1981), the standardization of the PIAT is superior in comparison to other individually administered achievement tests. Median reliabilities for the subtests are reported as ranging from .64 to .89, with concurrent validity estimates ranging from .58 to .95 when correlated with 1965 WRAT subtest scores.

The 1978 edition of the WRAT is the fourth revision (others being 1946, 1965, 1976) or the original test which appeared in 1936. The WRAT consists of two levels: Level 1 for students younger than 12 years and Level 2 for students aged 12 and older. Reading, spelling, and arithmetic subtests comprise the test at both levels.

Unlike the PIAT, which sampled students with respect to geographic region and community size, proper standardization was not attempted with the WRAT. The authors simply assumed that by sampling 400–600 students at each age level (at half-year intervals through age 13 and in one to 12-year intervals thereafter), that variables such as sex, race socioeconomic status, intelligence, geographic region, community size, etc., would naturally come to represent the population at large. The technical manual for the WRAT presents no data to this effect, however.

In addition, no reliability or validity data are presented for the 1978 WRAT. However, split-half reliability coefficients for the 1965 edition are reported at greater than .94, with concurrent validity estimates ranging between .58 to .95 when correlated with PIAT subtests, as mentioned above.

In general, although use of the PIAT and WRAT alone provide insufficient data bases for making major educational, treatment, and placement decisions, both tests are deemed adequate for screening purposes particularly when used as supplemental information sources to intelligence test data. It should be noted, however, that the PIAT is the superior of the two instruments, based largely on its approach to standardization and more comprehensive nature (five subtests *vs.* three subtests); and, that the 1965 edition of the WRAT is preferred over the more recent 1976 and 1978 revisions, for which no reliability and validity data are presented.

Adaptive Behavior Assessment

Primarily due to the problems associated with intelligence and achievement testing, and as an attempt to reduce the disproportionate labeling of minorities as mentally retarded, the American Association on Mental Deficiency (AAMD) in 1961 expanded its definition of mental retardation to include deficits in adaptive behavior as one of the criteria for its diagnosis (Heber, 1961). At that time, the AAMD proposed a definition in which adaptive behavior referred to ". . . the effectiveness with which the individual copes with the natural and social demands of his environment" (Heber, 1961, p. 61).

Several theoreticians (Leland, Nihira, Foster, Shellhaas, & Kagin, 1968; Mercer, 1973; Robinson & Robinson, 1976), as well as a number of governmental agencies and committees (Office of Civil Rights, 1976; President's Committee on Mental Retardation, 1975), have subsequently offered definitions for the term adaptive behavior. The definitions are similar, and all place varying emphasis on independent functioning, personal responsibility, and social responsibility. Currently the most widely accepted definition is that of the AAMD (Grossman, 1977), which defines adaptive behavior as ". . . the effectiveness of degree with which the individual meets the standards of personal independence and social responsibility expected of his age or cultural group" (p. 11).

Although a general definition for adaptive behavior seems to be agreed upon, it is somewhat vague and imprecise, and data from the empirical measurement of adaptive behavior are few. The various behaviors which comprise those classified as adaptive are often not easily specified, nor are they easily observed or measured. The specific behaviors considered as "adaptive", will always be socially determined, and as with indices of intelligence, will to some extent reflect the view of the particular test author.

As mentioned earlier, most definitions mandate the assessment of both intellectual functioning and adaptive behavior before an individual can be diagnosed as mentally retarded. In a study designed to survey state policies regarding the measurement of adaptive behavior, Morrow and Coulter (1978) asked agencies to list specific measures of adaptive behavior of which they were aware. The American Association on Mental Deficiency (AAMD) Adaptive Behavior Scale-Public School Version (Lambert, Windmiller, Cole, & Figueroa, 1974), Vineland Social Maturity Scale (Doll, 1965), the System of Multicultural Pluralistic Assessment-SOMPA (Mercer & Lewis, 1977), and the AAMD Adaptive Behavior Scale-1975 Revision (Nihira, Foster, Shellhaas, & Leland, 1975) proved to be the most frequently mentioned measures.

Vineland Social Maturity Scale (VSMS)

The oldest, if not the most well-known and widely used of these measures, is the Vineland Social Maturity Scale (Doll, 1965). The Vineland requires a recorder to evaluate client competencies as mastered, emergent, or latent within several classes of behavior (self-help, self-direction, occupation, communication, locomotion, and socialization), based on structured discussion with a knowledgeable informant. The Vineland is organized on the basis of developmental competencies (ages 0–30) and uses a hierarchical format to arrive at a measure of social age (SA). A ratio social quotient can also be caluculated, although the latter is usually ignored.

The norms for the VSMS were collected in 1935 and consist of 620 white, middle class individuals from greater Vineland, New Jersey. Both children with educational or mental retardation and those with physical handicaps were excluded.

Test-retest reliability estimates are provided in the test manual. The test-retest correlation for SA is .98. The manual also provides inter-interviewer and inter-respondent correlations; the pooled test-retest correlation being .92 for SA.

The validity of the VSMS is estimated to be over .80 when scores are correlated with subjective ratings of social competence made by those familiar with the subject. The content validity, however, must be questioned since the items and their placement at appropriate levels were determined nearly 50 years ago.

Although reliability and validity estimates are above average for a testing instrument, the VSMS is a dated scale. A revision of the scale, which is being prepared, is necessary before its value for use today can be assessed.

System of Multicultural Pluralistic Assessment (SOMPA)

The newest of the above mentioned measures is the System of Multicultural Pluralistic Assessment-SOMPA (Mercer & Lewis, 1977). Conceptualized as a total system of assessment, the SOMPA consists of nine sets of measures used within three separate assessment models: medical, social-system, and pluralistic. Among several measures within the social-system assessment model is the Adaptive Behavior Inventory for Children (ABIC), appropriate for use with children ages 5 through 11 years. Although it is important to note the ABIC was not designed for use outside of the total SOMPA package (Lewis & Mercer, 1978), it will be briefly discussed without reference to other measures because of its particular relevance to the topic under discussion.

The format of the ABIC is similar to that of the Vineland. A recorder categorically rates client competencies (latent, emergent, mastered) in relation to several classes of behavior (family role performance, community role performance, peer group role performance, non-academic school role performance, earner/consumer role performance, self-maintenance role performance) on the basis of information obtained through a knowledgeable informant (e.g., parent). As with the Vineland, the ABIC is organized using a developmental-hierarchical format, with items placed in chronological order from simplest to most difficult, within each age group. In addition, the ABIC contains a subset of items appropriate for use with clients of all ages. In total, the ABIC consists of 242 items distributed across the six role performance subscales. Raw scores are obtained for each of the subscales and converted to scaled scores ($\bar{x} = 50$, SD = 15) on the basis of normative data. Analysis of the scaled scores indicates the client's level of adaptive ability within each behavior class.

The great majority of the split-half estimates of reliability for the SOMPA subtests are below .9, although the correlation for the average scale scores is approximately .97. Moreover, statistical errors in computing interrater agreement preclude evaluation of that data. The test manual provides no data concerning validity.

The reliabilities reported in the SOMPA test manual for the ABIC are generally too low for use in making a major educational, placement, or treatment decision concerning the mentally retarded. The lack of validity data and limited norm sample requires the test user to exercise caution in administering and interpreting this newly developed test.

Adaptive Behavior Scales (ABS)

The "standard" for the assessment of adaptive behavior of the mentally retarded is the AAMD Adaptive Behavior Scales (ABS), the most recent of which is the 1975 Revision (Nihira et al., 1975). Originally developed in 1969 to provide operational descriptions and measurements of the adaptive behavior of mentally retarded individuals, the 1975 Revised edition of the ABS consists of two parts covering 24 behavioral domains. Part I includes 10 behavioral domains (independent functioning, physical development, economic activity, language development, numbers and time, domestic activity, vocational activity, self-direction, responsibility, and socialization) and 21 subdomains. These behavioral domains are organized within a developmental framework with information gathered in a manner similar to that used by the Vineland and ABIC (interviewing the most knowledgeable informant). Scoring is accomplished in step-wise fashion with the rater/recorder addressing individual items within each subdomain before computing subdomain totals, and finally, domain totals. The raw domain score for each behavior is then matched against normative data (for 4000 institutionalized mentally retarded individuals ages 3–69 years) and converted to decile ranks. The procedure for administering and scoring the 14 additional behavior domains of Part II of the ABS is identical to that used in Part I of the scale. However, since Part II addresses social expectations and the measurement of maladaptive behaviors (violent and destructive behavior, antisocial behavior, rebellious behavior, untrustworthy behavior, withdrawal, stereotyped behavior and odd mannerisms, inappropriate interpersonal manners, unacceptable vocal habits, unacceptable or eccentric habits, self-abusive behavior, hyperactive tendencies, sexually aberrant behavior, psychological disturbances, and use of medications), domains are not organized using a developmental format.

Only interrater agreement data is presented in the ABS manual in the form of correlation coefficients between ratings by attendants for 133 subjects. The mean reliability estimates ranged from .71 to .92 in Part I and from .37 to .77 in Part II.

Minimal validity data is presented by the test authors in the manual. A factor analysis indicates three factors are present in the ABS: personal independence; social maladaption; and personal maladaption. No evidence of content validity is provided by the authors.

Although the ABS was purportedly developed to aid in planning remedial programs, it is a norm-referenced device, usually thought to be inappropriate for such uses. Reliability estimates are low, and little data support the validity of the instrument. The AAMD Adaptive Behavior Scale does not appear adequate for use in making major decisions concerning the three groups of handicapped persons for which it was designed. However, this scale is currently being revised in an attempt to alleviate its shortcomings.

Discussion

With the mentally retarded, the traditional use of standardized intelligence tests such as the Stanford-Binet (L-M) and the Wechsler scales has involved applying the IQ for diagnosis and classification of intellectual ability. As noted in earlier sections, derived IQs greater than two standard deviations below mean performance for chronological age are indicative of mental retardation. Typically, the diagnosis of mental retardation is further classified according to levels of severity such as mild, moderate, severe, and profound (Grossman, 1977), the purpose of which is to standardize the interpretation of test performance vis-à-vis the IQ. Beyond its diagnostic function, however, the clinical utility of a standardized intelligence test is derived from its ability to accurately assess the categorical strengths and weaknesses of the individual tested and its assumed predictive validity with respect to school and vocational performance. Of the intelligence tests reviewed, the Wechsler scales (WPPSI, WISC-R, WAIS) were recommended as the strongest assessment instruments upon which to base major educational, treatment, and placement decisions. The Slosson Intelligence Test was noted as the weakest among the commonly used devices for such decision-making.

However, the Wechsler scales are not without their limitations. As stated earlier, these tests may be of questionable validity with individuals who obtain an IQ below 60. We caution the examiner to realize that the WAIS, WISC-R, and WPPSI assume basal mental age levels of 16, 6, and 4 ½ years, respectively. Thus, individuals with mental ages below these prerequisite basal levels will necessarily obtain deflated IQs. With individuals suspected of having a mental age lower than that assumed by a given Wechsler Scale, we recommend that the Stanford-Binet, McCarthy Scales, and/or Leiter be substituted. It is important to remember, however, that the substitute tests also present certain limitations, as reviewed earlier, and should be interpreted accordingly.

Among the individual achievement tests available, both the Peabody Individual Achievement Test and the 1965 edition of the Wide Range Achievement Test were recommended for use with children in the upper moderate and mild range of mental retardation. Both tests were deemed adequate as supplemental measures of cognitive skill when used in conjunction with standardized intelligence tests, such as the Wechsler scales. As with the intelligence tests, the clinical utility of the achievement test is derived from the accuracy with which it assesses the relative academic strengths and weaknesses of the individual tested. As such, these tests also may contribute useful information to the decision-making process surrounding educational, treatment, and placement planning with the mentally retarded. It should be noted, however, that intelligence and achievement test data does little in the way of providing the examiner with meaningful information about the individual tested. The diagnosis and classification of an individual based on mental age, IQ, and educational grade equivalents, does little more than project a hollow, stereotyped image of the tested individual. In no way does it impart the adaptive significance of the individual's intellectual or cognitive skills. Instead, the use of classification schemes implies fixed ability levels that may not be a true representation of intellectual or educational potential, and certainly not a valid predictor of the educational or vocational competencies that may be gained through intensive habilitation (Kazdin & Straw, 1976).

The Vineland, ABIC (SOMPA), and ABS were among the most frequently cited measures of adaptive behavior in the Morrow and Coulter (1978) survey of state policies. The Vineland is perhaps the most widely abused and outdated measure of the three. It has been severely criticized for its lack of usefulness in developing strategies for intervention and lack of comprehensiveness in assessing adaptive behavior. Despite these criticisms, psychologists often grossly misuse the Vineland by administering it as a substitute for intelligence tests to assess children found to be "untestable," and then use the overall social age as a measure to establish general cognitive levels. Even when the Vineland is used properly, in conjunction with a standardized measure of intelligence (and, if appropriate, an achievement test) in assessing the mentally retarded, psychologists frequently and wisely do not use the resultant social age in the decision-making process of diagnosing mental retardation. As originally designed, the Vineland is a structured interview technique with its clinical utility derived from gaining insight into the parents' or other third party informant's conceptualization of the presence or absence of adaptive behavior. This is not to say that the Vineland cannot function as an adaptive behavior rating scale when completed on the basis of direct observation. However, the limitations with this approach (e.g., lack of comprehensiveness, outdated norms, etc.) as discussed earlier, necessitate an extensive revision of the existing scale before its practical utility can be adequately assessed.

The ABIC is a relatively new instrument and has yet to be critically evaluated. However, because it is not recommended to be used apart from the total SOMPA system, the ABIC can only be relevant for those individuals for whom the entire SOMPA can be administered. Decisions based on the results of the SOMPA assessment measures are obtained from the combined information of the Parent

Interview, Student Evaluation, ABIC, the WISC-R, and the Bender-Gestalt. Since the entire SOMPA including the ABIC is normed only on nonretarded children between the ages of 5 and 12, and the WISC-R and Bender-Gestalt may not be valid for many mentally retarded children in that age group, the ABIC has very limited usefulness for assessing adaptive behavior of the mentally retarded. Future investigations should be directed toward determining if the ABIC can be used independently of the total SOMPA package without diminishing its predictive validity, as well as establishing norms for using the ABIC with mentally retarded children.

Potentially, the best instrument of the three for assessing adaptive behavior is the ABS. Comparisons of profiles derived from repeated administrations across time can be helpful in assessing the areas of relative strength and weakness necessary for developing strategies targeted at intervention/programming. However, since the ABS does not provide an overall rating of adaptive behavior, the scale has limited utility in the psychometric assessment (identification/classification) of mental retardation. In addition to this difficulty, the objectivity of some items on the ABS is questionable and reliability and validity coefficients are low, particularly on Part II. In truth, the ABS has potential, through its impending revision, to become a sound instrument for the assessment of adaptive behavior, given remediation of the weaknesses of test construction cited above.

It is important to note that like intelligence, adaptive behavior is a nebulous and ill-defined concept. Those who are required to administer measures of adaptive behavior and make diagnostic and/or treatment decisions concerning the mentally retarded based on the results must carefully examine the test for technical adequacy and the validity of purposes for which it is intended.

CONCLUSION

Throughout this chapter we have attempted to present the unique problems an examiner will likely face when performing and interpreting an intellectual assessment with a mentally retarded individual. It must be remembered that the majority of these tests were not designed with the mentally retarded in mind (e.g., standardization). Thus, at best, all intellectual test data obtained with mentally retarded individuals are of questionable validity. Nevertheless, many laws and regulations require test information in making diagnostic and treatment planning decisions and these tests can yield useful behavioral data. There is, we believe, nothing inherently wrong with the adjunct use of an intelligence test in comprehensively assessing an individual's behavioral strengths and weaknesses. The examiner must always be mindful however, that use of an intelligence test as the sole measure of an individual's adaptive behavior profile cannot be justified ethically, morally, or legally.

Acknowledgment

Preparation of this chapter was with support from grants MH-32206, MH-30915, and MH/HD-37449 from the National Institute of Mental Health; and, grant 300-82-0368 from the Department of Education.

REFERENCES

Anastasi, A. *Psychological Testing*. New York: Macmillan, 1976

Arthur, G. *The Arthur Adaptation of the Leiter International Performance Scale*. Chicago, IL: C.H. Stoelting, 1950

Ayllon, T, & Kelly, K. Effects of reinforcement on standardized test performance. *Journal of Applied Behavior Analysis*, 1972, *5*, 477–484

Bijou, SW. A functional Analysis of Retarded development. In NR Ellis (Ed.), *International review of research in mental retardation*. (Volume 1). New York: Academic Press, 1966

Binet, A. *Les idées modernes sur les enfants*. Paris: Flammarion, 1913

Binet, A, & Simon, T. "*Sur la necessité d'etablir un diagnostic scientifique des états inferieurs de l'intelligence,*" *L'année psychologique*, 1905, *11*

Blanton, RL. Historical perspectives on classification of mental retardation. In N Hobbs (Ed.), *Issues in the classification of children*. Volume 1. San Francisco: Jossey-Bass, 1975

Breuning, SE. An applied dose-response curve of thioridazine with the mentally retarded: Aggressive, self-stimulatory, intellectual and workshop behaviors—a preliminary report. *Psychopharmacology Bulletin*, 1982, *18*, 57–59 (a)

Breuning, SE. *Efficacy of methylphenidate with hyperactive mentally retarded individuals. A multidimensional analysis*. Presented at the American Association on Mental Deficiency Convention, Boston, May, 1982 (b)

Breuning, SE, & Davidson, NA. Effects of psychotropic drugs on intelligence test performance of institutionalized retarded adults. *American Journal of Mental Deficiency*, 1981, *85*, 575–579

Breuning, SE, & Davis, VJ. Reinforcement effects on the intelligence test performance of institutionalized retarded adults: Behavioral analysis, directional control, and implications for habilitation. *Applied Research in Mental Retardation*, 1981, *2*, 307–321

Breuning, SE, Davis, VJ, & Poling, AD. Pharmacotherapy with the mentally retarded: implications for clinical psychologists. *Clinical Psychology Review*, 1982, *2*, 79–114

Breuning, SE, Ferguson, DG, Davidson, NA, & Poling, AD. Effects of thioridazine on the intellectual performance of mentally retarded responders and non-responders. *Archives of General Psychiatry* (in press)

Breuning, SE, & Poling, AD. Pharmacotherapy with the mentally retarded. In JL Matson & RP Barrett (Eds.), *Psychopathology of the Mentally Retarded*. New York: Grune & Stratton, 1982 (a)

Breuning, SE, & Poling, AD. *Drugs and Mental Retardation*. Springfield, Illinois: Charles C. Thomas, 1982 (b)

Breuning, SE, & Zella, WF. Effects of individualized incentives on norm-referenced IQ test performance of high-school students in special education classes. *Journal of School Psychology*, 1978, *16*, 220–226

Bruner, JS. The course of cognitive growth. *American Psychologist*, 1964, *19*, 1–15

Cattell, RB. *Abilities: Their structure, growth, and action*. Boston: Houghton Mifflin, 1971

Clingman, JM, & Fowler, FL. The effects of primary reward on the IQ performance of grade-school children as a function of initial IQ level. *Journal of Applied Behavior Analysis*, 1976, *9*, 19–23

Dingman, HF, & Tarjan, G. Mental retardation and the normal distribution curve. *American Journal of Mental Deficiency*, 1960, *64*, 991–994

Doll, DA. *Vineland Social Maturity Scale*. Circle Pines, MN: American Guidance Service, 1965

Dunn, LM, & Markwardt, FC. *Peabody Individual Achievement Test*. Circle Pines MN: American Guidance Service, 1970

French, JL. *Pictorial Test of Intelligence*. Boston: Houghton-Mifflin, 1964

Goddard, HH. *The Kallikak Family*. New York: Macmillan, 1912

Goldstein, H. Social and occupational adjustment. In HA Stevens & RF Heber (Eds.), *Mental Retardation*. Chicago: University of Chicago Press, 1964

Grossman, HJ (Ed.). *Manual on terminology and classification in mental retardtion*. Washington, DC: American Association on Mental Deficiency, 1977

Guilford, JP. Intelligence has three facets. *Science*, 1968, *160*, 615–620

Halstead, WC. *Brain and intelligence: A quantitative study of the frontal lobes*. Chicago: University of Chicago Press, 1947

Hebb, DO. *The organization of behavior*. New York: Wiley, 1949

Heber, RF. A manual on terminology and classification in mental retardation. *American Journal of Mental Deficiency* (Monograph Supplement), 1961

Heber, RF. *Epidemiology of mental retardation*. Springfield, IL: Charles C. Thomas, 1970

Herrnstein, RJ. *IQ in the meritocracy*. Boston: Atlantic, Little, Brown, 1973

Hobbs, N. *The futures of children*. San Francisco: Jossey-Bass, 1975

Jastak, JF, & Jastak, CR. *The Wide Range Achievement Test*. Wilmington, DE: Guidance Associates of Delaware, 1965

Jastak, J & Jastak, S. *Wide range achievement test*. Wilmington, DE: Jastak Associates, 1978

Kamin, LJ. *The science and politics of IQ*. Potomac, MD: Erlbaum, 1974

Kazdin, AE, & Straw, MK. Assessment of the behavior of the mentally retarded. In M Hersen & AS Bellack (Eds.), *Behavioral assessment: A practical handbook*. New York: Pergamon, 1976

Krischell, CH. State laws on marriage and sterilization of the mentally retarded. *Mental Retardation*, 1972, *10*, 36–38

Lambert, NM, Windmiller, M, Cole, L, & Figueroa, R. *AAMD Adaptive Behavior Scale-Public School Version*. Washington, DC: American Association on Mental Deficiency, 1974

LeLand, H, Nihira, K, Foster, R, Shellhaas, M, & Kagin, E. *Conference on measurement of adaptive behavior: II*. Parsons, Kansas: Parsons State Hospital and Training Center, 1968

Lewis, JF, & Mercer, JR. The system of multicultural pluralistic assessment: SOMPA. In WA Coulter & HW Morrow (Eds.), *Adaptive behavior: Concepts and measurements*. New York: Grune & Stratton, 1978

Maloney, P, & Ward, M. *Mental retardation and modern society*. New York: Oxford, 1979

Masland, RL, Sarason, SB, & Gladwin, T. *Mental subnormality: Biological, psychological, and cultural factors*. New York: Basic Books, 1958

Matson, JL, & Barrett, RP (Eds.). *Psychopathology in the mentally retarded*. New York: Grune & Stratton, 1982

McCarthy, D. *Manual for the McCarthy Scales of Children's Abilities*. New York: Psychological Corporation, 1972

Mercer, JR. *Labelling and the mentally retarded*. Berkeley: University of California Press, 1973

Mercer, JR, & Lewis, JF. *System of multicultural pluralistic assessment: SOMPA*. New York: Psychological Corporation, 1977

Morrow, HW, & Coulter, WA. A survey of state policies regarding adaptive behavior. In WA Coulter & HW Morrow (Eds.), *Adaptive behavior: Concepts and measurements*. New York: Grune & Stratton, 1978

New York ARC v. Rockefeller, 357 F. Supp. 752 (E.D.N.Y., 1975)

Nihira, K, Foster, R, Shellhaas, M, & Leland, H. *American Association on Mental Deficiency Adaptive Behavior Scale, 1975* Revision. Washington, DC: American Association on Mental Deficiency, 1975

Nunnally, J. *Psychometric theory*. New York: McGraw-Hill, 1967

Office of Civil Rights. Memorandum from OCR to state and local agencies on elimination of discrimi-
    nation in the assessment of children to special education classes for the mentally retarded. In T
    Oakland (Ed.), *With Bias Toward None: Minority Group Children*. Lexington, KY: Coordinat-
    ing Office for Regional Resource Centers, 1976

Piaget, J. *The psychology of intelligence*. New York: Harcourt Brace, 1950

Poling, AD, & Breuning, SE. Overview of mental retardation. In SE Breuning & AD Poling (Eds.),
    Drugs and mental retardation. Springfield, IL: Charles C. Thomas Press, 1982

President's Committee on Mental Retardation. *Mental Retardation . . . the Known and the Unknown*.
    Washington, DC: Government Printing Office, 1975

Robinson, NM, & Robinson, HB. *The mentally retarded child*. New York: McGraw-Hill, 1976

Salvia, J, & Ysseldyke, JE. *Assessment in special and remedial education. Second edition*. Boston:
    Houghton-Mifflin, 1981

Salvia, J, Ysseldyke, JE, & Lee, M. 1972 revision of the Stanford-Binet: A farewell to the mental
    age. *Psychology in the Schools, 1975, 12*, 421–422

Sattler, JM. *Assessment of children's intelligence*. Philadelphia: W.B. Saunder 1974

Slosson, RL. *Slosson Intelligence Test (SIT) for Children and Adults*. East Aurora, NY: Slosson Edu-
    cational Publication, 1971

Spearman, C. General intelligence objectively measured and determined. *American Journal of Psy-
    chology,1904, 15*, 201–293

Sprague, RL. Litigation, legislation, and regulations. In SE Breuning & AD Poling (Eds.), *Drugs
    and mental retardation*. Springfield, IL: Charles C. Thomas, 1982

Terman, LM. *The measurement of intelligence*. Boston: Houghton-Mifflin, 1916

Terman, LM. Feeble-minded children in the public schools of California. *School and Society,
    1917, 5*

Terman, LM, & Merrill, MA. *Measuring intelligence*. Boston: Houghton-Mifflin, 1937

Terman, LM, & Merrill, MA. *Stanford-Binet Intelligence Scale*. Boston: Houghton-Mifflin, 1973

Thurstone, LL. *Primary mental abilities*. Chicago: Universityof Chicago Press, 1938

Tredgold, AF. *Mental deficiency*. New York: W. Wood & Co., 1929

Wechsler, D. *Manual for the Wechsler Adult Intelligence Scale*. New York: Psychological Corporation,
    1955

Wechsler, D. *Manual for the Wechsler Preschool and Primary Scale of Intelligence*. New York:
    Psychological Corporation, 1967

Wechsler, D. *Manual for the Wechsler Intelligence Scale for Children Revised*. New York: Psycho-
    logical Corporation, 1974

Welsch v. Likens, 550 F. 2d 1122 (8th cir. 1977)

Willis, J, & Shibata, B. A comparison of tangible reinforcement and feedback effects on the WPPSI
    IQ scores of nursery school children. *Education and Treatment of Children, 1978, 1*, 31–45

Wyatt v. Stickney, 344 F. Supp. 387 (1972)

Young, RM, Bradley-Johnson, S, & Johnson, CM. Immediate and delayed reinforcement on WISC-R
    performance for mentally retarded students. *Applied Research in Mental Retardation, 1982, 3*,
    13–20

PART 2

Psychiatric Problems

Johnny L. Matson
Cynthia Frame

5

Psychopathology

Diagnostic and related issues of assessing the mentally retarded can be traced as far back as the Greeks and Romans. At that time, such individuals, identified simply by slow development, were considered a burden to society to be disposed of by early death at the hands of their parents. Drowning such children was a readily accepted practice which fit well into the prevailing philosophy that children were the property of their parents. This philosophy briefly changed with the dawn of Christianity, when comfort and support were given to such unfortunates. The positive trend was short lived, though, and was soon replaced with a view of the mentally retarded as fools, a perspective that thrived in Western and Eastern cultures throughout the middle ages (Rosen, Clark, & Kivitz, 1976). From these early accounts, one cannot help but note that the future, particularly for more severely mentally retarded persons was bleak.

A timely and positive change in these long-held attitudes began to appear with the Reformation, forming the true beginning of the present-day position toward the mentally retarded. For the first time, education of afflicted individuals and scientific inquiry into mental retardation were introduced alongside the humanitarian concerns voiced previously at other points in history. Since that time, except for a few noted setbacks, the lot of these persons has steadily improved. In fact, in recent years, mental retardation has been one of the handicapping conditions receiving the most professional and lay attention, as evinced by the establishment of many well-organized advocacy groups.

Much has been done to educate the mentally retarded in self-help skills, educational and vocational tasks. Furthermore, great advances have been made in the treatment of stereotypic and self-injurious behaviors. Psychological disturbances of the mentally retarded, on the other hand, have been an infrequent topic of professional investigation of the mentally retarded. This fact would seem to indicate a general lack of interest in psychopathology of the mentally retarded. Such a trend is particularly discouraging, since mental health services for persons of normal intelligence have seen rapid expansion in the last 25 years, as is exemplified by the establishment of numerous community mental health centers throughout the United States over this period.

The lack of focus on psychopathology in the mentally retarded may be attributable to several factors. One important trend mitigating against attention to assessing, diagnosing and treating psychopathology in the mentally retarded has been the administrative structure of community mental health centers in the United States. Traditionally, the centers are divided into two units, one for mental health and a separate one for mental retardation. Such an approach suggests that by definition, a person can be either mentally disturbed or mentally retarded, but not both. Thus, mentally retarded individuals are automatically considered unlikely candidates for the diagnostic and treatment services provided through the mental health division.

It has also frequently been assumed that mentally retarded persons could not benefit from the psychotherapy and other forms of treatment that are used with emotionally disturbed persons. This traditional and long-held view can be traced to the development of psychodynamic approaches that required average or superior intellect, both for proper ego development and for the acquisition of insights during treatment. Such abilities have generally been deemed lacking in the mentally retarded by psychiatrists and clinical psychologists (Bialer & Sternlick, 1977).

A third reason for the general lack of interest in the emotional problems of mentally retarded persons stems from the historical lack of interest in the mentally retarded that has been shown by psychiatrists, clinical psychologists, and social workers. At least part of this reaction may be due to the previously noted assumption that mentally retarded individuals show a poor response to treatment. Since special educators have traditionally been the primary support group for the mentally retarded population, it is not surprising that most of the work with this population has focused on academic and self-help skills training to the exclusion of the treatment of psychological disturbances. Fortunately, this trend is beginning to change, with more emphasis currently being placed on emotional problems. Certainly, this area deserves much greater concern from professionals due to the high incidence of psychological problems of mentally retarded persons, which will be described below.

Incidence

A number of studies have been conducted to establish the incidence of various types of psychological disturbances in the mentally retarded. This data, however, is affected by two problems, which should be noted at the outset. First, the means of assessing emotional disorders in this population have varied widely and have not been considered particularly accurate (Matson, in press). Second most of the incidence studies have been with adult institutionalized populations or with individuals referred to mental health centers. Thus, a rather atypical group has been evaluated, leading to a biased view of the types and frequencies of various disorders. These data do suggest, though, that there is a wide range of psychopathology existing with respect to the mentally retarded population. The available data would seem to suggest that such problems occur quite frequently.

Most of the incidence data available in the English language has been obtained from Great Britain, beginning with the work of Penrose (1938) and Earl (1934). Penrose surveyed psychiatric patients at the Royal Eastern Counties Hospital and found that in about one-third of these mentally ill patients, mental retardation was a major factor in the problems that led to hospitalization. Among these mentally retarded persons, the types of psychopathology diagnosed ranged from psychoneurosis to affective psychosis and schizophrenia. In another early report, Earl (1934) noted catatonic psychotic episodes in mentally retarded patients. Included in the symptoms were signs of mental and physical deterioration, catatonic episodes (e.g., muscular stiffness or rigidity) and emotional dissociation from the outside world. The author hypothesized that this and many other forms of psychopathology might be present in the mentally retarded, but that overt manifestations of the disorders might differ somewhat from those observed in the intellectually normal person. Earl (1934) writes that "one might expect to find among the idiots larval or primitive prototypes of the emotional abnormalities, the psychosis and psychoneurosis of the intellectually normal" (p. 232). While these authors used clinical observation alone rather than formal methods to make their diagnoses, the problems were generally quite striking in terms of symptoms. Of course, only the most serious forms of emotional disorders were reported. These problems, therefore, were generally believed to be reliably described and that their presence was worthwhile for establishing that such problems did exist in mentally retarded individuals.

Following these early efforts, more systematic attempts were made to delineate the type and frequency of emotional disorders in the mentally retarded. The research of Primrose (1971), based on formal psychiatric criteria, studied the reasons for psychiatric hospital admissions in Scotland and reported that one-half of the admissions were mentally retarded. James and Snaith (1979) deduced that many patients from this group could be accounted for by the standard policy of admitting to the hospital patients with IQs between 50 and 70 who had been before the courts. They went on to note, however, that the primary reasons for the court trials of the mentally retarded patients involved psychiatric disturbances and gross deficits in social behavior.

In perhaps the most extensive series of reports on this topic (Reid, 1971, 1972, 1976; Reid & Angle, 1974; Reid & Naylor, 1976), Reid and his associates attempted to estimate the percentage of persons who were both mentally retarded and emotionally disturbed. As an example, in one of these studies Reid (1976) calculated the frequency of psychosis among hospitalized mentally retarded people at 1.2 percent for affectve psychosis and 3.2 percent for schizophrenia and paranoid psychosis. Reid further pointed out that these figures do not include non-psychotic disorders, which are much more numerous. Based on these and other reports, Heaton-Ward (1977) suggested that eight to ten percent of mentally retarded persons experience either psychotic or neurotic disorders. These rates parallel or exceed those of persons with normal intelligence and are backed up by the work of Rutter and his associates (Rutter, Tizard, Yule, Graham, & Whitmore, 1976). In a massive epidemiological study of children from the Isle of Wight, they determined that the incidence of emotional disturbance in the mentally retarded was four to five times more likely than it was the case with children of normal intelligence. Similarly, in a recent survey of 30,000 developmentally disabled persons published by Jacobson (1982), over half of the sample diagnosed as mentally retarded also displayed depression, schizophrenia, or conduct disorders, with the latter being the most frequent form of emotional disturbance. Teenagers and adults suffered from more problems than young children or the elderly. Mentally retarded persons were more likely to display problem behaviors than were other developmentally disabled people, and individuals in community settings were less likely to experience problems than people living in psychiatric hospitals or facilities for the mentally retarded. These latter two studies are particularly important, since they overcome some of the long-standing flaws mentioned earlier of epidemiological investigation with the mentally retarded. Given the large number of persons studied and the sampling of these individuals from the general population rather than from hospitals, it appears that the Rutter and Jacobson data would be far less biased than earlier reports and, thus, are fairly representative of the general population of mentally retarded individuals at large.

Problems in Differential Diagnosis

If one accepts that a wide range of emotional disorders is likely to be found in the mentally retarded and that such problems occur frequently, then assessments geared at identifying such problems should be made with this group on a routine basis. Unfortunately, this has not usually been the case to date. To accomplish this aim, some problems in differential diagnosis of mental retardation and emotional disturbance must first be addressed. Matson (in press) notes that most criteria for evaluating various forms of psychopathology are based on persons of normal or above normal intelligence and have relied on symptoms that occur with adults. Drawing parallels in mentally retarded persons using many established criteria of various psychological disorders may therefore be difficult. Differences in overt manifestations of psychopathology in mentally retarded patients may be due to cognitive deficits or lack of developmental maturation rather than a real psychological disturbance. Matson terms this the "developmental factor," which must be considered during the assessment of psychological problems of mentally retarded individuals. Such an argument parallels the general child psychiatric literature in which manifestations of most forms of psychopathology are also derived from a model based primarily on adults of normal intelligence. Lefkowitz and Burton (1978) aptly illustrate the pitfalls of using the normal adult standard by noting that increasing age in normal IQ children is the most important demographic factor associated with a decrease in their amount of deviant behavior. Similarly, Hetherington and Martin (1972) note that the length of time that symptoms are present is important. It has generally been shown that symptoms of psychopathology remit much faster among children than adults. These variables are also likely to differ for mentally retarded patients compared with individuals of normal intelligence and will differ even within the broad range of intellectual levels that are included in the category of mental retardation.

The developmental factor becomes even more important when mental retardation is combined with stressful situations and other handicaps. Many studies have shown that mentally retarded individuals process and retain information less efficiently than persons of normal intelligence, making their adjustment to stress less rapid than for persons of normal intelligence along the entire age spectrum (Ellis, 1970; Spitz, 1973). Clinicians and researchers interested in assessing psychopathology with the mentally retarded should anticipate this adjustment problem. This factor, along with age, level of mental retardation, and presence of other debilitating handicaps (e.g., vision or hearing problems) may further compound problems and the ways in which emotional disorders are manifested. This is highly likely, as multiple handicaps are also more prevalent in mentally retarded persons than in the general population.

The only way of dealing with this developmental factor in differential diagnosis is through the establishment of normative information based on age, sex, intellectual functioning and concomitant developmental delays and physical handicaps. This approach would provide an acceptable standard for differential diagnosis that would incorporate a wide variety of assessments for emotional disorders. Although this goal is far from being achieved, progress has occurred. The current status of psychopathology assessment with the mentally retarded forms the topic of the following sections.

TYPES OF ASSESSMENT

In general, assessment strategies can be broadly divided into at least three types. The first of these is the indirect assessment of psychopathology in which the patient and/or significant others give their reports through interview or written questionnaire about the patient's past and present symptoms. A second and more direct approach to assessment involves actual observations of the patient's behavior in either naturalistic or analogue situations. The third type of assessment is physiological, in which such subject responses as heart rate and skin conductance are measured. These three types of assessment and their applications to mentally retarded populations will be discussed below.

Indirect Methods of Assessment

Psychiatric Interviews

Probably the most frequently used assessment method is the psychiatric interview. This approach is partially based on the old notion that the patient, when directly questioned, is the best source of information about a problem. The interviewer asks the patient or his significant others about typical psychiatric symptoms the patient may be experiencing, such as changes in mood, perception, sleep, or appetite. One primary purpose of the interview is to obtain enough information for the assessment of a standard psychiatric diagnosis, such as those specified in the third edition of the *Diagnostic and Statistical Manual of Mental Disorders* (DSM-III; American Psychiatric Association, 1980).

Traditionally, interviewers have been permitted the freedom to elicit information in whatever areas they consider pertinent, although the psychiatric interview usually consists of inquiry and observation in the areas of appearance, thought processes, mood and affect, intellectual functioning, and sensorium. Recently, however, several structured psychiatric interviews have come into widespread use. Usually prepared in booklet form, structured interviews consist of groups of questions that are about various psychiatric disorders and that are to be asked in a standard order. Because reliability in the identification of many individual psychiatric symptoms is notoriously low, the interview manuals also provide explicit definitions and examples of such vague concepts as "thought disorder" or "loosening of associations." The interviewer rates the presence or absence of specified symptoms as he proceeds through the interview, after which the ratings may be tallied to obtain a diagnosis.

Structured interview schedules have several advantages over traditional interviews. First, both interviewer and interviewee bias are reduced. Two important sources of unreliability in interview data are the interviewer's line of questioning and the interviewee's topics of complaint. Some interviewers may concentrate on certain problems but miss others. In the same way, some patients may talk about one problem with one interviewer but present a different complaint to another interviewer. With structured interviews, the same types of information are obtained from every patient, thereby reducing the probability that a particular area of psychopathology will be overlooked or go unmentioned. Second, since standard questions and explicit definitions of terms are used, clarity of communication between professionals about the patient's presenting symptoms is enhanced. Finally, as a result of the first two points, the assignment of a particular diagnosis is easier and more reliable. Structured interview systems have become especially popular in clinical settings because they readily provide the DSM-III diagnoses legally required for financial reimbursement by third party payers, such as health insurance companies.

Typical examples of structured interviews are the Schedule for Affective Disorders and Schizophrenia (SADS; Spitzer & Endicott, 1978) and the Present State Exam (PSE; Wing, Cooper, & Sartorious, 1974), both of which yield research diagnoses that are close to those of the DSM-III for psychotic disorders. For other psychiatric disturbances and personality disorders, however, these interviews are less useful for assigning DSM-III diagnoses. Two new interviews, the Diagnostic Interview Schedule (DIS; Robins, Helzer, Croughan, & Ratcliff, 1981) and the Renard Diagnostic Interview (RDI; Helzer, Robins, Coughan, & Welner, 1981) are presently under development. They will cover a larger number of DSM-III categories and are designed for use by either clinicians or lay interviewers.

At times, the initial interview is chiefly a tool for making a standard diagnosis and for assigning the patient to an appropriate treatment facility or therapist. This situation is frequently the case when the diagnosis is sufficient for the development of an initial treatment plan. For instance, if a patient is given a careful diagnosis of mania, it may often be assumed that the treatment to which he will respond most rapidly is a drug called lithium carbonate. If his diagnosis is that of schizophrenia, he will probably be administered one of the antipsychotic medications as a first step in treatment. On the other hand, while diagnosis of certain disturbances may suggest a line of possible treatment techniques, diagnosis alone is not always sufficient for planning a specific intervention. When more detailed information must be collected, the next step often involves an assessment method termed behavioral interviewing.

Behavioral Interviews

In the behavioral interview, an attempt is made to carefully define the important elements of the problem situation. The questioning is not formally structured, since standard behavioral interviews have not been developed. The interviewer seeks to discover anything that may be maintaining the problem behavior. To this end, he inquires about events that typically occur before (antecedent) and after (consequent) the problem behavior. For example, if a child has temper tantrums, the interviewer tries to identify those situations which typically lead to tantrum behavior. For one child, the antecedent may be the parent's refusal to grant a candy snack, while for another child tantrums may be preceded by skipping naps. Consequent events may range from attempted punishment techniques, such as spanking or withdrawal of privileges, to "consoling" methods of soft talk, bargaining, or granting special privileges. While attempting to delineate the possible maintaining stimuli, the interviewer may discover that the problem behavior itself must be redefined. For instance, what an interviewee initially describes as simply a "fear of dog feces" may turn out to be an obsessive-compulsive disorder involving a broad range of obsessions about germs and illness. The final target behavior suggested by the interview is then further defined in terms of frequency, duration, and intensity by methods such as self-monitoring or direct observation (see the following sections). Assessment of these target behaviors provides not only an index of the severity of the problem, but also baselines for comparison of problem behavior before and after treatment. For a more detailed guide to behavioral interviewing, see Haynes and Jensen (1979), Meyer, Liddell and Lyons (1977) or Morganstern and Tevlin (1981).

Applications to the mentally retarded. Since they were developed for persons of average intelligence, the structured interviews described above have rarely been used with mentally retarded patients. Although it has not been done, restructuring of the SADS in a manner similar to its simplification for children (Kiddie SADS) might make this instrument suitable for interviewing mentally retarded persons. Some structured interview schedules do exist specifically for the assessment of mentally retarded patients. One, the Adaptive Behavior Scale of the American Association on Mental Deficiency (Nihira, Foster, Shellhaas, & Leland, 1974) provides an index of overall functioning, as well as a subscale describing psychopathology, albeit in a very general context. Another structured interview designed for the diagnosis of early childhood psychosis is currently being standardized by Wing and her colleagues (Wing, 1980; Wing, & Gould, 1978), and a scaling system by Matson and associates (1982) is being developed for assessing the wide range of psychopathology in mentally retarded adults and children. These interview systems are intended for use by highly trained professionals who rate the patient and/or obtain self-report data on a number of different behaviors. The ratings are based on interviews with significant others and teachers, and on relatively unstructured behavioral observations. As yet, however, the validity of these interview systems and the resulting diagnostic conclusions have not been tested.

Regardless of interview format, an interviewer should observe several important guidelines when working with mentally retarded individuals. Most of them were suggested some time ago by Menolascino and Bernstein (1970), and all of them stress flexibility as the keyword. The interviewer should keep in mind at least four characteristics of many mentally retarded individuals that could obstruct a successful interview: apprehension about unfamiliar situations, poor comprehension, poor retention, and short attention span. The interviewer can try to compensate for these problems in several ways.

In any interview, more accurate information is likely to be obtained when the interviewee feels comfortable disclosing facts to the interviewer. Rapport is also very important in interviewing mentally retarded persons. It can be enhanced through the generous use of smiles, praise, and even tangible positive reinforcement such as food. Additionally, some individuals will appreciate gentle physical contact in the form of a pat on the back or a touch on the arm. A careful and simple explanation of the interview's purpose given repeatedly also goes far toward alleviating anxiety. All of these techniques can be helpful in generally reassuring the patient and eliciting his or her cooperation.

Breaks and topic changes can be used as needed to accommodate the attention span of the interviewee. The interviewer should be alert to waning attention on the part of the patient, often indicated by increased fidgeting, decreased eye contact, or irrelevant responses. Obviously, the entire interview process must be adapted to the comprehenson and retention level of the patient. For instance, both questions and explanations should be worded using elementary vocabulary and short phrases. The patient should be encouraged to indicate when he does not understand something, although the interviewer cannot assume the patient will do so. Sometimes questions will require repeating several times, and rewording may be helpful. In fact, since some patients may have a bias toward answering in the affirmative (Sigelman, Budd, Spahel, & Schoenrock, 1981a, 1981b), it is desirable to reword the same question occasionally in ways requiring both yes and no replies. This approach will aid the interviewer in judging whether the patient seems to be responding to the content of the questions or simply has a tendence toward yes-saying. Finally, when the patient cannot seem to grasp a particular notion after repeated inquiry, it is best to introduce a new topic. Further insistence may increase the patient's anxiety and render him unable to complete the interview. It is often the case that the patient is simply unable to comprehend some questions, especially those dealing with a remote time-frame of days or weeks ago. As a result, it may also be necessary to interview a significant other to obtain a complete picture of the problem.

Summary.   An initial interview with a mentally retarded patient, when conducted with the special needs of the patient in mind, may provide a large amount of direct information about possible psychopathology. However, the usefulness of the interview is easily limited by the response bias and attention/comprehension problems of many mentally retarded persons, which comprise a major reason for the multiformat interview systems previously presented. Other limitations of psychiatric interviews in general, such as inaccurate responding, unknown reliability and lack of quantitative information, underline the need for a more complete evaluation by the addition of other assessment techniques.

Questionnaires

The written questionnaire is another indirect method for assessing psychopathology. The questionnaire is much like the structured psychiatric interview, in that the patient or significant other gives answers to questions about symptoms and behaviors, based on general perceptions of the patient over a specified time period. The main differences are that the questionnaire is usually written instead of given orally and that the answers are of a forced-choice nature. That is, the person must answer either true or false, pick one of several available answers in a multiple choice format, or answer on a Likert scale. With the latter format, the patient rates the characteristic that is in question on a numeric scale, such as from one to ten.

Questionnaires are most frequently used in conjunction with psychiatric interviews to corroborate a diagnosis or to quantify the severity of the psychopathology. Used as pre-and post-tests, they can also be helpful in the assessment of the effectiveness of treatment interventions. Most useful questionnaires have been standardized, their psychometric properties are known, and normative data are available. Two examples of standardized questionnaires for the global assessment of psychopathology are the Minnesota Multiphasic Personality Inventory (MMPI; Hathaway & McKinley, 1951) and the Eysenck Personality Inventory (EPI; Eysenck & Eysenck, 1968). For children, such scales include the Child Behavior Profile (Achenbach, 1978) and the Behavior Problem Checklist (Quay & Peterson, 1967). In addition to the global measures, questionnaires have been developed for specific problem areas such as depression (e.g., Beck Depression Inventory; Beck, Ward, Mendelson, Mock, & Erbaugh, 1961); fear (e.g., Fear Survey Schedule; Lang & Lazovik, 1963), and many anxiety disorders (e.g., Maudsley Obsessive-Compulsive Inventory; Rachman & Hodgson, 1980). (See Barlow [1981] and Hersen and Bellack [1981] for more complete information about the range of available self-report questionnaires and their descriptions.)

Applications to the mentally retarded. As with standard interviews, few questionnaires have been used for assessment purposes with mentally retarded psychiatric patients. Frequently, the wording of items written for persons of average intelligence is far too complex. The mentally retarded person can neither read the questions, understand them, nor write the answers. These problems have been surmounted in several ways. One strategy has been to ask a significant other to complete the questionnaire as he feels the items apply to the patient, or as he thinks the patient would reply. Some investigators (Guarnaccia & Weiss, 1974; Matson, 1981a) have assessed the fears of mentally retarded children in this manner. Parents were asked to rate items on the Louisville Fear Survey for Children (LFSC; Miller, Barrett, Hampe, & Noble, 1972) according to their perceptions of their mentally retarded child's fearfulness. This approach resulted in a broad range of fears being identified in a descriptive study by Guarnaccia and Weiss (1974). Matson (1981a) was able to use the parent-scored LFSC successfully as a treatment outcome measure. Two problems do exist with this type of assessment, however. First, the significant other may not always be sure of the actual nature or extent of the mentally retarded patient's fear or other target symptoms, resulting in a large margin of error from guessing or from misinterpretation of the patient's behavior. In addition, significant others' reports may be biased, either toward "normalizing" problems or toward "pathologizing" neutral events. In either case, the resulting data may not be valid.

To avoid these problems, another approach has been developed in which items from standard measures are first simplified and then read aloud to the mentally retarded person. To aid the patient in answering, cue cards or wall charts with symbolic drawings representing the various response possibilities may be provided. For example, brightly colored bar graphs can be shown to represent the Likert-scale ratings. In this way, the patient alone is responsible for describing his problem behavior. It should be noted, though, that this method involves many of the same issues as does psychiatric interviewing, and the same types of precautions should be taken, including some simple questioning to ensure the patient's ability to comprehend and to respond appropriately. For example, some investigators (Kazdin, Matson, & Senatore, 1983) routinely give a prescreening consisting of five multiple choice questions such as "Is it day or night now?" and six Likert items such as "How hot is a fire?" Patients who miss these questions must be assessed by other methods.

In addition to the aforementioned problems, the simplify-and-read-aloud approach introduces more serious complications in interpretation of responses. This is because the original versions of the measures were standardized using complex questions and persons of average intelligence. Changing both the questions and the target population renders the psychometric properties of the simplified instrument unknown. Comparisons with normative data become uninterpretable. Responses obtained from such modified measures may be useful for assessing changes within an individual patient over time, assuming adequate validity and reliability. Thus, they can be used pre- and post-treatment to help determine whether a patient has improved on some problems relative to his own baseline. Such measures, however, cannot be used to compare the patient to others who have answered the original questionnaire; in such cases it is unclear whether the mentally retarded patient's score is average or is pathological, relative to other mentally retarded individuals. As a result of this last problem, some authors have sought to standardize their simplifications of existing assessment measures with mentally retarded populations. For instance, Eysenck (1965) has developed a simplified version of the EEPI, called the Eysenck-Withers Personality Inventory, that is to be read aloud to mentally retarded patients. Although considered primarily a research instrument, normative data from mentally retarded patients are available. Matson and his colleagues (Kazdin, Matson, & Senatore, 1983) have recently obtained normative data from a large population of mentally retarded subjects for modified versions of several measures of depression. Their study typifies the type of work that must be done to render written instruments a useful assessment method with mentally retarded populations. Their subjects were 110 adult patients, ranging from borderline to severely mentally retarded, approximately half of whom were inpatients and half were outpatients. The scales that were simplified and read aloud to the patients included the Beck Depression Inventory, the Zung Self-Rating Depression Scale (Zung), the MMPI-Depression Scale, and the Hamilton Psychiatric Rating Scale for Depression. As described above, patients were shown a labelled bar graph on a wall chart to help them chose their desired responses. For comparison, staff members were also asked to complete the same measures on each patient. Results indicated that both patient and staff ratings on these instruments were viable means of assessing depression in mentally retarded adults, with relatively consistent agreement occurring between the patient and staff ratings. The BDI and the Zung were determined to be the most useful measures for distinguishing depressed from nondepressed patients, as defined by several sets of criteria. Most importantly, these authors provided descriptive statistics of the subjects' scores as a first step in establishing normative data for mentally retarded persons on these measures. In this way, a mentally retarded individual's score on each of these particular instruments may be interpreted in a meaningful way.

Summary. The questionnaire method has several problems as an assessment strategy for use with mentally retarded patients. In addition to the same type of considerations that must be observed during psychiatric interviews, questionnaires introduce problems of standardization of and interpretation of results. When simplified and used in conjunction with normative data for mentally retarded persons, however, the questionnaire shows great promise as a useful and an inexpensive assessment technique. The establishment of normative information for a variety of instruments covering various types of psychopathology presently remains the primary goal.

Direct Methods of Assessment

Direct Observation

Although interviews and questionnaires are initially useful for developing a broad notion of a patient's possible psychopathology, direct observation of the patient's behavior is often necessary to obtain an exact assessment of the problem. In addition to the previously discussed problems presented by indirect methods of assessment, the patient or significant other may simply be uncertain or mistaken when reporting the nature or extent of the psychological disturbance. A mother may maintain, for instance, that her child is "constantly on the go," while direct observation of the problem behavior indicates that his random activity increases only when he is faced with fine motor tasks, and that even this increase seems to be within normal limits. Or in a patient whose only complaint is that he does not "feel right physically," direct observation may reveal depressed facies, slowed motor behavior and reduced food intake, all characteristic of major depressive disorder. In these cases, although interview data may have suggested possible problem areas, direct observation is required to specify concrete targets for intervention.

There are several important steps in conducting a useful behavioral observation. The first and most crucial involves carefully defining the problem to be observed. This can often be difficult when the problem has been described in broad, general terms. For instance, the target behaviors of an "aggressive" child might include noncompliance, abusive language, destruction of property, or attempts to harm other people. If the problem behavior is not well defined, the validity of observational data will be low. That is, the behaviors under observation may be a poor representation of the problem the clinician wishes to measure. A good example of this would be defining aggressive behavior in the classroom as "time spent out of seat." While these two variables may be correlated, a child can engage in a great deal of aggressive behavior while remaining seated. Many aggressive behaviors would be missed by the "out of seat" definition. Instead, a better definition might read, "Physical aggression against others includes any bodily contact of the subject with another person that results in discomfort, pain, or injury to the other person. Throwing or shoving objects at another person are also considered physical aggression if contact is made with the victim." Note that this operational definition does not consider the intent behind the action; accidental contact would also be classified as aggression. Due to the great difficulty of inferring intent, definitions are often constructed in this way. The above definition also omits any "attempted" acts that do not inflict discomfort, such as swinging a fist and missing. Once again, definitions are frequently written this way, since attempted acts are more difficult to rate than completed ones. If the subject in question engages in many uncompleted attempts at aggression, the assessor might want to specify a definition for that problem and have observers rate attempted and completed aggressive behaviors separately.

Direct observation is best conducted by trained professionals, although significant others also may be taught to make reliable observations. After the problem behaviors are carefully defined, the patient is observed by two raters for a set period of time, and occurrences of the target behavior are noted. One observer becomes the primary rater and is present during every observation period. A second observer should rate at least 20 percent of the period to provide an estimate of rater agreement on the behavioral observations. This agreement, called reliability, is a crucial factor too frequently overlooked during assessment. If reliability is low or unknown, the observations are of little utility. Essentially, lack of reliability means that observers cannot agree as to what extent a problem behavior is present, rendering all measurements of the illusive behavior meaningless. This is just as true when a patient is seen in clinical practice as when the patient is assessed during a research project.

For best results, observers (whether professionals or significant others) should be trained to some specified criteria on practice subjects or behaviors before beginning the actual assessment. In addition, they should be retrained occasionally during repeated observations to prevent observer drift, in which raters may begin to change the definitions slightly or miss certain types of behaviors. In this way, agreement between raters will be maintained at an acceptable level. Videotaping the assessment situation makes reliability estimates even easier to obtain, since observers need not be present during the live sessions. The videotaped record also allows assessors to observe behaviors other than the original targets, or, if necessary, to redefine and rerate the target behavior.

Another step in behavioral observation involves deciding upon the sampling procedure to be used. Obviously, a patient cannot be observed on a continuous basis indefinitely. As a result, small samples are taken of the patient's behavior that are assumed to be representative of his typical manner of responding. To avoid influences that uncontrolled factors may have on behavior, repeated observations are usually collected in the same setting at the same time of day. Observations may also be collected in other settings, but should be interpreted separately, not in a combined manner. For instance, observation of the "aggressive" child might take place in the classroom every weekday for one hour after morning recess. Signals for starting and stopping observations are decided in advance, such as beginning when the teacher calls the class to resume work and ending one hour from that time. Actual behaviors may be measured in several ways. An observer can tabulate the number of occurrences of the target behavior, resulting in a frequency count, or the duration of each occurrence of the target behavior can be timed. Latency to respond, or the time lapse between a specific stimulus (such as a teacher's request) and a response (such as a child's compliance), can also be measured. While each of these measures may be appropriate for some situations, for statistical reasons, they all present problems in computing agreement between raters. An easier method to use is the interval procedure. Here, the total observation period is divided into some number of equal time intervals. The one-hour period described above might be broken into one-minute segments. Then, during each one-minute segment, the observer simply rates the target behavior as present or absent. The observer may use a stopwatch or headphones producing an audiotaped beep to mark the passage of time. The interval method is recommended for its ease in the recording, scoring, and interpretation of ratings.

Sometimes, as in the case of phobias, it is more appropriate to observe the distance of a patient's approach to a target object (called the Behavioral Avoidance Test, or BAT). The distance may actually be measured in feet and inches or in terms of completing each of several tasks in a hierarchy of increasing difficulty. For example, a spider phobic could be asked to touch or put his hand as close to a spider as possible. When he signals that he can approach no closer, the distance between his hand and the spider is to be measured. Alternatively, he might be asked to complete as many as possible of several steps of increasing contact with spiders, such as entering a room where a spider is boxed, touching the spider box, or removing the lid. He then receives a score corresponding to the highest step he could complete.

Sometimes patients complain that the behavior they exhibit in situations such as the BAT, or during other observations, is different from responses they typically experience when they are not being observed. This phenomenon is termed "reactivity" and is a final consideration in the use of behavioral observations. Although the extent to which direct observation results in subject reactivity is under debate, it is usually assumed that the more unobtrusive the observations, the more likely the patient is to exhibit typical behaviors. Unobtrusive measures can be made in several ways. Having raters present in the observation setting for some time before the actual assessment begins may give the subject a chance to "forget" about the raters' presence. Raters should also position themselves to the back and side of the subject and avoid eye contact or other interactions. When possible, direct observations can be made most unobtrusively through a one-way mirror. In most cases, it is an ethical requirement that subjects or significant others be informed that they may be observed at random during the assessment period. For a helpful guide to the many aspects of behavioral observations, see the chapter in this book on behavioral assessment.

Applications with the mentally retarded. The direct observation of behavior is an excellent technique for use with mentally retarded patients, since it does not depend on the patient's verbal abilities and does not require any major modifications of procedures for varying developmental levels. As mentioned before, the most difficult problem involves defining the behaviors or symptoms most indicative of psychopathology. Most of the reported cases with mentally retarded patients involve the assessment of fear and anxiety through approach or avoidance behaviors. For instance, to assess acrophobia, Guralnick (1973) asked a mentally retarded male to climb onto stacks of large blocks of increasing height. When the patient became too fearful to climb any higher, the number of inches from the floor he had climbed was recorded. Likewise, Peck (1977) counted the number of steps that mentally retarded acrophobics were able to climb before refusing to continue.

Matson (1981a) also assessed fear of strangers in terms of avoidance behaviors. He asked mentally retarded children who had been referred to a mental health clinic for debilitating fear of strangers to introduce themselves to an adult brought into the classroom. The adult was labelled as a "nice man". Raters measured the final physical distance left between the child and the adult as an indicator of the child's fear of strangers. Another study (Matson, 1981b) provides a good example of the use of the hierarchical BAT to measure fear of grocery stores. He worked with several mentally retarded adults who, out of fear, refused to enter grocery stores. Matson designed a set of actions of increasing difficulty to assess the patients before, during and after treatment. The steps included riding in the car to the grocery, entering the door of the store, pushing a cart through the store, placing specified items in the cart, and purchasing items by going through a check-out lane. Others fears that have been assessed using the physical distance or Hierarchical BAT include fear of rats (Peck, 1977) and store mannequins (Waranch, Iwata, & Wohl, 1981) and fear of leaving an institutional home (Mansdorf, 1976).

In other studies using direct observation, duration of a specific behavior or of its absence have been employed to assess various psychological disturbances. For example, Stoudenmire and Salter (1975) assessed hyperactivity in a three-year-old mentally retarded girl by summing the duration of instances of sitting or standing still during a 20-minute observation period. During the assessment, the child was in a playroom with her mother and one observer, while another observer watched from a one-way mirror. Mulhern and Baumeister (1969) used a similar approach to assess stereotypy in two mentally retarded males. Instead of observing the patients in their natural environment, these authors asked the patients to sit in a chair located in a soundproof chamber especially equipped to detect movement. Movement was automatically recorded by a mechanical device that had been shown to correlate highly with movement rates obtained during direct observation. Stereotypy was then measured by the percentage of time spent motionless by each patient. Cuvo (1976) used duration of problem behavior in a novel way to assess compulsive, repetitive backtracking by an elderly mentally retarded female. This woman would walk several feet forward and then turn to retrace her steps. Cuvo (1976) measured the amount of time the woman required to walk between two specified buildings on the hospital grounds as indicative of the compulsive behavior's extent.

In still other studies, behavioral observations have been conducted centering on patients' spontaneous verbal behavior as a correlate of psychopathology. For instance, Matson and his colleagues (Matson, Dettling, & Senatore, 1981) counted the number of suicidal and self-abusing statements made by depressed mentally retarded patients. They also noted the number and duration of fear complaints made by mentally retarded children suffering from intense fear of strangers (Matson, 1981a).

Summary.   All of these approaches to direct observation have proven to be very worthwhile in the assessment of psychopathology in mentally retarded individuals. Direct observation needs no modification for developmental level, and the cooperation of the patient is not required. While observational techniques may be somewhat time-consuming to conduct properly, they have no substitute. They can always, of course, be supplemented by other assessment information.

Self-Monitoring

Much like direct observations made by others, the patient may be asked to observe and report, or self-monitor, his own behaviors or feelings (e.g., anxiety level). Self-monitoring can be conducted with almost any behavior amenable to direct observation procedures and is also appropriate for assessing covert events such as fear or sadness, or private behaviors such as sexual response. As with direct observation, self-monitoring involves decisions about the definition of the target behavior and the selection of sampling procedures and recording instruments. Most self-monitoring practices have centered on recording the frequency or intensity of target behaviors, since they are simple to tally in the course of daily life. Unless there is a reason to select a specific time or location, self-monitoring is usually conducted in an on-going fashion. That is, behavior is not often time-sampled; instead, the target behavior is monitored continuously, with each occurrence recorded. For this reason, the type of recording instrument employed should be portable and easy to use, making paper and pencil tallies and wrist counters two of the most popular methods. Sometimes the recording method involves phoning a report to an answering machine.

As might be expected, self-monitoring is subject to major problems of accuracy, reliability and reactivity. Patients are frequently inaccurate in their reporting, which then tends to lower agreement with an independent rater. Nelson (1977) reports on several steps that can be taken to increase accuracy. First, the individual should be trained in the practice of self-monitoring before beginning the assessment. Reinforcement of correct recording, or even simple monitoring of the recording by the clinician will lead to improved accuracy. Problem behaviors are also less likely to be overlooked by the self-monitorer if they are recorded as they occur, rather than hourly or daily. Finally, the more accessible and easy to use the recording method, the more likely the patient will record the information correctly.

Unfortunately, some of the strategies leading to improved accuracy are also related to increased reactivity. Reactivity in self-monitoring usually involves the patient's inflation of the number of positive events and the under-reporting of undesirable behaviors. The greater the valence of the problem, the more likely this is to occur. In addition, the mere presence of the readily available recording device often seems to act as a discriminative stimulus to the patient to behave in a more appropriate or desirable manner, which then serves to deflate the rate of unwanted behaviors before treatment is begun. Obviously, this is a nuisance during attempts to establish an accurate baseline. It is therefore advised that self-monitoring be supplemented, whenever possible, by another assessment method. As a minimum, the patient or significant other should be asked, before commencement of self-monitoring, to estimate the rate of the target behavior.

Applications to the mentally retarded. Even more than with the indirect methods of assessment, the self-monitoring approach is limited by the patient's ability to understand the task and to provide the desired information. Developmental level is also important, as children have been found to be less accurate than adults when self-monitoring. Despite these facts, mildly and moderately mentally retarded patients seem to be surprisingly good at such self-ratings. Nelson, Lipinski, and Black (1976) have demonstrated that mentally retarded patients can self-monitor their own behaviors in a reliable manner. Similarly, Matson and Zeiss (1979) showed that chronic mentally retarded psychiatric patients were capable of monitoring the occurrence of both their own and a peer's inappropriate social behaviors. Zegiob, Klukas, and Junginger (1978) found that while mentally retarded patients were notoriously unreliable at recording the actual number of instances of problem behavior, they were able to accurately record the general direction of changes (e.g., reduction) in the unwanted behaviors. In terms of covert events, Matson (1981a) and Peck (1977) asked mentally retarded patients to rate their own levels of fear on four-point and seven-point visual scales, respectively, during presentation of feared objects. Although the patients' self-report correlated only .27 with observers' global ratings of the patients' fearful behaviors in the latter study, self-monitoring rates were more highly correlated (.43) with the patients' actual approach behaviors on a BAT.

Summary. In light of the research findings, self-monitoring appears to be an assessment approach of some value for use with mentally ratarded patients. In fact, its emphasis on patient responsibility makes it appropriate for many programs that emphasize independence skills for residents, as well as for institutional settings where overburdened staff cannot be asked to make frequent behavioral ratings. Although precautions must be taken to ensure that self-monitoring is being conducted as accurately as possible, and a supplementary assessment method should be used, self-monitoring is a simple, low-cost method of obtaining important information about problem behavior.

Global Ratings

A less exact method of direct observation that will be briefly described here can be conducted with global rating scales. Here, an observer watches the patient for a specified period of time and then rates him or her using a general scale or checklist. For example, observers have rated their perceptions of patients' fearfulness during exposure to a target object on a ten-point scale from "not at all afraid" to "extremely fearful" (Matson, 1981a). In the same manner, Worrall, Moody, and Naylor (1975) assessed aggression in affectively-disordered mentally retarded patients by having nurses rate the aggression of each patient on a seven-point scale approximately once every four hours. Detailed checklist of various behaviors and symptoms (such as activity level, mood, talking, crying, and sleeping) rated approximately once every eight hours, have also been used to assess manic-depressive affective disorder in mentally retarded patients (Reid & Naylor, 1976; Rivinus & Harmatz, 1979).

While global ratings are often easier and less expensive to obtain then direct observation data, they also tend to be much less reliable. The lower reliability stems from two factors. First, unlike direct observation in which ratings are made as the behaviors occur, some scales require memory of behaviors over a four or eight hour span of time, introducing a large potential for memory error. Second, the nature of the items often requires some arbitrary clinical judgment on the part of the rater (e.g., rating "six" versus "seven" on a ten-point scale), rather than a simple present/absent decision. Thus, global rating scales may be useful as supplementary information, but in most cases they should not be used as the only means of assessment. One exception might be the Nurses' Observation Scale for Inpatient Evaluation (NOSIE; Honigfeld, Gillis, & Kleff, 1966). This standard checklist of behaviors and symptoms reflecting general psychiatric and social functioning has acceptable reliability when staff members are thoroughly trained in its use. However, its application to some mentally retarded patients could require modification of items dealing with self-help skills that these patients might lack due to mental retardation rather than due to psychopathology. As a result, all global rating scales employed with mentally retarded populations should be interpreted with attention to the problems of the developmental factor, rater memory error, and subjectivity in rated items.

Role-Play

A final method of direct assessment does not involve observation in the natural environment. Instead, the patient is asked to pretend, or role-play, that he is involved in a particular situation and to react as he would normally. Observers then rate the appropriateness of the patient's response, just as they would during direct observation. This analogue approach is frequently employed for the assessment of social skills. While mildly mentally retarded patients can role-play adequately (see Matson, DiLorenzo, & Andrasik, 1982 for a review), more severely mentally retarded persons may find it difficult to imagine themselves in the role-play situations. In addition, questions remain as to both the validity and reliability of the role-play as an assessment method even for subjects of average intelligence (Van Hasselt, Hersen, & Bellack, 1981). Thus, its value as an assessment instrument may be limited, particularly with mentally retarded patients.

Summary of Direct Assessment Procedures

In review, direct observation and self-monitoring techniques appear to show much promise as useful assessment techniques with mentally retarded patients. Direct observation in particular has been used successfully to assess a number of psychological problems and requires few modifications for differing intelligence or developmental levels. Self-monitoring, when carefully supervised and supplemented by additional assessment data, can provide moderately reliable and inexpensive information about the patient's level of psychopathology. Other methods, such as global rating scales and role-play tasks should be employed with care due to their questionable validity and poor reliability.

One important issue relating to direct assessment techniques that has been largely overlooked involves the lack of normative data or standard behavioral criteria for comparison with the patient's responses. This issue is most easily illustrated through example. Suppose one mentally retarded patient's problem behavior has been defined as excessive complaining about physical ailments that actually do not require a doctor's care. During an hour observation period, the patient makes 30 complaints. This number is obviously excessive for a person who has been given a clean bill of health by her doctor. Consider, however, that the number of complaints drops to five after treatment. The problem lies in interpreting the importance of five medical complaints in a one-hour period. Is this still an excessive number, or is it within normal limits? This issue can occur during initial assessments, as well as during post-treatment. An absolute frequency count often has no meaning without some standard for comparison.

There are two ways to approach interpretation of such assessment data, both of which are termed types of social validation (Kazdin & Matson, 1981). The first method involves collecting normative data as a social comparison. In the problem discussed above, the clinician could observe other mentally retarded females of the patient's age and developmental level to determine the average number of complaints usually made by such persons during a one-hour time span. This would provide information to determine whether the patient's number of complaints were within normal limits. The underlying assumption of social comparison is that behaviors occurring at a "typical" rate are not problematic. Because this assumption may not always be true, a second approach to social validation can be used. Here, subjective evaluation is obtained from others who are in a position to judge the clinical significance or problematic nature of the existing problem. For example, 10 or 12 institutional staff members might be asked to rate the degree to which they thought ward activities or interpersonal relationships would be disrupted by the patient's present number of physical complaints. Thus, social validation techniques can be used both to investigate the usual level of occurrence of particular behaviors and to judge the extent of disruption expected from problem behaviors. Both of these procedures should be used whenever possible to complement the direct assessment techniques of psychopathology (see the chapter on behavioral assessment for a further discussion on social validation).

Physiological Assessment

A third general type of assessment involves monitoring the physiological responses of a patient across time and/or in reaction to target stimuli such as feared objects. Physiological assessment may vary from simple measures of temperature using a thermometer, or pulse rate using a wrist watch, to complex recordings of various responses obtained with electrodes and a polygraph. In most cases, the use of psychophysiological techniques requires special training in sophisticated instrumentation and methodology. Because psychophysiological assessment has provided some very useful information with subjects of normal intelligence, however, it will be discussed here at an elementary level. For more detail, see Kallman and Feuerstein (1977) or Ray and Raczynski (1981).

There are currently several ways available to measure the human body's many physiological responses. Some methods and responses can be more useful than others, depending on the particular psychological disturbance being assessed. In physiological assessment, the rule of thumb is to measure the response system that is most directly related to the problem behavior. Thus, respiration rate would be a better assessment variable for asthmatic patients who have problems in breathing, than blood pressure changes, which might be indirectly related to respiration. A brief review of the response systems and their assessment as indicators of psychopathology is given below.

Respiration

As a psychophysiological variable, respiration rate can be obtained in two ways. First, an elastic tube can be placed around the patient's chest, with the amount and frequency of stretching (mostly due to breathing) detected and recorded by the polygraph. A more sophisticated device is available that fits into the mouth and/or nose, but is not very comfortable for the patient to use. Generally, because of poor instrumentation and the limited relationship between breathing and most psychological disturbances, respiration rate is rarely used as the primary assessment measure.

Electrodermal Activity

Another infrequently used method involves the assessment of electrodermal changes such as skin conductance. As its name implies, the latter procedure records the skin's ability to conduct electricity and is related to sweat production. Because our knowledge about the function and significance of the electrodermal response is still limited, and due to its apparent lack of clear relationship to particular psychiatric problems, electrodermal recording has largely been replaced by measurement of other response systems such as cardiovascular, muscular, or thermal measures, in the assessment of psychopathology.

Temperature

Skin or body temperature is probably one of the easiest psychophysiological measures to obtain. Standard thermometers may be used for readings of oral or rectal temperature. Although rarely used in this manner, body temperature may correlate with manic-depressive cycling. A more common assessment variable is skin temperature obtained from small heat-sensitive devices that are taped to the skin. Raynaud's disease, in which poor circulation causes lowered temperature in the extremities, has been assessed through fingertip skin temperature. Hand temperature may also be a useful device in the assessment of migraine headaches.

Cardiovascular Measures

Skin temperature, as measured above is actually an indirect method of assessing the cardiovascular variable, blood flow. The cardiovascular system is frequently monitored in physiological assessment because of its quick response to stress. The simplest cardiovascular measure is pulse or heart rate. The time interval between heartbeats (called interbeat interval, or IBI) is a very sensitive measure of the cardiovascular system's response to stress. Another measure involves changes in blood pressure. A fourth technique, which takes into account both heart rate and blood pressure and is sensitive to change in either, is called pulse propagation time (PPT). In this case, the amount of time required for the blood to flow from the heart to a specified body part such as the ear lobe or fingertip is measured. Heart rate, IBI and PPT are all useful variables for assessing anxiety disorders (Mavissakalian & Barlow, 1981; Taylor & Agras, 1981).

Electromyography

Using sophisticated recording devices, the electrical activity of the muscles can also be assessed. Termed electromyography, or EMG, this procedure involves placing electrodes on the patient's skin to detect the electrical activity associated with muscle tension or movement. EMG has been used in the assessment of movement disorders, such as tics. In addition, some clinicians have reported elevated EMG activity in "muscle tension" patients. Finally, a possible relationship between excessive throat and mouth EMG activity and auditory hallucinations has been investigated in psychotic patients (Inovye & Schimizu, 1970).

Electroencephalography

Probably the most difficult psychophysiological technique to use and interpret is the electroencephalogram, in which the electrical activity of the brain is assessed through electrodes attached to the skull. Such readings have been helpful in the assessment of sleep disorders, depression, and actual physiological disorders such as epilepsy or brain tumor that may cause psychiatric symptoms.

Basic Procedures

In almost all psychophysiological assessment, the basic procedure that the patient undergoes is similar. The patient is asked to sit or recline in a comfortable chair while various recording devices such as electrodes are attached to his body. He then sits quietly for 20–30 minutes to habituate, or to become accustomed to the situation. At the end of this period a resting baseline is obtained, in which the patient's physiological responses are measured to reflect their rates during rest. A selected stimulus such as a feared object may then be introduced for a predetermined period of time, after which it is replaced with a neutral stimulus. The patient's physiological response during the target object presentation can be assessed in three ways: amount of change from the resting baseline, duration of the change, and recovery time. In most cases, these responses are recorded automatically by the polygraph by means of pens deflecting on paper and are later analyzed by computer or by hand.

Recently, portable units have been developed for the assessment of skin temperature, heart rate, and blood pressure. The portable heart rate monitor may be worn on the chest under clothing, making it possible to obtain measurements in the patient's natural environment.

Physiological assessment has been very useful in the assessment of some psychological problems. The clinician must be careful, however, to assess those variables that make sense in view of the presenting problem and not be overwhelmed by the technology of the field. Too often, literature reports are filled with detailed descriptions of sophisticated psychophysiological procedures, but provide scanty discussion of their meaning for the target problem purportedly being assessed. For example, presentation of a feared stimulus may simultaneously result in increased heart rate, decreased EMG activity, and no change in respiration. Without some rationale for the choice of a specific assessment technique, the resulting findings could be misleading. In those cases in which the choice of an appropriate physiological response system is not clear, the assessor may measure several systems simultaneously and report on all of them. He may also decide that a non-physiological assessment would provide more valuable information.

Applications with the mentally retarded. Because it does not rely on the patient's verbal report physiological measurement may initially appear to be very appropriate for use with the mentally retarded. In fact, Reid and his colleagues (Reid, 1976; Reid & Naylor, 1976) found the previously mentioned relationship between temperature readings and manic-depressive cycling in patients who were mentally retarded. This assessment was faster and much easier to conduct then either interviews or direct observations and provided important information. It must be noted, however, that obtaining pulse and temperature measurements are procedures that are familiar to most mentally retarded persons and that are not anxiety-provoking. Unfortunately, other types of physiological recording that involve the use of electrodes and a polygraph may be less successful with some mentally retarded patients. Such patients may be frightened and intimidated by the equipment, rendering recordings invalid or even impossible to obtain. Many mentally retarded patients may also be unable to sit quietly for the time required to conduct a physiological assessment, which often runs an hour or more and cannot be broken into smaller components. It may be for these reasons that reports of psychophysiological assessment with mentally retarded patients are virtually nonexistent in the literature. However, psychophysiological assessment may be possible with some patients, especially if the same guidelines used for interviewing are implemented. That is, the assessor should repeatedly give slow, simple explanations of the purpose and procedures of the assessment and use extensive praise and reassurance, as well as material rewards. It may be helpful to introduce the patient to the assessment situation in graded steps over several days, such as viewing the equipment on ''tour,'' then just chatting while sitting in the recliner, and permitting the patient to apply loose electrodes to himself. Sometimes the large polygraph can be placed in an adjoining room so that only the electrodes and their wires are visible to the patient. Finally, even those patients who are afraid of the regular physiological assessment situation may be able to wear the new portable monitors comfortably and successfully. This area of assessment with the mentally retarded has yet to be explored.

Summary. Physiological assessment has proven useful with individuals of normal intelligence for select psychological problems such as anxiety, sleep, and movement disorders. Although rarely tried to date, this approach may also be valuable for use with mentally retarded persons, especially since it requires no verbal response from the patient. The major problem lies in reducing the anxiety that may be generated in some patients by the rather intimidating assessment equipment.

CONCLUSION

Much is yet to be accomplished in assessing psychopathology with mentally retarded persons. Unlike what has been done with the measurement of intelligence and adaptive behavior, work in psychopathology has been far from systematic and little has been done to establish norm-referenced assessment methods. Thus, unlike assessment procedures with persons of normal intelligence, there are no analogous scales or normative data for the mentally retarded on measures such as the MMPI, Child Behavior Profile, or other general measures of psychopathology. The small amount of assessment that has been done has had to rely on modified versions of scales designed for persons of normal IQ. While such an approach is better than no assessment, mentally retarded persons present unique problems and require unique styles, particularly at the lower ranges of intellectual performance that make such assessments far from optimal.

Another point to consider in assessing psychopathology with the mentally retarded is the use of multiple assessment methods. Several self- and other-report rating scales and direct behavioral observations would thus seem optimal at this point. Perhaps later research will show that such elaborate methods are not necessary. However, this awaits empirical verification. In the meantime, the use of multiple measures would seem to afford a more conservative means of establishing differential diagnoses. Such efforts would also seem practical, at least with mildly and moderately mentally retarded patients, since ample evidence exists to demonstrate that at least under certain conditions these persons can provide accurate information on their own emotional problems. This point is important because such insight was considered lacking by clinical psychologist and psychiatrists in the field for many years (Matson & Barrett, 1982).

Another factor in assessing psychopathology with the mentally retarded that cannot be overlooked is the developmental factor. Cognitive level can and does markedly affect the rate of psychological and physiological development, which in turn affect the type and form by which psychopathology is manifested. This point has been recognized by researchers and clinicians for years (Penrose, 1938) but no one has made an effort to systematically incorporate these findings into differential diagnosis. Such an effort is greatly needed if adequate diagnosis and assessment of emotional disorders, particularly in the severely and profoundly mentally retarded, is to be achieved.

Another important factor to consider in future research is the optimal means for assessing psychopathology, relative to characteristics of the assessment situation and format. Sigelman and her colleagues (Sigelman, et al., 1981a, 1981b) are, to the knowledge of these reviewers, the only researchers who have attempted to evaluate this problem over a series of systematically planned studies. They have found, for example, that mentally retarded people are more likely to acquiesce than would persons of normal intelligence to interview questions. Yes-no question formats, thus, are less appropriate for this group than true-false questions, if the interviewee has sufficient cognitive skills to understand the more difficult true-false concept relative to yes-no. Additionally, the use of pictures that exemplify questions being asked increases accuracy and consistency of response. Breuning and his associates (Breuning & Davis, 1981) also found that reinforcement of responses, without giving any indication as to whether the response was correct, markedly increased motivation and enhanced performance on standard intelligence tests. Similar effects on self-ratings of psychopathology might be present as well, but await empirical validation. These initial data do point out the importance and necessity of further research in this area.

Despite the problems noted above, relate to the general shortage of information about psychopathology in the mentally retarded, there are a number of positive points. Perhaps the most useful of these is that despite the lack of sophisticated assessment techniques, professionals have been able to identify a variety of psychological disorders across the spectrum of mentally retarded persons (see incidence section). Additionally, the data that have been obtained are most encouraging relative to the likelihood that various forms of psychopathology can be accurately evaluated in this group. Thus, further efforts to develop assessment techniques with the mentally retarded should meet with considerable success.

REFERENCES

Achenbach, TM. The child behavior profile: I. Boys aged 6–11. *Journal of Consulting and Clinical Psychology*, 1978, *46*, 478–488

American Psychiatric Association. *Diagnostic and statistical manual of mental disorders* (3rd ed.). Washington, DC: American Psychiatric Association, 1980

Barlow, DH (Ed.). *Behavioral assessment of adult disorders*. New York: Guilford Press, 1981

Beck, AT, Ward, CH, Mendelson, M, Mock, J, & Erbaugh, J. An inventory for measuring depression. *Archives of General Psychiatry*, 1961, *4*, 561–571

Bialer, I, & Sternlick, M. *The psychology of mental retardation: Issues and approaches*. New York: Psychological Dimensions, Inc., 977

Breuning, SE, & Davis, VJ. Reinforcement effects on the intelligence test performance of institutionalized retarded adults: Behavioral analysis, directional control, and implications for habilitation. *Applied Research in Mental Retardation*, 1981, *2*, 307–322

Cuvo, AJ. Decreasing repetitive behavior in an institutionalized mentally retarded resident. *Mental Retardation*, 1976, *14*, 22–25

Earl, CJC. The primitive catatonic psychosis of idiocy. *British Journal of Medical Psychology*, 1934, *14*, 11–230

Ellis, NR. Memory processes in retardates and normals. In NR Ellis (Ed.), *International review of research in mental retardation* (Vol. 4). New York: Academic Press, 1970

Eysenck, SBG. *Manual for the Eysenck-Withers Personality Inventory for subnormal subjects (50–80IQ)*. London: University of London Press, 1965

Eysenck HJ, & Eysenck, SBG. *Eysenck Personality Inventory*. San Diego, CA: Educational and Industrial Testing Service, 1968

Guarnaccia, VJ, & Weiss, RL. Factor structure of fears in the mentally retarded. *Journal of Clinical Psychology*, 1974, *30*, 540–544

Guralnick, MJ. Behavior therapy with an acrophobic mentally retarded young adult. *Journal of Behavior Therapy and Experimental Psychiatry*, 1973, *4*, 263–265

Hathaway, SR, & McKinley, JC. *The Minnesota multiphasic personality inventory manual* (rev.). New York: The Psychological Corporation, 1951

Haynes, SN, & Jensen, BJ. The interview as a behavioral instrument. *Behavioral Assessment*, 1979, *1*, 97–106

Heaton-Ward, A. Psychosis in mental handicap. The tenth Blake Marsh lecture. *British Journal of Psychiatry*, 1977, *130*, 525–533

Helzer, JE, Robins, LM, Croughan, JL, & Welner, A. Renard Diagnostic Interview. *Archives of General Psychiatry*, 1981, *38*, 393–398

Hersen, M & Bellack, AS (Eds.). *Behavioral assessment: A practical handbook* (2nd ed.). New York: Pergamon Press, 1981

Hetherington, EM, & Martin, B. Family interaction and psychopathology in children. In HC Quay & JS Werry (Eds.), *Psychopathological disorders of children*. New York: John Wiley and Sons, 1972

Honigfeld, G, Gillis, RD, & Kleff, CJ. NOISE-30: A treatment sensitive ward behavior scale. *Psychological Reports*, 1966, *19*, 180–182

Inovye, T, & Schimizu, A. Electromyographic study of verbal hallucination. *Journal of Nervous and Mental Disease*, 1970, *151*, 415–423

Jacobson, JW. Problem behavior and psychiatric impairment within a developmentally disabled population I: Behavior frequency. *Applied Research in Mental Retardation*, 1983, *3*, 121–140

James, FE, & Snaith, RP. *Psychiatric illness and mental handicap*. London: Gaskell Press, 1979

Kallman, W.M., & Feuerstein, M. Psychophysiological procedures. In AR Ciminero, KS Calhoun & HE Adams (Eds.), *Handbook of behavioral assessment*. New York: Wiley, 1977

Kazdin, AE, & Matson, JL. Social validation with the mentally retarded. *Applied Research in Mental Retardation*, 1981, *2*, 39–54

Kazdin, AE, Matson, JL, & Senatore, V. Assessment of depression in mentally retarded adults. *American Journal of Psychiatry*, 1983, *140*, 1040–1043

Lang, PJ, & Lazovic, AD. Experimental desensitization of a phobia. *Journal of Abnormal and Social Psychology*, 1963, *66*, 519–525

Lefkowitz, MM, & Burton, N. Childhood depression: A critique of the concept. *Psychological Bulletin*, 1978, *85*, 716–726

Mansdorf, IJ. Eliminating fear in a mentally retarded adult by behavioral hierarchies and operant techniques. *Journal of Behavior Therapy and Experimental Psychiatry*, 1976, *7*, 189–190

Matson, JL. Assessment and treatment of clinical phobias in mentally retarded children. *Journal of Applied Behavior Analysis*, 1981, *14*, 145–152 (a)

Matson, JL. Use of independence training to teach shopping skills to mildly mentally retarded adults. *American Journal of Mental Deficiency*, 1981, *86*, 176–183 (b)

Matson, JL. Depression in the mentally retarded: Toward a conceptual analysis of diagnosis. In M Hersen, R Eisler & PM Miller (Eds.), *Progress in behavior modification*, New York: Academic Press (in press)

Matson, JL, & Barrett, R (Ed.). *Psychopathology in the mentally retarded*. New York: Grune & Stratton, 1982

Matson, JL, Dettling J, & Senatore, V. Treating depression of a mentally retarded adult. *The British Journal of Mental Subnormality*, 1981, *16*, 86–88

Matson, JL, DiLorenzo, TM, & Andrasik, F. A review of behavior modification procedures for treating social skill deficits and psychiatric disorders of the mentally retarded. In JL Matson & F Andrasik (Eds.), *Treatment issues and innovations in mental retardation*. New York: Plenum Press, 1982

Matson, JL, & Zeiss, RA. The buddy system: A method for generalized reduction of inappropriate interpersonal behaviour of retarded-psychiatric patients. *British Journal of Psychiatry*, 1979, *18*, 401–405

Mavissakalian, MR, & Barlow, DH. Assessment of abessive-compulsive disorders. In DH Barlow (Ed.), *Behavioral assessment of adult disorders*. New York: Guilford Press, 1981

Menolascino, FJ, & Bernstein, NR. Psychiatric assessment of the mentally retarded child. In NR Berstein (Ed.), *Diminished people*. Boston: Little Brown & Co., 1970

Meyer, V, Liddell, A, & Lyons, M. Behavioral interviews. In AR Ciminero, KS Calhoun, & HE Adams (Eds.), *Handbook of behavioral assessment.* New York: John Wiley & Sons, 1977

Miller, LC, Barrett, CL, Hampe, E, & Noble, H. Factor structure of childhood fears. *Journal of Consulting and Clinical Psychology,* 1972, *39,* 264–268

Morganstern, KP, & Tevlin, HE. Behavioral interviewing. In M Hersen & AS Bellack (Eds.), *Behavioral assessment: A practical handbook* (2nd Ed.). New York: Pergamon Press, 1981

Mulhern, T, & Baumeister, AA. An experimental attempt to reduce stereotypy by reinforcement procedures. *American Journal of Mental Deficiency,* 1969, *74,* 69–74

Nelson, RO. Methodological issues in assessment via self-monitoring. In JD Cone, & RP Hawkins (Eds.), *Behavioral assessment.* New York: Brunner/Mazel, 1977

Nelson, RO, Lipinski, DP, & Black, JL. The reactivity of adult retardates' self-monitoring: A comparison among behaviors of different valences, and a comparison with token reinforcement. *The Psychological Record,* 1976, *26,* 189–201

Nihira, K, Foster, R, Shellhaas, N, & Leland, H. *AAMD adaptive behavior scale* (manual). Washington, DC: American Association on Mental Deficiency, 1974

Peck, C L. Desensitization for the treatment of fear in the high level retardate. *Behaviour Research and Therapy,* 1977, *15,* 137–148

Penrose, LS. *A clinical and genetic study of 1280 cases of mental defect.* Special report of the medical research council, No. 229. London: HMSO, 1938

Primrose, PA. A survey of 502 consecutive admissions to a subnormality hospital from 1st January 1968 to 31st December 1970. *British Journal of Mental Subnormality,* 1971, *32,* 25–28

Quay, NC, & Peterson, DR. *Manual for the Behavior Problem Checklist.* Champaign, IL: University of Illinois, Children's Research Center, 1967

Rachman, SJ, & Hodgson, RJ. *Obsessions and compulsions.* Englewood Cliffs, NJ: Prentice-Hall, Inc., 1980

Ray, WJ, & Raczynski, JM. Psychophysiological assessment. In M Hersen & AS Bellack (Eds.), *Behavioral assessment: A practical handbook* (2nd ed.). New York: Pergamon Press, 1981

Reid, AH. *Mental illness in adult mental defectives with special reference to psychosis.* M.D. thesis. University of Dundee, Ireland, 1971

Reid, AH. Psychosis in adult mental defectives. I: Manic depressive psychosis. II: Schizophrenia and paranoid psychoses. *British Journal of Psychiatry,* 1972, *120,* 205–218

Reid, AH. Psychiatric disturbances in the mentally handicapped. *Proceedings of the Royal Society of Medicine,* 1976, *69,* 509–512

Reid, AH, & Angle, PG. Dementia in aging mental defectives. *Journal of Mental Deficiency Research,* 1974, *18,* 15–23

Reid, AH, & Naylor, GJ. Short-cycle manic-depressive psychosis in mental defectives: A clinical and physiologicl study. *Journal of Mental Deficiency Research,* 1976, *20,* 67–76

Rivinus, TM, & Harmatz, JS. Diagnosis and lithium treatment of affective disorder in the retarded: Five case studies. *American Journal of Psychiatry,* 1979, *136,* 551–554

Robins, LN, Helzer, JE, Croughan, J, & Ratcliff, KS. National Institute of Mental Health Diagnostic Interview Schedule. *Archives of General Psychiatry,* 1981, *38,* 381–389

Rosen, M, Clark, GR, & Kivitz, MS. *The history of mental retardation.* Baltimore: University Park Press, 1976

Rutter, M, Tizard, J, Yule, W, Graham, P, & Whitmore, K. Isle of Wight studies 1964–1974. *Psychological Medicine,* 1976, *6,* 313–332

Sigelman, CK, Budd, EC, Spahel, CL, & Schoenrock, CJ. Asking questions of retarded persons: A comparison of yes-no and either-or formats. *Applied Research in Mental Retardation,* 1981, *2,* 347–357 (a)

Sigelman, CK, Budd, EC, Spahel, CL, & Schoenrock, CJ. When in doubt, say yes: Acquiescence in interviews with mentally retarded persons. *Mental Retardation,* 1981, *19,* 53–58 (b)

Spitz, HH. Consolidating facts into the schematized learning and memory system of educable retardates. In NR Ellis (Ed.), *International review of research in mental retardation* (Vol. 6). New York: Academic Press, 1973

Spitzer, RL, & Endicott, J. *Schedule for affective disorders and schizophrenia (SADS)* (3rd ed.). New York: New York State Psychiatric Institute, Biometrics Research, 1978

Stoudenmire, J, & Salter, L. Conditioning prosocial behaviors in a mentally retarded child without using instructions. *Journal of Behavior Therapy and Experimental Psychiatry*, 1975, *6*, 69–42

Taylor, CB, & Agras, S. Assessment of phobia. In DH Barlow (Ed.), *Behavioral assessment of adult disorders*. New York: Guilford Press, 1981

Van Hasselt, VB, Hersen, M, & Bellack, AS. The validity of role play tests for assessing social skills in children. *Behavior Therapy*, 1981, *12*, 202–216

Waranch, HR, Iwata, BA, & Wohl, MK. Treatment of a retarded adult's mannequin phobia through *in vivo* desensitization and shaping approach responses. *Journal of Behavior Therapy and Experimental Psychiatry*, 1981, *12*, 359–362

Wing, JK, Cooper. JE, & Sartorious, N. *The measurement and classification of psychiatric symptoms*. Cambridge, England: Cambridge University Press, 1974

Wing, L. The MRC handicaps, behaviour and skills (HBS) schedule. *Acta Psychiatrica Scandinavica* (Suppl. 285), 1980, *62*, 241–247

Wing, L, & Gould, J. Systematic recording of behaviors and skills of retarded and psychotic children. *Journal of Autism and Childhood Schizophrenia*, 1978, *8*, 79–97

Worrall, EP, Moody, JP, & Naylor, GJ. Lithium in non-manic depressives: Antiaggressive effect and red blood cell lithium values. *British Journal of Psychiatry*, 1975, *126*, 464–468

Zegiob, L, Klukas, N, & Junginger, J. Reactivity of self-monitoring procedures with retarded adolescents. *American Journal of Mental Deficiency*, 1978, *83*, 156–163

Lori A. Sisson
Stephen E. Breuning

6

Medication Effects

Medication is a general term used to describe any drug or agent administered in the treatment of disease, illness, or injury. Within this definition, the possibilities of what is considered a medication are almost countless and we make no pretense that this chapter is intended to be applicable to each possibility. The scope of this chapter is limited to types of medication commonly used to treat behavior disorders displayed by mentally retarded individuals. These medications are synonymously called psychotropic, psychiatric, or psycholeptic drugs and refer to chemicals whose action is mediated physically but whose therapeutic target is a psychological or behavioral change (Werry, 1978).

The psychotropic drugs most frequently used with the mentally retarded are the neuroleptic drugs (also known as major tranquilizers and antipsychotics), which include the phenothiazines such as thioridazine (Mellaril, Sandoz) or chlorpromazine (Thorazine, Smith Kline & French) amd the butyrophenones such as haloperidol (Haldo, McNeil Pharmaceutical). Psychotropic drugs used much less commonly with the mentally retarded include the anxiolytics (minor tranquilizers, antianxiety drugs) such as chlordiazepoxide (Librum, Roche) and diazepam (Valium, Roche); the antidepressants including amitriptyline (Elavil, Merck Sharp & Dohme) and imipramine (Tofranil, Geigy); the antimanic drug lithium carbonate; and the stimulants such as dextroamphetamine (Dexedrine, Smith Kline & French) and methylphenidate (Ritalin, CIBA). We will also touch upon the antiepilepsy drugs because they are frequently used with the mentally retarded—often unjustifiably (Davis, Cullari, & Breuning, 1982), are behaviorally active, and are occasionally prescribed for behavioral control. A more specific listing of drugs and their representative classification appears in Table 6-1.

The chapter will begin with a brief historical review and discussion of the rationale and prevalence of psychotropic drug use with the mentally retarded.

143

Table 6-1
Classification of Psychotropic Drugs

NEUROLEPTICS
  Phenotiazines
    Chlorpromazine (Thorazine)
    Fluphenazine (Prolixin)
    Mesoridazine (Serentil)
    Thioridazine (Mellaril)
    Trifluoprazine (Stelazine)

  Butyrophenone
    Haloperidol (Haldol)

  Thioxanthenes
    Chlorprothixine (Taractan)
    Thiothixene (Navane)

ANXIOLYTICS
  Benzodiazepines
    Chlordiazepoxide (Librium)
    Diazepam (Valium)
    Oxazepam (Serex)

  Diphenylmethane Derivatives
    Diphenhydramine (Benydral)
    Hydroxyzine (Atarax, Vistaril)

  Glycerol Derivatives
    Meprobamate (Equanil, Miltown)

STIMULANTS
    Amphetamine (Benzedrine)
    Dextroamphetamine (Dexedrine)
    Methylphenidate (Ritalin)
    Magnesium Pemoline (Cylert)

ANTIDEPRESSANTS
  Tricyclics
    Amitriptyline (Elavil)
    Desipramine (Norpramine)
    Imipramine (Tofranil)
    Nortriptyline (Arentyl)

  Monoamine Oxidase (MAO) Inhibitors
    Nalamide (Niamid)
    Phenelzine (Nordil)
    Tranylcypromine (Parnate)

ANTIMANIC
  Lithium Carbonate

ANTIEPILEPTICS
  Barbiturates
    Phenobarbital (Luminal)
    Primidone (Mysoline)

  Benzodiazepines (see Anxiolytics)

  Carbamazepine (Tegretol)

  Hydantoins
    Ethotoin (Peganone)
    Methoin (Mesantoin)
    Phenytoin (Dilantin)

  Succinimides
    Ethosuximide (Zarontin)
    Methsuximide (Celontin)
    Phensuximide (Milontin)

  Sodium Valproate
    Valporic Acid (Depakene)

Ethical and legal reasons to utilize rigorous assessment standards will then be presented. This will be followed by sections concerned with the measurement of target behaviors and side effects, within-subject and between-subject assessment designs, and additional requirements for a valid assessment of drug effectiveness. Given the number of issues to be addressed, much of our coverage (particularly to non-assessment issues such as history, prevalence and pattern of drug use, and pharmacological properties of drugs) will be brief and occasionally redundent with our previous writings. However, we believe that a working knowledge of these briefly dicussed issues is necessary for one to adequately assess medication effects. For further coverage of these topics with the mentally retarded the reader is referred to Breuning and Poling (1982a. 1982b), Breuning, Davis, and Poling (1982), and Breuning,. Poling, and Matson (1983).

History

The use of drugs with mentally retarded individuals has become popular only within the past 25 years. Yet, there is evidence that sedatives such as bromide and chloral hydrate have been occasionally used since the late 1800s to reduce agitation and aggression in the mentally retarded living in institutions. In addition, antiepileptics have been used in attempts to control epileptic states and disorders, as well as to manage behaviors unrelated to seizures, for at least 50 years. There are few available data relating to the early use of behaviorally active drugs with the mentally retarded, and the little information that is available refers primarily to the neuroleptic drugs (see Table 6-1).

During the mid to late 1950s, studies of drug use with the mentally retarded began to appear in the published literature. The results of these studies were generally favorable to pharmacotherapy (see Breuning & Poling, 1982a, 1982b; Sprague & Werry, 1971, for a more complete review); however, methodological errors were abundant.

In the 1960s, the number of papers that reported the successful use of drugs for behavior control increased dramatically each year. Accompanying this increase in number of publications was a corresponding growth in the prevalance of pharmacotherapy with the mentally retarded. This trend was especially true for the use of the neuroleptics.

Besides the large number of papers supporting the use of psychotropic medications to alter troublesome behaviors exhibited by the mentally retarded, another factor seemed to contribute to increased drug use with this population. The use of pharmacotherapy with the mentally retarded appears to have gained much of its impetus from the growing literature that clearly indicated that neuroleptic drugs were effective, at least to some extent, in treating the symptomatology exhibited by adults with psychiatric disorders. Since many of the behaviors exhibited by adult psychiatric patients (e.g., behavioral stereotypies, failure to maintain good personal hygiene, aggressiveness, etc.) were similar to those exhibited by the institutionalized mentally retarded, there seemed to be a rationale for exposing mentally retarded individuals to neuroleptics and to other drugs as well. This rationale and practice was not seriously questioned for many years.

Freeman (1970) and Sprague and Werry (1971) were the first to raise questions concerning the efficacy of pharmacotherapy with the mentally retarded. For example, Sprague and Werry conducted an exhaustive review of the drug studies during the 1950s and 1960s, paying particular attention to the methodologies employed. They reached the distressing conclusion that with very few exceptions, these studies were methodologically inadequate; for this reason, the positive results reported were difficult to accept. Subsequent reviews have reached essentially the same conclusions (Aman, 1982; Aman & Singh, 1980; Breuning, Davis, & Poling, 1982; Breuning & Poling, 1982b; Ferguson & Breuning, 1982; Sprague & Baxley, 1978; Sulzbacher, 1973).

Other factors contributed to the realization that the issues surrounding the use of pharmacotherapy with the mentally retarded and mentally ill were not as clear-cut as they had once seemed. First, the discovery of debilitating, and some-times irreversible, side effects of long-term drug use (e.g., tardive dyskinesia with the neuroleptics) raised important questions concerning the costs of versus the benefits of pharmacotherapy. Second, in the early 1970s it became evident that certain behavior modification strategies were effective in improving the be-havioral repertoires of mentally retarded individuals. Finally, some authors boldly and specifically stated that drug effects in the mentally retarded were essentially unknown (Freeman, 1970; Lipman, 1970; Sprague & Werry, 1971), while others cautioned that drugs did not enhance, and might indeed diminish, the effective-ness of behavioral treatments (Breuning, O'Neill & Ferguson, 1980; McConahey, Thompson, & Zimmerman, 1977). A general skepticism concerning the use of pharmacotherapy with the mentally retarded continues to grow. Scientist have be-gun to call for appropriate evaluations of pharmacotherapy, citizens' groups have begun to demand accountability of those who treat the mentally retarded, and litigaton has supported both positions.

Since pharmacotherapy was first used with the mentally retarded, a great deal of clinical, and somewhat less scientific, attention has been directed toward this mode of treatment. It is clear that in some cases drugs have been shown to have a definite therapeutic effect. However, the parameters within which pharmacotherapy is likely to be most effective are often uncertain. This situation is due in part be-cause some issues have not been adequately addressed in the published literature (e.g., the efficacy of drugs versus alternative therapies), but also is the result of the use of inadequate assessment and research design strategies (Aman & Singh, 1980; Breuning, Davis, & Poling, 1982; Breuning & Poling, 1982a, 1982b; Breuning, et al., 1983; Freeman, 1970; Lipman, DiMascio, Reatig & Kirson, 1978; Sprague & Werry, 1971; Wysocki & Fuqua, 1982).

The data presented in several review articles sum up the state of the art in pharmacotherapy research. Klein and Davis (1969) found only 11 of over 12,000 published evaluations of chlorpromazine to be methodologically sound. In a later review Marholin and Phillips (1976) found even these 11 to involve serious meth-odological flaws, especially with regard to the definition and evaluation of thera-peutic change. In a similar vein, Sulzbacher (1973) found that 72.5 percent of published pharmacological studies with children were uncontrolled in that they lacked either double-blind conditions or a placebo phase.

Pharmacotherapy studies with the mentally retarded, older as well as many current studies, are plagued with methodological errors (Breuning & Poling, 1982b). This is a very distressing fact because: "Beyond rendering findings uninterpretable in the scientific sense, such methodological errors seem to increase the likelihood that a drug will reportedly produce beneficial effects in a given study (Sulzbacher, 1973). In a real sense poor research is worse than no research at all: uncontrolled investigations may indicate a particular drug to be effective (or ineffective), and subsequent clinical judgements may rest on this report, even though the findings are artifactual'' (Breuning, Davis & Poling, 1982, p. 97). Conversely, clearly specified and appropriate measurement procedures coupled with carefully conceived evaluation designs would promote confidence in obtained results. Such attention to experimental methodology would allow replication of procedures by clinicians and researchers in various settings, with various populations. Thus, the bounds of generalization of results could be established. It is in this way that the indications for effective use of pharmacotherapy with the mentally retarded can be made clear, making pharmacotherapy an efficient, data based treatment regimen.

Rationale and Prevalence

Neuroleptics

The neuroleptics, when effective, ''produce a specific improvement in the mood and behavior of psychotic patients without excessive sedation and without causing addiction'' (Goth, 1974, p. 221).

The primary group of patients for whom neuroleptics are prescribed are non-retarded ''schizophrenics''. Schizophernia is by no means a precise diagnostic category: schizophrenics are characterized by altered motor behavior, perceptual disturbances (hallucinations), disturbed thinking, altered mood (often flat affect), and unusual interpersonal behavior (Berger, 1978). Specific behavioral correlates of these general disturbances are not easily operationalized, nor homogeneous across patients. There are, for example, no unique patterns of motor behavior characteristic of all alleged schizophrenics—some are totally immobile, others engage in frantic and seemingly purposeless stereotypes. At present, the diagnosis of schizophrenia is typically based on clinical impression, not specific empirical signs, and is problematic at best.

The prescription of neuroleptics, like the diagnosis of schizophrenia, involves art quite as much as science. For example, at no point in The Physicians' Desk Reference, a main refernce for clinicians, are specific behavioral indications for neuroleptic treatment discussed, nor is there mention of the use of the drug with the mentally retarded. This latter oversight is of some interest, since it has been speculated for years that neuroleptics may be less useful in anergic, mentally retarded individuals, than in excited, non-retarded patients (National Institute of Mental Health, 1964).

Apparently, prescription of neuroleptics for the mentally retarded rests upon a superficial similarity between the behavior of the mentally retarded and that of the mentally ill (schizophrenic or otherwise psychotic). For example, the mentally ill often engage in stereotypic self-stimulation, speak in largely nonsensical phrases, avoid contact with others, and fail to maintain accepted standards of self-care. Similar behaviors are sometimes emitted by the mentally retarded, especially those in institutions. However, despite occasional similarities between the actions of the mentally ill and those of the mentally retarded, there typically are marked differences. In schizophrenic (and other psychotic) patients, the behavioral repertoire usually degenerates with the onset of the condition; no such degeneration is evident in most cases of mental retardation. Thus, the diagnosis of psychosis in this group is open to question. Further, perceptual disturbances (hallucinations) are commonly reported by the mentally ill, but not the mentally retarded. Even when there is a topographical resemblance between the responses of the mentally ill and mentally retarded, this does not necessarily imply a similar etiology, nor that the same treatment will be effective with both groups.

With the mentally retarded, the primary value of the neuroleptics seems to be their ability to produce a relatively nonselective sedation. A sedated person may be less likely to engage in undesired actions, but this hardly provides a compelling logical or empirical rationale for pharmacotherapy. At present, there are only a few specific target behaviors in the mentally retarded (e.g., aggression) that have been found to be selectively improved by any neuroleptic, and no known neuroleptic generally improves the deportment of the mentally retarded. The continued use of such drugs with this population seems to rest largely on positive findings with the mentally ill and a paucity of data concerning drug effects in the mentally retarded, coupled with a perhaps unfounded faith in the medical model, and a pragmatic need to provide some form of treatment.

Surveys spanning the past 10 years have consistently shown that 40–50 percent of the institutionalized mentally retarded are receiving neuroleptic drugs. In the first survey, Lipman (1970) found that 51 percent of the institutionalized mentally retarded were receiving a neuroleptic drug. Chlorpromazine, thioridazine, and haloperidol accounted for over 60 percent of this drug use. Sprague (1977) reported similar prevalence figures; 51 percent of the individuals in his survey received thioridazine or chlorpromazine. Analogous prevalence figures have also been reported by DiMascio (1975), Pullman, Pook, and Singh (1979), Sewell and Werry (1976), and Tu and Smith (1979). Most recently, Craig and Behar (1980) reported that psychotropic drug use may still be increasing as only 14.1 percent of the sample they surveyed was medication free. Common to all of these surveys is the finding that neuroleptic drugs are often used for extended periods of time and in doses exceeding those recommended by the drug's manufacturer. Comparable prevalence estimates and patterns of antipsychotic drug use have recently been reported with noninstitutionalized mentally retarded individuals. Davis et al. (1982) surveyed the prevalence and pattern of drug use with a random sample of 3500 mentally retarded individuals in community foster and group homes. It was found that 58 percent were receiving thioridazine, chlorpromazine, and/or haloperidol.

Anxiolytics

The anxiolytics are prescribed for nonretarded patients to treat a number of vaguely defined chronic conditions such as daytime anxiety, insomnia, night terrors, the tension associated with mild depression, and various neuroses. These drugs may also be used on a short-term basis to relieve stress associated with traumatic environmental events (e.g., divorce), and to decrease adverse reactions during withdrawal from alcohol and other central nervous system depressants.

As noted, the anxiolytics are used to treat a wide variety of patient reported distresses, most of which are not grossly debilitating. A usual measure of the success of treatment with anxiolytic agents is the patient's evaluation alone. Overt behavioral measures are rarely employed, either in prescribing anxiolytics for nonretarded patients, or for evaluating their effectiveness, which is apparently debatable (Garattini, Mussini, & Randall, 1973; Gittleman-Klein, 1978; Greenblatt & Shader, 1974).

When the mentally retarded are considered, the anxiolytics are less commonly prescribed than the neuroleptics. Apparently, the drugs are usually used to produce chronic sedation, although it is likely that anxiolytics are occasionally employed to reduce withdrawal symptoms in alcoholics, and to reduce anxiety during acute stress and disease states. Presumably, these latter usages would be confined to less severely retarded clients, who could develop an alcohol-abuse problem, or ask for stress relieving drugs. There is no reason to believe that anti-anxiety agents are of general value for improving the behavioral repertoire of the mentally retarded, although some patient-reported problems (i.e., states of "anxiety") might be temporarily alleviated.

Anxiolytic drugs are not used nearly as frequently as the neuroleptic drugs with the mentally retarded. In his 1970 survey, Lipman reported that chlordiazepoxide and diazepam were used with about 8 percent of the institutionalized mentally retarded. Cohen and Sprague (1977) report a slightly lower figure of 5 percent. Hughes (1977) found that as many as 23 percent of his sample received diazepam, primarily for seizure control. The use of these drugs with noninstitutionalized mentally retarded individuals appears to be even lower (Davis et al., 1982).

Antidepressants and Antimanics

Like the anxiolytics, the antidepressants are used to treat a wide and ill-defined range of disorders in the nonretarded. In general, depression involves self reports of sadness, guilt, and incompetency, coupled with observed and reported ahedonia. Weight loss and insomnia are common, as are disturbances in motor behavior, usually involving a general decrease in activity. Depressed people often report minor physical ailments, including constipation, dry mouths, headaches, and backaches; depressed women may stop menstruating. Severely depressed individuals often fail to maintain vocational and professional commitments; suicide becomes a real concern. Depression traditionally has been classified as exogenous (produced by obvious environmental changes, such as the death of a loved one) or endogenous (without obvious cause). Mild depression of the former, and probably the latter sort is common and usually does not require treatment. Severe and chronic depression is a very different matter, and demands attention. There are no conclusive data on the prevalence of depression in the mentally retarded (see Matson & Barrett, 1982).

In nonretarded individuals, antidepressants are effective in managing most cases of depression, although the conditions under which antidepressants are beneficial remain open to question. Berger (1978) has provided a careful review of antidepressant therapies. Antidepressants are rarely prescribed for the mentally retarded; when they are prescribed, the rationale is unclear. The mentally retarded assumedly suffer from depression (Gardener, 1967) and even though severely handicapped individuals may be unable to manage the self-reports indicative of the condition they might well benefit from antidepressants. In a recent review of antidepressant drug use with the mentally retarded, however, Gualtieri and Hawk (1982) note, "The only unequivocal indication for the use of tricyclic antidepressants in the mentally retarded is unipolar depression . . . They are effective for enuresis, but in most cases not necessary. Their use for the treatment of behavior disorders and/or hyperactivity cannot be recommended" (p. 231–232).

Most, perhaps 80 percent, of depressive illness is unipolar. However, bipolar manic-depressive disorders are not uncommon, and unipolar mania has occasionally been observed. During mania, patients are overly talkative, eat little, exhibit increased motor activity and brittle affect (rapid swings from elation to irritability), express seemingly divergent ideas as units in what is labeled "flight of ideas", and often engage in irresponsible social behavior. Hypomania may serve a person well in our society, but full blown manic episodes wreak havoc with jobs, friends, and family.

Lithium carbonate is the only known antimanic drug. In 1949, the Australian John Cade discovered that lithium salts are effective antimanic agents; this discovery has been heralded as the birth of modern psychopharmacology (Berger, 1978). Lithium was first used clinically in the United States in 1969, and several controlled studies attest to its effectiveness (Berger, 1978). However, acceptance of lithium as an antimanic is by no means unanimous. For example, Gualtieri and Hawk (1982) have cautioned that lithium should only be considered as a treatment measure for the mentally retarded when other, more conventional treatment approaches have failed and the situation is sufficiently grave to warrant a drug trial.

Lipman found that fewer than 4 percent of the mentally retarded individuals were treated with tricyclics and no mention was made of lithium treatment (Lipman, 1970). Sprague (1977) reported similar findings. Rimland (1974) reported use of only one tricyclic (nortriptyline) in 71 (3.5 percent) of over 2000 autistic children, while neuroleptics had been used in almost half of the children. Use of MAO inhibitors or lithium were not reported. In a survey of 184 studies of psychoactive drug treatment of the mentally retarded by Lipman, DiMascio, Reatig, and Kirson (1978), only 12 (6.9 percent) were concerned with tricyclics; none with MAO inhibitors or lithium. Virtually no use of these drugs was found in the survey of non-institutionalized individuals by Davis, et al. (1982).

Stimulants

The primary use of stimulants is in the treatment of nonretarded, hyperactive children, where the stimulants have some reported value (Walker, 1982). Hyperkinesis (also known as hyperactivity, minimal brain dysfunction, and attention deficit disorder) involves short attention span, aggression typically directed toward peers, impulsivity, and restlessness (Waldrop, Bell, McLaughlin, & Halverston, 1978; Walker, 1982). The etiology of the disorder is unknown. Several hypotheses have been advanced, but none have been clearly confirmed (Robinson & Robinson, 1976). Hyperkinesis is now generally not regarded as a distinct clinical entity, but rather as the upper end of a normally distributed behavioral dimension. Consequently, its assessment is problematic. Clinical evaluation and diffuse ratings by parents and teachers often enter into the diagnosis, although specific empirical criteria are occasionally employed.

Unfortunately, operational definitions of treated conditions are rare. At present, the stimulants are prescribed for a variety of behavioral problems, such as behavior that is disruptive in the opinion of parents and teachers, generally interfering in some manner with normal classroom or home activities. It should be noted that many of the behaviors exhibited by nonretarded children treated as hyperkinetic are commonly observed in mentally retarded children and adults. It is apparently on this basis that stimulants are used with the mentally retarded even though this use is infrequent. There is, by the way, no accepted biochemical explanation for the beneficial effects of stimulants in any population, although the mechanism of action of these drugs is rather well understood.

Stimulants have not been frequently used with the mentally retarded. Lipman (1970) reported that less than 3 percent of his sample were receiving drugs of this class. Cohen and Sprague (1977) found a similar prevalence with 2–3 percent of the sample receiving stimulant pharmacotherapy. In community foster and group homes, Davis et al., (1982) found that approximately 2.4 percent of the non-institutionalized individuals were receiving a stimulant drug. It is interesting to note that stimulant use was almost totally determined (about 95 percent) by males aged 5–16 having no history of institutionalization.

Antiepileptics

Unlike the drug classes discussed previously, the antiepileptics are not typically used for behavioral control per se, but rather to manage a variety of convulsive disorders known collectively as epilepsy. There are more than a dozen distinguishable forms of epilepsy, based upon seizure type and EEG pattern (Toman, 1965). Three of the most common forms are grand mal (generalized tonicclonic), petit mal (generalized absence), and psychomotor (complex partial focal) epilepsy (see chapter on Neurological Assessment).

Pharmacotherapy represents the primary treatment of epilepsy. Fortunately, such treatment usually is effective (Eadie & Tyrer, 1974; Gibbs, Gibbs, Gibbs, Gibbs, Dikman, & Hermann, 1982; Woodbury, Penry, & Schmidt, 1972). Seizure activity is relatively common among the mentally retarded, and in those instances where epilepsy is clearly evident, antiepileptics may prove invaluable. However, antiepileptics are sometimes used in an attempt to manage nonepileptic behavior and, more frequently, are prescribed to prevent seizures in mentally retarded persons who have never been observed to seize, or for whom the treatment is of no documented value. Further, it is becoming clear that antiepileptics may produce undesirable side effects, such that their use should be limited to situations where pharmacological management of epilepsy is both necessary and effective. Our coverage of the antiepileptics will focus on their behavioral effects, and use as behavior change agents. For more complete coverage see Gibbs et al. (1982)

The use of antiepilepsy dugs with the mentally retarded is second only to the neuroleptics. This is due to the fact that epilepsy is a predominant disorder with this population. For example, Corbett, Hariis, and Robinson (1975) present survey data suggesting that about 23 percent of the mildly/moderately mentally retarded, 28 percent of the severly mentally retarded, and 50 percent of the profoundly mentally retarded are likely to experience epilepsy. Phenytoin and phenobarbital are the most frequently used of the antiepilepsy drugs with both institutionalized and noninstitutionalized mentally retarded persons. Sprague (1977) reported that 39.7 percent of 1100 residents of a large state institution were receiving phenytoin and 38.4 percent were receiving phenobarbital. In a smaller institution he found phenytoin use to be 32.6 percent and phenobarbital use to be 28.3 percent. DiMascio found extremely large prevalence figures of 68 percent for phenytoin and 85 percent for phenobarbital. These figures appear to be extremes. Davis et al. (1982) reported that 34.7 percent of 3496 subjects were receiving phenytoin, 19.4 percent phenobarbital, and 6.9 percent diazepam. A combination of phenytoin and phenobarbital accounted for 53.9 percent of antiepilepsy drug use. The use of other antiepilepsy drugs in the Davis et al. survey included primidone (1.3 percent), carbamazene (1.1 percent) and ethasuximide (0.9 percent).

Ethics, Litigation, and Legislation

Many clinicians (regardless of discipline) are not trained in or shy away from rigorous assessment methods because they are clinicians not researchers. Sprague and Werry (1971) have made the case that from an ethical standpoint, there is less difference between the clinical and the research use of drugs than many people realize. This is because, given the lack of sophistication in this area, one cannot be entirely certain as to what drug should be administered, its safety, and the correct dosage level. Thus, the clinical use of psychotropic drugs involves some formal or informal experimentation. One can, and should, regard research on psychotropic drugs as simply the systematic investigation of some of these applied clinical problems, often with more than one subject at a time.

Perhaps the main impetus for the increase in quality clinical assessments are court orders and consent decrees. The most significant legal development in relation to the use of drugs for behavior management in the mentally retarded has been the courts' rejection of the idea that a state institution merely has to provide humane custodial care and consensus that residents of institutions have a right to treatment that is protected by the United States Constitution (Sprague & Baxley, 1978). One result of this change in attitude has been a substantial increase in successful litigation initiated by residents of state insitutions or their guardians who desire at least minimal constitutionally adequate treatment.

There have been more than 25 legal suits involving mentally retarded individuals and aspects of pharmacotherapy (see Sprague, 1982, for a comprehensive review). The first major case was that of *Wyatt v. Stickney* (1972). This case appeared before Federal District Court Judge Frank M. Johnson and concerned deplorable conditions at a state institution in Tuscaloosa, Alabama. Judge Johnson developed, with the aid of experts, an extensive set of standards that were agreed to be a constitutional minimum. The court ordered that these standards be implemented and created a ''human rights committee'' to ensure that the residents were afforded constitutional and humane habilitation. The 12-page ''Minimum Constitutional Standards for Adequate Habilitation of the Mentally Retarded'' included a section dealing with medication that called for:

1. Written prescriptions
2. 30-day termination/review dates on prescriptions
3. The right to be free from unnecessary or excessive medication
4. Documentation on medication changes and effects
5. Medication not to be used as punishment; for staff convenience; as a substitute for habilitative programs; or in quantities that interfere with habilitative programs
6. The drug regimen to be reviewed for adverse effects and contraindications
7. Interdisciplinary evaluations of drug effects
8. Drug administration only by properly trained staff

The *Wyatt* case was the cornerstone for most of the subsequent cases. The rulings from this case were upheld and extended in *Welsh v. Likens* (1974, 1977). The issue at hand in *Welsh v. Likens* concerned the indiscriminant use of pharmacotherapeutic agents in an institution in Minnesota, which the judge found to be ''cruel and unusual punishment'' of residents. In sum, it was ordered that:

1. The behaviors indicating pharmacotherapy must be described based upon direct staff observation and in terms of frequency of occurrence

2. Neuroleptics are to be used only to prevent injury to self or others, or when the behavior is found to impede the implementation of habilitative programs
3. There must be neuroleptic drug-free periods of at least 20 days (over an unspecified time period)

The same issues raised in the *Wyatt* and *Welsh* cases occurred in *New York ARC v. Rockefeller* (1973) and *New York ARC v. Carey* (1975). This case resulted in a consent decree which essentially repeated the previous orders on medication regulations and added few additional ones. These included the following requirements:

1. There must be weekly reviews of drug regimens by a physician
2. Written medication policies must be developed to govern safe administration and handling of all drugs
3. Medication errors and drug reactions must be recorded and reported to the prescribing practitioner

The orders of the *Wyatt, Welsh,* and *New York ARC* cases were upheld again in *Gary W. v. State of Louisiana* (1976) and *Doe v. Hudspeth* (1977). The *Doe* case, in Mississippi, added three new orders:

1. A single daily dose is to be used in neuroleptic maintenance pharmacotherapy
2. Polypharmacy was largely forbidden
3. Institutions must have seminars on pharmacotherapy

Perhaps the most comprehensive set of regulations on drug treatment for institutionalized populations was put forth by Judge Gigonux in a 1978 consent decree in Maine *(Wouri v. Zitnay,* 1978). In addition to all of the standards already mentioned, it was ordered that:

1. There must be monthly reviews of the number of residents receiving tranquilizers, phenothiazines, and antiepileptics
2. Pharmacotherapeutic agents must only be used as part of an individualized habilitative plan
3. There must be a statement explaining reasons for choice of a given medication including a balancing of expected therapeutic effects and potential adverse effects
4. There must be a statement regarding why nonpharmacotherapeutic treatments are inappropriate or inadequate
5. There must be an explanation to the residents and their advocates, in lay terms, regarding the reasons for pharmacotherapy, its possible benefits, and its possible adverse consequences
6. There must be careful monitoring of progress and side effects
7. There must be evaluations of pharmacotherapeutic effects on educational and habilitative performance

In the most recent case *(Clites v. Iowa, 1980, 1982)* a mentally retarded client of the Glenwood State Hospital-School in Iowa was awarded $760,165 in damages. Judge Martin concluded that,

> *For reasons which are noted in this opinion, the Court finds Tim has T.D. (tardive dyskinesia), the drugs caused it and it is permanent. . . . The Court wishes to state at the outset, however, that it finds Tim did not receive the standard of medical care that was acceptable as reasonable medical practice at that time with regard to the administration of major tranquilizers in an institutional setting such as Glenwood, and that this less than standard medical care resulted in injury to Tim. . . . For all the foregoing reasons the Court concludes that in Tim's case the major tranquilizers were given for the convenience of the staff and not as a part of a therapeutic program designed to provide Tim an opportunity for a better life.* (italics added)

Virtually none of the previously discussed standards of treatment and evaluation were used. This case was appealed to the Iowa Supreme Court where the initial judgment was affirmed.

The most pertinent legislation concerning pharmacotherapy is the *Developmentally Disabled Assistance Bill of Rights* (P.L. 95–187, 1975). All of the standards outlined above are generally encompassed in this document. Similar standards are also found in several sets of Federal Regulations such as the ICFMR (Intermediate Care Facilities for the Mentally Retarded), the ACMRDD (Accreditation Council for Services for the Mentally Retarded and other Developmentally Disabled), and JCAH (Joint Commission on Accreditation of Hospitals). Sprague (1982) has discussed these regulations in detail.

It is clear that a number of the standards which resulted from the court cases described above have great implication for the measurement of human behavior. First, the prescribing physician must ensure that objectionable behaviors to be modified are specified in the patient's record. This implies that global treatment goals are insufficient justification for drug use. Rather, target behaviors must be easily observed and operationally defined. Second, target behaviors must be counted and charted as a way of monitoring treatment progress. Third, monitoring medication effects must also involve ongoing assessment of physiological and behavioral side effects as well as any changes in performance in academic or work settings. Such multidimensional assessments allow for data-based decision making regarding the costs versus the benefits of pharmacotherapy. Finally, alternative treatment strategies must be evaluated for effectiveness prior to the introduction of drug therapies. The implication here is that appropriate measurement and design procedures must be employed in the justification of medication over other treatments for the behaviorally disordered mentally retarded patient.

Measurement of Target Behaviors

It is clear that more stringent requirements for drug evaluations are being called for by professional organizations, individual clinicians and researchers, judges, the FDA, and funding agencies. The sole objective of drug evaluation is to determine whether the independent variable, administration of a drug, significantly improves the dependent variable, some targeted aspect of the client's behavior. Deficits or excesses in the target behavior (with respect to rate, latency, magnitude, or stimulus control) constitute the problems that drugs are prescribed to treat; improvements in behavior that can be unambiguously ascribed to the drug are the only meaningful demonstration of clinical efficacy. Thus, integral to the assessment of drug effects are two components: the measurement of behaviors likely to be affected by the medication and the use of experimental designs to compare performance under conditions that assumedly differ only in whether or not a drug is administered. As detailed earlier in this volume, to obtain data that are useful, it is crucial that target behaviors are measured in ways that are repeatable over time or across observers (reliability), reflect what is actually being measured (validity), and involve assessment strategies that are sensitive to changes produced by the drugs. Beyond this, the assessment of clinical efficacy of a drug demands that the target behaviors bear some direct relationship to classroom or workshop performance, behavior in the home, school, or on the ward, or some other area of everyday functioning. Finally, measures of target behaviors should meet other obvious requirements such as practicality, economy, safety, and ethical acceptability. For further discussion of these topics, the reader is referred to Werry (1978).

There are a number of methods available for the assessment of target behaviors that meet some or all of these requirements. In an attempt to organize and standardize measurements in psychopharmacology, the National Institute of Mental Health (NIMH) set up an Early Clinical Drug Evaluation Unit (ECDEU now NCDEU) that reviewed and recommended instruments for assessing medication effects (see *Psychopharmacology Bulletin,* 1973; and the latest drug assessment manual, ECDEU, 1976). Although this battery is not without faults (e.g., some measures have not been used, others are too cumbersome for general use, and none of the measures provide an objective assessment of activity), it represents an important contribution to the field of psychopharmacology. Other reference sources for instruments and techniques used in the assessment of medication effects are reviewed by Werry (1978).

Global Impressions

Global ratings of overall client behavior defined along a continuum of drug response (e.g., from "marked improvement" to "marked deterioration") represent the most frequently used of the assessment strategies for drug effects. However, in spite of the usual impressive improvement percentages reported in research reports, global ratings of behavior change are grossly inadequate measures for describing drug effects for several reasons. First, such data reflect only the relative quality of any behavior change. Much information is lost. In particular, global ratings often do not capture day-to-day variability over the course of behavior change and never provide quantitative measures upon which to base statements about treatment effectiveness. More importantly, with global clinical impressions it is never clear what aspects of a patient's repertoire the clinician is evaluating nor if the assessment is unbiased. These factors undoubtedly contribute to the fact that the replicability of clinical impression across time or clinicians is rarely high. Because of these factors, it has been recommended that global clinical impressions as an index of drug effects can no longer be justified (Wysocki & Fuqua, 1982). At a minimum, whenever human observers are used to assess a drug effect, it must be clearly demonstrated that independent observers can agree in their evaluations (Marholin & Phillips, 1976).

Rating scales

A second very frequently used strategy for the assessment of medication effects is the problem-oriented checklist or rating scale. (See the chapter by Matson and Frame for further discussion of assessment methods that may be applicable during drug administration.) The basic format of the behavior problem checklist and rating scale requires a knowledgeable informant to evaluate, from memory or direct observation, various patient behaviors under given sets of conditions. Rating scales may be conceptualized as an attempt to systematize clinical impressions and make them objective, reliable, and quantitative. While rating scales are typically used in conjunction with other measures to diagnose psychopathology and monitor treatment gains, some drug studies have employed them as a primary or the only measure.

One of the advantages of rating scales is that they provide a quick and efficient survey of problem areas. They are inexpensive and practical. While rating scales represent a definite improvement over global impression in the assessment of medication effects, their reliability, validity, and sensitivity when used for this purpose with mentally retarded individuals remains to be established empirically. It is recommended that these measures be used in conjunction with other indices of behavior change.

Self-report

Self-reports of mood and image, often gathered via paper-and-pencil test, are particularly troublesome indices of change. One problem involves the logistics of data collection including making the instructions for test-taking and the concepts tested comprehensive to the mentally retarded patient. A further difficulty involves the discrepancies often observed between self-reports and other's estimates of behavior, an occurrence perhaps due to the intimate (non-public) nature of the material elicited. Finally, self-report measures are quite sensitive to non-drug factors, making it difficult to attribute changes in mood or self-image to the effects of pharmacotherapy. As a result, few studies with the mentally retarded have used self-report data.

One report does exist, however. Breuning (1982a) administered a modified self-report mood scale to institutionalized mildly retarded adolescents who exhibited frequent aggressive behavior before and during a trial of neuroleptic medication. Results were that self-ratings of feelings of "anger/frustration" and "apathy" corresponded well with more objective measures of aggression and workshop productivity in client's showing a theraputic response to the drug. This study suggests that self-reports are a potentially important data source in psychopharmacology with some mentally retarded individuals, meriting further consideration as selective, predictive, and effect measures.

Standardized tests

Standardized tests of personality (e.g., the Minnesota Multiphasic Personality Inventory, other behavior rating scales, and projective tests such as the Rorschach) and intellectual capabilities (e.g., the Stanford-Binet Intelligence Scale, and the various Weschler scales) represent another option in the assessment of medication effects. However, their role in psychopharmacology with the mentally retarded remains to be more clearly defined.

To date, there has been no real attempt to use personality or projective tests to assess medication effects in the mentally retarded. This is probably due at least in part to the lack of interest in this population and mode of treatment by most clinical psychologists and in part to some disenchantment with the whole notion of "personality" in general (Moos, 1973; Werry, 1978). Personality tests are cumbersome both to administer and to interpret, are of uncertain reliability and validity, and measure characteristics that have a questionable relationship to the condition drugs are intended to better.

Intelligence tests are frequently administered to mentally retarded individuals because the scores obtained are often necessary to justify school and/or institutional placements (Ciminero & Drabman, 1977). Relative to personality measures, they are more easily administered and scored and are generally considered to be more reliable and valid. However, intelligence tests are again indirect measures of the conditions of interest. Furthermore, these tests, when given under standarized conditions, are usually of limited drug sensitivity (Breuning, 1981; Breuning & Davidson, 1981; Breuning, Ferguson, Davidson, & Poling, in press).

Modification of intelligence test administration has been proposed by Breuning and colleagues (Breuning, 1981; Breuning & Davidson, 1981; Breuning, Ferguson, et al, in press) when these tests are to be incorporated into the drug evaluation protocol. It is advocated that reinforcement for correct responding be incorporated in testing procedures. These studies have been consistent in showing that mentally retarded individuals obtained improved IQs under reinforcement conditions more often than under standard conditions when off drugs. This differential effect was not apparent when subjects were receiving therapeutic doses of neuroleptics. In sum, the use of most standardized tests to assess drug effects in the mentally retarded cannot be recommended unless procedural modifications are incorporated.

Learning and Performance Measures

Other measurement strategies that may be employed to assess drug effects and are relevant to clinical management include measures of learning and task performance. Given that the notions of cognitive impairment and performance deficits are implicit in the definition and understanding of mental retardation, there are surprisingly few reports of drug studies that have used either learning or performance measures as dependent variables. The studies available can be separated into those that incorporated measures taken in applied (e.g., classroom or workshop) versus laboratory settings.

An example of how assessments of learning and performance in the classroom may be applied to the assessment of drug effects has been provided in an early study of Christensen (1975). Christensen compared the effects of methylphenidate to those of behavior modification on the cognitive performance of 16 mentally retarded boys. Through the administration of daily, individualized arithmetic quizzes, the investigator determined the effects of the drug on the number of problems attempted and the number of problems successfully completed. These indexes of learning yielded data suggesting that both drugs and behavior modification treatment enhanced learning, but the latter treatment had a greater effect.

More recently Breuning, Davis, Matson, and Ferguson (1982) assessed the effects of thioridazine and associated withdrawal dyskinesias on workshop performance of mentally retarded young adults. The workshop task was the assembly of a 15-part coaster bicycle brake, and the specific dependent measures included percentage of time on task, number of assemblies completed, and number and types of prompts required. These performance measures yielded data indicating that thioridazine can impair the workshop performance of mentally retarded persons; and decreases in workshop performance coincided with the onset of the dyskinesias while increases in performance occurred as the dyskinesias subsided.

Among the laboratory assays that have proven useful in the assessment of medication effects are performance under operant schedules of reinforcement (Breuning & Poling, 1982b; Hollis & St. Omer, 1972; Poling & Breuning, in press), delayed and non-delayed matching-to-sample tasks (Davis, Poling, Wysocki, & Breuning, 1981; Sprague, Barnes & Werry, 1970; Wysocki, Fuqua, Davis & Breuning, 1981), and repeated acquisitions of response sequences (Walker, 1982). These procedures enable the examiner to produce stable and enduring patterns of learning and performance against which drug effects may be evaluated. Examples of commonly used tasks are lever pressing and matching colors. These have been used in classroom and institutional settings. The utility of laboratory measures in drug evaluation is considered at length in several chapters in a recent text (Breuning & Poling, 1982a).

It should be noted that although measures of learning and performance provide potentially useful information regarding drug effects, certain problems surrounding reliability of observations and validity or relevance of the data obtained must be addressed. Measures taken in applied settings have good "face validity" (seeing is believing) and obvious relevance to adaptive functioning in various settings. However, the reliability of these observations must be established. This situation is typically handled by having two raters simultaneously and independently record the target behaviors during a certain proportion of observation sessions. Agreement between observers is then assessed via some statistical method, with calculation of interobserver agreement being the most common method used (Hartmann, 1977).

The issue of reliability is quite a different one in laboratory situations. Laboratory equipment often has the capabilities of measuring and recording responses. Thus, reliable data should be easy to ensure through careful calibration and periodic recalibration of measurement devices. However, the relationship between performance on laboratory tasks and performance in natural settings is frequently questioned (Sprague & Werry, 1971). This problem has been recognized and dealt with rather directly in a recent study by Davis et al. (1981). These researchers asessed the effects of phenytoin withdrawal on both matching-to-sample and workshop performance of mentally retarded persons. Behaviors exhibited in the laboratory and the applied settings were similarly negatively affected by the antiepilepsy medication. If researchers and clinicians continue to find such a correspondence between behavioral effects across these settings, the question of relevance of laboratory assessments will be resolved.

Behavioral Observations

Perhaps the most widely used and well-accepted strategy of behavioral assessment is one based on direct observation (see earlier chapters in this volume). According to this strategy, behavior is recorded as it happens, with a minimum of inference or data reduction, and ordinarily, in the client's natural environment. The development of direct observation procedures has progressed rapidly with the development and extended use of behavioral techniques to modify disordered behavior in a variety of populations and settings. Direct behavioral observation has been helpful to objectively determine the extent to which targeted behaviors occur; to control for reactive changes in the target behavior attributable to the assessment process; and to document changes in the target behavior as a function of treatment (Kazdin & Straw, 1976). Only recently have direct observational techniques been applied to psychopharmacological assessment.

Within the direct observation strategy of assessment, there are two well-known methods of measuring and recording behavior: event sampling and time sampling. To be effective as measuring devices, both methods require that the behavior being assessed possess characteristics of objectivity (clearly observable and without reference to inner states), and completeness (well delineated boundary conditions) (Kazdin & Straw, 1976). A third method, the use of mechanical recordings, will also be discussed.

Event sampling is a procedure wherein the frequency or duration of a specific behavior is measured for a given period of time. For example, in a study mentioned previously Breuning, O'Neill, and Ferguson (1980) compared the effectiveness of psychotropic drug, response cost, and psychotropic drug plus response cost procedures in reducing frequencies of several inappropriate behaviors (aggression, property damage, and yelling-screaming). Dependent measures were frequencies of each of the inappropriate behaviors recorded by staff members in 30-minute blocks, 24-hours per day.

Event sampling is usually considered to be appropriate only if the behavior in question has a clearly observable beginning and end. In cases where a specific behavior is not discrete, time sampling may yield more meaningful data. Time sampling is an assessment measure based on units of time rather than events. One of the most common forms of time sampling is interval recording, of which there are two types: continuous and non-continuous. In continuous interval recording, behavior is sampled for a given block of time (e.g., 15 min) each day with the time block being divided into shorter observation intervals (e.g., 10 sec). The targeted behavior is then scored as having occurred or not occurred within each separate interval of observation. Target behaviors are noted as occuring only once per interval and the data is expressed as a percentage across intervals. Non-continuous interval recording requires standardized departures from observation to allow the observer to record data. Christensen (1975) used non-continuous interval recording in the measurement of such behaviors as "out-of-seat," "disturbing others," "playing," and so forth.

The advantage of these techniques of direct observation lie in the relevance of the measured behavior to the child's actual problems. However, they require human observers. This procedure is expensive, and requires due caution, as Poling, Cleary, and Monaghan (1980) have emphasized:

As transducers, human observers are invariably suspect. Folklore suggests that lay observations are an imperfect reflection of actual happenings, and a large and growing body of data indicates that allegedly scientific observations sometimes provide an inaccurate index of the variables being considered. Among the factors demonstrated to influence reported observations are the observer's motivation and expectations, the specifics of the observational situation, the observational and data recording techniques that are being used, and the characteristics of the data being monitored.

In view of these considerations, researchers in applied behavioral analysis have gone to great lengths to ensure the believability of their observations. Beyond defining in detail the behavior(s) under consideration and carefully defining observational procedures, these investigators nearly always provide some measure of interobserver agreement, which specifies the correspondence obtained between the data recorded by each of two (or more) independent observers. Where feasible, "blind" observers—individuals not aware of the experimental conditions in effect—are employed, and video tapes of the subjects behavior are made subsequently used to check the accuracy of reported data (p. 243-244).

In an attempt to circumvent some of these problems, a few researchers and clinicans have developed and used mechanical devices in their assessments of drug effects. Primarily, these devices measure activity. One of the most frequently used mechanical devices is the stabilimetric chair (Sprague & Toppe, 1966), which has been described as, "inexpensive to construct, unobtrusive, produces simple numerical data and, in the originators' and the authors' hands, is highly drug-sensitive with intratask type motor overflow" (Werry, 1978, p. 63). Other, less frequently used devices include actometers, light grids focused on photoelectric cells, pressure sensors in the floor, pedometers, etc. Unfortunately, most devices are either cumbersome, expensive, or produce data which correlate rather poorly with other measures.

Measurement of Side Effects

So far, this section has emphasized the measurement of behaviors likely to be directly affected by administration or termination of a behaviorally active drug. The influence of drugs on behavior can be therapeutic (e.g., reduction in frequency of aggressive acts) or contratherapeutic (e.g., poorer performance on a habilitative task). It is clear that clinicians and researchers should assess for both effects in their evaluation of drugs in the mentally retarded in order to make a determination of the risk-benefit ratio of drug use.

While impaired habilitative performance is a side-effect (behavioral toxicity), there is a plethora of other possible side-effects that must be considered. For example, central nervous system effects such as acute dystonia (abrupt muscle spasms), akathisia (constant motor restlessness), parkinsonian reactions (body rigidity, masklike expression, shuffling gait), and dyskinesia (abnormal body movements); autonomic nervous system effects such as orthostatic hypotension (lowering of blood pressure upon standing), constipation, urinary retention, and dry mouth, blurred vision, and tachycardia (excessively rapid heartbeat); and endocrine and metabolic changes such as thyroid gland and hormone changes, and weight gain (with neuroleptics) or weight loss (with stimulants) may occur. There are hundreds of possible side-effects in addition to these and the reader is referred to Breuning and Poling (1982) and Campbell, Green, Perry & Bennett (1983) for a more complete discussion and specific references for additional information. Campbell et al. (1983) discuss the assessment of side-effects in detail so we will only review a few specific issues here.

The vast majority of side effects are well known by physicians and nursing staff and are generally identifiable by inquiry in combination with a simple physical examination. The ECDEU Dosage and Treatment Emergent Symptoms Scale (DOTES) provides a structured interrogation system which leaves no important area uncovered. Other side effects screening scales exist (e.g., the ECDEU Abnormal Involuntary Movement Scale; and, those described by Greenberg, Yellin, Spring & Metcalf, 1975; Saraf, Klein, Gittelman-Klein & Groff, 1974; and

Winesberg, Bialer, Kupietz & Tobias 1972), which also collect data through systematic interrogation plus physical and laboratory examinations. When the mentally retarded are patients or subjects, care must be taken to elicit relevant information from either themselves, if they are verbal, or a parent or guardian, if they are not.

Dyskinesias and withdrawal effects, which can often occur during or following neuroleptic treatment, are less well understood and more difficult to identify and assess. They are basically two types of dyskinesias—withdrawal and persistent.

Withdrawal dyskinesias. Involuntary movements of body parts and musculatures. The facial musculature (particularly oral-buccal-lingual) is most likely to be affected. Choreoathetoid and myoclonoic movements of the limbs and trunk also are common. Early indications include involuntary smacking and sucking of the lips, dartings and tremors of the tongue, lateral jaw movements, and purposeless movements of the extremities such as the fingers and wrists. These dyskinesias, like some of the extrapyramidal effects, are often mistakenly identified as hyperactive or stereotypic behaviors. Withdrawal dyskinesias may begin to appear within two or three days following an abrupt (e.g., all at once) discontinuation of the neuroleptic drug and may gradually appear throughout the course of a gradual (titrated) discontinuation of the drug (e.g., 8 weeks). Even with a gradual discontinuation dyskinesias typically do not appear until discontinuation is complete. These dyskinesias typically disappear within 12 to 16 weeks of drug discontinuation and are often accompanied by other withdrawal effects such as anorexia, nausea, vomiting, and weight loss.

The prevalence of withdrawal dyskinesias (and other withdrawal effects such as weight loss, nausea, vomiting) is not established with the mentally retarded. Preliminary data suggest a figure for dyskinesias of about 35 percent to 50 percent for gradual discontinuation and 45 percent to 65 percent for abrupt discontinuation. However, these figures are not firmly established (Gualtieri, Breuning, Schroeder, & Quade, 1982). In their most severe form, these abnormal movements can be very incapacitating. Even mild to moderate dyskinesias in the limbs have been found to interfere with adaptive behaviors such as the use of fasteners (e.g., buttons, snaps) and performance on workshop assembly tasks (Breuning, O'Neill, & Ferguson, 1980; Breuning, Davis, Matson, & Ferguson, 1982). Unlike extrapyramidal effects withdrawal dyskinesias may be aggravated rather than relieved by antiparkinsonian drug treatment.

Persistent dyskinesias (tardive dyskinesias). Topographically identical to the withdrawal dyskinesias described above. Differentiation between the two is based on length of occurrence. Withdrawal dyskinesias are those that disappear within 12 to 16 weeks after drug discontinuation, while persistent dyskinesias are those still present after this period. At present, this 12 to 16 week cutoff is largely arbitrary. Persistent usually appear either while the individual is on a stable maintenance dose of the drug (maintenance onset dyskinesia), or as the dose of the drug begins to be reduced. As the dose continues to be reduced, the movements often worsen. Recent estimates suggest the prevalence of persistent dyskinesias with the mentally retarded to be about 25 percent to 30 percent. Persistent dyskinesias may be irreversible and incapacitating, and they are typically aggravated by antiparkinsonian drug treatment. As with the withdrawal dyskinesias, mild to moderate limb movements have been found to interfere with adaptive behaviors such as performance on workshop assembly tasks. At the present time, an effective treatment is not available. Baldessarini and Tarsy (1978) discuss persistent dyskinesias in greater detail. In recent years several devices have become available for assessing dyskinesia. These include the Withdrawal Emergent Symptoms Checklist (WESC—Englehardt, unpublished*); Abnormal Involuntary Movement Scale (AIMS—available from the Pharmacological and Somatic Treatments Research Branch of the National Institute of Mental Health); the Simpson Tardive Dyskinesia Scale and the Smith Tardive Dyskinesia Rating Scale (both in Fann, Smith, Davis, & Domino, 1980); and the Dyskinesia Identification System—Coldwater (DISCO—Breuning, Kalachnik, Sprague, Davis, Ferguson, Cullari, Ullman, Davidson, & Hoffner, in press). Campbell et al. (1983) review these instruments in detail.

Recently, an additional side effect of neuroleptic drug use has been identified. This effect is termed "acute behavior deterioration" or "supersensitivity psychosis." It is posited that the neuroleptic drugs can cause a supersensitivity in the mesolimbic and mescortical dopamine systems. These systems have been functionally linked to the regulation of emotional behavior and intellectual functioning. Characteristics of acute behavior deterioration are primarily the occurrence of inappropriate behaviors after drug discontinuation that are qualitatively different from the inappropriate behaviors for which the drug was initially prescribed. For example, the initial inappropriate behavior might be hyperactivity while the inappropriate behavior after drug discontinuation might be aggression and screaming. Such acute behavior deterioration is not necessarily accompanied by other withdrawal effects such as anorexia, dyskinesias, or nausea and may be a short-term effect.

Recent research does suggest that this acute behavior deterioration will be highly correlated with the onset and disappearance of withdrawal dyskinesias (Gualtieri & Breuning, under review†). Gualtieri and Breuning also report the occurrence of this problem in eight of 51 mentally retarded individuals withdrawn from neuroleptic who became highly aggressive following neuroleptic discon-

---

*Englehardt, DA. WESC—Withdrawal Emergent Symptoms Checklist. Unpublished manuscript, 1974. Available from Dr. David A Engelhardt, Department of Psychiatry/Psychopharmacology, Downstate Medical Center, State University of New York, 450 Clarkson Avenue, Brooklyn, New York 11203

†Gualtieri, CT, & Breuning, SE. A behavioral analogue of tardive dyskinesia (under review)

tinuation. These subjects also had withdrawal dyskinesias. Both the aggressive behaviors and dyskinesias disappeared by the 16th week and were significantly correlated with each other ($+.84$).

Withdrawal effects, persistent dyskinesias, and acute behavior deterioration are often viewed as evidence that the individual requires continued antipsychotic drug treatment. This notion is usually confirmed, as reinstatement of the drug typically relieves the withdrawal effects. The problem is that the drug used to relieve the effects is very likely the initial cause of the effects and nothing more than a masking is occurring. Despite the fact that an effective treatment for many undesired effects such as dyskinesias and behavior deterioration is not available, the rapid reinstatement of the antipsychotic drug is ill-advised for two reasons. First, if the drug is the cause and only a masking is occurring, there is no way to assess a worsening of the effect or emergence of a new effect. Second, neuroleptic-free periods of 16 weeks will result in the disappearance of most withdrawal related problems (e.g., from 60 percent to 25 percent for dyskinesias and almost complete disappearance of acute behavior deterioration). In our opinion a 16 week drug-free period should in most cases be the minimum, following long-term chronic neuroleptic treatment.

ASSESSMENT DESIGNS

Controlled assessment, the defining feature of scientific analysis, clearly represents the most acceptable method for determining whether particular treatments (i.e., independent variables) are associated with lawful changes in the behavior of humans or other organisms (i.e., dependent variables). Central to the idea of controlled assessment is the use of various experimental designs that indicate the sequence of conditions to which individuals are exposed in treatment or a research investigation. This sequence of conditions is arranged such that meaningful comparisons of performance under the various conditions can be made and analyzed via statistical or graphic methods. The purpose of this section is to describe assessment strategies that may be appropriate for evaluating pharmacotherapies. This coverage will be necessarily brief; however, the interested reader is referred to the early chapters in this book and to several excellent texts (Hersen & Barlow, 1976; Kazdin, 1982; Keppel, 1973; Kirk, 1968) that cover topics related to experimental design in general and to a recent book (Breuning et al., 1983) for an overall discussion of issues in the evaluation of medication effects.

Between-Subjects Designs

Any experimental design set up to compare the behavior of individuals in two or more groups is referred to as a between-subjects or group comparison design. In the simplest case, two groups of individual considered to be equal in pertinent characteristics are used. This equivalence is obtained either by random assignment of individuals to conditions, in which case individual differences are hoped to average out, or by matching the individuals in the groups according to a priori selected criteria (e.g., age, sex, IQ, drug history). Individuals in one group are treated differently from those in the other group, with care being taken to ensure that all variables other than the treatment variable are held constant. For example, one group may be given a drug while the other group is provided with no treatment or placebo. The individual's behaviors are then measured and performance of the groups is compared via inferential statistics. Differences in the behavior of members of the two groups that are statistically significant can be attributed to the drug's actions. Whalen and Henker (1983) discuss the use of between-subject design in pharmacotherapy in detail.

Crossover and Counterbalanced Designs

The crossover design is a common between-subjects design that has been recommended for studies employing drugs as independent variables (Sprague & Werry, 1971). This design dictates that one group of individuals initially receives medication, while a second group receives placebo. Later, a second phase is instituted in which the conditions are reversed so that the initial placebo group receives the drug while the initial drug group receives placebo. The behaviors of interest are measured, usually repeatedly across time, during both phases of the study. If the medication is in fact effective, the performance of the group that receives the drug should be significantly different from the performance of the group that receives the placebo, in each phase.

This design can be extended by increasing the number of levels of the independent variable employed. For example, several different drugs or doses of the same drug plus placebo could be compared using a number of groups. In this case, the order of presentation of the different drugs or doses must be such that no group would receive the drugs or doses in precisely the same order. In addition, all possible combinations of orders must be arranged. This would control for any effects of order of presentation. If a given drug or dose condition produces an effect, the group receiving the condition, regardless of order, should be affected similarly. This more elaborate version of the crossover design is known as the counter-balance design.

Both the crossover and the counterbalanced designs are frequently used in drug research because all individuals receive all conditions, thus minimizing the ethical concerns generated by withholding treatment from the control group in a simple group comparison design. Such ethical considerations can be further circumvented by giving both groups medication at the end of experimentation if the drug actually has been shown to have beneficial effects. Additional advantages of the crossover and counterbalanced designs include the fact that each is sensitive to drug effects, and fewer individuals are required than in most other group designs. However, these designs require that the effects of a given treatment are reversible so as not to interact with subsequent treatments. If the proper response measures are used (non-permanent products), this problem can be avoided in most drug investigations by allowing a sufficient "washout" period between treatments. For example, stimulants require 24 hours to leave the system, while many investigators use a washout period of four weeks or longer with neuroleptics (Breuning & Poling, 1982b).

Limitations of Between-Subjects Designs

Between-subjects designs can yield meaningful evaluations of drug effects. However, in clinical assessment it is often difficult or impossible to find large and homogeneous subject populations from which to select experimental and control groups. The issues surrounding the use of untreated control groups, required by some between-subjects designs, have already been addressed. Finally, in a typical group study, some individuals improve during treatment, some worsen, and some remain unchanged. These differences, which are important to the clinician, are obscured in between-subject analyses. An example of such obscuring is reported by Breuning, Davis, Matson, and Ferguson (1982). These and other issues are discussed quite extensively by Hersen and Barlow (1976). Because of these problems, within-subjects comparisons have been strongly advocated for clinical drug evaluation (Breuning & Poling, 1982b; Breuning, Davis, & Poling, 1982; Poling & Cleary, 1983; Wysocki & Fuqua, 1982).

Within-Subjects Designs

In within-subjects or single-case designs, one or more individuals are studied intensively across treatment and no treatment conditions such that each individual's behavior in one condition is compared to his or her behavior in another condition (i.e., the individual serves as his or her own control). Typically, behavior is repeatedly measured in each condition under the empirically substantiated assumption that the more continuously behavior is sampled, the better the measure reflects the individual's usual behavior. Also, statistical evaluations are rarely employed with within-subjects designs. Instead, data are simply graphed and visually analyzed. This decreases the likelihood that statistical and clinical significance will be confused, but increases the probability that small treatment effects will go unnoticed. Recently single-subject statistical procedures have begun to emerge; these procedures are reviewed by Kazdin (1976,1982). There are many within-subject designs. These include the withdrawal design (Hersen & Barlow, 1976), the multiple baseline design (Baer, Wolfe, & Risley, 1968; Hersen & Barlow, 1976), and the alternating treatments design also known as the simultaneous-treatment design (Barlow & Hayes, 1979; Kazdin & Hartman, 1978).

Withdrawal Designs

In the withdrawal design (sometimes mistakenly called a reversal design), the individual's behavior is measured across no treatment (baseline), treatment, and no treatment conditions. Some authors refer to this sequence as A-B-A, with

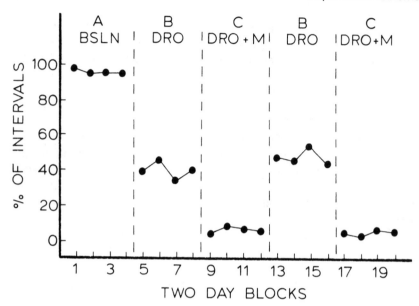

Fig. 6-1. Withdrawal design. Percentage of time-sample intervals target behaviors occurred plotted in two day blocks. Conditions were baseline, DRO, DRO plus methylphenidate, DRO, and again DRO plus methylphenidate.

A representing baseline conditions and B treatment conditions. If the dependent measure changes appreciably from the baseline level when treatment is implemented, and returns to at or near the intiial baseline level when treatment is withdrawn, there is good reason to believe that the observed changes in the target behavior reflect the actions of the treatment of interest. In the typical case in psychopharmacology research individuals are systematically exposed to baseline conditions involving no drug or placebo, and treatment conditions involving drug administration. Often, a final phase is added in which the individual again receives the treatment, provided the treatment has proven effective. This design would now be referred to as an A-B-A-B design. There are numerous variations and extensions of the withdrawal design (e.g., adding a second drug or dose could be an A-B-C-B-A design) and the reader is referred to Hersen and Barlow (1976) and Hersen (1982) for further illustration.

An example of application of the withdrawal design is presented in Figure 6-1. This data was gathered in our laboratory during an assessment of the effects of a behavior modification strategy versus behavior modification plus drug treatment in reducing disruptive behavior in a hyperactive mentally retarded child. The behavior modification procedure was differential reinforcement of other behavior (DRO) and the drug treatment involved administration of 0.5mg/kg methylphenidate.

It can be seen from the figure that measures of behaviors were taken across baseline (A), behavioral treatment (B), behavioral plus drug treatment (C), behavioral treatment (B), and behavioral plus drug treatment (C), phases (A-B-C-B-C). The important comparisons are between B-C-B-C phases and clearly show the superiority of the combined treatments.

This design is powerful, but the termination of effective medication or other treatment during the return-to-baseline phase may raise ethical and practical objections. Despite these concerns, one cannot be as sure that the treatment, as opposed to some other variable, caused the change unless the withdrawal and reinstatement occurs. Treatment (drug) effects also may be irreversible, which precludes evaluation via the withdrawal design. Finally, such designs require extended periods of time with many medications (e.g., neuroleptics).

Multiple Baseline Design

An alternative to the withdrawal design is the multiple baseline design. This design involves providing the treatment to several different individuals, to several behaviors of a single individual, or to the same behavior in the same individual across several different settings (Baer, Wolfe, & Risley, 1968). By showing that an effect repeats across individuals, behaviors, or settings, the multiple baseline design establishes the generality of, and confidence in, research results through replication of simple baseline-treatment (A-B) sequences. If used singularly these A-B sequences would yield minimally useful information. General issues pertaining to this design are discussed nicely by Kazdin and Kopel (1975) and Hersen (1982).

In one example of a multiple baseline across subjects design, the target behavior is first measured in a nondrug (i.e., no drug or placebo) baseline condition. Drug treatment is then begun with one individual at a time until all individuals are eventually receiving medication. Usually a drug is not administered to an individual until the previously treated individual's behavior has changed and/or stabilized. Thus, across individuals the length of baseline conditions varies. In this way, effects (or lack of) are evidenced by individual subjects after, and only after, drug treatment is introduced. Thus, reasonably powerful statements can be made.

This design is also very useful in evaluating drug effects as drug treatment is slowly and sequentially removed, again typically across several individuals. Figure 6-2, from Breuning, O'Neill, and Ferguson (1980) is a pictorial example of this application of the multiple baseline design. In this case, baseline frequencies of inappropriate behaviors were taken while the individuals were receiving psychotropic medication. Frequency counts were continued as response-cost procedures were implemented and then medication terminated, with both changes programmed according to multiple-baseline strategies. It is clear that withdrawal from psychotropic medication was the critical factor in achieving effectiveness of the response-cost procedure.

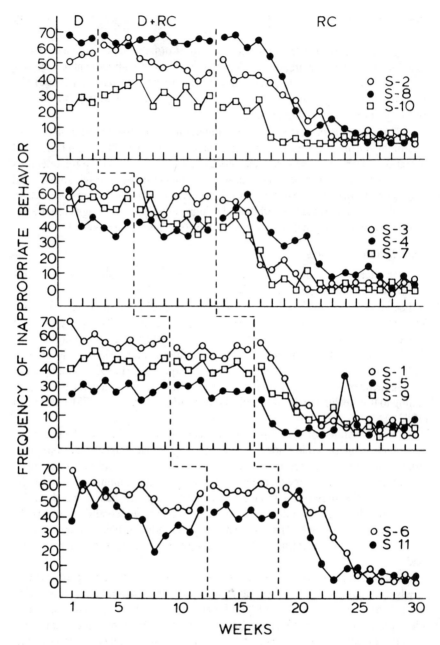

Fig. 6-2. Multiple baseline across subjects design. Weekly frequency of inappropriate behaviors as a function of psychotropic drug (D), response cost (RC), and combined (D + RC) procedures. [From Breuning, SE, O'Neill, MJ, & Ferguson, DG. Comparison of Psychotropic Drug, Response Cost, and Psychotropic Drug plus Response Cost Procedures for Controlling Institutionalized Retarded Persons. *Applied Research in Mental Retardation*, 1980, *1*, 253–268. Copyright by Pergamon Press, Ltd. With permission.]

The multiple baseline across subjects design is often effective in dealing with the problem of irreversible treatment effects, and eventually provides treatment for all individuals. This design should prove valuable for pharmacotherapeutic assessments. Recent investigators have documented the usefulness of this design in the assessment of drug effects (Breuning, O'Neill, & Ferguson, 1980; Davis et al., 1981; Wysocki et al., 1981).

Alternating Treatments Design

Within-subjects strategies for studying behavior change have been greatly enhanced by the advent of alternating treatments design that uniquely allows for a direct comparison of treatments within the same subject. According to this approach, which has been conceptualized as an A-B-B1 design (Shapiro & Barrett, 1981), a single target behavior is identified and observed for a baseline phase consisting of alternating stimulus conditions, usually time periods, which are in accordance with a planned schedule of intervention. After stable response levels across the alternating time periods of baseline (A) are established, two or more separate conditions of treatment are implemented. During this treatment phase (B), each of the separate treatment conditions is presented alternately and in counterbalanced fashion across the same stimulus conditions present during baseline. Often, the design is extended to include a final phase (B1) in which the most effective treatment, as determined in the B phase, is applied across all conditions. This design has been argued to be an extension of the withdrawal design where A-B-C conditions are rapidly alternated (Poling & Cleary, 1983), consequently, this design would appear to have the same advantages and disadvantages of the withdrawal design.

There are several additional problems associated with the use of the alternating treatments design. These involve the possible carryover of treatment effects in one condition to the second condition (multiple treatment interference) and the failure of the design to establish experimental control. The reader is referred to other sources for more thorough coverage of these issues (Barlow & Hayes, 1979; Kazdin, 1982; Shapiro & Barrett, 1981). Further, the applicability of the alternating treatment design to pharmacological research remains to be demonstrated (Breuning & Poling, 1982b; Poling & Cleary, 1983). Yet, one recent report shows that this design can provide great versitility in evaluating the effects of various behavioral procedures both alone and in combination with neuroleptic and stimulant medication (Breuning & Barrett, 1982). Figure 6-3 shows this design applied to the assessment of medication effects.

Initially the individual was observed during four time periods per day, and inappropriate behaviors were recorded according to an interval recording system. Subsequent to this, the treatments were introduced: response cost, visual screening, and control conditions for response cost and visual screening in which the discriminative stimuli for the treatments were presented, but the treatments were not. Meanwhile, the individual was slowly withdrawn from thioridazine. The data

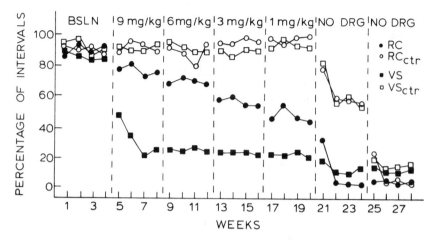

Fig. 6-3. Alternating treatments design. Percentage of time-sampled intervals target behaviors occurred plotted in one week blocks. Conditions were baseline (on 9 mg/kg), 9 mg/kg, 6 mg/kg, 3 mg/kg, and 1 mg/kg, and no drug conditions combined with response cost and visual screening procedures (treatment and control), and a final no drug condition where RC and VS control conditions became treatment conditions.

suggest that the two behavioral procedures were differentially effective in reducing inappropriate behavior while the individual was receiving thioridazine, with visual screening being the most effective, and with both treatments being more effective than control procedures. However, once a 0 mg/kg (no drug) level of drug was reached, both response cost and visual screening were highly effective in managing behavior problems. A final phase is also shown in which the behavioral treatments were applied in their respective control conditions. The resulting decrease in inappropriate behaviors in these latter conditions adds confidence to the finding of effectiveness of the behavioral treatments. Also, additional subjects were evaluated using the same procedure but with each phase lasting for a varying number of weeks. The same results were obtained and the variable of time was controlled for. Thus, the study shows how an alternating treatments design and multiple baseline design can be combined for a more complete assessment.

Caveat

As previously discussed (Breuning, Davis, & Poling, 1982; Breuning & Poling, 1982b) both between-and within-subjects design, used appropriately, allow for meaningful, and theoretically generalizable, evaluations of treatment efficacy, although generalizability is ultimately an empirical not a theoretical issue. Within-subjects designs are flexible, since they do not entail adherence to a fixed statistical model, and often allow for more intensive evaluations of drug effects, require fewer subjects, and may be more tenable with respect to clinical issues on a per client basis. Between subjects comparisons, however, are required to answer actuarial questions (e.g., what percentage of subjects improve when exposed to a particular drug?), and in some instances for the comparison of drug and nondrug treatments.

Our recommendation concerning choice of assessment strategy in evaluating medication effects is what has been voiced before. For the best results to be obtained clinicians and researchers should avoid dogma, be familiar with both between-subjects and within-subjects designs, and know the limitations of the setting where conditions are to be applied.

Once a design strategy has been selected, it is necessary to incorporate a number of general methodological criteria that are believed to represent the minimum requirements for a valid scientific study of the efficacy of psychotropic drugs. In particular, Sprague and Werry (1971) have specified six criteria that have been widely accepted. These criteria include:

1. *Placebo control.* To prevent nonspecific factors such as client or staff expectations and observer bias from confounding the drug effect, an inactive substance similar in size, shape, color, and taste to the drug being evaluated should be administered during nondrug conditions. A placebo phase allows for an evaluation of the possible placebo effects that appear in both placebo and drug conditions. Breuning, Ferguson, and Cullari (1980) have demonstrated the importance of using a placebo with the mentally retarded, including severely and profoundly retarded individuals.

2. *Double blind.* To further prevent bias and expectancy from confounding treatment effects, neither the client taking the medication nor the person evaluating the client's behavior should be aware of which is the placebo condition and which is the active medication condition. The importance of this is demonstrated in Breuning, Ferguson, and Cullari (1980). Unfortunately, double blind conditions may be difficult to maintain. For example, the discriminable effects of the drug itself may break the double blind. Some subjects probably can fairly readily ascertain whether they have received a drug such as amphetamine or an inert placebo.

3. *Standardized doses.* Doses should be clearly specified, preferably in units of drug per body weight (e.g., mg/kg/day for neuroleptics and stimulants), or amount of drug in the blood plasma (e.g., μg/ml for antiepileptics); and results reported separately for each dose. Each dose should be given for a sufficient period of time to allow for adequate evaluation. Different doses should be separated by nondrug periods (i.e., on drug or placebo) long enough to allow the effects of prior doses to disappear. When possible, other medications should be withheld during the period of evaluation. If this cannot be arranged, all drugs taken by a client should be carefully specified.

4. *Standardized evaluations.* Effects of treatment must be assessed by procedures of demonstrated sensitivity to drug effects (i.e., the instrument helps

discriminate drug conditions on some dimension), reliability (i.e., the instrument gives the same finding when repeated across testers and/or time), and validity (i.e., some independent evidence that the instrument is actually measuring what it proports to measure has been collected). Marholin and Phillips (1976), Breuning, Davis, & Poling (1982), and Breuning & Poling (1982b) have argued that adequate assessment must also include an evaluation of the medication's effects on appropriate as well as inappropriate target behaviors. The demonstration of a decrease in some undesired response is not a satisfactory demonstration of clinical efficacy. A drug might produce such an effect through generalized sedation, with a concomitant decrease in appropriate behaviors. For example, Breuning (1982b) has shown that regardless of whether or not an individual is showing a decrease in the targeted behavior, there will likely be decreases in workshop performances and responding to general reinforcement contingencies with the administration of neuroleptic drugs. The magnitude of these effects vary with dose (Breuning, 1982b). We have also found it very useful to analyze data in terms of percentage of change when we are comparing effects across groups or amongst individuals. Percentage of change analyses in conjunction with mg/kg doses nicely minimize idiosyncratic variability (Breuning, 1982b).

5. *Appropriate statistical analyses.*   The most acceptable way to evaluate between subject data is through the use of some kind of inferential statistical analysis. However, when inferential statistics are used, the assumptions underlying a particular test must not be violated. An additional caution regards the fact that statistically significant results cannot be automatically assumed to be clinically significant; and, similarly, clinically important effects may not reach statistical significance. Further, analysis of group data does not address the individual client's response to treatment. Therefore, it would seem important to at some point consider each client's data individually, if only to provide that individual with appropriate clinical care. If inferential statistics are used on a per client basis (e.g. time series analysis) underlying assumptions must also be met.

6. *Random assignment of subjects.*   Random assignment of clients or subjects to treatment conditions (as in matched groups designs) or to sequences of treatment (as in the crossover design) is necessary to meet the minimum assumptions of the statistical tests used to evaluate the research findings. It is also reasonable to use random assignment when a multiple baseline design is used. The order in which behaviors, clients, or settings are involved in treatment can easily be randomized. Random assignment of treatment presentations is required in the alternating treatments design.

Later, in a review of the potentially restrictive nature of the pharmacotherapies, Sprague and Baxley (1978) added a seventh criterion to the foregoing list. This criterion specifies that drug treatment be compared to some alternative treatment, preferably the best alternative available.

Recently, an eighth criterion has been espoused by Breuning, O'Neill, and Ferguson (1980) and Breuning, Davis, Matson, and Ferguson (1982). They have argued that the assessment of neuroleptic drug effects following drug discontinuation be ongoing for at least 12–16 weeks. This argument stems from their data indicating that the results of shorter evaluations can be confounded by various withdrawal effects such as the dyskinesias previously discussed.

CONCLUSION

We have emphasized what we (with strong clinical, scientific, legal, and legislative support) believe to be necessary procedures and designs for adequately assessing medication effects. At no point have we discussed procedures or designs that have not been successfully used in schools, institutions, or private practice. Occasionally, various aspects of what we have discussed will not be feasible. Lack of administrative support and/or uncooperative or improperly trained clinicians are most likely to account for this lack of feasibility. Nonetheless, it is apparent that quality clinical assessments of medication effects are very possible, and are occurring more and more frequently.

Acknowledgment

Preparation of this chapter was with support from NIMH grants MH-32206, MH-30915, and MH/HD-37449 from the National Institute of Mental Health; and grant 300-82-0368 from the Department of Education.

REFERENCES

Aman, MG. Psychoactive drugs in mental retardation. In JL Matson & F Andrasik (Eds.), *Treatment issues and innovations in mental retardation.* New York: Plenum Press, 1982

Aman, MG, & Singh, NN. The usefulness of thioridazine in childhood disorders—Fact or folklore? *American Journal of Mental Deficiency,* 1980, *84,* 331–338

Baer, DM, Wolf, MM, & Risley, TR. Some current dimensions of applied behavior analysis. *Journal of Applied Behavior Analysis,* 1968, *1,* 91–97

Baldessarini, RJ, & Tarsy, D. Tardive dyskinesia. In MA Lipton, A DiMascio, & KF Killiam (Eds.), *Pscychopharmacology—A generation of progress.* New York: Raven Press, 1978

Barlow, DH, & Hayes, SC. Alternating treatments design: One strategy for comparing the effects of two treatments in a single subject. *Journal of Applied Behavior Analysis,* 1979, *12,* 199–210

Berger, PA. Medical treatment of mental illness. *Science,* 1978, *200,* 974–981

Breuning, SE. *Drug use with the mentally retarded: Efficacy, behavioral effects, side effects, and alternative treatments.* Paper presented at the Ameircan Association on Mental Deficiency Conference, Detroit, May 1981

Breuning, SE. *The mentally retarded and the right to refuse: Pharmacotherapy and the law from a clinical perspective*. Paper presented at the American Association on Mental Deficiency Conference, Boston, May 1892 (a)

Breuning, SE. An applied dose-response curve of thioridazine with the mentally retarded: Aggressive, self-stimulatory, intellectual, and workshop behaviors—A preliminary report. *Psychopharmacology Bulletin*, 1982, *18*, 57–59 (b)

Breuning, SE, & Barrett, RP. *Effects of combined pharmacological and behavioral treatments with mentally retarded children: Relationship between different drugs and different behavioral procedures*. Paper presented at the American Association on Mental Deficiency Conference, Boston, May 1982

Breuning, SE, & Davidson, NA. Effects of psychotropic drugs on the intelligence test performance of mentally retarded adults. *American Journal of Mental Deficiency*, 1981, *85*, 575–579

Breuning, SE, Davis, VJ, Matson, JL, & Ferguson, DG. Effects of thioridazine and withdrawal dyskinesias on workshop performance of mentally retarded young adults. *American Journal of Psychiatry*, 1982, *139*, 1447–1454

Breuning, SE, Davis, VJ, & Poling, AD. Pharmacotherapy with the mentally retarded: Implications for clinical psychologists. *Clinical Psychology Review*, 1982, *2*, 79–114

Breuning, SE, Ferguson, DG, & Cullari, S. Analysis of single-double blind procedures, maintenance of placebo effects, and drug induced dyskinesia with mentally retarded persons. *Applied Research in Mental Retardation*, 1980, *1*, 237–252

Breuning, SE, Ferguson, DG, Davidson, NA, & Poling, AD. Effects of thioridazine on the intelligence test performance of mentally retarded drug responders and non-responders. *Archives of General Psychiatry*, (in press)

Breuning, SE, Kalachnik, JE, Sprague, RL, Davis, VJ, Ferguson, DG, Cullari, S, Ullman, RK, Davidson, NA, & Hoffner, BA. *Psychopharmacology Bulletin* (in press)

Breuning, SE, O'Neill, MJ, & Ferguson, DG. Comparison of psychotropic drug, response cost, and psychotropic drug plus response cost procedures for controlling institutionalized retarded persons. *Applied Research in Mental Retardation*, 1980, *1*, 253–268

Breuning, SE, & Poling, AD (Eds.). *Drugs and mental retardation*. Springfield, IL: Thomas, 1982 (a)

Breuning, SE, & Poling, AD. Pharmacotherapy with the mentally retarded. In JL Matson & RP Barrett (Eds.) *Psychopathology in the mentally retarded*. New York: Grune & Stratton, 1982 (b)

Breuning, SE, Poling, AD, Matson, JL (Eds.). *Applied psychopharmacology: Methods for assessing medication effects*. New York: Grune & Stratton, 1983

Campbell, M, Green, WH, Perry, R, & Bennett, WG. Assessment of side effects. In SE Breuning, AD Poling, & LL Matson (Eds.). *Applied psychopharmacology: Methods for assessing medication effects*. New York: Grune & Stratton, 1983

Christensen, DE. Effects of combining methylphenidate and a classroom token system in modifying hyperactive behavior. *American Journal of Mental Deficiency*, 1975, *80*, 266–276

Ciminero, AR, & Drabman, RS. Current developments in the behavioral assessment of children. In BB Lahey & AE Kazdin (Eds.). *Advances in clinical child psychology* (Vol. 1), New York: Plenum Press, 1977

Clites v. Iowa. No. 2-04/2-65599 (Court of Appeals, Iowa, filed June 29, 1982)

Cohen, MN, & Sprague, RL. *Survey of drug use in two midwestern institutions for the retarded*. Paper presented at the Gatlinburg Conference on Mental Retardation, Gatlinburg, TN, March 1977

Corbett, JA, Harris, R, & Robinson, RG. Epilepsy. In J Wortis (Ed.), *Mental Retardation* (Vol. 3). New York: Brunner/Mazel, 1975

Craig, TJ, & Behar, R. Trends in prescription of psychotropic drugs (1970–1977) in a state hospital. *Comprehensive Psychiatry*, 1980, *21*, 336–345

Davis, VJ, Cullari, S, & Breuning, SE. Drug use in community foster-group homes. In SE Breuning & AD Poling (Eds.), *Drugs and mental retardation*. Springfield, IL: Thomas, 1982

Davis, VJ, Poling, AD, Wysocki, T, & Breuning, SE. Effects of phenytoin withdrawal on matching to sample and workshop performance of mentally retarded persons. *Journal of Nervous and Mental Disease*, 1981, *169*, 718–725

Developmentally Disabled Bill of Rights. 42, U.S.C. 6010, 1975

DiMascio, A. *An examination of actual medication usage in retardation institutions*. Paper presented at the American Association on Mental Deficiency Conference, Portland, OR, May 1975

Doe v. Hudspeth. Civil No. J75-36 (S.D., Miss., filed Feb. 17, 1977)

Eadie, MJ, & Tyrer, JH. *Anticonvulsant therapy*. London: Churchill-Livingston, 1974

ECDEU. *Assessment Manual*. Rockville, MD: National Institute of Mental Health, 1976

Fann, WE, Smith, RC, Davis, JM, & Domino, EF (Eds.). *Tardive dyskinesia: Research and treatment*. Jamaica, New York: Spectrum Publications, Inc., 1980

Ferguson, DG, & Breuning, SE. Antipsychotic and antianxiety drugs. In SE Breuning & AD Poling (Eds.), *Drugs and mental retardation*. Springfield, IL: Thomas, 1982

Freeman, R. Psychopharmacology and the retarded child. In F Menolascino (Ed.), *Psychiatric Approaches to Mental Retardation*. New York: Basic Books, 1970

Gardener, WI. Social and emotional adjustment of mildly retarded children and adolescents. *Exceptional Children*, 1967, *33*, 106

Garattini, S, Mussini, M, & Randall, LO (Eds.). *The benzodiazepines*. New York: Raven Press, 1973

Gary, W. v. State of Louisiana. 437 F.Supp. 1209 (1976)

Gibbs, EL, Gibbs, TJ, Gibbs, FA, Gibbs, EA, Dikman, S, & Hermann, BP. Antiepilepsy drugs. In SE Breuning & AD Poling (Eds.), *Drugs and mental retardation*. Springfield, IL: Thomas, 1982

Gittelman-Klein, R. Psychopharmacological treatment of anxiety disorders, mood disorders, and tic disorders of childhood. In M Lipton, A DiMascio, & K Killam (Eds.), *A review of psychopharmacology: A second decade of progress*. New York: Raven Press, 1978

Goth, A. *Medical pharmacology*. St. Louis: Mosby, 1974

Greensberg, L, Yellin, A, Spring, C, & Metcalf, M. Clinical effects of imipramine and methylphenidate in hyperactive children. *International Journal of Mental Health*, 1975, *4*, 144–156

Greenblatt, DJ, & Shader, RJ. *Benzodiazepines in clinical practice*. New York: Raven Press, 1974

Gualtieri, CT, Breuning, SE, Schroeder, SR, & Quade, D. Tardive dyskinesia in mentally retarded children, adolescents, and young adults. *Psychopharmacology Bulletin*, 1982, *18*, 62–65

Gualtieri, CT, & Hawk, B. Antidepressant and antimanic drugs. In SE Breuning & AD Poling (Eds.), *Drugs and mental retardation*. Springfield, IL: Thomas 1982

Hartmann, DP. Considerations in the choice of interobserver reliability estimates. *Journal of Applied Behavior Analysis*, 1977, *10*, 103–116

Hawkins, RP, & Dobes, RW. Behavioral definitions in applied behavior analysis: Explicit or implicit. In BC Etzel, JM LeBlanc, & DM Baer (Eds.), New developments in behavioral research: *Theory, methods, and applications. In honor of Sidney W. Bijou*. Hillsdale, NJ: Lawrence Erlbaum Associates, 1975

Hersen, M. Single-case experimental designs. In AS Bellack, M Hersen, AE Kazdin, (Eds.), *International handbook of behavior modification and therapy*. New York: Plenum Press, 1982

Hersen, M, & Barlow, DH. *Single-case experimental designs: Strategies for studying behavior change*. New York: Pergamon Press, 1976

Hollis, JH, & St. Omer, VV. Direct measurement of psychopharmacologic response: Effects of chloropromazine on motor behavior of retarded children. *American Journal of Mental Deficiency*, 1972, *76*, 397–407

Hughes, PS. Survey of medication in a subnormality hospital. *British Journal of Mental Subnormality*, 1977, *33*, 88–94

Kazdin, AE. Statistical analyses for single-case experimental designs. In M Hersen & DH Barlow, *Single case experimental designs*. New York: Pergamon Press, 1976

Kazdin, AE. *Single-case research designs: Methods for clinical and applied settings*. New York: Oxford University Press, 1982.

Kazdin, AE, & Hartman, DP. The simultaneous treatment design. *Behavior Therapy*, 1978, *9*, 912–922

Kazdin, AE, & Kopel, SA. On resolving ambiguities of the multiple-baseline design: Problems and recommendations. *Behavior Therapy*, 1975, *6*, 601–608

Kazdin, AE, & Straw, MK. Assessment of the behavior of the mentally retarded. In M Hersen and AS Bellack (Eds.), *Behavioral assessment: A practical handbook*. New York: Pergamon, 1976

Keppel, G. *Design and analysis: A researcher's handbook*. Englewood Cliffs, NJ: Prentice-Hall, Inc., 1973

Kirk, RE. *Experimental design: Procedures for the behavioral sciences*. Belmont, CA: Brooks/Cole, 1968

Klein, D, & Davis, J. *Diagnosis and drug treatment of psychiatric disorders*. Baltimore: Williams & Wilkins, 1969

Lipman, RS. The use of pharmacological agents in residential facilities for the retarded. In F Menolascino (Ed.), *Psychiatric approaches to mental retardation*. New York: Basic Books, 1970

Lipman, RS, DiMascio, A, Reatig, N, & Kirson, T. Psychotropic drugs and mentally retarded children. In MA Lipton, A DiMascio, & KF Killian (Eds.), *Psychopharmacology: A generation of progress*. New York: Raven Press, 1978

Marholin, D, & Phillips, D. Methodological issues in psychopharmacological research. *American Journal of Orthopsychiatry*, 1976, *46*, 477–495

Matson, JL, & Barrett, RP. *Psychopathology in the mentally retarded*. New York: Grune & Stratton, 1982

McConahey, OL, Thompson, T, & Zimmerman, R. A token system for retarded women. Behavior therapy, drug administration and their combination. In J Thompson & J Grabowski (Eds.), *Behavior modification of the mentally retarded* (2nd Ed.). New York: Oxford, 1977

Moos, R. Conceptualizations of human environments. *American Psychologist*, 1973, *28*, 652–665

National Institute of Mental health, psychopharmacology Service Center Collaborative Study Group. Phenathiazine treatment in acute schizophrenia. *Archives of General Psychiatry*, 1964, *10*, 246–262

New York ARC v. Carey. 393 F. Supp. 715 (1975)

New York ARC v. Rockefeller, 357 F. Supp. 752 (1973)

Physicians' Desk Reference (34th ed.). Oradel, NJ: Medical Economics Co., 1980

Poling, A, & Breuning, SE. Effects of methylphenidate on the fixed-ratio performance of mentally retarded children. *Pharmacology, Biochemistry and Behavior* (in press)

Poling, AD, & Cleary, J. Single-subject designs. In SE Breuning, AD Poling, & JL Matson *Applied psychopharmacology: Methods for assessing medication effects*. New York: Grune & Stratton, 1983

Poling, AD, Cleary, J, & Monaghan, M. The use of human observers in psychopharmacological research. *Pharmacology, Biology and Behavior*, 1980, *13*, 243–246

Psychopharmocology Bulletin. *Special issue on pharmacotherapy of children*. 1973

Pullman, RM, Pook, RB, & Singh, N. Prevalence of drug therapy for institutionalized mentally retarded children. *Australian Journal of Mental Retardation*, 1979, *5*, 212–214

Rimland, B. Infantile autism: Status and research. In A David (Ed.), *Child Personality and Psychopathology: Current Topics* (Vol. 1). New York: Wiley, 1974

Robinson, NM, & Robinson, HB. *The mentally retarded child*. New York: McGraw-Hill, 1976

Saraf, K, Klein, D, Gittelman-Klein, G, & Groff, S. Imipramine side-effects in children. *Psychopharmacologia*, 1974, *37*, 265–275

Sewell, J, & Werry, JS. Some studies in an institution for the mentally retarded. *New Zealand Medical Journal*, 1976, *84*, 317–319

Shapiro, ES, & Barrett, RP. Behavioral assessment of the mentally retarded. In JL Matson & F Andrasik (Eds.), *Treatment issues and innovations in mental retardation*. New York, Plenum Press, 1982

Sprague, RL. Overview of psychopharmacology for the retarded in the United States. In P Mittler (Ed.), *Research to practice in mental retardation—Biomedical aspects* (Vol. 3). Baltimore: University Park Press, 1977

Sprague, RL. Litigation, legislation, and regulations. In SE Breuning & AD Poling (Eds.), *Drugs and mental retardation*. Springfield, IL: Thomas 1982

Sprague, RL, Barnes, KR, & Werry, JS. Methylphenidate and thioridazine: Learning, reaction time, activity, and classroom behavior in emotionally disturbed children. *American Journal of Orthopsychiatry, 1970, 40*, 615–628

Sprague, RL, & Baxley, GB. Drugs for behavior management with comment on some legal aspects. In J Wortis (Ed.), *Mental retardation* (Vol. 10), New York: Brunner/Mazel, 1978

Sprague, R, & Toppe, L. Relationship between activity level and delay of reinforcement in the retarded. *Journal of Experimental Child Psychology, 1966, 3*, 390–397

Sprague, RL, & Werry, JS. Methodology of psychopharmacological studies with the retarded. In NR Ellis (Ed.), *International review of research on mental retardation* (Vol. 5). New York: Academic Press, 1971

Sulzbacher, SI. Psychotropic medication with children: An evaluation of procedural bias in results of reported studies. *Pediatrics, 1973, 51*, 513–517

Toman, JEP. Drugs effective in convulsive disorders. In LS Goodman & A Gilman (Eds.), *The pharmacological basis of therapeutics* (3rd Ed.). New York: Macmillan, 1965

Tu, J, & Smith, JT. Factors associated with psychotropic medication in mental retardation facilities. *Comprehensive Psychiatry, 1979, 20*, 289–295

Waldrop, MF, Bell, RQ, McLaughlin,B, & Halverson, CF. Newborn minor physical anomalies predict short attention span, peer aggression and impulsivity at age 3. *Science, 1978, 199*, 563–564

Walker, MK. Stimulant drugs. In SE Breuning & AD Poling (Eds.), *Drugs and mental retardation*. springfield, IL: Thomas, 1982

Welsch v. Likins. 373 F. Supp. 487 (1974)

Welsch v. Likins. 550 F. 2d 1122 (1977)

Werry, JS. Measures in pediatric psychopharmacology. In JS Werry (Ed.), *Pediatric psychopharmacology: The use of behavior modifying drugs in children*. New York: Brunner/Mazel, Publishers, 1978

Whalen, CK, & Henker, B. Between-subjects designs. In SE Breuning, AD Poling, & JL Matson, *Applied psychopharmacology: Methods for assessing medication effects*. New York: Grune & Stratton, 1983

Winsberg, B, Bialer, I, Kupietz, S, & Tobias, J. Effects of imipramine and dextroamphetamine on behavior of neuropsychiatrically impaired children. *American Journal of Psychiatry, 1972, 128*, 1425–1431

Woodbury, DM, Penry, JK, & Schmidt, RP. *Antiepileptic drugs*. New York: Raven Press, 1972

Wouri v. Zitnay. No. 75-80-SD (Maine, 1978)

Wyatt v. Stickney. 344 F. Supp. 387 (1972)

Wysocki, T, Fuqua, RW. Methodological issues in the evaluation of drug effects. In SE Breuning & AD Poling (Eds.), *Drugs and mental retardation*. Springfield, IL: Thomas, 1982

Wysocki, T, Fuqua, RW, Davis, WJ, & Breuning, SE. Effects of thioridazine (Mellaril) on titrating delayed matching-to-sample performance of mentally retarded adults. *American Journal of Mental Deficiency, 1981, 85*, 539–547

Karen A. Christoff
Jeffrey A. Kelly

7

Social Skills

Workers in the field of mental retardation have discussed the importance of social norms, ability to adapt to the environment, and social skills since the early 1800s (Givens, 1978; Lambert, Wilcox, & Gleason, 1974). It is only in the relatively recent past, however, that a directive issued by the American Association on Mental Deficiency (AAMD) required that specific attention be paid to adaptive behavior in making the diagnoses of mental retardation (Grossman, 1973). Specifically, the AAMD has defined mental retardation as "significantly subaverage general intellectual functioning existing concurrently with deficits in adaptive behavior, and manifested during the developmental period" (Grossman, 1973, p. 11). They have further defined adaptive behavior as "the effectiveness or degree with which the individual meets the standards of personal independence and social responsibility expected of his age and cultural group" (Grossman, 1973, p. 11).

Heber (1959), in the AAMD-approved manual on terminology and classification in mental retardation, recommended the use of the Vineland Social Maturity Scale as the "best single measure of adaptive behavior currently available" (p. 61). The Vineland Scale is a checklist that is completed using information obtained in an interview with an informant who had presumably observed the subject over an extended period of time (i.e., a parent or primary caretaker). The scale assesses self-help, self-direction, occupation, communication, locomotion and socialization skills; and, items are arranged in chronological order from birth to 25 years of age. The obtained score is expressed as a Social Age (SA) and is computed like a ratio IQ (e.g., Social Age/Chronological Age, or, SA/CA) (Doll, 1953; 1965). Later, the National Institute of Mental Health funded an AAMD-sponsored project to develop the Adaptive Behavior Scale (Nihira, 1969; Nihira, Foster, Shellhaas, & Leland, 1969; 1974). This scale, which is completed by a parent, caretaker or teacher who has direct contact with the client, yields a score that places the client into one of four levels of adaptive functioning. These levels range from Level IV for individuals who require continuous medical and/or nursing care due to gross physical handicaps to Level I for individuals who can function effectively in low-demand environments with minimal supervision. However, the use of a single numerical score (Social Age or functioning level) is problematic for the same reasons that the IQ score is problematic. While it provides information for legislators and educators to use in identifying exceptional children for services planning and funds allocation, it provides only limited and highly summarized information regarding where an individual's specific deficits lie, in what situations the individual performs inadequately, and on what behaviors should social training effort be focused. The Vineland, in addition, was standardized on institutionalized mentally retarded populations and does not take into account the fact that different behaviors are adaptive in different settings. Clearly, not all mentally retarded persons currently reside in institutions. Many are now living with their families, in foster care homes and in group homes with minimal supervision. Assessment of deficits must necessarily take into account the skills needed by the client to function maximally within his or her own particular environment. It is impossible for any single instrument or scale to either determine all the settings within which a given individual will need to function socially, or for it to be able to evaluate all relevant areas of adaptive behavior (Baumeister & Muma, 1975). Weissman (1975), in a review of 15 available scales for assessing social adjustment, concludes that "none of the scales presently available will stand as the final instrument" (p. 364). Assessment efforts that rely on more direct, behavioral evaluation of a client's handling of social interactions may provide more precise, focused information relevant for treatment.

One alternative conceptual model for assessing the social behavior of mentally retarded individuals involves considering the specific interpersonal situations or contexts in which a given client will be expected to function, and closely examining the client's current performance in those situations. If specific deficits of performance can be identified, it then becomes possible to tailor interventions that remediate the client's current social skill difficulties. For example, if an institutionalized client is to move into the community and a group home living arrangement where the client will meet nonretarded people, those social skills necessary to converse appropriately with others will be needed. The extent that appropriate conversational behavior is presently deficient is an area of social functioning that merits close assessement and, presumably, treatment. Similarly, if a mentally retarded client is performing well in a sheltered vocational workshop and is a candidate for competitive employment in a nonsheltered setting, our conceptual analysis indicates that one should first identify the specific social interactions the person will have to handle in that new setting (such as interviewing for a job, conversing with co-workers, or asking a supervisor for directions) and then access how adequately the client exhibits these social skills. In essence, social skill assessment involves a form of task analysis in which relevant interpersonal situations or tasks for an individual are identified, the individual's current skill in those situations is specifically assessed, deficits or excesses of current performance in the situations are pinpointed, and a treatment plan to improve social skill is developed.

There are several reasons why close attention to the social skill of mentally retarded individuals is important. Mentally retarded persons often appear to exhibit relatively generalized, striking social skill impairment (Kelly, 1982). It has also been noted (Doll, 1953) that social functioning of mentally retarded persons, particularly those in the mild to moderate range of impairment, is a good predictor of interpersonal, vocational, and independent living adjustment. Several investigators have observed that rejection of mentally retarded persons by others can often be attributed to inadequate social behaviors rather than to intellectual handicaps (Blount, 1969; Dentler & Mackler, 1962; Johnson, 1950). With the present trend toward deinstitutionalization and integration of mentally retarded persons into community settings, provision of training in appropriate social and interpersonal behavior must be a priority (Bates, 1980; Brody & Stoneman, 1977; Strain & Shores, 1977).

It seems logical to assume that training to improve the social functioning of those mentally retarded persons with skills deficits will facilitate more successful integration into community settings and increased social acceptance by normal individuals within those settings. Since there is some evidence that responses to mentally retarded persons vary with the number of cues emitted that indicate that the individual is mentally retarded (Kelly & Drabman, 1977; Rosenberg, 1959), skills training to reduce the obvious deficits should facilitate community acceptance and formation of interpersonal relationships. Adequate assessment of the specific social skill deficits exhibited by the mentally retarded client is then of paramount importance in establishing the areas that are in need of training. The specific real life situations in which the client experiences difficulties should be obtained from the client, parent, and/or other persons familiar with the client. Assessment can then consist of observing the client directly in these situations or in a laboratory or office analog role-play, comparing the client's performance to "skillful" performance, and noting the specific deficits or excesses exhibited by the client. Once the client's specific deficits or excesses have been targeted, successful treatment will depend in part on adequate isolation of the factors that have led to or have maintained these behaviors. Some questions which need to be answered by assessment procedures follow. Is the appropriate behavior in the individual's repertoire (i.e., can the client behave in the desired manner when asked to do so in a structured setting such as a laboratory or office role-play)? Can the individual discriminate situations in which it is appropriate and inappropriate to perform the behavior? Is there something interfering with the individual's performance of the target behavior (such as anxiety or negative self-statements)? Lastly, is there something occurring in the individual's natural environment that serves to punish or suppress the desired behavior (such as parent or caretaker chastisement) or that serves to facilitate or maintain an inappropriate behavior (such as attention for whining or for helpless behaviors)? While other questions may be asked, thorough attention to those listed above should facilitate successful treatment planning and implementation, regardless of the targeted excess or deficit.

WHAT ARE SOCIAL SKILLS?

There are presently no generally agreed-upon social skills definitions that apply to all interpersonal situations. Hersen and Bellack (1977) suggest placing "focus on an individual's ability to express both positive and negative feelings in the interpersonal context without consequent loss of social reinforcement" (p. 512). Argyris (1965, 1968, 1969) defines social skills in terms of behaviors that enhance the individual's contribution to the larger network of which he or she is a part. Libet and Lewinsohn (1973) consider social skills to be the ability to behave in ways that elicit positive and negative reinforcement and to refrain from behaving in ways that elicit extinction or punishment. Although none of these definitions were formulated with special reference to the behavior of mentally retarded persons, their common theme should apply to all populations. In general it seems that social skillfulness can be defined functionally, in terms of effectiveness. In any situation, a response can be termed skillful if it serves to elicit a desired response from the environment. The critical defining factor of socially skillful behavior is the effectiveness of the behavior in social interactions. Determinations of effectiveness will necessarily vary with the context of the interaction and with the parameters of the specific situation. Skillful behavior will always involve the coordination of appropriate verbal and nonverbal responses.

Since different behavioral responses may be necessary components of skillful behavior in different kinds of situations, the remainder of this chapter will be devoted to discussions of several social skills that can be seen to be especially relevant to mentally retarded persons. Specifically, we will discuss grooming, dressing and self care skills; conversational skills; assertiveness skills; employment related social skills; problem solving skills; and dating or heterosocial skills. In all cases we will focus on behavioral rather than traditional assessment procedures since behavioral procedures have more heuristic value in that they relate directly to the development of viable treatment programs (Hersen & Bellack, 1976). Since the function of assessment presumably is to facilitate remediation of deficits, we believe the behavioral approach to be the most useful.

Grooming, Dressing, and Self-Care Skills

For normal individuals, social skills training and assessment seems to frequently focus on verbal and cognitive skills. While these are undoubtedly important for mentally retarded persons as well, members of this population may also require attention to more basic elements of self presentation, such as grooming, dress, and self care skills, prior to training in more complex verbal and interactive skills. Appearance is clearly important to social acceptance since impressions made on first sight may alter the opinions of others. This may be most obvious in the case of job interviews; however, it is also important for everyday interactions. The importance of clothing and appearance in impression management with normal persons has been well-documented (Molloy, 1976, 1977) and there is no reason to assume that this is not also the case for mentally retarded persons, albeit at a lower level of sophistication. One needs to consider the capabilities of the person being assessed and trained. At the lowest level exactly what behaviors the mentally retarded person is capable of emitting should be determined. Can the client dress, bathe, and groom appropriately within his or her particular environment? What behaviors require assistance to complete? Task analyses of these behaviors have been delineated elsewhere (Martin, Kehoe, Bird, Jense, & Darbyshire, 1971; Matson, DiLorenzo, & Esveldt-Dawson, 1981; Matson, Marchetti, & Adkins, 1980; Treffrey, Martin, Samels, & Watson, 1970), and the steps outlined can be used in checklist fashion while watching the person perform the behaviors. Alternately, one can ask the person, or his or her caretakers, how the client does these things if it appears that the person has some deficits in self-care and grooming. This is an area where the assessor can use personal judgment. If the mentally retarded client's appearance is deficient in some way, or if the assessor forms some negative impressions based on appearance, it can probably safely be assumed that these impressions will also be made on others in the community with whom the person interacts. Because dressing and grooming are very basic appearance-related aspects of social skill, and because others may respond very negatively to the individual with severe deficits in this area (dirty, unkept clothes; body odor; poorly-applied makeup; etc.), these problems may limit the practical impact of higher level training (such as conversational or assertiveness skills).

Kazdin, Matson, and Esveldt-Dawson (1981) have noted that it should not be assumed that appropriate behaviors are not contained in the repertoire of an individual simply because they do not occur spontaneously. A behavior may not be occurring simply because it has historically gone reinforced, or because other incompatible behaviors have been reinforced. A mentally retarded person may not bathe, groom, or dress properly simply because others have always done it for him or her; not because the person is incapable of exhibiting the behavior. Assessment must take this into account determine whether the skills need to be trained, or if reinforcers for incompatible behaviors (i.e., helplessness) should be withdrawn, or both.

Conversational Skills

Conversational skill refers to the ability to initiate and maintain informal conversations with others (Kelly, 1982). While these skills will facilitate acceptance in short-term interactions, they are also necessary to obtain longer-term positive outcomes such as obtaining employment, making dates, and establishing friendships. The additional, specialized skills required for obtaining these specific longer-term outcomes will be discussed in subsequent sections. Basic conversational skills, however, are prerequisites to competence in all of these areas. Trower (1980) suggests that conversational deficits are prominent determinants of impressions of social incompetence, and it has been suggested that the ability to converse in a cooperative manner facilitates social acceptance of mentally retarded persons (Chennault, 1967; Rucker & Vincenzo, 1970). Presumably, the ability to communicate verbally with others preceeds the ability to interact cooperatively. Mentally retarded persons have often been described as lacking effective communication skills (Longhurst, 1974; McClure, 1968; Rychtarik & Bornstein, 1979) and institutionalized or formerly institutionalized persons who lack conversation skills are perceived by others as peculiar, dull and sometimes threatening (Bellack & Hersen, 1978; Kelly, 1982; Kelly, Urey, & Patterson, 1980; Kelly, Wildman, Urey, & Thurman, 1979; Urey, Laughlin, & Kelly, 1979). Mentally retarded persons, if they appear overtly "retarded" will thus be likely to experience difficulty in establishing relationships with others in the community.

As is the case with any behavior, adequate assessment of conversational skills must necessarily take into account not only the environment in which the individual normally functions, but also other environments to which the client might reasonably aspire. Institutionalized retarded persons might well function adequately and quite appropriately within the institution. However, acceptable behaviors in an institution may not be acceptable in the community at large and may limit the individual's movement away from the institution. Adequate and functional communication skills within the institution may consist of grunts and pointing, if these facilitate fulfillment of needs. It might be argued that in the case of severely and profoundly mentally retarded persons without support systems external to the institution and for whom there is little hope of community placement, this skill level is appropriate and adequate, while it is inappropriate for those persons who are capable of more independent living situations. Lack of more generally accepted conversational skills will most certainly hinder movement from the institution, and we believe that development of conversational skills to the limits of the capabilities of the person being trained should be attempted. In general, conversational behavior should be evaluated with respect as to how closely it approximates that of age appropriate nonretarded persons.

Assessment of conversational behavior ordinarily focuses on evaluating the presence of behavioral components (or aspects) of the individual's conversational repertoire. Behaviors reported in the literature to be conversational skill components include: conversational questions, self-disclosing statements, reinforcing or acknowledging comments, speech duration and latency, eye contact, appropriate smiling, affect or emotionality, voice intonation, vocal fluency, posture, gesturing, and appropriate conversational content (Bradlyn, Himadi, Crimmins, Christoff, Graves, & Kelly, 1983; Kelly, 1982; Kelly, Furman, Phillips, Hathorn,

& Wilson, 1979; Kelly, Wildman, Urey, & Thurman, 1979; Minkin, Braukmann, Minkin, Timbers, Timbers, Fixsen, Phillips, & Wolf, 1976; Stalonas & Johnson, 1979; Urey, Laughlin, & Kelly, 1979). In order to adequately assess these components, they must be operationally defined as objectively as possible.

Behavioral assessments of skills in this area have typically consisted of having the client engage in an audio-or video-taped structured interaction with a confederate or with the therapist, and later the interaction is rated for some or all of the specific behaviors listed above. Typically these interactions consist of a series of scenes such as those contained in the Interpersonal Behavior Role Playing Test of Goldsmith and McFall (1975), or the revised Behavioral Assertiveness Test of Eisler, Hersen, Miller, and Blanchard (1975). Certainly these procedures provide a vehicle for assessing conversational abilities. It has been demonstrated, however, that behavior in structured role-plays does not necessarily correspond to behavior in the natural environment (Bellack, Hersen, & Lamparski, 1979; Bellack, Hersen, & Turner, 1978, 1979; Christoff & Edelstein, 1981). Moreover, the use of such a standard set of role-play scenes may lead to an inadequate assessment of the specific situations in which the person being assessed has problems. We have proposed, as an alternative, simply asking the client to interact with another person (either a mentally retarded peer or a nonretarded confederate) and ''get to know each other better'' (Bradlyn et al., 1983; Kelly, 1982; Kelly, Wildman, & Berler, 1980; Urey et al. 1979). This semi-structured interaction procedure seems intuitively to provide a better index of the client's general conversational skills. The behavioral components that are rated from tapes of these interactions are those presumed to be components of skillful performances. In initial assessments, it is critical to attend to all skill components, to ensure an adequate assessment. In later assessments of treatment effectiveness, it may only be necessary to attend to the specific behaviors that have been observed earlier to be deficient or excessive and are therefore the targets of training. It should be noted that numerous studies have demonstrated improved conversational skills in mentally retarded persons of all age-groups following training (Bornstein, Bach, McFall, Friman, & Lyons, 1980; Bradlyn et al., 1983; Gibson, Lawrence, & Nelson, 1976; Kelly, Furman et al., 1979; Kelly, Wildman et al., 1980; Longhurst, 1972, McClure, 1968; Nelson, Gibson, & Cutting, 1973; Rychtarik & Bornstein, 1979). In all cases, however, training was predicated on an objective assessment of baseline skill levels of component behaviors. While more extensive definitions of trained components are contained in these studies, it may be useful to provide general definitions and rationale for the commonly referenced components.

Conversational Questions

A conversational question can be defined as a question that serves to elicit information from the conversational partner. This category can also include statements that, although not grammatically phrased as questions, serve to elicit information. Question-asking has been validated as an important component of conversational effectiveness (Minkin et al., 1976). Asking questions obviously facilitates conversational flow and provides for more extended interactions. Conversational questions typically are simply counted over the course of the assessment interaction.

Self-Disclosing Statements

Self-disclosing statements are those that convey appropriate information about oneself to the conversational partner. Descriptions of thoughts, feelings, likes, hobbies, or background serve to allow the partner to get to know the speaker better and possibly establish common interests or ideas that may foster more lasting interpersonal relationships (Kelly, Furman et al., 1979; Urey et al., 1979). These also typically are rated for frequency.

Reinforcing or Acknowledging Comments

Reinforcing, acknowledging, or complimentary comments may be defined as verbalizations that serve to keep the partner talking by reinforcing the partner's verbalizations. These can be one-word acknowledgements such as "good," "Right!" or even "umm hmm," or more extended comments such as "That's nice," "You're fun to talk to," or "It sounds like you really enjoyed that." Acknowledging statements, by definition, facilitate more extended interaction by keeping the partner talking (Bradlyn et al., 1983). Again, these typically are rated for frequency of occurrence.

Speech Duration and Latency

These are time-based measures that have been associated with conversational competence. Specifically, longer durations of total speaking time, and shorter latencies from the time the partner stops speaking to the time the client begins to talk, in general, have been deemed more skillful. It may become obvious in assessment, however, that the client talks excessively and doesn't give the partner an opportunity to speak. Either excesses or deficiencies can be targeted for training. Duration is typically measured by activating a stopwatch whenever the client speaks during the assessment interaction. This can be reported cumulatively over an entire conversation, or for each individual verbalization made by the client. Latency is typically measured by activating the stopwatch when the partner stops speaking and turning the stopwatch off when the client begins to talk, and may be reported as a mean for all latencies during the conversation.

Eye Contact

This can be defined as the amount of time during the conversation that the client looks directly at the partner's face. It can be reported as a total duration for the entire conversation as measured cumulatively with a stopwatch, as a percentage of the total conversation time, or broken down into separate percentage for client talk time and partner talk time. Alternately, this can be rated on an occurrence, or on a nonoccurrence basis, as a subjective rating of percentage of conversation time or as a subjective rating of appropriateness.

Affect or Emotionality

Appropriate affect can be defined as the extent to which the client's nonverbal behaviors, tone, gesturing, and posture are congruent with his or her verbal content and with the situation at hand. This can be subjectively rated on a rating scale anchored, for example, from one, which represents an extremely inappropriate affect, to nine, which represents an extremely appropriate affect. Affect can also be rated on a scale anchored with negative one representing negative affect, zero representing neutral affect, and positive one representing positive affect.

Conversational Content

While many studies have demonstrated successful training of mentally retarded persons in specific conversational behaviors (such as asking questions and making eye contact), relatively little attention seems to have been directed toward assessing and training appropriate conversational topics or content. Retarded persons appear to frequently experience difficulty in selecting and talking about topics that would be of interest to nonretarded persons. In one attempt to assess this area, Bradlyn et al. (1983) polled nonretarded high school students regarding topics that they must enjoyed talking about with others. The five conversational topic areas (school activities, friends, movies, social events, and television shows) that were identified as most preferred then served as targets for training. While this procedure has not been documented with other age groups, data regarding valued conversational topics are needed to facilitate assessment and training of conversational skills.

Assertiveness Skills

Assertiveness has been considered an important skill for effective interpersonal functioning for at least the past two decades. Although many definitions of the term "assertiveness" have been proposed, it is generally construed to mean one's ability to express thoughts, feelings, beliefs, or opinions to another person in an effective and comfortable manner. The terms "social skills" and "assertiveness" have occasionally been used interchangeably. In contrast, we do not believe these terms are synonymous and we conceptualize assertiveness as a specialized subset of behavioral skills that facilitate attainment of specific objectives. Although there are many possible taxonomies of assertive behavior, we will address three general types or forms: refusal, request, and commendatory assertiveness.

Refusal Assertiveness

Assertive behavior may be an appropriate social skill within the context of a disagreement of dispute with another person, such as when one individual is attempting to block or interfere with another individual's on-going goal-directed behavior. In these cases, the appropriate assertive behavior may be termed refusal assertiveness since what is required is first a refusal to accept the interfering act or statement and, second, an attempt to prevent similar future occurrences. Refusal assertiveness has received the most attention of any behavior in the social-skills training literature (Kelly, 1982) and may be particularly important in the case of mentally retarded individuals who seem to be at high risk for ridicule and exploitation by nonretarded peers. In one investigation, Zisfein and Rosen (1974) found that of 25 institutionalized mentally retarded persons, all signed a "legal" document containing several blank spaces after being given no explanation of why they were being requested to do so, and 60 percent gave the experimenter a quarter. This occurred even though most of these individuals had earlier reported that they did not sign things or give money away indiscriminately. Since refusal assertiveness serves to prevent the loss of reinforcement for persons who might otherwise be taken advantage of, assessment of skills in this area seems particularly relevant for mentally retarded persons. Deficits in refusal assertiveness skills can be inferred from a client's direct self-reports of passivity, from staff or significant others' observations of non-assertive behavior, or from indications that the client has been exploited by others. Additionally, the study previously mentioned indicates that even self-reports of adequate refusal assertiveness skills may be invalid and should not necessarily be accepted as accurate since clients who reported that they didn't give away money or sign documents did do these things when confronted with the actual situations.

The client to be assessed for refusal assertion skills can be asked to role-play situations where the client is the recipient of an unreasonalbe request and his or her behaviorial responses are rated for assertive content (i.e., does the client refuse to comply with the request?), as well as are rated for style, the important elements of which are similar to those delineated in the previous section on conversational skills (e.g., eye contact, appropriate affect, loudness and fluency of speech, and latency to and duration of response). If the client cannot respond appropriately to a structured role-play situation it can probably be assumed that training is needed on whatever components are observed to be deficient. It should not be assumed, however, that demonstrations of skillful behavior in the laboratory or office on structured role-play situations indicate that the client will actually respond in a skillful manner in the natural environment. Close observation of how the individual handles actual conflict situations with others in the natural environment (for example, in a residential facility dayroom, a group-home living room, or at a sheltered workshop) is also needed. If instances of ineffective assertion skill are observed, an effort should be made to identify those deficient verbal, nonverbal and stylistic components that cause the client's behavior to be ineffective so these components can later be targeted for intervention.

Assessment of refusal assertiveness skill should also address the issue of whether a client can discriminate situations where refusal is appropriate, such as when asked to sign something or give away possessions or money, and situations where refusal is inappropriate, such as when asked to perform a job-related task by one's employer. Asking clients to role-play a variety of situations, some in which refusal assertiveness is appropriate and some in which it is not, can facilitate assessment of a client's ability to make such discriminations and provide information regarding whether or not training is needed in this area. Again, we prefer not to rely solely on the information obtained from structured role-plays in determining skill levels and do prefer to try to obtain more naturalistic data, including reports, whenever possible, from persons who observe the client's daily interactions. Role-play assessments, however, do provide important information since training will be different for individuals who cannot discriminate the appropriate situations in which to use the skills, than it would for those individuals who can discriminate but who do not demonstrate such skills in the natural environment.

Request Assertiveness

Another form of assertive behavior is the ability to make requests of others in order to facilitate meeting one's needs or attaining one's goals. These can occur in conjunction with refusal assertions, in which the individual turns down someone's unreasonable behavior and, in addition, requests a change in the antagonist's behavior ("No, I will not give you a quarter and *please don't ask me again.*") In this case, the request aspect of the assertive response serves not only to remove the immediate problem but presumably increases the likelihood that the problem will not occur in the future. A request can also exist by itself as a means to a specific goal, such as asking someone for the time, for directions, for assistance in locating a particular place or person, or for help in completing a particualr task. While request assertiveness has received relatively little attention in the research literature, the skills facilitate effective and efficient social functioning. Since helplessness, withdrawal from social interaction, and passivity have frequently been attributed to mentally retarded persons, particularly those with a history of institutionalization (Bates, 1980; Bornstein et al., 1980; Brody & Stoneman, 1977; Geller, Wildman, Kelly, & Laughlin, 1980; Zisfein & Rosen, 1974), assessment and training of request assertions seems warranted with this population. As has previously been discussed with respect to other skills, adequate assessment must not only take into account the issue of whether the individual can perform the requisite behaviors (i.e., has them in his or her repertoire), but also must consider if and when the client actually uses them in the natural environment, the client's ability to discriminate social situations in which the behaviors would be appropriate, and the persons to whom the behaviors might appropriately be directed. Again, reports of skill deficits can be obtained from the client directly, from others in the environment, or from direct observation of the client's behavior in the natural environment and/or structured role-played situations. Bates (1980) assessed skills in "asking for help" by giving clients money and instructing them to purchase a particular item that was hidden from view in the store by prior arrangement with the store management. Other similar situations can be structured by providing a block to completion of an assigned task, such as locking a door or removing a needed tool from the work area, and then observing how and if the client goes about dealing with the obstacle. As previously noted, however, one should be cautious in interpreting skillful behavior in a limited number of contrived situations as representative of generally skillful behavior in the natural environment. Particular situations, such as asking a stranger for directions, a landlord to make needed repairs, a store clerk to refund money on a defective purchase, or another person to accompany him or her to a social event, may be problematic and warrant assessment and intervention. Role-plays that sample such types of interactions may be the most feasible mode of assessment, since it would be difficult to directly observe a client's in vivo performance in them. While it is impossible to anticipate all situations which might be problematic for an individual, other living and adjustment difficulties may actually reflect a client's deficits in requisite assertion skills. One of the authors is aware of a mentally retarded client who was scheduled to be returned to a total care institution from a minimal care facility for failure to bathe. After close evaluation, it became clear that she was simply too obese to fit into the shower stall in her room. Had she been able to request a move to another room with a larger shower or tub, the presenting problem would have been eliminated. The client began bathing when the social worker noted the cause and moved her to another room. When questioned later the client reported that she was aware of the problem but was too embarrassed to ask for help. While this is an extreme example, it illustrates that deficits in request skills may manifest themselves in many ways. If a mentally retarded individual repeatedly does not perform a desired behavior, assessment should include exploration of possible blocks to performance, the individual's knowledge of these blocks, and his or her knowledge of how to remove them. Demonstrated failure to make appropriate request of others can result from simply never having learned how, from fear or embarrassment, from a lack of knowledge of what one needs to do in order to accomplish the goal (i.e., what to ask for), or from an inability to select the appropriate person to ask. Successful training in this form of assertiveness will depend on the adequacy of the assessment of the specific deficit.

Commendatory Assertiveness

Expressions of positive feelings such as praise, appreciation and liking can be seen as facilitative of positive interpersonal relationships (Kelly, 1982). In the child-behavior therapy literature, providing verbal expressions of praise for desirable behavior has repeatedly been shown to reinforce or to increase the occurrence of the behavior that has been praised. Similarly, persons who are skillful at commendatory assertion find that these expressions typically are very potent reinforcers for desirable behaviors of others in the environment and that frequent but genuine use of these skills facilitate positive interpersonal relationships. The ability to commend others in a warm, friendly, and sincere manner can be an extremely powerful interpersonal skill. While deficits in commendatory assertiveness are certainly not limited to mentally retarded persons, they stand to benefit maximally from training in these expressions. Increased ability to skillfully make positive statements to others should increase the reinforcement value of mentally retarded persons who have generally been noted to be unrewarding to interact with and, in fact, have sometimes been noted to be negatively reinforcing (Geller et al., 1980; Kelly, 1982). While this form of assertiveness has received relatively less attention in the literature than refusals and requests, training in its skillful use appears warranted for anyone who experiences difficulty in responding to the positive behaviors of others, or who exhibits deficits in interpersonal relationships that can be attributed to a failure to communicate positive feelings. Once this skill has been reported to be deficient by the client, or by others, or has been directly observed to be deficient by the assessor, the behavior can be analyzed with respect to specific components that have been described in the literature as important to overall performance. Skillfull commendatory assertions are believed to be comprised of many of the same components as refusals and requests (e.g., eye contact, appropriate affect, and speech loudness and duration). The content of the response, however, will differ in its specific inclusion of approval or praise (Geller et al., 1980; Kelly, Frederiksen, Fitts, & Phillips, 1978); in its inclusion of explicit statements that convey the assertor's positive feelings as a result of the other person's positive behavior (Schinke, Gilchrist, Smith, & Wong, 1979); and, perhaps, in its inclusion of an offer to return a positive act to the partner sometime in the future (Geller et al., 1980, Kelly et al., 1978; Skillings, Hersen, Bellack, & Becker, 1978). Demonstrated deficits in any of these components will imply the need for intervention, the nature of which will, again, depend on the observed deficit. A client might require either training in how to perform the behavior, instructions in situations for which it is appropriate, or both.

While it is normally the case that deficits in assertiveness skills are relatively situation-specific, mentally retarded individuals frequently seem to exhibit deficient behavior across a wide range of situations. For this reason, assessment of deficiencies for treatment planning should also take into account which specific situations are most problematic for the individual so that priorities for treatment can be established.

Employment Related Skills

While vocational skills assessment is addressed in another chapter, some employment related skills, particularly job finding, job interviewing, and employer-employee relationship skills are interpersonal in nature and therefore can be considered to be social skills. Vocational training has historically been an important component of habilitation programs for the mentally retarded. Attention has been directed only recently, however, toward the training of social skills necessary for locating potential jobs, convincing employers of vocational competence, and effectively interacting with co-workers and supervisors. While it has been estimated that 75 percent of mentally retarded adults could be trained to be financially self-supporting (President's Committee on Mental Retardation, 1969) this potential has undoubtedly not been reached. Even if a mentally retarded person is successful in a vocational skills training program, unless he or she can locate potential employment and can convince an employer of his or her vocational competence, the client will be unlikely to obtain work outside the sheltered setting.

Several component skills have been reported as particularly important to the job finding process. Locating and using information about potential jobs, initiating telephone and personal contacts with potential employers, completing job application forms, dressing and grooming appropriately for job interviews, and effectively presenting oneself in a positive manner in the interview have all been deemed relevant job finding skills (Azrin, Flores, & Kaplan, 1975; Clark, Boyd, & Macrae, 1975; Jones & Azrin, 1973; Perrin, 1977). Research, however, has consistently shown that hiring decisions are determined primarily by the performance of the applicant during job interviews (Cohen & Etheridge, 1975; Drake, Kaplan, & Stone, 1972; Kelly, 1982; Kelly & Christoff, in press; Springbett, 1958; Tschirgi, 1973).

Mentally retarded persons who are known to possess job performance skills by virtue of successful completion of a vocational training program, effective performance in a job workshop setting, or successful employment history, but who are unable to obtain gainful employment may be deficient in either job-finding or job interviewing skills and assessment of possible deficits in this area should be attempted. If the client is not obtaining interviews, assessment of what, if anything, he or she is doing in attempting to locate potential employers is warranted in order to determine which specific skills are deficient. Since Jones and Azrin (1973) found that two-thirds of job leads come from friends and relatives, individuals who are experiencing difficulty in locating job leads should be assessed for proficiency in the following social skills: asking others for job leads or openings; asking others if they would be willing to serve as a reference or to write an open letter of recommendation; and being able to target the appropriate people to ask. We have assessed these verbal abilities, which are actually a specific form of request assertiveness, in role-plays as well as by listening to the client actually make such a request of a friend, relative, or former employer on the telephone in our office. Skills in speaking with potential employers on the telephone can be assessed similarly and any noted deficits targeted for training.

Clearly, the ability to present oneself positively to prospective employers is crucial to job attainment, whether it occurs in initial telephone contact, by written material in job application forms, or in the employment interview. Since the interview has been reported to be the most crucial encounter, the main focus of most job finding programs is performance in the interview itself. Assessment of job interview skills typically involves observing the client's behavior in a role-play job interview and noting the presence, frequency, and/or appropriateness of component skills. Component behaviors of job interview skills are similar to those noted in the previous discussions of conversational and assertiveness skills and include: eye contact (Hollandsworth, Glazeski, & Dressel; 1978; Pinto, 1979); appropriate affect; and speech loudness, clarity, and fluency (Hollandsworth, Dressel, & Stevens, 1977; Hollandsworth et al., 1978; Pinto, 1979). Additional skills more specific to the job interview setting include: concise, direct answers to interviewer's questions (Barbee & Keil, 1973; Hollandsworth et al., 1978); job-relevant questions asked by the client to the interviewer (Barbee & Keil, 1973; Hollandsworth et al., 1978; Kelly, Laughlin, Claiborne, & Patterson, 1979); positive self-statements regarding past education, training, or work experience (Barbee & Keil, 1973; Furman, Geller, Simon, & Kelly, 1979; Kelly, Laughlin et al., 1979); positive self-statements regarding interests, hobbies, or activities (Kelly, Wildman, & Berler, 1980); and expressions of enthusiasm and interest in the prospective position (Furman et al., 1979; Kelly, Urey, & Patterson, 1980).

The job-interview role-play typically consists of an interview partner acting as an employer and delivering a series of predetermined questions and comments to the client. The questions asked should approximate those that the client might be expected to encounter on an actual interview and might be formulated following a survey of local personnel interviewers to determine what questions typically are asked of applicants who have experience and job aspirations similar to those of the clients. Some investigators (Hall, Sheldon-Wildgen, & Sherman, 1980; Kelly, Wildman et al., 1980) have assessed job interviewing skills in probe interviews with actual potential employers at the place of employment. In both of these studies, the interviewers were asked by the investigators to conduct the interviews as they normally would for any job interview.

Presumably, client behaviors exhibited in assessments conducted under these conditions will closely approximate the client's actual in vivo behavior. As has been previously noted, the more closely the assessment situation approximates the actual situations in which the client will be required to perform, the more likely it is that client performance in the assessment situation will be representative of his or her behavior in the natural environment. Assessment situations should, therefore, be structured with this in mind.

The assessment interview should include any difficult questions that the client might reasonably be expected to encounter, such as queries regarding work experience if the client has none, or why the client left his or her last job or if he or she was fired. Skillful interviewees are not likely to volunteer any information that will be potentially damaging to their chances of being hired. However, if they are asked directly, the best response seems to be an honest summary of the past problem followed by an elaboration of accurate reasons why the client is now able to work, is responsible and would be an asset to the employer (Kelly, 1982).

If a client has demonstrated ability to obtain employment but has a history of problematic relations with supervisors or co-workers, or has previously been fired, assessment of his or her skills in getting along with others is also warranted. The skills required to successfully interact with others in the work setting are a specialized subset of the relationship building, interpersonal, and conversational skills that have been previously discussed. Role-plays to approximate job site social interactions can be constructed to represent the situations that the client has actually encountered, and might reasonably be expected to tap such skills as commendatory assertiveness toward co-workers and supervisors, refusals of unreasonable requests, requesting assistance or time-off, handling criticism, and general abilities to carry on appropriate conversations with others in the job setting.

Social Problem-Solving Skills

Effective social behavior requires processing information about the environment, making inferences about possible course of action that are available and the consequences of each of these, and using this information to decide on the best possible course (Trower, Bryant, & Argyle, 1978). D'Zurilla and Goldfried (1971) have defined problem-solving as an overt or cognitive-behavioral process that consists of generating a number of alternative responses that might be effective for dealing with a particular problem and that increase the probability that the most effective alternative will be selected. These authors further suggest that training in general problem-solving strategies will facilitate interpersonal effectiveness by providing the individual with response options to be used in dealing with day-to-day problematic situations.

As we have discussed previously, the ability to discriminate situations in which the use of particular skills are appropriate is at least as critical to effective interpersonal functioning as is the ability to perform the skills. Brody and Stoneman (1977) have argued that social-competence training for developmentally disabled individuals should include not only training of the response itself, but also training in how to identify antecedent stimulus situations that occasion social responses, and training in selecting the appropriate responses to be used. These are essential components of problem-solving skills. While attention has been directed at assessing and training problem-solving skills in college students (Goldfried & D'Zurilla, 1969), in psychiatric patients (Platt & Spivack, 1972a; 1972b; 1977;* Trower et al., 1978), and in children and adolescents (Spivack & Shure, 1974), relatively little research on the problem-solving skills of mentally retarded persons is evident. It has been suggested, however, that while mentally retarded persons generally lack problem-solving skills and tend to exhibit avoidance behaviors and passivity when confronted with problematic situations, effective problem solving can be trained (Ross, 1969; Ross & Ross, 1973, 1978). Since skillful problem solving should facilitate effective independent social functioning as well as maximize the probability that trained behavior will be emitted in appropriate

---

*Platt, JJ, & Spivack, G. *Measures of interpersonal cognitive problem-solving.* Unpublished manuscript. Philadelphia, Pennsylvania: Hahnemann Medical College and Hospital, Department of Mental Health Sciences, 1977.

situations, assessment and training of these skills will be of great benefit to mentally retarded clients.

The basic problem-solving process involves five steps: general awareness that problematic situations are a normal part of day-to-day life and that they can be handled effectively, and recognition of a specific situation as a problem; definition of the particular problem at hand; generation of a variety of possible solutions to the particular problem; evaluation of the appropriateness and effectiveness of each possible solution, with particular attention given to the expected consequences of each solution and the selection of one alternative as the best one based on this evaluation; and implementing the chosen alternative and assessing the actual outcome (D'Zurilla & Goldfried, 1971). Since deficient problem-solving abilities may result from inability to perform any, all, or any combination of these steps, each step should be assessed. While problem-solving training will be useful to any client who is ineffective in handling a wide range of problematic situations, the particular focus and emphasis of training should depend on the specific difficulties or deficits exhibited by the client.

Assessment of social problem-solving skills has typically consisted of presenting the client with a written or oral description of a problem situation. A sample question may be: "You go to pay your rent and your landlord tells you that you may pay him $200 instead of the $150 you have been paying. He wants the money today." The client is then asked: what the problem is, what would be some possible ways of solving the problem, what the client thinks would happen if he or she did each of his or her proposed solutions, what the client thinks is the best solution, why the client thinks the chosen solution is the best one, and how the client would actually go about implementing the chosen solution. Answers to these questions can then be evaluated for accuracy of problem identification, adequacy of solutions generated, skills in evaluating the possible consequences of various actions and in deciding on the best course of action, and knowledge of how to actually go about solving the problem. The particular problem situations provided for the client can be selected from those already described in the problem-solving literature (Platt & Spivack, 1972a, 1977;* Spivack & Shure, 1974). We have also found it useful to develop problem situations that are likely to be relevant for the particular client being assessed.

Another method for assessing problem-solving skills is the means-ends problem-solving procedure (MEPS; Platt & Spivack, 1977*). This device consists of a series of vignettes that provide the client with a description of the problematic situation and the desired outcome. An example of this is: "He loved his girlfriend very much, but they had many arguments. One day she left him. He wanted things to be better. The story ends with everything fine between him and his girlfriend," (Platt & Spivack, 1977,* p. 2). The client is then asked to "make

---

*Platt, JJ, & Spivack, G. Measures of interpersonal cognitive problem-solving. Unpublished manuscript, Hahnemann Medical College and Hospital, Department of Mental Health Sciences, Philadelphia, 1977

up a story'' that describes the intervening events. Stories can be scored for relevant and irrelevant "means" or discrete steps the protagonist takes to reach the goal; described obstacles to reaching the goal such as anxiety, shyness, or some block external to the subject; and elaborations of means and obstacles (see Platt & Spivack, 1977,* for more detailed scoring procedures).

Other methods for assessing skills in the specific steps in problem-solving can also be used. The Optional Thinking Test (Platt & Spivack, 1977;* Spivack, Platt, & Shure, 1976) requires the client to generate as many solutions to a set of four situations in which the protagonist is faced with temptation (for example, opportunity to go off one's diet, or receiving too much money from a bank teller). The client is asked to describe the thoughts and actions of the protagonist in each situation. Responses are scored for reported awareness of the consequences of various courses of action. All of these measures tap skills relevant to social problem-solving, and can certainly be used in assessing individual client's general abilities in these areas. An important question one needs to consider, however, is whether the particular client being assessed can use these skills to solve the problems that arise in his or her own daily life. This question can probably best be answered by assessing abilities in situations that are observed or are reported to be problematic for each particular client. Standardized procedures for assessment can be useful, especially in determining whether the client has basic problem-solving skills that are independent of the problems he or she experiences. The content, or specific situation to which the procedures are applied might well be varied, however, to include some situations that are known to be problematic to the client, so that his or her abilities can also be assessed with respect to the specific problems he or she experiences.

Problem-solving training, by definition, is intended to increase the probability of dealing with problems effectively by increasing the chances that the individual so trained will select and implement the best available solution (D'Zurilla & Goldfried, 1971). It seems, therefore, to be a clinically useful component to any treatment program. If assessment of problem-solving abilities reveals that the client can generate reasonable alternative solutions to a social problem, can evaluate these solutions and can select one as the most appropriate, but cannot implement the chosen solution, training in this behavioral performance aspect of social functioning may be all that is needed. This, however, will probably not be the case with mentally retarded persons and it has been our experience that even persons without verbal and intellectual handicaps do not tend to use all of the steps without training.

Problem-solving training may well be the best vehicle for maximizing the probability that any skills taught in training programs will be used correctly in the natural environment. In addition, as D'Zurilla and Goldfried (1971) suggest,

---

*Platt, JJ, & Spivack, G. Measures of interpersonal cognitive problem-solving. Unpublished manuscript, Hahnemann Medical College and Hospital, Department of Mental Health Sciences, Philadelphia, 1977

problem-solving training, when implemented toward the end of more extensive long-term programs, will facilitate the client learning to rely less on the therapist's specific directions and more on his or her own skills and resources.

Thus, while problem-solving assessment and training with the mentally retarded has been an historically neglected area, the value of evaluating this skill, particularly in respect to social problems, seems apparent. Effective problem-solving abilities should lead to increased independence and more effective interpersonal functioning.

Dating or Heterosocial Skills

Another area of social skills that has long been neglected in mentally retarded persons involves dating or heterosocial skills. Mentally retarded persons have been recognized as deficient in this area and these deficiencies have been attributed, in part, to institutional living (Zisfein & Rosen, 1974). In the not-too-distant past, nearly all mentally retarded persons resided in institutional settings and were expected to remain in these settings for life. Institutional living settings often limit the opportunities of its residents to observe and engage in age-appropriate date initiation, dating, or other heterosocial skills, and the expectation that these residents would remain in the same setting indefinitely may have led to an implicit denial that these skills are necessary for mentally retarded persons. With the present emphasis on deinstitutionalization, however, increasing numbers of mentally retarded adolescents are being "mainstreamed" into regular classrooms and mentally retarded adults are being moved into community work and living settings where these skills are more relevant. As mentally retarded persons live in these settings, they have increasing opportunities to observe the heterosocial behavior of others and may express increasing interest in engaging in these dating behaviors. Although we are certain that some would disagree with our position, we believe that mentally retarded persons should be given the opportunity to approximate the age-appropriate social behavior of their nonretarded peers to the extent of their ability. This includes the development of heterosexual and heterosocial relationships. Like persons of normal intelligence, mentally retarded persons have sexual desires and needs, and we believe that they should be provided with the training necessary to fulfill them, including birth control counseling, as well as heterosocial skills training.

As in the case with normal adolescents, these issues should be dealt with when the individual expresses an interest or when it becomes apparent to someone in the environment that these issues are relevant. As with all of the social skills discussed previously, we believe that heterosocial skills should be assessed with respect to the degree to which they approximate the skills of same-aged nonretarded peers.

Date-initiation and heterosocial skills are, like job interviewing skills, specialized examples of conversational skills, directed at reaching a specific goal. In this case, the goal, presumably, is establishing an intimate sexual and/or social relationship with another person. Achieving this goal requires an individual to meet prospective dates, converse with them, and arrange for further social contacts. The term date-initiation skill refers specifically to the behavior of asking another person to accompany the requester in some prearranged social activity. Heterosocial skills represent the broader class of behaviors involved in initiating and maintaining conversations with persons of the opposite sex as well as represent affectionate motor behavior such as holding hands or touching. Date-initiation will necessarily occur within the context of heterosocial conversation.

It should not be surprising that the proposed components of heterosocial skills are, for the most part, the same as those believed to comprise conversational competence, albeit with a more specialized focus. These behaviors include: eye contact (Bander, Steinke, Allen, & Mosher, 1975; Heimberg, Madsen, Montgomery, & McNabb, 1980); appropriate affect (Bander et al., 1975; Heimberg et al., 1980); conversational questions (Heimberg et al., 1980); speech duration (Martinez-Diaz & Edelstien, 1979, 1980; Ziechner, Wright, & Herman, 1977); complementary comments (Curran, 1975; Farrell, Mariotto, Conger, Curran, & Wallender, 1979; Wessberg, Mariotto, Conger, Farrell, & Conger, 1979); requests for dates (Curran, 1975; Curran, Gilbert, & Little, 1976); and follow-up/acknowledgment statements such as questions, comments, or statements that indicate interest, attentiveness or a reaction to what the partner is saying (Heimberg et al., 1980; Kupke, Hobbs, & Cheney, 1979).

As we have discussed in previous sections of this chapter, assessment of the clients heterosocial skills occur within the context of sample behavior that can be observed by the assessor. This generally takes the form of a brief (eight to ten minute) semistructured or unstructured interaction with a person of the opposite sex. Instructions to the client can be as simple as "get to know your partner and ask him or her for a date." The interaction can then be audio- or video- taperecorded and rated later for the presence, absence and appropriateness of the above listed components skills; or, alternately, the client's performance can be rated as it occurs. Deficits found in any component indicate the need for targeting that particular component behavior for training. The client's performance in this observed interaction may reveal deficiencies in other areas beyond those specifically listed above. For example, stereotypic behaivor, strange mannerisms, speech dysfluencies, long silences, or negative self-disclosures may also be targeted for treatment if they appear to be problematic for the individual. As is presumably the case with all behavioral skills assessments, the more closely the assessment situation approximates the actual setting in which the behavior occurs, the more likely it is that the behavior observed will approximate the behavior in vivo. In the case of heterosocial skills assessment it is probably important that the partner be someone who is perceived by the client as a reasonable person to actually ask for a date, and the setting should be described as one in which the client might actually have occasion to meet appropriate persons of the opposite sex, such as a workshop break room, or in the hall or cafeteria at school. Assessment should also include knowledge of apropriate dating activities, and other behaviors required in actually carrying out a date, such as arranging a meeting time and place, dressing appropriately for the planned activity, arranging to pay for activities during the date, and planning transportation to and from the activity. Since all of these specific behaviors are required for dating, they are reasonable targets for training and should be assessed in mentally retarded person who are functioning relatively independently and express a desire to date.

CONCLUSIONS

The movement to "deinstitutionalize" mentally retarded persons, coupled with the AAMD-required focus on the adaptive behavior of such persons has led to an increasing interest in maximizing the social competence of the mentally retarded. As more mentally retarded persons move from institutions into the community, increasing attention has been paid to training programs that facilitate the development of skills necessary for effective functioning in these settings. If mentally retarded persons are to be successfully integrated into community settings, the training of appropriate social and interpersonal behavior is certainly important, and the aim of such programs must be to train mentally retarded persons in social and interpersonal skills that approximate those of the members of the community into which the mentally retarded persons are placed.

Since the adequacy of any training program depends to a large extent upon the adequacy of the assessment upon which it is based, the assessment of social competence is of critical importance. It is our suggestion that skills assessment should take place in the natural environment whenever possible and that the client's behavior should be observed and rated by as many persons as possible. We have asked trained observers to rate client behavior both in the natural environment and from audio- and video-taped role-play situations; we have asked employers, parents, teachers, counselors, and institutional staff to provide ratings of the clients behavior; and for clients who are capable, we often requested specific self-evaluation and description of their own behavior. We have conducted observations in homes, classrooms, school cafeterias, work environments, and office or laboratory settings. We recommend that those who are assessing behavior be innovative in incorporating as many settings, situations, and significant others as possible into the assessment procedures. Obviously this should all be done with the knowledge and consent of the client and his or her legal representative, and while attending to the client's right to confidentiality.

In this chapter we have provided descriptions and definitions of several classes of social skills. This review is not exhaustive, but rather is intended to be representative of some of the skills required of most people in their daily lives. Any situation that requires interpersonal interaction may require specialized social skills; close assessment of a client's social behavior in the environments where he or she will need to function is a necessary step that precedes training to facilitate attainment of the client's goals. The notion that it is important to behaviorally assess and train social skills in the mentally retarded is relatively new and the application of these procedures to the behaivor of mentally retarded persons is even newer. The future is promising .

REFERENCES

Argyris, C. Explorations in interpersonal competence—I. *Journal of Applied Behavioral Science,* 1965, *1,* 58–83

Argyris, C. Conditions for competence acquisition and therapy. *Journal of Applied Behavioral Science,* 1968, *4,* 147–177

Argyris, C. The incompleteness of social-psychological theory: Examples from small group cognitive, consistency, and attribution research. *American Psychologist,* 1969, *24,* 893–908

Azrin, NH, Flores, T, & Kaplan, SJ. Job-Finding club: A group assisted program for obtaining employment. *Behaviour Research and Therapy,* 1975, *13,* 17–27

Bander, KW, Steinke, GV, Allen, GJ, & Mosher, DL. Evaluation of three dating-specific treatment approaches for heterosexual dating anxiety. *Journal of Consulting and Clinical Psychology,* 1975, *43,* 259–265

Barbee, JR, & Keil, EC. Experimental Techniques of job interview training for the disadvantaged: Videotape feedback, behavior modification, and microcounseling. *Journal of Applied Psychology,* 1973, *58,* 209–213

Bates, P. The effectiveness of interpersonal skills training on the social skill acquisition of moderately and mildly retarded adults. *Journal of Applied Behavior Analysis,* 1980, *13,* 237–248

Baumeister, AA, & Muma, JR. On defining mental retardation. *Journal of Special Education,* 1975, *9,* 293–306

Bellack, AS, & Hersen, M. Chronic psychiatric patients: Social skills training. In M Hersen & AS Bellack (Eds.), *Behavior therapy in the psychiatric setting.* Baltimore: Williams & Wilkins, 1978

Bellack, AS, Hersen, M, & Lamparski, D. Role play tests for assessing social skills: Are they valid? Are they useful? *Journal of Consulting and Clinical Psychology,* 1979, *47,* 335–342

Bellack, AS, Hersen, M, & Turner, SM. Role play tests for assessing social skills: Are they valid? *Behavior Therapy,* 1978, *9,* 448–461

Bellack, AS, Hersen, M, & Turner, SM. The relationship of role playing and knowledge of appropriate behavior to assertion in the natural environment. *Journal of Consulting and Clinical Psychology,* 1979, *47,* 670–678

Blount, WR. A comment on language, socialization, acceptence, and the retarded. *Mental retardation,* 1969, *7,* 33–35

Bornstein, PH, Bach, PJ. McFall, ME, Friman, PC, & Lyons, PD. Application of a social skills training program in the modification of interpersonal deficits among retarded adults: A clinical replication. *Journal of Applied Behavior Analysis,* 1980, *13,* 171–176

Bradlyn, AS, Himadi, WG, Crimmins, DB, Christoff, KA, Graves, KG, & Kelly, JA. Conversational skills training for retarded adolescents. *Behavior Therapy,* 1983, *14,* 314–325

Brody, GH, & Stoneman, A. Social Competencies in the developmentally disabled. *Mental Retardation,* 1977, *15,* 41–43

Chennault, M. Improving the social acceptance of unpopular educable mentally retarded pupils in special classes. *American Journal of Mental Deficiency,* 1967, *72,* 455–485

Christoff, KA, & Edelstein, BA. *Functional aspects of assertive and aggressive behavior: Labora-*

tory and in vivo observations. Paper presented at the meeting of the Association for Advancement of Behavior Therapy, Toronto, 1981

Clark, HB, Boyd, SB, & Macrae, JW. A classroom program teaching disadvantaged youths to write biographic information. *Journal of Applied Behavior Analysis*, 1975, *8*, 67–75

Cohen, BM, & Etheridge, JM. Recruiting's main ingredient. *Journal of College Placement*, 1975, *35*, 75–77

Curran, JP. An evalution of a skills training program and a systematic desensitization program in reducing dating anxiety. *Behaviour Research and Therapy*, 1975, *13*, 65–68

Curran, JP, Gilbert, FS, & Little, LM. A comparison between behavioral replication training and sensitivity training approaches to heterosocial dating anxiety. *Journal of Counseling Psychology*, 1976, *23*, 190–196

Dentler, RA, & Mackler, B. Mental ability and sociometric status among retarded children. *Psychological Bulletin*, 1962, *59*. 273–283

Doll, EA. *The Measurement of Social Competence*. Minneapolis, Minnesota: Education Publishers, 1953

Doll, EA. *Vineland Scale of Social Maturity*. Minneapolis, Minnesota: American Guidance Service, 1965

Drake, LR, Kaplan, HR, & Stone, RA. How do employers value the interveiw? *Journal of College Placement*, 1972, *32*, 47–51

D'Zurilla, TJ, & Goldfried, MR. Problem solving and behavior modification *Journal of Abnormal Psychology*, 1971, *78*, 107–126

Eisler, RM, Hersen, M, Miller, PM, & Blanchard, EB. Situational determinants of assertive behaviors. *Journal of Consulting and Clinical Psychology*, 1975, *43*, 330–340

Farrell, AD, Mariotto, MJ, Conger, AJ, Curran, JP, & Wallender, JL. Self-ratings and judges' ratings of heterosexual social anxiety and skill: A generalizability study. *Journal of Consulting and Clinical Psychology*, 1979, *47*, 164–175

Furman, W, Geller, M, Simon, SJ, & Kelly, JA. The use of a behavior rehearsal procedure for teaching job-interviewing skills to psychiatric patients. *Behavior Therapy*, 1979, *10*, 157–167

Geller, MI, Wildman, HE, Kelly, JA, & Laughlin, CS. Teaching assertive and commendatory social skills to an interpersonally-deficient retarded adolescent. *Journal of Clinical Child Psychology*, 1980, *9*, 17–21

Gibson, FW, Jr., Lawrence, PS, & Nelson, RO. Comparison of three training procedures for teaching social responses to developmentally disabled adults. *American Journal of Mental Deficiency*, 1976, *81*, 379–387

Givens, T. The current status of three major techniques for the assessment of social competence in the diagnosis of the potentially retarded child. *Southern Journal of Educational Research*, 1978, *12*, 75–84

Goldfried, MR, & D'Zurilla, TJ. A behavioral-analytic model for assessing competence. In CD Speilberger (Ed.), *Current topics in clinical and community psychology* (Vol. 1). New York: Academic Press, 1969

Goldsmith, JB, & McFall, RM. Development and evaluation of an interpersonal skill-training program for psychiatric inpatients. *Journal of Abnormal Psychology*, 1975, *84*, 51–58

Grossman, HJ. *Manual on terminology and classification in mental retardation*. Washington, DC: American Association on Mental Deficiency, 1973

Hall, C, Sheldon-Wildgen, J, & Sherman, JA. Teaching job interview skills to retarded clients. *Journal of Applied Behavior Analysis*, 1980, *13*, 433–442

Heber, R. A manual on terminology and classification in mental retardation. *American Journal of Mental Deficiency* (Monograph suppl.) 1959

Heimberg, RG, Madsen, CH, Montgomery, D, & McNabb, CE. Behavioral treatments for heterosocial problems: Effects on daily self-monitored and role played interactions. *Behavior Modification*, 1980, *4*, 147–172

Hersen, M, & Bellack, AS. *Behavioral Assessment: A practical handbook*. Oxford: Pergamon Press, 1976

Hersen, M, & Bellack, AS. Assessment of social skills. In AR Ciminero, KS Calhoun, & HE Adams (Eds.), *Handbook for behavioral assessment*. New York: Wiley, 1977

Hollandsworth, JG, Jr., Dressel, ME, & Stevens, J. Use of behavioral versus traditional procedures for increasing job interview skills. *Journal of Counseling Psychology*, 1977, *24*, 503–510

Hollandsworth, JG, Jr., Glazeski, RC, & Dressel, ME. Use of social-skills training in the treatment of extreme anxiety and deficient verbal skills in the job-interview setting. *Journal of Applied Behavior Analysis*, 1978, *11*, 249–269

Johnson, GO. A study of the social position of mentally handicapped children in the regular grades. *American Journal of Mental Deficiency*, 1950, *55*, 60–89

Jones, RJ, & Azrin, NH. An experimental application of a social reinforcement approach to the problem of job-finding. *Journal of Applied Behavior Analysis*, 1973, *6*, 345–353

Kazdin, AE, Matson, JL, & Esveldt-Dawson, K. Social skill performance among normal and psychiatric inpatient children as a function of assessment conditions. *Behaviour Research and Therapy*, 1981, *19*, 145–152

Kelly, JA. *Social Skills Training: A practical guide for interventions*. New York: Springer, 1982

Kelly, JA & Christoff, KA. Job interview training for the mentally retarded: Issues and applications. *Applied Research in Mental Retardation* (in press)

Kelly, JA, & Drabman, RS. The modification of socially detrimental behavior. *Journal of Behavior Therapy and Experimental Psychiatry*, 1977, *8*, 101–104

Kelly, JA, Frederiksen, LW, Fitts, H, & Phillips, J. Training and generalization of commendatory assertiveness: A controlled single subject experiment. *Journal of Behavior Therapy and Experimental Psychiatry*, 1978, *9*, 17–21

Kelly, JA, Furman, W, Phillips, J, Hathorn, S, & Wilson, T. Teaching conversational skills to retarded adolescents. *Child Behavior Therapy*, 1979, *1*, 85–97

Kelly, JA, Laughlin, C, Claiborne, M, & Patterson, J. A group procedure for teaching job interviewing skills to formerly hospitalized psychiatric patients. *Behavior Therapy*, 1979, *10*, 299–310

Kelly, JA, Urey, JR, & Patterson, J. Improving heterosocial conversational skills of male psychiatric patients through a small group training procedure. *Behavior Therapy*, 1980, *11*, 179–188

Kelly, JA, Wildman, BG, & Berler, ES. Small group behavioral training to improve the job interview skills repertoire of mildly retarded adolescents. *Journal of Applied Behavior Analysis*, 1980, *13*, 461–471

Kelly, JA, Wildman, BG, Urey, JR, & Thurman, C. Group skills training to increase the conversational repertoire of retarded adolescents. *Child Behavior Therapy*, 1979, *1*, 323–336

Kupke, TE, Hobbs, SA, & Cheney, TH. Selection of heterosocial skills. I. Criterion-related validity. *Behavior Therapy*, 1979, *10*, 327–335

Lambert, NM, Wilcox, MR, & Gleason, WP. *The educationally retarded child*. New York: Grune & Stratton, 1974

Libet, J, & Lewinsohn, PM. Concept of social skill with special reference to the behavior of depressed persons. *Journal of Consulting and Clinical Psychology*, 1973, *40*, 304–312

Longhurst, TM. Assessing and increasing descriptive communication skills in retarded children. *Mental Retardation*, 1972, *10*, 42–45

Longhurst, TM. Communication in retarded adolescents: Sex and intelligence level. *American Journal of Mental Deficiency*, 1974, *78*, 607–618

Martin, GL, Kehoe, B, Bird, E, Jensen, V, & Darbyshire, M. Operant conditioning in dressing behavior of severely retarded girls. *Mental Retardation*, 1971, *9*, 27–31

Martinez-Diaz, JA, & Edelstein, BA. Multivariate effects of demand characteristics on the analogue competence. *Journal of Applied Behavior Analysis*, 1979, *12*, 679–689

Martinez-Diaz, JA, Edelstein, BA. Heterosocial competence: Predictive and construct validity. *Behavior Modification*, 1980, *4*, 115–129

Matson, JL, DiLorenzo, TM, & Esveldt-Dawson, K. Independence training as a method of enhancing self-help skills acquisition of the mentally retarded. *Behaviour Research & Therapy*, 1981, *19*, 399–405

Matson, JL, Marchetti, A, & Adkins, JA. Comparison of operant-and independence-training procedures for mentally retarded adults. *American Journal of Mental Deficiency*, 1980, *84*, 487–494.

McClure, RF. Reinforcement of verbal social behavior in moderately retarded children. *Psychological Reports*, 1968, *23*, 371–376

Minkin, N, Braukmann, CJ, Minkin, BL, Timbers, GD, Timbers, BJ, Fixsen, DF, Phillips, EL, & Wolf, MM. The social validation and training of conversational skills. *Journal of Applied Behavior Analysis*, 1976, *9*, 127–139

Molloy, JT. *Dress for success*. New York: Warner Books, 1976

Molloy, JT. *The woman's dress for success book*. Chicago: Follett Publishing Company, 1977

Nelson, RO, Gibson, F, Jr., & Cutting, DS. Video taped modeling: The development of three appropriate social responses in a mildly retarded child. *Mental Retardation*, 1973, *11*, 24–28

Nihira, K. Factorial dimensions of adaptive behavior in mentally retarded children and adolescents. *American Journal of Mental Deficiency*, 1969, *74*, 130–141

Nihira, K, Foster, R, Shellhaas, M. & Leland, H. *AAMD adaptive behavior scale*. Washington, DC: American Association on Mental Deficiency, 1969

Nihira, K, Foster, R, Shellhaas, M. & Leland, H. *AAMD adaptive behavior scale*. (rev. ed.) Washington, DC: American Association on Mental Deficiency, 1974

Perrin, TO. Job seeking training for adult retarded clients. *Journal of Applied Rehabilitation Counseling*, 1977, *8*, 181–188

Pinto, RP. An evaluation of job-interview training in the rehabilitation setting. *Journal of Rehabilitation*, 1979, *45*, 71–76

Platt, JJ, & Spivack, G. Problem-solving thinking of psychiatric patients. *Journal of Consulting and Clinical Psychology*, 1972, *39*, 148–151

Platt, JJ, & Spivack, G. Social competence and effective problem-solving thinking in psychiatric patients. *Journal of Clinical Psychology*, 1972, *28*, 3–5 (b)

President's Committee on Mental Retardation. *MR 69: Toward progress: The story of the decade*. Washington, DC: President's Committee on Mental Retardation, 1969

Rosenberg, S. *Interpersonal processes in the perpetuation and reduction of language retardation: Some speculations and some data*. Paper presented at the American Association on Mental Deficiency, Milwaukee, Wisconsin, May 1959

Ross, DM, & Ross, SA. Cognitive training for the EMR child: Situational problem solving and planning. *American Journal of Mental Deficiency*, 1973, *78*, 20–26

Ross, DM, & Ross, SA. Cognitive training for EMR children: Choosing the best alternative. *American Journal of Mental Deficiency*, 1978, *82*, 598–601

Ross, SA. Effects of intentional training in social behavior on retarded children. *American Journal of Mental Deficiency*, 1969, *73*, 912–919

Rucker, CN, & Vincenzo, FM. Maintaining social acceptance gains made by mentally retarded children. *Exceptional Children*, 1970, *36*, 679–680

Rychtarik, RG, & Bornstein, PH. Training conversational skills in mentally retarded adults: A multiple baseline analysis. *Mental Retardation*, 1979, *17*, 289–293

Schinke, SP, Gilchrist, LD, Smith, TE, & Wong, SE. Group interpersonal skills training in a natural setting: An experimental study. *Behaviour Research and Therapy*, 1979, *17*, 149–154

Skillings, RE, Hersen, M, Bellack, AS, & Becker, MP. Relationship of specific and global measures of assertion in college females, *Journal of Clinical Psychology*, 1978, *34*, 346–353

Spivack, G, Platt, JJ, & Shure, MB. *The problem-solving approach to adjustment: A guide to research and intervention*. San Fransisco: Jossey-Bass, 1976

Spivack, G, & Shure, MB. *Social adjustment of young children: A cognitive approach to solving real-life problems*. San Fransisco: Jossey-Bass, 1974

Springbett, BM. Factors affecting the final decision in the employment interview. *Canadian Journal of Psychology*, 1958, *12*, 13–22

Stalonas, PM, & Johnson, WG. Conversation skills trainings for obsessive speech using an aversive-cueing procedure. *Journal of Behavior Therapy and Experimental Psychiatry*, 1979, *10*, 61–63

Strain, PS, & Shores, RE. Social reciprocity: A review of research and educational implications. *Exceptional Children*, 1977, *43*, 526–530

Treffry, D, Martin, G, Samels, J, & Watson, C. Operant conditioning of grooming behavior of severely retarded girls. *Mental Retardation*, 1970, *8*, 29–33

Trower, P. Situational analysis of the components and processes of behavior of socially skilled and unskilled patients. *Journal of Consulting and Clinical Psychology*, 1980, *48*, 327–339

Trower, P, Bryant, B, & Argyle, M. *Social skills and mental health*. Pittsburgh: University of Pittsburgh Press, 1978

Tschirgi, HD. What do recruiters really look for in candidates? *Journal of College Placement*, 1973, *33*, 75–79

Urey, JR, Laughlin, CS, & Kelly, JA. Teaching heterosocial conversational skills to male psychiatric patients. *Journal of Behavior Therapy and Experimental Psychiatry*, 1979, *10*, 323–328

Weissman, MM. The assessment of social adjustment. *Archives of General Psychiatry*, 1975, *32*, 357–365

Wessberg, HW, Mariotto, MJ, Conger, AJ, Farrell, AD, & Conger, JC. Ecological validity of role plays for assessing heterosocial anxiety and skill of male college students. *Journal of Consulting and Clinical Psychology*, 1979, *47*, 525–535

Ziechner, A, Wright, JC, & Herman, S. Effects of situation on dating and assertive behavior. *Psychological Reports*, 1977, *40*, 375–381

Zisfein, L, & Rosen, M. Effects of a personal adjustment training group counseling program. *Mental Retardation*, 1974, *12*, 50–53

PART III

Community Adaptation

Jan L. Wallander
Nancy C. Hubert
Carolyn S. Schroeder

8

Self-Care Skills

The ability to demonstrate appropriate self-care skills of feeding, dressing, toileting, and grooming is of paramount importance because of their central role in any individual's life. For a mentally retarded individual, the implication of not being able to attend to these immediate and basic daily personal needs may be even more devastating than for other populations. With appropriate intervention, however, most retarded individuals, even those who are profoundly handicapped, can learn at least some self-care skills. The implications of this training are important, since with every skill an individual acquires, he or she becomes more nearly "normal," and this can result in a beneficial change in people's attitudes towards him or her. The individual may gain great satisfaction from this process, which can be demonstrated repeatedly throughout the day; the workload of those caring for the individual is lightened; and, not the least important, the ability of the individual in these areas may determine to some extent whether community living is feasible. To help mentally retarded individuals develop self-care skills, the level of deficiency must first be documented, factors contributing to this state identified, and change as a function of intervention monitored. Assessment methods that target specific self-care skills are needed for these purposes.

This chapter will critically review current methods and suggest future directions for the assessment of self-care skills. However, self-care skills are usually assessed as one part, or domain, of the more general construct of adaptive behavior and, therefore, this review will also include some methods for assessing general adaptive behavior. To provide a perspective for the specific assessment of self-care skills, a general discussion of adaptive behavior and its relationship with self-care skills will precede the review of assessment methods.

ADAPTIVE BEHAVIOR

The long-existing discontent with measuring only intelligence when determining presence and degree of mental retardation has resulted in an interest, which has consistently increased over several decades, in measuring adaptive functioning. With the American Association on Mental Deficiency (AAMD) formally adding the adaptive behavior component to the definition of mental retardation (Grossman, 1973, 1977; Heber, 1961), this interest has been intensified in the last 15 years. In a survey of various definitions of adaptive behavior, two elements typically are included: standards of performance that are socially and culturally defined, and the extent to which the individual meets these standards (Coulter & Morrow, 1978b). The AAMD definition of adaptive behavior, "the effectiveness or degree to which an individual meets standards of personal independence and social responsibility expected for age and cultural group" (Grossman, 1977, p. 11), typifies most definitional attempts. As Meyers, Nihira, and Zetlin (1979) have pointed out, adaptive behavior is thus a socially defined construct. The degree of impairment in adaptive behavior depends not only on the behavioral characteristics of an individual, but also on the social and cultural norms of the environment to which the individual is attempting to adjust. This fact creates obvious problems for developers and consumers of standardized tests of adaptive functioning.

In spite of these problems, numerous investigators guided by these definitions have developed a variety of instruments for measuring adaptive behavior, beginning with Doll (1947), who developed the Vineland Social Maturity Scale. Reflecting the diversity of environmental adaptive behavior demands that individuals are likely to encounter in their respective life situations, these instruments target several behavior domains. The most commonly included behavior domains are: self-care skills, physical development, communication skills, cognitive functioning, domestic and occupational activities, self-direction and responsibility, and socialization. Several instruments have also included domains of maladaptive behavior that focus on the increasing concern for social-emotional adjustment and correlated display of problem behaviors in mentally retarded individuals.

The relevance of self-care skills for adaptive functioning may seem obvious, given that the latter is, in part, defined as personal independence, but there are also empirical data supporting this relationship. Different factor analyses of adaptive behavior instruments (Guarnaccia, 1976; Lambert & Nicoll, 1976; Nihira, 1969a, 1969b, 1976, 1978) have consistently yielded a factor representing personal independence (e.g., functional autonomy, self-sufficiency). Items addressing self-care skills, as well as neuromotor and sensory development, always emerge as part of this factor. The face validity of including self-care skills as an important adaptive function is indisputable, a point also supported by the fact that every adaptive behavior instrument has included items addressing these skills.

Reflected in definitions of adaptive behavior, which typically are stated within the context of age, is the widely-held assumption that it is an age-related developmental attribute. This has indeed been substantiated in normative studies as well as in follow-up studies to the factor analyses described above. Nihira (1976) has described the development of adaptive behavior in mentally retarded populations in terms of factors delineated from multivariate studies. From Nihira's work, it becomes evident that the development of self-care skills, as part of the factor of personal self-sufficiency, is characterized by an initial rapid growth in early childhood, followed by slower increments of growth during adolescence, reaching the asymptote at young adulthood and remaining stable until old age. Most other adaptive behaviors follow a similar function in mildly, moderately, and severely mentally retarded populations; for profoundly mentally retarded individuals, however, adaptive behavior continues to develop into adulthood (Nihira, 1976).

While this increased emphasis on adaptive functioning has been welcomed by many in the field of mental retardation, some have objected to it, in part on the grounds that it is not sufficiently independent from the construct of intelligence. In fact, correlations *(r)* between measures of adaptive behavior and intelligence vary considerably from .09 to .83, with an average of about .50 (Meyers et al., 1979). In contrast to correlations between IQ and the adaptive domains of cognitive and language development, the correlations with self-care skills are in the lower end of this range, and similar to those with occupational, self-directional, and social skills. At a conceptual level, intelligence is distinguished from adaptive behavior in that measures of the former are always interpreted in terms of a trait system, while this is not necessarily the case for the latter. At a more practical level, measurement of adaptive behavior emphasizes everyday behavior and, in particular, the ability to cope with environmental demands, as opposed to emphasis on thought processes and potential for academic achievement.

To a large extent, self-care skills, and especially their assessment, have been viewed within the context of adaptive behavior. With increased emphasis on measuring adaptive behavior, more attention has also been paid to the measurement of self-care skills. The recent vigorous development of methods for assessing adaptive behavior and, thus, self-care skills, have occurred primarily for three reasons (Meyers et al., 1979): the AAMD included adaptive behavior in its formal definition of mental retardation, creating the need for this construct to be quantified; institutions have focused on programming, as opposed to custodial care and, thus, target behaviors and entry level skills need to be documented; and, behavioral methods have proven to be widely effective for improving adjustment and, thus, more formalized methods for measuring target behaviors to gather baseline and post-intervention data have been needed. Self-care skills have been assessed for the first two reasons primarily as one of several domains of the broader construct of adaptive behavior. Consequently, to review methods for assessing self-care skills, general adaptive behavior instruments must be inspected. This will be accomplished in the next section. Self-care skills have been assessed more independently, however, when the intent has been to apply behavior modification techniques to change them. The assessment procedures used for this purpose will be reviewed separately in a subsequent section.

ASSESSMENT OF SELF-CARE SKILLS AS AN ADAPTIVE BEHAVIOR DOMAIN

A plethora of adaptive behavior instruments exists. Walls, Werner, and Bacon (1977) listed 136 without being all-inclusive. Most of these instruments included at least some items addressing self-care behavior. For this review, 29 instruments were considered because they were published, they provided sufficient information for an evaluation of their quality and utility, and they targeted self-care skills.

In almost all instances, self-care skills are included in one or more of several domains of behavior assessed. The Balthazar Scales of Functional Independence represent the only exception, where only self-care domains are sampled. Aside from the range of adaptive behaviors measured, these instruments also vary along several other major dimensions: the *populations* for which they are intended, including age range, level of mental and physical functioning, and population setting; the *nature of the data produced* in terms of the source of information, range of behavior sampled, level of behavioral specificity, psychometric quality, and interpretation with respect to normative and/or criterion referencing; and, the related dimension of instrument *utility* at either or both the individual client and program levels.

Information pertaining to these dimensions was sought for the 29 selected adaptive behavior instruments. In addition to test manuals, previous reviews of adaptive behavior instruments were relied upon in compiling this information, summarized in Table 8-1 (Coulter & Morrow, 1978a; Doucette & Freedman, 1980; Mayeda, Pelzer, & Van Zuylen, 1978; Meyers et al., 1979; Walls et al., 1977).

General Review of Instruments

In terms of the populations targeted, the entire age range is represented across instruments, with the majority focusing either on childhood or on all age groups. A range of functioning levels is also represented, with some instruments designed for measurement of age-appropriate functioning through all levels of mental retardation, particularly for children (e.g., AAMD Adaptive Behavior Scale—School Edition, Lambert & Windmiller, 1981; Denver Developmental Screening Test, Frankenburg & Dodds, 1975; Learning Accomplishment Profile, Sanford, 1974). Others are focused on specific levels of mental retardation, such as mild to moderate (e.g., Community Adjustment Scale, Seltzer & Seltzer, 1978; Fairview Social Skills Scale, Giampiccolo & Ross, 1971; Mid-Nebraska Independent Living Screening Test, Schalock, 1975), or severe and profound (e.g., O'Berry Developmental Tests—Behavior Maturity Checklist II, Soule, Bell, & Smith, 1977;

Ohio Performance Scale, Niesen, Mays, Hardesty, & Pranitch, 1976). Self-care assessments, furthermore, often focus on behavior within the context of specific settings. A number of measures were developed and remain applicable in institutional settings (e.g., Balthazar Scales of Adaptive Behavior, Balthazar, 1973, 1976; Fairview Self-Help Scale, Ross, 1970; O'Berry Developmental Tests— Behavior Maturity Checklist II, Soule et al., 1977); these measures also frequently apply to severely or profoundly mentally retarded populations. Fewer scales were specifically designed for assessment in school settings (e.g., AAMD Adaptive Behavior Scale—School Edition, Lambert & Windmiller, 1981; TMR School Competency Scales, Levine, Elzey, Thormahlen, & Cain, 1976). Several measures for developmentally delayed and other handicapped children, however, would appear useful in a range of educational settings, including developmental daycare centers (e.g., Learning Accomplishment Profile, Sanford, 1974; Lexington Developmental Scales, Irvin, Ward, Deen, Greis, Cooley, Auvenshine, & Taylor, 1977; Progress Assessment Chart of Social and Personal Development, Gunzberg, 1977). Finally, a limited number of measures were intended for assessment of mentally retarded individuals living in community residences or group homes (e.g., Community Adjustment Scale, Seltzer & Seltzer, 1978; Social and Prevocational Information Battery—Form T, Irvin, Halpern, & Reynolds, 1977). With the increasing number of mentally retarded persons being placed in community group residences, the need for assessment of the self-care domain of adaptive functioning, which is critical to adjustment within this setting, is obvious.

The current assessment of self-care skills utilizes a variety, and often a combination, of data sources and collection procedures. The most common method involves either data obtained through interview with an individual regarded as a knowledgeable informant (e.g., parent, teacher, staff member), or a combination of interview with an informant and direct observation of the client. The client alone is far less frequently relied upon to obtain data, either by interview or by direct observation. Understandably, client report of self-care skills is not a practical approach in most cases within a mentally retarded population. Although data obtained through direct observation by trained observers, such as that yielded by the Balthazar Scales, are highly desirable for the purpose of assessing self-help "micro-behaviors," the utility of this approach is clearly limited by cost considerations. The response format of most instruments includes either behavioral ratings, checklists, or a combination thereof. Typically, responses require a judgment of the presence or absence of specific behaviors, the frequency of specified behaviors, or the highest level of performance of given behaviors. Considerable variability is found across instruments in terms of the fineness of judgment and level of inference required of the rater, characteristics that have an impact on reliability. The range and specificity of behavior sampled within the self-care and other domains of adaptive functioning also varies tremendously across instruments, as indicated by the range in number of items. Clearly, instruments such as the Minnesota Developmental Programming System—Behavioral Scales, (Bock & Weatherman, 1976) containing 80 items related to self-care, and the Balthazar Scales of Func-

Table 8-1

A Review of 29 Selected Adaptive Behavior Instruments

Instrument	Domains	Ages (years)	Data Source	Format	Products
AAMD Adaptive Behavior Scale (Nihira, Foster, Shellhaas & Leland, 1974)	24 domains (21 subdomains): Part I (10 developmental domains)—independent functioning; physical and language development; numbers and time; vocational, economic, and domestic activity; self-direction; responsibility; socialization. Part II (14 maladaptive behavior domains)—violent and destructive, antisocial, rebellious, untrustworthy, self-abusive, and sexually aberrant behavior; withdrawal; stereotyped behavior and odd mannerisms; inappropriate interpersonal manners; unacceptable vocal habits; unacceptable or eccentric habits; hyperactive tendencies; psychological disturbances; use of medications (110 items)	6 to adult	direct observation, completion and/or interview with informant	ratings, checklists	domain, subdomain scores; norms for institutional population
AAMD Adaptive Behavior Scale—School Edition (Lambert & Windmiller, 1981)	21 domains (18 subdomains): Part I (9 normal development domains as above; domestic activity not included). Part II (12 adaptive behavior domains)—aggressiveness, antisocial vs. social behavior, rebelliousness, trustworthiness, withdrawal vs. involvement, mannerisms, interpersonal manners, acceptability of vocal habits, acceptability of habits, activity level, symptomatic behavior; use of medications (95 items)	7 to 13	direct observation, completion by parent or teacher, interview with informant	ratings, checklists	domain, subdomain scores; percentile scores; factor scores and profile; comparison score
Adaptive Behavior Inventory for Children (Mercer & Lewis, 1977)	6 domains: role-performance in family; community, peer relations; nonacademic school roles; earner/consumer; self-maintenance (242 items)	5 to 11 years, 11 months	interview with informant	ratings	domain scores, total score; norms

| Standardiza-tion Sample | Reliability | | | Validity | Utility Purported by Developer | |
	Interrater	Test-Retest	Internal Consistency		Population	Purpose
4014 institution residents, 3 to 69 years of age	(Part I) $r = .71$ to .93, $\bar{r} = .86$; (Part II) $r = .37$ to $> .70$, $\bar{r} = .57$ ($n = 133$)	———	———	Part I domains correlate with IQ significantly; lower (NS) correlations with achievement tests; Part II independent of IQ and achievement scores	MR, DD, emotionally maladjusted; moderately to profoundly MR adults; all levels of children in institutions	program development, placement and evaluation; differentiation among levels and types of handicap
6500 normal, EMR, and TMR, 3 to 16 years of age, in California and Florida public	———	———	generally high $\alpha =$ coefficients of factors	domain and factor scores correlate low to moderately with IQ and achievement scores; discriminates children by placement (special education vs. regular) and classification (normal, EMR, TMR)	MR, LD, emotionally handicapped and normals in school setting	suggest areas of remediation within an educational setting; limited diagnostic value
2085 California public school children in regular classes; 3 ethnic groups	———	———	$r = .78$ to .92 for odd-even items	minimal correlations with IQ, achievement scores, and sociocultural variables	normal and mild to moderate MR from multiple cultures	individual placement, descriptive information

continued

Abbreviations key: CA—Chronological Age; DD—Developmentally Disabled; EMR—Educable Mentally Retarded; ILST—Independent Living Screening Test; ITPA—Illinois Test of Psycholinguistic Ability; MA—Mental Age; MR—Mentally Retarded; NS—non-significant; TMR—Trainable Mentally Retarded; WAIS—Wechsler Adult Intelligence Scale.

Table 8-1 (continued)

Instrument	Domains	Ages (years)	Data Source	Format	Products
Adaptive Functioning Index (Marlett, 1976)	15 domains (68 subdomains): Social Education Test—reading, writing, communication, concept attainment, number concepts, time, money handling, community awareness, motor movements; Vocational Checklist—basic work habits, work and acceptance skills; Residential Checklist—personal routines, community awareness, social maturity (274 items)	14 and older	any informant	direct test, ratings, checklists	profile, no norms
Balthazar Scales of Adaptive Behavior I. Scales of Functional Independence (Balthazar, 1976)	4 Self-Help domains (22 subdomains): eating, dressing, toileting, supplementary eating (132 items)	5 to 57	direct observation, interview with informant	ratings	domain, subdomain scores; no norms
Balthazar Scales of Adaptive Behavior II. Scales of Social Adaptation (Balthazar, 1973)	8 domains (20 subdomains): unadaptive self-directed behavior, unadaptive interpersonal behavior, adaptive self-directed behavior, adaptive interpersonal behavior; verbal communication, play activities, response to instructions, personal care and other behaviors (84 items)	all	direct observation by trained raters	checklist	domain, subdomain scores; no norms
Behavior Development Survey Individualized Data Base project; shortened version of the Adaptive Behavior Scale (1977)	6 domains: Part I (adaptive behaviors)—personal and community self-sufficiency; personal-social responsibility. Part II (maladaptive behaviors)—personal and social maladaptation; other (66 items)	all	interview with informant	ratings, checklist	domain scores; percentiles and profile histogram; norms based on Adaptive Behavior Scale

Standardiza-tion Sample	Reliability				Utility Purported by Developer	
	Interrater	Test-Retest	Internal Consistency	Validity	Population	Purpose
National norms not available; data for 5 groups are presented ($N = 524$)	$p<.05$ for all items	$r = .96$ to .99 (2-week interval)	———	———	mild, moderate and severe MR in the community or rural institutions	group and individual needs assessment, program planning, evaluation of progress
451 institution residents, 5 to 57 years of age	high using trained observers	high using trained observers	———	moderate correlations between total self-help scores and Vineland Social Maturity Scale ($r = .59$ to .67)	severely or profoundly MR in institutional setting	discriminates microbehaviors of eating, dressing and toileting; utility limited by training needed; needs assessment, program planning, evaluation and research
288 institution residents, 5 to 57 years of age	high using trained observers	high using trained observers	———	———	severely or profoundly MR in institutional setting	individual program planning
———	———	———	———	———	MR, DD	summary information for programming, planning and evaluation; utility limited by lack of data

continued

Abbreviations key: CA—Chronological Age; DD—Developmentally Disabled; EMR—Educable Mentally Retarded; ILST—Independent Living Screening Test; ITPA—Illinois Test of Psycholinguistic Ability; MA—Mental Age; MR—Mentally Retarded; NS—non-significant; TMR—Trainable Mentally Retarded; WAIS—Wechsler Adult Intelligence Scale.

Table 8-1 (continued)

Instrument	Domains	Ages (years)	Data Source	Format	Products
Cain-Levine Social Competency Scale (Cain, Levine & (Elzey, 1977)	4 domains: self-help, initiative, social skills, communication (44 items)	5 to 13	interview with informant	ratings	domain scores, percentile ranks (normed)
Camelot Behavior Checklist (Foster, 1977)	10 domains (40 subdomains): self-help; physical development; home duties; vocational, economic, and social behavior; independent travel; numerical and communication skills; responsibility (399 items)	2 to adult	direct observation or interview with informant	checklist	domain and total scores, norms available
Community Adjustment Scale (Seltzer & Seltzer, 1978)	8 domains (each by 4 dimensions—skill, performance, environmental opportunity, motivation): advanced personal care, housekeeping, communication, social adjustment, community participation, economic management, work, agency utilization (452 items)	adult	completion by informant	ratings, open and closed-ended questions	no scoring, no norms
Denver Developmental Screening Test (Frankenburg & Dodds, 1975)	4 domains: personal-social; fine motor-adaptive; language; gross motor (105 items)	birth to 6	direct observation, interview with informant	pass/fail items	age norms
Fairview Self-Help Scale (Ross, 1970)	5 domains: motor dexterity, self-help skills (toilet-training, dressing, eating, grooming), communication, social interaction, self-direction (34 items)	2 to 9	direct observation and/or completion by informant	ratings	domain and total scores; behavioral age, quotient, and level

Standardization Sample	Reliability			Validity	Utility Purported by Developer	
	Interrater	Test-Retest	Internal Consistency		Population	Purpose
716 TMR children in California, 5 to 13 years of age	$r = .94$ ($n = 23$)	$r = .88$ to .97 ($n = 35$) (3-week interval)	high for self-help and communication	discriminates severely and profoundly MR from TMR, correlates moderately with Vineland, equivocal correlation with Stanford-Binet	TMR	screening device to identify deficits for group, rapid assessment of relative standing of TMR children
revisions based on sample of 624 institutional MR	overall $r = .93$	——	——	scores correlated with measures of intelligence and adaptive behavior	not specified but assumed to be mildly to profoundly MR	group program planning
field tested on 34 clients	——	——	generally acceptable ($n = 34$)	discriminates performance between adults living in institutions vs. less restrictive environments; items rated for appropriateness by 18 experts	mild to moderate MR adults living in community residences	assessment of skill development and utilization; motivation; environment; and their interactions
1036 children in the Denver population, 2 weeks to 6.4 years of age	81 to 100%, $M = 98\%$ ($n = 72$)	$r = .66$ to .93 ($n = 175$) (1-week interval)	——	correlates highly with Revised Yale Developmental Scale, identifies high percentage of children who subsequently obtain IQ scores <70 (92%), or ≥ 70 (97%)	normal and delayed children	screening instrument, limited program planning
341 residents in state hospital	$\bar{r} = .91$ ($n = 70$)	$\bar{r} = .87$ ($n = 70$) (3-month interval)	——	for normal children, CA relates to scaled scores in curvilinear pattern; high correlations with Vineland & Cain-Levine	mildly to profoundly MR, institutionalized	screening, needs assessment, individual program planning

continued

Abbreviations key: CA—Chronological Age; DD—Developmentally Disabled; EMR—Educable Mentally Retarded; ILST—Independent Living Screening Test; ITPA—Illinois Test of Psycholinguistic Ability; MA—Mental Age; MR—Mentally Retarded; NS—non-significant; TMR—Trainable Mentally Retarded; WAIS—Wechsler Adult Intelligence Scale.

Table 8-1 (continued)

Instrument	Domains	Ages (years)	Data Source	Format	Products
Fairview Development Scale (Ross and Boroskin, 1971)	5 domains: perceptual and motor skills; self-help skills (toilet-training, dressing, feeding, grooming); language, social interaction, self-direction (26 items)	birth to 2	direct observation and/or completion by informant	ratings	domain, subdomain and total scores; developmental age, quotient, and level
Fairview Social Skills Scale (Giampiccolo & Ross, 1971	5 domains: self-help skills (locomotion, toilet-training, dressing, eating, grooming), communication, social interaction, occupation, self-direction (36 items)	10 and older	direct observation and/or completion by informant	ratings	subdomain and total scores; social age, quotient, and level
Learning Accomplishment Profile (Sanford, 1974)	6 domains: gross and fine motor, social, self-help, cognitive, language (481 items)	birth to 6	direct observation, interview with client	pass/fail items	developmental age for each domain, developmental profile
Lexington Developmental Scales (Irvin, Ward, Deen, Greis, Cooley, Auvenshine & Taylor, 1977)	4 domains (47 subdomains): motor, language, cognitive, personal-social development (424 items)	birth to 6	direct observation, parent or other report	ratings	developmental age and quotient norms in 4 areas
Mid-Nebraska Independent Living Screening Test (Schalock, 1975)	9 domains (26 subdomains): personal and home maintenance; clothing care and use; food preparation; time management; social behavior; community utilization; communication; functional academics (88 items)	18 and older	direct observation, completion of test items by client	pass/fail items	circle graph of areas and subareas, criterion-referenced
Minnesota Developmental Programming System—Behavioral Scales (Bock & Weatherman, 1976)	18 domains: gross and fine motor development; eating; dressing; grooming; toileting; receptive and expressive language; social interaction; readiness in reading; time; money; writing; numbers; domestic behavior; community orientation; recreation/leisure time activities; vocational (360 items)	all	direct observation supplemented by informant	ratings	scale bar graphs and total scores, no age norms

220

	Reliability				Utility Purported by Developer	
Standardiza-tion Sample	Interrater	Test-Retest	Internal Consistency	Validity	Population	Purpose
127 non-handi-capped chil-dren, 4 to 71 months of age	$\bar{r} = .71$ to $.94$ ($n = 163$)	$\bar{r} = .85$ to $.97$ ($n = 163$) (2-month interval)	———	for normal chil-dren, CA re-lated to total score in non-linear pattern	severely and profoundly in-stitutionalized	screening, needs assessment, in-dividual program planning
341 residents in state hospital	$r = .64$ to $.87$ ($n = 105$)	$r = .71$ to $.96$, sub-scales; $r = .84$ to $.93$, total scores ($n = 105$) (2-month interval)	———	correlates mod-ately with Vine-land Social Quotients, cur-vilinear rela-tionship between CA and social skills score	mildly and moderately MR, institutionalized	screening, needs assessment, in-dividual program planning
———	———	———	———	———	normal and DD	individual pro-gram planning and evaluation
———	$r \geqslant 90$	———	———	cognitive do-main correlates highly with Stanford-Binet, language domain correlates mod-erately with ITPA	cerebral palsied, MR, multiply handicapped	global assessment and evaluation of progress
48 individuals, 18 to 52 years of age, IQ scores 40 to 79	$r = .31$ to $.77$ (NS); $n = 8$)	———	———	significant cor-relations be-tween WAIS subscales and approximately half of the ILST areas	borderline to moderate MR	individual needs assessment, spe-cific program-ming, program and individual evaluation
1975 edition standardized on 2535 state hos-pital residents and 1877 com-munity residents	$r \geqslant .90$	———	$r \geqslant .90$	———	MR	screening instrument

continued

Abbreviations key: CA—Chronological Age; DD—Developmentally Disabled; EMR—Educable Mentally Retarded; ILST—Independent Living Screening Test; ITPA—Illinois Test of Psycholinguistic Ability; MA—Mental Age; MR—Mentally Retarded; NS—non-significant; TMR—Trainable Mentally Retarded; WAIS—Wechsler Adult In-telligence Scale.

Table 8-1 (continued)

Instrument	Domains	Ages (years)	Data Source	Format	Products
O'Berry Developmental Tests—Behavior Maturity Checklist II (Soule, Bell & Smith, 1977)	8 domains (11 subdomains): dressing, grooming, eating, toileting, communication, social interaction, ambulation, supported mobility (15 items)	children	interview with informant	ratings	behavior age and quotient (comparable to IQ score), conversion to functioning levels
Ohio Performance Scale (Niesen, Mays, Hardesty & Pranitch, 1976)	5 domains (20 mandatory subdomains): caring for self, motor development, social interaction, communication, self-maintenance	all	direct observation	ratings	domain profile, no norms
Pinecrest Behavior Meters of Primary Functioning (Cassel, 1967)	8 domains (21 subdomains): locomotion, eating, self-cleaning, self-drying, evacuation, communication, dressing and undressing, dressing and undressing motivation (138 items)	all	interview with informant	yes/no items	subdomain, domain and overall scores, no norms
Progress Assessment Chart of Social and Personal Development (6 versions—P-P-A-C, P-A-C 1, P-A-C 1A, P-A-C 2, M/P-A-C1, S/P-A-C 2 (Gunzburg, 1977)	4 domains (subdomains vary): self-help, communication, socialization, occupation (items vary)	birth to adult (6 versions target different ages)	direct observation supplemented by interview with informant	yes/no items	circular graph by domain, Progress Evaluation Index and age norms
Social and Prevocational Information Battery (Halpern, Raffeld, Irvin & Link, 1975)	9 domains: purchasing habits, budgeting, banking, job-related behaviors, job search skills, home management, physical health, personal hygiene and grooming, functional signs (277 items)	14 to 20	client responses to oral administration	true/false items	domain and total scores, percentile rank
Social and Prevocational Information Battery—Form T (Irvin, Halpern & Reynolds, 1977)	9 domains (same as above): (291 items)	14 to 20	client responses to oral administration	true/false items	domain and total scores, percentile rank

	Reliability				Utility Purported by Developer	
Standardiza-tion Sample	Interrater	Test-Retest	Internal Consistency	Validity	Population	Purpose
731 institutional mentally retarded	———	$r = .88$ ($n = 30$) (1-month interval) $r = .87$ ($n = 103$) (1-year interval)	split-half $r = .96$	moderate correlations obtained with IQ measures	institutionalized severely and profoundly MR	screening, needs assessment and individual program development
———	———	———	———	———	institutionalized severely and profoundly MR	program unit placement, group and individual program development
———	85 to 100% agreement ($n = 28$)	75 to 100% agreement ($n = 34$)	———	———	institutionalized severely and profoundly MR	individual placement, planning and evaluation of progress
4 of 6 versions standardized on different samples ranging in size from 144 to 337	total battery $= .97$	———	———	P-A-C1 and M/P-A-C domain scores correlate moderately with Stanford-Binet and Peabody scales, correlates highly with Vineland	institutionalized and non-institutionalized MR	individual assessment and evaluation of progress
reference group data obtained from 453 Junior High and 453 Senior High students in Oregon	———	$r = .70$ to .79; .94 overall (Junior High); $r = .62$ to .78; .91 overall (Senior High) ($n = 253$; 1-week)	Kuder-Richardson $= .78$ to .82; .94 overall	moderate correlation between pre-publication version and 5 criterion vocational rehabilitation subscales over one year	EMR	evaluation for training and community placement, planning programs, evaltion of progress
186 residents of 25 group homes in 6 northwestern states and 200 in TMR classes in Pennsylvania	———	———	α-coefficient $= .78$ to .87 (homes); .68 to .82 (TMR)	moderate correlations with corresponding domains of the Behavior Rating Form	TMR	evaluation of training and community placement, planning programs, evaluation of progress

continued

Abbreviations key: CA—Chronological Age; DD—Developmentally Disabled; EMR—Educable Mentally Retarded; ILST—Independent Living Screening Test; ITPA—Illinois Test of Psycholinguistic Ability; MA—Mental Age; MR—Mentally Retarded; NS—non-significant; TMR—Trainable Mentally Retarded; WAIS—Wechsler Adult Intelligence Scale.

Table 8-1 (continued)

Instrument	Domains	Ages (years)	Data Source	Format	Products
The TARC (Topeka, Kansas, Association for Retarded Citizens) Assessment System Sailor & Mix, 1975)	4 domains (12 subdomains): self-help, motor, and communication skills; social behavior (26 items)	3 to 16	interview with informant	ratings; checklists	profile of domain and subdomain scores; total inventory score; standard scores available
TMR School Competency Scales— Form I & Form II (Levine, Elzey, Thormahlen & Cain, 1976)	5 domains: perceptual motor, initiative-responsibility, cognition, personalsocial, language Form I—91 items; Form II—103 items	Form I— 5 to 10 Form II— 11 and older	direct observation	ratings	domain score and percentile; full scale percentile and norms
Uniform Performance Assessment System— Birth to Six Years Scale Bendersky, 1977)	4 domains (25 subdomains): pre-academic, communication, social/self-help, gross motor (265 items)	birth to 6	direct observation	checklist	criterion-referenced, no norms
Vineland Social Maturity Scale (Doll, 1965)	8 domains; self-help general, eating, and dressing; locomotion; occupation; communication; self-direction; socialization (117 items)	3 months to adult	interview with informant	ratings	total score converted to social age and quotient, norms available
Vulpé Assessment Battery (Vulpé, 1977)	8 domains (43 subdomains): basic senses and functions; gross motor behaviors; cognitive processes and specific concepts; organization of behavior; activities of daily living; environment (1127 items)	birth to 6	direct observation or interview with informant	ratings	profile, no summary scores or norms

<table>

| | Reliability | | | | Utility Purported by Developer | |
Standardiza-tion Sample	Interrater	Test-Retest	Internal Consistency	Validity	Population	Purpose
283 severely handicapped, 3 to 16 years of age, moderate to profound MR	r = .63 to .95, overall = .85 (n = 66)	r > .80 (n = 66) (6-month interval)	———	———	severely and profoundly MR	individual pro-gram planning and monitoring of progress
302 TMR stu-dents rated by 80 teachers in California schools, 5 to 17 years of age and older	———	———	split-half = .80 to .98	———	TMR	assessment and development of school instruc-tional plan
———	———	———	———	———	normal and handicapped	assessment of developmental status, program development
620 white rural and community residents of New Jersey, birth to 30 years	high	r = .98 (n = 250) 1.7–1.9 year interval	———	correlates with CA, moderately to highly related to Binet MA scores, differen-tiates MR from non-MR, and handicapped vs. nonhandicapped	all disabilities	selection of group training programs and planning
———	———	———	———	———	developmen-tally handi-capped	planning and evaluation of individual programs

Abbreviations key: CA—Chronological Age; DD—Developmentally Disabled; EMR—Educable Mentally Retarded; ILST—Independent Living Screening Test; ITPA—Illinois Test of Psycholinguistic Ability; MA—Mental Age; MR—Mentally Retarded; NS—non-significant; TMR—Trainable Mentally Retarded; WAIS—Wechsler Adult Intelligence Scale.

tional Independence, (Balthazar, 1976) containing 132 such items, represent a greater range and specificity in assessment than, for example, the Fairview Social Skills Scale, or the Cain-Levine Social Competency Scale, (Cain, Levine, & Elzey, 1977) containing 7 and 13 self-care items, respectively. As will be discussed shortly, these differences across instruments should be considered in the selection of measures for specific purposes.

Table 8-1 summarizes data that were found pertaining to instrument reliability (including inter-rater, test-retest, and internal consistency estimates), validity (particularly construct and predictive validities) and utility. The majority of instruments have some relevant psychometric data, with inter-rater reliabilities and validity data reported most frequently. In the vast majority of cases where inter-rater reliability data are reported, moderate to high levels are found. Validity data typically involve correlations with IQ measures (such as the Stanford-Binet), achievement scores, or other scales of adaptive behavior (e.g., Vineland Social Maturity Scale). Correlations with IQ generally yield moderate values, although in some cases, equivocal results have been obtained (e.g., AAMD Adaptive Behavior Scale—School Edition, Cain-Levine Social Competency Scale). Moderate to high correlations are generally obtained when comparing scores (e.g., Balthazar Scales of Social Adaptation, Balthazar, 1973; Cain-Levine Social Competency Scale; Fairview Self-Help Scale; Progress Assessment Chart of Social and Personal Development) with another measure of self-care, particularly the Vineland. In a few reported cases, lower values are obtained for correlations with achievement test performance (e.g., AAMD Adaptive Behavior Scale, Nihira, Foster, Shellhaas, & Leland, 1974; AAMD Adaptive Behavior Scale—School Edition). This pattern of validity findings, whereby overall the highest correlations are obtained with another measure of self-care and the lowest correlations with a measure of academic achievement, is not at all surprising considering the differential degree of content overlap in these comparisons.

A surprising number, nearly one-quarter, of the adaptive behavior instruments that include self-care skills, do not have information relevant to standardization. A slightly higher portion do not have associated normative data with which the total and/or domain scores of individuals can be compared. Clearly, the lack of such information prohibits the generalizability of tests across situations, or the comparability of test scores across individuals for purposes of program placement or large-scale evaluation of multiple programs. One must consider in evaluating these instruments: the scores yielded by various measures, the availability of normative data, and the corresponding interpretability of scores vis-à-vis a standard population, prior to instrument selection.

Closely related to the dimensions of targeted populations and data characteristics is the consideration of instrument utility. Utilization of specific measures is dependent upon the population or individual in need of assessment, as well as the data the examiner wishes to obtain and the interpretability desired. An additional aspect of utility is, of course, the purpose or goal intended by the assessment.

Whereas some measures are more useful for evaluation at an individual client level, others provide important data relevant to programming for groups of individuals. Major factors that differentiate these functions include: behavioral specificity of test items, reliability, aggregation of data into total and standard scores, and time and cost involved in data collection and interpretation. Instruments characterized by greater behavioral specificity and item reliability are generally better designed for individual clinical application, whereas those conducive to comparability of scores across programs and cost effectiveness are frequently more useful at the program level (Doucette & Freedman, 1980). The instruments reviewed in Table 8-1 are purported by their developers to be appropriate for different purposes. Specification of the behavioral deficits of individuals and training objectives may be well achieved, for example, using the Adaptive Functioning Index (Marlett, 1976), the Mid-Nebraska Independent Living Screening Test, or the Social and Prevocational Information Battery—Form T. These measures represent a deliberate attempt to develop behavioral training programs on the basis of assessment data. The Adaptive Functioning Index also includes guidelines for the use of incentives for goal attainment. Other measures may be particularly useful for evaluation of client progress at a very fine level (e.g., Balthazar Scales), or at a more global though behavioral level (e.g., Learning Accomplishment Profile; Pinecrest Behavior Meters of Primary Functioning, Cassell, 1967; Progress Assessment Chart of Social Personal Development; and the Topeka, Kansas Association for Retarded Citizens (TARC) Assessment System, Sailor & Mix, 1975). Instruments such as the Learning Accomplishment Profile, the TMR School Competency Scales, and Uniform Performance Assessment System (Bendersky, 1977) have been regarded as useful in developing Individual Educational Plans, or in the case of adults, the Mid-Nebraska is recommended for outlining Individual Habilitation Plans (Doucette & Freedman, 1980). Selection and placement in community vocational settings would appear aided by the Social and Prevocational Information Battery—Form T. Finally, several measures have been designed specifically as screening instruments (e.g., Denver Developmental Screening Test) to determine the need for further individualized assessment.

At the program level, behavioral objectives may be defined and curricula planned using a variety of the individualized instruments noted above. Selection of individuals for appropriate program units and the establishment of unit-by-unit program objectives are goals specifically intended by the Ohio Performance Scale. Large-scale research or evaluation projects may best utilize relatively low cost and more gross measures, such as the Behavior Development Survey (1977) and the Minnesota Developmental Programming System.

Selected Instruments

Although many instruments are available for the measurement of adaptive behavior and, in part, self-care skills, only a few are used with any degree of generality across sites. Survey data obtained from professionals working in the field of mental retardation in Texas, for example, indicate that the AAMD Adaptive Behavior Scale and its public school version, together with the Vineland Social Maturity Scale, were the most frequently used measures (Coulter & Morrow, 1978c). These three scales, in addition to the Adaptive Behavior Inventory for Children (Mercer & Lewis, 1977) and the Balthazar Scales of Adaptive Behavior, which represent more recent and alternative approaches to adaptive behavior measurement, will be reviewed in more detail, with emphasis on their assessment of self-care skills.

AAMD Adaptive Behavior Scale. The AAMD Adaptive Behavior Scale (ABS) Nihira, Foster, Shellhaas, & Leland, 1974) is a behavior rating scale for use with mentally retarded, emotionally maladjusted, and developmentally disabled individuals, ages 3 to 69 years of age, who are institutionalized. The first part, organized along developmental lines, covers 10 behavioral domains important to the maintenance of personal inependence, including self-care skills. In the second part, the 14 domains focus primarily on maladaptive behavior related to personality and behavior disorder. Three administration methods are permissible: the informant can complete it, the informant is interviewed and the interviewer completes it, or several informants provide the desired information which is synthesized by the interviewer. Using the interview format, it takes between 30 to 60 minutes to complete.

The ABS was standardized on approximately 4,000 individuals residing in 68 mental retardation facilities in the United States. Based on these data, percentile norms are presented in the manual for 11 age groups. These norms, however, do not take into account differing cognitive levels (Sundberg, Snowden, & Reynolds, 1978). A serious limitation is the lack of test-retest and internal consistency reliability estimates in the manual. Interrater reliabilities, on the other hand, appear acceptable across domains for Part I (mean $r = .86$), but appear questionable for Part II domains (mean $r = .57$). Some of the Part II domains have been noted to correlate highly with each other, suggesting considerable redundancy in those domains (Leva, 1976). A fair amount of data exist supporting the validity of the ABS such as the following observations: it discriminates between individuals who are judged to be at different adaptive functioning levels and who are in different placements within the institution (Nihira et al., 1974); it is sensitive to changes resulting from interventions (Sattler, 1982); it relates to measures of intelligence (Christian & Malone, 1973); and it yields a reliable factor structure consistent with expectations (Nihira, 1969a, 1969b).

With respect to self-care skills as conceived in this chapter, the ABS covers all the major ones including: eating (items targeting skills with utensils, independence in eating in public, level of table manners); toileting (frequency of accidents, independence at toilet); hygiene for overall body, skill with tooth brushing, independence with menstruation if applicable); and dressing (skill at dressing appropriately, level of care for clothes, independence with dressing, independence with undressing, independence with use of shoes). The formal ABS domain of independent functioning, for which a separate score is obtained, also includes items targeting posture, sense of direction, use of public transportation, use of telephone, and miscellaneous functions (e.g., bed making, use of mail service). While the inter-rater reliability for this domain is reported to be very good ($r = .92$), to our knowledge separate item reliabilities are not available. This limitation unfortunately prohibits the use of specific item data for programming or evaluation. This is unfortunate because the items targeting the various self-care skills appear potentially useful for this purpose; that is, for the most part, they are specific, objective, and structured in such a fashion as to suggest criterion-referenced possibilities.

In summary, the ABS appears to be a clinically useful scale for the purpose of classification, but not for specific programming or evaluation. This is in contrast to its purported utility, as noted in Table 8-1. Both practitioners and researchers have found the scale useful for describing the adaptive performance of mentally retarded individuals in terms of daily living skills and complex social and interpersonal skills. Drawbacks have been noted, however, with the standardization sample, which includes only institutionalized individuals, and with the reliability data being limited both in kind and, for part of the scale, in quality. Finally, the lack of a summary score, although theoretically understandable, makes practical decision-making difficult since a complex profile of 25 points must be interpreted.

AAMD Adaptive Behavior Scale—School Edition (ABS-SE). The ABS has been restandardized for use with school children, first as the AAMD Adaptive Behavior Scale—Public School Version (Lambert, Windmiller, Cole, & Figueroa, 1975) and recently as the AAMD Adaptive Behavior Scale—School Edition (ABS-SE) (Lambert & Windmiller, 1981). The following description will pertain to the current revision. The ABS-SE is used with children ages 3 years, 3 months, to 17 years, 2 months. Otherwise it is similar to the ABS, except that those domains not applicable to the school setting have been eliminated and several summary scores can be calculated. That is, instead of solely yielding domain scores, like the ABS, the ABS-SE also yields five empirically derived factor scores (Personal Self-Sufficiency, Community Self-Sufficiency, Personal-Social Responsibility, Social Adjustment, and Personal Adjustment) and a comparison score, which is a single score based on an empirically validated weighted combination of the first three factor scores.

The ABS-SE was standardized on 6,500 children, primarily from California, who were of appropriately varied ethnic, socioeconomic, and living environment groups and who were enrolled in regular, Educable Mentally Retarded (EMR), and Trainable Mentally Retarded (TMR) school programs. Rather than providing percentiles, the manual now provides tables for converting raw scores into scaled factor scores for three comparison groups, representing regular, EMR, or TMR placements. Population distributions of factor scores and the comparison score are also provided. The only reliability data reported in the manual were in the form of internal consistency indices for the different factor scores, which varied as a function of the specific factor, as well as with the age and school placement of the evaluation sample. Whereas the majority of the internal consistency indices were reported to be above .60, there was a range between .27 and .97. Validity data are more abundant, however. Correlations of ABS-SE domain scores and factor scores with IQ vary, but for the most part have remained below .40. Further, domain scores predicted, independently and in the form of regression equations, the classroom placements of students 7 through 12 years of age. Data also showed that children assigned to regular, EMR, and TMR programs were significantly different with respect to adaptive behavior, as measured by the ABS-SE. Moreover, within these classifications, boys and girls from different ethnic groups had, on the average, similar levels of adaptive behavior. The comparison score, finally, correctly classified an average of 74 percent of the students into current school placements. Given the recency of the ABS-SE, it must be realized that the psychometric data provided are all by the scale developers.

The same self-care skills are included in the ABS-SE as in the ABS. No reliability data for these items nor for the domain of independent functioning, however, are reported. This prohibits the reliable use of information obtained from the ABS-SE with respect to self-care behaviors and presents a problem for the use of the ABS-SE for the specific assessment of self-care skills.

In summary, the ABS is attractive from a consumer's point of view, is easy to use, and is practical with the various scores it yields. There is even a separate manual to aid in instructional planning based on the ABS-SE (Lambert, Windmiller, Thoringer, & Cole, 1981). Unfortunately, as it stands now, there is little to support the use of the ABS-SE other than for classification purposes. The domain scores are without sufficient psychometric support, not to mention the item scores, making programming and evaluation based on these scores currently indefensible. Investigators are urged to remedy this situation quickly, because on the surface of it, the ABS-SE appears promising.

Vineland Social Maturity Scale.   The forerunner to adaptive behavior measurement is the Vineland Social Maturity Scale (VSMS) (Doll, 1947, 1965). It is a developmental schedule purported to measure social competence from birth to maturity with 117 items. These items are divided into eight categories, three of which target self-care skills: Self-Help General, Self-Help Dressing, and Self-Help Eating. The majority of the self-care items are found in the age range up to and including early childhood. Inferences about the presence or absence of certain behaviors relevant to the items are made based on an interview with the caretaker. This takes between 15 to 30 minutes. The VSMS yields a Social Age (SA) that is based upon the raw number of items passed, and that is often then used to calculate a Social Quotient ratio.

The standardization sample for the VSMS is quite limited as it consists of only ten males and ten females at each age level from birth to 30, all caucasian and living in New Jersey. Test-retest reliability over a period of two as well as three years has been good based on Social Age ($r \geqslant .94$). Comparisons between information obtained from mothers and teachers have indicated discrepancies, however, with mothers reporting higher levels of competence (Kaplan & Alatishe, 1976). In terms of validity, the VSMS has been reported to differentiate mentally retarded from nonretarded individuals, as well as other handicapped from non-handicapped individuals; to be substantially correlated with changes in chronological age, and to be moderately to highly related to intelligence, as assessed by Stanford-Binet Mental Age scores (Doucette & Freedman, 1980).

Although separate categories on the VSMS exist corresponding to certain self-help skills, no technical data are available for these or, for that matter, for the other categories. The Self-Help General category includes items primarily targeting motor skills, but also inludes two items addressing toileting. The Self-Help Eating category appears rather complete in its coverage of utensil use and a few other relevant eating skills (e.g., discriminates edibles, masticates food). The Self-Help Dressing category, aside from covering various dressing skills, deals as much with hygiene skills. A major problem with the first two of these developmental scales is that, while they include a good number of items up through age two or three, there are very few items beyond that age. This makes the VSMS insensitive to behavior changes in relatively short periods of time. (There is a downward extension and expansion of the VSMS for the preschool level, the Preschool Attainment Record [Doll, 1966], which might be better suited for this purpose.) Furthermore, the criteria for the items in these three categories, as is the case for many of the rest of the items, are often vague and imprecise.

In conclusion, the major difficulties with the VSMS are the inadequate standardization and relatively limited psychometric properties. The use of the ratio SQ also presents problems since, as with a ratio IQ, the standard deviation is not comparable at different ages. Silverstein (1971) has, however, provided tables for the conversion of the SQ into a deviation score, thereby standardizing the variability at each age. In light of these problems, nonetheless, it is questionable for what purposes the VSMS can currently be recommended. Its strength seems to lie in that, unlike most other adaptive behavior scales, it is a developmental scale with age norms, which can be informative at a descriptive level. It certainly is not an adequate instrument for assessing self-care skills at this point. It may be that the revision of the VSMS currently under development can overcome the noted deficiencies.

Adaptive Behavior Inventory for Children. (ABIC) (Mercer & Lewis, 1977) is a relatively recent addition to the adaptive behavior instruments, but it has already created a great amount of controversy. This is probably due more to the theoretical conceptions of the authors guiding the development of their comprehensive system of Multicultural Pluralistic Assessment (Lewis & Mercer, 1978), of which the ABIC is a part, rather than any characteristic of the scale itself. It attempts to provide a multidimensional view of the child's role-functioning across the family, school, and community systems of which the child is a part. The ABIC yields separate scaled scores based on its 242 items for six areas of adaptive functioning, as well as yielding a Total Score. The Self-Maintenance area comes closest to the self-care skills domain addressed in this chapter, but also covers ability to cope with unfamiliar social situations and to maintain control under stress or distractions. The ABIC is administered as an interview questionnaire with the primary caretaker and is available in both English and Spanish. As the name implies, it is intended for use with children 5 to 12 years of age. The standardization sample consists of 2085 California public school children, 5 to 12 years of age, approximately equally distributed across the three primary ethnic groups. The manual reports odd-even reliabilities of satisfactory quality across ages, ethnic groups, and behavior domains (median $r = .86$), but other reliability data are lacking. The relatively high intercorrelations (median $r = .77$) among domain scores, however, call into question the independence, and therefore the utility of these separate domains. Consistent with their attempts to maximize the independence between measures of adaptive and intellectual functioning, very low correlations between the total scores and various IQ scores have been reported ($r \leq .19$) (Sapp, Horton, McElroy, & Ray, 1979). Further construct validity support was provided by the insignificant correlations ($r \leq .19$) obtained between the ABIC and sociocultural variables (e.g., family size, socioeconomic status (SES), living environment), regardless of ethnic group (Mercer & Lewis, 1977). No criterion-referenced validity data could be found, which is needed.

Since the ABIC is a norm-referenced instrument intended solely for classification purposes, it only samples some of the self-care behaviors and does not describe level of functioning in behavioral terms. The items sampling self-care skills, like most others, are relatively specific and objective. They are often answered in terms of how independently or how often the child demonstrates the skill. The answer format generally attempts to discriminate latent, emergent, and master proficiency. In spite of these good features, though, specific self-care skills cannot be assessed with the ABIC and, even though the subscale of Self-Maintenance has good reliability ($r \geq .81$), it is confounded with skills in other than the self-care area.

In summary, the principal strength of the ABIC appears to be its format, content validity, and good psychometric properties for those that have been assessed thus far. Several reviewers have concluded that it is a potentially strong instrument (Oakland, 1979; Sattler, 1982), some even proposed that it is better than its competitors, the ABS-SE and the VSMS (Scott, 1979). It must be emphasized, however, that these statements rest more on its potential rather than on its demonstrated strength at this point. On the negative side, besides lacking much psychometric information, the ABIC norms may not be applicable nationwide (Buckley & Oakland, 1977). The ABIC is also only useful for a relatively small age range. Finally, the function of ABIC is limited to classification, with no apparent utility for programming or evaluation, and it is not a good instrument for the specific assessment of self-care skills.

Balthazar Scales of Adaptive Behavior. (BSAB) (Balthazar, 1973, 1976) represent a more objective, but also more limited, approach to the assessment of adaptive behavior. This system consists of two parts: Part I. Scales of Functional Independence (BSAB-I) (Balthazar, 1976), and Part II. Scales of Social Adaptation (BSAB-II) (Balthazar, 1973). They were designed for the assessment of severely and profoundly mentally retarded institutionalized individuals. Both scales are completed following direct observation, over several days if necessary, by the rater. Scores therefore represent the actual display of the behavior in question, for example, in frequency out of a sample of ten occurrences, or in frequency rate per minute. The scales are intended specifically for evaluating the effectiveness of an intervention, being very suitable for yielding pre- and post-scores. They are also intended for measuring the functioning level of a limited range of adaptive skills.

The BSAB were standardized on severely and profoundly mentally retarded residents at only one institution in Wisconsin. They ranged in age from 5 to 57 and numbered between 122 and 288, depending on the specific subscale. Interrater reliability is reported to exceed .93 for BSAB-I, but ranges much lower for BSAB-II (median = 81 percent). Presumably because results from these scales are not intended to be used for inferential or predictive purposes and solely as measures of the specific target behaviors, validity data were not in the manual.

The BSAB-I appears to sample rather exhaustively from the self-care subdomains of toileting, feeding, and dressing, but does not target grooming. The rater directly observes eating and dressing behaviors, while an informant is questioned about toileting behavior. With respect to feeding skills, opportunities to display 58 separate behaviors relevant to dependent feeding, spoon usage, fork usage, finger foods, and drinking are observed ten times and the number of occurrences of each behavior is tallied. In addition, the presence or absence is noted regarding 32 other feeding behaviors in a total of seven categories (i.e., self service, assistance devices, type of food, positioning, rate of eating, advanced utensil usage, supervision). Opportunities to display 32 dressing behaviors (30 for females) are similarly observed and the number of successes out of ten attempts is recorded (e.g., "tie single bow—right/left," "unfasten belt," "button blouse"). The toileting subscale is divided into day-time and night-time behavior and separately targets bladder and bowel elimination, as well as some general toileting behaviors (e.g., adjusts clothing, indicates accident). A total of 12 toileting behaviors thus are assessed in terms of the number of times out of ten opportunities these behaviors were displayed. The manual (Balthazar, 1976) provides detailed criteria and instructions for scoring these self-care behaviors.

The Balthazar scales, in summary, are intriguing instruments. Clearly, they do not appear useful for a broad-based assessment of adaptive behaviors. However, the BSAB-I should yield very detailed information about three of the primary self-care subdomains and prove useful for treatment planning and evaluation. Unfortunately, the target behaviors are relevant primarily for institutionalized populations. The utility for the assessment of community-based individuals remains to be seen. Psychometric data are scant. While the premise for not providing validity data is in part understandable, it would still be good to have data for constrasted groups and pre- and post-intervention, for example, to support the utility of these scales. In spite of this lack of data, several investigators have supported the use of the BSAB (Meyers, 1978; Proger, 1973). It is our feeling that, while much more research is needed on these scales, the BSAB-I appears to have the best potential for fine-grained and treatment-relevant assessment of self-care skills of the instruments reviewed.

DIRECT MEASUREMENT OF SELF-CARE SKILLS

Self-care skills have been assessed more independently when the purpose has been to provide objective information for specific behavior modification programs. From this standpoint, the relatively global categories of behavior typically measured with adaptive behavior instruments are not sufficiently precise to be useful. In order for self-care behaviors to be developed they must first be carefully specified and, therefore, observable overt responses must be assessed. Kazdin and Straw (1976) noted three purposes of assessing overt behavior directly: to reveal the precise extent to which the target behavior is performed, partly in order to establish its baseline prior to intervention; to test whether mere observation temporarily changes behavior since assessment often is reactive (Webb, Campbell, Schwartz, & Sechrest, 1966); and, to reflect behavior change after treatment has been implemented through comparison with baseline performance.

The first step in direct observation is to select the target behavior. This behavior needs to be described in terms so that few inferences are required to detect a response. It is often helpful to observe the client informally in order to accomplish this. In the case of self-care skills, this rather global concept needs to be broken down into components (e.g., feeding, toileting), which in turn are further broken down into specific target behaviors (e.g., spoon behavior, cup behavior) that can be reliably observed. These behaviors then become the object of assessment and behavior change, rather than the global concept. Three criteria have been suggested for an adequate response definition (Hawkins & Dobes, 1975). First, the definition should be objective and refer to observable characteristics of the behavior and, if applicable, environmental events. Second, it should be clear and unambiguous so that it could be read, repeated, and paraphrased accurately. Finally, it should be complete, with the boundary conditions of the definition delineated so that the responses that are to be included and excluded are enumerated.

The extent to which a response definition is objective, clear, and complete determines, in part, whether observers will agree in scoring the behavior, as well as whether the behavior of the client or the perceptions of the observers are changing over the course of treatment.

Although the assessment of target behaviors is necessary, it is not always sufficient. The assessment of antecedent and consequent events that may be associated with the target behavior is also important (Kazdin & Straw, 1976). In the case of feeding skills, for example, intervention would focus on this behavior in response to the particular stimuli of lunch time or food on the plate. Performing the target behavior per se may not be of interest unless some event has preceded it. Furthermore, assessing stimulus events is important in evaluating intervention. Antecedent and consequent events are always manipulated to alter the target behavior, as in the case of a shaping program intended to teach dressing skills. The failure to assess the events that will be used in designing a program to alter a client's behavior can make the basis for behavior change unclear.

There are several strategies for directly assessing behaviors such as self-care skills. The most common way is a simple frequency-count of the specific target behavior. As an alternative, in particular when several behaviors are targeted, interval recordings can be conducted, where the presence or absence of behaviors is noted for time intervals of a predetermined length. A duration measure also can be obtained, although for the behaviors involved in the various self-care skills, which typically are discrete, this is less applicable. Finally, the number of individuals can be counted who display a particular skill, according to a strict definition. This may be relevant when evaluating ward programs, for example. Selecting among these strategies is dictated by such factors as the goals of the intervention, the behaviors to observe, the rate of responding, the ease with which the behaviors can be detected, and a variety of practical concerns. For a further review of these strategies see Kazdin and Straw (1976).

Rather extensive literature exists describing behavioral interventions for self-care skills including feeding, toileting, hygiene, and dressing. The direct observation methods of assessing these self-care skills in the context of behavior modification programs are reviewed in the following sections.

Feeding

The self-care skill of feeding can be defined to include a range of behaviors at different levels of complexity. The most common way of measuring feeding skills has been to focus on inappropriate feeding behaviors. Azrin and Armstrong (1973), for example, counted the number of time intervals eating errors were observed. These were defined to include spilling, use of inappropriate utensil, oversize bites, eating spilled food, handfeeding, throwing food, stealing food, and drooling. They reported an overall interobserver agreement of 96 percent for this rather comprehensive system. Christian, Holloman, and Lanier (1973) represent a simpler approach as they counted the following as inappropriate eating behaviors: hand-to-food eating, eating directly from a tray, and stealing. In addition, they measured eating time. Another example is Martin, McDonald, and Omichinski (1971), who calculated the rate per minute from interval recordings of slopping food, eating with hands, playing with utensils, and yelling. Although these categories were defined further, reliability probes yielded highly variable interobserver agreement from 50 to 100 percent between checks. Other listings of inappropriate feeding behaviors have included food-throwing (Hamilton & Allen, 1967) and fast eating (Henriksen & Doughty, 1967).

In contrast, other investigators have focused on appropriate behaviors. Song and Gandhi (1974) calculated the percentage of correct feeding responses during meals out of the total number of feeding responses. Nelson, Cone, and Hanson (1975) calculated the percentage of intervals when correct use of utensil was observed. Both of these groups reported reliabilities above 90 percent. Richman, Sonderby, and Kahn (1980) provided a highly objective definition of correct use of a fork: the ability to grip the fork in one of the standard, socially acceptable positions depicted by Nelson et al. (1975), impale the presented material securely on the tines, and bring the fork to within three inches of the mouth. Observers agreed in scoring this response during training meals at an average of 94 percent.

Still other investigators have assessed both appropriate and inappropriate feeding behaviors, representing more inclusive approaches. O'Brien, Bugle, and Azrin (1972) targeted both correct feeding, defined as the taking of food from a bowl with a spoon held right side up by the handle and bringing food to the mouth without spilling, and incorrect feeding, defined as an error in correct feeding. Interobserver agreements of 97 and 94 percent, respectively, were reported. Miller, Patton, and Henton (1971) used a similar approach, but they defined appropriate feeding as when the food reached the client's mouth by spoon for non-finger food or by the fingers in the case of finger food (e.g., fruit).

Two teams of investigators have approached the task of observing feeding behavior in a more comprehensive fashion. Barton, Guess, Garcia, and Baer (1970) counted the number of intervals in which any of seven behaviors occurred: stealing, finger feeding, messy utensil use (spilling, face-to-plate, finger-to-utensil), neat utensil use (not messy), pigging (eating spilled food, eating without use of fingers or utensil), other behavior, and no behavior. They reported an average of 90 percent interobserver agreement for this system. Finally, O'Brien and Azrin (1972) probably represent the most comprehensive observation system of feeding behavior, consisting of ten categories. They recorded separately correct use of spoon, glass, fork, and hand in eating; meat cutting; use of napkin; and butter transport. They also recorded incorrect eating responses, incorrect preparatory feeding responses, and other inappropriate responses. The last category was defined as any other response that would be determined improper if performed by a customer in a restaurant. They reported an impressive 99 percent agreement between independent observers using this system.

Toileting

Toileting is a more discrete and limited behavior than feeding. Consequently, more circumscribed observational systems have been used to measure toileting for purposes of behavioral interventions. Most approaches have obtained a frequency count of accidents in bowel movements and/or urination (Doleys & Arnold, 1975; Levine & Elliot, 1970), and voids in toilet (Baumeister & Klosowski, 1965; Raborn, 1978). Smith, Britton, Johnson, and Thomas (1975) counted the number of self-initiated voiding episodes in the toilet, as well as the number of accidents. Dayan (1964) and Kimbrell, Luckey, Barbuto, and Love (1967) represent a different, less direct, but also ingeniously unobtrusive approach. They measured and reported the weight of the laundry generated per a specified time unit by each resident or living unit. Dayan (1964) also counted the number of outbreaks of shigella dysentery, which is transmitted by bacteria growing in human waste. These investigators argued convincingly that their measures are directly correlated with toileting skills and showed changes occurring as a function of intervention. While well-suited as general outcome measures, these indirect measures do not provide information on the person's skill level for planning an intervention program. The few behavior modification programs targeting nighttime toileting skills have relied on simple measures of frequency of wet nights (Azrin, Sneed, & Foxx, 1973; Sloop & Kennedy, 1973; Smith, 1981).

As with feeding skills, a few investigators have developed more detailed and objective observational methods to monitor toileting skills. Smith (1979), measured several variables of importance including the frequency of urinary incontinence, the proportion of trials when urine was passed while seated on the toilet as part of the training and, as a general outcome measure, independence with toileting. The last variable was defined as consistently self-initiated continent toileting. In addition, Smith is one of the only investigators who reported amount of staff time needed to train the clients, an important comparative outcome measure. Dissatisfied with the reliability of staff recorded toileting accidents as they occurred (50 percent agreement), Azrin and Foxx (1971) had the staff check whether the clients' pants were wet or dirty every hour for one eight-hour shift each day of training. They reported an agreement of 100 percent on all checks. Not only is this an impressive observer reliability, it is also the only reliability figure reported for the direct observation of toileting behavior. Finally, Mahoney, Van Wagenen, and Myerson (1971) presented a very detailed and highly treatment-relevant observation system. Through a rating from one to ten, which was assigned for each trial, they communicated the toileting behavior displayed by the clients (e.g., walk to commode, lower pants, position, urination) and the level of prompting needed from staff to achieve this behavior (i.e., physical, verbal, none). Through this criterion-referenced observation system, they were able to effectively trace the acquisition of toileting behavior as well as determine the appropriate entry level of training for each client.

Hygiene

Although many skills are involved in the display of hygiene and undoubt-edly much effort is expended on teaching these skills in various institutions, re-markably few behavior modification programs with these skills have actually been published. Two could be found that relied upon observations in developing an operational definition of toothbrushing, one subarea of hygiene skills. Hamilton and Allen (1967) had staff rate the amount of effort needed to get the clients to come to the bathroom to brush or to have their teeth brushed. The rating scale values had behavioral anchors to facilitate their objective assignment (e.g., comes when called). Horner and Keilitz (1975) developed a criterion-referenced obser-vation system in which toothbrushing was broken down into 15 steps (e.g., pick up and hold toothbrush, brush the inside surfaces of the teeth, rinse the sink). They then recorded the type of prompting needed to get the clients to emit each of these steps (i.e., no help, instruction, demonstration and instruction, physical aid and instruction). An agreement of 97 percent was noted between observers. Their system appears well-suited for both programming and evaluation, as dem-onstrated in their study. Treffry, Martin, Samels, and Watson (1970) studied hands and face washing, using a criterion-referenced approach. They developed a sys-tem of recording both the amount and type of prompting needed for the clients to display each of the 12 steps involved in washing hands and face. While specific information obtained from this system provided good programming data, they also used a summary score, based on the number of steps performed without physi-cal or verbal prompts, as the outcome measure in their evaluation of a behavioral training program. Finally, Matson, DiLorenzo, and Esveldt-Dawson (1981) de-veloped a 27-step sequence to showering (e.g., acquire wash cloth, wash left arm, rinse off soap), of which some steps had to be carried out in a particular order. Trained observers then scored clients who participated in a training pro-gram as to which steps they performed correctly or incorrectly. They agreed on an average of 96 percent of all responses.

Dressing

Dressing skills have not been the object of many published behavioral inter-ventions either. Azrin, Schaeffer, and Wesolowski (1976) defined a criterion for their training (i.e., dress in each of five garments to criterion without assistance after one verbal prompt, and remove them after one verbal prompt) and noted only its achievement. Since this complete behavior was not broken down further, their approach offers little for a finer assessment of dressing skills. In contrast, Ball and his colleages (Ball, Serie, & Payne, 1971; Minge & Ball, 1967) have provided a novel approach to this end. They developed a "situation test," con-sisting of 11 items relating to dressing, undressing, and attention. In this procedure, clients are prompted to emit each of 11 relevant behaviors (e.g., unbutton shirts) and their performance on each is rated. Since no psychometric data were reported, this approach cannot be formally evaluated, but it appears conceptually promising. Other constructs, representing response capabilities, have been successfully assessed in this manner (e.g., social skills), arguing for further work using a situation test format for assessing self-care skills.

SUMMARY AND RECOMMENDATIONS

This overview of methods and principles for the assessment of self-care skills as an adaptive behavior domain leads to the following summary statements:

1. Adaptive behavior has become an increasingly important variable in the definition of mental retardation. Cognitive skills are no longer seen as the sole basis for determining a person's level of functioning and potential for independent living.
2. Adaptive behavior is defined by specific behaviors in specific social contexts and the acquisition of adaptive skills is age-related.
3. The self-care skills of feeding, dressing, toileting and rooming are included at some level in virtually all definitions of adaptive behavior and of assessment instruments for adaptive behavior. Self-care proficiency level has a considerable impact on a person's daily living and a certain level is often viewed as a prerequisite for normalization.
4. One of two approaches generally have been followed in assessing self-care skills: they have been assessed as one type of adaptive behavior, along with many others, in general surveys of adaptive functioning, primarily for purposes of classification; or, they have been assessed as the specific target behaviors in direct observational systems, primarily for purposes of developing and evaluating behavioral interventions. This chapter reviewed specific techniques within both of these assessment approaches.
5. In terms of assessing self-care skills as an adaptive behavior, 29 instruments were reviewed chosen on the basis of published information. Five currently popular instruments were reviewed in more detail. The adaptive-functioning assessment instruments varied along several dimensions that were considered, including target population, setting, format, psychometric quality, and utility, as well as in their coverage of self-care skills.
6. In general, these instruments assessing adaptive behavior currently lack much-needed psychometric support, in particular for the specific measurement of self-care skills. Most of the instruments notably have not been standardized on a representative sample.
7. The observational systems assessing specific self-care skills have tended to

be narrowly focused and idiosyncratically developed to suit certain purposes. Therefore, they lack general utility, although there are a few comprehensive systems that may have potential for more general use.

8. Given the importance of self-care skills in the conception of overall level of functioning, it is surprising that no comprehensive system has yet been developed that meets all the needs for assessment: classification, program development, and treatment evaluation. No attempt has been made at combining or dovetailing the two separate approaches reviewed into a system where an individual's level of functioning could be determined, intervention planned with entry target behaviors delineated, and treatment evaluated.

These summary statements naturally give rise to recommendations for the advancement of self-care assessment. It should be obvious from this review that adaptive behavior assessment in general is still in its infancy and this applies even more to the assessment of self-care skills. Much more work is needed in both of these areas. A primary concern should still be the psychometric status of available instruments. Even some of the better-developed and better-researched instruments, like the AAMD Adaptive Behavior Scale—School Edition, still lack basic properties, including inter-rater reliabilities. Other instruments are in much worse condition, even lacking fundamental standardized norms.

The psychometric quality must first be demonstrated for any instrument before it should be allowed to be used as a basis for decisions. The specific criteria for this process are set forth in *Standards for Educational Psychological Tests and Manuals* (American Psychological Association, 1974). Furthermore, when information about self-care skills is sought from general adaptive assessment instruments, either subscale or item data have to be employed. In this case, these data also must meet certain minimum psychometric criteria. Since most of the instruments reviewed fail in this consideration, because they lack psychometric data, self-care skills strictly speaking should not be assessed with these instruments. Clearly, these deficiencies must be repaired soon.

As was noted, there usually seems to be very little relationship between assessment for classification and treatment, at least in the way self-care skills are being assessed. The adaptive behavior instruments are useful for establishing an adaptive level of functioning and, possibly, a self-care level of proficiency in general terms. The specific observational systems, in contrast, can specify target behaviors for treatment and provide means for evaluating treatment. Effort must now be put into combining these two approaches. First, adaptive behavior instruments could be used to isolate problem domains, such as self-care skills, which then are followed up by direct observations of only the problem domains. In other words, the two approaches can dovetail each other. Such a hierarchical assessment system obviously would need to be formalized and evaluated first.

Along similar lines, the relationship between data from interview scales and observational systems need to be investigated. That is, can interview data obtained from a caretaker be relied upon to represent actual behavior? Of course, since the interview scales are likely to draw information from an extended time period, in contrast to typical observations, this comparison is confounded. Through appropriate time sampling in conducting the observations, however, this confound could be minimized, especially in lower-functioning populations. The concern is that second-hand report is as much, if not more, a measure of the perceptions of the interviewee, rather than of the behavior itself. These perceptions admittedly are important, since they shape the attitudes and behaviors of others towards the mentally retarded individual. Nonetheless, if there is only a small relationship between interview data and actual display of behavior, the former cannot be considered a measure of the latter. Empirical results bearing upon this concern, thus, are sorely needed.

It was refreshing to see amidst the prevalent interview scales the commercial publication of a naturalistic observational approach to the assessment of self-care skills in the form of the Balthazar Scales of Adaptive Behavior. While clearly more limited in scope than the interview scales, the introduction of these observational scales allows comparisons of different assessment approaches. Possibly there are still other approaches to the assessment of adaptive behavior in general, and in self-care skills specifically. A test format perhaps could be explored, for example, in which items could be presented that would adequately represent an area or domain, much like what is done on an individual IQ-test. It seems that most self-care skills could be relatively conveniently assessed in this manner, while more complex adaptive behaviors admittedly could create problems. In any event, it is felt the overreliance on secondary report in the assessment of adaptive behavior needs to be decreased.

Finally, one may ask whether developing potentially more time-consuming and more involved assessment procedures for adaptive behavior is justified. We know that many professionals, including ourselves, at times behave in a manner suggesting that the assessment of adaptive behavior is not an important endeavor, at least not in relative terms. In an evaluation of possible retardation, adaptive functioning often seems to be assessed as an afterthought, if at all, and then typically only in a cursory fashion. The investment in time and energy to this end frequently is dwarfed compared to that put into the assessment of cognitive functioning. How many of us will routinely spend on adaptive assessment the hour or two we typically spend on administering, scoring, and interpreting an IQ-test? While the portion of the professionals who do this undoubtedly is increasing, in light of changing regulations and new awareness, we are afraid it still is too small. However, given the comparable weight now afforded adaptive and cognitive functioning in considering level of retardation and, ultimately more important, the sizable documented relationship between adaptive functioning and life adjustment (Robinson & Robinson, 1976), should we even question the utility of adaptive behavior assessment? If we no longer do, our behavior needs to change to reflect that positive attitude as well, and much more attention will need to be paid to adaptive behavior assessment, both on the research-development end and the professional practice end.

Acknowledgment

The helpful comments provided by Betty Conover on an earlier draft of this chapter are acknowledged.

REFERENCES

American Psychological Association. *Standards for educational and psychological tests and manuals.* Washington, DC: American Psychological Association, 1974

Azrin, NH, & Armstrong, PM. The "mini-meal"—A method for teaching eating skills to the profoundly retarded. *Mental Retardation,* 1973, *11,* (2), 9–13

Azrin, NH, & Foxx, RM. A rapid method of toilet training the institutionalized retarded. *Journal of Applied Behavior Analysis,* 1971, *4,* 89–99

Azrin, NH, Schaeffer, RM, & Wesolowski, MD. A rapid method for teaching profoundly retarded persons to dress by a reinforcement-guidance method. *Mental Retardation,* 1976, *14* (6), 29–33

Azrin, HN, Sneed, TJ, & Foxx, RM. Dry bed: A rapid method of eliminating bedwetting (enuresis) of the retarded. *Behaviour Research and Therapy,* 1973, *11,* 427–434

Ball, TS, Serie, K, & Payne, LG. Long-term retention of self-help skill training in the profoundly retarded. *American Journal of Mental Deficiency,* 1971, *76,* 378–382

Balthazar, EE. *Balthazar scales of adaptive behavior—scales of social adaptation.* Palo Alto, CA: Consulting Psychologists Press, Inc., 1973

Balthazar, EE. *Balthazar scales of adaptive behavior for the profoundly and severely mentally retarded—scales of functional independence.* Palo Alto, CA: Consulting Psychologists Press, Inc., 1976

Barton, ES, Guess, D, Garcia, E, & Baer, DM. Improvement of retardates' mealtime behaviors by timeout procedures using multiple baseline techniques. *Journal of Applied Behavior Analysis,* 1970, *3,* 77–84

Baumeister, AA, & Klosowski, R. An attempt to group toilet train severely retarded patients. *Mental Retardation,* 1965, *3*(6), 24–26

Behavior Development Survey. Pomona, CA: University of California—Los Angeles, Neuropsychiatric Institute, 1977

Bendersky, M (Ed.), *Uniform performance assessment system—birth to six years scale.* Seattle, WA: Child Development and Mental Retardation Center, 1977

Bock, WH, & Weatherman, RF. *Minnesota developmental programming system—Behavioral scales.* St. Paul, MN: Outreach Training Project, 1976

Buckley, KJ, & Oakland, TP. *Contrasting Localized Norms for Mexican-American Children on the ABIC.* Paper presented at the meeting of the American Psychological Association, San Francisco, CA, August, 1977

Cain, LF, Levine, S, & Elzey, FF. *Cain-Levine social competency scale.* Palo Alto, CA: Consulting Psychologists Press, Inc., 1977

Cassell, RH. *Pinecrest behavior meters of primary functioning.* Bossier City, LA: R. H. Cassell, 1967

Christian, WP, Holloman, SW, & Lanier, CL. An attendant operated feeding program for severely and profoundly retarded females. *Mental Retardation,* 1973, *11*(5), 35–37

Christian, WP, & Malone, DR. Relationships among three measures used in screening mentally retarded for placement in special education. *Psychological Reports,* 1973, *33,* 415–418

Coulter, WA, & Morrow, HW. A collection of adaptive behavior measures. In WA Coulter & HW Morrow (Eds.), *Adaptive behavior: Concepts and measurements.* New York: Grune & Stratton, 1978 (a)

Coulter, WA, & Morrow, HW. A contemporary conception of adaptive behavior within the scope of psychological assessment. In WA Coulter & HW Morrow (Eds.), *Adaptive behavior: Concepts and measurements.* New York: Grune & Stratton, 1978 (b)

Coulter, WA, & Morrow, HW. One year after implementation: Practitioners' views of adaptive behavior. In WA Coulter & HW Morrow (Eds.), *Adaptive behavior: Concepts and measurements.* New York: Grune & Stratton, 1978 (c)

Dayan, M. Toilet training retarded children in a state residential institution. *Mental Retardation,* 1964, *2,* 116–117

Doleys, DM, & Arnold, S. Treatment of childhood encopresis: Full cleanliness training. *Mental Retardation,* 1975, *13*(6), 14–16

Doll, EA. *Social maturity scale.* Circle Pines, MN: American Guidance Service, 1947

Doll, EA. *Social maturity scale.* Circle Pines, MN: American Guidance Service, 1965

Doll, EA. *DAR, Preschool attainment record, research edition manual.* Circle Pines, MN: American Guidance Service, 1966

Doucette, J, & Freedman, E. *Progress tests for the developmentally disabled: An evaluation.* Cambridge, Massachusetts: Abt Books, 1980

Foster, R. *Camelot behavior checklist.* Lawrence, KS: Camelot Behavioral Systems, 1977

Frankenburg, W, & Dodds, J. *Denver developmental screening test.* Denver, CO: LADOCA Project and Publishing Foundation, 1975

Giampiccolo, JS, & Ross, RT. *Fairview social skills scale.* Westminster, CA: Giampiccolo and Ross, 1971

Grossman, H (Ed.). *Manual on terminology and classification in mental retardation* (special publication No. 2). Washington, DC: American Association on Mental Deficiency, 1973

Grossman, H. *Manual on terminology and classification in mental retardation,* (1977 rev.). Washington, DC: American Association on Mental Deficiency, 1977

Guarnaccia, V. Factor structure and correlates of adaptive behavior in noninstitutionalized retarded adults. *American Journal of Mental Deficiency,* 1976, *80,* 543–547

Gunzberg, HC. *Progress assessment chart of social and personal development.* Briston, IN: Aux Chandelles, 1977

Halpern, A, Raffeld, P, Irvin, LK, & Link, R. *Social and prevocational information battery.* Monterey, CA: CTB/McGraw-Hill, 1975

Hamilton, J, & Allen, P. Ward programming for severely retarded institutionalized residents. *Mental Retardation,* 1967, *5*(6), 22–24

Hawkins, RP, & Dobes, RW. Behavioral definitions in applied behavior analysis: Explicit or implicit. In BC Etzel, JM LeBlanc, & DM Baer (Eds.), *New developments in behavioral research: Theory, methods, and applications. In honor of Sidney W. Bijou.* Hillsdale, NJ: Lawrence Erlbaum, 1975

Heber, RA. A manual on terminology and classification in mental retardation (2nd ed.). *American Journal of Mental Deficiency,* 1961, *66,* (monograph suppl.)

Henriksen, K, & Doughty, R. Decelerating mealtime behavior in a group of profoundly retarded boys. *American Journal of Mental Deficiency,* 1967, *72,* 40–44

Horner, RD, & Keilitz, I. Training mentally retarded adolescents to brush their teeth. *Journal of Applied Behavior Analysis,* 1975, *8,* 301–309

Irvin, JV, Ward, MN, Deen, CC, Greis, AB, Cooley, V, Auvenshine, A, & Taylor, FC. *The Lexington developmental scales.* Lexington, KY: The United Cerebral Palsy of Bluegrass Child Development Centers, Inc., 1977

Irvin, LK, Halpern, AS, & Reynolds, WM. *Social and prevocational information battery—Form T.* Monterey, CA: CTB/McGraw-Hill, 1977

Kaplan, HE, & Alatishe, M. Comparison of ratings by mothers and teachers on preschool children using the Vineland Social Maturity Scale. *Psychology in the School,* 1976, *13,* 27–28

Kazdin, AE, & Straw, HK. Assessment of behavior of the mentally retarded. In M Hersen & AS Bellack (Eds.), *Behavioral assessment: A practical handbook.* New York: Pergamon, 1976

Kimbrell, DL, Luckey, RE, Barbuto, PFP, & Love, JG. Operation dry pants: An intensive habit-training program for severely and profoundly retarded. *Mental Retardation,* 1967, *5*(2), 32–36

Lambert, N, & Nicoll, R. Dimensions of adaptive behavior of retarded and nonretarded public school children. *American Journal of Mental Deficiency,* 1976, *81,* 135–146

Lambert, N, & Windmiller, M. *AAMD adaptive behavior scale—school edition.* New York: McGraw-Hill, 1981

Lambert, N, & Windmiller, M, Cole, LJ, & Figueroa, R. *AAMD adaptive behavior scale* (rev. ed.). Washington, DC: American Association on Mental Deficiency, 1975

Lambert, N, Windmiller, M, Thoringer, D, & Cole, L. *AAMD adaptive behavior scale—school edition: Administration and instruction planning manual.* New York: McGraw-Hill, 1981

Leva, RA. Relationships among the self-direction, responsibility, and socialization of the Adaptive Behavior Scale. *American Journal of Mental Deficiency,* 1976, *81,* 297–298

Levine, MN, & Elliot, CB. Toilet training for profoundly retarded with a limited staff. *Mental Retardation,* 1970, *8*(3), 48–50

Levine, S, Elzey, FF, Thormahlen, P, & Cairn, LF. *TMR school competency scales.* Palo Alto, CA: Consulting Psychologists Press, Inc., 1976

Lewis, JF, & Mercer, JR. The system of multicultural pluralistic assessment: SOMPA. In WA Coulter & HW Morrow (Eds.), *Adaptive behavior: Concepts and measurements.* New York: Grune & Stratton, 1978

Mahoney, K, Van Wagenen, RK, & Mayerson, L. Toilet training of normal and retarded children. *Journal of Applied Behavior Analysis,* 1971, *4,* 173–181

Marlett, NJ. *Adaptive functioning index social education test, vocational checklist, residential checklist.* Calgary, Alberta, Canada: The Vocational Rehabilitation Research Institute, 1976

Martin, GL, McDonald, S, & Omichinski, M. An operant analysis of response interactions during meals with severely retarded girls. *American Journal of Mental Deficiency,* 1971, *76,* 68–75

Matson, JL, DiLorenzo, TM, & Esveldt-Dawson, K. Independence training as a method of enhancing self-help skills acquisition of the mentally retarded. *Behaviour Research and Therapy,* 1981, *19,* 399–405

Mayeda, T, Pelzer, I, & Van Zuylen, JE. *Performance measures of skill and adaptive competencies in the developmentally disabled.* Los Angeles, CA: University of California, 1978

Mercer, JR, & Lewis, JF. *System of multicultural pluralistic assessment.* New York: The Psychological Corporation, 1977

Meyers, CE. Review of the Balthazar Scales of Adaptive Behavior. In OK Buros (Ed.), *The eighth mental measurement yearbook.* Highland Park, NJ: Gryphon Press, 1978

Meyers, CE, Nihira, K, & Zetlin, A. The measurement of adaptive behavior. In NR Ellis (Ed.), *Handbook of mental deficiency.* Hillsdale, NJ: Lawrence Erlbaum, 1979

Miller, HR, Patton, ME, & Henton, KR. Behavior modification in a profoundly retarded child: A case report. *Behavior Therapy,* 1971, *2,* 375–384

Minge, HR, & Ball, TS. Teaching of self-help skills to profoundly retarded patients. *American Journal of Mental Deficiency,* 1967, *71,* 864–868

Nelson, GL, Cone, JD, & Hanson, CR. Training correct utensil use in retarded children: Modeling vs. physical guidance. *American Journal of Mental Deficiency,* 1975, *80,* 114–122

Niesen, N, Mays, M, Hardesty, K, & Pranitch, C. *Ohio performance scale.* Columbus, OH: Office of Habilitation Services, 1976

Nihira, K. Factorial dimensions of adaptive behavior in adult retardates. *American Journal of Mental Deficiency,* 1969, *73,* 868–878 (a)

Nihira, K. Factorial dimensions of adaptive behavior in mentally retarded children and adolescents. *American Journal of Mental Deficiency,* 1969, *74,* 130–141 (b)

Nihira, K. Dimensions of adaptive behavior in institutionalized mentally retarded children and adolescents. *American Journal of Mental Deficiency,* 1976, *81,* 215–226

Nihira, K. *Dimensions of maladaptive behavior in institutionalized mentally retarded persons.* Paper presented at the 4th annual Western Conference on Mental Retardation, ''The Profoundly Mentally Retarded,'' Corpus Christi, TX, May, 1978

Nihira, K, Foster, R, Shellhaas, M, & Leland, H. *AAMD adaptive behavior scale.* Washington, DC: American Association on Mental Deficiency, 1974

Oakland, T. Research on the ABIC and ELP: A revisit to an old topic. *School Psychology Digest,* 1979, *8,* 209–213

O'Brien, F, & Azrin, NH. Developing proper mealtime behaviors of the institutionalized retarded. *Journal of Applied Behavior Analysis,* 1972, *5,* 389–399

O'Brien, F, Bugle, C, & Azrin, NH. Training and maintaining a retarded child's proper eating. *Journal of Applied Behavior Analysis,* 1972, *5,* 67–72

Proger, BB. Review of the Balthazar Scales of Adaptive Behavior. *Journal of Special Education,* 1973, *7,* 95–101

Raborn, J. Classroom applications of the Foxx-Azrin toileting program. *Mental Retardation,* 1978, *16,* 173–174

Richman, JS, Sonderby, T, & Kahn, JV. Prerequisite vs. *in vivo* acquisition of self-feeding skill. *Behaviour Research and Therapy,* 1980, *18,* 327–332

Robinson, NM, & Robinson, HB. *The mentally retarded child* (2nd ed.). New York: McGraw-Hill, 1976

Ross, RT. *Fairview self-help scale.* Westminster, CA: RT Ross, 1970

Ross, RT, & Boroskin, A. *Fairview development scale.* Westminster, CA: Ross and Boroskin, 1971

Sailor, W, & Mix, BJ. *The TARC Assessment System.* Lawrence, KS: H & H Enterprises, Inc., 1975

Sanford, AR. *Learning accomplishment profile.* Chapel Hill, NC: Chapel Hill Training Outreach Project, 1974

Sapp, GL, Horton, W, McElroy, K, & Ray, P. An analysis of ABIC score patterns of selected Alabama school children. In *Proceedings of the National Association of School Psychologists/California Association of School Psychologists and Psychometrists,* San Diego, CA, April 1979

Sattler, JM. *Assessment of children's intelligence and special abilities* (2nd ed.). Boston: Allyn & Bacon, 1982

Schalock, RL. *Mid-Nebraska Independent Living Screening Test.* Hastings, NE: Mid-Nebraska Mental Retardation Services, 1975

Scott, LS. *Texas Environmental Adaptation Measure: Its Use in Classification and Planning.* Paper presented at the meeting of the National Association of School Psychologists, San Diego, CA, 1979

Seltzer, MM, & Seltzer, G. *Community Adjustment Scale.* Cambridge, MA: Educational Projects, Inc., 1978

Silverstein, AB. Deviation social quotients for the Vineland Social Maturity Scale. *American Journal of Mental Deficiency,* 1971, *76,* 348–351

Sloop, EW, & Kennedy, WA. Institutionalized retarded nocturnal enuretics treated by a conditioning technique. *American Journal of Mental Deficiency,* 1973, *77,* 717–721

Smith, L. Training severely and profoundly mentally handicapped nocturnal enuretic. *Behaviour Research and Therapy,* 1981, *19,* 67–74

Smith, PS. A comparison of different methods of toilet training the mentally handicapped. *Behaviour Research and Therapy,* 1979, *17,* 33–43

Smith, PS, Britton, PG, Johnson, M, & Thomas, DA. Problems involved in toilet-training profoundly mentally handicapped adults. *Behaviour Research and Therapy,* 1975, *13,* 301–307

Song, AJ, & Gandhi, R. An analysis of behavior during the acquisition and maintenance phases of self-spoon feeding skills of profound retardates. *Mental Retardation*, 1974, *12*,(7), 25–28

Soule, D, Bell, J, & Smith, D. *O'Berry Developmental Tests: Behavior Maturity Checklist II*. Goldsboro, NC: O'Berry Center, 1977

Sundberg, ND, Snowden, LR, & Reynolds, WM. Toward assessment of personal competence and incompetence in life situations. In MR Rosenzweig & LW Porter (Eds.), *Annual review of psychology*, 1978, *29*, 179–221

Treffry, D, Martin, G, Samels, J, & Watson, C. Operant conditioning of grooming behavior of severely retarded girls. *Mental Retardation*, 1970, *8*(4), 29–33

Vulpé, SG. *Vulpé Assessment Battery*. Downsview, Ontario, Canada: National Institute of Mental Retardation, 1977

Walls, RT, Werner, TJ, & Bacon, A. Behavior checklists. In JD Cone & RP Hawkins (Eds.), *Behavioral assessment: New directions in clinical psychology*. New York: Brunner/Mazel, 1977

Webb, EJ, Campbell, DT, Schwartz, RD, & Sechrest, L. *Unobtrusive measures: Nonreactive research in the social sciences*. Chicago: Rand McNally, 1966

Bruce M. Menchetti
Frank R. Rusch
Sister Diane M. Owens

9

Vocational Training

Vocational competence is associated with mentally retarded persons' successful community integration and therefore represents an important ingredient in their education and development (Baker, Seltzer, & Seltzer, 1977; Cobb, 1972; Mithaug, 1981; O'Connor, 1976; Rusch & Mithaug, 1980; Schalock & Harper, 1978; Schalock, Harper, & Carver, 1981; Scheerenberger, 1976; Scheerenberger & Felsenthal, 1977). In fact, today educators recommend vocational preparation be the primary goal toward which all educational experiences lead (Bates & Pancsofar, 1981; Rusch, Rusch, Menchetti, & Schultz, 1980; Wilcox & Bellamy, 1982). Awareness of the importance of vocational preparation has facilitated development of the more traditional rehabilitation counseling approach (Brolin, 1976; Wright, 1980), as well as the behavior analytic approach (Bellamy, Horner, & Inman, 1979; Rusch & Mithaug, 1980; Wehman, 1981).

All approaches to vocational training, regardless of their orientation, share the need for some preliminary information about an individual. Brolin (1976) stated that vocational assessment should be a comprehensive process that includes the interactions and expertise of many professionals to assure that all services, educational and rehabilitational, are coordinated to best serve each individual. As a result of the importance of vocational assessment, information is collected from various sources (e.g., interests batteries, manual dexterity tests, work samples, adaptive behavior scales) and used for different purposes (e.g., determining eligibility for services, identifying training needs, developing individual program plans).

Recently, Halpern, Lehmann, Irvin, and Heiry (1982) delineated two different types of assessment approaches, each with its own instrumentation and purpose. These include the traditional and contemporary assessment approaches. Traditional assessment refers to those approaches that employ measures such as intelligence tests, aptitude tests, and interest surveys for the purpose of classifying individuals. Typically, traditional assessment data are utilized to determine eligibility for services. Contemporary assessment, on the other hand, utilizes measures of targeted work and social behaviors. The purpose of collecting contemporary assessment data is to facilitate identification of an individual's training needs. Halpern et al. (1982) suggested the emergence of contemporary assessment as the most pragmatic means of assessing the educational needs of mentally retarded individuals.

A similar trend toward more program-related assessment information has developed in vocational assessment (Schalock & Karan, 1979). Program-related assessment promotes opportunity for entry and potential for success within the vocational training system. Identifying vocational needs is especially crucial for individuals with severe mental retardation since these individuals require the greatest concentration of training resources (Gold, 1973). Schalock and Karan (1979) called for the improvement of vocational assessment procedures, beginning with a close, interactive relationship between assessment and training activities. They suggested a shift in the focus of assessment, away from a prediction orientation toward a skill deficit identification orientation.

We also recommend replacement of the psychometric approach and its prediction emphasis with an edumetric approach and its emphasis upon the development of functional skills. The movement of vocational assessment from the traditional, psychometric to the contemporary, edumetric purposes is the organizational theme of this chapter, which overviews various vocational assessment approaches and examines their utility for the purposes of training.

TRADITIONAL APPROACHES TO VOCATIONAL ASSESSMENT

Three approaches, which reflect the traditional classification purpose of assessment, are currently used to assess vocational performance of mentally retarded adults. These approaches include a psychological measurement approach, a motor measurement approach, and a work sample approach. Earlier vocational assessment approaches emphasized the use of psychological variables as measures of workers' performance. Baumeister (1967) concluded that attitudes toward users of the traditional measurement approach indicated they were valued as testers but not as contributors to the remediation of problems associated with mentally retarded individuals.

Psychological Measurement Approach

Several psychological variables have been used in an attempt to predict the performance of mentally retarded workers. These variables include intelligence, occupational interest, and aptitude. Table 9-1 lists several of the more popular

Table 9-1

Representative Tests Measuring Psychological Variables

IQ TESTS

Instrument	Brief Description	Author	Publisher
Revised Beta Exam	A strictly timed, non-verbal measure of general intelligence.	Kellogg & Morton (1978)	The Psychological Corporation, New York
Slosson Intelligence Test	An individually administered test used to screen mental ability.	Slosson (1981)	The Psychological Corporation, New York
Wechsler Adult Intelligence Scale-Revised	An individually administered intelligence test for persons 16 years and and older, yielding a verbal, performance and full scale IQ.	Wechsler (1980)	The Psychological Corporation, New York
Wide Range Intelligence and Personality Test	An instrument that measures verbal, pictorial, numerical, muscular, spacial, and perceptual abilities.	Jastak (1978)	Guidance Associates of Delaware, Inc., Wilmington, DE

INTEREST TESTS

Instrument	Brief Description	Author	Publisher
AAKID-Becker Reading Free Vocational Interest Inventory	An objective inventory that assesses an individual's work preference.	Becker (1975)	American Association on Mental Deficiency, Washington, D.C.
Geist Picture Interest Inventory	An interest test, which is primarily pictorial, with a minimum of verbal questioning.	Geist (1978)	Western Psychological Services, Los Angeles
Kuder Preference Record	An instrument designed to assess interests in activities covering 10 occupational areas.	Kuder (1976)	Science Research Associates, Inc., Chicago
Picture Interest Inventory	A nonverbal interest survey of six fields of interest including interpersonal natural, mechanical, business, esthetic, and scientific.	Weingarten (1958)	CTB/McGraw-Hill Monterey, CA

continued

Table 9-1 (continued)

IQ TESTS			
Instrument	*Brief Description*	*Author*	*Publisher*
Vocational Interest and Sophistication Assessment (VISA)	A nonverbal pictorial inventory that measures selected vocational in-interests and awareness of career options.	Parnicky, Kahn, Burdett (1970)	Ohio State University Columbus, OH
Wide Range Interest and Opinion Test	A pictorial instrument that determines voca-cational and educational interest of individuals; unbiased with regard to age, sex, mental ability, cultural background, and educational history	Jastak & Jastak (1979)	Guidance Associates of Delaware, Inc., Wilmington, DE
APTITUDE TESTS			
Bennett Mechanical Comprehensive Test	An instrument designed to measure ability to understand the relation-ship between physical laws and mechanical ele-ments in practical studies	Bennett (1969)	The Psychological Corporation, New York
General Clerical Test	A test that measures clerical speed and accuracy, numerical ability, and verbal skills.	no authors (1972)	The Psychological Corporation, New York
Minnesota Clerical	An instrument designed to measure aptitude for clerical work and to select personnel whose jobs consist of quick recognition of numbers and letters.	Andrews, Patterson, & Longstaff (1961)	The Psychological Corporation, New York
Revised Minnesota Paper Form Board	A nonverbal, mechanical ability test that requires the capacity to visualize and to manipulate ob-jects in space.	Likert & Quasha (1970)	The Psychological Corporation, New York

and currently available intelligence tests, interest tests, and aptitude tests. This list is not intended to present readers with a complete index of available tests. Our inclusion of any one particular test in Table 9-1, or subsequent tables, does not constitute an endorsement nor does omission of any one test imply our dissatisfaction.

Intelligence tests, such as the Wechsler Adult Intelligence Scale (WAIS) and the Stanford-Binet, have been shown either to discriminate between different worker groups (Appell, Williams, & Fishell, 1962) or to correlate with other measures of work performance (Wagner & Hawver, 1965). For example, Tobias and Gorelick (1962) found "planfullness" scores on the Porteus Maze Test (Porteus, 1965) correlated with success in competitive employment. Additionally, the proponents of the psychological approach to assessment have utilized IQ tests to predict vocational potential of mentally retarded people. Gold (1973) pointed out, however, that these tests were validated by studies investigating concurrent validity, rather than predictive validity. Cronbach (1960) suggested the concurrent validation information has limited generality when tests are used to make predictions regarding potential performance. The limited generality relates to temporal differences betweeen concurrent and predictive validation. Concurrent validity refers to a test's ability to correlate with an individual's current performance on some criterion measure. In the case of intelligence tests, scores have been typically correlated with workers' current vocational performance. Predictive validity, on the other hand, refers to a test's ability to correlate with future performance on a criterion measure. Thus, concurrent validation results suggest little about an individual's future vocational performance. As Gold (1973) suggested, the distinction between concurrent and predictive validity must be made when tests are used to assess the vocational behavior of workers because training can substantially alter their performance level. Psychological measures reporting only concurrent validity, therefore, have limited usefulness for predicting work performance.

Other psychological measures, which have been used to predict mentally retarded workers' future performance, include occupational interest tests such as the Kuder Preference Record (Kuder, 1934), the Wide Range Interest and Opinion Test (Jastak & Jastak, 1970), and the AAMD—Becker Reading Free Vocational Interest Inventory (Becker, 1975). Two of these tests, the Wide Range Interest and Opinion Test and the Kuder Preference Record, included scores from a nonretarded population as the criteria in their standardization process. Including a normative group with quite different characteristics from those with whom the test is intended to be used is a second general limitation of the psychological measurement approach. In order to make relevant comparisons the normative group must resemble individuals with whom a test will be used (Cronbach, 1960). Obviously, this is not the case when comparing nonretarded and retarded groups.

Interestingly, Becker, Schull, and Cambell (1981) suggested a functional use for interest tests in the vocational assessment process. Becker et al. (1981) validated the AAMD—Becker Reading Free Vocational Interest Inventory (Becker,

1975) for the moderately mentally retarded, adult population. This inventory includes a pictorial, vocational interest inventory designed to assess job preference. Becker et al. (1981) measured mentally retarded adults' vocational interests several times throughout their participation in job training programs via a structured interview and with the responses on the inventory. A five-year follow-up study investigated the job retention of individuals placed in the community. Statistically significant relationships between a person's expressed and inventoried interests led Becker et al. (1981) to suggest that moderately mentally retarded adults can discriminate between occupational likes and dislikes. The reliability coefficients obtained through repeated administrations of the inventory were in the .60 to .80 range, the majority being significant at the .05 level. Finally, the results of the five-year follow-up found that of the 50 original subjects, 32 were still employed in the jobs for which they originally indicated a preference. These results suggest the ability of the AAMD-Becker Reading Free Vocational Interest Inventory to predict employment retention. Becker et al. (1981) suggested that vocational interest inventories have utility for counseling and guidance decisions. As more vocational training opportunities are provided to mentally retarded adults, interest inventories may play an important role in the vocational assessment process.

Psychological measures of aptitudes, such as spatial perception as measured by the Minnesota Paper Form Board Test (Patterson, Elliott, Anderson, Toops, & Heidbreder, 1920), the ability to understand mechanical relationships as measured by the Bennett Mechanical Comprehension Test (Bennett, 1940), and the quick recognition of numbers or letters as measured by the Minnesota Clerical Test (Andrews, Patterson, & Longstaff, 1933) have also been applied to the problem of assessing the vocational performance of mentally retarded adults. Aptitude tests share many of the weaknesses of interest and intelligence tests including the use of nonretarded comparison groups and validation studies that investigated concurrent rather than predictive validity issues. These weaknesses limit the ability of aptitude measures to predict the future vocational performance of mentally retarded workers or, more importantly, to identify their training needs.

Summary

Tests that have been developed via the psychological measurement approach have little usefulness in identifying mentally retarded adults' training needs. As a result, their role in the vocational assessment process should be limited to selection, identification, and classification functions only. The ability of psychological measures, like intelligence aptitude tests, must be evaluated in light of what is measured by their content. If it is useful to identify a worker as having a low aptitude for spatial relationships or to classify workers as mildly, moderately, or severely mentally retarded, then these measures may have a function in the assessment process. Becker et al. (1981) suggest that information obtained by interest inventories, such as the AAMD—Becker Reading Free Vocational Interest Inventory, is related to job retention; such information may be helpful in selecting vocational training alternatives for mentally retarded individuals. A training-oriented approach to vocational assessment, however, must emphasize the collection of information directly related to work skills.

Motor Measurement Approach

The motor measurement approach focuses upon the assessment of motor skills, which, on the surface, appear to be related to work performance. Advocates of the motor measurement approach to vocational assessment typically measure motor performance in an effort to predict work performance. Manual dexterity tests including the Purdue Pegboard Test (Tiffen, 1968), the Minnesota Rate of Manipulation Test (Minnesota Employer Stabilization Research Institute, 1969), and the Pennsylvania Bi-Manual Work Sample (Roberts, 1969) measure fine and gross motor movements. The motor measurement approach to vocational assessment represents the first movement away from psychological variables toward more work-related behavior in the area of vocational assessment. Table 9-2 lists several tests measuring fine and gross motor movements that are often used to assess vocational behavior.

Manual dexterity tests have been validated in a number of ways. Wagner and Hawver (1965) correlated scores for five manual dexterity tests. They found that each test correlated highly with the others. Manual dexterity scores have also been correlated with mental age (Distefano, Ellis, & Sloan, 1958), intelligence tests (Elkin, 1967), and work potential as measured via assembly task proficiency (Tobias & Gorelick, 1962). These methods of validating manual dexterity test, however, are limited in generality. The criterion measures (i.e., intelligence, age) used in manual dexterity validation studies are not related to general work behavior. Assembly task proficiency, alone, represents a relatively small component of overall work behavior. Evidence of the concurrent validity of dexterity tests using these criteria are not meaningful in light of a contemporary assessment focus on identifying training needs. For a test to be useful in the educational/rehabilitation process, its content should represent the skills it is purporting to measure. For example, knowledge of the skill requirements for specific jobs in a community should be known in advance and used as the criteria for determining placement readiness. Manual dexterity tests tend to examine only gross and fine motor movements of the individual. Gross and fine motor movements represent only a fraction of the activities related to vocational success. Manual dexterity assessments are also subject to the same general criticisms as the psychological measurement approaches to vocational assessment (Brolin, 1976; Gold, 1973). For instance, the majority of manual dexterity tests are normed using nonretarded populations and their validation studies investigate concurrent, not predictive, validity issues. Therefore, these measures are not appropriate for determing the training needs of the mentally retarded population. It is quite possible that a mentally retarded per-

Table 9-2

Test Representing the Motor Measurement Approach

Instrument	Brief Description	Author	Publisher
Bennet Hand-Tool Dexterity Test	A measure of proficiency in ordinary mechanical tool usage	Bennett (1965)	The Psychological Corporation, New York
Crawford Small Parts Dexterity Test	A test measuring eye-hand coordination	Crawford & Crawford (1956)	The Psychological Corporation, New York
Minnesota Rate of Manipulation	A test used to select applicants for jobs requiring gross arm-hand motor movements.	Minnesota Employment Stabilization Institute (1969)	American Guidance Service, Inc., Circle Pines, MN
O'Connor Finger Dexterity Test	A test designed to measure dexterity and coordination predicting success in some assembly jobs.	O'Connor (1926)	Stoelting Co., Chicago
O'Connor Tweezer Dexterity Test	A test that measures finger and manual dexterity and coordination in order to assess manual aptitude for work involving precision and steadiness in the use of small hand tools.	O'Connor (1928)	Stoelting Co., Chicago
Pennsylvania Bi-Manual Work System	A test measuring finger dexterity, gross movements, eye-hand coordination, and bi-manual coordination related to simple work situations.	Roberts (1969)	American Guidance Service, Inc., Circle Pines, MN
Purdue Pegboard	A test designed to measure fine and gross hand, finger, and arm movements to determine potential for industrial jobs.	Tiffen (1968)	Science Research Associates, Inc., Chicago
Stromberg Dexterity Test	A test used to select workers for jobs requiring speed and accuracy of arm and hand movements.	Stromberg (1957)	The Psychological Corporation, New York

son could score quite low on any one or all of these tests, and yet be quite capable of learning tasks associated with diverse jobs.

Summary

Tests representing the motor measurement approach also have limited value in assessing the vocational training needs of mentally retarded adults. There are two major limitations posed by relying solely on this approach. The first relates to the content measured in any one of the tests displayed in Table 9-2. Fine and gross motor movements, although related to work behavior, are not representative of the complexities of a real life employment setting. The second limitation relates to the weak methodology used to validate the psychometric properties (e.g., validity, reliability) of these tests.

Work Sample Approach

The use of work samples as vocational assessment tools has increased rapidly in recent years and represents the most popular vocational assessment strategy in use today. Wright (1980) referred to a work sample as "a sampling of the activity and other demands of a real job or occupation" (p. 415). The primary impetus for the rapid growth of the work sample approach to vocational assessment derived from the growing awareness that psychological and manual dexterity testing methods failed to measure the vocational needs of a large number of the severely disabled, including mentally retarded, individuals (Pruitt, 1970). Table 9-3 lists several of the more popular work samples currently available.

The work sample approach relies heavily on normative data taken from typical work tasks. Some popular work sample systems include the McCarron-Dial Work Evaluation System (McCarron & Dial, 1976), the Vocational Information and Evaluation Work Samples (Jewish Employment and Vocational Service, 1976), the Tower System (Institute for the Crippled and Disabled, 1967), the Micro-Tower System (Institute for the Crippled and Disabled, 1977), and the Valpar System (Valpar Corporation, 1974, 1977, 1978). These work sample systems allow mentally retarded individuals to participate in work by manipulating various tools and displaying the worker characteristics that the samples are designed to simulate. Consequently, there are several advantages to using a work sample approach to assess mentally retarded adults' training needs. These include: (1) they approximate real-life work situations that isolate specific skills within the reach of severely disabled persons; (2) they assess worker characteristics (e.g., following directions, tool usage, attitudes) associated with the work sample; and (3) they are relatively unbiased, in that they are less likely to be influenced by such factors as insufficient motivation, anxieties, language ability, and cultural influences (Sinick, 1962).

Table 9-3
Tests Representing the Work Sample Approach to Vocational Assessment

Instrument	Brief Description	Author	Publisher
JEVS Work Samples	JEVS includes 28 work samples designed to assess vocational skills (i.e., dexterity, perceptual abilities, direction following abilities, numerical abilities); work related behaviors (i.e., punctuality, attention span, supervisory and co-worker interactions); and interests (i.e., preferences for working with tools, clerical detail, routine work, problem solving work.	no author (1973)	Jewish Employment and Vocational Service, Philadelphia
MacDonald Vocational Capacity Scale (VCS)	This scale consists of eight tests administered during a 2-week period. The eight factors assessed include: work habits, physical capacities, social maturity, general health, manual dexterity, arithmetic achievements, motivation, and the ability to follow directions. The VCX utilizes both commercially-produced tests as well as instruments developed and standardized at the MacDonald Training Center in Tampa.	no author (1972)	MacDonald Training Center, Tampa, FL
McCarron-Dial Work Evaluation System	This system utilizes psychological tests (WAIS or Stanford-Binet), behavior rating scales, and manual dexterity tests measuring the following factors: verbal cognition, sensory, motor and emotional ability, and integrating-coping skills. Evaluation of emotional stability and integrating-coping skills requires two weeks of systematic observation in a work setting, commonly a rehabilitation workshop. The other components can be assessed in a day.	McCarron & Dial (1976)	Common Market Press, Dallas, TX

Micro-Tower	This test consists of 13 work samples measuring aptitudes required in many skilled and unskilled jobs. The test utilizes group discussions, audiovisual presentations of occupational information, and attitudinal and behavioral scales for comprehensive evaluation. MICRO-TOWER may be used with educable mentally retarded persons and takes 3–5 days to complete.	no author (1977)	Institute for the Crippled and Disabled, New York
Singer Vocational Evaluation System (VES)	A test designed to determine vocational aptitude, interests, and work tolerance of individuals as they explore the world of work. VES utilizes an audiovisual teaching machine to present programmed instruction on how to perform specific tasks in the work evaluation process; the presentation is completely controlled by the client. VES introduces a self study component with the client participating in the assessment whereby the client evaluates his or her own interests and aptitude along with the evaluator. There is an occupational exploration segment that helps the client determine interests by describing a number of actual jobs related to various occupational clusters. Administration time takes approximately 3 weeks; however, the work samples are usually administered selectively (the average number of work samples per client is 5 to 7).	Singer (1977)	The Singer Educational Division, Rochester, New York

continued

Table 9-3 (continued)

Instrument	Brief Description	Author	Publisher
Talent Assessment Program (TAP)	TAP consists of 10 subtests that measure characteristics of work in industrial technical, and service occupations (i.e., visual and tactile discrimination, physical dexterity, mechanical serialization). This system is individually administered in approximately 3 hours and is often used in conjunction with other work evaluation/assessment programs.	Nighswonger (1981)	Ideal Systems, West Allis, WI
The Comprehensive Occupational Assessment and Training System (COATS)	This package takes approximately one week to complete and focuses primarily upon the nonhandicapped but may have potential usefulness with mildly mentally retarded persons. This system evaluates employability attitudes, work samples, job matching and living skills.	no author (1978)	Prep Incorporated, Trenton, NJ
VALPAR Component Work Sample Series	VALPAR consists of 16 work samples designed to assess universal worker characteristics based on realistic job settings. Each work sample has a manual that lists related jobs found in the	no author (1974, 1977, 1978)	VALPAR Corporation, Tucson, AZ

Dictionary of Occupational Titles. The *Pre-Vocational Readiness Battery (#17)*, utilizes a work sample format designed to assess one's ability to function in competitive employment and independent living situations.

Vocational Information and Evaluation Work Samples (VIEWS)	no author (1976)	Jewish Employment and Vocational Services, Philadelphia	This assessment instrument consists of 16 work samples that take approximately 4–5 days to complete. Each work sample is related to the Work and Worker Trait Groups found in the *Dictionary of Occupational Titles*. The individual learns each task before assessment begins.
Wide Range Employment Sample Test (WREST)	Jastak & King (1979)	Guidance Associates of Delaware, Inc., Wilmington, DE	A short battery of 10 work samples including single and double folding, pasting, labeling, stuffing, stapling, bottle packaging, rice measuring, screw assembly, tag stringing, and pattern matching. Each represent simple tasks that assess manipulation and dexterity ability. The entire battery of work samples can be administered to a group of three to six persons in 2 hours.

The content of most work samples is more work related than that of either psychological or motor measures. For example, these work samples typically include tasks such as folding table cloths, sorting buttons, packaging poker chips, and assembling key chains (Tobias, 1960). Other work related content assessed by such samples include dexterity, coordination, ability to follow verbal directions, and the ability to count. Work samples provide the opportunity to observe actual work and work related behavior in a controlled setting (Neff, 1968). Employers also tend to accept evaluations based upon work samples more readily than evaluations based upon psychological tests (Sakata & Sinick, 1965). The work sample approach to vocational assessment represents an improvement in content validity of vocational assessment instrumentation.

An additional advantage of the work sample approach relates to the use of appropriate normative information. Originally, norms for work samples were determined via Method-Time-Measurement, Master Standard Data, or similar industrial techniques (Botterbusch, 1981). Collection of such information requires the expertise of an industrial engineer. Furthermore, this type of data collection system is based upon the performance of skilled, nonretarded workers. As indicated above, such information may have limited value when compared to the work behavior of mentally retarded individuals because such comparisons may inaccurately represent the mentally retarded individual's actual potential for learning. (Gold, 1973; Timmerman & Doctor, 1974). Botterbusch (1981) has suggested that mentally retarded workers must be included in the original normative sample to provide accurate and useful information. These norms provide information about how an evaluee's performance on a work sample compare to performance of other similarly handicapped persons who may have varying levels of vocational competence. In summary, the major advantages of the work sample approach are its higher content validity and its use of appropriate normative groups. Although these advantages represent an improvement over the psychological and motor measurement approaches to assessment, the work sample approach has some limitations. In particular, the use of work samples may have limited predictive validity for a mentally retarded population since setting characteristics associated with job clusters cannot be easily simulated (Timmerman & Doctor, 1974). Another limitation related specifically to mentally retarded individuals and some of the available work samples (e.g., the Jewish Employment and Vocational Service Work Sample Evaluation System [JEVS]) include an instructional format that relies upon higher level reading and comprehension abilities. In addition, many work samples require the client to draw a comparison between the work sample and potential jobs. Finally, work sample assessment data may be confounded by motivational variables since many samples include methods such as disassembling parts once they have been assembled. Wolfensberger (1967), Gold (1973), and Brolin (1976) have criticized the continued use of work samples in the absence of process evaluation techniques (e.g., training time, reinforcer preference).

Summary

There are problems associated with a work sample approach that limit its generality for the purpose of contemporary assessment. The greater majority of work samples measure production related work behavior, such as folding, sorting, and assembling. Other skills assessed include counting, measuring, and reading. There is little or no measurement of social skills, such as grooming and interpersonal skills. Interestingly, Schalock and Harper (1978) found job retention among mentally retarded workers was related to appropriate social skills. Others have also suggested that inappropriate social behaviors are associated with job loss (Greenspan & Schoultz, 1981; Greenspan, Schoultz, & Weier, 1982). It would appear, then, that work samples have not included a very critical component of work behavior, i.e., social competence. Numerous critics have suggested other problems associated with work samples, including the methods used to administer the work samples and the difficulty of simulating pressures in everday work settings (Gold, 1973; Timmerman & Doctor, 1974; Wolfensberger, 1967). Typically, work samples are administered in a sheltered workshop environment by a familiar workshop employee. Usually the sample is administered early in the person's employment. This initial performance on work samples may reveal little about later performance or, more importantly, how skills are learned. Effective assessment of the training needs of mentally retarded individuals requires information about social skills and skill acquisition. The use of work samples does not guarantee this information will be provided.

CONTEMPORARY APPROACHES TO VOCATIONAL ASSESSMENT

There are three newly developed approaches to vocational assessment of mentally retarded adults; the adaptive behavior approach (Nihira, Foster, Shellhaas, & Leland, 1974), the survival skill approach (Rusch & Mithaug, 1980), and the process assessment approach (Irvin & Halpern, 1979). These approaches reflect the contemporary purpose of assessment (Halpern et al., 1982). The unique characteristic of the information provided by these approaches is its direct relationship to the vocational training needs of the individual.

The Adaptive Behavior Approach

As assessment approaches moved away from the traditional trait identification and classification purpose toward a more functional training related focus, there was a parallel trend toward a definition of mental retardation that emphasized the alterable nature of adaptive behavior (Schalock & Karan, 1979). The concept of adaptive behavior has played an important role in the development of the contemporary assessment purpose (Halpern et al., 1982). Adaptive behavior refers to a wide range of appropriate and inappropriate behaviors in diverse social contexts. Goldfried and D'Zurilla (1969) defined adaptive behavior as behavioral "competence" or the "effectiveness or adequacy with which an individual is capable of responding to the various problematic situations which confront him" (p. 161). Meyers, Nihira, and Zetlin (1979) suggested that definitions of adaptive behavior have two elements: (1) standards of performance that are socially defined, and (2) a statement of the extent to which the individual meets these standards. There are at least ten current definitions of adaptive behavior offered by various professional associations and governmental agencies (Coulter & Morrow, 1978). The definition posed by the American Association on Mental Deficiency (AAMD) is representative of these separate attempts. AAMD defines adaptive behvior "as the effectiveness or degree to which an individual meets the standards of personal independence on social responsibility expected for age and cultural group" (Grossman, 1977, p. 11). Adaptive behavior became an important component of the definition of mental retardation.

Recognition that the phenomenon known as mental retardation could, in part, be defined as a deficit in adaptive behavior suggested retardation could be changed through skill training. This emphasis on skill training changed the requirements for assessment information for mentally retarded individuals. The most functional assessment approaches provide information about adaptive behavior deficits rather than retardation level. As a result, there has been a proliferation of assessment instruments designed to measure an individual's adaptive behavior. For example, Walls, Werner, Bacon, and Zane (1977) reviewed 132 currently available adaptive behavior scales. Walls and Werner (1977) listed 39 vocational behavior checklists now on the market.

Adaptive behavior scales are typified by their measurement of appropriate and/or inappropriate behavior. The behaviors are usually clustered into domains that are often interpreted separately to assess a certain type of behavioral response exhibited by an individual. In most cases, each item on an adaptive behavior scale reflects a range of behavior to differentiate an individual's skill level. Since most adaptive behavior scales include a separate vocational behavior domain, these instruments have become popular vocational assessment supplements to larger assessment efforts.

In this section, two popular adaptive behavior scales are presented in detail: the American Association on Mental Deficiency Adaptive Behavior Scale (Nihira et al., 1974), and the San Francisco Vocational Competency Scale (Levine & Elzey, 1968a). Both include a vocational behavior domain, and more importantly, are representative of the large number of adaptive behavior scales used to assess vocational behavior of mentally retarded adults. Other adaptive behavior scales, not reviewed here, include: the Three Track System (Schalock & Harper, 1977), the Work Adjustment Rating Form (Bitter, 1969), the Street Survival Skill Questionnaire (Linkenhoker & McCarron, 1980) the Social and Prevocational Information Battery (SPIB; Halpern, Raffeld, Irvin, & Link, 1975), the SPIB Form T (Irvin, Halpern, & Reynolds, 1979), the Vocational Behavior Checklist (Walls, Zane, & Werner, 1978), and the Progress Assessment Chart of Social and Personal Development (Gunzburg, 1976). Table 9-4 provides a brief description of each of these scales.

The Adaptive Behavior Scale

The Adaptive Behavior Scale (ABS) was developed for the American Association on Mental Deficiency in 1969. There is a 1975 revision of the test manual. The scale consists of a test booklet and manual. The price is $1.50 for each booklet and a starter set, including manual and 5 scale booklets, costs $14.50. The ABS is a behavioral rating scale designed primarily for use among mentally retarded, emotionally maladjusted, and developmentally disabled children and adults, ages 3 to 69.

The ABS is designed to provide objective descriptions of an individual's adaptive behavior. The ABS consists of two parts. Part I includes 66 items across 10 general behavior or skill areas "considered important to the development of personal independence in daily living" (Nihira, Foster, Shellhaas, & Leland, 1975, p. 6). These include the domains of independent functioning, physical development, economic activity, language development, numbers and time, domestic activity, vocational activity, self direction, responsibility, and socialization. Six of these domains are further divided into subdomains. The vocational activity domain consists of only three items: job complexity, job performance, and work habits.

Part II of the ABS includes 44 items across 14 domains, providing measures of maladaptive behavior. Once again, several of the domains are subdivided. The 14 domains of Part II are: violent and destructive behavior, anti-social behavior, rebellious behavior, untrustworthy behavior, withdrawal, stereotyped behavior and odd mannerisms, inappropriate interpersonal manners, unacceptable vocal habits, unacceptable or eccentric habits, self abusive behavior, hyperactive tendencies, sexually aberrant behavior, psychological disturbance, and use of medication.

The ABS is designed to be administered by people without a great deal of special training, as well as by professionals. It may be used by institutional aides and nurses, parents, outreach workers, community service technicians, teachers, workshop supervisors, home trainers, as well as by psychologists, social workers, speech and hearing personnel and other more specially trained professionals. However, the ABS was standardized on individuals residing in institutional settings and administered by institutional staff (e.g., nurses, aides, social workers). Interestingly, in the description of the methods for administration, the authors state that the first person assessment method requires enough professional or on-the-job training to judge the relevance of the scale. Three different types of administration procedures are presented. The authors suggest that the rater use his

Table 9-4
Tests Representing the Adaptive Behavior and Survival Skill Approaches to Vocational Assessment

ADAPTIVE BEHAVIOR TESTS

Instrument	Brief Description	Author	Publisher
AAMD Adaptive Behavior Scale (ABS)	A behavior rating scale designed to provide a description of the ability to adjust to the demands of the general environment. Part I of the scale includes ten general behavior or skill areas related to achieving independent living status while Part II covers maladaptive social or personal characteristics.	Nihira, Foster, Shellhaas, & Leland (1975)	American Association on Mental Deficiency, Washington, DC
Mid-Nebraska Mental Retardation Services Three Track System	An assessment system that includes 3 distinct components for measuring mentally retarded examinees' competencies: the Basic Skills Screening Test, the Community Living Skills Screening Test, and the Vocational Training Screening Test. This system is based on an Adult Developmental Model that assumes that achievement of basic skills should precede achievement of domestic and community adjustment skills and both should precede development of employment skills.	Schalock, Ross, & Ross, (1976); Schalock & Gadwood, (1980); Schalock (1981)	Mid-Nebraska Mental Retardation Services, Hastings, NB
Progress Assessment. Chart 2 of Social and Personal.	An assessment system that provides a comprehensive overview of social functioning by measuring social knowledge and skills along four major domains: self help, communication, socialization, and occupation. The PAC 2 is designed for use with mildly and moderately	Gunzburg (1976)	SEFA, Ltd. London

Instrument	Description	Author (Date)	Publisher
	mentally retarded adolescents and adults while the S/PAC 2 is designed for use with the severely mentally retarded adults.		
San Francisco Vocational Competency Scale (SFVCS)	A behavior rating scale assessing vocational competence in either a sheltered workshop or prevocational classroom. The four areas of the VCS are motor skills, cognition, responsibility, and social-emotional behavior.	Levine & Elzey (1968)	The Psychological Corporation, New York
Social and Prevocational Information Battery. (SPIB)	A a group administered paper and pencil test, completed by the client, assessing social and prevocational knowledge in areas important to community adjustment (i.e., purchasing skills, budgeting, banking, job-related behaviors, job search skills, home management, physical health, personal hygiene and grooming, functional signs). This instrument designed for use with mildly mentally retarded adolescents and adults.	Halpern, Raffeld, Irvin, & Link (1975)	Publishers Test Service, Monterey, CA
Social and Prevocational Information Battery—Form T	A downward extension of the SPIB designed to assess social and prevocational knowledge of moderately mentally retarded persons in areas important to their community adjustment. The SPIB—Form T, which is administered orally, contains items across the same nine domains as those that comprise the original SPIB. The SPIB—Form T includes two pretest administered to all examiners to determine whether the individual can respond to the yes/no format.	Irvin, Halpern, & Reynolds (1979)	Publisher's Test Service—California Test Bureau, McGraw-Hill, Monterey, CA

continued

265

Table 9-4 (continued)

ADAPTIVE BEHAVIOR TESTS

Instrument	Brief Description	Author	Publisher
Street Survival Skills Questionnaire (SSSQ)	A questionnaire designed to assess community-relevant adaptive behavior of adolescents and adults who are suspected of lower intellectual functioning, psychiatric disorders, or cultural deprivation. Domains assessed include: basic concepts, functional signs, tool identification and use, domestic management, health, first aid, and safety, public services, time, money, and measurement.	Linkenhoker & McCarron (1979)	Common Market Press, Dallas, TX
Vocational Behavior Checklist (VBC)	A checklist that evaluates an individual's vocational skills, provides input for designing individual program plans (i.e., identification of training objectives) and evaluates program effectiveness. Areas assessed include: prevocational skills, job seeking skills, interviewing skills, job related behavior work performance, on-the-job skills, and union-financial-security related concerns.	Walls, Zane, & Werner (1978)	West Virginia Rehabilitation Research and Training Center, Morgantown, WV
Work Adjustment Rating Form (WARF)	A rating scale designed to provide an objective measure of job-readiness for clients ages 16–29.	Bitter & Bolanovich (1969)	Educational Testing Service, Princeton, NJ

SURVIVAL SKILLS TESTS

Prevocational Assessment and Curriculum Guide (PACG)	A behavior rating scale designed to assess and identify the prevocational training needs of handicapped persons, analyze behavior and skill deficits in terms of sheltered employment expectations, prescribe training goals, and determine progress toward training goals. Items assessed include attendance/endurance, independence, production, learning, behavior, communication, social grooming-eating skills, and toileting skills.	Mithaug, Mar, & Stewart (1978)	Exceptional Education, Seattle, WA
Vocational Assessment and Curriculum Guide (VACG)	The VACG assesses and identifies skills relevant to competitive employment expectations. The VACG includes a curriculum guide to assist in developing training goals. Areas assessed include attendance/endurance, independence, production, learning, behavior, academic skills, communication skills, social skills, grooming-eating skills.	Rusch, Schutz, Mithaug, Stewart, & Mar (1982)	Exceptional Education, Seattle, WA
Vocational Problem Behavior Inventory (VPBI)	An inventory designed to assess specific interpersonal situations and problems that may interfere with an individual's vocational adjustment. The VPBI is useful for establishing interpersonal skills training programs.	LaGreca, Stone, & Bell (1982)	Department of Psychology, University of Miami, Coral Gables, FL

or her own judgment as to which procedure would be most appropriate for obtaining the necessary information. These include the first person, third party, and interview assessment procedures. With the first person assessment procedure the evaluator fills out the scale when sufficiently familiar with the individual. This assessment procedure also requires enough professional, on-the-job training to judge the relevance of the scale items. The second method, the third-party-assessment procedure, requires asking a person who is knowledgeable about the mentally retarded individual each of the scale items. This method is recommended whenever detailed information is required. A less structured assessment procedure, the interview method, is an efficient method to use to acquire much of the same information as the third party assessment procedure.

In Part I of the ABS, each domain represents a specific area with questions regarding an individual's range of performance. For example, in the "Job Complexity" subdomain the following three questions are posed: (a) "performs a job requiring use of tools or machinery," (b) "performs simple work," and (c) "performs no work at all." In Part II, multiple questions query whether any problems are present within that area. Part II differs from Part I in that maladaptive behaviors, which may be present in any one or several social settings, are measured. For example, in the area of "following instructions, requests, or orders," the following behaviors are listed and require a frequency score: (1) "gets upset if given a direct order," (2) "plays deaf and does not follow instructions," (3) "does not pay attention to instructions," (4) "refuses to work on assigned subject," (5) "hesitates for long periods before doing assigned tasks," and (6) "does the opposite of what was requested."

In Part I of the ABS there are two different types of items requiring three different scoring procedures. The first type of item asks the rater to select one of several alternative statements best describing the evaluee's behavior. The second type of item requires multiple scoring in which the tester checks all appropriate items. In most cases the rater sums up the number of checks to arrive at an item score. Since some of the items are negatively worded, the rater subtracts the number of such checked items according to a formula provided next to the item. The third type of item is found only in Part II of the ABS. Here, the rater checks items corresponding to frequency of occurrence. Each item occurring "frequently" is assigned a score of 2; each item occurring "occasionally" is assigned a score of 1. Any item for which none of the above has been checked is scored with a 0. Any entry for "other" is counted once for each item no matter how many different behaviors have been entered. Each item score in Part II is then summed.

Several factor analytic studies have been conducted using the ABS for the purpose of providing information regarding the salient dimensions of individual differences (Guarnaccia, 1976; Lambert & Nicoll, 1976; Nihira, 1969a, 1969b; Nihira, 1976). There appear to be two common dimensions of appropriate behavior measured by Part I of the ABS (Meyers et al., 1979). These include functional autonomy or independence, and social responsibility. In Part II of the ABS, which identifies maladaptive behavior, the factors of social maladaption and personal maladaption were identified as contributing to the majority of within group variance. These findings suggest adaptive behavior is multidimensional and cannot be adequately described in terms of a single score such as those obtained with intelligence tests or tests of social maturity (Meyers et al., 1979).

The San Francisco Vocational Competency Scale (SFVCS)

The SFVCS (Levine & Elzey, 1968a) primarily assesses vocational competence of mentally retarded adults. The SFVCS is comprised of 30 items relating to four domains of vocational behavior. These four domains include motor skills, cognition, responsbility, and social/emotional behavior. The scale booklet and manual are available for a minimal fee, approximately $7.00. Like the ABS, the recommended scoring procedures for the SFVCS are the first person assessment procedure or the third party assessment procedure. Administration time is estimated to be about 15 minutes. Each item included on the SFVCS is stated in terms of observable behavior, followed by four to five statements that describe different degrees of performance regarding that item. The evaluator is instructed to rate the degree of competency demonstrated by the mentally retarded individual by circling the number of statements representing general performance level. The scores for each item are then summed, yielding a total vocational competency score.

Levine and Elzey (1968b) factor analyzed the SFVCS with a population of mentally retarded adults working in a sheltered workshop setting. Analysis of the 30 SFVCS items suggested four factors accounted for the differences between individuals. These included: (1) cognitive competence, such as a reading level, recall of previously learned tasks, and following verbal instructions; (2) cognitive interpersonal flexibility represented by error correction behavior, reorientation behavior, reactions to changes in the work routine and frustration, and acceptance of criticisms and supervision; (3) cognitive-motor ability as measured by behaviors such as equipment use; and finally, (4) initiative-dependability, which included such behavior as requesting materials and assistance. Meyers et al. (1979) suggested the VCS factors of cognitive interpersonal flexibility and initiative-dependability are analogous to the ABS autonomy factor while cognitive competence and cognitive responsibility are related to the other ABS factor of social responsibility.

Both the ABS and SFVCS have been standardized and validated in typical, psychometric fashion. For example, the percentile ranks for the ABS were determined using 4,000 mildly to profoundly mentally retarded residents of residential facilties in the United States (Nihira, Foster, Shellhaas, & Leland, 1975). Nihira et al. (1975) did not examine the concurrent validity of the ABS by, for example, demonstrating a correlation between Part I of the Scale and IQ ratings. Lambert, Windmiller, Cole, and Figueroa (1975) differentiated mildly to moderately mentally retarded students from nonretarded students by sex and ethnicity using ABS profiles. The SFVCS was validated by utilizing school and sheltered workshop experiences as criteria (Levine & Elzey, 1968b). The normative group in the SFVCS standardization was comprised of 562 mentally retarded sheltered workshop employees. Reported reliabilities for both the SFVCS and the ABS appear to be satisfactory (Meyers et al., 1979). Validation studies examining predictive validity of the ABS and the SFVCS have not been conducted (Meyers et al., 1979).

Summary

The inclusion of adaptive behavior in the definition of mental retardation significantly changed the purpose and function of assessment activities. Conceptualization of mental retardation as socially defined behavioral excesses and deficits suggested the utility of systematic skill training programs. Consequently, a need arose for assessment information that identified the training needs of mentally retarded individuals. Adaptive behavior scales, with their socially defined standards of performance, filled this need. Adaptive behavior scales, like the ABS and SFVCS, reflect the contemporary approach to assessment by facilitating direct identification of training needs. Because many adaptive behavior scales include a sample of vocational behavior, these scales have some utility for assessing the vocational training needs of mentally retarded adults.

The Survival Skill Approach

Discussion of validation issues in connection with vocational assessment of mentally retarded adults must include an examination of social validity. The intent of social validation is inclusion of members of society, who have a vested interest in training, in the determination of training objectives and procedures, as well as in the evaluation of training outcomes (Kazdin, 1977; Kazdin & Matson, 1981; Van Houten, 1979; Wolf, 1978). Social validation methodology provides researchers with the means to empirically identify important vocational skills, assess the acceptability of training procedures, and evaluate the significance of research findings. Applied to the problem of validating assessment instruments, social validity requires that an instrument's content be determined empirically; for example, by surveying employers' perceptions of desirable work-related behavior (Rusch & Mithaug, 1980).

Rusch (1979b) conceptualized important vocational behavior in terms of the skills necessary to obtain and maintain employment. Rusch (1979b) and Rusch and Schutz (1981) referred to these behaviors as survival skills. They distinguished between technical work behavior, or vocational survival skills, and the more social aspects of work, i.e., the social survival skills. The concept of survival is defined as those behaviors that, when acquired, facilitate entry into employment (Rusch, 1979b).

The suggestion by Rusch and his colleagues to socially validate survival skills (Menchetti, Rusch, & Lamson, 1981; Rusch, 1979b; Rusch & Schutz, 1981) has important implications for vocational assessment. First, social validity issues, specifically the empirical identification of assessment instrumentation content, must be viewed as an important validity concern. Social validity information becomes as important as an instrument's concurrent and predictive validity, reliability, and standardization data. Furthermore, the relationship between social validity and predictive validity, although currently uninvestigated, presents intriguing possibilities for researchers. For instance, it would be interesting to examine the impact of an instrument's predictive power when social validation of its content had been conducted prior to its development. The final, and most important implication of social validation for vocational assessment is that instrument design and development is based upon the expectations of employers. Empirical identification of an instrument's content is prima facie evidence of program relatedness, and hence satisfies contemporary assessment requirements of functional assessment and facilitation of program planning.

Currently, there are three social validation vocational assessment instruments available. Described in Table 9-4, they include: (1) the Prevocational Assessment and Curriculum Guide (PACG); (2) the Vocational Assessment and Curriculum Guide (VACG); and (3) the Vocational Problem Behavior Inventory (VPBI).

The Prevocational Assessment and Curriculum Guide (PACG)

An excellent example of social validation survey methodology applied to the identification of the skills needed for employment in sheltered workshop settings has been provided by Dennis E. Mithaug and his colleages (Johnson & Mithaug, 1978; Mithaug & Hagmeier, 1978; Mithaug & Hanawalt, 1977; Mithaug, Mar, Stewart, & McCalmon, 1980). Mithaug (1979) initially developed a survey questionnaire that included items addressing skill areas such as social interaction, personal hygiene, productivity, and endurance. Mithaug and Hagmeier (1978) asked supervisory personnel in several sheltered workshops in the Pacific Northwest to indicate the necessity and optimal performance level of each of the items for successful employment. Later, Johnson and Mithaug (1978) replicated the findings in another geographic area (Kansas). These data were used by Mithaug, Mar, and Stewart (1978) to develop the PACG. The PACG is designed to assess the presence and level of a mentally retarded individual's skill with regard to what sheltered workshop supervisors considered to be critical for entrance into their work environments. In addition to providing a method of identifying prevocational training needs and a means of analyzing behavior and skill deficits in terms of sheltered employment expectations, the PACG is designed to prescribe training goals to reduce identified deficits. The PACG can also be administered periodically to measure student progress toward attainment of these goals.

The PACG contains 46 items within nine subcategories. These subcategories include: attendance/endurance, independence, production, learning, behavior, communication, social skills, grooming/eating, and toileting. Each item requires the evaluator to answer one or more questions about how a student behaves in different work or classroom situations. Each item begins with the statement, "Does the student . . .", with the behavior to be assessed described in a completed phrase. A range of alternative answers are provided that indicate the level of response occurring in a specified time period or the existence of the behavior (e.g., yes the behavior is present or no it is not).

The PACG consists of a teacher's manual, a student inventory, a curriculum guide that lists the training goals for each assessment item in the inventory, and a summary profile sheet comparing summary scores in each subcategory with sampled, sheltered workshop supervisors' expectations. The cost of the teacher's manual and ten copies of the inventory, the curriculum guide, and the profile sheet is $8.00. Ten copies of the inventory, curriculum guide, and profile sheets, without the teacher's manual, cost $3.50 (1982 prices).

The PACG may be administered by professionals or paraprofessionals familiar with the student's behavior patterns in the work situations described. Information for completing the inventory can be obtained either through direct observation of the student or by interviewing someone who is familiar with the individual's performance in the work setting. Once the inventory has been completed, the evaluator can identify the skill deficits that require training by reviewing the answers to each item.

Once the skill deficits have been identified, the evaluator can check corresponding training goals in the curriculum guide. These goals can then be used to develop training programs. To compare the student's PACG scores with the score expected of a person typically entering sheltered employment, the evaluator summarizes and charts the score totals on the Summary Profile Sheet. Estimated time for completion of administration and scoring is 45 minutes.

Mithaug, Mar, Stewart, and McCalmon (1980) conducted two studies validating the PACG. The results of the first study indicated that workshop clients do, in fact, display those skills previously specified by workshop administrators as being crucial for entry into sheltered employment. In a second study, Mithaug et al. (1980) assessed the vocational competence of moderately, severely, and profoundly mentally retarded persons who were not employed in a workshop. These groups were found to possess 76, 60, and 50 percent of skills needed to enter into the workshop, as indicated by the PACG. Mithaug et al. (1980) interpreted these findings as indicative of the high content validity of the PACG. A split-half reliability coefficient, calculated by correlating scores on even numbered PACG items with the odd numbered items, resulted in a Pearson's r of .92, which was significant at the .001 level. These data were interpreted as further indicators of the validity and reliability of the PACG.

The Vocational Assessment and Curriculum Guide (VACG)

The VACG (Rusch, Schutz, Mithaug, Stewart, & Mar, 1982) is also a socially validated instrument assessing broad classes of vocational and social skills of individuals preparing for employment in competitive settings. The skills assessed are those that employers in food, janitorial and maid services, and light industrial occupations indicated were important for entry. Its major functions include assessing and identifying skill deficits in terms of competitive employment expectations, prescribing training goals designed to reduce identified deficits, and evaluating program effectiveness by periodically assessing progress toward identified goals.

The VACG Inventory contains 42 items within 10 subcategories. These subcategories include Attendance/Endurance, Independence, Production, Learning, Behavior, Communication Skills, Social Skills, Self Help Skills, Grooming/eating Skills and math. Each item requires that one or more questions be answered regarding how the worker characteristically responds in a given work situation. Each item begins with the phrase, "The worker. . . ," and is completed with a phrase describing the behavior. Alternative answers indicate a level of response (e.g., the number of responses within a specified time period) or answer the question "does the behavior/skill exist?" (i.e., Yes or No).

The VACG consists of a manual, an Inventory, a Curriculum Guide, a Summary Profile Sheet. The VACG may be purchased as a package containing the manual, 10 inventories, 10 curriculum guides, 10 profile sheets or the package of 10 inventories, curriculum guides and profile sheets without the manual. The cost of the packages are $8.00 and $3.50, respectively.

The VACG must be administered by someone who is familiar with the worker's behavior in the work settings. The evaluator simply marks with a check the answer that best describes the worker's behavior or skills. After the inventory has been completed, the skill/behavior deficits that require training are identified. After training needs within a specific area have been identified, the evaluator checks the corresponding training goals in the Curriculum Guide. These goals serve as a basis for developing individual training programs. To compare the worker's VACG scores with scores expected of persons entering competitive employment, item scores must be summarized within each of the subcategories and score totals charted on the Summary Profile Sheet.

Rusch and his colleagues at the University of Illinois embarked upon a program, similar to Mithaug's work on the PACG, of research in their validation of the VACG. First, Rusch, Schutz, and Agran (in press) surveyed employers representing service occupations. Employers were asked to respond to 47 questions derived from the Mithaug and Hagmeier (1978) study. The survey respondents suggested 70 behaviors as survival skills necessary for entry into food service, maid service, and janitorial service occupations. Changes in the original item listings were made based upon input from an expert panel comprised of representative community employers. A 47 item questionnaire resulted. Potential employers were requested to indicate which skills/behaviors they considered important for entry into unskilled or semi-skilled positions. The initial survey (Rusch et al., in press) included 55 service industry employers (i.e., food service, maid service, janitorial occupations) in six midwestern communities and yielded information concerning the worker behaviors and skills that employers considered important for entry into their respective businesses. A second survey (Schutz, 1983) yielded similar information from 53 light industrial employers within the same six midwestern communities. A comparison of identified requisite skills and corresponding behavioral standards obtained from the two surveys yielded a Pearson r of .66 (significant at the .001 level). The combined results of these two surveys provided the basis for selecting items to include in the VACG. Each item was derived from the items that 85 percent or more of the combined respondents considered to be important for entry into competitive employment. A Spearman r of .62 was found to be significant for the ranking of these two surveys.

Finally, Menchetti (1983) established, in a manner similar to Mithaug's work with the PACG, the validity and reliability of the VACG by assessing its ability to discriminate between workers representing four employment groups: (1) mentally retarded workers with only sheltered workshop experience ($N = 61$), (2) mentally retarded workers in competitive employment who lost their jobs and returned to sheltered workshops ($N = 37$), (3) mentally retarded workers who had been in competitive employment for more than four months ($N = 20$), and (4) nonhandicapped workers employed in service and light industrial occupations ($N = 27$). The instrument discriminated between those persons who were competitively employed and those who were not. Menchetti (1983) also checked the reliability of the VACG scores for the three mentally retarded groups, and it was significant well beyond the .001 level for each group. For example, the reliability coefficient for the mentally retarded workers who returned from competitive employment to work in sheltered workshops was .96.

The Vocational Problem Behavior Inventory (VPBI)

The VPBI is another socially validated survival skill assessment instrument (LaGreca, Stone, & Bell, 1982a). It is designed to provide information on problem situations and behavior that could potentially interfere with mentally retarded workers' performance in work settings. The inventory includes 48 problem behaviors grouped in six areas. The larger areas are inappropriate interpersonal behavior, aggressive interpersonal behavior, inappropriate reaction to frustration or anger, attention/memory problems, inappropriate personal habits and mannerisms, and inappropriate work habits. The purpose of the inventory is to provide a focus for training efforts.

LaGreca et al. (1982b) conducted two studies validating the VPBI. In the first study, social validity issues, specifically the empirical identification of problematic situations and behavior, were addressed. Traditional psychometric validity concerns such as concurrent validity, predictive validity, interrater reliability, and test-retest reliability were addressed in the second study. In study 1, LaGreca et al. (1982b) employed the behavior analytic model for assessing social competence that was suggested by Goldfried and D'Zurilla (1969) to identify problematic situations occurring in two work settings (i.e., prevocational classrooms and sheltered workshop). The model includes situational analysis, response enumeration, and response evaluation. The situational analysis consists of naturalistic observation of workers in the work settings and interviews with prevocational teachers, a principal, an educational coordinator, and sheltered workshop evaluators and work supervisors. These individuals represented the people most familiar with the demands of the work settings and the behavior of mentally retarded adolescents and adults. During the interviews, these professionals generated a list of problem behaviors and situations that they had observed in their respective settings. Information from the interviews was compiled into lists of common problem situations and behavior.

The second component of the situational assessment, naturalistic observations of mentally retarded persons' behavior, was conducted in both the prevocational classes and the sheltered workshop. In the classroom, seven students were observed for a total of 50 minutes over 10 observation days. A similar procedure was employed to observe four workshop employees. A descriptive recording procedure was selected as the recording technique in this phase of the study to generate lists of problem situations and behaviors occurring in the two settings.

The response enumeration phase of the behavior analytic assessment model (Goldfried & D'Zurilla, 1969) consisted of data based categorization of the problem behavior lists. LaGreca et al. (1982b) compiled lists of problem situations and behaviors based upon the earlier interviews and naturalistic observations. The main purpose of these lists was to generate situations and behaviors that could become the focus of training efforts.

The last component of the behavior analytic assessment model, response evaluation, analyzed the behaviors and situations in terms of frequency of occurrence and seriousness in the work settings. The 48 problem behaviors comprising the VPBI were presented to raters. A four-point scale (i.e., 1 = never occurs, 2 = sometimes occurs, 3 = frequently occurs, 4 = always occurs) was used to measure frequency of occurrence of the behaviors. A five point scale was used to measure the seriousness (i.e., how likely the behaviors would lead to job termination) of each of the behaviors. The obtained ratings were averaged across three raters. The averages became the empirical criterion for the formation of four skill training priority categories. These categories included behaviors rated as frequent and serious, behaviors rated as low in frequency but high in seriousness, behaviors rated high in frequency but low in seriousness, and behaviors rated low on both frequency and seriousness. This response evaluation concluded the social validation of the VPBI.

In Study 2, LaGreca et al. (1982b) attempted to assess the psychometric properties on the VPBI. VPBI ratings on 40 mentally retarded students were collected prior to their placement in a sheltered workshop. Other adaptive behavior measures, such as the ABS and the SFVCS, were collected to assess the concurrent validity of the VPBI. Predictive validity was assessed by collecting data on work attendance after students were placed in the workshop. It was hypothesized that individuals with high behavior problems as rated on the VPBI would work fewer days than those receiving low scores. Data analysis revealed that individuals with high VPBI scores (i.e., high behavior problem individuals) also scored high on the antisocial behavior and rebellious behavior domains of the ABS. Moderate correlations were found between the VPBI and the SFVCS suggesting high behavior problem workers are likely to have lower vocational competence. The VPBI also correlated with the number of days mentally retarded individuals worked during a seven week period after their placement in a workshop.

Reliability issues assessed by LaGreca et al. (1982b) included test-retest and interrater reliability. Correlation for 8 week and 10 week test-retest intervals were .40 and .72, respectively. Both coefficients were statistically significant. Interrater reliability was determined by correlating ratings between teachers and supervisors. The .51 correlation coefficient was statistically significant, suggesting the interrater reliability of the VPBI.

Summary

The last three vocational assessment instruments reviewed, the PACG (Mithaug et al., 1978); the VACG (Rusch et al., 1982); and the VPBI (LaGreca et al., 1982a) represent a major advance in vocational assessment methodology. Like the adaptive behavior scales that preceded them; the PACG, VACG, and VPBI offer an improvement over traditional instrumentation (i.e., intelligence tests, interest tests, aptitude tests, manual dexterity tests, work samples) for identifying the vocational training needs of mentally retarded individuals. This improvement is related to the use of social validation methodology in their development. This process, usually incorporating input by employer, possesses the most promise for the identification of relevant vocational assessment items and categories.

Process Assessment Approach

Knowledge of an individual's vocationally-relevant behavior, as measured by survival skill assessment instruments, is a major step toward merging assessment and training processes. Clearly, evaluating an individual's vocational survival skill repertoire facilitates functional program planning. This close, functional relationship between assessment and program development represents an improvement in vocational assessment (Irvin & Halpern, 1979; Schalock & Karan, 1979), reflecting a trend toward contemporary evaluation of the behavior of mentally retarded persons (Halpern et al., 1982).

There is another important dimension related to the vocational training process that, if assessed, would further increase the relevance of assessment efforts. Several investigators have suggested the importance of training to the performance of mentally retarded workers (Baumeister, 1967; Bellamy, Horner, & Inman, 1979; Brolin, 1976; Gold, 1973; Rusch & Mithaug, 1980). Knowledge about the type of training (e.g., verbal instruction, modeling, physical assistance) needed to increase a mentally retarded worker's performance, is important for program planning. Combined with knowledge about survival skill deficits, this process assessment provides information about what skills/behaviors need to be developed and how those skills/behaviors can be effectively trained. Process assessment, then, accompanied by survival skill assessment, represents a vocational assessment approach with optimal utility for educational/rehabilitational efforts.

In one effort, Budoff and Hamilton (1976) suggested a procedure referred to as the learning potential format to assess the relationship between instructional processes, such as the use of modeling and physical assistance, and skill acquisition. Sackett (1977) suggested that process assessment can be accomplished most effectively by continuous observation of behavior and environmental events in the natural setting. This naturalistic observational methodology permits statements to be made about functional relationships between a mentally retarded individual's behavior (i.e., work performance) and specific environmental events (i.e., verbal instruction, modeling, physical assistance). These approaches to process assessment have great potential as sources of program-related data regarding mentally retarded workers' behavior.

Table 9-5 briefly describes the only two assessment instruments designed for use with mentally retarded individuals that incorporate a process assessment component: (2) the Learning Potential Assessment Device and (2) the Trainee Performance Sample (TPS). The Learning Potential Assessment Device (LPAD), developed by Feuerstein, Rand, and Hoffman (1979), is designed to assess the cognitive deficits of mentally retarded adolescents. Some of the cognitive skills assessed include number series completion, verbal and figure analogy ability, and stencil design skill. The Feuerstein et al. (1979) assessment model involves combining testing and teaching to include task presentation, training designed to improve cognitive functioning in the area, and presentation of progressively more complex and dissimilar tasks to assess learning. If a mentally retarded adolescent's performance improves during the instructional period the tester considers the amount and nature of instruction required and makes empirically-based placement recommendations.

The second process assessment instrument, the Trainee Performance Sample, was specifically designed for vocational assessment use. Bellamy and Snyder (1976) developed the Trainee Performance Sample to assess specifically the benchwork assembly skills of mentally retarded workers, and also the individual's ability to benefit from training. An assessment of the relationship between various training processes and assembly skill is also provided in the TPS by including commonly used training and correction procedures in each of the 25 test items. The process assessment approach represents a promising addition to vocational assessment instrumentation. Inclusion of information about those training procedures that are related to skill improvement or learning advance the program relatedness of vocational assessment efforts. In summary, we believe that the survival skill approach

Table 9-5

Tests Representing the Process Assessment Approach to Vocational Assessment

Instrument	Brief Description	Author	Publisher
Learning Potential Assessment Device (LPAD)	An assessment instrument designed to assess cognitive deficits of mentally retarded adolescents. Cognitive skills assessed include number series completion, verbal and figure analogy ability, and stencil design skill.	Feuerstein, Rand, & Hoffman (1979)	Requests should be addressed to: Reuven Feuerstein Director, Hadassah-WizoCanada Research Institute, 6 Karmon St., Beit Hakerem, Jerusalem, Israel
Trainee Performance Sample (TPS)	An assessment instrument designed specifically to determine a client's responsiveness to various training procedures while completing benchwork. The training procedures include modeling and physical assistance. The TPS consists of 25 items.	Bellamy & Snyder (1982)	Ideal Developmental Labs, Milwaukee, WI

in combination with the process assessment approach to vocational assessment will yield information that has the greatest potential for best serving mentally retarded individual's preparation for employment.

REFERENCES

Andrews, DM, Patterson, DG, & Longstaff, HP. *Minnesota Clerical Test.* (1st ed.) New York: The Psychological Corporation, 1933

Andrews, DM, Patterson, DG, & Longstaff, HP. *Minnesota Clerical Test.* New York: The Psychological Corporation, 1961

Appell, MJ, Williams, CM, & Fishell, KN. Significant Factors in placing mental retardates from a workshop situation. *Personnel and Guidance Journal,* 1962, *41,* 260–265

Baker, BL, Seltzer, G, & Seltzer, M. *As close as possible.* Boston: Little, Brown, and Company, 1977

Bates, P, & Pancsofar, E. Longitudinal vocational training for severely handicapped students in the public schools. Springfield, IL: Illinois State Board of Education, Department of Adult, Vocational and Technical Education. 1981

Baumeister, AA (Ed.). *Mental retardation: Appraisal, education, rehabilitation.* Chicago: Aldine, 1967

Becker, RL. *The AAMD-Becker Reading Free Vocational Interest Inventory.* Washington, DC: American Association on Mental Deficiency, 1975

Becker, RL, Schull, C, & Cambell, K. Vocational interest evaluation of TMR adults. *American Journal of Mental Deficiency,* 1981, *85,* 350–356

Bellamy, GT, Horner, RH, & Inman, DP. *Vocational habilitation of severely retarded adults: A direct service technology.* Baltimore: University Park Press, 1979

Bellamy, GT, & Snyder, S. The trainee performance sample: Toward the prediction of habilitation costs for severely handicapped adults. *AAESPH Review,* 1976, *1,* 17–36

Bellamy, GT, & Snyder, S. *Trainee Performance Sample.* Milwaukee, WI: Ideal Development Labs, 1982

Bennett, GK. *Bennett Mechanical Comprehension Test* (1st ed.) New York: The Psychological Corporation, 1940

Bennett, GK. *Bennett Mechanical Comprehension Test.* New York: The Psychological Corporation, 1969

Bennett, GK. *Hand Tool Dexterity Test.* New York: The Psychological Corporation, 1965

Bitter, JA, & Bolanovich, DJ. *Work Adjustment Rating Form.* Princeton, NJ: Educational Testing Service, 1969

Botterbusch, KF. *Work sample: Norms, reliability and validity.* Menomonie, WI: Materials Development Center, 1981

Brolin, DE. *Vocational preparation of retarded citizens.* Columbus, OH: Charles E. Merrill Publishing Company, 1976

Budoff, M, & Hamilton, J. Optimizing test performance of moderately and severely mentally retarded adolescents and adults. *American Journal of Mental Deficiency,* 1976, *81,* 49–57

Cobb, HV. *The forecast of fulfillment.* New York: Teachers College Press, 1972

Comprehensive Occupational Assessment and Training System. Trenton, NJ: Prep, Inc.

Coulter, WA, & Morrow, HW (Eds.). *Adaptive behavior: Concepts and measurements.* New York: Grune & Stratton, Inc., 1978

Crawford, JE, & Crawford, DM. *Crawford Small Parts Dexterity Test.* New York: The Psychological Corporation, 1956

Cronbach, LJ. *Essentials of psychological testing.* New York: Harper & Row, Publishers, 1960

Distefano, MK, Ellis, NR, & Sloan, W. Motor proficiency in mental defectives. *Perceptual and Motor Skills,* 1958, *8,* 231–234

Elkin, L. Predicting productivity of trainable retardates on experimental workshop tasks. *American Journal of Mental Deficiency,* 1967, *71,* 576–580

Feuerstein, R, Rand, Y, & Hoffman, MB. *The dynamic assessment of retarded performers: The learning potential assessment device theory instruments, and techniques.* Baltimore: University Park Press, 1979

Geist, H. *The Geist Picture Interest Inventory.* Los Angeles: Western Psychological Services, 1978

General Clerical Test. New York: The Psychological Corporation, 1972

Gold, MW. Research on the vocational habilitation of the retarded: The present, the future. In N Ellis (Ed.), *International review of research on mental retardation* (Vol. 6). New York: Academic Press, Inc., 1973

Goldfried, MR, & D'Zurilla, TJ. A behavior-analytic model for assessing competence. In CD Spielberger (Ed.), *Current topics in clinical and community psychology* (Vol. 1). New York: Academic Press, 1969

Greenspan, S, & Shoultz, B. Why mentally retarded adults lose their jobs: Social competence as a factor in work adjustment. *Applied Research in Mental Retardation,* 1981, *2,* 23–38

Greenspan, S, Shoultz, B, & Weir, MM. Social judgment and vocational adjustment of mentally retarded adults. *Applied Research in Mental Retardation,* 1982, *2,* 335–346

Grossman, H. *Manual on terminology and classification in mental retardation.* Washington, DC: American Association on Mental Deficiency, 1977

Guarnaccia, V. Factor structure and correlates of adaptive behavior in noninstitutionalized retarded adults. *American Journal of Mental Deficiency,* 1976, *80,* 543–547

Gunzburg, HC. *Progress Assessment Chart of Social and Personal Development.* England: SEFA Ltd., 1976

Halpern, AS, Lehmann, JP, Irvin, LK, & Heiry, TJ. *Contemporary assessment for mentally retarded adolescents and adults.* Baltimore: University Park Press, 1982

Halpern, A, Raffeld, P, Irvin, LK, & Link, R. *Social and Prevocational Information Battery.* Monterey, CA: Publishers Test Service, 1975

Irvin, LK, & Halpern, AS. A process model of diagnostic assessment. In GT Bellamy, G O'Connor, & OC Karan. *Vocational rehabilitation of severely handicapped persons.* Baltimore: University Park Press, 1979

Irvin, LK, Halpern, A, & Reynolds, WM. *Social and Prevocational Information Battery Form T.* Monterey, CA: Publishers Test Service, 1979

Jastak, JF. *Wide Range Intelligence and Personality Test (WRIPT),* Wilmington, DE: Guidance Associates of Delaware, Inc., 1978

Jastak, JF, & Jastak, SR. *Wide Range Interest and Opinion Test (WRIOT).* (1st ed.). Wilmington, DE: Guidance Associates of Delaware, Inc., 1970

Jastak, JF, & Jastak, SR. *Wide Range Interest and Opinion Test (WRIOT).* Wilmington, DE: Guidance Associates of Delaware, 1979

Jastak, JF, & King, DE. *Wide Range Employment Sample Test (WREST).* New Wilmington, DE: Guidance Associates of Delaware, 1979

JEVS Work Sample Evaluation System. Philadelphia: Jewish Employment and Vocational Service, 1973

Johnson, JL, & Mithaug, DE. A replication of sheltered workshop entry requirements. *AAEPH Review,* 1978, *3,* 116–122

Kazdin, AE. Assessing the clinical or applied importance of behavior change through social validation. *Behavior Modification,* 1977, *1,* 427–451

Kazdin, AE, & Matson, JL. Social validation in mental retardation. *Applied Research in Mental Retardation,* 1981, *2,* 39–54

Kellogg, CE, & Morton, NW. *Revised Beta Examination*. New York: The Psychological Corporation, 1978

Kuder, GF. *Kuder Preference Record: Vocational*. Chicago: Science Research Associates, Inc., 1934

Kuder, GF. *Kuder Preference Record*. Chicago: Science Research Associates, Inc., 1976

LaGreca, AM, Stone, WL, & Bell, CR. *Vocational Problem Behavior Inventory*. Coral Gables, FL: Department of Psychology, University of Miami, 1982 (a)

LaGreca, AM, Stone, WL, & Bell, CR. Assessing the problematic interpersonal skills of mentally retarded individuals in a vocational setting. *Applied Research in Mental Retardation*, 1982, *3*, 37–53 (b)

Lambert, N, & Nicoll, R. Dimensions of adaptive behavior of retarded and nonretarded public school children. *American Journal of Mental Deficiency*, 1976, *81*, 135–146

Lambert, N, Windmiller, M, Cole, LJ, & Figueroa, R. *AAMD Adaptive Behavior Scale Manual*. Washington, DC: American Association on Mental Deficiency, 1975

Leland, H, Nihira, K, Foster, R, Shellhaas, M, & Kagan, E. *Conference on measurement of adaptive behavior: II*. Parsons, KS: Parsons State Hospital and Training Center, 1966

Levine, S, & Elzey, FF. *San Francisco Vocational Competency Scale*. New York: The Psychological Corporation, 1968 (a)

Levine, S, & Elzey, FF. Factor analyses of the San Francisco vocational competency scale. *American Journal of Mental Deficiency*, 1968, *73*, 509–513 (b)

Likert, R, & Quasha, WH. *Revised Minnesota Paper Form Board* (1st ed.). New York: The Psychological Corporation, 1970

Linkenhoker, D, & McCarron, LT. *Street Survival Skills Questionnaire*. Dallas: Common Market Press, 1980

McCarron, LT, & Dial, JG. *McCarron-Dial Work Evaluation System*. Dallas: Common Market Press, 1976

Menchetti, BM. *Assessing the nonsheltered employment survival skills of mentally retarded adults*. Doctoral Dissertation, Champaign, IL: University of Illinois, 1983

Menchetti, BM, Rusch, FR, & Lamson, DS. Employers' perceptions of acceptable training procedures for use in competitive employment settings. *Journal of the Association for the Severely Handicapped*, 1981, *6*, 6–16

Meyers, CE, Nihira, K, & Zetlin, A. The measurement of adaptive behavior. In NR Ellis (ed.), *Handbook of mental deficiency, psychological theory and research*. Hillside, NJ: Lawrence Erlbaum Associates, 1979

Micro Tower. New York: Institute for the Crippled and Disabled, 1977

Minnesota Employment Stabilization Research Institute, *Minnesota Rate of Manipulation Test*. Circle Pines, MN: American Guidance Service, Inc., 1969

Mithaug, DE. Critical steps in developing a prevocational training program for severely handicapped young adults. In L York and E Edgar (Eds.), *Teaching the severely handicapped* (Vol. 4). Columbus, OH: American Association for the Education of the Severely/Profoundly Handicapped, 1979

Mithaug, DE. *Prevocational training for retarded students*. Springfield, IL: Charles C. Thomas, 1981

Mithaug, DE, & Hagmeier, LD. The development of procedures to assess prevocational competencies of severely handicapped young adults. *AAESPH Review*, 1978, *3*, 94–115

Mithaug, DE, & Hanawalt, DA. Employing negative reinforcement to establish and transfer control of a severely retarded child and aggressive nineteen year old girl. *AAESPH Review*, 1977, *2*, 37–49

Mithaug, DE, Mar, DK, & Stewart, JE. *The Prevocational Assessment and Curriculum Guide*. Seattle, WA: Exceptional Education, 1978

Mithaug, DE, Mar, D, Stewart, J, & McCalmon, D. Assessing prevocational competencies of profoundly, severely and moderately retarded persons. *Journal of the Association for the Severely Handicapped*, 1980, *5*, 270–284

Neff, W. *Work and human behavior*. New York: Aldene-Atherton, 1968

Nihira, K. Factorial dimensions of adaptive behavior in adult retardates. *American Journal of Mental Deficiency*, 1969, *73*, 868–878 (a)

Nihira, K. Factorial dimensions of adaptive behavior in mentally retarded children and adolescents. *American Journal of Mental Deficiency*, 1969, *74*, 130–141 (b)

Nihira, K. Dimensions of adaptive behavior institutionalized mentally retarded children and adults: Developmental perspective. *American Journal of Mental Deficiency*, 1976, *81*, 215–226

Nihira, K, Foster, R, Shellhaas, M, & Leland, H. *AAMD Adaptive Behavior Scale*. Washington, DC: American Association on Mental Deficiency, 1974

Nihira, K, Foster, R, Shellhaas, M, & Leland, H. *Manual for AAMD Adaptive Behavior Scale*. Washington, DC: American Association on Mental Deficiency, 1975

O'Connor, J. *O'Connor Finger Dexterity Test*. Chicago: Stoelting Co., 1926

O'Connor, J. *O'Connor Tweezer Dexterity Test*. Chicago: Stoelting Co., 1928

O'Connor, G. *Home is a good place: A national perspective of community residential facilities for developmentally disabled persons*. Washington, DC: American Association on Mental Deficiency, Monograph No. 2, 1976

Parnicky, JJ, Kahn, H, & Burdett, AD. *Vocational Interest and Sophistication Assessment*. Columbus, OH: Ohio State University, 1970

Patterson, DG, Elliott, RM, Anderson, LD, Toops, NA, & Heidbreder, E. *Minnesota Paper Form Board Test*. Marietta, OH: Marietta Apparatus Co., 1920

Porteus, SD. *Porteus Maze Test*. New York: The Psychological Corporation, 1965

Pruitt, W. Basic assumptions underlying work sample theory. *Journal of Rehabilitation*, 1970, *36*, 24–26

Roberts, JR. *Pennsylvania Bi-Manual Work Sample*. Circle Pines, MN: American Guidance Service, Inc., 1969

Rusch, FR. A functional analysis of the relationship between attending to task and production in an applied restaurant setting. *The Journal of Special Education*, 1979, *13*, 399–411 (a)

Rusch, FR. Toward the validation of social/vocational survival skills. *Mental Retardation*, 1979, *17*, 143–145 (b)

Rusch, FR, & Mithaug, DE. *Vocational training for mentally retarded adults: A behavior analytic approach*. Champaign, IL: Research Press, 1980

Rusch, FR, Rusch, JC, Menchetti, BM, & Schutz, RP. *Survey-train-place: Developing a school-aged vocational curriculum for the severely handicapped student*. Champaign, IL: Department of Special Education, University of Illinois, 1980

Rusch, FR, & Schutz, RP. Vocational and social work behavior: An evaluative review. In JL Matson and JR McCartney (Eds.), *Handbook of behavior modification with the mentally retarded*. New York: Plenum Press, 1981

Rusch, FR, Schutz, RP, & Agran, M. Validating entry level survival skills for service occupations: Implications for curriculum development. *Journal of the Association for the Severely Handicapped* (in press)

Rusch, FR, Schutz, RP, Mithaug, DE, Stewart, JE, & Mar, DE. *Vocational Assessment and Curriculum Guide*. Seattle, WA: Exceptional Education, 1982

Sackett, G. *Observing behavior: Volume II*. Baltimore: University Park Press, 1977

Sakata, R, & Sinick, D. Do work samples work? *Rehabilitation Counseling Bulletin*, 1965, *8*, 121–124

Schalock, RL. *Mid-Nebraska Vocational Training Screening Test*. Hastings, NE: Mid-Nebraska Mental Retardation Services, 1981

Schalock, RL, & Gadwood, LL. *Mid-Nebraska Community Living Skills Screening Test*. Hastings, NE: Mid-Nebraska Mental Retardation Services, 1980

Schalock, RL, & Harper, RS. Three track approach to programming in a rural community-based mental retardation program. In P Mittler (Ed.), *Research to practice in mental retardation* (Vol. 1). Baltimore: University Park Press, 1977

Schalock, RL, & Harper, RS. Placement from community-based mental retardation programs: How well do clients do? *American Journal of Mental Deficiency*, 1978, *83*, 240–247

Schalock, RL, Harper, RS, & Carver, G. Independent living placement: Five years later. *American Journal of Mental Deficiency*, 1981, *86*, 170–177

Schalock, RL, & Karan, OC. Relevant assessment: The interaction between evaluation and training. In GT Bellamy, G O'Connor, & OC Karan (Eds.), *Vocational rehabilitation of severely handicapped persons*. Baltimore: University Park Press, 1979

Schalock, RL, Ross, BE, & Ross, I. *Mid-Nebraska Basic Skills Screening Test*. Hastings, NE: Mid-Nebraska Mental Retardation Services, 1976

Scheerenberger, RC. *Deinstitutionalization and institutional reform*. Springfield, IL: Charles C. Thomas, 1976

Scheerenberger, RC, & Felsenthal, D. Community settings for mentally retarded persons: Satisfaction and activities. *Mental Retardation*, 1977, *15*, 3–7

Schutz, RP. *Assessing light industry employers' expectations for entry into competitive employment*. Doctoral dissertation, Champaign, IL: University of Illinois, 1983

Singer, T. *Vocational Evaluation System*. Rochester, NY: The Singer Educational Division, 1977

Sinick, D. Client evaluation: Work task approach. *Rehabilitation Record*, 1962, *3*, 6–8

Slosson, RL. *Slosson Intelligence Test for Children and Adults*. New York: The Psychological Corporation, 1981

Stromberg, EL. *Stromberg Dexterity Test*. New York: The Psychological Corporation, 1951

Talent Assessment Program. Jacksonville, FL: Talent Assessment, Incorporated, 1981

Terman, LM, & Merrill, MA. *Stanford Binet Intelligence Scale* (Manual for the Third Edition L-M). Boston: Houghton Mifflin, 1973

Tiffen, J. *Purdue Pegboard*. Chicago: Science Research Associates, Inc., 1968

Timmerman, WJ, & Doctor, AC. *Special applications of work evaluation techniques for prediction of employability of the trainable mentally retarded*. Menomonie, WI: University of Wisconsin-Stout, Materials Development Center, 1974

Tobias, J. Evalution of vocational potential of mentally retarded young adults. *Training School Bulletin*, 1960, *56*, 122–135

Tobias, J, & Gorelick, J. The Porteus Maze Test and the appraisal of retarded adults. *American Journal of Mental Deficiency*, 1962, *66*, 600–606

TOWER (Testing Orientation and Work Evaluation in Rehabilitation System). New York: Institute for the Crippled and Disabled, 1967

Valpar Component Work Sample Series: #1-13. Tucson, AZ: Valpar Corporation, 1974

Valpar Component Work Sample Series: #14-16. Tucson, AZ: Valpar Corporation, 1977

Valpar Component Work Sample Series: #17 Prevocational Readiness Battery. Tucson, AZ: Valpar Corporation, 1978

VanHouten, R. Social validation: The evolution of standards of competence for target behaviors. *Journal of Applied Behavior Analysis*, 1979, *12*, 581–592

Vocational Capacity Scale. Tampa, FL: McDonald Training Center, 1972

Vocational Information and Evaluation Samples (VIEWS). Philadelphia: Jewish Employment and Vocational Services, 1976

Wagner, EE, & Hawver, DA. Correlations between psychological tests and sheltered workshop performance for severely retarded adults. *American Journal of Mental Deficiency*, 1965, *69*, 685–691

Walls, RT, & Werner, TJ. Vocational behavior checklists. *Mental Retardation*, 1977, *15*, 30–35

Walls, RT, Werner, TJ, Bacon, A, & Zane, T. Behavior checklists. In JD Cone & RP Hawkins (Eds.). *Behavioral assessment: New directions in clinical psychology*. New York: Bruner/Mazel, 1977

Walls, R, Zane, T, & Werner, T. *Vocational Behavior Checklist*. Morgantown, WV: West Virginia Rehabilitation Research and Training Center, 1978

Wechsler, D. *Wechsler Adult Intelligence Scale* (revised). New York: The Psychological Corporation, 1980

Wehman, P. *Competitive employment.* Baltimore: Paul H. Brookes, 1981

Weingarten, KP. *Picture Interest Inventory.* Monterey, CA: CTB/McGraw Hill, 1958

Wilcox, B, & Bellamy, GT. *Design of high school programs for severely handicapped students.* Baltimore: Paul H. Brookes Publishing Co., 1982

Wolf, MM. Social validity: The case for subjective measurement or how applied behavior analysis is finding its heart. *Journal of Applied Behavior Analysis,* 1978, *11,* 203–214

Wolfensberger, W. Vocational preparation and occupation. In AA Baumeister (Ed.), *Mental retardation.* Chicago: Aldine, 1967

Wright, GN. *Total rehabilitation.* Boston: Little, Brown, & Company, 1980

Mark L. Sundberg

10
Language

Effective communication plays a very important role in human affairs. It can provide a person with a great deal of reinforcement (e.g., the ability to ask for help or for a drink of water), and it can allow one to avoid possible punishment (e.g., reading "walk" versus "don't walk"). The outstanding problem for most mentally retarded individuals usually involves some degree of delayed or inappropriate communication skills. For some, emphasis should be placed on developing the rudiments of language while others need to acquire verbal repertoires such as those concerning current events, society, mathematics, or reading. The function of a language assessment is to determine which repertoires are weak, and where to begin instruction.

A person without language is at a great loss (Lovaas, 1977). Many problems and discomforts are experienced but are never understood and it becomes reasonable to expect that various inappropriate behaviors might occur in the absence of language. For example, aggressive behavior such as hitting and kicking may be emitted if a response similar to "Leave me alone," is not in a person's repertoire. Inappropriate social behavior may likewise result from unsuccessful attempts at communication. And after several years, these behaviors become a strong part of a person's repertoire and are difficult to change. Unfortunately, many behavior change programs focus on modifying a certain behavior (e.g., head banging) without considering its possible link to defective verbal skills.

Linguists and cognitive psychologists may de-emphasize actual language instruction by viewing mental retardation and delayed language as by-products of defective cognitive processes. Salzinger (1978) points out in his analysis of the current state of psycholinguistics that "the cognitive psychologists and the generative grammarians have abandoned language as behavior . . . by focusing their interests on the mental events assumed to underlie it" (p. 277). As a result, when language is delayed, emphasis is often placed on developing the "prerequisite" cognitions rather than developing language behavior.

Skinner (1957) presented an alternative view of language in his *Verbal Behavior*. Basically, Skinner analyzes language as behavior that is controlled by its relation to antecedent and consequent events, as well as to motivational variables (Michael, 1982a). The unique feature of Skinner's approach is his ability to explain language without the use of any mediating or cognitive variables. The body of the book consists of a careful analysis and classification of the independent variables mentioned above, and of how they control verbal behavior. The following program for language assessment is based on Skinner's book. There are six sections: receptive language, duplic, mand, tact, intraverbal and codic. Each section contains a definition and overview of the repertoire being tested, methods of assessment, and guidelines for interpreting the assessment (including suggested sources for training materials).

The Definition of Verbal Behavior

Prior to discussing the specific features of the classification scheme, it is important to point out two features of Skinner's approach. First, he defined verbal behavior as behavior that achieves its effect on the environment through the behavior of some other person (Skinner, 1957, pp. 1–2). For example, one can open a box by the appropriate hand and arm movement, which achieves this effect directly; or one can say, "Open the box," in the presence of an appropriate listener, and achieve the same effect indirectly. It is this indirect reinforcement that characterizes verbal behavior and is responsible for many of the important features that distinguish verbal from non-verbal behavior. This use of "verbal" is not synonymous with "vocal"; nor is it defined here as "verbal" contrasted with "quantitative" or "mathematical." Second, Skinner analyzed language as the behavior of a speaker (Skinner, 1957, p. 2) and not as the behavior of a listener. What is typically called receptive language is not technically verbal behavior from Skinner's point of view. This will be discussed in more detail in the receptive language section.

The Parsons Language Sample

The first published attempt to use Skinner's analysis to assess verbal skills was the Parsons language sample (Spradlin, 1963). The assessment concerned several different kinds of verbal behavior: Tact, Echoic, Echoic Gesture, Comprehension, Intraverbal, Intraverbal Gesture and Mand. Spradlin's program was quite different from most language assessments and it was never adopted (nor well understood) by most speech and language clinicians. There were however, as Spradlin (1967) pointed out, several problems with the assessment program. First, it was not clearly stated how the behavior sample related to language usage in the natural environment. This issue was amended by Spradlin (1966), but it seemed that the main problem was that most people were unfamiliar with Skinner's *Verbal Behavior* and didn't know what such things as mands, tacts, and intraverbals were. Another issue was that the results of the test did not indicate where training should begin; specifically, the test was not in any clear way connected to a language curriculum. Also, the test only required single-word responses and most speech and language therapists could not accept such fragmentation as any indication of language ability. A final point discussed by Spradlin (1967) was that the Parsons language sample did not contain any predictions as to which students could be trained by a given procedure and which could not. In general, the results of the sample did not help the teacher or parent design an individualized training program. In retrospect, Spradlin* felt that his heavy emphasis on statistics was also a major deterrent to his program. However, Spradlin's assessment program was clearly a step in the right direction. Most of the problems can be rectified since the theoretical basis upon which Spradlin operated seems quite sound. Spradlin was a pioneer in the application of Skinner's analysis and there were few precedents in the literature to support this work. Now, however, a number of theses, dissertations, research projects and books have been written about Skinner's analysis of verbal behavior and its application is becoming more widespread (Sundberg & Partington, 1982).

Pre-Assessment Activities

Prior to the actual assessment of a mentally retarded person's verbal repertoires it is important to establish rapport with the individual. This aspect of assessment is usually viewed as somewhat of a luxury and dealt with hastily because of the cost of the speech therapist's time. However, failure to know the person who is being assessed will most likely result in an inefficient assessment and an inadequate program, and ultimately greater overall costs.

It is essential that the tester have stimulus control over the person's behavior. That is, the person being assessed must be willing to respond in the best possible way. Such control develops as a function of reinforcement and usually over an extended period of time. The failure to obtain this control will result in an assessment of a very atypical verbal repertoire. This is usually one of the main contributors to the often large discrepancies found between formal speech and language reports and informal observations by parents.

Usually it is easy to establish a positive relationship with a mentally retarded individual. The best procedure seems to be one that utilizes a large amount of reinforcement. The first step, therefore, (after reviewing the case and considering possible etiologies) should be the assembly of potential forms of reinforce-

---

*Spradin, JE. Personal Communication, 1982

ment (e.g., food, drinks, toys, tickling) to be used during the assessment. Each individual is susceptible to different types of reinforcements. These may be identified by asking questions and carefully observing what activities or items the person seems to prefer. Skillful use of the identified reinforcers will be helpful in obtaining an accurate measure of verbal behavior. The tester should ask those most familiar with the person for descriptions of items and activities that seem to interest (reinforce) the person. In addition, the tester should conduct independent observations.

The next step involves the tester's actual development of rapport with the person. The first contact should be extremely positive and the tester should be paired with the student's most powerful reinforcers and deliver them contingent on any appropriate behavior (e.g., following eye contact: praise, tickle, and give some food to the person). Slowly, the tester should make the delivery of reinforcement contingent upon some requested behavior (e.g., "look at me"). The key is for the tester to become a conditioned reinforcer for the student so the student will listen and respond to instructions. These techniques for developing rapport and stimulus control should occur in the student's most typical environment and in a very unstructured and unthreatening way.

There are several other aspects of the student's behavior and living environment that will provide useful information to those conducting the assessment. First, a measure of inappropriate behavior (e.g., excessive crying, tantrums, aggression, withdrawal) along with its antecedents and consequences can help in understanding the person's current method of communication. These data can also serve as a baseline of the current level of functioning. The lack of verbal skills is closely related to behavior problems and an effective language assessment and intervention may help to reduce these inappropriate behaviors. It is also important to observe the student's social interaction and regular behavior patterns in the natural environment. For example, you may note that the person approaches several people, although not saying anything, and may give them things or sit next to them. Knowledge of such social behavior can be very useful. A careful observation of several aspects of the student's environment will also be helpful. For example, with what objects does the person regularly come in contact? What actions does the student prefer to do or observe? What people or animals evoke interest? These data are critical for determining the first words or signs to teach a student and to further individualize the language program.

All of these preliminary observations can be conducted while establishing rapport with the student. These activities can be time-consuming and it is tempting to skip them; however, without them the results of the assessment can only be less than optimal. If one is pressed for time and money, an attempt should be made to approximate this procedure, even for higher-functioning individuals. If a tester presents the first test item shortly after meeting a person he will observe behavior that reflects that short and uncertain relationship.

The Form and Function of Language

At this point it is important to make a distinction between two major aspects of language—form and function. The form of language concerns the topography or structure of language. The form can be auditory (e.g., English, Spanish, Mandarin), visual (e.g., writing, sign language, fingerspelling, pointing) or tactile (e.g., braille). Thus, asking for water can involve many different response forms (languages), all of which will result in receipt of water given the appropriate conditions and audiences.

The functional aspect of language concerns the environmental circumstances under which a form is emitted. For example, one may say (sign, or write) "water" (the form) because someone else says (signs, or writes) "water"; the behaver wants some water; or, sees or hears a river or stream; or is asked, "What else do you need to make coffee?" and so on. In all examples the same form or word is emitted for different reasons, that is, for different functions (to get water, or to get someone to look at water, etc.). The functional aspects of language can become quite complex and elusive, but it is important to account for as much of the functional environment as possible. The goal of this assessment is to provide the reader with a behavioral account of the different circumstances under which language occurs. These different conditions or functions make up the basic outline of Skinner's book *Verbal Behavior*. Michael (1982b) has suggested some alterations in Skinner's categories and the current assessment will make use of those changes (Table 10-1).

THE RECEPTIVE REPERTOIRE

Receptive Language and Its Relation to Expressive Language

It is typical to view language development as occurring in two major steps: receptive, then expressive (Piaget, 1926, Kent, 1974). Receptive language is characterized as reacting to items such as the expressive commands, instructions, or directions, of others (Table 10-1). That is, one stands up because he was asked to do so. Expressive language is, of course, the actual emission of words or signs. A speaker is engaging in expressive language when he asks someone to "Stand up." It is common to equate these two repertoires by referring to them as part of the "understanding of the meaning of words"; and, expressive and receptive skills are viewed as the two ways to demonstrate such understanding. If one of these language skills fails to develop, usually expressive, then extensive training is often given to further strengthen the "good" repertoire with the general notion that the two are somehow equivalent. The two repertoires, however, are actually quite

Table 10-1
Skinner's Verbal Relations

Controlling Variables	Response	Consequence
Verbal stimulus with point-to-point correspondence and formal similarity	Duplic (echoic, imitation copying a text)	Social, educational, facilitative
Establishing operation (deprivation, aversive stimulation) or establishing stimulus	MAND (asking)	Specific thing or action manded
Non-verbal stimulus (an object, action, relation, property)	TACT (naming)	Social, educational facilitative
Verbal stimulus without point-to-point correspondence and formal similarity	Intraverbal word associations	Social, educational, facilitative
Verbal stimulus with point-to-point correspondence without formal similarity	Codic (reading aloud, taking dictation)	Social, educational, facilitative
Verbal stimulus (usually a mand)	Receptive Behavior* (compliance to the speaker's mand)	Social

Modified by Michael, J.L. Skinner's verbal operants: Some new categories. VB News, 1982, *1*, 2.(b)
*A special non-verbal relation

different (Guess, 1969; Sundberg, Ray, & Rueber, 1980), but they may facilitate one another. The current assessment approaches receptive language as an additional repertoire that a student must acquire. No attempt is made to equate it with expressive language or to consider it verbal behavior.

Assessing Receptive Language

To assess the receptive repertoire one should start with very simple commands such as, "Look at me," or "Come here." Then, complexity should be increased to include multiple component commands such as, "Pick up the book and touch the pen." The objective is to determine the degree to which the student complies with the tester's instructions.

Data collection is a very important aspect of a language assessment. A data sheet should be used that allows one to record the antecedent events, the actual behavior (i.e., correct, approximation, wrong or no response) and the consequences. The tester should present the antecedent stimulus, reinforce correct responses or approximations and record the data. It is extremely important to reinforce during the assessment. A more accurate assessment of a person's skills is possible when correct responses are reinforced rather than ignored as is suggested in the instructions for most standardized tests (Breuning & Davis, 1981; Breuning & Zella, 1978; Young, Bradley-Johnson, & Johnson, 1982).

Interpreting the Receptive Assessment

If a person readily complies with the tester's requests, but has a weak expressive repertoire, then little time should be spent on teaching more complex aspects of the receptive repertoire. Emphasis should instead be placed on developing the expressive skills, even if the person can only comply with simple commands. It is important, however, for a person to continue to develop his or her receptive repertoire but it should not be viewed as a prerequisite to expressive behavior. Instead, both repertoires should be developed simultaneously. In a session, for instance, receptive and expressive trials should be interspersed with each other. Techniques and procedures for teaching instruction-following can be found in the behaviorally-oriented journals (e.g., Zimmerman, Zimmerman, & Russell, 1969; Striefel & Wetherby, 1973), and language programs (e.g., Engelmann & Osborn, 1969; Guess, Sailor & Baer, 1976).

THE DUPLIC REPERTOIRE

The duplic (Michael, 1982b) is a type of verbal relation in which the form of the response (what is said, signed, written, etc.) is controlled by a verbal stimulus that has point-to-point correspondence, and in which there is formal similarity between the stimulus and the response product (i.e., they are in the same sense mode and the stimulus and the response resemble each other). The consequences for duplic behavior usually involve some kind of conditioned reinforcement (Table 10-1). Two types of duplic behavior will be covered in this assessment; echoic, which involves the vocal muscles and auditory response products; and imitation, which involves the appendage muscles and visual response products.

Assessing Echoic Behavior

The tendency to emit a vocal response (e.g., "late") that matches an auditory stimulus (e.g., "late") exemplifies the echoic relation. The objective for this part of the assessment is to find out what sounds a person can copy and if he can continue to do so when the sounds are blended together, or when they occur in larger units. Echoic behavior plays a very important function in language instruction, and knowledge of the strength of this repertoire is necessary to determine an appropriate language curriculum. There are four general levels to the echoic evaluation: phonemes, blends, words, and phrases.

The easiest type of echoic relation to produce is usually a single phoneme that matches the presented stimulus (e.g., say "mmm," can you say "mmm?") There are 42 phonemes in the English language and it is important to be able to echo or duplicate each one. Some sounds are easier than others, for example, "ah," "mmm," "oh," and "e" are easy because there are very few muscles involved. Other sounds such as, "f," "ch," "s," and "j" involve more muscles and more complex responses, hence, they are more difficult to say. For an individual who has very little vocal behavior, a good place to start is with the sounds he emits in the natural environment. In the phonetic section of the evaluation the tester is interested in identifying which sounds can be echoed in isolation. (Note: Many mentally retarded individuals can easily copy sounds. For these persons little time should be spent on this aspect of the assessment.)

The ability to blend sounds is a more difficult skill. A person may be able to emit an "s" sound in isolation but not when followed by a "p" phoneme (e.g., "spill" becomes "pill"). Combining sounds requires some fine muscle movements from one vocal position to another and is generally more difficult than emitting sounds in isolation. Some blends are much easier than others and the trials should be arranged in a simple-to-complex order. It is important to note that the assessment only samples behavior, thus, it is not necessary to assess all possible vocal combinations. The objective is to assess the strength (not the size) of a person's echoic repertoire. If a person can copy phonemes and blends, often whole words and phrases are not much more difficult. The presentation of words in the assessment should be ordered from simple (e.g., say "hat") to complex (e.g., say "exasperate"). Phrases can also be ordered from simple (e.g., say "red car") to complex (say "the big yellow ball fell into the old gutter"). The tester should collect data in the manner previously suggested and reinforce each correct response or approximation.

Assessing Imitative Behavior

The tendency to emit motor responses (e.g., clapping) that match visual stimuli (e.g., clapping) exemplifies the imitation relation. The objective for this part of the assessment is to determine if the person can copy physical movement modeled by the tester. The stimulus, "Do this," should be presented in conjunction with the movement (be careful not to include a specific instruction like, "Do this, touch your nose," because that involves the blending of two repertoires (i.e., imitative and receptive) and will confound the results of the assessment). Data should be collected and both correct responses and approximations reinforced. The tester should begin with very gross motor movement (e.g., clapping, raising hands over the head) and progress to finer movements (e.g., touching the fingertips together, picking up small objects). The task is not to determine the total number of imitative responses, but rather the strength of the imitative repertoire in terms of stimulus control (i.e., do visual stimuli appropriately control matching motor responses and at what level of complexity does stimulus control weaken?).

Interpreting the Duplic Assessment

The echoic evaluation is basically an articulation test, although it is much less formal. If the person has a strong echoic repertoire, this will be detected early in the assessment and the tester should move on to other sections. If echoic behavior is weak, then upon completion of the assessment, techniques should be used to strengthen such behavior (Lovaas, Berberich, Perloff, & Schaeffer, 1966; Sundberg, Ray, Braam, Stafford, Rueber, & Braam, 1980).

If the student can't make any vocal sounds or does very poorly on an echoic evaluation it may be reasonable to consider sign language as an alternative to vocal behavior. In terms of the effect, there is not much difference between signing "water" and saying "water." The form is not as important as the function. Unfortunately, some form is necessary to serve a function. If vocal behavior is delayed or somehow impaired and imitative behavior is strong (or even somewhat stronger than echoic behavior), one should not hesitate to consider sign language (Sundberg, 1980*). However, if imitative behavior is impossible because of physical impairments, then other non-vocal systems such as symbol boards or electronic devices should be considered (Partington & Sundberg, 1977).

There are several reasons why a mentally retarded individual can often acquire sign language more quickly than vocal speech. First, it is much easier to teach the person sign as a response form. The hands can be placed in the appropriate position and prompts can be easily faded out. Sign language allows the trainer to make clear and unambiguous examples of the appropriate response form and the shaping process is much quicker and more positive. The vocal apparatus on the other hand, cannot be manipulated into correct position sufficiently to produce desired sounds. Therefore, indirect speech therapy usually develops new skills slowly and is often aversive for the learner.

Another advantage of a signing system is that the form of a large number of signs closely resemble features in the environment. The sign for "cup" for example, which looks somewhat like a cup, is made by placing a C-shaped hand on a flat palm. This relation results in a powerful prompt already in existence between the controlling variable (e.g., the object) and the form (the signed response "cup"). English has only a few of these iconic or onomatopoetic relations (e.g., "buzz," "hiss") and they are of little help in early language instruction.

A final, and more subtle, issue deals with the history of reinforcement and

---

*Sundberg, ML. *Developing a verbal repertoire using sign language and Skinner's analysis of verbal behavior.* Unpublished doctoral dissertation, Western Michigan University, 1980

punishment, related to vocal behavior, that has prevailed for many of the individuals with weak vocal skills. Such histories typically involved frequent failure to communicate vocally and considerable urging on the part of others to attempt communication. This is a situation that has a high probability of developing various negative emotional reactions and similarly a variety of inappropriate behaviors. Effective instruction in signing may, to some extent, avoid involvement in this undesired social and emotional repertoire.

The decision to use a sign system should be a careful one. The main problem is that the success of the program is largely dependent on developing a signing environment for the person (Sundberg, Milani, & Partington, 1977). That means other people must learn and use sign language with the student. Most schools, parents, and programs approach this as a difficult task, which indeed does involve some effort; however, the gains of successful communication and intellectual development are sufficiently important and reinforcing to justify the effort. Trainers, parents, siblings, and staff should be able to learn the signs at least as fast as students with defective verbal skills.

THE MAND REPERTOIRE

The mand (Skinner, 1957, p. 35) is a type of verbal relation in which the form of the response is controlled by motivational variables, or what Michael (1982a) calls establishing operations (EO) and establishing stimuli (S^E). The consequences for the mand are quite different than those for the other types of verbal relations in that the mand specifies what would function as reinforcement for the speaker (Table 10-1). For example, under conditions of food deprivation, a person may mand, "Food please," which specifies to the listener the reinforcing value of food. If the speaker receives food it will strengthen such behavior, if not, the hungry person will probably seek another listener or engage in non-verbal methods to obtain food.

Establishing operations and establishing stimuli are very important in controlling verbal behavior. Michael (1982a) defines the EO as "any change in the environment which alters the effectiveness of some object or event as [unconditioned] reinforcement and simultaneously alters the momentary frequency of the behavior that has been followed by that reinforcement" (pp. 150–151). While the EO is restricted to unconditioned reinforcement (e.g., food, water, heat), the S^E deals with conditioned reinforcement. Michael (1982a) defines the S^E as

a stimulus change which establishes another stimulus change as conditioned reinforcement without altering the effectiveness of the relevant unconditioned reinforcement. If the behavior which has previously obtained such conditioned reinforcement now becomes strong we have an evocation relation like that produced by the establishing operation but where the effect depends upon an organism's individual history rather than the history of the species. (p. 152)

For example, the first stimulus change might be the receipt of a taped box, which might establish a knife as conditioned reinforcement, and behavior that has been reinforced in the past comes to strength, such as the mand, "Please give me a knife." The relevant source of control here involves conditioned reinforcement (obtaining the knife) rather than unconditioned reinforcement (obtaining food). For a typical speaker, a large amount of verbal behavior is controlled by the EO and S^E. Asking for help, directions, instructions, locations, and so on exemplify manding, as do all the "question words" (who, where, when, why, etc.).

Assessing the Mand Repertoire

The natural environment provides the best circumstances to assess the strength of verbal behavior, especially responses controlled by EO and S^E. The objective is to assess the person's tendency to emit a verbal response when the motivational variable is present. First, we will consider verbal behavior controlled by the EO. For example, when an individual is thirsty, does he ask for a drink? When he is hurt, does he ask for help? When he has a full bladder, does he ask for a restroom? When he is cold, does he ask for a coat? EOs occur throughout the day and many language-delayed individuals simply do not have the verbal skills to respond appropriately in these situations. Usually, the response emitted by these persons is non-verbal, non-existent, or some general response form (e.g., crying when any of the above mentioned EOs are in effect). A specific response is of course essential to the listener so that specific reinforcement can be delivered. A person who has learned to cry when EOs are present creates a situation in which a caretaker may find himself guessing as to which EO, if any, is controlling the crying behavior. The ability to emit a specific response for each EO is essential to effective communication and will greatly improve a person's probability of obtaining the desired reinforcement.

The natural environment is also useful in assessing a person's tendency to emit verbal behavior under the control of S^Es. For example, if you give a person who eats with a spoon both a plate and food without a spoon, does he ask for a spoon? Or does he cry, wtihdraw, or just look at you? There are naturally occurring S^Es in the environment and the assessment should be conducted across a variety of settings and time. Also, the S^E can be contrived or arranged for testing purposes. This type of mand assessment involves direct intervention by the tester, who sets up certain conditions in order to assess the existence and strength of the mand repertoire. The procedure begins with a chain of behaviors that the person being assessed can emit non-verbally. For example, putting dry Tang in a cup, adding water and drinking it. After the person has demonstrated the ability to complete the chain and name all the objects, remove one of the objects (e.g., the water) and ask the child to complete the chain. The question of interest is, will the person ask for the water? If so, give them the water and score the mand response correct. Another example of a contrived S^E is a chain of behaviors involving the assembly of a toy car, which includes the body, wheels and battery. After the person has demonstrated the ability to complete the chain and name the objects, remove one of the pieces. Does the person ask for the missing item?

Manding is often quite weak for a language-delayed person because the majority of traditional language instruction mainly involves receptive language and procedures for teaching the names of objects and actions. Thus, the verbal behavior that does exist is almost entirely under the control of non-verbal stimuli. When those non-verbal stimuli are removed, so is the verbal behavior. A person's response, "wheels," may be strong when the wheels are present but non-existent when the wheels would be reinforcing but are absent.

Questions are also mands, and it is important to assess the person's ability to ask questions under the control of the relevant EOs and S^Es. The natural environment constitutes the best circumstances for assessing a person's tendency to appropriately emit the responses: who, what, which, when, where, how, and why; when the relevant EOs and S^Es are present. Since the variable that controls the mand is less concrete than other controlling variables (e.g., objects), the mand assessment should be conducted across a variety of settings and people.

Interpreting the Mand Assessment

The objective of the mand assessment is to examine the degree to which verbal behavior is controlled by EOs and S^Es or motivational variables as opposed to non-verbal stimuli or verbal stimuli. If a person fails to mand in the natural environment or under contrived conditions, then procedures should be used to transfer control to those motivational variables (Guess et al., 1976; Hall, Sundberg, & Stafford, 1979; Halle, Baer, & Spradlin, 1981; Sundberg, Ray, Braam et al., 1980). If a person already mands then techniques for strengthening this repertoire should be implemented (Hart & Risley, 1978, 1980; Rogers-Warren & Warren, 1980; Sundberg, Ray, Braam et al., 1980).

THE TACT REPERTOIRE

The tact (Skinner, 1957, p. 82) is a type of verbal relation in which the form of the response is controlled by a prior non-verbal stimulus (e.g., an object, action, relation, property). The consequences for the tact usually involve some type of conditioned reinforcment (Table 10-1). In common sense terms, tacting can be thought of as the naming of items such as things, actions, and relations in the environment. Because non-verbal stimuli can effect any one, or more, of the senses and because there are a great number of non-verbal stimuli in the world, the tact repertoire can be quite large. Like the other aspects of the assessment, non-verbal stimuli should be arranged in a progression from simple to complex. The following assessment items proceed in such a manner, beginning with single component visual stimuli, then progressing to compound stimuli, and then to stimuli that affect the other sense modes.

Assessing the Tact Repertoire

Responses controlled by visual, non-verbal stimuli make up a large part of the tact repertoire, and the most basic of these stimuli are common objects in a person's environment. Such objects might be items such as books, shoes, paper, cups, or spoons. It is important that the person eventually learn the names of these items so that he can ask for them or talk about them in a conversation.

The objective of this assessment is to test the strength of the tact repertoire, that is, the degree to which non-verbal stimuli control verbal behavior. The evaluation should begin with common objects (nouns) and slowly progress to complex items. The common objects should consist of those items that are familiar to the student (i.e., those items that were noted in the pre-assessment observation). The person should be presented with the object (e.g., a toy car) while the tester says, "What's that?" Correct responses or approximations should be reinforced and the relevant data recorded.

Pictures can be used during the assessment of common objects but the tester should note that pictures are more difficult to identify than real objects. However, for complex items (e.g., circus, supermarket), pictures are often necessary and can vary from a silhouette to a color photograph.

The next level of complexity consists of visual actions (verbs). Since actions are transitory they may represent a more difficult type of stimulus control. The assessment should contain samples of actions ranging from simple movements (e.g., jumping) to more complex ones (e.g., adjusting). The student should be presented with the action (e.g., pushing) while the tester says, "What am I doing?" Correct responses or approximations should be reinforced and the relevant data recorded.

A combination of objects and actions (or multiple features of one object) should be assessed next. For example, a trial may consist of placing several objects on a table and asking the person, "What do you see?" The aim is to determine the extent to which the individual can emit multiple responses (e.g., "book and shoe," "blue hat," or, "girl jump").

Prepositions are even more complex than nouns and verbs because they represent relations such as those that exist between nouns, verbs, or nouns and verbs. A spoon and a table can easily be seen and identified, but what about the word "on"? It cannot be touched or picked up because it is a non-verbal spacial relation between two items. Thus, the stimuli controlling such responses as "in," "on," or "above" are more vague than those of "book," or "jump." As a result, they usually develop later in a typical child's repertoire. Combinations of nouns, verbs, and prepositions should also be tested. For example, place a red ball in a green cup, and a blue car on a white plate, and ask the person, "Where is the _____?"

Adjectives and adverbs represent properties or specific features of objects and actions. Many adjectives are relative in nature. A pencil might be long compared to a toothpick, but that same pencil is short when compared to a baseball bat. Acquiring this relative discrimination can be difficult and usually takes considerable time to learn (Skinner, 1957, p. 107). Learning colors involves the acquisition of behavior which is controlled by a single feature of an object (its redness versus its squareness, texture, size, etc.). An object can have many different attributes; it can be clean, dry, fast and blue or it can be old, sick, and tired. Learning to name these properties of objects and actions often requires many training trials and these tacts do not develop until nouns and verbs are strong in a person's repertoire. Again, combinations should be presented to assess the person's ability to emit multiple responses.

It is also important to be able to name things or events that affect the other sensory systems. First, there can be many tacts under the control of non-verbal auditory stimuli. Hearing a phone ring and saying "phone," or hearing an airplane and saying, "plane," are examples. Visual stimuli are not always present when talking, so if one only learns to tact objects and actions visually (i.e., the object itself), then he may not react effectively when just the auditory stimulus is present (i.e., the noise produced by the object). To assess this repertoire the tester should block the visual system (e.g., turn out the lights, use a blindfold) and ask the person, "What do you hear?" Auditory tacts of common sounds (e.g., water running) are more easily acquired than those of less common sounds (e.g., a falling tree). Auditory discriminations, like visual discriminations, are behaviors that are learned by contact with the environment (shaping). An example of a strong auditory tact repertoire is that of a musician who can discriminate among slight tone differences.

The tactile sensory system also plays a role in language. Often a person must know the names of things without the benefit of seeing or hearing them. In a dark room, for example, a parent may ask a child to help her find the cat and to reach under the bed and to tell her if he feels it. Tactile stimuli can range from simple to complex. During the assessment, the tester should block the visual system (e.g., having the person reach into a box, turning off the lights) and ask the question, "What do you feel?" Examples of simple tactile items might be cups, balls, or books, while more difficult items might involve textures, shapes and mechanical objects. An example of a strong tactile repertoire is that that is obtained by a blind person who must depend heavily on tactile stimulation for survival. The blind person acquires these skills not because of any extra biological equipment but because of the environmental contingencies (e.g., a blind person quickly learns to feel his way around because it allows him to successfully get places without being hurt).

Language also occurs under the control of olfactory (smell) stimuli. These make up a much smaller part of a typical verbal repertoire. A person usually acquires the names for common smells such as cake, soap, or flowers. But it is important that the person eventually have names for other smells such as spoiled meat, gas or smoke. The olfactory tact repertoire can be assessed in the same manner as the others (i.e., blocking off the other senses) and going from simple to complex. The tester should present the person with the stimulation and say, "What do you smell?" Correct responses or approximations should be reinforced and the relevant data recorded.

The last of the more common sensory systems to be assessed is the gustatory (taste) system. These tacts comprise only a small part of our language skills but are still important. Consumption of some poisons and harmful substances may be prevented if the taste can be identified. The four basic tastes that affect the human are sweet, sour, bitter, and salt. The combinations of these are almost endless. We can name many of the foods we eat by taste alone; some, we cannot identify in this way. Assessment of the gustatory tact repertoire should be conducted while the other senses are blocked. The tester should present the person with a specific taste and ask, "What does that taste like?" As always, appropriately consequate the response and record the data.

A final, and complex, aspect of the tact repertoire involves the ability to tact stimuli that arise within the body. Inside a person's skin there are sensory systems (e.g., mechanoreceptors, thermoreceptors, free nerve endings) that are affected by various environmental changes. For example, improper eating and dental care can result in aversive stimulation arising from the free nerve endings in the teeth and gums. This stimulation can control several different forms of non-verbal behavior (e.g., holding the jaw, clenching the teeth) and, for an advanced speaker, several forms of verbal behavior (e.g., "My tooth hurts," or, "I need a dentist"). The non-verbal behavior presents no special problem but the verbal behavior does.

How does a person learn to tact this private stimulation? The problem is that only the person with the toothache is affected by the stimulus, hence, how does the trainer know when to punish incorrect responses and reinforce correct ones? It is much easier to teach a person to tact objects that both the teacher and the student have access. For example, to teach a person to tact "book," a trainer has access to the presence or absence of the book. When the stimulation is private, differential shaping is impossible. Yet, typical children and mentally retarded persons do acquire verbal behavior that is controlled by private events (albeit the behavior is weak in many cases).

Skinner (1945, 1953, & 1957) has described four methods that the verbal community uses to teach people to tact private stimuli. These four are called public accompaniment, collateral responses, common properties, and response reduction. The methods will be described and offered as a tool for assessing the level of a person's verbal behavior under the control of private events.

Frequently a private event is accompanied by an observable public stimulus. For example, a painful internal stimulus may be accompanied by blood or bruises. Or, an observer may see a person fall down, bump into something, or poke themselves, all of which usually accompany painful stimuli. The verbal community uses these circumstances to teach people to correctly identify painful sensations.

A language assessment can make use of these public stimuli to determine if

an individual appropriately tacts private events. The natural environment constitutes the best conditions for assessing this repertoire. The tester should observe
the person during typical activities and determine if accurate verbal behavior is
emitted (e.g., "ouch") when the public stimulus is observed (e.g., pricking himself with a pin). If not, can the person emit the response with a prompt such as,
"What's wrong?" If so, mark it as correct and record the occurrence of the prompt.

A person may also engage in specific collateral behavior (e.g., holding the
stomach) when a private stimulus is present (e.g., stomachache). These collateral behaviors can also be used to teach and assess verbal behavior controlled by
private stimulation. The tester should watch for these collateral behaviors and
record the relevant verbal behavior. If no responses occur when, say, a person is
pacing by a locked bathroom door (collateral behavior), the tester should prompt
by asking, "What's wrong?" or, "What do you want?" If the response "bathroom" or something similar occurs it should be scored as correct and the prompt
noted.

The final two methods, common properties and response reduction, are relevant for those persons who already have a fairly complex verbal repertoire. Common properties involve circumstances where private stimuli share some of the
features of public stimuli. A sensation in the leg may be described as, "a mushy
leg with tingles." Thus, metaphors may be used to describe private stimulation
(exemplified by the responses often emitted by a patient who is asked by a physician to describe his pain). Some higher-functioning mentally retarded individuals
may emit metaphors to describe these stimuli. If so, the responses should be recorded and appropriately consequated.

Response reduction consists of conditions in which a response is learned
under public conditions and is later transferred to private conditions. For example,
the verbal community may teach a student to tact his arm as "moving in circles."
Along with the visual (public) stimuli there are kinesthetic (private) stimuli (i.e.,
the sensations from the muscles, tendons, and joints). A student may initially be
able to say, "moving in circles," when both visual and kinesthetic stimuli are
present, but eventually the response can come under the control of the kinesthetic
stimuli alone, which are always present. For example, a student may look, see
his arm rotating, and feel his muscles moving in a similar manner. Soon, he learns
that he doesn't need to check his arm because whenever his muscles move in that
manner his arms rotate, and eventually there is no need to check the public stimulus because the private ones are usually reliable. This is the process by which one
learns to describe his bodily conditions in the absence of visual stimuli (e.g., in a
dark room).

Assessing a person's ability to tact kinesthetic stimulation can be done by
blindfolding the person and asking them to identify their body position or movement (e.g., sitting, standing, jumping, squatting, etc.). The limbs can be moved
up, down, or rotated, and the tester should ask, "What are your arms doing?"
Correct responses or approximations should be reinforced and the data recorded.

Accurate verbal behavior under the control of private stimulation represents a rather advanced form of communication. Many mentally retarded individuals suffer from the inability to tact bodily conditions. Such obvious suffering often encourages trainer to immediately begin a language program with procedures to teach this behavior. Frequently, the need to tact private events is given as the rational for a language program (e.g., "He needs to learn language so he can express his wants and needs."). However, tacting private events is complicated and a person should have a fair amount of simple mands and tacts before such training is heavily emphasized. The reader who is interested in the study of private events is encouraged to read the relevant sections in Skinner's writings.

Interpreting the Tact Assessment

Often, weaknesses in the tact repertoire are very obvious. A person may be able to tact objects and actions but not relations. The individual may be only able to emit single tacts under the control of visual stimuli. The results of the tact assessment can clearly suggest areas of intervention. This repertoire (except private events) has received a great deal of professional attention (unfortunately, at the expense of the other repertoires), and the literature contains several procedures and methods to teach this behavior (Engelmann & Osborn, 1969; Guess et al., 1976; Sundberg, Ray, Braam et al., 1980; Welch & Pear, 1980).

THE INTRAVERBAL REPERTOIRE

The intraverbal (Skinner, 1957, p. 71) is a type of verbal relation in which the form of the response is controlled by antecedent verbal stimuli that lack point-to-point correspondence to the verbal response (approximately the opposite of the duplic relation). The consequences for the intraverbal usually involve some form of conditioned reinforcement (Table 10-1). Word associations like a tendency to say, "cat," when someone says, "dog and ———," exemplifies intraverbal behavior. The ability to fill in the missing words, as in, "put on your shoes and ———," or, "you wake up in the ———," depends on the strength of one's intraverbal repertoire.

In the early stages of eductional training, a considerable amount of intraverbal behavior is developed in activities such as counting, reciting the alphabet, singing songs, listing the colors, or listing types of animals. Eventually educators work on the development of more complex intraverbal repertoires (e.g., conversations, mathematics, history, political science, psychology). This training usually results in fairly strong tendencies for certain verbal stimuli to evoke verbal responses other than echoic responses. Some are relatively trivial in their communicative effect, such as tendencies to say "pool" on hearing or seeing the word "swimming." These word associations are not trivial, however, in their role in facilitating effective verbal behavior by a speaker or signer. The intraverbal repertoire is quite important for rapid and effective speaking and listening. For example, it is relatively important that verbal responses such as, "pool," "sun," "cooler," "towels," and "beach," be readily available when "swimming" is introduced into a conversation.

Assessing the Intraverbal Repertoire

The task for a tester is to determine the strength and complexity of the intraverbal repertoire. As with the other aspects of the assessment, a careful analysis of the stimulus control involved and the response unit emitted will provide a frame for the intraverbal assessment.

The most basic form of a verbal stimulus is probably one that contains a single feature or unit such as "bread and ———," and is somewhat relevant to the person being tested. The tester should begin by presenting the person with open-ended phrases and recording the topography of the person's responses. The point is to see if a word (e.g., eat) evokes a related responses (e.g., apple). Examples of single controlling variables might be ones such as asking the person to name a food, drink, animal, color, body part, or clothing item. These single stimuli should then be increased in complexity of content to include such items as naming a state, president, or automobile. A person's ability to emit an appropriate response is dependent on his verbal history, as well as the current contingencies. A careful sequencing of stimuli will provide the tester with some indication of the strength of that history.

Another indication of the strength of the intraverbal repertoire is the number of responses that the person is able to emit when presented a single verbal stimulus. For example, given the verbal stimuli, "Name some vegetables," how many can the person name? A strong history regarding talking about vegetables should allow one to easily emit several appropriate responses. Note that this part of the assessment is concerned with verbal behavior that is controlled by other verbal behavior, not by non-verbal stimuli, EOs or S^Es, thus the tester should be careful that such variables are not present during this aspect of the assessment.

The verbal stimuli that control verbal behavior in day-to-day conversations usually involve more than one component. For example, a teacher might ask a student, "Did you see the baseball game last night?" To respond correctly the student's behavior must be appropriately controlled by the three main variables in the questions (i.e., see versus go, baseball versus football, last night versus last week). An incorrect response may be emitted if one or more of the variables fail to control the student's response. An assessment of a person's ability to respond to multiple verbal stimuli should begin with two or three components on an easy topic (e.g., name some hot foods, cold drinks, or land animals) and progress to several components (e.g., "Name some hot foods that you eat in the morning," or, "What do you wear on your hands when it's cold?"). Then the topics should be increased in complexity, for example, "What's seven plus seven?" or, "What's your home address?"

A final method to assess the strength of a person's intraverbal repertoire is to pick a topic and ask a series of questions (what, when, which, where, who, how, and why) about that topic. This can be done with easy topics (e.g., ice cream, chairs, paper) and more difficult topics (e.g., fish tanks, stores, machines). The tester should pick a topic, for example, "cars" and ask, "What is a car?" "Where do you see cars?" "When do you need a car?" or, "How do you drive a car?" This procedure can be conducted with any number of different topics and at varying levels of complexity. The entire verbal episodes should be recorded and responses appropriately consequated.

Interpreting the Intraverbal Assessment

The intraverbal repertoire, like the mand repertoire, is often quite weak for a language-delayed person. A person may have hundreds of tacts but only a few intraverbal responses. This situation is usually due to ineffective training as opposed to a lack of ability to acquire such behavior. The assessment will provide the language trainer with the strength of this repertoire and will suggest a starting point for training. For example, if the person can only make single responses to a few verbal stimuli, then training should begin at that level. However, if the person can easily respond to compound stimuli, then developing an intraverbal repertoire for specific topics would be appropriate.

The basic procedure for teaching intraverbal behavior involves the transfer of stimulus control from non-verbal or duplic sources to verbal stimuli (Braam, Sundberg, Ray, Braam, Stafford, Rueber, Thompson, Stang, & Jackson, 1979; Raymore & McLean, 1971, Partington & Bailey, 1980; Sundberg, 1980; Sundberg, Ray, Braam et al., 1980).

THE CODIC REPERTOIRE

The codic repertoire (Michael, 1982b) includes what Skinner (1957, pp. 65–71) calls "textual behavior" and "taking dictation," as well as some additional relations. Michael (1982b) defines the codic as a type of verbal behavior in which the

response form is controlled by 1) a verbal stimulus, with which it 2) has point-to-point correspondence, but there is NO formal similarity between stimulus and response product. Formal similarity is Skinner's term for the case where the controlling stimulus and the response product are 1) in the same mode (both are visual, auditory, tactile, etc.) and 2) resemble each other in the physical sense of resemblance. *Textual* and *taking dictation* are special types of codic behavior. the textual relation is where the stimulus is visual (written or printed "words") and the response consists of speaking. In common sense terms textual behavior is reading aloud (without the implication that the reader "understands" what is being read). Taking dictation is where the stimulus is auditory (the result of someone's vocal behavior) and the response consists of writing what is heard. (p. 1)

The consequences for codic behavior usually consist of some type of conditioned reinforcement (Table 10-1).

Michael's broadening of Skinner's categories allows us to include such verbal relations as reading written sign language (Stokoe, Casterline, & Croneberg, 1965), and reading Braille. In written sign language, the stimulus is visual (as in textual behavior) but the response is also visual (Skinner's definition restricts the use of textual to only those conditions in which the response is vocal). In Braille, the stimulus is tactile (as opposed to visual) but the response is still "reading aloud."

In some respects, codic behavior is like duplic behavior except the response does not produce a stimulus that matches the controlling stimulus. When you read aloud, you do not produce a written visual stimulus, but produce instead an auditory stimulus. This auditory stimulus matches the written one, but not in the strict use of "match" since they are in different sense modes. Still, saying "hat" as a result of seeing "hat" written on a chalkboard seems more of a match than saying "shoes" as a result of seeing "hat." Skinner used the term "point-to-point correspondence" to refer to this "lesser" type of matching, thus, in codic behavior the beginning of the stimulus, for example, is closely related to the beginning of the response, and the middle of the stimulus is closely related to the middle of the response.

Reading and writing are often viewed as complex behaviors that are beyond the reach of many mentally retarded individuals. Unfortunately, this position is maintained by psychologists and generative grammarians who have focused "their interest on the mental events assuming to underly [language]" (Salzinger, 1978, p. 277). As a result, many programs focus on developing cognitive "reading readiness skills" that are viewed as necessary before actual reading instruction can begin. Furthermore, when it does begin, it is usually of poor quality (Engelmann, 1975).

Sundberg (1980,* experiment 8) conducted a study to determine if two mentally retarded 4.5-year-old girls could acquire the basics of a textual repertoire. Six months prior to the start of the study, both girls had virtually no functional language. Earlier experiments in the Sundberg study described the procedure that was used to teach sign language to the girls. Both acquired a fairly large sign repertoire and some vocal behavior during the six months of training; they began the textual study with that signing history. During approximately one month of echoic-to-textual transfer training, the girls were able to produce the sounds for 15 to 20 fingerspelled letters and sight-read two to four words. Sundberg (1980) concludes the following.

---

*Sundberg, M. *Developing a verbal repertoire using sign language and Skinner's analysis of verbal behavior.* Unpublished doctoral dissertation, Western Michigan University, 1980

Perhaps the most interesting aspect of these data were that such individuals could acquire basic letter discrimination in such a short period of time. This may simply point out that the procedure of transferring stimulus control from an echoic stimulus to a manual stimulus is an effective procedure for generating a type of textual behavior. The procedure makes no appeal to "cognitive levels" or "reading readiness," both of which would have predicted failure. (p. 102)

Assessing the Codic Repertoire

The aim of this assessment is to determine the degree to which an individual can produce sounds (or fingerspelled letters) that correspond to a presented written (or Braille) letter; produce words that correspond to presented written (or Braille) words; write a letter (fingerspell it, or punch it in Braille) that corresponds to a vocal phoneme; and write words (fingerspell them, or punch them in Braille) that correspond to vocal words (spelling).

There are two general approaches to teaching reading. They have been called the "phonetic approach" and the "whole word approach." In phonetic reading, the student learns specific sounds for each letter in a word and then blends them together. Since English is a non-phonetic language (i.e., we have 42 phonemes and only 26 letters) a fair amount of whole word reading is also necessary for effective reading. Whole word reading consists of emitting a response that is controlled by the configuration of the word rather than that of each individual phoneme.

Since whole-word reading is often easier, many mentally retarded individuals can acquire this faster than phonetic reading. Although, as mentioned previously, a combination of both repertoires will eventually be necessary. The reading assessment should consist of presenting the student with the letters and asking "What sound is that?" and presenting the student with a sample of whole words and asking "What word is that?" Correct responses or approximations should be reinforced and the data recorded.

Reading comprehension is often referred to as a person's ability to understand what he has read. This repertoire is usually assessed by further tests consisting of questions (e.g., "Whose ball was it?" or pictures (e.g., "What word is that? Touch the ———.") Reading then involves two repertoires: emitting the correct textual response, and being able to react effectively to the verbal stimuli in other ways. The effectiveness of the reaction depends on the strength of the student's mand, tact, and intraverbal repertoires and these should be assessed as well.

Writing can be assessed by using paper and pencil or a typewriter. There are two basic repertoires involved in writing: the ability to write the letters, and the ability to write a specific letter when requested to do so. Emphasis is, unfortunately, usually placed on "writing form" and often becomes aversive for the student. Thus, he may have little tendency to write because of this aversive history. The use of a typewriter may allow one to by-pass the requirement that a person be able to write letters before he can be taught how to take dictation (or self-dictation).

The assessment of these repertoires can consist of presenting the student with letters and words and ask them to write or type them. Correct responses or approximations should be reinforced and data recorded.

Interpreting the Codic Assessment

If a student cannot emit vocal responses under the control of written stimuli, then transfer of stimulus control procedures should be implemented (Braam, Daeshlein, & Braam, 1979; Corey & Shamow, 1972; Engelmann & Bruner, 1974; Sundberg, 1980*). It is suggested that a trainer begin a reading program using words that are relevant and, even better, are reinforcing to the student. That is, do not use commercial readers; design one that is directly relevant to the person you are teaching (Engelmann, 1975). If a person can emit textual responses but fails to respond correctly on tests of comprehension, then training on those repertoires should occur. Since spelling and reading involve different contingencies (Lee & Pegler, 1982; Skinner, 1957) specific training for spelling should occur (Dixon & Engelmann, 1979; Dixon, Engelmann, Meier, Stecly, & Wells, 1980).

CONCLUSIONS

Several issues concerning the nature of this assessment need to be addressed. First, the program is not a "cookbook" that contains step-by-step instructions as to what words or items to assess. Rather, the goal of this chapter is to facilitate a thorough and integrated understanding of the components of language so that a tester is in an informal and flexible position to individualize the assessment, and hence, develop the most beneficial language program for a student. The author has, in some cases, suggested certain words, but these are only given as examples since it is impossible to specify which words are relevant to a particular student. Each has a different history and interaction with his current environment. The reader has access to some of these data and should incorporate them into a particular student's assessment.

Second, the assessment is only a sample of a person's verbal repertoire. It is impossible to determine all the verbal relations in a given speaker's repertoire (unless it is extremely limited). Verbal responses occur under such a wide variety of circumstances that, even if a tester followed someone all day for several weeks, all possible responses probably would not occur. Traditional assessments recognize this problem and only a sample of words are tested. But most programs fail to distinguish between the five verbal repertoires, and results are usually lumped together into one or two categories, thus, providing less useful information to the language programmer.

---

*Sundberg, M. *Developing a verbal repertoire using sign language and Skinner's analysis of verbal behavior.* Unpublished doctoral dissertation, Western Michigan University, 1980

Third, the best conditions for conducting an assessment probably consist of a blend of natural and contrived situations. Several types of verbal behavior may never occur under formal testing conditions, and observations in the student's natural environment will allow the tester to obtain these data. Contrived conditions are useful because a tester can evoke a large amount of behavior in a short period of time, and control the antecedents much better, which allows for more appropriate sequencing of the material.

Fourth, it is not necessary to conduct every phase of the assessment for each person. For example, if one fails to tact objects and actions, then he probably cannot tact properties or private events, or read. Once a general functioning level has been determined (i.e., the strength of each of the verbal repertoires) then training on the weak areas should begin. Note that the order of items presented in this assessment should not imply that receptive behavior occurs, for example, before mands, or that mands occur before tacts. Rather, that language is made up of all these different repertoires and training should be conducted on them simultaneously (although, perhaps at different intensities).

Finally, language assessment is an ongoing process. In a good environment, new behaviors are acquired every day and a trainer needs to know what to teach next. Table 10-2 contains an overview of the assessment program and can be used as a quick guide for the major parts of each repertoire.

Acknowledgments

I would like to acknowledge Dr. Jack Michael for his numerous contributions to this chapter and Dr. A. Charles Catania for reviewing the manuscript. Also, I thank my research associates David Ray, Steven Braam, Mark Stafford,

Table 10-2
Assessment Overview
___

Pre-Assessment Activities
  Establish rapport
    collect list of reinforcers
    deliver reinforcers contingent on appropriate behavior
    deliver reinforcers contingent on a requested response

  Acquire baseline measures of inappropriate behavior and social behavior.

  Make a list of items and actions that are relevant to person being tested. These words will eventually be used as the initial vocabulary for language training.

Assessment of Non-Verbal Behavior
  The receptive repertoire
    follows simple commands, instructions
    follows compound commands, instructions
    follows complex commands, instructions   continued

Table 10-2 (continued)

Assessment of Verbal Behavior
The duplic repertoire
can echo:
phonemes
blends, words
phrases
can imitate:
gross movements
fine movements

The mand repertoire
In the natural environment can ask:
for unconditioned form of reinforcement (EO)
for the removal of unconditioned forms of punishment (EO)
for types of conditioned reinforcement (S^E)
appropriate questions
In a contrived situation can ask:
for missing items
appropriate questions

The tact repertoire
can visually tact:
objects
actions
combinations of actions or objects
relations
combinations of relations
properties
combinations of properties
private events
can auditorily tact same items listed above
can tactilely tact same items listed above
can tact gustatory stimuli
can tact olfactory stimuli

The intraverbal repertoire
can provide a single response given a single verbal stimulus
can provide a multiple response given a single verbal stimulus
can provide a single response given a multiple verbal stimulus
can provide a multiple response given a multiple verbal stimulus
can appropriately respond to a series of questions on a simple topic
can appropriately respond to a series of questions on a complex topic

The codic repertoire
can produce sounds (or fingerspelled letters) that correspond to presented written (or braille) letters
can produce words that correspond to presented written (or braille) words
can write a letter (fingerspell it, or punch it in braille) that corresponds to a vocal phoneme
can write words (fingerspell them, or punch them in braille) that correspond to vocal words

Thomas Rueber, Cassandra Braam, James Partington and Gerald Shook for their contributions. Support for writing this chapter was provided by the Regional Center of the East Bay, Oakland, California; Jose Maltos, Executive Director, and Mike Weber, Program Director.

REFERENCES

Braam, CA, Daeschlein, M, & Braam, SJ. *Mediated transfer in reading instruction with special populations*. Paper presented at the Fifth Annual Association for Behavior Analysis Convention, Dearborn, MI, June 1979

Braam, SJ, Sundberg, ML, Ray, DA, Braam, CA, Stafford, MW, Rueber, TM, Thompson, T, Stang, S, & Jackson, B. *Recent procedural developments in teaching an intraverbal repertoire.* Paper presented at the Fifth Annual Association for Behavior Analysis Convention, Dearborn, MI, June 1979

Breuning, SE, & Davis, VI. Reinforcement effects on the intelligence test performance of institutionalized retarded adults: Behavior analysis, directional control, and implications for habilitation. *Applied Research in Mental Retardation,* 1981, *2,* 307–321

Breuning, SE, & Zella, WF. Effects of individualized incentives on norm-referenced IQ test performance of high school students in special education classes. *Journal of School Psychology,* 1978, *16,* 220–226

Corey, JR, & Shamow, JC. The effects of fading on the acquisition and retention of oral reading. *Journal of Applied Behavior Analysis,* 1972, *5,* 311–315

Dixon, B, & Engelmann, S. *Corretive spelling through morphographs.* Chicago: Sicence Research Associates, 1979

Dixon, B, Engelmann, S, Meier, MY, Stecly, D, & Wells, T. *Mastery Spelling.* Chicago: Science Research Associates, 1980

Engelmann, S. *Your child can succeed!* New York: Simon and Schuster, 1975

Engelmann, S, & Bruner, E. *Distar reading.* Chicago: Science Research Associates, 1974

Engelmann, S, & Osborn, J. *Distar language.* Chicago: Science Research Associates, 1969

Guess, D. A functional analysis of receptive language and productive speech: Acquisition of the plural morpheme. *Journal of Applied Behavior Analysis,* 1969, *2,* 55–64

Guess, D, Sailor, WS, & Baer, DM. *A functional speech and language training program for the severely handicapped.* Lawrence, KS: H & H Enterprises, Inc., 1976

Hall, G, Sundberg, ML, & Stafford, MW. *Teaching a mand repertoire to deaf individuals: Transfer of stimulus control from imitative or tact variables to the establishing operation.* Paper presented at the Fifth Annual Association for Behavior Analysis Convention, Dearborn, MI, June 1979

Halle, JW, Baer, DM, & Spradlin, JE. Teachers' generalized use of delay as a stimulus control procedure to increase language use in handicapped children. *Journal of Applied Behavior Analysis,* 1981, *14,* 389–409

Hart, By, & Risley, TR. Promoting productive language through incidental teaching. *Education and Urban Society,* 1978, *10,* 407–429

Hart, B, & Risley, TR. In vivo language intervention: Unanticipated general effects. *Journal of Applied Behavior Analysis,* 1980, *13,* 407–432

Kent, LR. *Language acquisition program for the retarded or multiply impaired.* Champaign, IL: Research Press, 1974

Lee, VL, & Pegler, AM. Effects on spelling of training children to read. *Journal of the Experimental Analysis of Behavior,* 1982, *37,* 311–322

Lovaas, OI. *The autistic child: Language development through behavior modification.* New York: Irvington Publishers, 1977

Lovaas, OI, Berberich, JP, Perloff, BF, & Schaeffer, B. Acquisition of imitative speech by schizophrenic children. *Science,* 1966, *151,* 705–707

Michael, JL. Distinguishing between discriminative and motivational functions of stimuli. *Journal of the Experimental Analysis of Behavior,* 1982, *37,* 149–155 (a)

Michael, JL. Skinner's verbal operants: Some new categories. *VB News,* 1982, *1,* 2 (b)

Partington, JW, & Bailey, JS. *Teaching an intraverbal repertoire to normal preschool children.* Paper presented at the Sixth Annual Association for Behavior Analysis Convention, Dearborn, MI, May 1980

Partington, JW, & Sundberg, ML. *Bliss Symbolics.* Paper presented at the Third Annual Association for Behavior Analysis Convention, Chicago, IL, May 1977

Piaget, J. *The language and thought of the child* (M. Cook, trans.). London: Routledge and Kegan Paul, Ltd., 1926

Raymore, S, & McLean, JE. A clinical program for carry-over of articulation therapy with retarded children. In JE McLean, DE Yoder, & RL Schiefelbusch (Eds.), *Language intervention with the retarded: Developing strategies.* Baltimore: University Park Press, 1971

Rogers-Warren, A, & Warren, S. Mands for verbalizations: Facilitating the display of newly trained language in children. *Behavior Modification* 1980, *4,* 361–382

Salzinger, K. Language behavior. In AC Catania, & TA Brigham (Eds.), *Handbook of applied behavior analysis: Social and instructional processes.* New York: Irvington Publishers, 1978

Skinner, BF. The operational analysis of psychological term. *Psychological Review,* 1945, *52,* 270–277

Skinner, BF. *Science and Human Behavior.* New York: Free Press, 1953

Skinner, BF. *Verbal Behavior.* Englewood Cliffs, NJ: Prentice-Hall, 1957

Spradlin, JE. Assessment of speech and language of retarded children: The Parsons language sample. In RL Schiefelbusch (Ed.), Language studies of mentally retarded children. *Journal of Speech and Hearing Disorders Monograph,* 1963, *10,* 8–31

Spradlin, JE. Environmental factors and the language development of retarded children. In S Rosenberg (Ed.), *Developments in Applied Psycholinguistic Research,* Riverside, NJ: The MacMillian Company, 1966

Spradlin, JE. Procedures for evaluation processes associated with receptive and expressive language. In R Schiefelbusch, R Copeland, & J Smith (Eds.), *Language and mental retardation.* New York: Holt, Reinhart and Winston, 1967

Stokoe, WC, Casterline, D, & Croneberg, C. *A dictionary of American sign language based on linguistic principles.* Washington, DC: Gallaudet College Press, 1965

Striefel, S, & Wetherby, B. Instruction—following behavior of a retarded child and its controlling stimuli. *Journal of Applied Behavior Analysis,* 1973, *6,* 663–670

Sundberg, ML, Milani, I, & Partington, JW. *The use of sign language with hearing, non-vocal mentally impaired persons.* Paper presented at the 85th Annual Meeting of the American Psychological Association, San Francisco, CA, August 1977

Sundberg, ML, & Partington, JW. Skinner's Verbal Behavior: A reference list. *VB News,* 1982, *1,* 3–5

Sundberg, ML, Ray, DA, Braam, SJ, Stafford, MW, Rueber, TM, & Braam, CA. A manual for the use of B. F. Skinner's analysis of verbal behavior for language assessment and programming. *Western Michigan University Behavioral Monograph,* (No. 9), 1980

Sundberg, ML, Ray, DA, & Rueber, TM. Issues in language research. *Western Michigan University Behavioral Monograph,* (No. 7), 1980

Welch, SJ, & Pear, JJ. Generalization of naming responses to objects in the natural environment as a function of training stimulus modality with retarded children. *Journal of Applied Behavior Analysis,* 1980, *13,* 629–643

Young, RM, Bradley-Johnson, S, & Johnson, CM. Immediate and delayed reinforcement on WISC-R performance for mentally retarded students. *Applied Research in Mental Retardation,* 1982, *3,* 13–20

Zimmerman, EH, Zimmerman, J, & Russell, CD. Differential effects of token reinforcement on instruction-following behavior in retarded students instructed as a group. *Journal of Applied Behavior Analysis,* 1969, *2,* 101–112

Michael L. Jones
Todd R. Risley
James E. Favell

11
Ecological Patterns

The goal of most, if not all, treatment efforts with the mentally retarded is to ameliorate skill deficits. To date, the most effective techniques for achieving this have been derived from applied behavior analysis (i.e., behavior modification). Inherent in this behavioral approach is the premise that behavior is controlled largely by the environment in which it occurs, and consequently that behavior may be modified by systematic manipulation of environmental determinants. The effectiveness of behavior modification techniques is determined by such factors as the degree of stimulus control, the influence of other (facilitating or competing) setting events, and the nature and degree of control over contingencies; all factors that are primarily environment-mediated. Moreover, the generalization and maintenance of treatment effects are determined by the influence of these environmental factors across settings and over time.

Despite the successes of behavioral treatment technology, it does not always work and when it fails, we are often less likely to fault the technology than the persons with whom it is attempted. This is particularly apparent in attitudes toward the more severely disabled and the ongoing argument over their educability. Some experts argue that our best technology has been employed with this population and it has failed to improve skill deficits; therefore these individuals are ineducable (Bailey, 1981; Ellis, 1979, 1981; Professional Advisory Committee, 1979). The counterargument is that exhaustive efforts have not been made to employ our best technology (e.g., Baer, 1981; Favell, Risley, Wolfe, Riddle & Rasmussen, 1981). We support the latter argument and suggest that, not only have these efforts been non-exhaustive, but relatively little attention has been given to where these efforts have been made. Quite often habilitation is attempted in nonconducive environment. Therefore, when treatment fails, fault lies not only with the technology but also in settings that don't support the treatment. If researchers hope to understand why treatment fails, then it is necessary to gain a better understanding of how the environment influences treatment effectiveness. Professionals will undoubtedly find some settings (e.g., institutions) in which efforts to provide effective treatment will be fruitless until the environment is able to support these efforts.

The deinstitutionalization movement has expanded the variety of treatment environments in which mentally retarded persons may reside. Although a burgeoning literature exists on the impact of transitions from institutional to non-institutional or less restrictive environments, there is still little empirical data regarding functional differences between various setting alternatives, or among settings of a particular type (Crawford, Aiello, & Thompson, 1979). There is also little data to suggest the type of treatment setting that is most appropriate for individuals with different characteristics. If the unique nature and type of disabilities exhibited by an individual warrant the development of an individualized treatment plan, then they should also warrant the selection of the most appropriate environment for providing this treatment. In addition as the treatment needs of the individual change with progressive development, so too must his or her environmental needs (Rosen, 1977).

With a growing variety of settings available to an expanding range of mentally retarded persons, behavioral scientists are increasingly called upon to determine the probable behavioral effects of different settings. They are asked to advise on the design or modification of settings that will optimize treatment effectiveness. Although it is common to engage in practical modification of settings in order to facilitate behavior change, there is little in the way of a data base on environmental design.

It appears that a strong case can be made for greater attention to the environment's influence on the behavior of the mentally retarded. Systematic analysis of environment-behavior relationships is necessary: (1) to improve the effectiveness and applicability of treatment technology, both in terms of behavior modification interventions and in the development of environmental design interventions; (2) to aid in the prescriptive placement of mentally retarded persons in the most suitable treatment environment for the type and degree of their disability and their changing environmental needs over time; and, (3) to evaluate the overall quality of treatment settings in order to improve existing environments and shape the design of future environments that will maximize adaptive functioning.

Analyses of the sort required to attain these goals necessitate studying behavior from a more ecological perspective. While these analyses are useful in evaluating treatment effectiveness and quality of treatment environments, the focus should remain on the behavioral functioning of mentally retarded individuals. Thus, the perspective is more ecobehavioral in nature; one that goes beyond traditional behavior analysis to include measurement of both behavior and the environment where it occurs (Rogers-Warren, 1982; Rogers-Warren & Warren, 1977; Willems,

1977). This chapter will describe such a perspective assessing the mentally retarded. In the sections that follow, we will attempt to distinguish the ecobehavioral approach to assessment from more traditional assessment strategies, discuss some issues related to the development of ecobehavioral assessment strategies, and describe some applications of these strategies.

The Ecobehavioral Perspective in Assessment

Traditional psychological assessment may be characterized by its primary concern for measuring intraorganismic traits and events (e.g., personality, intelligence, cognitive processes). In traditional assessment, overt behavior is interpreted as a sign of these internal processes; these processes are presumed to be the primary mediators of behavior that are relatively stable over time and situations. Accordingly, there is little concern for situational or setting variables in traditional assessment. Events observed in the test situation are assumed to signify processes operating within the individual regardless of the situation.

In contrast and in reaction to traditional assessment, behavioral assessment has emerged, which is concerned with the quantifiable measurement of overt behavior. In addition to diagnostic, prescriptive, and evaluative utility, behavioral assessment may also serve a descriptive function by characterizing behavior in relation to the assessment setting. The focus on varying environmental factors in traditional behavioral assessment is usually limited to the immediate interface between environment and behavior. Only those factors that are temporally and spatially contiguous with the target behavior(s) are assessed, and although behavior may be studied under differing environmental conditions, these conditions are rarely described adequately. As Willems (1977) remarks, "Behavior analysts are notorious for ignoring the nature of the environmental settings with which they work" (p. 49).

Willems (1977) also notes that the setting-specificity of behavior creates the assessment problem of describing and classifying the types and patterns of interaction between behavior and environment. He advocates developing an ecobehavioral technology to deal with this problem, and suggests that understanding the congruence between environment and behavior must be accomplished. Although Willems offers some general methodological guidelines for initiating an ecobehavioral assessment strategy (i.e., increase the number of behaviors and persons observed, observe other dimensions of behavior in addition to its type, lengthen the time period of observations, increase the number of settings in which behavior is observed), he admits that the technology for investigating behavior-environment relationships is far from complete.

How then should researchers and clinicians proceed? What descriptions and codes for environmental variables are necessary? In what settings should these be applied and to what ends? Perhaps a more basic question is how do we conceptualize the environment in order to catalog the almost infinite number and variety of environmental variables? Further, what are the functional criteria, if any, for selecting the environmental and behavioral variables to assess?

Conceptualization of the Environment

Moos (1973) notes that as yet there is no model that fully conceptualizes the broad range of environmental variables and systematically relates them to behavior. A problem for any attempt to study the relationship between environment and behavior is describing the various dimensions of the environment in commonly understood terms. In the broadest sense, environment may refer to any external factors (some would include intraorganismic factors as well) that act upon an organism and ultimately determine its form (behavior). Classification of this multitude of variables seems to be a preliminary step toward description and ultimate understanding of the interaction between these variables as they influence behavior.

It is important to note that by classification, we are referring only to the simple categorization of environmental variables according to some descriptive criterion, and not to comparisons between or qualitative judgements about different variables. A descriptive classification scheme does not necessarily make judgments about the goodness of particular variables; additional evaluative criteria are required for that purpose. Rather, descriptive classification permits the sorting of variables so that evaluations and comparisons may be made. For example, the sorting of variables as stimuli and responses is a simple descriptive classification; a more evaluative (and explanatory) classification of stimuli defines them as discriminitive, reinforcing, punishing, etc. However, this higher-order classification requires the use of some evaluative criterion (i.e., the impact of a stimulus on behavior).

Moos (1973) describes six traditional methods by which enviromental variables have been categorized and related to indices of human functioning:

1. *Ecological variables* include the geographic-meterological and architectural-physical design dimensions of the environment; what may be referred to as the physical environment, consisting of luminous, sonic, thermal and atmospheric as well as structural-spatial dimensions.
2. *Behavior settings* are the units of analysis developed by Barker and his colleagues in ecological psychology. According to Barker (1968), behavior settings are distinguishable ecological units that consist of one or more, "standing patterns of behavior and milieu, with the milieu circumjacent and synomorphic to the behavior." The standing pattern of behavior refers to the molar behavior of individuals, en mass, in a given setting, and with a specific time-space locus (e.g., the worship service in church on Sunday morning). In behavior setting research, focus on the behavior of individuals is limited to the extent that a behavior setting affects compliance with the standing pattern of behavior.

Barker argues that methodogically, environment-behavior relationships cannot be described or explained by focusing on the environment's influence on individual behavior.

3. *Factors of organizational structure* deal with the interrelatedness of various structural dimensions of organizations. Attempts are made to relate these dimensions to the behavior and attitudes of organization members. Dimensions of organizations that have been examined include: organizational and subunit size, number of organizational levels, centralization of control, span of control (e.g., size of supervisory units), cost expenditures, staffing ratios, average salary levels, staff turnover rate, and population density.

4. *Dimensions of personal/behavioral characteristics of milieu inhabitants* include variables such as age, ability level, socioeconomic background and educational attainment. These are characterized as situational variables that define the social and cultural environment, with the assumption that the character of an environment is partly dependent upon the typical characteristics of its inhabitants.

5. *Psychosocial characteristics and organizational climate* differ from factors of organizational structure in that they include the dynamic psychosocial processes operating within the organizational structure. In their work on social ecology, Moos and colleagues (Moos, 1973) have identified three dimensions by which to characterize the social and organizational climate of an environment: (1) *relationship dimensions*—that assess the degree to which individuals are involved in the environment and provide mutual support and assestance; (2) *personal development dimensions*—the level and direction in which personal growth and self-enhancement occur in the environment; and (3) *system maintenance and system change dimensions*—the level of order and organization, and clarity and control exerted by the environment.

6. *The functional analysis of environments* is derived from behavioral modification and involves identifying the controlling stimulus conditions for particular behaviors.

Moos (1973) emphasizes that these six broad classification schemes are nonexclusive, overlapping and mutually interrelated. he concludes that the classification of environmental variables into these categories may or may not have general utility. Clearly, the categories are overlapping, and certain variables may easily fit into a number of categories (i.e., certain categories are simply different conceptualizations of the same variables). Further, the purpose of a descriptive classification scheme is to sort common environmental variables into as few descriptive categories as possible, without making judgements about or attempting to interpret effects of different variables.

Perhaps the simplest descriptive scheme is one derived from Moos' later conceptualization of the environment (1979). This approach involves classifying environmental variables into one of three interrelated categories. The first category, physical factors, is essentially identical to Moos' category of ecological factors. The second category is the social dimension of the environment, which includes the behavior of and interactions with others as they influence the individual. The social environment would also include the dynamic aspects of the psychosocial and organizational climate. The third category of variables is what Moos (1979) refers to as organizational factors, but what may be more generally described as the program characteristics of the environment. These include the formal and informal policies and procedures of the setting as well as the non-physical dimensions of its organizational structure (e.g., administrative hierarchy, staffing patterns, scheduling of activities). Barker (1968) refers to the "program" of a behavior setting as the rules governing the activity within the setting (e.g., the rules of a baseball game), which may be conveyed in written or verbally-conveyed policy and/or may be implicit in the physical dimensions of the setting (e.g., the layout of a baseball diamond). Program characteristics may have a formal and informal component. For example, in a residential care setting, there are formal administrative policies regarding client care practices. There are also informal care policies adopted by direct-care staff (i.e., what they perceive as the minimum they must abide by), however, that override the formal policies to the extent that these formal policies go unenforced.

In many cases, it is differences in program characteristics of the environment that distinguish the quality of one setting from another; these program variables may also greatly influence the impact of behavior on the physical and social environment. Some examples from previous research may help to clarify the distinctions between these three categories of variables and point out their interrelationship. These examples are drawn from our work on the improvement of the quality of living environments for profoundly mentally retarded clients in an institution. In a group care setting such as this, it is important that staff members can always monitor and supervise client activity, provide assistance and encouragement, prevent possible injury, and intervene in emergencies. It is also important that the direct-line supervisor is able to monitor staff activity, provide direction and assistance, and intervene when problems occur. Research has shown that these conditions can best be met with an open environmental design—an environment with a minimum of physical and visual barriers, with most activities occurring within a single large setting. This open environment does not greatly interfere with training or other activities that require a minimum of distractions. The open design has also been shown to greatly improve caregivers' supervision of clients and the supervisor's ability to monitor staff (Twardosz, Cataldo, & Risley, 1974). It should be noted that the open design referred to here is not unlike that of the typical large dayroom in an institution. However, the differences between a workable open environment and a barren dayroom are largely determined by the program characteristics of the setting. It is the program, in terms of the assignment and monitoring of staff responsibilities, the sequencing of activities, etc., that makes the open environmental design work.

Another example, in this case involving the social environment, is the specification of how staff should conduct activities with clients. Based on our work in a number of settings, we have developed explicit procedures describing the manner in which care and training activities should be conducted. This includes providing clients with a maximum of opportunities to participate in the activity, incorporating training into care routines, and ensuring that the activity is completed safely and thoroughly. By training staff to perform routines this way, we have been able to greatly increase both the frequency and quality of social interactions between staff and clients, and the frequency of training activities available for clients. These improvements, however, are maintained only by incorporating changes in the program environment. The improved social environment is heavily dependent upon factors such as the scheduling of activities (allowing ample time for their completion in the prescribed manner), assignment of staff responsibilities, and policies mandating client engagement that are explicitly enforced through monitoring and feedback from the supervisor.

Using this simple conceptual scheme, professionals can sort environmental variables and begin to determine the physical, social, and program characteristics of a setting that are important to optimal client functioning. There must, however, still be some criteria for determing the favorable and unfavorable characteristics of an environment. Numerous criteria have been proposed for evaluating the quality of environments; the most notable among these is normalization, (Wolfensberger, 1972) which stresses that all aspects of the environment should be as culturally normative as possible. Evaluation of environments via normalization involves cultural norm as the standard for evaluation (Wolfensberger & Glenn, 1975). Critics of normalization, however, argue that it addresses the appropriate end (culturally normative functioning), but provides the wrong means for achieving it (Throne, 1975). These critics argue that the mentally retarded are by definition not normal, and exposure to a normal environment may only maintain subnormal functioning (Throne, 1975; Mesibov, 1976). Therefore, a "supernormal" environment to produce normal functioning is suggested. Further, there is little empirical evidence to support the position that a normalized environment substantially contributes to appropriate functioning of all mentally retarded persons (Balla, 1976; Landesman-Dwyer, 1981).

Ultimately, the criteria for evaluating settings should be related to their actual impact on client functioning. Assessing the quality of the environment should be based on the functional analysis of behavior within that environment and the extent to which desirable client outcomes are obtained. But in order to assess environmental impact on client functioning, professionals must have some notion of what behavioral outcomes are desirable. Once these outcomes are determined, professionals can identify client behaviors that indicate progress toward achieving these outcomes, and focus on the environmental factors that influence these behaviors.

Selecting Behavioral and Environmental Variables to Assess

Notions of desirable client outcomes have changed dramatically over the past 30 years. Historically, treatment for the mentally retarded focused on reasonably acceptable custodial care and the desired outcomes were low mortality rates, good health care, protection from harm, etc. Educational and vocational goals were reasonable expectations only for the mildly disabled. With the advent of effective treatment technology and the realization that virtually all mentally retarded persons are "trainable", the emphasis in treatment became habilitation. While habilitation is a desirable goal for all mentally retarded persons, the reasonably expected outcome of habilitative treatment will certainly vary for each individual. What then is an appropriate measure of client functioning that takes into account the broad range of current levels of functioning among the mentally retarded? A review of recent studies investigating the relationship between various environmental factors and the functioning of mentally retarded persons reveals a remarkable diversity in the type of client variables that are assessed. Traditional, standardized measures of intellectual functioning (MA, IQ) have been employed (Balla, Butterfield, & Zigler, 1974; Felce, Kushlick, & Smith, 1980; Grant & Moores, 1977), as have measures of client performance on standardized tasks (Balla et. al, 1974). Self report measures of client self-image (Birenbaum & Re, 1979) and preferences for community residences (Aninger & Bolinsky, 1977) have been employed. The impact of the environment on clients' mortality rate (Carsrud, Carsrud, Henderson, Alisch, & Fowler, 1979; Felce et al., 1980), weight change (Carsrud et al., 1979), frequency of illness and injury (Heller, 1982; Lawrence, 1977), and frequency of defecation/urination and seizures (Lawrence, 1977) have also been assessed.

By far, the most common measures of client functioning used in these studies relate to adaptive behavior, and the AAMD Adaptive Behavior Scales (Nihira, Foster, Shellhaas, & Leland, 1974) have been the measure of choice in assessing such functioning.

The Adaptive Behavior Scales (ABS) have been used to assess the impact of transitions from an institution to supervised apartments (Aninger & Bolinsky, 1977), from larger to smaller institutions (Cohen, Conroy, Frazer, Snelbecker, & Spreat, 1977), from an institution to community-based residential facilities (Conroy, Efthmiou, & Lemanowicz, 1982), and from one living unit to another within an institution (Spreat & Isett, 1981) on clients' adaptive functioning. Eyman and colleagues have used versions of the ABS to examine differences in behavior problems among mentally retarded persons residing in institutions, community residences, and at home (Eyman & Call, 1977), differences in the adaptive behavior of persons residing in foster homes and those residing in board-and-care facilities (Eyman, Demaine, & Lei, 1979), and in the adaptive behavior of persons residing in institutions versus selected community-based facilities (Eyman, Silverstein, McClain, & Miller, 1977). Grant and Moores (1977) used the ABS to compare differences in the social competency of clients residing in institutional settings with varied staffing levels and patterns. Hull and Thompson (1980) employed components of the ABS to compare behavior problems exhibited by clients residing in settings with varying residential and community characteristics.

The ABS has also been used to assess the impact of residing in a nursing home (Aanes & Moen, 1976), the relationship between home environment, family adjustment to a mentally retarded child, and the adaptive behavior of the child (Nihira, Meyers, & Mink, 1980), and differences in clients who were successfully and unsuccessfully placed in the community (Sutter, Mayeda, Call, Yanagi, & Yee, 1980). Similar in content to the ABS, The Progress Assessment Chart (Gunzburg, 1969), or P-A-C, has been used to compare the adaptive functioning of clients transferred to group homes with matched clients remaining in the institution (Schroeder & Henes, 1978).

Both the ABS and the P-A-C rely on caregivers as informants to assess client adaptive behavior. Numerous other indirect measures have been employed, which rely on information provided by staff (e.g., questionnaires, checklists and interviews) to assess clients' adaptive functioning. These include measures of:

1. Client autonomy and degree of independent functioning (Aninger & Bolinsky, 1977; Brown & Guard, 1979; Hull & Thompson, 1980; McClain, Silverstein, Hubbell, & Brownlee, 1975)
2. Maladaptive behavior (James, Spencer, & Hamilton, 1975; Willer & Intagliata, 1981, 1982)
3. Extent of community involvement (Pratt, Luszcz, & Brown, 1980; Willer & Intagliata, 1982)
4. Social competency (Hull & Thompson, 1980; Reizenstein & McBride, 1978; Willer & Intagliata, 1982)
5. Overall quality and appropriateness of client activity (Brown & Guard, 1979; James et al., 1975; McClain et al., 1975; O'Neil, Brown, Gordon, Schonhorn, & Greer, 1981; Reizenstein & McBride, 1978; Tognoli, Hamad, & Carpenter, 1978).

Though extensively employed and relatively inexpensive to obtain, there is some concern over the veracity of indirect measures of client adaptive functioning. For example, research has shown that measures of client functioning obtained with the ABS correlate poorly with observed client behavior (Marks & Rodd-Marks, 1980) and direct measures of client gains (King, Soucar, & Isett, 1980). Alternatively, numerous investigators have advocated the use of direct observations of client behavior as the most valid measure of the environment's influence on adaptive functioning (Berkson, 1978; Butler & Bjaanes, 1977; Cataldo & Risley, 1974; Cruickshank & Quay, 1970; Pratt et al., 1980). Almost half of the studies reviewed have employed direct observations of client behavior as it occurs in the natural environment. The most commonly targeted behaviors include: maladaptive behaviors such as stereotypes, aggression and anti-social behavior, leisure activity, personal care, object contact and use, and work and domestic activity. All but one of the studies employing direct observations have included some measure of social interactions between staff and clients.

These studies suggest that adaptive behavior may be a useful and universal measure of client functioning in relation to the environment. It is clearly relevant to the definition of mental retardation (Grossman, 1977), and is the usual goal of treatment for the mentally retarded (Kazdin & Matson, 1981). As Brooks and Baumeister (1977) suggest, adaptive behavior may be the most ecologically valid dimension upon which to investigate the phenomenon of mental retardation. However, adaptive functioning includes a wide array of skills and behaviors, the appropriateness of which is determined in part by the situational context. Traditional measures of adaptive behavior may be too limited in the range of skills they assess. Kazdin and Matson (1981) note that, "no single test or scale can fully assess the range of adaptive behaviors appropriate to all contexts" (p. 40). Likewise, no existing measure is available that can assess the range of adaptive responses exhibited by persons throughout the entire range of mental retardation. What is considered appropriate adaptive behavior should be determined as much by the characteristics of the individual (i.e., type and severity of disabilities) as by the environmental context in which it occurs.

Behaviors reflecting adaptive functioning may range from any interaction with the environment for profoundly multi-handicapped persons to independent participation in the community for borderline or mildly mentally retarded persons. The common element throughout this continuum of adaptive functioning appears to be the extent to which the individual is actively engaged with (attending to, interacting with, participating in) the environment. Interactive engagement with the environment is a process that directly relates to the outcome of adaptive functioning, for adaptation occurs in response to interaction. Engagement may consist of simply attending to events in the environment, active manipulation and exploration of features in the environment, and interacting with others in the environment. In whatever form, the process of engagement may be directly measured by monitoring the individual's interactions with the environment. The appropriateness of environmental engagement in any context may be judged by the extent to which it occurs independently of extensive prompts or assistance, and conforms to culturally/developmentally appropriate norms.

Further, the use of environmental engagement as a measure of client functioning has direct relevance for selecting those aspects of the environment to examine in assessing environment-behavior relationships. Quite simply, the important features of an environment are those that promote appropriate, independent engagement with the environment. These features may be directly contiguous with behavior (i.e., stimulus-response relationships) or spatially/temporally removed setting events that influence the occurrence of existing stimulus-response functions (Wahler & Fox, 1981). The primary task of ecobehavioral assessment is to identify, to the extent possible, those salient (and therefore manipulable) characteristics of the environment influencing independent engagement.

It is probably safe to assume, and there is growing evidence to suggest, that engagement with the environment is largely a function of the opportunities provided by the environment for engagement (Delquadri, Greenwood, & Hall, 1979[1]; Hall, Delquadri, & Harris, 1977[2]). In this vein, Landesman-Dwyer (in press) has suggested that the quality of a setting should not necessarily be judged by a prior or absolute criteria (e.g., smaller, homelike living units, higher staff-client ratios, individual privacy, interdisciplinary planning). Instead she suggests that the efficacy of the environment should be determined by the match between three elements: the availability of resources (objects, people, events), the demands of the environment, and the ability of the inhabitants to perceive and respond to these resources and demands. It is the match between the available resources and environmental demands that comprise the opportunities for engagement and, as Landesman-Dwyer points out, these in turn must be matched to the individual's abilities. In contrast to normalization, this assumption implies that an environment with culturally-normative resources and demands may not invoke culturally-normative engagement by mentally retarded persons. A normalized environment may in fact constitute an overly restrictive environment for many mentally retarded persons in terms of the opportunities available for engagement.

We suggest that a potentially useful framework for assessing the influence of the environment on behavior is to examine the relationship between individuals' engagement with the environment and the immediate opportunities provided for engagement. The nature of these opportunities (i.e., the features of the environment to assess) will be largely determined by the nature of engagement appropriate to the individual and situation. It may be, as Rogers-Warren (see footnote 1) has suggested, that the best way to determine the optimal features of the environment is to begin with an individual analysis of environment and behavior. Once this analysis is complete and the functional link between environment and behavior has been established, then the analysis may be expanded to look at the general features of the environment that influence the opportunities available for engagement.

---

[1]Delquadri, J, Greenwood, C, & Hall, R. *Opportunity to respond: An update.* Invited address at the fifth annual meeting of the Association for Behavior Analysis, Dearborn, MI, June 1979

[2]Hall, R, Delquadri, J & Harris, J. *Opportunities to respond: A new focus in the field of applied behavior analysis.* Invited address at the annual meeting of the Midwest Association for Behavior Analysis, Chicago, IL, May 1977

Considerations in Developing Ecobehavioral
Assessment Strategies

The primary consideration in planning and conducting ecobehavioral assessment strategies should be the purpose of assessment. Assessment of environment-behavior relationships may be undertaken to plan interventions for modifying the behavior of a particular individual or improving the quality of the overall environment to impact the behavior of its inhabitants. Each case requires a somewhat different strategy. If the intent is individual assessment and intervention, the basic strategy is to assess the individual's behavior in varying environmental contexts; if the purpose is to modify the setting, then an effective strategy might involve assessing the behavioral reaction of different individuals to the features of the particular setting.

A noteworthy example of an individual assessment strategy is provided in a recent study by Iwata, Dorsey, Slifer, Bauman and Richman (1982) that examined environmental determinants of self-injurious behavior in mentally retarded children and adolescents. Iwata et al. observed subjects' self-injurious behavior in four analogue environments. The four environmental conditions were: (1) *social disapproval*—remarks of concern and social disapproval paired with nonpunitive physical contact provided contingent upon self-injury; (2) *academic demands*—structured academic task provided and instructional demands terminated contingent upon self-injury, simulating a negative reinforcement condition (i.e., escape/avoidance of demands); (3) *unstructured play*—a no demand, enriched environment condition with praise and physical contact contingent upon the absence of self-injury; (4) *alone*—subject placed alone in a barren room, simulating an impoverished environment. With six of the nine subjects studied, levels of self-injury were consistently associated with specific environmental conditions and the authors were able to determine whether self-injury was maintained by social attention, reduced demands, or as a form of self-stimulation. Assessment strategies of the sort used here and in other studies to assess the environmental determinants of deviant behavior (Adams, Tallon, & Stangl, 1980) have obvious utility in planning interventions to modify the behavior of specific individuals.

More actuarial interventions, those with the aim of modifying the environment to impact behavior of all inhabitants, may best be exemplified by research in environmental design. A notable example of these environment-based interventions is the research of Sommer (1969) that investigated the effects of modifying the seating arrangement in the dayroom of a psychiatric ward on the social behavior of patients. Sommer observed substantially higher socialization when seating was arranged in clusters versus lined up around the perimeter of the dayroom.

Similar examples of environmental design interventions are provided in the research of Proshansky and colleagues (reviewed in Wolfe & Proshansky, 1974) investigating the influence of setting design on patient and staff behavior in psychiatric settings. Using the observational technique of behavior mapping (i.e., noting the type, location and context of behavior), these investigators have documented a variety of changes in behavior patterns within living units as a result of the reorganization and refurnishing of these units. Additional examples are available in the work of our own research group, investigating the optimal design of group care settings for a variety of populations (for reviews of this research see Risley, 1977, and Jones, Favell, & Risley, 1982).

A common element in this research is the modification of specific (physical, program, or social) environmental features to influence a particular global behavior of the inhabitants. The more central concern in assessment, however, is determining what environmental modifications are warranted in a given setting. What is an effective strategy for planning actuarial interventions? As suggested earlier, one strategy might involve assessing the behavior of different (or all) individuals in a particular setting. This strategy is likely to yield data with considerable variance across individuals because different individuals will be affected to different degrees by environmental characteristics. An alternative and less costly strategy is to select those individuals with the greatest sensitivity to the influences of the environment—the "canaries in the coal mine"; in most instances, these will be the individuals who exhibit the least adaptability or most problematic behavior. By monitoring their behavior in relation to the environment, the investigator may determine with some degree of confidence those features of the environment that will have an impact, though to a lesser degree, on all inhabitants of the setting.

Whether the purpose of assessment is to design individual or actuarial interventions, there are a number of methodological concerns which should be considered in developing ecobehavioral assessment strategies. These are related to selecting the locus, level and units of measurement to be employed.

The Locus of Measurement

The locus, orientation, or reference point for measuring environment-behavior relationships may be either environment-centered or person-centered. Environment-centered measures involve ignoring the specific behavior of individuals and focusing on the surrounding environment and the more global (i.e., standing) patterns of behavior. This is the approach traditionally employed in ecological psychology. Measures using the individual as the referent focus on behavior and the individual's interactions with the surrounding environment. The environment is defined as that with which the individual comes into contact, the external inputs to the subject that represent those environmental features he or she selects or invites (Gump, 1977). An example may help clarify this distinction. In examining the social interactions between caregivers and clients, two strategies might be employed: focusing on the behavior of caregivers in the setting to determine the proportion of their behavior directed to clients (an environment-centered measure with respect to clients), or focusing on the behavior of clients to determine the extent to which each client is contacted by caregivers (i.e., person-centered with respect to clients). We have simultaneously employed both measures in our evaluations of living environments for mentally retarded clients and noted that staff spend approximately 40 percent of their time contacting clients but individual clients are contacted an average of about six percent of the time (Harris, Veit, Allen, & Chinsky, 1974). Of course much of the disparity is due to the ratio of staff to clients, but we have also noted that staff's social attention is not equitably distributed among all clients. This should come as no surprise as it is a common finding in studies of the social environment of settings (Prior, Minnes, Coyne, Golding, Hendy, & McGillivary, 1979). The point here is that the social environment for a particular client can only be determined by focusing the measurement on individual clients. Environment-centered measurement is largely irrelevant to a functional analysis of the individual client's social environment.

Both environment-centered and person-centered approaches have inherent advantages and limitations, and both measures may be necessary for a comprehensive evaluation of behavior and setting. Environment-centered measures are needed to obtain global, descriptive information about the environment; they may also be useful in assessing environmental factors that would not be detected by focusing on individual behavior. However, a person-centered orientation would seem to be essential for a more functional assessment of the opportunities for engagement that are available to individual clients. This would be true regardless of the purpose of assessment, be it individual or actuarial intervention. Even in actuarial studies, assessment from the perspective of individuals may be a more valid basis for determining the salient features of the environment for those individuals.

The Level of Measurement

Behavior may be conceptualized on a continuum from molecular, singular responses to molar behavior events. Similarly, environmental units that influence behavior may range from temporally and spatially immediate to remote. This poses the dual problem in ecobehavioral assessment of selecting the appropriate level of behavior and environment to investigate. Applied behavior analysis has traditionally been concerned with investigation of molecular response units in the context of immediate environmental variables. Conversely, ecological psychology has been concerned with molar behavior events and environmental influences.

To some extent, the level of behavioral measurement may be determined by the purpose of inquiry and the extent to which behaviors have already been targeted for change. If assessment is undertaken to identify the determinants of a specific problem behavior, the behavior may be measured at a more molecular level. If the purpose is to identify problem behaviors, however, a molar level of analysis may be initially required, proceeding to a molecular analysis when intervention is necessitated. As Wahler and Fox (1981) have recommended, attention to molar events may be useful in the preliminary analysis of environment-behavior relationships but, "one must eventually conduct *experimental* analysis dealing with *molecular* units comprising the chosen problem" (p. 334).

The apropriate level of environmental analysis should be determined primarily by the locus of the controlling environmental variables. This locus may best be determined inductively by assessing the immediate context of behavior and proceeding to temporally/spatially more distant phenomena until controlling variables are identified. Again, Wahler and Fox (1981) offer cogent advice in suggesting that in cases where behavior is "not largely controlled by its temporally close stimulus associations, a setting event search ought to be initiated . . . (and when a) researcher manipulates these stimuli and finds no change, or highly variable change, the control locus may lie at a more temporally distant point" (p. 337).

Thus, with respect to behavior, a general strategy might be to proceed from molar patterns to more detailed, molecular analyses. In contrast, the search for controlling environmental variables may best proceed from the immediate to more distant context.

The Units of Measurement

By units of measurement, we are referring to the unit of behavior selected for measurement that may range from discrete, arbitrarily defined target responses to the ongoing stream of behavior. Ecological psychology is concerned with the analysis of ongoing behavior streams, which involves collecting detailed and continuous accounts of behavior. As noted by Gump (1977), the assumption is that discrete units of behavior are imbedded in behavior streams and their structure can only be delineated by observing the ongoing stream, not by imposing arbitrary units of behavior. In principle, the authors concur with Gump's caution against the use of arbitrary units of behavior in the study of environment-behavior relationships. However, an acceptable alternative to the costly and phenomenological methods of behavior-stream analysis exists in the method of instantaneous time-sampling of behavior.

Ongoing behavior may be accurately assessed by taking periodic samples of behavior and without imposing arbitrarily defined behavior units. Several methodological conditions must be met, however, in order to obtain accurate samples of the ongoing behavior stream. First, time-sampling must be relatively instantaneous so that discrete samples rather than multiple episodes of behavior are observed. In this manner, behaviors may be quantified by their duration rather than their rate since the proportion of times a behavior is seen during these time-lapse observations corresponds directly with the absolute proportion of time occupied by the behavior.

Second, time samples of behavior must be made with sufficient frequency to minimize sampling error. As with any sampling procedure, the number of samples required to obtain a representative sample will be determined by the heterogeneity of the population, in this case the behavior of the individuals observed. A related issue is the latency between samples of behavior, which should be determined by the relative interest in the sequential nature of behaviors.

A third consideration in using time samples of behavior is whether arbitrary units of behavior should be employed. Traditionally, time-sampling is used to assess pre-selected target behaviors (i.e., recording only whether one of the target behaviors occurs during each observation). An alternative method is that employed in the Resident Activity MANIFEST (Cataldo & Risley, 1974), in which any behavior that is occurring during the time-sampling observation is described in detail. The resulting behavior record reflects an accurate sample of the ongoing stream of behavior.

In summary, there are a number of methodological issues that should be considered in conducting ecobehavioral assessment. The particular assessment strategy employed will depend to some extent on the underlying purpose of assessment. Regarding locus of measurement, person-centered strategies may reveal the most useful information on the direct impact of the environment on behavior but also acknowledge that envionment-centered strategies have utility in describing extra-individual environmental features. Another concern is for the level of analysis of both behavioral and environmental variables. It is suggested that there may be general utility in proceeding from a molar to molecular analysis of behavior and from the level of immediate to more distant environmental variables. With respect to the units of analysis, we recommend the use of an open data system—one that is not constrained by the focus on arbitrary units of behavior—that employs the sampling of ongoing behavioral and environmental events.

An Example of Ecobehavioral Assessment

To illustrate the potential utility of an ecobehavioral perspective in assessment, we would like to provide an example from our ongoing research with nonambulatory, profoundly multi-handicapped clients. This research is being conducted in a large residential facility for the mentally retarded. The facility is licensed as an intermediate care setting and provides residence for approximately 400 clients. Approximately 160 multi-handicapped clients reside in two buildings of the facility, both constructed in the past four years. The living units in these buildings house 16 clients each, and are almost identical in structure. They were designed with the intent of creating as ''homelike'' an atmosphere as possible (e.g., absence of a large dayroom, nurses' stations, dormitory-style bedrooms), in contrast to the former hospital environments in which clients resided.

The purpose of this research is to improve clients' independent exploratory behavior, or the manipulation and investigation of stimulus materials in the environment. As part of this project, we are conducting an ecobehavioral analysis of clients' independent engagement with the environment, specifically during times when no habilitative programming is provided; we are concerned with improving the environment to maintain appropriate engagement during nonprogramming or leisure time. By observing clients in their living environment, we hope to determine: the opportunities for engagement provided by the environment in terms of the availability of engaging materials (e.g., toys) and structured activities, and the frequency and nature of social interactions provided to clients; and the nature and extent of clients' behavioral engagement with the environment. This information is being used to identify environmental deficiencies (i.e., lack of opportunities for engagement) and develop interventions to alleviate them.

The study involves direct observations of clients using an adapted version of the resident activity MANIFEST. The MANIFEST employs instantaneous time-sampling observations whereby 10 categories of client and environmental variables are assessed. These categories are described in Table 11-1. Client variables include noting their body position and motion, the objects or features in the environment to which they are visually attending, what they are contacting/manipulating with their hands, a description of the specific behavior(s) they are engaged in during the abservation, and whether they are vocalizing. From assessment of these variables, clients' activity levels (i.e., changes in position, motion) and visual and behavioral engagement with the environment can be determined.

Environmental factors include material availability, structured activity availability and staff-client and client-client social interactions. The MANIFEST is a client-centered procedure; both client and environmental variables are assessed by observing the client and the immediate environmental context. For example, these clients are non-ambulatory so material availability is limited to the presence of appropriate materials within reach of the client.

In the present setting, MANIFEST observations have been conducted at six week intervals for the past 1.5 years. At each interval, observations are made during a three day period (including one weekend day). Each client is observed once every 30 minutes, from 2:30–6:00 PM on weekdays and from 9:00 AM–6:00 PM on weekends.

A full summary of the results is not feasible here but some of the data that reflect quality of the environment and client engagement are worth noting. MANIFEST data have been obtained for a total of 65 clients; however, for purposes of comparison to a later study, we will present data for only 22 of the most active clients. In almost 6000 observations made thus far, clients had appropriate materials available less than 8 percent of the time. This ranged from 0 to 61 percent per client. Only five of the 22 clients noted here had materials available more than 10 percent of the time, and with a few exceptions, materials were available to clients primarily during care routines (e.g., a cup or spoon within reach during mealtimes).

Structured activities were available to clients an average of 0.4 (range = 0–2) percent of the time, and were never available to 10 of these 22 clients. Virtually all structured activities observed were mealtimes for clients who fed themselves; no formal training or organized leisure/recreational activities were observed.

Clients were engaged in some form of interaction with others during less than 6 (range = 2.5–12) percent of the observations, with approximately 12 percent of these interactions occurring between clients (physical contact only). Approximately 70 percent of the interactions between staff and clients were classified as nonsocial-custodial in nature (no positive social interaction: caregiver is per-

Table 11-1
MANIFEST Observation Categories

Category	Description
MATERIAL AVAILABILITY	A manipulable stimulus material (e.g., toy, training equipment) is within arm's reach of the subject.
STRUCTURED ACTIVITY AVAILABILITY	Any organized, staff-directed activity in which the subject can actively participate, and for which a staff member is in the immediate vicinity to provide assistance and encouragement.
POSITION	The specific body position of the subject (e.g., sitting, lying, slumping over).
MOTION	The most prominent body movement(s) observed (e.g., head, leg, arm, hand).
ATTENTION	The object, environmental feature or person that the subject appears to be attending to (i.e., looking at) most prominently.
HANDS	The object or environmental feature that the subject is contacting with his or her hands (may be two objects).
BEHAVIOR	A brief description of the behavior the subject is emitting at the instant of observation.
VOCAL	Is the subject vocalizing (yes/no)?
INTERACTION	Subject's involvement in a social interaction, the person involved and the type ("C": another client; "SA": social assistive with staff; "NA": nonsocial assistive with staff; "SC": social custodial with staff; "NC": nonsocial custodial with staff). *Social*—caregiver is positively talking to, smiling at, etc. client. *Custodial*—caregiver is performing some activity for client and not providing an opportunity for independent responding. *Assistive*—caregiver is providing client with an opportunity to respond.
LOCATION	Location of the subject in the environment (e.g., Dayroom).

forming some activity for the client and not providing an opportunity for independent responding). Only 5 percent of the staff-client interactions were assistive in nature (giving the client an opportunity to respond), and only 23 percent included any positive social contact. Most of the contacts between staff and clients occurred in the context of feeding, diapering, or transporting clients in their wheelchairs. Interactions for the sake of social stimulation (e.g., hugging, rocking,

Table 11-2
MANIFEST Summary: Behavior Codes

Categories	Number of Behavior Codes	Example
1.0 OBSERVE		
1.1 People	5	1.12—"Look at observer"
1.2 Objects	7	1.23—"Look at plate"
1.3 Specific Environment	5	1.33—"Watch TV"
1.4 Self	5	1.42—"Look at hand"
1.5 Scan Environment	1	1.50—"Look around room"
2.0 MANIPULATE BY HAND		
2.1 People	5	2.13—"Play with client's hair"
2.2 Objects	7	2.21—"Play with rattle"
2.3 Specific Environment	5	2.34—"Bang on tray top"
2.4 Self	5	2.41—"Pat head"
3.0 MANIPULATE BY MOUTHING		
3.1 People	5	3.13—"Bite client"
3.2 Objects	7	3.26—"Chew on towel"
3.3 Specific Environment	5	3.32—"Chew on mat"
3.4 Self	5	3.42—"Mouth hand"
4.0 TALK TO	5	4.10—"Talk to caregiver"
5.0 RECEIVE		
5.1 Care	7	5.11—"Being fed by caregiver"
5.2 Social Interaction	6	5.22—"Held and rocked by staff"
6.0 "NON-BEHAVIOR"	3	6.10—"Stare"
7.0 GROSS MOTION		
7.1 Non-repetitive	10	7.11—"Turn head"
7.2 Repetitive	5	7.24—"Rock upper torso"
8.0 EXPRESS EMOTIONS	5	8.10—"Smile"
9.0 SELF CARE	6	9.10—"Feed self"

playing with a client) accounted for less than 10 percent of all interactions, with half of these contacts directed to a single client.

The relevant client variable for this discussion is observed behavior. We have developed acoding system of 114 behaviors to summarize the descriptive entries of behavior recorded with the MANIFEST. The categories and subcategories of behavior codes are presented in Table 11-2. These codes are not mutually exclusive by observation since more than one behavior can occur simultaneously.

However, a single behavior can only occur once during an observation and can only be scored with a single code. The data presented here are based on all observations with these 22 clients during a recent three-day observation period. Although this is a small sample of all the data collected thus far, the patterns noted here have been relatively stable over successive observation periods.

The category of "non-behavior" (6.0) was scored for 26 percent of the behavior entries. This category is used if "sleep," "stare," or nothing is entered under behavior, indicating that no discernible behavior was noted during the observation. It is a mutually exclusive category. Another frequently scored category was 7.0—non-repetitive and repetitive gross motion. This category includes simple motor responses that do not constitute any apparent, purposeful behavior; 32 percent of all the behavior entries were scored in this category. Based on the number of behaviors scored in these two categories, it appears that clients spend well over half of their leisure or non-programming time not engaged in any purposeful behavior.

The most frequently occurring "purposeful" category of behavior was (1.0) observing people, objects, etc. and visually scanning the environment. The category was used to score 23 percent of all behavior entries. A measure of active behavioral engagement can be derived by combining the categories of (2.0) manipulation by hand, (3.0) manipulation by mouthing, (4.0) talking to others, and (9.0) self care. Altogether, these categories account for 20 percent of the behaviors scored. Manipulation of objects by hand (2.2) was scored for 6.5 percent of the observations; however, manipulation of appropriate stimulus materials was scored for less than 3 percent of the observations, and all but two occurrences were by a single client.

This brief summary demonstrates the general lack of opportunities for engagement afforded to even the most active multi-handicapped clients in this setting. The lack of opportunity is apparent in the immediate physical, program, and social dimensions of the environment. These data also reflect the lack of active, purposeful behavior exhibited by profoundly multi-handicapped clients. The lack of responding observed here, however, is not entirely due to the clients' functioning ability.

A recent study with these 22 clients examined their independent exploratory contact with various stimulus materials. A variety of manipulable objects were systematically presented to clients in a controlled setting, during a total of four hours of direct observation with each client. The results of this study indicate that clients contacted objects 68 percent of the time (range = 38–98 percent). These clients engaged in active tactile exploration of objects (versus simple contact or repetitive play) 49 percent of the time (range = 9–84 percent).

These results suggest that the lack of engagement noted with the MANIFEST may be largely due to the lack of opportunities for engagement and point out the need for improved material availability. Beyond this, additional chages are warranted in the level of structured activities for clients and in the frequency and quality of social interactions between staff and clients. Our experiences suggest that such improvements will only result from more global modifications of the setting. For example, changes in program characteristics such as staff training, better scheduling of staff and activities, and improved monitoring and supervision within the setting are required.

One shortcoming of the MANIFEST is its failure to assess these features of the environment. However, descriptive information about these variables can be obtained with relative ease, and correlated with the functional ecobehavioral information provided by the MANIFEST to suggest those characteristics of the setting that warrant change. Measures such as those obtained with the MANIFEST may serve as the basis for evaluating the impact of these changes on client functioning.

CONCLUSION

In this chapter, an attempt has been made to point out the importance of studying the relationship between the environment and the behavioral functioning of mentally retarded persons. This relationship should be considered in assessment in order to improve and evaluate the effectiveness and applicability of treatment, to improve the match between a mentally retarded persons and the environment they inhabit, and to evaluate and ensure the quality of present and future environments for the mentally retarded.

An ecobehavioral assessment strategy that has its basis in applied behavior anlysis but goes beyond traditional behavioral assessment in attempting to evaluate the relationship between environment and behavior is proposed, and some general and specific recommendations on how to proceed with the development of an ecobehavioral technology provided. In making these recommendations, we must caution that there are currently few empirically demostrated principles or techniques for an ecobehavioral technology. Many of the suggestions here come from our own experience and informal strategies for assessing environments for dependent populations. The general utility of these strategies must still be determined. We also share Willems' (1977) optimism however, that an ecobehavioral technology will emerge. Its potential contribution to assessment of the mentally retarded is unquestionable, and when and how this technology will emerge is uncertain.

Acknowledgment

Preparation of this manuscript was funded in part by a grant from the Office of Special Education and Rehabilitation Services (#G008101010). We would like to thank Jennifer Lattimore for her comments on an earlier draft of this paper, and Susan L. Dewey for her assistance in preparation of the manuscript.

REFERENCES

Aanes, D, & Moen, M. Adaptive behavior changes of group home residents. *Mental Retardation,* 1976, *14,* 36–40

Adams, G, Tallon, R, & Stangl, J. Environmental influences on self-stimulatory behavior. *American Journal of Mental Deficiency,* 1980, *85,* 171–175

Aninger, M, & Bolinsky, K. Levels of independent functioning of retarded adults in apartments. *Mental Retardation,* 1977, *15,* 12–13

Baer, D. A hung jury and a Scotch verdict: "not proven". *Analysis and Intervention in Developmental Disabilities,* 1981, *1,* 91–97

Bailey, J. Wanted: a rational search for the limiting conditions of habilitation. *Analysis and Intervention in Developmental Disabilities,* 1981, *1,* 45–52

Balla, D. Relationship of institution size to quality of care: A review. *American Journal of Mental Deficiency,* 1976, *81,* 117–124

Balla, D., Butterfield, E, & Zigler, E. Effects of institutionalization on retarded children: a longitudinal cross-institutional investigation. *American Journal of Mental Deficiency,* 1974, *78,* 530–549

Barker, R. *Ecological Psychology: Concepts and Methods for Studying the Environment of Human Behavior.* Stanford, CA: Stanford University Press, 1968

Berkson, G. Social ecology and ethology in mental retardation. In G Sackett (Ed.), *Observing Behavior* (Vol. 1). Baltimore: University Park Press, 1978

Birenbaum, A, & Re, M. Resettling mentally retarded adults in the community—almost 4 years later. *American Journal of Mental Deficiency,* 1979, *83,* 323–329

Brooks, P, & Baumeister, A. A plea for consideration of ecological validity in the experimental psychology of mental retardation: A guest editorial. *American Journal of Mental Deficiency,* 1977, *81,* 407–416

Brown, J, & Guard, K. The treatment environment for retarded persons in nursing homes, *Mental Retardation,* 1979, *17,* 77–82

Butler, E, & Bjaones, A. A typology of community care facilities and differential normalization outcomes. In P Mittler (Ed.), *Research to practice in mental retardation, Vol. I. Care and Intervention.* Baltimore: University Park Press, 1977

Carsrud, A, Carsrud, K, Henderson, D, Alisch, C, & Fowler, A. Effects of social and environmental change on institutionalized mentally retarded persons: The relocation syndrome revisited. *American Journal of Mental Deficiency,* 1979, *84,* 266–272

Cataldo, M, & Risley, T. Evaluation of living environments: The MANIFEST description of ward activities. In P Davidson, F Clark, & L Hamerlynck (Eds.), *Evaluation of Social Programs in Community, Residential and School Settings.* Champaign, IL: Research Press, 1974

Cohen, H, Conroy, J, Frazer, D, Snelbecker, G, & Spreat, S. Behavioral effects of interinstitutional relocation of mentally retarded residents. *American Journal of Mental Deficiency,* 1977, *82,* 12–18

Conroy, J, Efthimiou, Jr, & Lemanowicz, Jr. A matched comparison of the developmental growth of institutionalized and Deinstitutionalized mentally retarded clients. *American Journal of Mental Deficiency,* 1982, *86,* 581–587

Crawford, J, Aiello, Jr, & Thompson, D. Deinstitutionalization and community placement: Clinical and environmental factors. *Mental Retardation,* 7979, *17,* 59–63

Cruickshank, W, & Quay, H. Learning and physical environment: The necessity for research and research design. *Exceptional Children,* December 1970, 261–268

Ellis, N. The Partlow Case: A reply to Dr. Roos. *Law and Psychology Review,* 1979, *5,* 15–49

Ellis, N. On training the mentally retarded. *Analysis and Intervention in Developmental Disabilities,* 1981, *1,* 99–108

Eyman, RK, & Call, T. Maladaptive behavior and community placement of mentally retarded persons. *American Journal of Mental Deficiency,* 1977, *82,* 137–144

Eyman, R, Demaine, G, & Lei, T. Relationship between community environments and resident changes in adaptive behavior: A path model. *American Journal of Mental Deficiency,* 1979, *83,* 330–338

Eyman, R, Silverstein, A, McClain, R, & Miller, C. Effects of residential settings on development. In P Mittler (Ed.), *Research to Practice in Mental Retardation,* (Vol. I). Baltimore: University Park Press, 1977

Favell, J, Risley, T, Wolfe, A, Riddle, I, & Rasmussen, P. The limits of habilitation: How can we identify them and how can we change them? *Analysis and Intervention in Developmental Disabilities,* 1981, *1,* 37–43

Felce, D, Kushlick, A, & Smith, J. An overview of the research on alternative residential facilities for the severely mentally handicapped in Wessex. *Advances in Behavioural Research and Therapy,* 1980, *3,* 1–4

Grant, G, & Moores, B. Resident characteristics and staff behavior in two hospitals for mentally retarded. *American Journal of Mental Deficiency,* 1977, *82,* 259–265

Grossman, H. *Manual on Terminology and Classification in Mental Retardation,* Washington, DC: American Association on Mental Deficiency, 1977

Gump, P. Ecological psychologists: critics or contributors to behavior analysis. In A Rogers-Warren, & S Warren (Eds.), *Ecological Perspectives in Behavior Analysis.* Baltimore: University Park Press, 1977

Gunzburg, H. *Progress Assessment Chart manual.* 3rd edition. Birmingham, England: SEFA Publications, Ltd., 1969

Harris, J, Veit, S, Allen, G, & Chinsky, J. Aide-resident ratio and ward population density as mediators of social interaction. *American Journal of Mental Deficiency,* 1974, *79,* 320–326

Heller, T. Social disruption and residential relocation of mentally retarded children. *American Journal of Mental Deficiency,* 1982, *87,* 48–55

Hull, J, & Thompson, J. Predicting adaptive functioning of mentally retarded persons in community settings. *American Journal of Mental Deficiency,* 1980, *85,* 253–261

Iwata, B, Dorsey, M, Slifer, K, Bauman, K, & Richman, G. Toward a functional analysis of self-injury. *Analysis and Intervention in Developmental Disabilities,* 1982, *2,* 3–20

James F, Spencer, D, & Hamilton, M. Immediate effects of improved hospital environment on behavior patterns of mentally handicapped patients. *British Journal of Psychiatry,* 1975, *126,* 577–581

Jones, M, Favell, J, & Risley, T. Socioecological programming. In J Matson, & F Andrasik (Eds.), *Treatment Issues and Innovations in Mental Retardation,* New York: Plenum Press, 1982

Kazdin, A, & Matson, J. Social validation in mental retardation. *Applied Research in Mental Retardation,* 1981, *2,* 39–53

King T, Soucar, E, & Isett, R. An attempt to assess and predict adaptive behavior of institutinalized mentally retarded clients. *American Journal of Mental Deficiency,* 1980, *84,* 406–410

Landesman-Dwyer, S. Living in the community. *American Journal of Mental Deficiency,* 1981, *86,* 223–234

Landesman-Dwyer, S. Residential environments and the social behavior of handicapped individuals. In M Lewis, & L Rosenblum (Eds.), *Beyond the Dyad,* New York: Plenum Press (in press)

Lawrence, W. Relationship of climatological and behavioral variables among profoundly retarded males. *American Journal of Mental Deficiency,* 1977, *82,* 54–57

Marks, H, & Rodd-Marks, J. On an attempt to assess and predict adaptive behavior of institutionalized mentally retarded. *American Journal of Mental Deficiency,* 1980, *85,* 195

Mesibov, G. Alternatives to the principle of normalization. *Mental Retardation,* 1976, *14,* 30–32

Moos, RH. Conceptualizations of human environments. *American Psychologist,* 1973, *28,* 652–665

Moos, R. *Evaluating Educational Environments.* San Francisco: Jossey-Bass Publishers, 1979

McClain, R, Silverstein, A, Hubbell, M, & Brownlee, L. The characterization of residential environments within a hospital for the mentally retarded. *Mental Retardaton,* 1975, *13,* 24–27

Nihira, K, Foster, R, Shellhaas, M, & Leland, H. *AAMD Adaptive Behavior Scales,* 1974 edition, Washington, DC: American Association on Mental Deficiency, 1974

Nihira, K, Meyers, CE, & Mink, I. Home environment, family adjustment, and the development of mentally retarded children. *Aplied Research in Mental Retardation,* 1980, *1,* 5–24

O'Neil, J, Brown, M, Gordon, W, Schonhorn, , & Greer, E. Activity patterns of mentally retarded adults in institutions and communities: A longitudinal study. *Applied Research in Mental Retardation,* 1981, *2,* 367–379

Pratt, M, Luszcz, M, & Brown, M. Measuring dimensions of the quality of care in small community residences. *American Journal of Mental Deficiency,* 1980, *85,* 188–194

Prior, M, Minnes, P, Coyne, T, Golding, B, Hendy, J, & McGillivary, J. Verbal interactions between staff and residents in an institution for the young mentally retarded. *Mental Retardation,* 1979, *17,* 65–69

Professional Advisory Committee. A note on professional testimony and opinions in the Partlow case. *Mental Retardation,* 1979, *17,* 165–166

Reizenstein, J, & McBride, W. Designing for mentally retarded people: A social-environmental evaluation of New England Villages, Inc. In A Friedmann, C Zimring, & E Zube (Eds.), *Environmental Design Evaluation.* New York: Plenum Press, 1978

Risley, T. The ecology of applied behavior analysis. In A Rogers-Warren, & S Warren (Eds.), *Ecological Perspectives in Behavior Analysis.* Baltimore: University Park Pres, 1977

Rogers-Warren, A. *Ecobehavioral analysis: Some working definitions.* Paper presented at the eighth annual meeting of the Association for Behavior Analysis, Milwaukee, WI, May 1982

Rogers-Warren, A, & Warren, S. The developing ecobehavioral psychology. In A Rogers-Warren, & S Warren (Eds.), *Ecological Perspectives in Behavior Analysis.* Baltimore: University Park Press, 1977

Rosen, D. Alternative patterns of care for the mentally retarded. In P Mittler (Ed.), *Research to Practice in Mental Retardation,* (Vol. I). Baltimore: University Park Press, 1977

Schroeder, S, & Henes, C. Assessment of progress of institutionalized and deinstitutionalized retarded adults: A matched control comparison. *Mental Retardation,* 1978, *16,* 147–148

Sommer, R. *Personal Space: The Behavioral Basis of Design.* Englewood Cliffs, NJ: Prentice-Hall, Inc., 1969

Spreat, S, & Isett, R. Behavioral effects of intra-institutional relocation. *Applied Research in Mental Retardation,* 1981, *2,* 229–236

Sutter, D, Mayeda, T, Call, T, Yanagi G, & Yee, S. Comparison of successful and unsuccessful community placed mentally retarded persons. *American Journal of Mental Deficiency,* 1980, *85,* 262–267

Throne, J. Normalization through the normalization principle. *Mental Retardation,* 1975, *13,* 23–25

Tognoli, J, Hamad, C, & Carpenter, T. Staff attitudes toward adult male residents' behavior as a function of two settings in an institution for the mentally retarded people. *Mental Retardation,* 1978 *16,* 142–146

Twardosz, S, Cataldo, M, & Risley, T. Open environment design for infant and toddler day care. *Journal of Applied Behavior Analysis,* 1974, *7,* 529–546

Wahler, , & Fox, J. Setting events in applied behavior analysis: Toward a conceptual and methodological expansion. *Journal of Applied Behavior Analysis,* 1981, *14,* 327–338

Willems, E. Steps toward an ecobehavioral technology. In A Rogers-Warren, & S Warren (Eds.), *Ecological Perspectives in Behavior Analysis.* Baltimore: University Park Press, 1977

Willer, B, & Intagliata, J. Social-environmental factors as predictors of adjustment of deinstitutionalized mentally retarded clients. *American Journal of Mental Deficiency,* 1981, *86,* 252–259

Willer, B, & Intagliata, J. Comparison of family-care and group homes as alternatives to institutions. *American Journal of Mental Deficiency,* 1982, *86,* 588–595

Wolfe, M, & Proshansky, H. The physical setting as a factor in group functions and process. In A Jacobs, & W Spradlin (Eds.), *The Group as Agent of Change.* New York: Behavioral Publications, 1974

Wolfensberger, W. *Normalization.* Toronto, Canada: National Institute of Mental Retardation, 1972

Wolfensberger, W, & Glenn, L. *PASS 3: A Method for the Quantitative Evaluation of Human Services.* Toronto, Canada: National Institute of Mental Retardation, 1975

Paul Weisberg
Edward V. Sims, Jr.
Bruce A. Weinheimer

12

Academic Skills

The search for those features that distinguish the evaluation of academic behavior with low-performing individuals from the evaluation of nonacademic behavior is not likely to find differences in the kind of research methodology employed, the processes or phenomena studied, or the dimensions of the dependent variable measured. A broad spectrum of experimental designs and procedures concerning research methodology have been employed with both kinds of behaviors. Those for academic behavior have included: between group (Abt Associates, 1977; Becker & Gersten, 1982; Sindelar & Wilson, 1982); within group (Bracey, Maggs, & Morath, 1975a, 1975b); single subject, including treatment reversal designs (Dixon, Spradlin, Girardeau, & Etzel, 1974; Paine, Carnine, White & Walters, 1982); and multiple baseline approaches (Carnine, 1980; Johnson & Newman, 1982); as well as normative comparisons (Gersten, 1981; Gersten & Maggs, 1981[1]). That the academic-nonacademic distinction is also not peculiar to the behavioral processes or the phenomena examined is apparent from the fact that the target behaviors from both realms have been investigated in experiments dealing with discrimination, generalization, and maintenance, as well as with other psychological topics. The interested reader will find the journals replete with experiments on these topics for academic and nonacademic behavior; the few given here are intended as representative samples of the academic domain, namely, discrimination learning (Dixon et al., 1974; Englemann & Rosov, 1972; Gersten, White, Falco, & Carnine, 1982); transfer or generalization (Gersten et al., 1982; Johnson & Newman, 1982; Packer, 1982[2]; Sindelar & Wilson, 1982); and maintenance (Carnine, 1980; Johnson & Newman, 1982; Paine et al., 1982).

---

[1]Gersten, R, & Maggs, A. *Five year longitudinal study of moderately retarded children in a direct instruction program.* Unpublished manuscript, University of Oregon, 1981

[2]Packer, RA. *The Role of the instructional model and level of intelligence on word acquisition and transfer for beginning readers.* Unpublished doctoral dissertation, University of Alabama, 1982

Finally, the aspects of behavior selected as the dependent variable are irrelevant to behavior type. Measures, such as the rate, amount, duration, and "correctness" of behavior, are used to evaluate the effects of a treatment independent of whether the target behavior is academic or otherwise. The same is true of other indices (percent on target, trials to criteria, time taken to learn, number of steps completed in a multi-step task, etc.).

We usually think of academic behavior and its evaluation as that that occurs in a particular place, for instance, the classroom or the resource room of a public school, day care or residential facility. Though classification by place probably embraces much of where academic behavior would be found, there are a host of other behaviors in that situation not likely to fit that description, for example, dressing skills, self management, having snacks, lining up, and a large number of social behaviors. Many will furthermore claim, quite appropriately, that critical and everyday academic performances for the mentally retarded are now commonly taught and better practiced in nonclassroom learning contexts, such as in the natural settings of the home, work sphere and other important sectors of the community. Indeed, the value of the school context is frequently judged by how well it provides the learner with preparatory and functional behavior to operate in these other settings.

Classification may also be based upon which features and relationships of the familiar A-B-C sequence (antecedent-stimulus-behavior-consequence) are emphasized. Since many of the consequences given for academic and nonacademic behaviors are one and the same, the B-C contingency is not a viable basis for differentiation. Rather, we may look at academic behavior by the nature of the controlling antecedent stimulus dimensions or more precisely, the "content" that we want the students to learn. For reading and writing, part of the controlling stimulus dimension might be the arrangement of prescribed textual and verbal stimuli; for mathematical behaviors, it might be the arrangement of certain numeral symbols or the translation of verbal statements to those numeral symbols; and for language behaviors, it might be the arrangement of verbal stimuli according to the conventional standards of a group or society. We can readily define what constitutes the nature of the controlling relationship by examining the statements of objectives of state and local curricula, and by sorting them into categories that emphasize the stimulus side (e.g., the words in Wilson's [1963] Essential Vocabulary List, and those corresponding to the behavioral side, (e.g., read, write, spell and/or tell what the words mean). The same analysis can be done for statements of objectives of teachers, supervisors, and curricula specialists as well as those of publishers of textbooks and those of assessment instruments.

It could be argued that evaluation of how much and how well the student learned the prescribed content is an incomplete picture of academic assessment. Other variables need assessment, namely, characteristics of the teacher and the learner, type of classroom structure, teacher management and efficiency in the presentation of the content, and the role played by significant others (the principal and other building personnel, supervising and supportive staff, school administrators and board members, parent groups, volunteers, etc.). This point is well taken and to be sure, there is a burgeoning literature that links some of these variables to student performance (Bushell, 1973; Charters & Jones, 1973; Engelmann, 1982; Loucks & Hall, 1977; Rosenshine & Berliner, 1978; Tawney, 1982b). Space limitation, however, restricts description to the role of only a few variables, which are summarized in the section on evaluating classroom performance.

There is also the issue of what stimuli are deemed academic in nature. Suppose an educator posits that performance of the ''three Rs'' is substantially influenced by prior locomotor training or by perceptual-motor training using stimuli ordinarily not cast as academic. Though evaluation of the tool subjects would certainly qualify as being academic in scope, it is unclear whether evaluation of changes in the other, possibly correlated, behaviors would qualify. For many low-performing handicapped individuals, presenting academic content suitable for the child entering nursery school or kindergarten would prove too imposing for them, many of whose entire ''academic'' curriculum consists of learning what is otherwise simple attentional and motor skills. Attempting to develop a data base on the educability of very low-functioning individuals, Tawney (1982b) could only locate ten studies based altogether on 30 subjects. Acceleration of ''academic'' behavior ranged from shaping tongue thrusts, to social play, to shaping specific motor skills. Tawney (1982b) concluded that, functionally, there is no academic data base for the extremely handicapped. Carrying the issue one step further, there are some (Kauffman, 1981) who are doubtful whether academic training, even of the most minimum sort, should be contemplated with these individuals.

A major purpose of academic evaluation is to improve the decision-making process regarding instructional planning, implementation, and remediation. In this regard, some version of a diagnostic-prescriptive approach is usually taken with the handicapped individual (Bushell, 1973; Haring & Schiefelbusch, 1976; Pasanella & Vokmor, 1977). Sometimes, a first step is to identify the relevant atributes or characteristics of various students that pertain to the entry behaviors of the greatest concern to the teacher. Partly toward this end, this chapter will review traditional norm-referenced assessment in the form of achievement and related measures, with some of the limitations and uses of this approach highlighted. Since a second step is to specify curriculum/teaching goals and to translate them into instructional objectives, a review of this process will be given, as well as the rationale and characteristics of criterion-referenced testing, which is a newer kind of assessment that is more closely tied to behaviorally stated objectives and to the instructional tasks to be taught. Additional steps include the selection and implementation of appropriate instructional programs and strategies. At some point, the teacher or program evaluator will need to develop evaluative items to be given periodically during the instructional process to determine how firm the learner is on the concepts and operations taught and what, if any, remedial procedures are necessary. To help with item construction, several guidelines will be discussed and specific examples mentioned to indicate the "dos and don'ts" associated with this process.

Engelmann (1980) has proposed that more attention be given to the evaluation of the instructional format used to communicate concepts to the low performer. Tasks in a program very often are selected and sequenced in a faulty way so that not only is the target concept not taught, but it is mistaught; in other words the learner comes up with an incorrect interpretation that is not easily spotted during the original demonstration of the concept. By the time the misrule is noticed, it is hard to rectify. To take a simple example, a program/teacher that attempts to teach "redness" might show all examples of the concept by using red flannel squares and all examples of "not-red" by using differently colored plastic circles. Such a presentation cannot clearly teach the naive learner, since "red" could refer to color, certain shapes and materials, or any combination thereof. A more sophisticated illustration of misinterpretation, and one that Engelmann (1982) has in fact found to be prevalent in classroom practice is provided by a poorly designed series of examples to teach the main idea of a story. If the main idea in the first few examples is expressed by the first sentence in a passage, the students will perform admirably. If, however, the next passage contains no sentence that expresses the main idea, the learner will likely and, with good reason, continue to select the first sentence.

Engelmann's (1982) contention that many programs fail to promote acquisition and generalization of the concept has major implications for the evaluation process. Typically, the characteristics of the learner are examined first when learning failure is encountered. Unable to associate the names of colors with their physical referents, a student is diagnosed for attentional deficits, response deficiencies and, possibly, for sensory handicaps. In addition, if the learner's response system is inadequate, corrective methods are instituted entailing, perhaps, response prompts, shaping procedures, special forms of practice and/or changes in the type and schedule of reinforcement. Hardly any attention, however, is given to diagnosing the instructional program; that is, the selection and sequencing of tasks to teach the concept. Concerned with diagnosing the learner, the evaluator is frequently unaware of the details of the instructional programs and, if instructional flaws exist, they certainly would not be detected by the evaluator, especially when that person doubles as the unknowing teacher of the flawed program.

Engelmann and Carnine (1982) suggest that a necessary first step in the evaluation process is to diagnose the instructional program in order to rule out the possibility of faulty programming variables. The analysis of a program can be done on logical grounds without involving the learner. If the tasks are sequenced in such a way as to promote misrules, like the "main idea" illustration, or to create different interpretations of the concept, like the "redness" illustration, these possibilities can be detected from a step-by-step analysis of the program. This means that an instructional program will need to be highly specified (Weisberg, Packer, & Weisberg, 1981), which is the way it should be, since the low performer is apt to become confused if the wrong or insufficient "details" are presented. Engelmann and Carnine (1982) have described specific criteria for the design of "faultless" instructional programs for different types of concepts. Once the programming deficiencies are removed and replaced by a faultless program, the newly arranged format is taught to the learner. If the learner fails with this revised program or with a similar program that attempts to teach a new concept, then blame cannot be placed upon instructional variables and diagnosis is focused upon those characteristics of the learner that impede learning.

How to design instructional programs so that concepts will be communicated in the most consistent and efficient manner will not be the province of this chapter. The interested reader is referred to some excellent treatments on this subject (Carnine & Silbert, 1979; Engelmann & Carnine, 1982). Nevertheless, the theme running through this chapter is that academic evaluation must always be formulated in a way that considers the instructional content and program the student has experienced and soon will experience.

MAKING INSTRUCTIONAL DECISIONS

Norm- and Criterion-Referenced Tests

Interpreting an individual's test score ultimately involves making comparisons. Assessment instruments, such as standardized achievement and intelligence tests, that make comparisons of a person's score to the distribution of scores obtained by other persons belonging to a norm or reference group are known as norm-referenced tests. These tests usually describe the relative standing of individuals with each other in terms of differences in standard scores, percentiles, stanines, and age or grade equivalents.

A score may also be judged without regard to individual differences. Instead, comparisons can be made with respect to some specified criterion or standard of performance. For example, can the individual pass an oral reading test, which contains a 100-word paragraph taken from an end-of-second grade reader, with a reading rate of at least 40 words per minute and fewer than six errors? Given a 25-item, multiple-choice test, can the individual recognize, with at least 80 percent correct performance, which of four clocks illustrated matches a dictated time stated in digital form? Judgments such as these, in which the absolute level of skill mastery is of primary consideration, are determined from criterion-referenced tests (Glaser & Nitko, 1971; Popham, 1973). Minimum competency tests, also called basic skills tests, fit this designation. An individual's performance is judged not by how well it compares to other individuals taking the tests, but by how well it compares to the criteria set for the attainment of the minimal competencies. Thus, unlike norm-referenced tests, how well one individual does on a criterion-referenced test does not determine the score or placement of another individual.

Content Validity and Transfer

In a norm-referenced test, the goal is to write and select items that appropriately cover the objectives of the academic content area or domain being evaluated. To the extent that the items provide a representative sample of the domain in question, the test is said to have content validity. Unlike the estimates of a test's predictive and concurrent validity, in which the magnitude of a correlation coefficient provides a quantitative yardstick of the adequacy of validity, the assessment of content validity is largely a judgmental affair.

Test publishers generally go to great lengths to ensure that their test is judged high in content validity. They typically assemble a panel of curriculum specialists in a particular content area to examine a wide variety of curricular material from leading basal tests, syllabi, and State guidelines. The final test objectives stemming from such an extensive search results in a set broader in scope than the objectives of any single curriculum. Discussing the test objectives of reading comprehension subtests, Davis (1968) claims they measure a fairly mixed bag of language skills, and Carroll (1970) agrees that the tests are aimed at a more general "common denominator" kind of curriculum.

Besides needing to be appropriate samples of the academic subject matter, the items are constructed to reflect different psychological processes, more or less guided by Bloom's (1956) taxonomy of the cognitive domain. In order of increasing complexity, these cognitive levels are: knowledge (recognition of content), comprehension (translation, interpretation, and extrapolation), application, analysis, synthesis, and evluation (making judgments as to the accuracy and value of ideas, methods, solutions, and products).

Selecting a wide range of items to ensure test completeness, and evaluating at several cognitive levels, serves to emphasize further the discrepancy between an achievement test and any given instructional program. Additionally, the tasks included in an achievement test are often different in content, directions, and response conventions than those taught, and because the test comes at the end of the school year, it will contain many early tasks long since reviewed. To the extent that it samples material unlike that in an instructional program, a standardized achievement test represents a procedure for evaluating transfer or generalization phenomena across several dimensions. Using Stokes' and Baer's (1977) terminology, such a test probes for generalization of different stimulus events (unfamiliar content and directions) and conditions (the testing situation), across different responses (new response requirements) and over time (the degree of long-term control by early, nonreviewed content and nonpracticed responses).

To highlight the transfer problem of instructional program-test differences, the following scenarios are presented. Some of the illustrations may appear to represent trivial differences, but to the low-performing child they could pose substantial obstacles.

Many kindergarten and first grade math programs use real coins to teach coin identification and value. When pictures of coins are displayed, it is on their front-side. Both real and pictorially displayed programs do not provide explicit discrimination training of information appearing on the back-side. However, it is the back-side of coins that tests generally display.

One beginning reading program uses diacritical markers to distinguish long from short vowels and alters the orthography of letters similar in appearance to ease letter discrimination. Tests neither present the markers nor modify letter orthography.

A program identifies mathematical operations by their signs, such as "plussing" and "minusing" problems, whereas the directions of a test refer to them as "addition" and "subtraction." One test identifies a problem of the form $5 + \square = 8$ as a "number sentence" whereas the program refers to it as a plus (or minus) problem.

Upon encountering difficulty with their seat work assignments, children are taught to flag the teacher, who provides the necessary remediation; and, for many tasks, they are instructed not to go on to the next problem until they have correctly completed the present one. Both of these general work directions are contradicted in the test-taking situation.

The steps for doing computational problems with a multiple-choice format, as practiced in a classroom workbook, are to: work the problem, write the answer, match the written answer with the appropriate answer from among the printed choices, and fill in the circle next to that choice. The directions of a leading test instructs the students not to mark up (or write in) the test booklet. The apparent justification of the test designers is that, since the answer sheets are scored by machine, students who write answers for the problem may neglect to fill in any blank spaces. In effect, this prevents the child from writing the answer and forces the child to work the entire problem covertly ("in one's head"), a response sequence foreign to doing workbook problems. The proctors are requested to hand out scratch paper, but this is not always done, and even when it is, it requires yet another set of responses for which beginning students are ill-trained. They must take the time to copy each computation problem exactly from the test booklet and to make sure that their written scratch paper answers are synchronized with the right set of choices from which the problem was copied.

It should be apparent that an instructional program whose content, response conventions, and sequence of task presentation more nearly resembles those of a particular achievement test should be associated with higher test scores than programs less perfect in these matches. A comparison of the content of four fourth-grade standardized achievement tests in mathematics, with the percent of tested topics covered in three popular mathematic textbooks, showed wide variation in tested content (Test-Text, 1981–82). One achievement test covered no more than 53 percent of the topics of any textbook, while another test covered as much as 71 percent of the topics. A similar analysis, done for various reading series-test combinations for hypothetical first and second graders, that also found wide performance discrepancies (Jenkins & Pany, 1978), will be discussed later.

Judging the worth of a program by how well its participants will do on norm-referenced tests can greatly discourage the development of new and innovative programs for special students. Sometimes, designing a program that accommodates low performers may need to contain programming elements that represent significant departures from the common core of programs used with average and higher performers. This departure is likely to be greatest in the first few years of its development, after which the program may increasingly come to resemble the common core. If standardized achievement tests are employed to validate atypical programs during their infancy, when the program-test match is most discrepant, it is unlikely that the new program, no matter how innovative and workable with low performers in the long run, will ever get off the ground. Under these circumstances, evaluation of the new program is best done through self-developed criterion-referenced instruments that directly test whether the students have learned the content and response conventions taught.

General Limitations of Norm-Referenced Tests

From the foregoing, it should be obvious that a test item can be failed for many reasons. The smaller the overlap between an instructional program and the test, the lower the likelihood that the teacher will be able to pinpoint the reasons for item failure. Coupled with this problem is that, although it is available, teachers often do not use the item-by-item pass/fail account of each child's performance on an achievement test. Instead, norm-referenced scores are preferred (grade equivalents, percentiles, stanines, etc.), but they are insufficient for specific remediation purposes. Moreover, with end-of-school outcome scores, the teacher cannot make remedial plans for immediate use. With respect to locating specific academic weaknesses and suggesting remedial procedures, Becker and Engelmann (1976) contend that norm-referenced achievement batteries are of little value and mainly serve as rough initial screening devices.

Norm-referenced tests are also inadequate for use in process evaluation that deals with the measurement of what are believed to be the critical components of an instructional package. Process evaluation, or "formative measurement," typically involves continuous measurement of the hypothesized important elements taken one at a time to ensure that the components "fit together" and are properly implemented before the final outcome or "summative evaluation" is conducted (Scriven, 1967). The design, sequencing and integration of the curricular components as well as teacher effectiveness, management, and degree of program implementation are all assessment targets for process evaluation. In effect, process evaluation provides a mechanism for fine tuning the instructional system. Norm-referenced tests simply lack the necessary precision for making fine-grained statements about the status of instructional components. Should students perform much lower than expected on an appropriately selected test, all that may be said is that one or more elements of the instructional package must be weak, but determination of specific shortcomings is left for some other form of analysis (Bereiter, 1972).

Grade equivalent scores. Because of their widespread use in describing grade achievement in commonly taught academic subjects and in possibly tracing academic growth across different grade levels, grade equivalent scores (GES) are intuitively very appealing. According to Anastasi (1976), these scores enjoy the same popularity in academic settings as does the mental age index in traditional intelligence assessment. However, lest one be drawn to these scores because of their ubiquitousness and their apparent ease of interpretation, a strong word of caution needs to be issued.

Grade scores are scale scores assigned on the basis of the average raw score attained by a group of students of a given grade. A student with a GES of 2.0 has a score earned by the average beginning second-grader; one with a 4.0 as the average beginning fourth-grader. Since test constructors divide the school year into ten months (nine academic months plus one summer month), which starts in September and ends in June, intermediate months can be expressed in decimals. Thus, to give a few representative scores, the average GES of 2.1 equals the average achievement after the first month of second grade, 2.2 equals that after the second month, and 2.9 equals that after the end of second grade.

Students who obtain average raw scores that convert into grade equivalents of 2.0, 2.5, and 2.9, respectively, for the beginning, middle and end of second grade should similarly obtain values at or close to the 50th percentile for each of those time frames. This degree of comparability in the average GES and the average percentile value should hold for all grade levels on which an achievement test was standardized. To discover whether there is close accord between the GES at the different grades and the expected 50th percentile equivalent, the norm tables for grades one to nine of four widely used achievement tests were consulted. For present purposes, only the reading subtests were considered, but the findings and conclusions are true for mathematics and the total battery of each test. The norm tables were entered by looking first for the appropriate grade equivalent, i.e., 1.9 for the end of first grade and 2.9 for the end of second grade and so forth. Then, the corresponding raw scores and percentile values were located. For three tests, the Wide Range Achievement Test, the Stanford Achievement Test, and the Metropolitan Achievement Test, the fit was very good with the end-of-year grade equivalents at each grade falling between the 48th and 52nd percentile. For the California Achievement Test (CAT), the fit was good at the sixth to the ninth grade, but it was relatively less adequate at the earlier grades, and most inadequate at the first grade. More specifically, GES of 6.9, 7.9, 8.9, and 9.9 each corresponded to the 52nd percentile, whereas for 5.9, 4.9, 3.9, 2.9, and 1.9, the corresponding percentiles were the 54th, 55th, 56th, 55th, and 66th.

The discrepancy at the first grade is serious, enabling one to employ different standards about what constitutes average first grade performance. A child with a GES of 1.9, by typical achievement test yardsticks, would be judged as showing average first grade performance. Yet, that raw score could be considered above average if the percentile for that score which is the 66th on the CAT, is reported. (The difference between the 66th and 50th percentile is substantial, amounting to almost 0.50 standard deviation units on the normal curve.) If the 50th percentile on the CAT was defined as average first grade performance, the child could now be considered below average if that percentile's raw scores were converted to a

GES. The GES at the 50th percentile is .7, which is two months below grade expectation.

For the most part, grade equivalents are interchangeable with other norm-derived scale scores because the scores are stretched or compressed so as to conform to normal curve parameters. In cases where the interchange is less than perfect, as with the CAT and perhaps with other tests, the evaluator should be cautious when average achievement is defined. Had a more liberal definition of average been chosen, say the fifth stanine which spans the 41st to the 59th percentile, then average GES for end-of-first-grade CAT reading would be even lower, including GESs from 1.6 to 1.8.

Other grade equivalent characteristics are highlighted in Table 12-1, which was developed by R.S. Weisberg.

Except for first grade, the total number of reading-related items on the CAT is consistently around 70 for each grade. Since the number of correct items necessary to attain the average GES is quite variable across grades, the percentage of correct items also fluctuates. It is higher for the early grades, with the highest at grade three being 83 percent (61 correct out of 73 items) and it is lower for the later grades, with the lowest at grade nine being 51 percent (36 correct out of 70 items). The relatively higher performance levels for the first three grades, particularly at grade three, is also true of the reading sections of other achievement tests, although their absolute level is from eight to fifteen percentage points lower than the CAT. Generally speaking, getting from 55 to 70 percent of the items correct will place a student from the first six grades at the 50th percentile whereas from 50 to 60 percent is necessary for the next three grades.

The point to be made is that although these levels of achievement are considered acceptable for norm-referenced assessment, they would be most unacceptable if one subscribed the concept of mastery as 85 to 100 percent correct performance, a standard commonly set for criterion-referenced instruments. Since the rationale behind norm-referenced tests is not to evaluate the degree of mastery of a particular set of skills in depth, but rather to compare individuals on a broad range of skills; the definition of acceptable achievement is determined by average group performance. This means that it is relative performance that is the important feature of norm-referenced testing; the absolute level attained is of little consequence except in the preliminary tryout phases of item selecion where extremely easy and extremely difficult items are weeded out in order to maintain moderate levels of item difficulty (Anastasi, 976; Salvia & Ysseldyke, 1981).

It is instructive to ask what can be said of students who do less well than their same grade peers on an achievement test. As an index of poor performance, the raw scores of hypothetical students guessing according to chance on the reading items at each grade were converted into grade equivalents. Consider such a student taking the seventh grade CAT. His or her ''guessing'' grade equivalent falls between 4.0 and 4.2 (Table 12-1). Does the score imply placement at the beginning of fourth grade? An educator who thinks so is exhibiting one of the most fun-

Table 12-1
Normative Scores for Total Reading on the California Achievement Test for Grades One to Nine

	Number of Items		Expected GES		If 40% Items Correct			If 75% Items Correct		
						Percentile			*Percentile*	
Grade	*on test*	*to reach normative year end GES**	*by year end*	*by guessing*	*GES*	*beginning of year*	*end of year*	*GES*	*beginning of year*	*end of year*
1	60	43	1.9	.6	1.2	56	17	2.0	97	70
2	71	57	2.9	1.0	1.7	30	14	2.7	72	48
3	73	61	3.9	1.5	1.9	18	9	3.4	60	41
4	70	48	4.9	2.5–2.6	3.6	35	25	5.3– 5.4	77	62
5	70	49	5.9	2.7–2.8	4.0	26	21	6.3– 6.4	74	62
6	70	47	6.9	3.1–3.3	4.6	25	20	7.7– 8.0	75	64
7	70	40	7.9	4.0–4.2	6.1	36	30	9.3– 9.6	81	74
8	70	40	8.9	4.3–4.6	6.9	33	28	11.1–11.3	84	76
9	70	36	9.9	5.0–5.3	8.0	35	33	12.9	86	84

Developed by Robert S. Weisberg; Tuscaloosa, Alabama; Tuscaloosa City Board of Education.
*GES = Grade Equivalent Score

damental misconceptions about the use of GES. The content of the seventh grade test is largely derived from traditional seventh grade reading sources, such as basal readers or state curricula. None or very little of the content is derived from fourth grade material. Without knowing the scope of the reading material that the low performing seventh grader is able to understand, a deviant GES is meaningless and does not enable proper grade placement. What needs to be remembered is that the 4.0 asigned to a seventh grader is derived simply from the low end of the raw score distribution, and that both extreme raw scores and grade scores are merely convenient benchmarks on the test constructor's quantitative scale. Other than signaling poor seventh grade performance, an extremely low GES furnishes no more functional information with regard to grade or instructional placement as, for example, the report that the student placed at the 5th percentile, or was in the second stanine, or was -1.50 standard deviation units below the group mean. For extreme scores, the term, "grade equivalent," is an unfortunate misnomer that could best be discarded or supplamented by psychometric scores devoid of any mention of the word, "grade."

Similar problems in making valid instructional decisions emerge for a student getting a very high raw score that converts into an extremely high grade euivalent. That is, if a second grader obtains a 4.8 on a reading or any other subtest, it does not imply mastery of all of the pre-requisites necessary to do satisfactory work in the eighth month of fourth grade. It is only in the theoretical sense that the second grader's performance is equivalent to the typical performance of those in the norm group who have completed eight months of fourth grade. The possibility of functional equivalency is unlikely due to the incomplete overlap of content between second and fourth grade. In other words, we cannot be any more confident in placing a second grader who is awarded 4.0 into a fourth grade reading group than placing the eighth grader who achieved the same GES into that same fourth grade group.

To make a proper decision, both the low and high performers could be given an informal, comprehensive test containing reading content sampled from all school grades. The student could be placed in that grade or reading group in which reading is found to be accurate and fluent. Many achievement tests now have locator tests designed to facilitate functional level placement. Probably, the best policy is to ask the skill-deficient students to read from the various readers in use at the school they attend, and to place them in the grades (readers) where accuracy, speed, and comprehension reaches an acceptable level.

It is well known that the most reliable score in a normal distribution are those near the middle of the distribution. Publishers of the CAT Test Coordinator's Handbook (1978) have set the reliability zone for each grade as extending from those scores where 40 percent to 75 percent of the items were answered correctly. The grade equivalents defining the boundary of this interval are presented in Table 12-1. Considering the results of the third grade test, this means that grade equivalents from 1.9 to 3.4 are the most dependable upon which to make instructional decisions. Scores lower and higher than this range are not very meaningful.

Also given are the percentile equivalents for the 40 and 75 percent points for students taking the reading test at the beginning and end of each grade level. These values have particular significance for showing the sensitivity of percentiles to instructional efforts. A group of beginning fifth grade students passing 40 percent of the items and improving to 75 percent by the end of the grade would progress from the 26th to 62nd percentile. Similar sensitivity to instruction is possible for all other grades, although the magnitude of potential change is greater for the upper than the lower grades. Percentiles are also receptive to decrements in performance, as when within-grade correct mastery is lowered from 75 to 40 percent. What about the "stagnant" student whose performance is not materially changed during the school year? Curiously enough, the percentiles are not equally sensitive across grade levels for such students. And the amount of possible change diminishes with an increase in grade level. Note the ninth grader in Table 12-1 getting 40 percent of the items correct both at the start and end of school. The drop is only two percentile points. Meanwhile, the percentile drop in a similar unchanging second grader is 16 points. Evaluators, educators, and researchers alike should extend this same kind of psychometric analysis to other achievement tests.

A further problem is that beginning percentile values at the 40 percent correct point are different for different grades. They are highest for the first grade (56th percentile) and lowest for the third grade (18th percentile). To discover whether true changes have occurred within grades, one could take the initial and final raw scores of a target group and transform the scores into standard scores. (Test constructors will furnish the mean beginning and end score for each grade level to enter into the standard score formula.) Once derived, the initial and final standard scores of the target group(s) can be converted into percentiles based on the area under the normal curve. Done for each grade for which data is available, the amount of percentile change from the beginning to the end of the grade can then be assessed.

Interrelations among achievement tests: The Jenkins and Pany study. How some of the already discussed limitations of norm-referenced tests can be exploited is revealed by Jenkins and Pany's (1978) simulated study of word recognition. These investigators asked how a hypothetical first or second grade reader, who mastered all of the content words from each of several commercial reading series, would fare on word recognition sections of various achievement tests. If the same word appeared in both the reading series and the test, the hypothetical reader was scored as getting the word "correct." Raw scores were converted into GES for each test. Table 12-2 shows the discrepancies between five reading programs and four tests for each grade level.

Table 12-2

Grade Equivalent Scores Obtained by Matching Specific Reading Text Words to Standardized Reading Test Words

Reading Curriculum	Publisher	PIAT*	MAT* Word Knowledge	MAT* Word Analysis	SORT*	WRAT*
Bank Street Reading Series	Macmillan, 1965					
Grade 1		1.5	1.0	1.1	1.8	2.0
Grade 2		2.8	2.5	1.2	2.9	2.7
Keys to Reading	Economy, 1972					
Grade 1		2.0	1.4	1.2	2.2	2.2
Grade 2		3.3	1.9	1.0	3.0	3.0
Reading 360	Ginn, 1969					
Grade 1		1.5	1.0	1.0	1.4	1.7
Grade 2		2.2	2.1	1.0	2.7	2.3
Science Research Associates Reading Program	Science Research Associates, 1970					
Grade 1		1.5	1.2	1.3	1.0	2.1
Grade 2		3.1	2.5	1.4	2.9	3.5
Sullivan Associates Programmed Reading	McGraw-Hill, 1978					
Grade 1		1.8	1.4	1.2	1.1	2.0
Grade 2		2.2	2.4	1.1	2.5	2.5

Reprinted from Jenkins, J., & Pany, D. Standardized achievement tests. How useful for special education? *Exceptional children*, 1978, *44*, 448–453. With permission.

*The achievement tests were the Peabody Individual Achievement Tests (PIAT; Dunn & Markwardt, 1970), the Metropolitan Achievement Test (MAT; Durost, Bixler, Wrightstone, Prescott, & Balow, 1970), the Slosson Oral Reading Test (SORT; Slossen, 1963), and the Wide Range Achievement Test (WRAT, Jastak, Bijou, & Jastak, 1965).

The data should caution one not to assume that GES of different tests are interchangeable or that curriculum bias is uniform across all tests. The simulated data, together with the discussion in connection with the data in Table 12-1, also show that the tests are not useful for measuring growth, evaluating teacher effectiveness, and determining specific curriculum placement.

The measurement of the amount of growth of a student over some time period, as expressed in GES, is difficult to accurately determine. At the end of first grade, the average child is expected to obtain a score of 1.9 and, thereafter, to advance one full grade unit for each year in school. This linear rate of progress from first to second grade is neither found for a single program judged by different tests, nor for several programs judged by a single test.

Inconsistencies are also evident in evaluating teacher effectiveness based on student performance on different tests. A first grade teacher using the Sullivan Series would be judged as acceptable by the Peabody Individual Achievement Tests (PIAT; Dunn, & Markawardt, 1970) or by the Wide Range Achievement Test (WRAT; Jastak, Bijou, & Jastak, 1965) evaluation, but as inadequate by the Metropolitan Achievement Test (MAT; Durost, Bixler, Wrightstone, Prescott, & Balow, 1970) or by the Slosson Oral Reading Test (SORT; Slossen, 1963) evaluation (note that perfect mastery of any program words was assumed, which should qualify that teacher as outstanding).

Specific curriculum (or reading) placement is difficult to determine from series-test comparisons. According to one series-test combination, a first grade child might be labeled as a nonreader (a GES of 1.0 with the Sullivan Series and the SORT) and by another as on-grade level (a GES of 1.8 with the Bank Street Series and the SORT). The possibility of making incorrect placement decisions, say, for a transfer child coming from a school where Sullivan was taught to one using Bank Street, are obvious.

Several comments concerning Jenkins and Pany's (1978) selection of programs and tests are in order. Except for the MAT, the other achievement tests examined were not among the six leading ones used to assess end-of-grade reading in the U.S. schools, but were selected because they are individually administered, require oral reading, and provide a wide range of GES. These tests probably reflect the kind of selections upon which a school system bases decisions. When a counselor or administrator is faced with a suspect score from a leading test, for example, a second testing is commonly done, not with another leading test, but with one of the oral reading tests selected by Jenkins and Pany (1978).

The consistently lower outcome score of the MAT needs to be considered. Although such low scores would seem to indicate insensitivity to instruction, a large scale intervention project known as "Follow Through" found the MAT to be very sensitive to different forms of reading instruction with low-performing children (Abt Associates, 1977).

The words used as distractors also need to be considered. The two MAT subtests evaluated by Jenkins and Pany (1978) incorporate a multiple-choice format containing four words. In word knowledge, a picture must be recognized, and in word analysis a dictated word must be identified. It appears that Jenkins and Pany's (1978) definition of "correct" words included only those words represented by the pictures or those dictated; that is, words listed in a reading series that served as distractors or choices in the MAT had no bearing on the raw score. Consequently, a strategy by which a hypothetical reader rules out known incorrect choices in the search for a correct answer is not helpful.

Additionally, the lowest possible first grade GES, as reported in the MAT norms (Prescott, Balow, Hogan, & Farr, 1978) is 1.0. This means that a hypothetical non reader, who simply guesses according to chance on both subtests, and is thus exposed to none of the reading programs, is credited with almost the same GES as that obtained by "proficient" readers in the other programs.

The three other tests in Table 12-2 are essentially word lists, having error ceilings that, if reached, signal the conclusion of testing. It appears that testing in the simulated situation was not concluded until the entire word list from a reading series for a particular grade was exhausted. This scoring technique would greatly inflate the GES for the PIAT, SORT, and WRAT. Nevertheless, the higher GES of these tests might portray what occurs in actual practice. Weisberg (1981) found that for first grade readers, the WRATs grade level score overestimates that found by the MAT by an average of 1.8 school years (one year, eight months).

One would expect from the Jenkins and Pany (1978) simulation that one way to elevate the GES is to program more sight words in a reading series. Not only is this wishful thinking, because of the high memory load it imposes on the learner, especially the low performer, the proposition fails to recognize what some have thought to be the central programming principle underlying a beginning reading program (Carnine & Silbert, 1979; Weisberg et al., 1981). That is, words explicitly taught in beginning series should be those that enable application of functional word-attack skills to a generalizable set of nontrained words larger in range than the teaching set. There is no empirical support for word list size per se to index the worth of a reading program. Barnard and De Gracie (1976) found that the leading basal readers in the 1970s had 56 percent more words than those ten years prior, yet reading achievement, judged by whatever yardstick, has not improved appreciably.

A further word about the implications of grade scores. Although these scores may increase in a linear manner from one grade to the next or over several grades, the actual amount of learning that takes place may not parallel the unit increase in grade scores. Some skills may develop rapidly in the early grades and then level off, so that a GES change from 4.0 to 8.0 might represent very little new learning. The number of new reading and mathematical skills taught during the first four grades, for example, far overweighs those taught in the next four grades, the latter of which is often a time to consolidate previously taught skills. In the same vein, even with an academic subject taught in every grade, a rapid acceleration that represents the accumulation of a great amount of knowledge can occur for a selected period of time, as is the case for the intensification of social studies learning during grades six through twelve.

Because of the unevenness in the distribution of newly introduced skills during the school years, ceiling and floor effects in skill acquisition, therefore, can occur within different grades. As noted by Becker and Engelmann (1976), unless achievement test items can somehow be weighted in terms of such criteria as time-to-teach, scales based upon changes in grade scores can give deceptive results with respect to the amount of progress the learner has made in learning new and functional skills.

Evaluation problems using relative scores. Several major limitations of norm-referenced procedures have already been discussed and it is worth considering still others that have lead to the widespread interest in criterion-referenced testing. Donlon (1975) noted that descriptions and interpretations based upon relative scores derived from norm-referencing procedures can misrepresent or hide performance characteristics.

Specifically, psychometrically derived scores such as percentiles can divert attention from the actual behaviors that are the underpinnings of norm-ranked scores. One can talk about a person's relative standing with respect to a hypothetical variable, such as "reading ability" or "achievement in mathematics," without really knowing the logic of the measurement of these inferred qualities (Glaser & Nitko, 1971). Criterion-referenced scores, on the other hand, are constructed to support generalizations derived from known behavioral domains (e.g., letter discrimination, letter blending, reading aloud, etc.). Statements about how much reading ability a student possesses gives the mistaken impression that one has directly measured a known aspect of behavior when, in truth, one is making inferences about hypothetical ability dimensions.

Psychometrically derived scores can also impart imperfect definitions of excellence. A high percentile can be taken to mean exceptional performance when, in an absolute sense, it may not be. Attaining the 70th percentile in a standardized physical fitness test may seem relatively high but, as Dolon (1975) notes, given the reportedly poor physical condition of American children, that same performance might reach the 30th percentile in some more active country. Conversely, the tenth percentile should not always carry negative connotations; a mentally retarded adult scoring at the tenth percentile on a standardized twelfth-grade reading test may be limited in certain kinds of academic skills, but may possess the necessary behavioral repertoires to hold a job. Decision-makers must resist the temptation to overgeneralize from psychometrically derived scores that lack information about particular skill proficiencies.

Lastly, these scores can mask academic progress because of the changing norm populations during the school years. A child consistently between the 20th and 30th percentile on most achievement tests learns he is constantly outdone by others although he is not given precise information about what he is doing wrong.

Although his academic performance is changing in an absolute sense, and he, for example, is making the necessary progress to maintain his percentile ranking, the amount of this growth is hidden because the child is locked into a normative and relative system at each school grade that emphasizes not how much he did but how many he outdid.

Norm-Referenced Comparisons

Making within-program and between-program comparisons with norm-referenced tests to judge program effectiveness constitutes two widespread test uses. When a control group is lacking, the most common educational design for within-program evaluation is "norm-referenced comparison" (Horst, Tallmadge, & Wood, 1975). Here the pretest and posttest scores of a program are expressed as standard scores and compared to the test constructor's norm group at pretest and posttest. This procedure assumes that without the special program, relative standard score positions will remain the same, and that posttest scores are best predicted from pretest scores. In contrast, a gain in the standard score would indicate that the program is working better than the hypothesized average program used for similarly performing students in the normative sample.

By scaling the pre-post data in equal standard deviation units and plotting the scale points in more familiar percentile values, the magnitude of the program gain of each norm-referenced subtest can be displayed. Within-program gains of one-fourth standard deviation or greater are considered to be educationally significant (Abt Associates, 1977). Stated in terms of percentiles on the normal curve, this means that a pre-post gain of 0.25 standard deviation units is equally as educationally important whether the advance is from the 16th to the 23rd percentile, the 50th to the 60th percentile, or from the 77th to the 84th percentile.

Gersten and Maggs (1982) compared the norm group of the Stanford-Binet against the within-program IQ changes of pre-adolescent, mentally retarded public school students in Australia. Mean pretest IQs were 41.9 and, after almost five years of continuous training with the Direct Instruction Language and Reading programs, the posttest IQs rose to 50.6, which, when corrected for regression effects, resulted in a "true" IQ gain of seven points. Relative to IQ changes made by comparable students in the Binet standardization sample, the obtained gain proved to be statistically significant. Moreover, snce the pre-post gain in standard deviation units was 0.44, well above the conventional 0.25 unit change, the magnitude of the effect was considered educationally significant. Unfortunately, data on year-to-year changes in IQ were not collected, so the course of cognitive growth is unknown. To provide concurrent validity measures, posttest program data were also collected on the Peabody Picture Vocabulary Test. The mean IQ was 54.9, which, in standard score units, was comparable to that of the posttest Binet IQ. Aside from the Binet, norm-referenced comparisons were done with the Baldie Language Ability test (Baldie, 1978), an objective-based criterion-referenced instrument that reports scores in terms of the percentage of Australian school children mastering each of 66 objectives. The program group was found to do equally well on these objectives as a random sample of nine year-old, non-handicapped children did, serving as a representative norm sample.

Norm-referenced designs can also be judiciously applied to between-program comparisons. Maggs and Morath (1976) evaluated the amount of mental age gain on the Stanford-Binet of two groups of institutionalized moderately mentally retarded children who were provided with language training that involved either Direct Instruction (Engelmann & Osborn, 1976) or the Peabody Language kit (Dunn & Smith, 1976). Knowing that the annual expected mental age (MA) gain is 12 months, the finding of a 22.5 month gain over a 24-month instructional period for the Direct Instruction group was deemed exceptional in light of the children's level of functioning, and the instructional program was lauded. The other group gained 7.5 months over the two-year period, exemplifying the usual intellectual decline in institutional settings.

In the Follow Through Project (Abt Associates, 1977), the academic progress of over 15,000 educationally "at risk" children was evaluated from first grade or kindergarten through third grade using the MAT. These children normally place at the end of the 20th percentile by the end of the third grade (Becker, 1977; US Office of Education, 1976), which is equivalent to being three-quarters of a standard deviation unit below the 50th percentile norm. Such a low standing for third grade students translates, depending upon the achievement subtest, into grade levels of from 0.75 to 1.5 years below norm. By providing different intervention programs, running the instructional gamut from Open Education, Responsive Environment, Cognitive-Piagetian, Behavior Analysis, and Direct Instruction (just to mention six of the twelve major Follow Through programs), it was possible to access program effectiveness by comparing children's scores to normative academic functioning on the third-grade MAT. As it turned out, not many programs succeeded in reaching the 50th percentile. The Direct Instruction model came closest: percentile values were at the 41st on Total Reading, the 48th on Total Math, the 51st on Spelling, and the 50th on Language (grammar and sentence structure). Behavior Analysis scored at the 49th percentile on Spelling. The normative performance of the children in many of the other programs hovered around the 20th percentile baseline.

When using normative information, it is important that the program and norm groups agree on such characteristics as time of testing, duration of the program year, and subtest composition. Normative testing for the leading achievement tests is currently conducted during early Fall and Spring and, sometimes, a third time in mid-year. Becker and Engelmann (1976, p. 275) summarize these dates for tests published prior to 1973; more current listings are available in the most recent norm manuals of each test. Pretesting and posttesting of a program should correspond to these dates. The time period between the first and last testing period is usually ten months, which, for proper norm comparison, should also define the duration of a full program "year."

Virtually every standardized test is normed on a nonhandicapped population. Evaluators of a program for the mentally retarded or for other special group have no choice but to use these inappropriate norms. The situation is slowly changing. Gersten (1981) reports that the state of Oregon is collecting normative data on a curriculum-referenced instrument for trainable mentally retarded students. Until similar efforts are completed nationwide, making norm-referenced comparisons using leading achievement tests will apply an overly stringent standard that will make it harder for special programs to show gains against the norm group. Sometimes, with the mentally retarded, slight, nonsignificant declines against the norm group may even be found (Lloyd, Cullinan, Heins, & Epstein, 1980; Maggs & Morath, 1976).

Criterion-Referenced Tests

The 1960s were marked by a growing recognition that assessment procedures predicated on traditional, norm-referenced test theory and practices were either inappropriate or not sufficiently informative to meet the evaluation demands of the newer emerging forms of behavioral-oriented technologies. The movement away from global, nonspecifiable academic objectives toward more detailed and behaviorally worded statements (Glaser & Klaus, 1962) required a set of test items of much greater specificity than those that were included in existing achievement tests. The items were to be keyed to the academic objectives and were to provide a direct test of whether those objectives being met. A related development was individually prescribed instruction (Glaser, 1963), which emphasized a different part of the instructional process; but, it too required the construction of a special and ever-changing set of evaluative items, the performance on which was to be intimately tied to instructional decisions about what program components to alter or retain.

A hallmark of both technologies was the design of evaluative tasks that yielded information that was directly interpretable in terms of a specified performance standard or criterion (Glaser & Nitko, 1971). As used by Glaser (1963), the term criterion stemmed from the experimental psychology of learning in which it meant a critical level of mastery beyond which additional learning trials are not helpful. Decisions based on criterion-referenced data should thus always be tied to some level of mastery. This definition should not be confused with another well-known meaning of criterion provided by the educational testing literature. Here, to validate the scores of a test, another instrument is chosen, called a criterion measure or scale, and the scores of the two tests are compared. Fremer (1972) has attempted to link the two meanings of criterion by arguing that any behavioral output can be graded in terms of some yardstick of performance that can then serve as a basis for validating another instrument.

Domains and Mastery Levels

Central to the definition and interpretation of performance standards is the concept of a domain of related tasks. In the field of education, the domains of related behaviors are commonly called academic content or subject matter areas. The domain can be identified in a very general terms, (e.g., reading, mathematics, language, etc.), but when instructional goals and teaching procedures are described, they are typically given narrower focus, as indeed they should be (e.g., decoding skills, identifying the main idea of a story, numeral identification, two-column addition computations, pluralization, discrimination of present, past, and future tense, etc.). Once the domain is prescribed, representative samples of related tasks are drawn up and are given to learners as test items. Measurements of behavior are taken and, in the case of criterion-referenced assessment, statements about the individual's performance are referenced directly to the domain under examination. These statements should include descriptions of the individual's level of proficiency, derived either by using a preset cutoff score that pronounces competency in the domain (e.g., by passing a driver's test or a high school minimal competency test) or by using absolute scores, such as percent correct performance, which in turn provides some basis for the steps to take in the learning sequence (such as to switch the learner to a higher/lower skill level or to give additional practice on the present skill). At first, the guidelines for setting mastery levels are probably based upon conventional standards and, if none are available, then on arbitrary but logical grounds. One deciding and ultimate factor is the empirical demonstration of whether a previously "mastered" component skill facilitates the learning of more complex skills of which the component is a part.

Objective-Based Criterion-Referenced Tests

Becker and Engelmann (1976) have pointed to two sources from which test items are constructed and are administered to students. First, items may emanate from a set of behavioral objectives or statements that specify what performances should be attainable after instruction. Test items are then developed to measure each stated objective. Criterion-referenced tests following this approach are called objective-based. The second source is a clearly delineated instructional program that specifies the kind and sequence of concepts and skills to be taught. Test items are constructed to parallel the program with the goal of evaluating whether the components of the program that are said to be taught actually are taught. Criterion-referenced testing following this approach is called instructional-program based.

Objective-based tests have grown in popularity ever since the beginning of the behavioral objectives movement in education (Bloom, 1956; Mager, 1962). Popham (1973) has worked out a simple four-step procedure in planning for assessment. The test developer, whom Popham envisioned was typically the classroom teacher, should: state objectives in terms of the observable performances the students will be expected to do before instruction; develop a sample of objective-based test items and pretest for the presence of the relevant skills; develop daily lesson plans and/or more long-term teaching units that teach the relevant skills; and, posttest and evaluate how many students met some performance standard.

Additionally, several factors must be considered when writing complete and clearly delineated academic objectives. According to Pasanella and Volkmor (1977), a behaviorally written objective should: describe the terminal behavior in terms of what behavioral operations will be displayed; describe the conditions of learning, which includes listing any special materials (Language Masters, special work sheets, Bliss Symbols, words written in Distar orthography or taken from the Dolch sight word list, etc.), and describe how the student will perform the terminal act (read aloud, write sentences, reading by Braille, filling in the space, reproduce by drawing, etc.); and, offer a criterion for success. Criterion statements can concentrate on the number of behaviors, the time it takes, as well as certain characteristics related to the process or products of academic performance. Further consideration given to the construction of appropriate test items will be discussed throughout this chapter.

One problem with many academic objectives is that they are often written in such summary form that teahers will differ greatly in their versions of what concepts and skills the objective entails. To some teachers, fulfilling a generally worded objective will be a rather simple affair; whereas, for others, interpretation of that same objective will be more difficult. A case in point is the goal, ''to develop auditory discrimination skills'' an objective appearing in many checklists. Although this seemingly suggests an unambiguous behavioral entity, it is actually inconsistently measured in the reading research literature. At least four different interpretations of that single objective have been uncovered (Samuels, 1970), as described in Table 12-3.

By describing the behavioral operations and providing sample tasks appropriate for each objective, teachers will be in a better position to judge whether each objective was met. The importance of providing a range of sample evaluative tasks must be emphasized. The inclusion of only one in Table 12-3 is simply to raise the same doubts in the reader as in a teacher as to whether any single task actually fulfills the objectives. Providing a host of illustrative tasks would lend precision to the measurement of each skill, and, when coupled with criteria statements about mastery performance (also excluded from Table 12-3), the set of sample tasks can assist in indexing the level of skill difficulty for each objective. The objectives, as presently described and with single sample tasks, leave a teacher uncertain as to the permissibility of using: for objective one, multi-syllable words or nonsense words; for objective two, consonants that do not vary in the sounds they make (l, m, r) or do vary (c as in come or c as in cent), or using vowels for that matter; and, for objective three, beginning stop sounds (c-a-t) and nonsense words. For objective four, there are a whole host of uncertainties related to story content, position of the target sound in a word, and the comprehension level of the words used as choices for answers. Indeed, many learners may be ill-equipped

Table 12-3
Four Possible Interpretations and Sample Tasks for the Objective:
To Develop Auditory Discrimination Skills

Behavioral Operation	Sample Task
1. Distinguishing whether word pairs are similar or different	Told word paris (tat-dat, cup-cup, salt-sought, jaw-jar), student appropriately says "same" or "not same"
2. Matching letter sounds to letter configurations	Told a consonant sound (s, m, l, etc.), the student must circle a letter corresponding to that sound from four written choices
3. Blending sounds to form words	Told the sound components of a consonant-vowel-consonant (CVC) word, the student must blend them to form the word (m-a-t: "mat!")
4. Combining content and phonological cues	Examiner: "Listen, when Gus started to school, he forgot to shut something. What Gus forgot to shut begins with the first sound in his name. Circle the picture of what he forgot to shut." Picture Choices: door, garden, gate

to deal with objective four and a task analysis to pinpoint and describe in sequence the critical subskills would be a logical next step. The result of such analysis would be the generation of new objectives, each with its own set of sample tasks. It should be obvious that thoughtful objective writing is an unending affair that demands continual scrutiny and revision; and (as will be amplified later) in an objective-based program, the range of sample skills will signal what tasks to teach.

To carry the analysis of specifying objectives to a larger domain, that of reading, Table 12-4 is provided. As with Table 12-3, the procedure for specifying objectives in Table 12-4 is at best a necessary first step, and more information is needed before sufficient evaluation of each objective is possible. However, the intent is to reveal the gamut of some frequently-mentioned reading objectives required of handicapped individuals in school settings. The first three objectives stem from the *Observation Manual of the Behavioral Characteristics Progression* (1977), which targets some 50 reading objectives for developmentally impaired individuals. The next three were devised by the present authors. They typify objectives universally stated by school systems and frequently evaluated in reading research studies. For example, Sidman, Cresson, and Wilson-Morris (1974) taught a 20-word reading comprehension task (picture-word matching) to severely

Table 12-4
Sample Reading Objectives and Related Tasks

Objective/Skill Desired	Task Requirements or Sample Item	Mastery Level
1. Can open book and turn it right side up	Student (resident) presented with an upside-down positioned book must open it, then turn it right-side up	Correct repositioning of three different books (all less than one inch thick)
2. Names capital letters	Shown a flash card of *M*, says its name within five seconds	Identifies at least 23 of 26 capitals
3. Orally reads pre-primer words from Dolch word list	Given the 40 pre-primer Dolch words (e.g., blue, for, look, one, said, two, you), reads them aloud without hesitating and within ten seconds	Reads 36 or more of the 40 words
4. Can answer picture-vocabulary questions	Shown a sample picture (e.g., cat) can select the appropriate word (choices: car, ear, cat, cow)	Given 20 items, gets 18 or more correct
5. Reads sentences and answers literal questions	Student must silently read and answer: "The cow jumped out of the boat and the boy stayed inside. Who jumped out of the boat?" (boy, cow, cat)	Given ten similar sentences, gets eight or more correct
6. Reads sentences and answers simple inferential questions	Student must silently read and answer: "My job is to fix teeth. Who am I?" (toothbrush, dentist, diver)	Given ten similar sentences, gets eight or more correct

| 7. | Recognizes compound words | Teacher: "Fill in the space next to the compound word." Student's choices: happy 0, saw 0, maybe 0, want 10 | Given a set of ten single compound words, can identify eight or more words |
| 8. | Recognizes and understands "safety" words | Given "safety-related" terms from Wilson's Essential Vocabulary (e.g., caution, fire exit, noxious, thin ice, proceed at your own risk, etc.) can read them aloud and answer yes/no questions. For instance, shown *combustible*, the student must read it and answer: 1. Does it mean broken? 2. Is it something you use to comb your hair? 3. Is it something that burns easily? (If unable to read, student is told the word and then asked yes/no questions) | Able to read 90% of words and comprehension is 90% or higher. Maintains 90% level over six follow-up periods spaced three months apart. |

Objectives 1–3 modified from *Observation manual of the behavioral characteristics progression.* Austin, Texas: Texas Department of Mental Health and Mental Retardation, 1977

Objectives 4–6 developed by the authors

Objective 7 modified from *Minimum standards and competencies (reading, language, mathematics) for Alabama schools* (Bulletin No. 25). Montgomery, Alabama: Alabama State Department of Education, 1982

Objective 8 modified from Foster, RW. *Camelot behavioral checklist.* Lawrence, KS: Camelot Behavioral Systems, 1974 mentally retarded Down's-syndrome children using some of the sample words shown for objective five. Objectives six and seven reflect more difficult comprehension tasks and embody typical objectives dealing with who-questions and knowledge of occupations. Objective seven was elected as an example of one of the 22 reading objectives listed for the first-grade level of the *Minimum Standards and Competencies (reading, language, mathematics) for Alabama Schools* (1982). Special education students have the opportunity to participate in this basic competency program. Objective eight comes from the *Camelot Behavioral Checklist* (Foster, 1974), an evaluation system intended for the mentally retarded. It contains 40 behavior classes; the one for reading lists ten items.

Since none of the sources gave criteria performance, the mastery level statements were written by the present authors to serve as prototypes. When a source did not refer to the kind of permissible material to use in evaluation, the authors supplied material. For example, for objective eight, the Camelot checklist reports, "recognizes safety words," (Foster, 1974, p. 10) but it does not provide any actual words, and so the Wilson (1963) list was added by us. Obvious advantages of citing already established lists of materials, such as the Wilson (1963) and the Dolch (1936) Word lists, are to shorten the process of constructing evaluative items and to add objectivity to evaluation.

Problems with objective-based evaluation. A reputed feature of objective-based tests is that the objectives should not bind one to adopt any particular instructional program. Faced with an objective, the teacher is supposedly free to select any program, curriculum material, resource, or activity as long as it helps to tech the skills implied by the objective. If criterion-referenced testing, however, is to contribute to instruction, it should reveal where instruction has succeeded or failed. Ideally, an appropriate evaluative task is one that is passed because of successful instruction and failed because of inadequate instruction. As elaborated earlier in discussing achievement test items, an item may be failed for many reasons. If an objective, therefore, is written without regard to an instructional program, it becomes difficult to tell a well-constructed evaluative item from a poorly constructed one (Becker & Engelmann, 1976). In other words, a worthwhile program developed by Teacher A might enable all children to pass difficult tasks of the kind set for objective four in Table 12-3. Under these circumstances, correctly answering such evaluative tasks would be judged as fulfilling the objective because they reflect a teachable program. Suppose Teacher B, given the same class of children as Teacher A, but adopting a different instructional program, fails to teach even ten percent of the class to mastery. If Teacher B, and possibly hundreds of others using uniquely different teaching tactics, each produce learning failures, one possible fallacious conclusion might be that the evaluative task and not the instructional program is poorly developed.

The assumption that statements of academic objectives do not hamper the choice of instructional program and the kinds of teaching methods to use is a myth that continues to be supported by those who set objectives for the classroom teacher. Suppose objective three in Table 12-4 is universally adopted by a school district or state agency, which is a very reasonable proposition since the Dolch Sight Word List is a widely cited, objective-based source. The basis for selection of the 40 pre-primer words (as well as higher–grade-level words) stems from a frequency count of words in basal readers and in children's literature. The words, however, do not necessarily represent regular, decodable words whereby each letter in a word is represented by its most common sound (Carnine & Silbert, 1979). In fact, of the 40 words, 28 of them are highly irregular (e.g., blue, one, said, where, you), making it extremely difficult to teach students to apply consistent phonic rules for sounding out or decoding them. Judged during or at the end of the school year by whether his or her class can master these sight words, a teacher will, in all likelihood, dispense with early phonics training and instead opt for sight word training and adopt a whole-word, meaning-emphasis approach, which is at the heart of basal readers (Flesch, 1979; Terman & Walcutt, 1958; Weisberg et al., 1981).

Unfortunately, it is the low performer who is likely to suffer by the imposition of sight-word emphasized objectives. Unable to employ a consistent strategy to decode words, the low-IQ reader taught by whole-word methods will likely guess at previously taught words and have trouble decoding new words (Packer, 1982*). In Sidman et al. (1974), in which whole-word training was provided to Down's-syndrome children, hundreds of extra training trials had to begiven before consonant-vowel-consonant (CVC) words similar in appearance (e.g., bed, bug, box, boy; hat, hen, hut, hoe) could be mastered. Even with highly dissimilar words (apple, ball, horse, dog, elephant), severe and moderately mentally retarded children taught by a whole-word method, which was aided by a faded picture-prompt procedure, forgot over 50 percent of the sight words upon removal of the prompts (Dorry & Zeaman, 1973). Examining the decoding strategies of educable mentally retarded teenagers, Mason (1978) discovered that they converted unfamiliar words into familiar words (ship for skimp, coat for coax), read only a shorter, familiar word unit embedded in an uncommon word (ear for earl, eyes for yeast), committed more errors on the endings of words rather than on the beginning (seem for seep), often guessed at words, and discounted letter-sound relationships. Since this error pattern is typical of whole-word trained readers, Weisberg et al. (1981) speculated that they were taught by this reading approach in grade school. Still further, once a whole-word–induced error pattern is set into motion, it becomes difficult to correct part or all of the errors, even with phonics-based remediation (Terman & Walcutt, 1958); and the longer the whole-word training, the harder it is to correct (Carnine, 1980).

In contrast, synthetic phonics programs, such as Direct Instruction (Distar), premised upon the postponement of teaching irregular words until a decoding strategy is firmly established have greatly advanced the word attack skills of low

---

*Packer, RA. *The role of the instructional model and level of intelligence on word acquisition and transfer for beginning readers.* Unpublished doctoral dissertation, University of Alabama, 1982

IQ children (Becker & Engelmann, 1976; Bracey et al., 1975a; Gersten, Heiry, Becker & White, 1981; Packer, 1982*). And, if a phonics-first program is employed and continued into the primary grades, the decoding performance will remain strong later when the students are evaluated in the middle grades (Becker & Gersten, 1982).

The sequence of skills taught in Distar do not necessarily follow those emphasized by whole-word objectives. It is not until the second year of Distar training when the names of the letters of the alphabet, capital letters, contractions and the rules for many vowel digraphs *(ea, oi, ou)* are introduced. Objectives biased in favor of teaching these skills earlier load the dice against the selection of particular programs (such as Distar).

Some advocates of Objective-based testing (Popham, 1973) have urged the use of objectives that possess content generality. That is, those objectives that describe behaviors that can generalize across a range of content. The objectives, "can read any CVC word," or, "can add any pair of single-digit numbers," fit this designation. On the other hand, objectives that are essentially redundant with the test items devised to measure them are called test item equivalents (e.g., test items are developed to match such single-purpose objectives as "can red six, hot, mud," or "can add four plus two, four plus three). It is unfair, however, to favor the construction of evaluative items of one sort or another without knowing anything of the instructional program used to satisfy the objectives. When programs teach general case strategies of such types that, after problem-solving routines are taught with some members of a set, then any new member belonging to that set should be performed (Becker & Engelmann, 1976), then presenting items with content generality (items belonging to the set) is a legitimate form of evaluation. When programs teach linear additive skills, such that each member of a set must be explicitly taught, evaluative test items that are equivalents of the particular skill taught are not only fair but are necessary, whereas items testing content generality are not justifiable.

Evaluating the oral reading of low IQ children, Packer (1982*) used evaluative items of both the equivalent item and content generality forms. Children taught by whole-word methods did well on items of the first kind, but did poorly on the second kind. Children taught by a synthetic phonics method did reasonably well on both kinds. These and similar findings (Engelmann, 1982) should serve to caution instructional supervisors and administrators to learn about the kinds of skills taught in various programs before they set policies in force about academic objectives and evaluation. Developers of objectives oriented toward the evaluation of content generality are too often the very same persons who advise teachers to adopt instructional programs or curriculum packages that leave children unable to deal with items that generalize across a range of content.

---

*Packer, RA. *The role of the instructional model and level of intelligence on word acquisition and transfer for beginning readers.* Unpublished doctoral dissertation, University of Alabama, 1982

A final problem concerns the task of selecting objectives and devising or searching for appropriate evaluative measures. There is no doubt that techers should be knowledgeable about how to develop and measure simple objectives that reflect day-to-day classroom activities. Hofmeister (1975) has shown how this could be done with a few tasks, and there is a wealth of guidelines on how to devise criterion-referenced test items (Dillman & Rahmlow, 1972; Gronlund, 1970; Kemp, 1977; Mager, 1962; Popham, 1973), although these are largely intended for student evaluation at the high school and college level. There are, nevertheless, literally hundreds of major academic objectives that could be developed and an even larger number of corresponding assessment procedures. The process of writing relevant objectives and test items is an arduous, time-consuming, and often wasteful affair (Becker & Engelmann, 1976) and there is no reason to expect the already burdened classroon teacher to spend valuable instructional time in this endeavor.

To lighten the load, Popham (1974) launched an Instructional Objective Exchange in 1958, the major purpose of which was to develop, and distribute to teachers, booklets containing collections of measureable instructional objectives and related test items. The test material usually came in the form of preprinted spirit masters that could be duplicated and distributed to a class of students. Ever since Popham's Exchange, scores of worksheets, not tied to any explicit instructional program, have become commercially available for the claimed purpose of providing teachers with convenient material to assess students on skills related to various objectives. If teachers think the worksheets are largely evaluative in nature, to be used as independent seatwork, they are in for a big surprise. Some worksheet concepts may be within the student's repertoire, but because many are not, the teacher will often end up doing some unexpected teaching. For example, to test whether students have benefited from instruction on the difference between short versus long vowels, suppose a commercially prepared worksheet is selected and distributed by the teacher. Each of eight rows might show four pictures; the one at the left is a sample and the others are choices. The instructions might be to find the word that goes with these pictures (choices) that makes the same vowel sound as the vowel sound in the word that goes with this picture (sample). A secondary task might be to mark the short or long vowel sound.

The degree to which a child succeeds on this task depends upon how well the worksheet content and response conventions are congruous with the teacher's original instructions on short-long vowels. Since commercial distributors cannot know these facts, these "all purpose" worksheets may backfire. Low-performing children, while able to recognize all the pictures if the words for the pictures are given, often cannot come up with the names themselves (Willows, 1975). Or, if they arrive at a word, it may be the wrong choice among several possible word meanings derived from a picture (Samuels, 1970). Or, pictures may convey a silent vowel sound *(Leaf, gate)* whereas these kind of vowels were not presented in original training. If this is the case, the evaluative worksheets should certainly not be considered as review or as "busy" work. Unfortunately, such supplementary materials, being handy and apparent time-savers, sometimes become the primary instructional tools even though they were not prepared in a way that represents a logically sequenced and empirically validated program.

Instructional-Program Criterion-Referenced Tests

In the words of Becker and Engelmann (1976), "When tests are directly geared to an instructional program, it is easier to write test items that are logically valid measures of what is taught, to show that the test items are sensitive to instruction, and to use the tests to carefully monitor the process of instruction" (p. 6). Under these circumstances, it is possible to show pre-to-post gains for the program skills, to show continuity in skill development from grade to grade (assuming use of the same program series), and to analyze and remediate weaknesses for specific children and teachers. Instructional-program based tests, however, are usually inappropriate forcomparing different programs; whereas objective-based tests are appropriate if each program deals with the same objective.

More and more teaching systems now contain a set of criterion-referenced tests that are given at different points in the curriculum. Placement tests describe the general level of the student's present proficiency and predict the optimal point of entry into the program. If there are separate program objectives, pretests can be given to provide details on what the student should learn to satisfy each objective. There are curriculum-embedded tests in the form of very specific questions that are asked daily throughout the process of instruction, as well as in the form of general review questions that are interspersed periodically at longer intervals. These signal whether learning is occurring and provide feedback for possible remediation. Finally, there are end-of-year posttests to check performance of each objective and to compare it with pretest scores.

Almost all curriculum-embedded tests in commercial programs, especially in reading, contain prearranged evaluative formats for teachers to use. These vary in teacher directions from general suggestions that leave the questioning up to the teacher to scripted programmed material that lead the teacher and children along each step of some prescribed learning process. An example of the latter is Science Research Associates' *Reading Mastery III* (Engelmann & Hanner, 1982). It consists of a carefully sequenced questioning strategy, whereby comprehension questions about a reading passage are broken into skill areas (main idea, sequencing cause-and-effect, fact versus opinion, taking one's perspective, interpretation of feelings, information recall, reality versus fantasy, literal comprehension) and, during each reading lesson, specified questions from some or all of these areas are asked. In addition, there are correction procedures classified into four types of task errors: recall of literal information from the present passage; recall of literal information presented in earlier passages; having to infer some perspective (imagining some story detail or imagining themselves in the story); and, having to infer judgments (how something works or why something happened).

Table 12-5
Summary Continuous Progress Test Pattern for Lessons 61–80

	Students					
Skills Tested	A	B	C	D	E	F
1. Symbol Identification (Identifies: 2, =, 4, 6, □, +, 7, 5)	+	+	–	+	–	+
2. Rote Counting by One (up to 23)	+	+	+	–	–	+
3. Rote Counting (from 7 to 11)	+	–	+	+	–	+
4. Lines to Numeral (Given four lines under a box, counts each and writes 4 in the box; repeats by writing 6 for six lines)	+	+	+	+	–	+
5. Numeral to Lines (Given the numerals 2 and 5, makes two and five lines, respectively, under the numeral)	+	+	+	+	–	+
6. Equality—Same Number (Answers questions about whether same number is on both sides of the equal sign)	–	–	–	–	–	–

Adapted from Becker, WC, Carnine, D, and Davis, G. *Continuous progress tests for Distar language, reading and arithmetic.* Eugene, OR: Engelmann-Becker Corp., 1978

An essential evaluation feature of any instructional program is the opportunity to probe the students throughout the academic year on the major skills taught, not just at the end of the year. The Distar program contains supplementary review subtests, known as Continuous Progress Tests (CPTs) for each of the content areas of language, reading and arithmetic (Becker, Carnine, & Davis, 1978). These tests are divided into equal lesson segments and are given every two or four weeks following each 10th or 20th lesson to all students in an instructional group, but particularly are given to the lowest performers. A digest of how six hypothetical students did in the arithmetic skills taught for lessons 61–80 in the Distar I program is provided in Table 12-5.

By looking at the pattern of errors, it is possible to prescribe the kind of remedial steps to take. There are specified remedial tasks (not shown) that correspond to each failed skill that are to be re-taught to those students in need of them (e.g., remedial tasks are needed for students C, D, and B, for skills 1, 2, and 3 respectively). When that is done, the skill-deficient student is given the opportunity to try again (Hively, 1974). Since student E is not being taught effectively, one tactic is to have a supervisor observe a teaching lesson to check the nature of the problem (e.g., the teacher fails to deal with student inattention, does not give enough practice, does not check student accuracy, (etc.). It is possible that skill six was failed by everyone because the program, not the teacher presentation, was at fault. A look at the same CPTs of other children taught by the same teacher and by different teachers using the same program could provide a decisive answer regarding whether program modification or teacher training is necessary.

Between-Program Comparisons

Norm-referenced testing continues to be the major means of evaluating the impact of different instructional programs. There are several comparative studies representative of this approach with special education and learning disability students (Gersten, 1981; Gersten & Maggs, 1982; Lloyd et al., 1980). A problem is that such tests may not provide a valid and meaningful index of the skills taught; and, there is always the possibility that the program that "failed" did so because of a program-test mismatch.

Another approach is to compare programs on common objectives. This is not easy to do because programs may differ in ways other than in common objectives. One important research question is the equivalency of the different programs in relevant student characteristics; and in this case, random assignment of subjects is the best policy, but is not one easily obtainable in educational research. Two other questions are: did the implementation of each program into the classroom faithfully represent what the designer said should be done; and, was the time devoted to teaching comparable among programs (Bloom 1971; Rosenshine & Berliner, 1978)?

When programs have common content but differ on directions and response conventions, it is possible to design tests with program-specific formats (Becker & Engelmann, 1976). If three programs differ on division computation methods (e.g., $8/4 = \Box$; $8 \div 4 = \Box$; and $4/8 = \Box$), then these response forms would be preserved and the students from different programs tested on the same numerical problems. The rule is to search for common elements among programs and to test for them. If two phonic reading programs differ in the specific words taught, the common sounds of both programs could be used to design a test of word reading that contains regular and nonsense words based on these sounds The specific words tested, however, would not belong to either program.

Programs frequently differ not only on the type of material but also the amount taught. When this occurs, each program could be evaluated on the common and uncommon elements as well as how well each element is taught. Suppose Spelling Program A contains 750 words and Program B contains 500 words. If there are 100 common words, a random sample of 40 common words could be given to students from both A and B. Specially derived tests, based on a random sample of the 650 words unique to program A (750 – 100) and of the 400 words unique to program B (500 – 100), could also be given. Should students from both programs spell equally well on the common and uncommon word tests, for example, getting 90 percent correct on each one, program A would be considered superior to B since students from A would be estimated to know 675 words (0.90 × 100 + 0.90 × 650) whereas those from B would know only 450 words (0.90 × 100 + 0.90 × 400). Program A would be even more powerful if the time devoted to teaching was the same as it was for B.

EVALUATING CLASSROOM PERFORMANCE

With the swing toward the back-to-basics movement during the past decade, there has been an increasing emphasis on looking at what classrom practices should be undertaken by teachers to ensure that every student is given sufficient opportunity to learn and practice the "tool" subjects in elementary school. Studies with this aim have been mostly of a correlational nature, in which variations in student classroom performance are recorded on such variables as amount of time on-task and the kind of questions asked, and determination is made of the overlap of these measures with gains in achievement in reading, math, and language (Rosenshine, 1979; Rosenshine & Berliner, 1978). Sometimes, specially designated classrooms and teachers are required to follow a particular educational philosophy; hence, it is possible to evaluate experimentally how this philosophy, when translated into a unique kind of classroom practice, affects achievement outcomes and how it compares with other philosophies (Stallings & Kaskowitz, 1974).

Although the subjects of these studies have commonly included hard-to-teach children in regular classrooms but seldom, if ever, in special educational settings, the methods of instruction that are proving to be effective could have application to teaching basic skills to handicapped students (Stevens & Rosenshine, 1981).

Classroom Time

High on the list of advantages in using time as an index of school performance are its attractive measurement features. As a unit of measurement, time has an absolute zero point for example, one can meaningfully say that Teacher A (or Student B) spends zero minutes daily, teaching (or attending to) math computational problems. Time also possesses ratio scale characteristics, for example, each day, School A allots twice as much time to Spelling as does School B. Temporal measures are easily recorded and can be employed both as dependent variables, by providing information about the range of effectiveness of various teaching practices, and as independent variables, by systematically varying some aspect of classroom time and determining its effect on learning. Furthermore, since individuals differ in time taken to learn a skill, an unambiguous measure of individual differences is made possible by recording the temporal aspects of learning academic behaviors.

Finally, by knowing various temporal parameters, such as time taken to learn, one has a yardstick to calculate cost efficiency. The time needed to bring students up to some acceptable level of performance can be converted, for example, into wages paid to special staff and into the purchase of special equipment and materials; these time and cost figures are known to have a major impact on funding agencies.

Allocated Time

When applied to classroom settings, three measures of time are commonly reported. Allocated time is what the teacher or school system claims to devote to a particular academic domain. It may refer to the length of the school year, the school day, or the amount of time appropriated for instruction in particular content areas. The latter value is made most readily available by examining the teacher's daily lesson plans, which are usually posted or kept on file by the school principal. As such, the reporting of allocated time may simply reflect compliance with an administrative request. The amount of allocated time can sometimes express what a teacher or project director thinks are the important concepts, skills, and/or activities to be promoted in a school setting, for example, a Montesorri teacher might plan for 50 percent of the day in individualized, sensory-motor activities, whereas a Direct Instruction teacher might allocate that time to academically structured, group learning tasks.

Although some studies have found positive correlations of allocated time and achievement test scores (Rieth, Polsgrove & Semmel, 1982), not too much reliance should be placed on an individual teacher's report of allocated time since it can misrepresent what actually goes on in the classroom. Investigators (Engelmann, 1982; Rosenshine, 1979) have reported gross discrepancies between what teachers say they are doing and what, in fact, is done during instruction. By way of a case history (Tawney, 1982a), a parent asked a special educator to record the amount of learning time the school provided to her low IQ child. Despite posted plans of sizeable amount of allocated time, the total amount of actual instructional time for the single day observed was 86 seconds!

Academic Engaged Time

Even when a devoted teacher's best intentions are to spend every minute of planned time in instruction, the important question is how much time the student is involved in instruction. For this reason, academic engaged time has become a central index of classroom observational studies. Simply put, it is on-target performance that is related to the successful completion of academic tasks and, in classroom behavior modification experiments, it is most commonly measured by the percent of time the student or class attends to a teacher, instructional materials, and/or worksheets. Measurement of student attention involves making difficult decisions concerning what should be measured, for example, should reading, listening to the teacher, writing, or keeping track of another student reading count equally as "attentive"? In addition, the procedures used to gather data are frequently crude and varied. Despite these difficulties, the correlations between student attention and academic gain based on 15 studies was about 0.40 when the student was the unit of analysis, and was about 0.52 when the class was the unit of analysis (Rosenshine, 1979). In a large-scale observational study of different first and third grade classrooms for low-performing children who belonged to one of the eight Follow Through models, Stallings and Kaskowitz (1974) recorded every 15 minutes what every child in the class was doing and whether the content area was reading or math. The resulting percentage of time during which the average class was productively engaged in reading and math revealed great inter-model variability. The models with the highest academic engaged time were those emphasizing a small-step programming and reinforcement approach (Direct Instruction and Behavior Analysis). These classrooms spent an average of close to 60 percent of the time in reading, and of about 27 percent of the time in math. The model with the lowest engaged time emphasized a developmental, inquiry-oriented approach. Classrooms adhering to the same philosophy spent an average of 29 percent and 37 percent, respectively, in first and third grade reading and 14 percent and 24 percent, respectively, in math. The rank order correlations between the relative standing of the model in engaged time and its corresponding achievement gain on the MAT was as follows: for first and third grade reading, it was .99 and .80, respectively; for math, it was .17 and .78, respectively.

Variation in engaged time, by itself, is probably not the critical variable. Rather, it is the nature of the instructional program used during the time in which the children are engaged. It is possible to observe two well-managed classrooms, both revealing high levels of on-task performance, that, because the instructional programs are not the same, can end up with vastly different levels of learning and achievement outcomes. School-wise children can learn to ''look attentive'' or ''busy'' when the demands call for those superficial behaviors and yet learn very little about the relevant instructional content. Observers of classroom learning are now beginning to talk about ''academic success time,'' meaning that not only should the students' engaged time be high, but that the student, by virtue of brief questions asked during teaching or shortly thereafter, must evidence some acceptable level of mastery performance on the content taught.

Elapsed Time

The amount of time spent in reaching a level of proficiency in some new task or unit is a common evaluative measure of classroom learning. The time needed to learn may be short, consisting of a few minutes or hours, or much longer, comprising weeks or an entire school year. Bloom (1974) referred to this larger interval as elapsed time and has used it to assess how individuals differ in the learning of relatively large academic units, for example, mastering sequential material such as each chapter of a book or a number of hierarchically arranged objectives from a high school or college course.

Integration of Time Measures

Additional measures of time can be derived by the integration of allocated time, engaged time, and elapsed time. Rosenshine (1982) developed an index called "productive minutes" in which allocated time, expressed in minutes, is multiplied by the percent of engaged time. Teacher A, who allocates 30 minutes to reading and whose students are academically engaged 80 percent of the time, woudl be spending 24 productive minutes. Teacher B, whose class is only half as academically engaged as that of Teacher A, would need to plan a 60-minute reading lesson to be equally as productive (60 minutes × 40 percent = 24 minutes). It is unknown how many productive minutes are currently spent in each content area across different grades, and we probably know less about what is being done with low-performing students in special classes. Indeed, calculating productive minutes spent with students functioning at different levels under different instructional procedures would provide valuable baseline information about the proper allocation and utilization of time for special students.

By having normative data on the expected elapsed time needed by various students to master a learning unit or to complete an entire content area, and contrasting that time with the time currently being allocated to them, one can make reasonable judgments of who will finish the work. In each of the Distar (Level I and II) programs, there are 160 lessons that can be completed in a nine-month school year, allowing room for shool closing, absences, and some instructional inefficiency. Field data has shown that most students can safely finish the program in a year by doing one lesson per day, assuming that they are firm on what was already taught. Lower-performing students, however, will need more time, possibly taking three weeks to accomplish what the majority can do in two weeks. By knowing the rate at which the low performer is currently learning, the teacher (and parent) can project the last lesson number to be completed before the year ends. If promotion or satisfaction of some criterion performance is based upon learning the skills covered up to a certain lesson, teachers can work to accelerate that rate, perhaps by scheduling extra time, doing lessons in tandem with a resource teacher, and/or starting the instructional process earlier, in kindergarten or preschool.

Nature of Content and Mode of Presentation

Classroom investigators exploring the relationship between the nature of content covered and achievement gain of regular students have consistently yielded a simple and seemingly obvious conclusion, which was succinctly summarized by Rosenshine (1978), "what is not taught and attended to in academic areas is not learned" (p. 6). This means tht students who are not taught some concept or operation will not do well on those portions of an achievement or any other test containing that content or procedure. Although this message follows from plain common sense, it is far from rigorously adhered to in regular and special classrooms. How many times have students, who are ostensibly doing reading exercises, been noted to spend a considerable portion of their time in activities clearly unrelated to reading? Based on the Stevens and Rosenshine (1981) review of teacher effectiveness variables, those teachers directing students to spend more time focused on reading and mathematical activities using tests, workbooks, and instructional materials, and less time on nonacademic activities, such as arts and crafts and the asking of open-ended, nonacademic questions about the student's personal feelings, were regarded as the most effective teachers. These teachers put students into contact with curriculum materials and found ways to sustain the academic engaged time in these activities.

Instruction centered on academic involvement does not imply that teachers are to be harsh and impersonal, never allowing affective aspects of the curriculum to enter into their teaching of academic skills. To the contrary, high-achieving classrooms are observed as being convivial, cooperative, and warm, whereas lower-achieving classrooms showed more belittling, shaming, and use of sarcasm (Rosenshine, 1978). Reith, et al. (1981) suggest that if teachers incorporate affective components within the framework of academic tasks, they could increase academic engaged time and achievement gain and also develop affective behaviors. Fisher (in Reith et al., 1981) found that systems in which teachers polarized the school day into separate periods for academic and affective content had a negative impact on academic achievement. In the Follow Through project, those models with a primary academic focus, but having a built-in component of frequent positive feedback during the instructional process, turned out third grade students with higher self-esteem scores than models predicated on the prior and separate development of strong affective behaviors.

The kinds of questions asked during instruction have proven to be significant predictors of test achievement. Two kinds have generally been coded. One calls for a verifiable factual answer, consisting of a single word or a simple phrase, which involves recalling, searching, or reviewing the just-presented instructional material in order to derive the answer (e.g., ''What did the rabbit [in the picture] do after it saw the horse?'' or, ''What word in the story tells that John felt good?''). These questions are classified as low in cognitive content in Bloom's (1956) taxonomy and, since only one answer is appropriate, they are convergent in nature. The other kind of question is divergent and allows for the possibility of more than one answer, which is derivable from sources outside the instructional context. Asked in an open-ended manner, these questions are based on personal experiences, judgments, and opinions, and involve cognitive processes higher in Bloom's taxonomy (e.g., ''If you were the rabbit, what would you do after you saw a horse and why would you do it?'' or, ''If you were John, how do you think you would feel?'').

Correlational and experimental studies have shown that the frequency of asking lower-level questions results in better acquisition of basic reading, arithmetic, and instruction-following skills (Stevens & Rosenshine, 1981). In contrast, the higher-level questions are negatively correlated with these basic achievement measures. The benefits of asking a great number of lower-level cognitive questions is that they permit a high continuous rate of successful answers, keep the student actively engaged in the task, and simplify the process of correction. In addition, successful learning of low cognitive content is often a prerequisite for dealing with more complex forms.

A three-step procedure is usually followed in teaching lower-order concepts (Stevens & Rosenshine, 1981). First, teacher-led demonstration or modeling of concept examples or nonexamples is provided. The second step is a large amount of controlled student practice and review in the identification and discrimination of concept examples as well as in making concept statements. If an error occurs, the answer is supplied, then the concept is sometimes re-demonstrated and the task is re-presented immediately, as well as again at some later point in the lesson. The third step is independent student practice in concept usage. The same basic procedure is used in teaching simple rule statements (e.g., ''If you use it to hold things, it is a container.''), except that during corrections of errors, the answer is withheld and the learner is prompted to apply the rule statement or strategy in answering the question.

The teaching of tasks involving higher order cognitive content, such as complex critical and interpretive thinking, is extremely difficult partly because of the many and varied substeps necessary to achieve the end-product. Many of the steps, moreover, cannot be taught simply through modeling. A more fundamental problem is that open-ended, divergent questions require a broad range of language comprehension and inferential skills that low IQ students do not have or are not being taught in school settings. Carrying out such teaching becomes an imposing feat, especially when the student does not understand the intent of a question, has little world knowledge and a limited vocabulary, gets trapped by irrelevancies, and interprets metaphors literally. Even regular classroom students who were frequently asked higher level questions did not show that this questioning technique had had a measureable effect on their essay performance or on their performance on tests containing these same kinds of higher level questions (Stevens & Rosenshine, 1981).

There is, however, an intermediate ground of skills between those of the learning of simply concepts and those of the learning of very complex reasoning skills, that could and should be taught. These are skills that enable the learner to go moderately beyond the information immediately before him and require more than just literal translations. One such set of skills is involved in reading comprehension. Here, the learner must often make inferences from the passage to understand its meaning. Durkin's (1978-79) data suggest that either teachers are not spending their time teaching comprehension skills or that they are ill-prepared to teach them. Observing 24 fourth-grade reading teachers for an average of 200 minutes each, the proportion of time spent in giving assistance to comprehension difficulties, defined as specific instruction in working out the meaning of more than a single word in a textbook, occurred less than one percent of the time. Techniques for teaching comprehension are just emerging (Carnine & Silbert, 1979) and, hopefully, the systematic training of vocabulary (Becker, 1977) will go hand-in-hand with comprehension training.

Another critical comprehension skill is learning how to derive the main idea of a passage. Students need to learn that the main idea is not necessarily contained in the first sentence and, in fact, not even in any single sentence. Sometimes, the main idea is to be inferred from reading the entire passage and, when that is the case, strategies for learning how to do this must be explicitly taught. Engelmann (1982) analyzed how five different basal reading programs advised teachers to teach the main idea of a passage. Based on the sets of examples presented by the different programs, the correct interpretation of the main idea could be expected only 27 percent of the time. Texts were found to overprompt the main idea in the students' workbooks 49 percent of the time, to allow an average of 62 days to intervene before two or more examples of a main idea format were presented, to schedule a long time interval between the teaching of main ideas and when they next appeared in the students' workbooks, and to provide absolutely no specific correction procedures for main idea errors.

Engelmann (1982) further videotaped how 17 experienced teachers, familiar with their particular reading series, taught the main idea to a class of regular students. Despite the possibility that teachers will recognize program deficiencies in the text and will hasten to modify and improve upon the program, not one teacher deviated in any way from the specifications for the primary part of the lessons. One of the major problems the teachers had was in the area of corrections. When errors were made, only 37 percent were corrected; when appropriate corrections were provided, the students were retested on only ten percent of the items to see if the information contained in the correction was adequately communicated. After they had been taught, the students were tested on how well they understood the lesson. The results were frightening: no more than one-third of the students correctly identified more than 75 percent of the topics the teachers had just taught, and only one-half of the students got 50 percent of the material correct. If these are the performance standards expected of a regular student in learning as critical a skill as appreciating the main idea of a passagge, one can easily imagine the dismal results of mildly handicapped students, not to mention the hard-to-teach learner.

Mastery Performance

A key component of the task analysis movement (Block, 1971; Haring & Schiefelbusch, 1976) is that the learning of a complex skill rests upon the learning of a sequence of less-complex component skills. Theoretically, by breaking a complex behavior down into a chain of component behaviors and by ensuring student mastery of each link in the chain, it should be possible to teach even the most complex skills. Mastery learning procedures are most effective for school subjects consisting of a number of well-defined units the learning of which is cumulative in that the learning of any one unit builds upon the learning of all prior units. If at each stage in the sequence the student learns the material that is the prerequisite for the next unit, then his learning throughout the sequences is likely to be adequate.

Bloom and his co-workers (Block, 1971) found some very interesting relationships between learning or elapsed time and individual differences. Although not all individuals learn a new unit at the same rate, given enough time and help, 90 percent or more will finally attain mastery performance. The difference in learning rate, moreover, between the fastest and slowest learners is likely to be greatest on the first unit of a series of related tasks. Here, it takes the slowest five percent of the learners approximately five times as much time to learn as the fastest five percent. Continuing to give extra time and help, however, to those who need it over the remaining learning units, the five to one ratio eventually reaches a value of three to one. As Bloom (1974) notes, "student variation in elapsed time keeps decreasing over successive units" (p. 685).

When a more precise measure of academic learning is used, namely that of academic engaged time, variation between the highest and lowest learners in time-on-task for the early learning tasks is approximately three to one. If the students receive training under favorable mastery learning conditions, the ratio for on-task time for units toward the end of a curriculum is reduced to 1.5 to 1.0. These findings do not hold unless mastery learning conditions are maintained throughout the course of learning. In another study (Bloom, 1974), two groups of students each had an initial time-on-task baseline of 65 percent. A group trained continuously under mastery learning conditions, who did not move to the next unit until they were firm on the previous unit, steadily increased in time-on-task over several tasks to 85 percent. The engaged time of the other group, trained under conventional nonmastery conditions, fell to 50 percent.

Under nonmastery conditions of learning, pretest measures involving intelligence or aptitude tests can safely predict posttest measures of achievement in some academic skills. The correlations vary from .55 to .70 and are greatly influenced by the relatively high common verbal component found in the pre-and posttests. If mastery conditions are imposed, however, affording each student to receive the extra time and help to achieve mastery levels at each step along the way, especially in verbal skills, the correlations between pretest verbal indices and posttest academic performance should approach zero. In the case of a moderately loaded verbal task, as in constructing block patterns to match pictorial representations, the correlation between the pretest IQ measures of moderately and severely mentally retarded individuals and their pretest block scores is approximately .50, which is significant (Budoff & Hamilton, 1974). If mastery training is provided for the matching task, however, the correlation between initial IQ scores and amount of gain is small and nonsignificant ($r = .12$).

These findings suggest that not much headway is to be expected in advancing academic skills that are verbally weighted unless a systematic and sustained approach in teaching the necessary verbal components is undertaken (Becker, 1977). There are many academic skills, nevertheless, requiring less verbal competency that can be taught without spending time to develop strong verbal behaviors. Teaching math computations, time-telling, and handwriting are three such examples. What frequently happens, however, is that these skills are evaluated by unfair verbal standards. For example, having been successfully taught how to calculate time, a learner is asked time-related questions, such as, "Is it dark at midnight?" or, "Who gets up earliest in your house?" Similar unfavorable evaluative circumstances are obtained when verbal constraints are placed on math computation problems. Able to do basic computations, the learner should not be expected to do math story problems, unless the key operative words (e.g., buy, sell, lost, found, etc.) are part of the instructional regime. Naive learners can begin to write manuscript letters if verbally simple instructions are used (Weisberg, 1982). If terms such as baseline, midline, three-quarter line, slanted, or reversal, however, become part-and-parcel of the instructional format, the handwriting progress of low-performing individuals without such knowledge will be dead-ended.

It is practically and logically impossible to train all classroom skills to mastery. The teacher must be sensitive in choosing a certain set of skills to teach, and hopefully selects those that will be most relevant for future academic success. Counting by fives to 60, for example, is a relevant skill for counting nickels and, as such, mastery performance is most critical. To take valuable classroom time, however, to achieve high levels of proficiency in learning to memorize all of the inscriptions on the coin (e.g., *E Pluribus Unum*, Monticello, etc.) is instructionally wasteful.

Given these qualifications, the following are general recommendations for enhancing student academic time and overall classroom efficiency.

1. Reduce the number of time-consuming activities that interfere with academic engaged time. These usually include transitional activities, such as lining up, moving to different sections of the room or to different places inside and outside of the school building.
2. Children with behavior problems should be separated from the rest of the class and, along with low performers, should be seated near the teacher.
3. If possible, group students ccording to the level of skill difficulty and use unison responding procedures to increase the amount of active participation by each child and to give needed practice in oral language skills.
4. Give priority to teaching the most critical skills, and whenever possible, teach general case strategies.

5. Coordinate efforts with the resource teacher so that rather than introducing new skills, added practice is provided for skills already being taught.
6. Have an experienced person objectively observe the organizational structure of the classroom and determine how well the teacher engages the children academically.
7. Provide academically relevant seatwork when children are not engaged in small group instruction, especially during administrative home-room time, and when assigned work has been completed.
8. Monitor seatwork performance by moving among the students and giving brief feedback of no more than 30 seconds per child.
9. Praise hard work when it occurs, but not to the extent that it interferes with the ongong academic performance of the praised student and others as well.
10. Get parents and responsible volunteers to assist not only in the management of the children but also to help in such academic endeavors as listening to the students read, evaluating spelling performance, or firming-up counting activities.
11. Define desireable academic performances, provide specific feedback when they occur and, whenever possible, make the products of these achievements public. Examples of chartable performances are: number of errors made on some task, speed of task performance, amount of time on-task, last lesson completed, and any measure specific to the desired objective. Seatwork exercises meeting some acceptable criterion could also be posted.
12. In multi-step tasks, such as long division, provide oral speed drills throughout the day on those steps that slow down overall performance. Instructionally "dead" times, such as transitional activities, should be used for these drills.

BASIC CONCEPTS AND OPERATIONS

To understand task evaluation, some consideration of the structure of teaching concepts and operations is in order. A concept consists of a class of stimulus examples that share one or more common qualities or features (Becker, Engelmann, & Thomas, 1975). For example, the concept "triangle" refers to those examples of two-dimensional object forms that have three joined sides; the concept "adjective" consists of words that modify nouns. A major goal in teaching is to communicate to the learner in the most consistent and efficient manner the common stimulus quality (or qualities) that defines the concept. In the case of a naive learner, the essential quality cannot be conveyed through elaborate verbal descriptions in the form of rules or definitions. Instead, the communication must be done through concrete presentations of examples of the concept (positive examples) and of non-examples of the concept (negative examples). Concepts conveyed through direct, concrete experiences are called basic concepts. As elaborated by Engelmann and Carnine (1982):

We cannot explain *red* to a blind person in a way that would permit the person to discriminate between red and not-red objects. Similarly, concepts such as *smooth, heavy, over, toward, happy,* etc. require concrete examples unless the learner already knows the concept by a different label *(unrough, unlight, above, closer, glad).* Examples are needed to teach these concepts because the words that we use are not containers of the concept. They are merely symbols that stand for particular qualities. Unless the communication presents the learner with the actual experience of the quality being symbolized, the communication provides no basis for understandig which quality or property the symbol represents. (p. 10)

There are three types of basic concepts: non-comparatives, comparatives, and nouns. Table 12-6 summarizes the distinctions among them.

Non-Comparative Concepts

Positive and negative examples of non-comparative concepts, which include prepositions, most adjectives, adverbs, and action verbs, are distinguished from each other on the basis of a single stimulus dimension. Something that is *under* (in the spatial sense) is differentiated from things that are *in, above,* and *on,* only by the relative location of that object in space; something that is *long* is differentiated by its size; something that is *turning,* by its movement in a particular direction. The defining properties of *under* are judged in an absolute sense because they are independent of a preceding example, or are defined in relation to the example with which it is currently being compared. And, we can be fairly certain whether a non-comparative is a positive or negative example. Either it is *under* or it is *not-under;* there are no in between values.

Comparative Concepts

Like non-comparatives, comparative concepts similarly involve making changes in a single stimulus dimensions in order to create positive and negative examples. That is, comparative concepts, such as *heavier than, sweeter, moving slower,* and *getting steeper,* involve making sensory discriminations along single dimensions that vary quantitatively in the examples in weight, sugar concentration, movement, and orientation, respectively. Unlike non-comparatives, judgments about whether the comparative example is a positive or a negative instance cannot be made in isolation; all comparative concept judgments entail relative comparisons. A six-inch–wide space becomes a positive example of "wider" if the previous space was five inches wide; however, that same six-inch–wide space would be a negative instance of "wider" if the previous space were eight inches wide. (The relative nature of comparatives holds whether the comparisons are based on successive or on simultaneous presentations). Another consideration is that positive examples of comparatives can be distinguished from negative ones fairly easily, even if the stimulus differences are small. We would have no trouble reporting whether the space between our hands increased or decreased in distance. The psychophysical literature (Kling & Riggs, 1971) attests to man's ability to make very good comparative-based judgments in the middle range of a stimulus continuum for all sense modalities.

Table 12-6
Parameters of Basic Concepts

Type of Basic Concept	Common Examples	Number of Relevant Differences Between Positive and Negative Examples	Concept Properties are:	Classification of Positive and Negative Examples is:
Non-comparatives	on, big, red, running, gradually	one	absolute	fairly precise
Comparatives	bigger, fatter than, louder, more slanted	one	relative	very precise
Nouns	quarter, weapons, shoe, M	many	absolute	sometimes imprecise

Adapted from Engelmann, S & Carnine, D. *Theory of instruction: Principles and applications.* New York: Irvington Publishers, Inc., 1982

Noun Concepts

Finally, with noun concepts, there is not one but many reliable dimensions that enable us to differentiate positive from negative examples. The concept *dogs* is distinguishable from *cats* in any number of ways, as is *cars* from other vehicles. Some noun concepts, such as numerals and alphabet letters, have fewer relevant dimensions upon which to form a discrimination between positives and negatives. As with non-comparatives, noun concepts have fixed or absolute properties. The boundary line, however, between positives and negatives of some common nouns is very thin, making it difficult to obtain a consensus of judgments about what to call certain objects. Show various examples of footwear (sandals, moccasins, tennis shoes, cowboy boots, flats, ice skates, high heels) to a group of individuals and many will disagree whether all are in the same class of *shoes* or *not-shoes*. This same group will have no trouble organizing and labeling examples of non-comparatives (*on* versus *not-on*) or comparatives *(brighter than* versus *not-brighter than).*

Concepts and Operations

Whereas concepts refers to what is common to a set of stimulus instances, operations refers to what is common to a set of response instances (Becker et al., 1975). Operation, like operants, are responses under stimulus control. Touching things, adding two numbers in a column, tying shoelaces, drawing a picture of a tree, and sounding out words all involve operations. Concepts and operations are contrasted in Table 12-7.

Table 12-7
Stimulus and Response Properties of Concepts and Operations

Type of Instructional Element	Illustration	Stimulus Properties	Response Properties
Concept	the color "red" red truck red ball red flower	A class of stimulus examples that have some essential feature(s) in common (their color), and vary in other ways (size, shape, location, texture, etc.)	All examples are somewhat responded to in the same way (learner says "red" to all examples)
Operation	"pushing" pushing a ball pushing a can pushing a person	The same instructional stimulus is present in all examples (teacher says "push it" to all examples)	A class of response examples that have some essential or functional effect in common (pushed object moves in opposite direction of force), and vary in other ways (direction, force, arm used, object pushed, etc.)

Adapted from Becker, WC, Engelmann, S, & Thomas, DR. *Teaching 2: Cognitive learning and instruction. Chicago: Science Research Associates, 1975*

Test items involve evaluation of both concepts and operations; the concept usually being the stimulus features or the stimulus examples of the task, and the operation being the response(s) required to demonstrate knowledge of the concept.

GUIDELINES FOR CONSTRUCTING EVALUATIVE TASKS

The principles described below were gleaned from several sources dealing with instructional design: Becker et al. (1975); Becker and Engelmann (1976); Carnine and Silbert (1979); Englemann and Carnine (1982); Engelmann (1980); and Weisberg et al. (1981). The guidelines contain principles that are not completely independent of each other; rather, each one is meant to stress different aspects of the overall evaluation picture.

Test Only Previously Taught Concepts and Operations

Concept examples presented in test items must be familiar to the learner. An evaluative task requiring one to identify which of various objects are *on, under, in, over,* and *next to* a car must utilize objects previously encountered in instruction. By testing with different and possibly unfamiliar objects, it is difficult to disentangle whether student failure is due to poor object identification or to a poor understanding of key prepositional terms.

Another illustration of the violation of an evaluation task is to test reading comrehension by presenting a passage that includes previously taught vocabulary words, but involves an ancilliary set of pictorial scenes, some of which contain unfamiliar content, stress difficult language concepts, and are open to several interpretations. A great injustice is done if reading comprehension is judged, not so much by questions based on the words and syntax read, but mainly upon the ability to describe and analyze the untaught picture content.

A confounding in the analysis of errors is also produced when new or unusual response conventions (or operations) are introduced into the evaluation context. Although this practice is commonplace in norm-referenced test formats, it is to be avoided when one wishes to know when students have benefited from instruction, which is the primary reason for criterion-referenced testing. As part of the task, the wording of the instructions or directions must also be controlled. A student taught what is meant by the directions, "Read these words to yourself," by watching a teacher demonstrate scanning printed material and "reading" in an inaudible manner punctuated by occasions of audible reading and commenting, "I am not reading to myself," will probably be baffled by the directions of an unknowing evaluator that request the student to "read in your mind's eye," or "read silently."

SAD

SAM

MOM

Fig. 12-1. Ambiguous instructions: "Circle the word that tells about the picture." [Adapted from Carnine, D, & Silbert, J. *Direct instruction reading.* Columbus, Ohio: Charles E. Merrill, 1979]

Some variation of task details, however, may be desirable to test for transfer or generalization. The details are varied, but they are still controlled. As discussed earlier, transfer tasks are acceptable only when a general case strategy has been taught. An untaught word would not be presented unless a general word-attack strategy applicable to that word had been taught. In short, the student must have the skills which would lead the tester to expect transfer.

Tasks Should Be Consistent With Only One Interpretation

Once the target concept is taught, test for that concept, making sure no other competing interpretations are possible. The instruction, to find the "smallest" coin, accompanied by the choices of a quarter, a dime, a nickel, and a penny, is likely to be ambiguous. Is the penny correct due to its smaller monetary value or the dime due to its smaller size? The direction, "Count from one to five," might produce the strange answer pattern, "one, to, five," because of the misinterpretation of the homonyms, *to* and *two*. A better direction might be, "count from one and end up with five." The demonstration in Figure 12-1, from Carnine and Silbert (1979), illustrates that any one of the three choices could reasonably be selected as the answer.

We have no way of knowing the misrule responsible for an error and, worse yet, how to correct for it. By changing to the less ambiguous instructions, "How does the boy feel?" and knowing beforehand that a face like this has been called *sad,* we can more readily pinpoint the source of an error.

Finally, the learner might produce the appropriate response because a spurious prompt was given. If the learner is to name an object outlined in the form of a fish, the outline is a spurious prompt. Testing for knowledge about an object's size by asking, "Touch the big, green one," a learner could easily identify it by attending to the color prompt. Similarly, when stuck on reading the word, *rabbit,* the learner is spuriously prompted if told to think about the animal with long ears that hops. Or, to help read *feet,* legs and feet are drawn underneath the *ee;* or an *e* in the word *eye* is converted into an eyeball. Sometimes an unintentional prompt is given by acting with certain facial expressions and voice inflections to yes or no questions. In questioning handicapped children for difficult word discriminations, Engelmann and Rosov (1972) had the examiners stand behind the subjects, presumably to remove mouthing and related cues.

Determine Concept Difficulty and Test for the Highest Difficulty Level

All things being equal, concept difficulty is determined by the number of different concepts included in the task and how many of them are familiar to the learner. The number of concepts is found simply by counting how many different ones there are. The multiple-concept task, "Circle the red trucks over the table," contains four concepts: red, trucks, over, table. As such, it should be harder than the single-concept task, "Circle the trucks." Given two or more multiple-concept tasks, each having an equal number of concepts, the easiest one of the set should be that containing the highest proportion of trained or already familiar concepts. In the case of two tasks, equal in concept number and concept familiarity, it remains for future research to determine what variables would cause the greatest hardship. For example, it is unknown which of the three-concept tasks is harder: "Touch the *boy* with the *biggest cats,"* or "Touch the *boy* that is *big* and *wet."* Until there is firm data on the teachability or the relative difficulty level of various concept attributes (e.g., size, number, color, relative location, pluralization, conjunctions, etc.), it is probably best to treat difficulty as a function of the number of concepts and the amount of previous training (see Palmer, 1971,* for a beginning in this direction).

Following the instruction and evaluation of separate concepts, it is important to teach and test for concept integration. This can be done by teaching a multiple-concept rule and having the learner apply it in various contexts. If the rule is, "The *wet bird* will *fly,"* three birds could be shown, only one of which looks wet, with the learner being asked logically structured yes-no questions about each bird: "Is this bird wet? So, will it fly?" These predictions should immediately be confirmed after the questioning process. If a worksheet shows wet and dry children, the learners can be directed: "Color the wet children orange." As newer concepts are introduced and mastered, succeeding concept application tasks

---

*Palmer, FH. *Concept training curriculum: For children ages two to five* (Vols. 1–5). Unpublished manuscript, State University of New York at Stony Brook, 1971

should be structured to include them to reflect the growing complexity in task evaluation: "The *fat bird* that is *wet* and *next to* the *log* will *eat* the *worm.*"

A particularly useful multiple-concept task is one that requires an implied conclusion. In this task, the learner must utilize information about two concepts: the target concept and another already familiar concept. The target concept is indirectly evaluated by requiring the learner to apply information about the other concept. If the target concept is *bigger* and *not-bigger,* one could evaluate this discrimination by asking: "What color is the *bigger* object?"; "Name the object that is *not-bigger"*; "What is the *bigger* child doing?"; "Where is the *bigger* ball?"; and, "Touch the container that is *not-bigger.*" It is important that in each case the incorrect choices consist of one or more negative instances for both the target and the other concept. That is, for the first task listed above, the incorrect object must consist not only of a smaller object but one that is also of a different color.

Implied conclusion tasks afford considerable economy in testing situations because knowledge of two concepts can be probed with a single question. These, along with concept application tasks, are the kind commonly found in evaluation instruments because they feature the integration of several concepts (Moss, 1970).

Use Familiar Response Conventions and Evaluate at the Most Difficult Level

Table 12-8 shows a useful taxonomy of response requirements for evaluating basic concepts.

There are two broad types of response requirements: choice responses, which include yes-no questions, choice-of-examples, and choice-of-labels; and production responses, which include production-of-label and production-of-example (Engelmann & Carnine, 1982). In choice response formats, the key concept is prompted by being specifically mentioned or embedded in the task frame. This means the learner can emit the correct answer by attending closely to the content of the question. Often, incorrect alternatives or distractors are included as part of the task frame. In production response tasks, the correct concept is not specifically mentioned in the frame; rather, it is up to the learner to produce or construct the label or example.

Choice response tasks are generally earier than production tasks because they only require recognition of the correct answer. Production tasks, however, more closely resemble real-life demands and, as such, are preferable in assessment whenever possible. As McCoy and Buckhalt (1981) point out, since verbally expressed and written behaviors permit greater opportunity to control the academic and social environment, these behaviors should receive greater priority in instructional settings. It is also the case that the cognitive sophistication of individuals is commonly judged by the adequacy of oral and written expression. Although the appropriate production of verbal statements is the ultimate goal of instruction,

Table 12-8
Type of Questions for Basic Concepts

	Response Requirements (ordered from low to high difficulty)			
Yes/No	Choice of Example	Choice of Label	Production of Label	Production of Example
		Non-Comparative ("on")		
Is the ball *on*?	Cross out the balls that are *on* the line	The ball is: o on o over o under o above	Where is the ball?	Make a ball *on* the line
		Comparative ("bigger than") Circle the correct answer		
Is A *bigger than* B?	Make an X on the one that is *bigger*	o bigger o not bigger	Boy A is _____ than Boy B	Make a square that is *bigger than* this one

384

Nouns ("quarter")

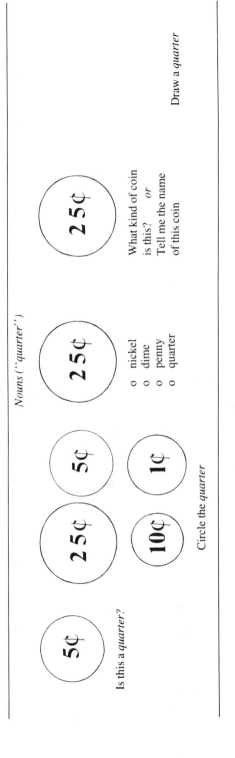

5¢

Is this a *quarter?*

25¢   5¢

10¢   1¢

Circle the *quarter*

25¢

o nickel
o dime
o penny
o quarter

25¢

What kind of coin
is this?   *or*
Tell me the name
of this coin

Draw a *quarter*

evaluation of learning must always be done using the learner's existing predominant response conventions in order to properly interpret the source of errors. For example, if during the evaluation of prepositions the understanding of where-questions is clearly weak, its usage should be postponed, and teaching the concept, "where," should become an instructional goal. Evaluation of prepositions, meanwhile, could shift to yes-no questions or to simple manipulative requests.

Bereiter and Engelmann (1966) point out that instructionally naive learners, after a few minutes of verbal exercises, may show honest signs of fatigue, and with it comes an increasing number of errors. When this occurs, the teacher should employ a less demanding task and should remember to reinstate the verbal presentations very soon afterwards. Once the learner becomes more facile in verbal tasks, instruction should increasingly shift toward more elaborate verbal presentations. At this point, returning to simpler response forms, like pointing or head nodding, is instructionally wasteful and, if the opportunity to engage in easier verbal routines becomes a viable consequence to escape from verbally more demanding ones, unintended contingencies can develop in the learning situation (Sailor, Guess, Rutherford, & Baer, 1968). The occurrence of these same problems in the evaluation situation is a distinct possibility and is one to be watched carefully. For example, the evaluator will need to know how to spot legitimate forms of fatigue, when to schedule breaks, how to maintain prolonged independent work, and so forth.

Choice responses. Considering choice response tasks (Table 12-8), yes-no questions and choice-of-example tasks are useful for the evaluation of basic concepts at the initial stages of istruction. In yes-no questions, there is the opportunity to dichotomize concept instances, which are presented one at a time, into positive and negative examples. Verification of the correctness of yes-no answers is an absolute necessity. Blank and Solomon (1969) provide one among many incidents of nonverification in their report of how teachers can inappropriately appraise academic behavior. Upon entering the classroom, a student is asked if he saw a flower on the way. After an affirmative gesture, he is then probed, "Oh, was it yellow? Was it a dandelion?" From those nonsubstantiated answers it will remain unclear whether the target concepts, "flower," "yellow," and "dandelion," are understood.

The choice-of-example task consists of presenting positive and negative examples of the concept and presenting a single concept label. This task, if patterned after the manner in which the concept was taught, will yield information about how well the learner has attended to the stimulus features of the positive and negative examples. Choice-of-example tasks are well-designed for the non-reader with the evaluator able to present the instructions verbally.

In the the choice-of-label task, a single stimulus example, usually a positive one, is presented; and, there are several different labels serving as choices. This format is structurally the reverse of the choice-of-example task. Its purpose is to evaluate how firm the learner is with respect to the use of different labels. It is most appropriate for learners who can read and it is the kind of task found in the reading vocabulary and math concept sections of achievement tests.

As always, all of the choice labels should be familiar to the learner, but which labels are selected depends upon the purpose of the task. For instance, if the objective is to measure whether one knows that one of the attributes distinguishing a tree from other plants is its trunk-like quality, then given a picture of a tree, the choice labels, *bush, tree, flower,* and *vine,* are more appropriate than *girl, tree, box* and *nine.* If the purpose, however, is to test the decoding of words, the choices, *truck, tree, spree,* and *tee,* would suffice.

Choice-of-example and choice-of-label items can be altered to conform to the matching-to-sample tasks frequently used in discrimination research (Sidman et al., 1974). The sample may be presented in any of three modes: pictures or concrete objects; symbolic (letters, numerals, words, etc.); and, dictated verbal instructions. The choices can consist of examples or labels. To test for the concept "red" using the choice-of-example format, the following choices can be used: a red square, a blue triangle, and a green circle. The sample may be in the form of a picture of a red circle, the word "red," or the instructions, "Find the one that is red." With choice-of-label matching tasks, all of the choices would be words and the samples can be, as just described, visual, symbolic, or dictated expressions of the choices. It should be noted that when the sample and choice are not in the same sense modality, the matching task is referred to as cross-modality matching.

Production responses. Concerning production response tasks, the most common form is the production of a label. In this task, a learner may be asked to verbally identify a particular object (i.e., "What is this?"), the class to which it belongs (i.e., "What class is an apple in?), or some fact (i.e., "What do you call a person who puts out fires?"). The form of the response may be verbal or written.

Production-of-example tasks require the learner to create an example to fit a label or fact. These could include: "Draw a cat"; "Draw a glass that is full"; and "Make a box on the left end of the line." Production-of-example tasks are useful for the evaluation of instruction-following behaviors, particularly when the task involves "low probability" items; that is, the answers are not readily apparent unless the learner attends very carefully to the directions.

When the task concept contains many attributes, as is the case for many nouns, requesting the learner to produce or construct all of them is likely to pose difficulties. For this reason, the task, "draw a quarter" (Table 12-8), which requires the organization and combination of many attributes, is extremely complex and a possibly unfair item, unless the learner has been given extensive practice in attending to and constructing the relevant attributes. On the other hand, testing for the non-comparative, "make a ball on the line," calls for the discrimination of a single attribute and we are likely to accept crude constructions as long as they touch the line.

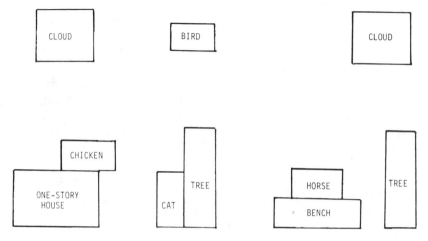

Fig. 12-2. Verbal description of a scene for a multiple question format. In the actual picture, the chicken is standing on the roof of the house, the cat is climbing up the tree, and the horse is standing on top of the bench. [Adapted from Engelmann, S, & Carnine, D. *Theory of Instruction: Principles and applications.* New York: Irvington Press, Inc., 1982]

Complex Tasks

Matching labels and examples is a complex form of choice response task. In this task, a number of labels and examples are presented, requiring the learner to indicate the correct association of respective label-example pairs. An important consideration for using matching tasks is that sophisticated learners may use an elimination strategy as a means of increasing their chance of making correct responses. One way to discourage elimination strategies is to present an unequal number of labels and examples.

There are two types of complex production response tasks that are frequently used: multiple questions about a single example, and multiple questions about multiple examples. For the first kind, a blue truck could serve as the single example and the learner would be queried by this battery: "What color is this object? Touch a part of the object that is round. Is this object a vehicle? What kind of vehicle is it? What would you use this truck for?"

For a multiple examples-multiple questions task, the "scene" in Figure 12-2 could be presented and the learner asked: "What kind of animal is over the tree? What animal is climbing something? What is it climbing? Where is the chicken? What is between the two clouds? What is the horse on? What animal is between two trees? What is the horse doing? Name the animals the cat is between."

As long as the students are well-practiced on the concepts and on the different response conventions employed, asking a range of questions centered on a single or many examples can provoke and challenge the students to show how smart they are in dealing with diverse information. Done incorrectly, without enough training in concept mastery and in handling the assorted question forms, this tactic could lead to disastrous results and greatly baffle the students. New teachers, hoping to "draw out" as much information as possible from instructionally naive students by using a scatter-gun questioning procedure, should seriously consider postponing its use until their students are firm on both the content and the means by which they are evaluated.

Present at Least One Task for Each Concept or Operation Taught

As stated earlier, to tie assessment as closely as possible to teaching, ideally there should be a one-to-one correspondence between the concepts and the operations taught to those tested. An important point is that each concept taught should be sampled in direct proportion to the amount of instruction provided. A quick index of the number of tasks needed for adequate evaluation may be obtained by listing all the concepts and operations introduced since the last test. At least one item should then be constructed for each member of the list.

It is important to note that not every exemplar used in instruction need appear on the tests. For example, if "carrying to the tens place" is to be tested, it would be unreasonable and unwieldly to include all possible problems requiring carrying to the tens place, and unnecessary to include all the sample problems introduced during instruction. Rather, only a well-selected sample of items is necessary. Novick and Lewis (1974) have outlined procedures for determining the appropriate selection of items for criterion-referenced tests as well as for making decisions about the length of a test.

Intersperse Recently Taught Information With Old Information

About 25 to 30 percent of the tasks comprising a test should be review items (Weisberg & Sims, 1982). Mixing in "old" tasks will lessen the overall difficulty of the test as well as maintain high levels of performance on previously taught material. While teaching sound-symbol correspondences to preschoolers, Kryzanowski and Carnine (1978) found that an interspersed presentation pattern, although prone to producing more errors during training, resulted in significantly better posttest performance (72 percent versus 38 percent correct). Similarly, Neef, Iwata, and Page (1977) reported that both the acquisition and the retention of the spelling and sightreading of words by six mentally retarded adolescents were facilitated by an interspersal procedure. These authors attributed the effectiveness of the procedure (in how it created improved attending behavior from the students regarding the new material) to be the result of the high rates of reinforcement acquired by the correct spelling of the familiar material. Fink and Brice-Gray

(1979) found that a cumulative review procedure, in which each new functional word (e.g., exit, danger, poison, etc.) was reviewed in a context of all previously taught words, produced better acquisition and recall performance in handicapped children than a review procedure consisting of word pairs.

Give Preference to Recently Taught and/or Highly Similar Material

Recent and thus less-practiced items need to be tested whenever possible to prevent forgetting, and to keep the learner always firm on the old material in case new and similar material is to be taught in the near future. In this way, the learner will need to master only one piece of information, the new material, since the old material will already be intact.

What constitutes recent material? Generally, "recent" refers to any concepts or operations introduced since the last test. In addition, Becker and Engelmann (1976) suggest that, as a rule of thumb, skills should not be tested until they have been taught for three days.

Inclusion of highly similar items is important for detecting possible confusion errors. For example, in the Distar Reading I: Continuous Progress Tests (Becker et al., 1978) given during lessons 51–61, five letter-sounds are tested. Three are sounds taught within the last ten days (t, n, and c). Two are sounds taught earlier, but are similar to the first two recent sounds (th and m). Thus, the most critical discriminations are evaluated. If these discriminations have been mastered, chances are that other, easier discriminations have also been mastered.

Do Not Test Trivial or "Dead End" Skills

A trivial skill is one that is taught, but is not integrated with other skills or is not used later in the instructional program. Becker and Engelmann (1976) note that in one reading program, children are asked to indicate whether a particular letter-sound appears at the beginning, middle, or end of the word. This skill is subsequently dropped from the instructional program, and, as such, is a trivial skill.

Trivial skills generally bear no relationship to the final target skill. Describing the position of a sound in a word has little to do with reading the words. The student may be perfect on locating the sound's position but may still be unable to read. Each skill introduced into an instructional program should be logically evaluated as to whether it is a critical subskill for later learning, and assessment should reflect the logical selection of material.

Textbooks and curricular material would be of great benefit to the teacher if they stressed what skills should receive top priority and which are of lesser importance. The relationship of the "critical" preskill to other performance, moreover, should be made clear. Too often, teachers are handed a laundry list of skills to teach, many of which are recycled out of tradition and have little functional value for the low performer.

Analyze Tasks in Multi-Step Operations and Test for the Component Skills

When a learner commits one or more errors on a task containing many component skills, the source of the mistake must be immediately traced. Given a passage to read, a student could fail to arrive at the meaning for several reasons, some of which could be: the words could not be decoded; statement repetition or memory of what was read was insufficient; the words were not understood; the sequence of important concepts was lost; or pausing at critical places in a sentence was neglected.

To determine to what extent such basic skills in language and reading have been taught, Engelmann and Hanner (1976) developed the *Survival Skills Reading Test*. The skills tested represent minimum common standards to be mastered by all students, no matter what the instructional program. The test is broken down by grade, starting at kindergarten. For grades 2 to 12, there is a Screening Test that, for the early grades, measures following instructions and the decoding of often-missed words (e.g., *the, then, left, felt, where, were*, etc.). In the later grades, screening is done for reading rate, accuracy, and comprehension. Diagnostic Tests are available for those failing the Screening Test and, at each grade, there are different prescriptions offered depending upon the nature of the deficient skill. For those passing the Screening Test, there is an Elaborated Test that examines advanced skills, such as deduction, induction, reading for information, sequencing of ideas, and following difficult instructions. The reader interested in other diagnostic reading tests should consult Anastasi (1976), Carnine and Silbert (1979), or Salvia and Ysseldyke (1981).

Frequently, the nature of the student's answers can provide a clue as to what was done wrong. Multiple-choice formats readily allow this opportunity, and this is most apparent in math computational problems. For example, to diagnose whether addition or subtraction operations have been adequately taught, problems of the form illustrated below could be given. The proviso is that the larger number always appears in the top part of the problem and that the problems do not entail borrowing or carrying skills. The answers summarize the type of suspected incorrect operations.

$$
\begin{array}{r}
55 \\
+41 \\
\hline
\end{array}
$$

o   14   (both columns subtracted)
o   16   (added numbers in ones column; subtracted in tens column)
o   94   (subtracted numbers in ones column; added in tens column)
o   96   (correct answer; both columns added)

Similarly, to detect whether the advanced student who was taught four basic arithmetic operations is attending to the appropriate sign, problems of one type, for example, 6 ÷ 3, would have these alternative answers: 2, 3, 9, and 18; whereas, those of another type, for example, 9 − 3, would have as alternatives 3, 6, 12, 27, and so on.

If the accuracy of a particular operation is in doubt, that could be evaluated by including several answers close in value to the correct one, for example, for 8 + 5, possible alternatives are 12, 13, 14, and 15; for 9 × 4: 27, 36, 37, and 45. It goes without saying that unless there are specific remedial procedures dealing with each component skill, diagnosing for the sake of exposing the faults of the learner is of little value and serves to give parents and others false hopes that something will be done.

Acknowledgments

Support was furnished in part by the University of Alabama Office of Contracts and Grants, under the direction of Dr. Robert L. Wells. The authors are grateful to Roberta Weisberg of the Tuscaloosa City Board of Education for reading an earlier draft and to Connie Sulentic for the careful preparation and typing of this chapter.

REFERENCES

Abt Associates. *Education as exerimentation: A planned variation mmodel* (Vol. 4). Cambridge, MA: Abt Associates, 1977

Anastasi, A. *Psychological testing*. New York: MacMillan, 1976

Baldie, B. *Baldie language ability test*. North Ryde, Australia: Macquarie University, 1978

Barnard, DP, & DeGGracie, V. Vocabulary analysis of new primary reading tests. *The Reading Teacher*, 1976, *30*, 177–180

Becker, WC. Teaching reading and language to the disadvantaged: What we have learned from field research. *Harvard Education Review*, 1977, *47*, 518–543

Becker, WC, Carnine, D, & Davis, G. *Continuous progress tests for Distar language, reading and arithmetic*. Eugene, OR: Engelmann-Becker Corp., 1978

Becker, WC, & Engelmann, S. *Teaching 3: Evluation of instruction*. Chicago: Science Research Associates, 1976

Becker, WC, Engelmann, S, & Thomas, DR. *Teaching 2: Cognitive learning and instruction*. Chicago: Science Research Associates, 1975

Becker, WC, & Gersten, R. A follow-up of Follow Through: The later effects of the Direct Instruction Model on children in fifth and sixth grades. *American Educational Research Journal*, 1982, *19*, 75–92

Bereiter, C. An academic preschool for disadvantaged children: Conclusions from evaluation studies. In JC Stanley (Ed.), *Preschool programs for the disadvantaged: Five experimental approaches to early childhood education*. Baltimore: Johns Hopkins University Press, 1972

Bereiter, C, & Engelmann, S. *Teaching disadvantaged children in the preschool.* Englewood Cliffs, NJ: Prentice-Hall, 1966

Blank, M, & Solomon, F. How shall the disadvantaged child be taught? *Child Development,* 1969, *40,* 47–61

Block, JH. *Mastery learning: theory and practice.* New York: Holt, Rinehart & Winston, 1971

Bloom BS. *Taxonomy of educational objectives: The classification of educational goals. Handbook I: Cognitive domain.* New York: McKay, 1956

Bloom, BS. Mastery learning. In JH Block (Ed.), *Mastery learning: Theory and practice.* New York: Holt, Rinehart & Winston, 1971

Bloom, BS. Time and learning. *American Psychologist,* 1974, *29,* 682–688

Bracey, S, Magggs, A, & Morath, P. The effects of a direct phonic approach in teaching reading with six moderately retarded children: Acquisition and mastery learning stages. *The Slow Learning Child,* 1975, *22,* 83–90 (a)

Bracey, S, Maggs, A, & Morath, P. Teaching arithmetic skills to moderately mentally retarded children using direct verbal instruction: Counting and symbol identification. *Australian Journal of Mental Retardation,* 1975, *3,* 200–204 (b)

Budoff, M, & Hamilton, JL. Learning potential among the moderately and severely retarded. *Mental Retardation,* 197, *12,* 33–36

Bushell, D, Jr. *Classroom behavior: A little book for teachers.* Englewood Cliffs,NJ: Prentice-Hall, 1973

California Achievement Tests: Test coordinator's handbook. Monterey, CA: CTB/McGGraw-Hill, 1978

Carnine, D. Phonic versus whole-word correction procedures following phonic instruction. *Education and Treatment of Children,* 1980, *3,* 323–330

Carnine, D, & Silbert, J. *Direct instruction reading.* Columbus, OH: Charles E. Merrill, 1979

Carroll, JB. Problems of measurement related to the concept of learning for mastery. *Educational Horizons,* 1970, *48,* 71–80

Charters, WW, & Jones, J. On the risk of appraising non-events in program evaluation. *Educational Researcher,* 1973, *2,* 5–7

Davis, FB. Research in comprehension in reading. *Reading Research Quarterly,* 1968, *3,* 499–545

Dillman, CM, & Rahmlow, HF. *Writing instructional objectives.* Belmont, California: Fearon Publishers, 1972

Dixon, L, Spradlin, J, Girardeau, G, & Etzel, B. Facilitation of acquisition of an "in front" spatial discrimination. *Acta Symbolica,* 1974, *5,* 1–22

Dolch, EW. A basic sight vocabulary. *Elementary School Journal,* 1936, *36,* 456–460

Donlon, TF. Referencing test scores: Introductory concepts. In W Hively, & M Reynolds (Eds.), *Domain-referenced testing in special education.* Minneapolis, MN: Council for Exceptional Children, 1975

Dorry, G, & Zeaman, D. The use of a fading technique in paired-associate teaching of a reading vocabulary with retardates. *Mental Retardation,* 1973, *11,* 3–6

Dunn, LM, & Markwardt, F. *Peabody individual achievement test.* Circle Pines, MN: American Guidance Service, 1970

Dunn, LM, & Smith, JC. *Peabody early experiences kit.* Circle Pines, NM: American Guidance Services, 1976

Durkin, D. What Classroom observation reveals about reading comprehension instruction. *Reading Research Quarterly,* 1978–1979, *14,* 481–533

Durost, W, Bixler, H, Wrightstone, JW, Prescott, G, & Balow, I. *Metropolitan achievement test.* New York: Harcourt, Brace, Jovanovich, 1970

Engelmann, S. Toward the design of faultless instruction: The theoretical basis of concept analysis. *Educational Technology,* 1980, *20,* 28–36

Engelmann, S. A study of fourth to sixth grade basal reading series. *Direct Instruction News*, 1982, *1*, 1, 4–5, 9

Engelmann, S, & Carnine, D. *Theory of instruction: Principles and applications*. New York: Irvington Publishers, Inc., 1982

Engelmann, S, & Hanner, S. *Survival skills reading test*. Eugene, OR: Engelmann-Becker Press, 1976

Engelmann, S, & Hanner, S. *Reading Mastery III*. Chicago: Science Research Associates, 1982

Engelmann, S, & Osborn, J. *DISTAR langguage level I*. Chicago: Science Research Associates, 1976

Engelmann, S, & Rosov, R. Tactual hearing experiment with deaf and hearing subjects. *Exceptional children*, 1972, *41*, 243–253

Fink, W, & Brice-Gray, K. The effects of two teaching strategies on the acquisition and recall of an academic task by moderately and severely retarded preschool children. *Mental Retardation*, 1979, *17*, 8–12

Flesch, R. Why Johnny can't read. *Family Circle*, 1979, *26*, 43–45

Foster, RW. *Camelot behavioral checklist*. Lawrence, KS: Camelot Behavioral systems, 1974

Fremer, J. *Criterion-referenced interpretations of survey achievement tests*. Princeton, NJ: Education Testing Service, 1972

Gersten, RM. *Direct instruction programs in special education settings: A review of evaluation research findings*. Paper presented at the Annual Conference of the Council for Exceptional Children, New York, NY, April 1982

Gersten, RM, Heiry, TJ, Becker, WC, & White, WA. *The relationship of entry IQ level and yearly academic growth rates of children in a Direct Instruction Model: A longitudinal study of over 1,500 children*. Paper presented at the Annual Conference of the American Educational Research Association, Los Angeles, CA, April 1981

Gersten, RM, & Maggs, A. Teaching the general case to moderately retarded children: evaluation of a five-year project. *Analysis and Intervention in Developmental Disabilities*, 1982, *2*, 329–343

Gersten, RM, White, WAT, Falco, R, & Carnine D. Teaching basic discriminations to handicapped and non-handicapped individuals through a dynamic presentation of instructional stimuli. *Analysis and Intervention in Developmental Disabilities*, 1982, *2*, 1–13

Glaser, R. Instructional technology and the measurement of learning outcomes: Some questions. *American Psychologist*, 1963, *18*, 519–521

Glaser, R, & Klaus, DJ. Proficiency measurement: Assessing human performance. In R Gagne (Ed.), *Psychological principles in system development*. New York: Holt, Rinehart and Winston, 1962

Glaser, R, & Nitko, AJ. Measurement in learning and instruction. In RL Thorndike (Ed.), *Educational measurement*. Washington, DC: American Council on Education, 1971

Gronlund, NE. *Stating behavioral objectives for classroom instruction*. New York: MacMillan, 1970

Haring, BG, & Schiefelbusch, RL. *Teaching special children*. New York: McGraw-Hill, 1976

Hively, W. Domain-referenced testing. *Educational Technology*, 1974, *14*, 5–10

Hofmeister, A. Integrating criterion-referenced testing and instruction. In W Hively & MC Reynolds (Eds.), *Domain-referenced testing in special education*. Minneapolis, MN: University of Minnesota, Leadership Training/Special Education, 1975

Horst, DP, Tallmadge, GK, & Wood, CT. *A practical guide to measuring project impact on student achievement*. Washington, DC: US Government Printing Office, 1975

Jastak, J, Bijou, S, & Jastak, S. *Wide range achievement test*. Wilmington, DE: Guidance Associates, 1965

Jenkins, J, & Pany, D. Standardized achievement tests. How useful for special education? *Exceptional Children*, 1978, *44*, 448–453

Johnson, JM, & Newman, M. *Procedures for teaching and generalizing subtraction with regrouping*. Paper presented at the Conference on Behavior Analysis in Education, Columbus, Ohio, September 1982

Kauffman, JM (Ed.) Are all children educable? *Analysis and Intervention in Developmental Disabilities* (Special issue), 1981, *1*, 1–108

Kemp, JE. *Instructional design: A plan for unit and course development.* Belmont, CA: Fearon Publishers, 1977

Kling, JW, & Riggs, LA. *Experimental psychology.* New York: Holt, Rinehart and Winston, 1971

Kryzanowski, JA, & Carnine, DW. The effects of massed versus distributed practice schedules in teaching sound-symbol correspondences to young children. *Formative Research on Direct Instruction Technical Report 1978-82.* Eugene, OR: University of Oregon, 1978

Lloyd, J, Cullinan, D, Heins, ED, & Epstein, MH. Direct instruction: Effects on oral and written comprehension. *Learning Disabilities Quarterly,* 1980, *3,* 70–76

Loucks, S, & Hall, GE. A developmental model for determining whether the treatment is actually implemented. *American Educational Research Journal,* 1977, *14,* 263–276

Mager, RF. *Preparing instructional objectives.* Belmont, CA: Fearon Publishers, 1962

Maggs, A, & Morath, P. The effects of direct verbal instruction on intellectual development of institutionalized moderately retarded children: A two-year study. *American Journal of Special Education,* 1976, *10,* 357–364

Mason, JM. Role of strategy in reading by mentally retarded persons. *American Journal of Mental Deficiency,* 1978, *82,* 467–473

McCoy, JF, & Buckhalt, JA. Language acquisition. In JL Matson & JR McCartney (Eds.), *Handbook of behavior modification with the mentally retarded.* New York: Plenum, 1981

Minimum standards and competencies (reading, language, mathematics) for Alabama schools (Bulletin No. 25). Montgomery, AL: Alabama State Department of Education, 1982

Moss, MH. *Tests of basic experiences.* Monterey, CA: CTB/McGraw-Hill, 1970

Neff, NA, Iwata, BA, & Page, TJ. The effects of known item interspersal on acquisition and retention of spelling and sightreading words. *Journal of Applied Behavior Analysis,* 1977, *10,* 738

Novick, MR, & Lewis, C. Prescribing test length for criterion-referenced measurement. In CW Harris, MC Alkin, & WS Popham (Eds.), *Problems in criterion-referenced measurement* (Monograph series, No. 3). Los Angeles, CA: Center for the Study of Evaluation, 1974

Observation manual of the behavioral characteristics progression Austin, TX: Texas Department of Mental Health and Mental Retardation, 1977

Paine, SC, Carnine, DW, White, WAT, & Walters, G. Effects of fading teacher presentation structure (covertization) on acquisition and maintenance or arithmetric problem-solving skills. *Education and Treatment of Children,* 1982, *5,* 93–107

Pasanella, AL, & Volkmor, CB. *Coming back or never leaving: Instructional programming for handicapped students in the mainstream.* Columbus, OH: Charles E. Merrill, 1977

Popham, WJ. *Criterion-referenced instruction.* Belmont, CA: Fearon Publishers, 1973

Popham, WJ. Selecting objectives and generating test items for objectives-based tests. In CW Harris, MC Alkin, & WJ Popham (Eds.), *Problems in criterion-referenced measurement* (Monograph series, No. 3). Los Angeles, CA: Center for the Study of Evaluation, 1974

Prescott, GA, Balow, IH, Hogan, TP, & Farr, RC. *Metropolitan Achievement Tests.* New York: Harcourt Brace Jovanovich, Inc., 1978

Reith, HJ, Polsgrove, L. & Semmel, MI. Instructional variables that make a difference: Attention to task and beyond. *Exceptional Education Quarterly,* 1982, *2,* 61–71

Rosenshine, BV. The third cycle of research on teacher effects: Content covered, academic engaged time, and quality of instruction. In *Seventy-eighth Yearbook of the National Society for the Study of Education.* Chicago: University of Chicago Press, 1978

Rosenshine, BV. Content time and direct instruction. In P Peterson, & H Walberg (Eds.), *Research on teaching: Concepts, findings, and implications.* Berkeley, CA: McCutchan, 1979

Rosenshine, BV, & Berliner, DC. Academic engaged time. *British Journal of Teacher Education,* 1978, *4,* 3–16

Sailor, WS, Guess, D, Rutherford, G, & Baer, DM. Control of tantrum behavior by operant techniques during experimental verbal training. *Journal of Experimental Analysis of Behavior*, 1968, *1*, 237–244

Salvia, J, & Ysseldyke, JE. *Assessment in special education and remedial education*. Boston: Houghton Mifflin, 1981

Samuels, JS. Effects of pictures on learning to read, comprehension and attitudes. *Review of Education Research*, 1970, *40*, 397–407

Scriven, M. The methodology of evaluation. In RW Tyler (Ed.), *Perspectives of curriculum evaluation*. Chicago: Rand McNally, 1967

Sidman, M, Cresson, O, Jr, & Willson-Morris, M. Acquisition of matching to sample via mediated transfer. *Journal of the Experimental Analysis of Behavior*, 1974, *22*, 261–273

Sindelar, PT, & Wilson, RJ. *Acquisition of academic skills as a function of teacher-directed instruction and seatwork*. Paper presented at the Conference on Behavior Analysis in Education, Columbus, Ohio, September 1982

Slossen, R. *Slossen oral reading test*. East Aurora, NY: Slossen Educational Publications, 1963

Stallings, J, & Kaskowitz, D. *Follow-through classroom observational evaluation* (1972–1973). Menlo Park, CA: Stanford Research Institute, 1974

Stevens, R, & Rosenshine, BV. Advances in research on teaching. *Exceptional Education Quarterly*, 1981, *2*, 1–10

Stokes, TE, & Baer, DM. An implicit technology of generalization. *Journal of Applied Behavior Analysis*, 1977, *10*, 349–367

Tawney, JW. *Empirical verification of instruction: An impossible dream?* Paper presented at the Conference on Behavior Analysis in Education, Columbus, ohio, September, 1982 (a)

Tawney, JW. *The pragmatics of the educability issue: Some questions which logically precede the assumption of ineducability*. Paper presented at the Conference on Behavior Analysis in Education, Coumbus, OH, September 1982 (b)

Terman, S, & Walcutt, CC. *Reading: Chaos and cure*. New York: McGraw-Hill, 1958

Test-text match. *Research for Better Schools*, Winter 1981–1982, *3*, 2, 6

US Office of Education. *Annual evaluation: Report on programs administered by the US Office of Education*. Washington, DC: Capitol Publications, Educational Resources Division, 1976

Weisberg, P. *Direct instruction in the preschool—logical and empirical validation*. Invited address for the Association for Behavior Analysis, Milwaukee, WI, May 1981

Weisberg, P. *Mythical variables in the teaching of beginning handwriting*. Invited address for the association for Behavior Analysis, Milwaukee, WI, May 1982

Weisberg, P, Packer, RH, & Weisberg, RS. Academic training. In JL Matson & JR McCartney (Eds.), *Handbook of behavior modification with the mentally retarded*. New York: Plenum, 1981

Weisberg, P, & Sims EV, Jr. Tokens that teach. *Directive Teacher*, 1982, *4*, 16–18

Willows, DM. *Influences of background pictures on children's decoding of words*. Paper presented at the Biennial Meeting of the Society for Research in Child Development, Denver, Colorado, April 1975

Wilson, CT. An essential vocabulary. *Reading Teacher*, 1963, *17*, 94–96.

PART 4

Medical Concerns

Edward Page-El
Bruce P. Hermann

13

Neurologic Disorders

Within the past decade, major developments in the elucidation of biochemical pathways, the emergence of refined analytical techniques, and the reclassification of known degenerative diseases on a biochemical basis have resulted in a formidable array of information available to those clinicians involved in the identification, prevention, and treatment of developmentally disabled persons. Mental retardation, cerebral palsy, epilepsy, and autism are examples of developmental disabilities with the implied concept of neurological dysfunctioning.

More than 100 new diseases have been discovered during the past 10 years and the biochemistry of many other diseases are being elucidated, which have important prognostic and therapeutic implications. Consequesntly, the traditional "sign and symptom" approach to the diagnosis of a disease process must be modified to established a rational approach to the sorting out of disease processes. This situation is especially true for those disorders in which the biochemical disorder preceeds the appearance of symptons (Adams & Lyon, 1982).

This chapter will attempt to focus on those disease processes where mental retardation is the primary result of the presenting manifestation of the disease and the screening and diagnostic procedures necessary for diagnostic accuracy will be described. Since this chapter cannot adequately cover the entire available literature, references are provided for those individuals seeking more detailed and precise information.

Those diseases in which mental retardation and early developmental lags are suspected include five categories. These are the metabolic encephalopathies, chromosomal disorders, development morphologic anomalies of the brain, heredodegenerative disorders, and acquired lesions of the brain.

Table 13-1
Mental Retardation With
Skeletal and Somatic
Abnormalities

Mucopolysaccharidoses
Mucosulfatidosis
Mucolipidosis
    Type I   Sialidosis
    Type II   I-cell Disease
    Type III
    Type IV
Mannosidosis
Aspartylglucosaminuria

METABOLIC ENCEPHALOPATHIES

The genetic transmission of these disorders implies that they are directly or indirectly the result of inborn enzymatic defects. The metabolic inherited disorders, as a group, represent only a small fraction of the known causes for mental retardation. Because of their dire prognostic and therapeutic implications, however, a sense of urgency is lent to their early recognition (Hanley, Linsao, & Netley, 1971; Scriver, Mackenzie, Clow, & Delvin, 1971). The metabolic disorders can be separated into two groups: a) mental retardation with skeletal and somatic (physical) anormalies, and b) mental retardation without somatic abnormalities. Examples of the first group are shown in Table 13-1.

Mental Retardation with Cranial-Skeletal and Somatic Involvement

Mucopolysaccharidoses

This group of diseases is characterized by varying degrees of mental retardation, and hepatic (liver) and ocular (eye) involvement with gross skeletal disorders. This group includes several unique types of diseases. To date, all enzymatic and metabolic pathways have been elucidated (see Table 13-2). Enzyme assays, urine screening for the mucopolysaccharides, electromyograms, peripheral blood examination, bone marrow examinations, and cranial and skull x-rays may assist in separating and identifying the specific variants of the mucopolysaccharidoses.

Mucolipidoses

These disorders similarly present with mental retardation, and visceral and skeletal abnormalities. These disorders include two types. Mucolipidosis, Type III, has normal urinary mucopolysaccharide excretion and an elevation of serum

Table 13-2
Clinical Types of Mucopolysaccharidosis*

Name	Class	Enzyme defect	Excreted product (urine)	Mental retardation	Cloudy cornea	Skeletal dysplasia
Hurler's disease	I (H)	α-L-Iduronidase	Dermatan sulfate, heparan sulfate	++	+	+++
Scheie's disease	I (S)	α-L-Iduronidase	Dermatan sulfate, heparan sulfate	-	++	+
Hunter's disease Severe	II	Iduronate sulfatase	Dermatan sulfate, heparan sulfate	++	-	++
Mild	II	Iduronate sulfatase	Dermatan sulfate, heparan sulfate	+	-	+
Sanfilippo's disease	III					
	A	Heparan N-sulfatase	Heparan sulfate	+++	-	++
	B	N-acetyl-α-D-glucosaminidase	Heparan sulfate	+++	-	++
Morquio's disease	IV	Hexosamine-6-sulfatase	Keratan sulfate, chondroitin-6-sulfate	-	-	+++
Maroteaux-Lamy disease	VI	Galactosamine-4-sulfatase	Dermatan sulfate	-	+	++
Sly's disease	VII	β-glucuronidase	Dermatan sulfate	+	±	+
Mucosulfatidosis		Multiple sulfatases	Dermatan sulfate, heparan sulfate, cholesterol sulfate sulfatide	++	-	+

Courtesy of Dr. E. H. Kolodny
*Type V of older classifications has been eliminated. A new finding is the milder form of Hunter's disease.

hydrolases. Mental retardation occurs late. Mucolipidosis, Type IV, is associated with mental retardation and developmental delays during the first year of life. Corneal clouding occurs early. Bone marrow histiocytes have a weal metachromasia. Skin fibroblast and liver calls contain lipidlike bodies. the lysosomal enzyme responsible for this variant is unknown. Mannosidosis, aspartylglucosaminuria, and fucosidosis are other disorders associated with mental retardation and facial dysmorphism and can be diagnosed by enzyme assays of white blood cells and other tissues (Gautieres, Arasenio-Nunes, & Acardi, 1979; Loeb, Tondeur, Toppet, & Clemer, 1969; Norden, Lundblad, Svensson, & Autio, 1974).

Mental Retardation Without Somatic Involvement

Defects in Amino Acid Metabolism

The aminoacidopathies comprise a complex group, which makes it difficult to recognize individual entities and to separate them from the degenerative diseases of the central nervous system. Though relatively rare as a cause of mental retardation, most of the inherited disorders of amino acid metabolism have been discovered by systematic screening of handicapped children.

Mental retardation or neurologic signs appearing in the period of infancy and early childhood should raise the suspicion of an aminoacidopathy. Further clues from the history and physical examination may suggest the possibility of such a disorder. Unusual har, unusual body odor, unexplained acidosis, seizures, or a combination of various disturbances of mental or motor function (i.e., exaggeration or diminution of muscle tone) may be present.

Some of the specific disorders categorized under this heading include: phenylketonuria, Maple Syrup Urine Disease, homocystinuria, histidinemia, argininosuccinicaciduria.

Various attempts to classify the aminoacidpathies into meaningful disgnostic approaches have proven useful. From a biochemical viewpoint they may be classified into: (1) those in which the transport of an aminoacid is impaired, (2) those in which there is an enzyme or cofactor deficiency, or (3) those grouped around certain chemical components such as sulfur-containing amino acids (Farmer, 1975).

Phenylketonuria (PKU) is an inborn error of metabolism characterized by the inability of the body to convert phanylalanine to tyrosine. Untreated, it produces a syndrome of mental retardation, seizures, and hair pigmentation dificiency. It is the most common of the aminoacidopathies with a frequency of 1 in 14,000 (Berman, Cunningham, Day, Ford, & Hsia, 1969). Neonatal screening programs and the early implemetation of a phenylalanine restricted diet have reduced the incidence of mental retardation in this disease. A small group of children have

Table 13-3
Screening Tests for Detection of Hereditary Metabolic Diseases

Test	Compounds or Diseases Detected
Ferric Chloride Test (Phenistix)	Phenylalanine tyrosine histidine, certain other Amino Acids, Phenothiazines, Salicylates isoniazid
2,4,-Dinitrophenylhydrazine	Alpha-heto acids
Cyanide-Nitroprusside	Homocystine, disulfide
Clinitest	Reducing sugars
Berry Spot Test	Mucopolysaccharides

hyperphenylalaninemia and fail to respond to the diet (Table 13-3). These patients have normal levels of liver phenylalanine hydroxylase, the dificiency enzyme in classical PKU, but cannot produce the active cofactor tetraphydrobipterin. The use of L-dopa and 5-hydroxytryptophan is beneficial in these cases (Kaufman, Holtzman, Milstien, Buteer, & Krumholz, 1975; Niederwieser, Curtius, Bettonio, Bieri, Schricks, Viscontini, & Schauls, 1979).

A recent study of clinically normal phenylketonuric mothers revealed a high percentage of mentally retarded offspring. The frequency of microcephaly, mental retardation, and congenital heart disease was greatly increased over those in the normal population. There was no evidence that dietary treatment before and during pregnancy was effective in preventing the disorders seen in the offspring (Leuke & Levy, 1980).

Maple Syrup Urine Disease, phenylketonuria, and homocystinuria are examples of an enzyme or cofactor deficiency and are typical of the overflow aminoacidopathies with resultant abnormal serum and urine amino acids. Hartnup's Disease is an example of impaired transport of amino acids with aminoaciduria but normal blood levels of aminoacids. Therefore, both urine and blood are examined in suspected aminoacid disorders (Table 13-3).

Table 13-4 provides some examples of aminoacidopathies and enzymatic defects associated with mental retardation.

Hyperlysinemia, saccharopinuria, and carnosinemia are other examples of aminoacidopathies (Ghadini et al., 1965; Perry, Hansen, Tischler, Bunting, & Berry, 1967; Simell, Visakorpi, & Donner, 1972). Mental retardation, often with seizures and other neurologic signs has been seen in other aminoacidurias such as cystathioninuria, persistent hyperlysinemia, hydroxyprolinemia, iminoglycinuria, and histidemia (Kolodny & Cable, 1977). The disorders of amino acid metabolism discussed above represent only a few of the varieties that can threaten the developing brain and emphasize the importance of systematic screening of all newborn infants, the mentally retarded, and mothers with two or more mentally retarded children.

Table 13-4
Aminoacidopathies and Enzyme Defects

Disease	Enzyme Defect
Phenylketonuria	(a) Phenylalanine Hydroxylase
	(b) Dihydropteridine Reductase
Phenylalanemias	(a) Phenylalanine Hydroxylase
Maple Syrup Disease	Decarboxylases of Alpha-keto isocaproic acid, alpha-keto beta-methylvaleric acid and alpha-ketoisovaleric acid
Arginino Aciduria	Arginosuccinaie
Citrullinemia	Argininosuccinic acid Synthetase

Defects in Carbohydrate Metabolism

Galactosemia

Mild to moderate mental retardation, evidence of liver dysfunction, ocular abnormalities, and failure to thrive are findings seen in galactosemia, an autosomal recessive disorder of carbohydrate metabolism. The incidence varies between 1:100,000–1:500,000. The basic enzymatic defect is the absence of galactose-1-phosphate uridyl transferase. The degree of mental retardation varies with the length of exposure of the brain to the toxic effect of galactose. The therapeutic effect of a low galactose diet has been difficult to assess (Komrower & Lee, 1970; Nadler, Inouye & Hsia, 1979).

Fructose Intolerance

Fructose intolerance, though relatively rare in the United States, is frequently associated with mild mental retardation. The enzymatic defect is due to a deficiency of fructose-1-phosphate in the liver and kidney (Nikkila, Somersalo, Pitkanen, & Perheentupá, 1962; Jeune et al., 1961). Treatment is relatively simple and involves avoiding the intake of fruits and cane or beet sugar (Corblath & Schwartz, 1976).

Defects in Lipid Metabolism (Lysosomal Storage Disease)

The term lysosomal storage has supplanted the group of disorders formerly called the lipidoses because each of the diseases in this group can be traced to a missing lysosomal enzyme. Simply put, the lysosomes are vesicles within the cell whose primary function is to degrade the breakdown products of cellular metabolism. Twenty-five to 30 or more enzymes within the lysosome participate

Table 13-5
Lysosomal Storage Disease

Disease	Age of Onset	Enzyme Deficienty	Store Metabolities
Glycogenoses			
Type 2—Pompe's disease			
Infantile	1	α-Glucosidase	Glycogen
Adult	>20	α-Glucosidase	Glycogen
Krabbe's disease			
Infantile	1	Galactocerebrosidase	Galactocerebroside
Juvenile	4	Galactocerebrosidase	Galactocerebroside
Fabry's disease	>10	α-Galactosidase A	Ceramide trihexoside
Gaucher's disease			
Type 1—adult form	1–70	β-Glucosidase	Glucocerebroside
Type 2—infantile form	1	β-Glucosidase	Glucocerebroside
Type 3—juvenile form	>10	β-Glucosidase	Glucocerebroside
Niemann-Pick disease			
Type A—late infantile, neuropathic	1	Sphingomyelinase	Sphingomyelin
Type B—juvenile, non-neuropathic	2	Sphingomyelinase	Sphingomyelin
Type C—without sphingomyelinase deficiency	1–2	Activating factor	Sphingomyelin
Type D—Nova Scotia type	Childhood	Unknown	Sphingomyelin
Farber's disease	1	Ceramidase	Ceramide

in the breakdown of lipids, carbohydrates, proteins, and proteolipids. A missing or defective enzyme results in an excessive accumulation of a particular metabolite with resulting impairment of the cell function. The enzyme defect may occur in the brain, liver, spleen, bone, and lung, may involve several organ systems. Therapy to date has been unsuccessful.

More than 50 varieties of lysosomal storage diseases have been identified due to the use of the electron microscope, the availability of artificial substrates, the use of cultured fibroblasts from the skin, and the increased potential for carrier detection and prenatal diagnosis. Tables 13-5 and 13-6 represent some of the known lysosomal storage diseases with the exception of the mucopolysaccharidoses and related disorders referred to in earlier sections, which are also lysosomal storage disorders.

The lipidoses are generally classified into the sphingolipidoses, with at least 10 types (e.g. glycogenoses, sulfatidoses, mucopolysaccharidoses, aligosacchar-

Table 13-6
Lysosomal Storage Diseases

Disease	Age of Onset	Enzyme Deficiency	Stored Metabolites
Sphingolipidoses			
GM$_1$gangliosidosis			
Type 1—infantile			
generalized	1	β-Galactosidase	GM$_1$ganglioside, olgosaccharide
Type 2—juvenile	1–2	β-Galactosidase	GM$_1$ganglioside, olgosaccharide
GM$_2$gangliosidosis			
Tay-Sachs disease	1	Hexosaminidase A	GM$_2$ganglioside
Sandhoff's disease	1	Hexosaminidases A & B	GM$_2$ganglioside, globoside, oligosaccharide
AB variant	1	GM$_2$ activator factor	GM$_2$ganglioside
Juvenile Tay-Sachs disease	>2	Hexosaminidase A	GM$_2$ganglioside
Juvenile Sandhoff's disease	>2	Hexosaminidases A & B	GM$_2$ganglioside, globoside
Adult Tay-Sachs disease	>15	Hexosaminidase A	GM$_2$ganglioside,
Sulfatidoses			
Metachromatic leukodystrophy			
Late-infantile	1–3	Arylsulfatase A	Sulfatide
Juvenile	4–15	Arylsulfatase A	Sulfatide
Adult	>16	Arylsulfatase A	Sulfatide
Activator factor deficiency	1–2	Cerebroside sulfate sulfatase activator factor	Sulfatide

idoses), and other enzyme deficient specific disorders. Other disorders are classified and identified on the basis of the enzyme deficiency and major accumulating metabolitics.

Sphingolipidoses

The sphingolipidoses, as a group, are characterized by predominantly early onset of symptoms ranging from birth to two years of age, although late infantile, juvenile, and adult age of onset may occur. All of the early onset disorders show progressive deterioration and loss of previously acquired skills or regression in motor and mental development.

Tay-Sachs Disease (Early Infantile GM$_2$-Gangliosidosis)

Tay-Sachs disease is an autosomal recessive hereditary disorder seen primarily in Jewish children and caused by a deficiency of hexosaminidase A that results in the accumulation of GM$_2$-Ganglioside in the neural cells. Tay-Sachs disease is one of several disorders characterized by the accumulation of ganglio-sides (Kolodny & Cable, 1977). The reader is referred to the text by Farmer (1975) for clinical descriptions of these disorders.

The diagnosis of lysosomal storage diseases includes the use of a computer-ized tomographic (CT) scan and evoked potential recordings for those disorders characterized by leucodystrophy (breakdown of white matter) before symptoms of neural storage dysfunction are seen. Electron microscopic study of skin, con-junctiva (mucous membrane covering the anterior surface of the eyeball and lin-ing of the lids), circulating blood cells may identify the curvilinear bodies and finger print structures seen in neuronal ceroidlipofuscinosis and other disorders with vacuolated (a clear space in the substance of a cell, sometimes degenerative in character) lymphocytes (Bauman & Markesberry, 1978). Stored material in nerve cells on axonal inclusions can be identified by skin biopsy (Lasser, Carter, & Mahoney, 1975; Martin & Centrick, 1978; Sipe & O'Brien, 1979).

Amniotic fluid and cultured fibroblasts can be examined for various ultra-structural abnormalities in patients with storage diseases (Kohn, Ornoy, Sekeles, Cohen, & Sekeles, 1978). The exmination of cultured amniotic fluid cells by electron microscopy has been of value in the screening of mothers with suspected storage diseases (Kohn, Livni, Ornoy, Sekeles, Legum, Bach, & Cohen, 1977).

Thin layer chromotography (TLC), a new technique, has been developed to detect the accumulating substances and to determine the amount. This procedure can separate the substances excreted in the urine of patients with various lyso-somal storage diseases. The TLC patterns are distinctive for each disease and require only a minute amount of urine (Holmes & O'Brien, 1979; Humbel & Collart, 1974).

High performance liquid chromatography (HPLC) is another new procedure. HPLC detects and separates small amounts of oligosaccharides (a compound made up of the condensation of a small number of monosaccharide units) and gly-colipids from tissue, plasma, and urine. The plasma glycolipids in Sandhoff's disease and Fabry's disease, as well as gangliosides in cultured fibroblasts from patients with Tay-Sachs can be quantitated (Kolodny, Rachavan, Ellison, Lyerla, & Biemer, 1980; Ullman, Pyeritz, Maser, Wenser, & Kolodny, 1980).

Lysosomal enzyme activity can be determined by using artificial substrate with chromogenic (pigment producing) or flurogenic properities. Radioactive la-beled natural substrates are also commercially available. Solid tissue biopsies are no longer needed in most instances since body fluids (plasma) and tissue (leucocytes and cultured fibroblasts) are readily accessible.

Metabolic screening should be perfomed in patients within the following categories: (1) infants with recurrent episodes of unexplained vomiting or altered consciousness, (2) recurrent unexplained spasticity or ataxia, (3) mental retarda-tion in a sibling or close relative, (4) mental retardation in the absence of major congenital anomalies, (5) neurological disorder replicated in a sibling or close relative, and (6) progressive central nervous system degeneration.

The processing of lysosomal enzymes in Inclusion cell disease (I-cell disease) and the identification of activator dificiency diseases lend hope that further research may open up modalities for effective treatment of these disorders in the future.

CHROMOSOMAL DISORDERS

Mental retardation is the most common neurologic finding in chromosomal abnormalitiies and the intellectual deficit associated with chromosomal aberration is accompanied by either gross anatomic or microsopic malformations of the central nervous system. The small fraction of abnormal chromosomes in children with mental retardation and multiple congenital anomalies as compared to a large proportion of normal adults found to have chromosomal abnormalities is an obvious sampling bias (Tharapal & Summitt, 1977). The significance of some of the chromosomal abnormalities and many of the minor chromosomal variations is still uncertain (Miller & Breaj, 1976).

Though human genetics is a relatively new discipline, the pace of its development was extremely slow until the 1950s when technical improvements (Hsu & Pomerat, 1953; Makino & Nishimura, 1951) aided in definitely establishing the diploid (two haploid sets of 23 chromosomes each) number of chromosomes in man as 46 (Tijo & Levan 1956).

The discovery of an extra chromosome in patients with Down's snydrome or mongolism was reported by Lejeune, Gautier and Turpin in 1959 in France, and Jacobs, Baike, Court-Brown, McGregor and Strong (1956). Following the revelation that chromosomal aberrations could cause disease in man, gigantic strides were made in the correlation of distinct clinical syndromes with recognizable changes in the chromosomes.

New staining procedures were developed in the 1970s, which produced patterns of bright and dark bands that are characteristic for each chromosome. These are G banding, Q banding, R banding and bromodeoxyuridine (BUdR) (Caspersson, Lindsten, & Zech, 1970; Latt, 1974; Schneider, Chaillet, & Tice, 1976). It is now possible to identify every single chromosome. More than 300 regions in the human gene can be distinguished, which has greatly facilitated the study of human chromosomes.

The classification of chromosomal disorders is based on: (1) variations in chromosomal length, (2) abnormalities in satellite size or location, (3) variations in secondary constrictions, (4) forms of mosaicisms, (5) balanced translocations, and (6) differences in the intensity and appearance of bands. These abnormalities will be referred to throughout this section. The reader is referred to several excellent texts for the basic principles of cytogenetics (deGrouchy & Turleau, 1977; Priet, 1977).

Table 13-7
Major Signs in Newborns with Down's Syndrome

Signs	Down's syndrome Frequency (%)
Slanting palpebral fissures	80
Dysplastic ears	60
Abundant nuchal skin	80
Flat face (hypoplastic maxilla)	90
Simian crease (at least of one hand)	50
Dysplastic middle phalanx of fifth finger	60
Hyperextensibility of joints	80
Muscular hypotonia	80
Dysplastic pelvis	70
Absent Moro reflex	80

Down's Syndrome (mongolism)

This disorder represents one of the more classical and well known cyto-genetic disorders. It is due to an extra chromosome or at least parts of an extra chromosome belonging to a chromosome 21. Clinical features include mental re-tardation, epicanthal folds (mongoloid configuration), brachycephaly (dispropor-tionate shortness of head), moderate growth retardation, and various stigmata such as shallow orbits, large tongue, simian creases, incurving of the fifth digits and others. Congenital heart lesions are also often found. Blood ab-normalities and malformations of the intestinal tract are more frequent than in euphoid (normal chromosome complement) people. The incidence of Down's syndrome is about one in 800 to 1000 live births (Table 13-7).

There are 3 types of cytogenetic types of Down's syndrome: trisomy 21 (two sets of 23 chromosomes plus one chromosome for a total of 47 chromosomes), translocation (transfer of a piece of one chromosome to another), and mosaicism with a 21-trisomic clone (two or more cell-populations-clones, each with a differ-ent type). Trisomy 21 accounts for 95 percent of all cases. Translocations ac-count for four percent and mosaics occur in about one to two percent of all Down's syndrome cases.

Down's syndrome has been reported in all ethnic groups and most countries. Several investigations (Hug, 1951; Zellweger, 1965) found Down's snydrome to be more common in males, however, this finding was not confirmed by Collman and Stoller (1963) or Wahrman and Fried (1970).

As previously mentioned, mental retardation is the most consistent symp-tom of Down's syndrome. The majority of patients are moderately mentally re-tarded with scores in the 36 to 55 IQ range. Those persons with complications of epilepsy or brain abscesses may be profoundly mentally retarded. Individuals with IQs of 56 to 69 are common but those in the dull-normal or normal ranges are extremely rare. Individuals with mosaicism have been reported with IQ scores of 80 but more often are seen in the ranges of 43 to 92 (Fishler, Koch, & Donnell, 1976).

Premature aging in Down's syndrome was first noticed by Fraser and Mitchell in 1876. Although intellectual deterioration, a major sign of senile dementia, is difficult to detect, abrupt or gradual behavior changes may signal the process of early senescence (Rollins, 1946). Senile plaques and neurofibrillary tangles, typical Alzheimer lesions, can be found in the brains of young adults with Down's syndrome (Haberland, 1969).

The diagnosis of Down's syndrome is made prima vista on the basis of well known stigmata and presents as an "all-or-none" condition as opposed to some single-gene autosomal dominant conditions where a spectrum of intermediate cases may occur with only a few known stigmata present. Chromosomal analysis will identify the specific chromosomal abnormality.

Chromosomal Disorders with Mental Retardation

Following the discovery of an extra chromosome in patients with Down's syndrome by Lejeune and his associates in 1959, a number of chromosomal aberrations have been identified, in some of which mental retardation is a constant feature (Table 13-8). Some of the more prevalent of these disorders will be discussed below.

Trisomy 8

Since the advent of chromosomal banding, more than 30 patients have been identified as having trisomy 8 (Riccardi, Atkins, & Holmen, 1970). The cardinal clinical features include mental retardation, anteverted (tilted foward) nose, absent patellae (knee cap), long philtrum (the groove in the midline of the upper lip) and malformed ears. In early childhood, children with trisomy 8 tend to resemble each other. Unusual skeletal anomalies occur. The absent patellae is one; another is a cleft between the first and third interdigital web of the foot and is associated with retroflexion (backward bending) of the great toe. Limitation of mobility may occur in the large joints. Congenital heart disease and urinary tract anomalies are common.

This disorder should be detectable using anmiocentesis and chromosomal naryotyping for prenatal diagnosis.

4p-Syndrome (Partial Depletion of Short Arm of No. 4 Chromosome)

The 4p-syndrome also known as the Wolf-Hirschhorn snydrome, was first described by Wolf, Beinwein, Porsch, Schroter, and Baitsch (1965) in a patient presenting with a high prominent glabella (forehead), hypertelorism (extreme width between the eyes), and antimongoloid slant (downward slant of the eyes and promi-

Table 13-8
Chromosomal Disorders With Retardation

Name	Mental Retardation	Clinical Features	References
(109) Trisomy 8	$+ +$ to $+ + + +$*	Absent patellae Anteverted nose, micrographia malformed ears	Riccardi, et al (1970) Casperson, Lindstein, Zech, Bucieton, & Price (1972)
4p-Syndrome Partial deletion of Short Arm of No. 4 Chromosome (Wolf-Hirschhorn Syndrome)	$+ + + +$	Unusual facies with marked hypotelorism, antimongoloid slant; misshapen nose.	Wolf, et al (1965) Hirschhorn, Copper, & Firscher (1965)
5p-Syndrome The Cat Cry Syndrome CRI-DU-CHAT Syndrome	$+ + + +$	Characteristic cry infancy (meowing of a cat; microcephaly, hypotelorism, epicanthic, antimongoloid slant.	Lejeune, Lafourcade, Berger, Vialett, Boeswilloughby, Seringe, & Ruptin (1963) German, et al. (1964)
13q-Syndrome	$+ + + +$	Absent thumbs, severe cerebral defect, eye abnormalities, congenital cardiac disease dysmorphic facies.	Bain & Gauld (1963)
18Q-Syndrome Deletion of the Long Arm of Chromosome 18	$+ + +$ to $+ + + +$	Microcephaly, carpmouth, large low set ears, short stature.	deGrouchy, et al. (1964) Lejeune, Berger, Lafourcase, & Rethove (1966)

*Levels of Retardation
    0 = Normal
    + = Mild
    + + = Moderate
   + + + = Severe
  + + + + = Profound

nent epicanthal folds). The nose is misshapen and the ears are low set. Undescended testes and hypospadium (abnormal urethral openings) may be present. Midline fusion defects such as cleft lip or palate are seen. Congenital heart disease is a leading cause of death. Mental retardation is profound. The diagnosis of the syndrome at birth is possible on clinical grounds alone. However, the use of fluorescent or Giemsa staining techniques easily identifies the deletion of the short arm.

5p-Syndrome (Cri Du Chat)

Lejeune, Berger, Lafourcad, and Réthoré (1966) described a syndrome of low birth weight, microcephaly and profound mental retardation. A characteristic cry in infancy similar to a mewing cat occurs and disappears as early as two weeks of age. Additional clinical features include antimongoloid slant, hypertelorism and epicanthi.

Patients with the cat cry syndrome have a deletion of the short arm of chromosome no. 5. Chromosome no. 5 is similar to chromosome no. 4 but the two can be distinguished by autoradiography (German, Lejeune, Maintyre, & de Grouchy, 1964). Fluorescent technique and Giemsa banding readily differentiate between chromosomes 4 and 5.

13q-Syndrome (Ring D Chromosome)

The cardinal signs of Ring D chromosome include absent thumbs, severe cerebral defects in the form of a large single ventricle (holoprosencephaly), or markedly reduced cerebral substance and microcephaly. The mental retardation is severe. Occular anomalies and antimongoloid slant, epicanthal folds, ptosis (drooping of the upper eyelid) and narrow palpebral (eyelid) fissures are typically noted. The bridge of the nose is depressed. The palate is high arched and the ears are low set and malformed.

Ring D chromosome has been reported in 50 or more patients with a wide range of variation of the phenotypes. Since the formation of the ring shaped chromosome results from the partial deletion of chromatid material at the ends of the long and short arms of the chromosome with the subsequent sticking of the ends together to form a circle or ring, it has been suggested that variation in the amount of chromatid material lost could account for the variability in the observed congenital malformations (Wang, Melnyk, McDonald, Ulchida, Carr, and Goldberg, 1962).

18q-Syndrome (Deletion of the Long Arm of Chromosome 18)

In 1964, a patient with microcephaly, mental retardation, and deafness was described by de Grouchy, Royer, Salmon and Lamy (1964). Other features included a characteristic carp-mouth, large malformed ears and midfacial dysplasis (LeJeune, et al., 1966). In patients with this disorder, profound retardation is present with IQs ranging from 20 to 30. Hypotonia may be severe and seizures with abnormal electroencephalogram (EEG) may complicate the picture.

The characteristic facial features include prominent forehead, hypoplasia of the supraorbital ridges with deep set eyes. Prominent epicanthal folds and hypertelorism is a constant finding. The nose is upturned, small, with a depressed nasal bridge. The mouth has downward slanted carriers below the midpoint of the lower lip. The upper lip appears rolled when viewed in profile. The size of the

Table 13-9

Chromosomal Disorder With Retardation Klinefelter's Disease
and Variants

Name	Mental Retardation*	Clinical Features	References
Klinefelter's XXY	0 to + +	Gynecomastia, small testes, tall, slim, eunuchoid appearance, decubitus varus, azoospermia.	Bronstein (1939) Klinefelter, et al. (1942)
XXXY	+ + to + + +	Hypoplasia of Scrotum, small testes, hypotonia. Undescended testes.	Zollinger (1969) Greenstein, et al. (1970)
XXXXY	+ + +	Growth failure hypo-telorism, mongoloid slant of eyes, sunken nose, prognathia con-genital heart lesions, muscular hypotonia, seizures.	Moric-Petrovic, et al. (1973) Cunningham and Ragsdale (1972)

*Levels of Retardation
    0 = Normal
    + = Mild
   + + = Moderate
  + + + = Severe
+ + + + = Profound

deletion on the long arm of the no. 18 chromosome (18q-) varies from one third to one fourth of the length of the long arm. Quinacrine mustard staining produces a characteristic banding pattern by which the 18th chromosome can be identified (Parker, Mavalwala, Koch, Hatashita & Derencsenyl, 1972).

Klinefelter's Snydrome (XXY)

Klinefelter's snydrome is a sex chromosome abornmality in contrast to the previously discussed autosomal abnormalities. Klinefelter's syndrome is one of the more common forms of hypogonadism is males. Although retardation is rare in the classical syndrome with one extra X chromosome (X/XY or XXY), the incidence of mental retardation increases with karyotypes showing two (XXXY) or three (XXXXY) extra chromosomes Table 13-9.

The first probable case of Klinefelter's syndrome was that of a 17 year old youth with gynecomastia (large breasts), excessive arm span, small testes, azoo-spermia (absence of living spermatozoa in the semen), normal penis and increased urinary gonadotropins (Bronstein, 1939). Klinefelter, Reifenstein and Albright

(1942) presented the classical paper confirming the clinical symptoms described by Bronstein and describing the gonadal histology. Following the discovery of the presence of a sex chromatin or Barr body in somatic cells of the female and its absence in the males (Barr & Bertram, 1949), the issue of the "femaleness" in Klinefelter's syndrome was resolved by the finding of an extra X-chromosome (Jacobs et al., 1956).

The XXXY variant of Klinefelter's snydrome is rare but when seen, the mental retardation is more severe (Zollinger, 1969). The clinical picture is similar to that of the XXY Klinefelter's snydrome (Greenstein, Harris, Luzzatti, & Cann, 1970).

The XXX XY variant is more frequent than the XX XY and about 90 cases have been reported (Moric-Petrovic, Laca, Markovic, & Markovic, 1973). Growth failure is common. Many of the XXX XY show facial dysmorphism with mongoloid slant of the eyes, hypertelorism, depressed nasal bridge and a high arched palate. Mental retardation is a constant feature. Hypoplasia of the genitalia is also a constant finding.

Indications for sex chromatia studies (nuclear sexing) include infants and children with ambiguous genitalia, hypospadius or undescended testes, short stature, or lax or superfluous neck skin. Primary amenorrhea, absence of secondary sex characteristic, gynecomostia in the male, infertility, and eunuchoid body proportions during puberty or in the adult age are indication for sex chromatin studies. Amniotic fluid cell studies are indicated where the mother is suspected of being a gene carrier for X-linked diseases, or if the parent is a rare fertile Klinefelter syndrome.

Indications for chromosomal analysis include the above indications described above. Tall men with behavioral disorders should be studied. Every case of Down's syndrome should be evaluated including cases with multiple congenital anomalies. Persons with mental retardation and growth failure for which there are no other genetic or environmental causes should have chromosomal analysis.

The Fragile X Chromosome

Despite the fact that mentally retarded males have outnumbered females in a ratio of 3 to 2, it was only after a published report (Lubs, 1969) that shed light on a specific abnormality of the X chromosome as a major chromosomal defect associated with mental retardation in males, for the most part, and occasionally mild mental retardation in females. Lubs, after studying 3 generations of a family with mental retardation of unknown cause, found that all male members of the family had constriction near the end of the X-chromosome which he referred to as a "fragile X." A subsequent review of a population of mentally retarded individuals in Australia revealed that 30 to 50 percent more males than females were mentally retarded and that 32 percent of the males had more affected brothers than the females with affected sisters and suggested an X-linked mental retardation

(Turner & Turner, 1974). The inability of early investigators to duplicate the initial findings by Lubs was resolved by using folic acid deficient media for chromosome culture (Sutherland, 1977).

Physical characteristics of the fragile X chromosome defect include macroorchism (large testes) (Turner, Gill, and Daniel, 1978), prognathia (projecting jaw), midline facial defects and speech defects. Others with the fragile X defect may appear normal (Turner, Turner, & Collins, 1971). There is no current treatment though investigators are attempting to elucidate the relationship of folic acid to the fragile X defect.

DEVELOPMENTAL ANOMALIES OF THE BRAIN

The developing brain undergoes a variety of structural and biochemical processes in rapid succession from its early embryonic origin to the postnatal period. Consequently, it is highly vulnerable to injury from different sources. The high incidence of congenital malformations of the central nervous system attest to its susceptability to damage during this period. Metabolic and biochemical changes during the continued growth, maturation, and myelination of the nervous system may affect the brain with diseases related to metabolic disturbance of the neurones.

The critical timing of morphogenic (differentiation of cells and tissues) events in the embryonic brain will determine the nature and type of the malformation irregardless of the etiologic report. Experimentally, numerous agents are capable of causing cerebral anomalies including radiation, viral infections, vitamin deficiencies, hormonal changes, and a variety of toxic compounds.

A major cause of developmental disorder of the brain is chromosomal aberration. Those malformations of the brain that are lethal with early demise are omitted. Four of the more common developmental anomalies will be reviewed.

Holoprosencephalophy (Holotelencephaly)

The defect in holoprosencephaly is a large single ventricle due to the failure of the primary cerebral vesicle (telencephalon) to split and expand bilaterally and it is associated with midline facial defects (Yakovlev, 1959). The olfactory bulbs and tracts may be absent or rudimentary (archinenecephaly). Less extensive anomalies include a median cleft lip, hypotelorism (abnormal closeness of eyes) and a depressed nose. Occasionally, a single orbital fossa and eye (cyclopia) is seen.

The timing for the defect is specific (23 to 24 days gestation) and the short vulnerable period accounts for its relative sporadic occurrence (Millen, 1963). The disorder may be associated with trisomies 13, 18 and, C trisomy and deletion of short arm 18 chromosome (Ming, Goodner, & Park, 1976).

Mental retardation is severe. Seizures, rigidity, and rarely hydrocephalus may be present. Diagnostic studies should include a computerized axial tomography (CAT) scan, x-rays of the skull and face, and chromosomal analysis.

Porencephaly and Schizencephalies

The term porencephaly has been used to describe a variety of lesions with gross cerebral defects in the cerebral hemispheres. The cyst-like lesions, which may communicate with the ventricles and occur in late fetal and neonatal life, are appropriately termed encephalomalacic porencephaly (Yakovlev & Wadsworth, 1946). The schizencephalies result from injury to developing cerebral vesicles during the second month of gestation.

Individuals with schizencephaly have spastic double hemiplegia (paralysis) or are nonambulatory, quadraparetic, and unable to talk. Seizures are common. Persons with porencephaly, depending on the location and the size of the lesion, may have hemiplegia, variable mental retardation, seizures, and visual field defects. If the cavity is in the frontal or temporal areas, convulsions may be the only feature. The diagnosis may be possible with a CAT scan and the lesions may be undetected with present neurological procedures.

Hydranencephaly

This disorder is characterized by the almost complete absence of the cerebral hemisphere with remnants of the brainstem allowing for the maintenance of vital functions for extended periods. The child has a normal external appearance.

Several mechanisms have been suggested as to the basic etiology. First, it has been suggested that hydranencephaly is a type of early hydrocephalus that has run its course. In other instances, a genetic defect involving vascular development has been proposed, with occlusion (blockage) of both internal carotid arteries (Lindenberg & Swanson, 1967; Vogel & McClenahan, 1942). Schizencephaly and cortical agenesis (absence) has been caused by defects in embryogenesis and subsequent cellular migration (Yakovlev & Wadsworth, 1946).

The infant may have a somewhat large head. Spontaneous and reflex activity is usually normal. Failure in the development of cortical inhibition results in exaggeration and persisting reflexes. Subsequently, increased muscle tone, hyperactive reflexes, quadraplegia, and decerebration (spastic posturing) develop with infantile spasms and disconjugate (impaired) eye movements. The EEG eventually reveals an isoelectric (flat) pattern because of the absence of cortical neurons.

The diagnosis is based on transillumination of the head in a darkened room using a flashlight projected against the head. Computerized tomography is necessary to rule out expanding large parencephalic cysts or severe obstructive hydrocephalus (Matson, 1969). Massive bilateral subdural collections of fluid can be ruled out by carotid angiography. No treatment is available and some individuals survive for several years (Hoffman & Liss, 1969).

Microcephaly

Microcephaly is defined as a head measuring 2 standard deviations below the mean for age, sex, and gestation (Nelhaus, 1968). Measurement is made around the gabella (forhead) and the occipital protuberance. The small size of the skull usually reflects a small brain except for those instances of premature closure of the sutures (craniosynostosis).

The microcephalies can be divided into primary or secondary categories. Primary microcephaly is caused by abnormal development during the first seven months of gestation and include a variety of insults. Secondary microcephaly is the result of an insult occurring during the last months of gestation or during the perinatal period.

Primary Microcephaly

Primary microcephaly may be transmitted as an autosomal recessive disorder (Benda, 1952; Book, Shut, & Reed, 1953). Numerous migration anomalies are present including macrogyria (see Other Cerebral Defects), micropolygyrias, lissencephaly and schizencephaly. The external skull, small at birth, is characterized by a narrow receding forehead, flat occiput and head circumference more than 3 standard deviations below the mean. Mental retardation, hyperkinetic behavior and deficits in gross and fine motor coordination are seen. Mild to severe spasticity, seizures, and visual defects with cataracts may be additional clinical findings (McKusik, Stauffer, Knox, & Clark, 1966; Scott-Emuakpor, 1977). Consanguineous parents are seen in about 10 percent of cases.

Numerous chromosomal disorders including trisomies, deletions, and translocation syndromes are associated with microcephaly. There are approximately 20 well-defined dysmorphic syndromes with normal karyotype (chromosome characteristics) such as the Cornelia de Lang and Hallerman-Strieff syndromes (Smith, 1976).

Irradiation during the first two trimesters may cause microcephaly; particularly between 4 and 20 weeks gestation (Dekaban, 1968; Hicks, 1953). a variety of infectious agents such as cytomegalic inclusion disease, toxoplasmosis and rubella are resonsible for microcephaly. In experimental animals a wide variety of chemical agents have been implicated including cortisone, nitrogen mustard and sulfhydryl inhibitors. Diabetes mellitus may produce a similar disorder (Ford, 1973).

Secondary Microcephaly

Secondary microcephaly can result from a variety of agents during the last part of the third trimester of the perinatal period and early infancy. Anoxia, infections, trauma, and metabolic disorders all have been implicated with destruction of brain tissue, subsequent poor brain growth, and early closure of small sutures. Both types of microcephaly display a wide spectrum of neurologic disorders ranging from mild to severe mental, motor, and behavioral dysfunctioning.

Serologic studies for intrauterine infections, karotyping with banding, amino acid screening, and skull x-rays are utilized in providing an accurate diagnosis.

Other Cerebral Defects

One group of individuals presenting with retardation and abnormal muscle tone may have hidden cerebral anomalies involving the cerebral convolutions (gyri). Lissencephaly (Aqyria) literally means a "smooth brain" without convulsions. The defects occurs before the end of 3 months gestation. Clinically, one may see severe mental retardation, spastic quadraplegia, microcephaly, seizures, or hypotonia.

Macrogyria (pachygyria) is characterized neuropathologically by coarse and few gyral patterns. The insult inducing this defect occurs up to the fifth month of gestation. The clinical picture is similar to that of lissencephaly.

Micropolygyria results from an insult sustained prior to the fifth month of gestation. The suli (space between gyri) are widened and the gyri are small and numerous. The abnormality may be generalized or only affect focal areas of the cerebral cortex. The clinical picture is that of mental retardation, spasticity, and hypotonia.

HEREDODEGNERATIVE DISORDERS WITH MENTAL RETARDATION

Many of the genetically transmitted neurologic diseases may involve one or more specific areas of the brain. Although the pattern of inheritance may be known, the metabolic defects have not been elucidated to date in most instances. The grouping or classification of these disorders is based on the primary sites of involvement. These are generally referred to as heredodegenerative disease of (1) the basal ganglia; (2) cerebellum, brain stem, and spinal cord; (3) peripheral and cranial nerves; and (4) diffuse cerebral degernerative diseases. With the exception of childhood Huntington's chorea, mental deterioration is usually a late finding relative to the early onset of severe motor and movement disorders in the first three categories. Those hereditary disorders of the central nervous system with characteristic associated skin lesions (neurocutaneous syndromes) will be included in this section.

Huntington's Chorea—Childhood Type

This is an autosomal dominant chronic progressive degenerative disease characterized by choreiform movements (irregular, spasmodic, and involuntary) and mental deterioration (Huntington, 1872). The disease has been found in all races and nationalities (Stevens & Parsonage, 1969) although all early cases in

America were traced to two English brothers. Spontaneous mutations have been documented.

The metabolic error is unclear, but considerable evidence points to a disorder in cerebral monamine metabolism (Barbeau, Chase, & Paulson, 1973) and specifically to an imbalance of the relationship between dopamine and acetylcholine with the brain (Klawans & Rubovits, 1972). Pathologically, the frontal lobes show marked atrophy of the gyri (convolutions) and shrinkage of the straitum (caudate nuceus and putamen) (McCaughey, 1961).

The clinical picture in children differs from that of adults and presents with seizures, rigidity, hyopkinesia (diminished or slow movement), and mental deterioration (Jervis, 1963; Collman & Stoller, 1963). Cerebellar symptoms and choreoathetosis (abnormal movements of the body) may also occur. The occurence in children under 14 years of age is about 5 percent and in about 70 percent of cases the child received the gene from his father.

The EEG is often abnormal and the CAT scan may demonstrate ventricular dilatation that is most marked in the region of the caudate nucleus (Terrence, Delany & Albert, 1977). Reserpine or phenothiazines may alleviate the choreiform movements and antiparkinson drugs may benefit the rigidity (no treatment has been found effective in reversing the dementia).

Familial Calcification of Basal Ganglia (Fahr's Disease)

This disorder is characterized by mental deterioration, seizures, and rigidity appearing early in life and was first described by Baumberger in 1855. The outstanding feature is the deposition of large quantities of calcium within the walls of the cerebral blood vessels, specifically those of the dentate and lenticular nuclei. Hypoparathyroidism can be ruled out by normal blood calcium and phosphorus levels.

Sudanophilic Cerebral Sclerosis

This disorder usually occurs between five and eight years of age with onset of mild intellectual impairment and disturbance of gait. Early seizures are common, as well as attacks of crying and screaming. Swallowing is disturbed in about 30 percent of the children. Visual impairment occurs later in the course of the disease. Abnormal pigmentation or classic adrenal insufficiency may be associated with this disorder (Schaumberg, 1975).

Chemical analysis of the brain demonstrates an accumulation of longchain fatty acids suggesting a deficit in an enzyme system responsible for the degradation of the long chain fatty acids (Menkes & Corbo, 1977).

The CAT scan may demonstrate a bilateral symmetric decrease in the density of periventricular white matter (Robertson, Gomez, Reese, & Okazaki, 1977).

Pelizaeus-Merzbacher Disease

This rare disorder, a slowly progressive demyelinating (destruction or loss of myelin) condition (Merzbacher, 1910; Pelizaeus, 1885) may appear in infancy or early childhood with roving eye movements and dysrhythmic trembling. Cerebellar symptoms, involuntary movement, and spasticity may appear as the disease progresses. Mental degeneration may be an early or late feature. Pathologically, the loss of myelin is scattered giving a "tigroid" appearance on microsopic examination. The white matter lipids may be normal or reduced on chemical analysis of the brain. In the absence of other affected members of the family, the diagnosis is difficult to make with certainty during the lifetime of the patient.

Other Cerebral Defects of Myelin

The following diseases are characterized by pathological changes involving the cerebral white matter, early onset in the first two years of life, mental retardation, and their relatively low incidence.

Spongy Degeneration of the Cerebral White Matter (Canavan's Sclerosis)

Spongy degeneration of the cerebral white matter (Canavan, 1931) appears between the second and fourth month of life and includes mental retardation, optic atrophy, and hypotonia. A progressive and significant enlargement of the head is often seen by six months of age. Though death usually occurs prior to 5 years the onset may not occur until after 5 years (Adachi et al., 1973). Pathologically, the white matter is replaced by a network of fluid containing cystic spaces giving the characteristic sponge-like appearance.

Cultured skin fibroblasts reveal an elevation in the activities of several lysosomal enzymes; alpha-galactosidase, xylosidase, and beta-glucosidase (Milunsky, Kanter, Spielvogel, Shahood, 1972). The significance of this observation is obscure. The diagnosis of Canavan's disease can be made on the basis of progressive neurologic deterioration, megalocephaly (enlarging head) and CAT scan findings, which demonstrate the cystic appearance of white matter.

Alexander's Disease

Seizures, macrocephaly, and spasticity occurring in the first year of life is a leukodystrophy associated with mental retardation (Alexander, 1949). An esoinophilic material is found in the cytoplasm of nerve cells and along the surface of the brain. The nature of the deposit and relation to the disease is unknown (Sherwin & Berthrong, 1970).

Cockayne's Syndrome

This syndrome of unusual facies (sunken eyes and large ears), growth failure, and mental retardation was first described in 1936 by Cockayne. Lack of subcutaneous fat, retinal deterioration, and skin photosensitivity are associated findings (Macdonald, Fitch, & Lewis, 1960). Thickening of the skull bones and deformities of the spine (kyphoscoliosis) are evident on radiographic examinations. Patchy demyelination of the white matter similar to that seen in Pelizium-Merzbacher's disease is seen pathologically. The fact that skin fibroblasts show sensitivity to ultraviolet light can be utilized in the prenatal and postnatal diagnosis (Schmikel, Chu, Trosko, & Chang, 1977).

Chediak-Higashi Syndrome

This syndrome is characterized by mental retardation, partial albinism, sensitivity to light, enlargement of the liver or spleen, and enlarged lymph nodes. Abnormal leucocytes and disorders of platelet and white cells comprise the hematologic picture. A progressive spinocerebellar degeneration may be present (Donohue & Bain, 1957). Intracytoplasmic inclusions within the neurons are found throughout the nervous system including the peripheral nerves. The cause is unknown.

Mental Retardation With Cutaneous Lesions (Neurocutaneous Snydromes)

The term "neurocutaneous" is used to describe a group of diseases with neural and cutaneous involvement, associated with mental retardation, and of hereditary or embryonic origin. In most instances, the diagnoses are made by characteristic skin lesions and associated clinical findings.

Tuberous Sclerosis

Tuberous sclerosis is an autosomal dominant inherited disorder manifested chiefly by mental retardation, epilepsy, and skin lesions. The frequency is 1 in 30,000 and has variable penetrance and expressivity and spontaneous mutations may occur.

Pathologically, abnormalities may be found in the brain, eyes, skin, kidneys, bones, heart, and lungs. In the brain, numerous hard areas of gliotic tissue of varying size (tubers) may be found. Some project into the ventricles and appear like "candle drippings." Obstructive hydrocephalus may occur from interference with the flow of cerebrospinal fluid.

The characteristic skin lesions of adenoma sebaceum (angiofibroma) occur as a papular (elevated) rash over the nose, chin, cheeks, and malar areas. These may vary in size from pinhead to pea size and appear between 1 and 5 years of age (Pampiglione & Moynahan, 1976). Depigmented nevi (birthmarks) resembling vitiligo occur over the trunk and extremities appearing at birth or before the age of 2 (Gold & Freeman, 1965). Flattened fibromata may appear on the trunk, gingivae, and around toe and finger nails. Coffee colored spots (café au lait) and areas of gray-green thickened skin (shagreen patch) are also observed.

The degree of mental retardation varies widely. About two-thirds of patients diagnosed as tuberous sclerosis may be retarded while others may have normal intelligence with few characteristic lesions.

Seizures are frequent in all patients with tuberous sclerosis. Infantile spasms (infantile polymyoclonus) with a grossly abnormal electroencephalogram (hypsarythmia) may present as the initial finding in infants (Roth & Epstein, 1971). Tumors occur intracranially in about 15 percent of patients with tuberous sclerosis: flattened ocular tumors are seen, tumors of the kidney, bones, and lungs may show neoplastic changes (Dawson, 1954).

The diagnosis of tuberous sclerosis is based on the characteristic skin lesions, mental retardation, and epilepsy. Radiography and CAT scan may reveal scattered calcium deposits, tubers, or obstructive hydrocephalus if present. Ocular examination is indicated in all instances where the diagnosis is suspected. One must remember that because of the variable degrees of penetrance and expressity, numerous patients with incomplete forms of tuberous sclerosis have been documented (Bundey & Evans, 1969; Lagos & Gomez, 1967).

Encephalotrigeminal Angiomatosis (Sturge-Weber-Dimitri Syndrome)

The classic description of Sturge-Weber-Dimitri syndrome consists of a port wine vascular nevus often in the distribution of the first division of the trigeminal nerve. Contralateral focal seizures, contralateral hemiparesis or visual field defects, and ipsilateral intracranial calcifications are often seen (Sturge, 1879). Mental retardation may occur in 60 percent of the cases. It is a dominantly inherited disorder with varying degrees of expressivity although recessive inheritance has been postulated for a number of families.

The essential pathologic feature of the condition is an angioma of the leptomeninges (soft membranes enveloping brain) on the side of the face where the port wine lesion is located and involves the occipital and parietal areas. Calcifications are usually formed under the vascular malformations and present on x-rays as sinusoid, linear streaks of calcium deposits.

The cutaneous port wine nevus is present at birth and involves the supraorbital region of the face (Alexander, 1949; Alexander & Norman, 1960) and may be associated with unilateral congential glaucoma due to angiomatous lesions in the choroid membrane of the eye. Seizures occur in 90 percent of affected persons and the seizures may appear in the first year of life. The diagnosis is usually made from the physical findings. The CAT scan will reveal calcifications unilaterally and cortical atrophy with ventricular dilation on the affected side. Treatment is symptomatic, although successful cases of early surgery have been reported (Falconer & Ruschworth, 1960).

A somewhat similar syndrome of scattered cutaneous vascular nevi over various parts of the body with hypertrophy of the bone and occasional seizures with intracerebral calcification has been described as the Klippel-Trenaunay syndrome (Heuser, 1971; Kramer, 1968).

Neurofibromatosis (von Recklinghausen's Disease)

Mental retardation occurs in only approximately 10 percent of persons affected by this disorder of multiple tumors of the central nervous systems and peripheral nerves, cutaneous pigmentation, and lesions of the vascular systems and organs (von Recklinghausen, 1882). It is the most common single gene defect affecting the nervous system and has a frequency of 1 in 2000.

Neurofibromatosis occurs along major peripheral and cranial nerves, primarily the optic and acoustic nerves with visual and auditory defects. Meningiomas and gliomas may occur in the cerebrum, cerebellar, and spinal cord.

Children with major complications of neurofibromatosis (severe mental retardation, seizures, scoliosis, and intracranial masses) tend to have a higher incidence of affected mothers (Miller & Hall, 1978). The most common skin lesions are the café au lait spots. Various types of cutaneous tumors may be observed. The diagnois is based on the presence of 5 or more café au lait spots one cm or more in diameter (Crowe, School, & Neel, 1956) and associated physical findings.

Ataxia-telangiectasis (Louis-Bar Syndrome)

This disorder is a recessively inherited condition associated with progressive ataxia, occulocutaneous lesions, and increased susceptibility to bronchopulmonary infections (Bodero & Sedgwick, 1958; Louis-Bar, 1941; Syllabu & Henner, 1926). Cerebellar signs (ataxia) appear in early infancy with subsequent appearance of an intention tremor, dysarthric speech, and choreoathetoid movements. The characteristic superficially dilated blood vessels appear between 4 and 6 years of age and exhibit a "butterfly" distribution, the pattern over the bridge of the nose. Ears and neck may also be involved. The telangiectatic lesions of the bulbar conjunctiva (eyeballs) is especially striking. Frequent upper respiratory tract infections are a common occurrence and thought to be related to a decreased serum gamma-1A globulin (Peterson, Kelly, & Good, 1964). Mental retardation occurs as the disease progresses.

The diagnosis is not difficult when the occulocutaneous lesions, neurologic status, and the characteristic defect in serum immunoglobulin are present.

Other cutaneous syndromes with mental retardation include incontinentia pigmenti (Block-Sulzberger syndrome), keratosis follicularis (Darier's disease), anhidrotic ectodermal dysplasia, chondro-ectodermal dysplasis (Ellis-van Creufel syndrome), centrofacial lentiginosis and albinism (Aita, 1966).

ACQUIRED LESIONS OF THE BRAIN

Cerebral Birth Injury

The incidence of intracranial cerebral injury at birth has been greatly reduced by modern obstetric techniques. Complications such as abnormal fetal presentation, prolonged or precipitate labor, and trials of labor, can theoretically be prevented or resolved by frequent prenatal examinations, ultrasound imaging and fetal monitoring techniques.

Physical trauma to the fetal head may produce extracranial lesions such as cephalohematoma and *caput succedaneum*. Cephalohemotoma indicates a hemorrhage under the periosteum (fibrous membrane) of the bone produced by differences in the intra and extrauterine pressure and is rarely associated with permanent sequelae. *Caput succedaneum* represents an area of swelling due to edema of the scalp and microscopic hemorrhages and is usually begnign. Subdural hematomas in the newborn tend to be acute and may result in shock and death within 36 hours. Those infants who survive after 36 hours may present with increasing signs of cerebral injury. Subdural taps are usually positive (Schrieber, 1959) and surgical evacuation is indicated. Normal development of the infant is possible after surgery, in the absence of other serious cerebral injuries (Schipke, Riege, & Scoville, 1954).

Physical trauma with secondary cerebral circulatory disturbances such as shock or vascular insufficiency alone is rarely the cause of brain injury. More often metabolic disorders—hypoxia, acidosis and hypoglycemia—may injure the brain directly or result in edema, swelling, and secondary circulatory disturbance (Brann & Myers, 1975; Myers, 1977). The relative resistance of the newborn brain to lack of oxygen has been known for years (Fazekas, Alexander, & Himwich, 1941) in the absence of antecedent brain damage. This resistance to anoxia or oxygen lack has been attributed to a greater dependance on glycolytic metabolism and decreased energy demands in comparison to the adult brain. One report (Gilles & Murphy, 1969) revealed evidence of white matter defects of the brain in 53 percent of infants who has expired with no known evidence of central nervous system disease. Comparison with controls failed to identify any single specific etiology. It was concluded that the changes in white matter could be the results of several nonspecific insults or combination of insults that produced damage during the critical period of myelinization. These white matter defects could potentially disrupt synaptic connections and lead to a variety of intellectual deficits ranging from severe retardation to various types of learning disabilities.

Infections of the Nervous System

Infections of the nervous system are a major cause of mental retardation and are significant because of preventative and therapeutic implications. This section will be concerned with infections of maternal origin (congenital) and those acquired postnatally.

Maternal infections may pass from the mother to the fetus by way of the placenta. Those diseases that are transferred that affect the nervous system of the immature fetus include: rubella, cytomegalovirus infection, toxoplasmosis, and herpes simplex virus. The majority of women infected during pregnancy have no apparent signs of the disease.

Table 13-10

Diagnostic Features of Neonatal Infections Compared to Erythroblaslosis Fetalis

	Jaundice	Anemia	Hepato-Splenomegaly	Thrombocytopenia	Purpura	Chorioretinitis	Intracranial Calcification
Toxoplasmosis	+	+	+	+	+	+	+
Cytomegalic Inclusion disease	+	+	+	+	–	+	+
Rubella syndrome	+	+	+	?	+	+	?
Herpes simplex	+	+	+	?	?	?	?
Septicemia	+	+	+	+	+	–	–
Congenital Syphillis	+	+	+	+	+	+	–
Erythroblastosis fetalis	+	+	+	+	–	–	–

Modified from Oski and Naiman (1966)

+ Present in 1–25% of cases or more; –, not described; ?, anecdotal reports.

Table 13-11

Incidence of Mortality and Residua After Various Forms
of Meningitis

Infection	Number of Cases	Deaths	Mental Retardation or Major Neurologic Residua	Minor Neurologic Residua
Hemophilus influenzae (1961–1964)	40	7	4	11
Diplococcus pneumoniae (1960–1964)	10	2	0	1
Neisseria menigitidis (1960–1964)	12	0	1	3
Mixed infections (1948–1963)	20	7	6	0

From Menkes. *Textbook of Child Neurology* (2nd Ed.). Philadelphia: Lea & Febiger, 1980

Diagnostic features of some transplacentally acquired infections are generalized in the neonatal period, and are not specific for any particular infection, hence the reliance on specific laboratory tests to establish the etiology. Within the TORCH Complex toxoplasmosis, cytomegalovirus, rubella, herpes simplex, and others common symptoms and signs include: (1) jaundice, (2) anemia, (3) hepatosplenomegaly (disease of liver and spleen), (4) aremia, (5) chorioretinitis (inflammation of the retina and choroid), (6) anemia, (7) thromobocylopenia, (8) purpura (a condition characterized by hemorrhage into the skin), (9) skin rash, and (10) intracranial calcifications (Oski & Naiman, 1966). Septicemia (systemic disease caused by multiplication of microorganisms in the blood), congenital syphilis, and erthroblastosis fetalis must be considered in the differential diagnosis of the above diseases.

Postnatally, bacterial meningitis is quite different clinically from that of older children and adults and the sequelae and mortality is much greater than that of any other age. The incidence of meningitis in the premature is 1 in every 450 cases as compared to 1 in every 7700 cases in the full term infant (Groover, Sutherland, & Handing, 1961). The cases of high morbidity and mortality are attributed to the delay in diagnoisis, rare organisms that are lethal, and difficulty ascertaining potency of conventional antibiotics with freedom from toxicity (Shen, 1978).

The diagnosis of meningitis in the newborn is difficult. The signs and symptoms are subtle, nonspecific, and deceptive. Fever, convulsions, anorexia, vomiting, respiratory distress, lethargy, or irritability may be the earliest clues to indicate the initiation of laboratory tests to confirm the diagnosis of meningitis.

The diagnosis of meningitis requires prompt examination and culture of cere-

Table 13-12
Major Complications Seen in
71 Children After Recovery
from Meningitis*

Complication	Number of Cases
Mental retardation	3
Seizures	3
Hemi- or quadriparesis	1
Bilateral deafness	4
Vestibular disturbance	1
Hydrocephalus	1
TOTAL	13 (18%)

From Menkes. *Textbook of Child Neurology* (2nd Ed). Philadelphia: Lea & Febiger, 1980

brospinal fluid. Examination of cerebrospinal fluid glucose, protein, sodium chloride, and white cells aid in establishing the diagnosis. Test for fungi may be appropriate in the differential diagnosis.

The outcome of meningitis depends on several factors. The age of the patient, nature of the infectious agent, duration of symptoms prior to treatment, and the type and amount of antibiotic used. A high residual of complications is still observed although the mortality rate from all forms of meningitis has decreased (see Table 13-11).

Major complications still occur and include mental retardation, epilepsy, deafness, and cerebral palsy (see Table 13-12).

In long term followup studies on patients with H influenza meningitis, 29 percent had significant handicaps, and 48 percent were apparently free of sequelae (Sell, Webb, Pate, & Doyne, 1972).

Mental retardation, epilepsy, gait disturbances, and difficulties with speech and vision are sequelae common to all of the viral encephatides.

REFERENCES

Adachi, M, et al. Spongy degeneration of the central nervous system (Van Bogaert-Bertrand Type): Canavan's disease. *Journal of Human Pathology*, 1973, *4*, 331

Adams, DA, & Lyon, G. *Neurology of Hereditary Metabolic Diseases in Children*. New York: Hemisphere Publishing Corp., 1982

Aita, J.A *Neurocutaneous Diseases*. Springfield: Charles C. Thomas, 1966

Alexander, GL, & Norman, RM. *The Sturge-Weber Syndrome*. Bristol: John Wright and Co., Ltd., 1960

Alexander, WS. Progressive fibrinoid degeneration of fibrillary astrocytes associated with mental retardation in hydrocephalic infant. *Brain*, 1949, *72*, 373–381

Bain, AD, & Gauld, IK. Multiple congenital abnormalities associated with ring chromosomes. *Lancet*, 1963, *2*, 304–305

Bamberger, H. Beobachtugen und Bemerkugen über Hinkrankheiten. *Verh. Phys. Med. Ges. (Wurzburg),* 1856, *6,* 283

Barbeau, A, Chase, TN,.& Paulson, GW. *Huntington's Chorea 1872–1972.* New York: Raven Press, 1972

Barr, ML, & Bertram, EG. A morphological distinction between neurones of the male and female and the behavior of the nucleolar satellite during accelerated nucleo protein synthesis. *Nature,* 1949, *163,* 676–679

Bauman, RJ, & Markesberry, WB. Juvenile amaurotic idiocy (neuronal ceroidlipofuscinosis) and lymphocytic fingerprint profiles. *Annals of Neurology,* 1978, *4,* 531–536

Benda, CE. *Developmental Disorders of Mentation and Cerebral Palsies.* New York: Grune & Stratton, Inc., 1952

Berman, JL, Cunningham, GC, Day, RW, Ford, R, & Hsia, DY. Causes for high phenylalanine with normal tyrosine. *American Journal of Diseases of Children,* 1969, *117,* 54–56

Bodero, E, & Sedgwich, RP. Ataxiatelangiectasia: A familial syndrome of progressive cerebellar ataxia, oculocutaneous telanglectasia and frequent pulmonary infection. *Pediatrics,* 1958, *21,* 526–554

Book, JA, Shut, JW, & Reed, AC. A clinical and genetical study of microcephaly. *American Journal of Mental Deficiency,* 1953, *57,* 637–652

Brann, AW, & Myers, RE. Central nervous system findings in the newborn monkey following severe *in utero* partial asphyxia. *Neurology,* 1975, *25,* 327

Bronstein, TP. Gynecomastia. *Endocrinology,* 1939, *24,* 274–277

Bundey, S, & Evans, K. Tuberous sclerosis: A genetic study. *Journal of Neurology, Neurosurgery and Psychiatry,* 1969, *32,* 591–603

Casperson, T, Lindsten, J, & Zech, L. The nature of structural X chromosome aberrations in Turner's Syndrome as revealed by quinacrine mustard fluorescence analysis. *Heredity,* 1970, *60,* 287–291

Casperson, T, Lindsten, J, Zech, L, Bucleton, KE, & Price, H. Four patients with Trisomy 8 indentified by fluorescence and giemsa banding techniques. *Journal of Medical Genetics,* 1972, *9,* 1–7

Chediak, M. Nouvelle anomalic leucocytaire de caractére constitutionnel et familial. *Revue D'Hematologie,* 1952, *7,* 362–367

Cockayne, EA. Dwarfism with retinal atrophy and deafness. *Archives of Disease in Childhood,* 1936, *11,* 1–8

Collman, RD, & Stoller, A. A life table for mongols in Victoria, Australia. *Journal of Mental Deficiency Research,* 1963, *7,* 53–59

Cornblath, M, & Schwartz, R. *Disorders of Carbohydrate Metabolism in Infancy.* (Second ed.), Philadelphia: W. B. Saunders, 1976

Crower, F, Scholl, W, & Neel, J. *Clinical, Pathological and Genetic Study of Multiple Neurofibromatosis.* Springfield: Charles C. Thomas, 1956

Cunningham, MD, & Ragsdale, JL. Genital anomalies of an XXXXY male subject. *Journal of Urology,* 1972, *107,* 872–874

Dawson, J. Pulmonary tuberous sclerosis. *Quarterly Journal of Medicine,* 1954, *47,* 113–145

de Grouchy, J, Royer, P, Salmon, C, & Lamy, M. Délétion partielle des bras longs de chromosome 18. *Pathologia et Microbiologia,* 1964, *12,* 579–585

de Grouchy, J, & Turleau, C. *Clinical Atlas of Human Chromosomes.* New York: John Wiley, 1977

Dekaban, A. Abnormalities in children exposed to x-radiation during various stages of gestation: Tentative timetable of radiation injury to the human fetus. *Part I. U. Nuelean Medicine,* 1968, *9,* 471

Donohue, WL, & Bain, HW.: Chediak-Higashi syndrome. *Pediatrics,* 1957, *20,* 416–430

Falconer, MA, & Ruschworth, RG. Treatment of encephalo-trigeminal angiomatosis (Sturge-Weber Disease), by hemispherectomy. *Archives of Disease in Childhood,* 1960, *35,* 433–447

Farmer, TW. *Pediatric Neurology.* New York: Harper & Row, 1975

Fazekas, JF, Alexander, FA, & Himwich, HE. Tolerance of the newborn to anoxia. *American Journal of Physiology,* 1941, *139,* 281–288

Fishler, K, Koch, R, & Donnell, GN. Comparison of mental development in individuals with mosaic and trisomy 21, Down's snydrome. *Pediatrics*, 2976, *58*, 744–748

Ford, FR. *Diseases of the Nervous System in Infancy, Childhood and Adolescence* (6th ed.). Springfield: Charles C. Thomas Publisher, 1973

Fraser, MB, & Mitchell, A. "Kalmuc idiocy." *Journal of Mental Science*, 1876, *22*, 169–179

Gautieres, F, Arasenio-Nunes, ML, & Aicardi, J. *Mucolipidosis IV*, 1979, *10*, 321–331

German, J, Lejeune, J, Macintyre, MN, & de Grouchy, J. Chromosomal autoradiography in the *cri du chat* syndrome. *Cytogenetics*, 1964, *3*, 347–352

Ghadini, H, et al. Hyperlysinemia associated with retardation. *New England Journal of Medicine*, 1965, *273*, 723

Gilles, FH, & Murphy, SF. Perinatal telen-cephalic leucoencephalopathy. *Journal Neurology, Neurosurgery and Psychiatry*, 1969, *32*, 404–413

Gold, AP, & Freeman, JM. Depigmented nevi: The earliest sign of tuberous sclerosis. *Pediatrics*, 1965, *35*, 1003–1005

Greenstein, RM, Harris, DJ, Luzzatti, L, & Cann, H. Cytogenetic analysis of a boy with the XXXY syndrome: Origin of the X chromosomes. *Pediatrics*, 1970, *45*, 677–686

Groover, RV, Sutherland, JM, & Landing, BH. Purulent meningitis of newborn infants: Eleven year experience in the antibiotic era. *New England Journal of Medicine*, 1961, *264*, 1115–1118

Haberland, C. Alzheimer's disease in Down's syndrome. *Acta Neurologica Belgica*, 1969, *69*, 369–380

Hanley, WB, Linsao, LS, & Netley, C. The efficacy of dieting therapy for phenyketonuria. *Cananadian Medical Association Journal*, 1971, *104*, 1089–1092

Heuser, M. De L'entité nosolo qique des angiomatose neurocutanées (Sturge-weber et Klippel-Trenaunay). *Nevue Neurologique*, 1971, *124*, 213–228

Hicks, SP. Developmental malformations produced by radiation. *American Journal of Radiology*, 1953, *69*, 272–280

Hirschhorn, K, Copper, HL, & Firesehen, JL. Deletion of short arms of chromosome 4–5 in a child with defects of midline fusine. *Human Genetics*, 1965, *1*, 479–483

Hoffman, J, & Liss, L. Hydranencephaly. *Acta Paeiatria Scandanavica*, 1969, *58*, 297

Holmes EW, & O'Brien, JS. Sepration of glycoprotein-derived oligosaccharides by thin layer chromatography. *Annals of Biochemistry*, 1979, *93*, 167–170

Hsu, TC, & Pomerat, CM. "Mammalian chromosome *in vitro:*" II: A method for spreading the chromosomes of cells in tissue cultures. *Journal of Heredity*, 1953, *44*, 23–29

Hug, E. Das geschlectsv erhaltnus beim Mongolismus. *Annale Paediatrici*, 1951, *177*, 31–54

Humble, R, & Collart, M. Oligosaccharides in urine of patients with glycoprotein storage diseases. I. Rapid detection by thin layer chromatography. *Clinica Chimica Acta*, 1974, *60*, 143–145

Huntington, G. On chorea. *Medical Surgical Reporter*, 1872, *26*, 317

Jacobs, RA, Baikie, AG, Court-Brown, WM, McGregor, TN, & Strong, JA. The somatic chromosomes in mongolism. *Lancet*, 1956, *2*, 423–425

Jervis, GA. Huntington's chorea in childhood. *Archives of Neurology*, 1963, *9*, 244–257

Jeune, M., et al. Hereditary inteolerance to fructose: Apropos of a ruse. *Pediatrics*, 1961, *16*, 605

Kaufman, S, Holtzman, A, Milstien, S, Butler, IJ, & Krumholz, A. Phenylketonuria due to a deficiency of dihydropterine reductase. *New England Journal of Medicine*, 1975, *293*, 785–790.

Klawans, HL, & Rubovits, R. Central cholinergic-anticholinergic antagonism in Huntington's chorea. *Neurology*, 1972, *22*, 107–116

Klinefelter, HF, Reifenstein, EC, & Albright, F. Syndrome characterized by gynaecomastia, aspermatogenesis without A-leydigism and increased excretion of follicle stimulating harmoné. *Journal of Clinical Endocrinology*, 1942, *2*, 615–627

Kohn, G, Livni, N, Ornoy, A, Sekeles, E, Legum, C, Bach, G, & Cohen, MM. Prenatal diagnosis of mucolipidosis IV by electronmicroscopy. *Journal of Pediatrics*, 1977, *90*, 62–66

Kohn, J, Ornoy, A, Sekeles, B, Cohen, R, & Sekeles, E. Electron microscopy of cultured skin fibroblasts and amniotic cells in the diagnosis of hereditary storage diseases. *Monographs of Human Genetics*, 1978, *10*, 32–39

Kolodny, EH, & Cable, WJ. Inborn errors of metabolism. *Annals of Neurology*, 1977, *3*, 221–232

Kolodny, EH, Rachavan, SS, Ellison, PH, Lyerla, TA, & Biemer, EG. AB variant of GM_2 gangliosidosis: Diagnosis by *in vivo* assay of GM_2 clearing activity in clutured skin fibroblasts. *Annals of Neurology*, 1980, *8*, 215 (abstract)

Komrower, GM, & Lee, DH. Long term follow up of galactosemia. *Archives of Diseases in Children*, 1970, *45*, 367–374

Kramer, W. Klippel-Trenaunay syndrome. In PJ Vinken, & GW Bruyn, (Eds.), *Handbook of Clinical Neurology*. Amsterdam: North Holland Publishing Co., 1968

Lagos, JC, & Gomez, MR. Tuberous sclerosis: reappraisal of a clinical entity. *Mayo Clinic Proceedings*, 1967, *42*, 26–49

Lasser, A, Carter, DM, & Mahoney, MJ. Ultrastructure of the skin in mucdopholysacchararidosis. *Archives of Pathology*, 1975, *99*, 173–176

Latt, SA. Localization of sister chromatid exchanges in human chromosomes. *Science*, 1974, *185*, 74–76

Lejeune, J, Berger, R, Lafourcade, J, & Réthoré, MO. La délétion partielle de bras long du chromosome 18. Individualisation d'un nouvel état morbide. *Annales de Genetique*, 1966, *3*, 32–36

Lejeune, J, Gautier, M, & Turpin, R. Le mongolisme, premier exemple d'abberration autosomique humaine. *Competes Rendus Hebdomadaires des Séances de l'Academie des Sciences*, 1959. *248*, 1721–1722

Lejeune, J, Lafourcade, J, Berger, R, Vialette, J, Boeswillwald, M, Seringe, P, & Rutpin, R. Trois cas de délétion partialle du bras cour d'un chromosome 5. *C.R. Acad. Science* [D] (Paris), 1963, *257*, 3098

Leuke, RR, & Levy, N. Maternal phenylketonuria and hyperphenylalaninemia: An international survey of the outcome of untreated and treated pregnancies. *New England Journal of Medicine*, 1980, *303*, 1202–1208

Lindenberg, R, & Swanson, PD. Infantile hydrancephaly, report of five cases of infarction of both cerebral hemipheres in infancy. *Brain*, 1967, *90*, 839–850

Loeb, H, Tondeur, M, Toppet, M, & Clemer, N. Clinical biochemical and ultra structural studies of an atypical form of mucopolysaccharidosis. *Acta Pediatrica Scandinavica*, 1969, *55*, 220–228

Louis-Bar, D. Sur un syndrome progressif comprenant des telangiectasies cappallaires cutanées et conjunctiva symetriques à disposition naevoide et des trouble cerebelleux. *Confinia de Neurologica*, 1941, *4*, 32–42

Lubs, HA. A marker X chromosome. *American Journal of Human Genetics*, 1969, *21*, 231–244

Macdonald, WB, Fitch, K, & Lewis, IC. Cockayne's syndrome. *Pediatrics*, 1960, *25*, 997–1007

Makino, S, & Nishimura, E. Water pretreatment swuash technique: A new and simple practical method for the chromosome study of animals. *Stain Technology*, 1952, *27*, 1–7

Martin, JJ, & Centrick, C. Morphologic study of skin biopsy specimens: A contribution to the diagnosis of metabolic disorders with involvement of the nervous system. *Journal of Neurology, Neurosurgery and Psychiatry*, 1978, *41*, 232–248

Matson, DD. *Neurosurgery of Infancy and Childhood* (2nd Ed.). Springfield; Charles C. Thomas-Publisher, 1969

McCaughey, WTE. Pathologic spectrum of Huntington's chorea. *Journal of Nervous and Mental Disease*, 1961, *133*, 91–103

McKusik, VA, Stauffer, M, Knox, DL, & Clark, DB. Chrioretinopathy with hereditary microcephaly. *Archives of Opthalmology*, 1966, *75*, 597–600

Menkes, JH, & Corbo, LM. Adrenoleuko dystrophy: Accumulation of cholesterol esters with very long chain fatty acids. *Neurology*, 1977, *27*, 928–932

Merzbacher, L. Eine eigenartigo familiär hereditäre Erkrankungsform. *Z. Ges. Neurol. Psychiat.*, 1910, *3*, 1

Millen, JW. Timing of human congenital malformations. *Developmental Medicine and Child Neurology*, 1963, *5*, 343–350

Miller, M, & Hall, JG. Possible maternal effect on severity of neurofibromatosis. *Lancet*, 1978, *2*, 1071–1073

Miller, OJ, & Breaj, WR. Current concepts in genetics: Autosomal chromosomal disorders and variations. *New England Journal of Medicine*, 1976, *294*, 596–597

Milunsky, A, Kanfer, JN, Spielvogel, C, & Shahood, JM. Elevated lysomal enzyme activities in Canavan's disease. *Pediatric Research*, 1972, *6*, 425

Ming, PL, Goodner, DM, Park, TS. Cytogenetic variants in holoprosencephaly. *American Journal of Diseases of Childhood*, 1976, *130*, 864–867

Moric-Petrovic, S, Laca, Z, Markovic, S, & Markovic, V. "49, XXXXY karotype in a mentally retarded boy." *Journal of Mental Deficiency Research*, 1973, *17*, 73–80

Myers, RE. Experimental models of perinatal brain damage: Relevance to human pathology. In L. Gluck, (Ed.), *Intrauterine Asphyxia and Developing Fetal Brain*. Chicago: Year Book Medical Publishers, 1977

Nadler, HL, Inouye, I, & Hsia, DY. Clinical galactosemia: A study of 55 cases. In DY Hsia, (Ed.), *Galactosemia*. Springfield: Charles C. Thomas, 1979

Nelhaus, G. Head circumference from birth to eighteen years. *Pediatrics*, 1968, *41*, 106–114

Niederwieser, A, Curtius, HS, Bettonio, J, Bieri, J, Schircks, B, Viscontini, M, & Schauls, J. Atypical phenylketonuria caused by 7–8, dihydrobioterine synthetase deficiency. *Lancet*, 1979, *1*, 131–133

Nikkila, EA, Somersalo, O, Pitkanen, E, & Perheentupa, J. Hereditary fructose intolerance: An inborn deficiency of liver adolase complex. *Metabolism*, 1962, *11*, 727–731

Oskin, FA, & Naiman, JL. *Hematological Problems in the Newborn*. London: Saunders, 1966

Norden, NE, Lundbald, S, Svenson, & Autio, S. Characterization of two mannose containing oligosaccharides isolated from the urine of patients with mannosidosis. *Biochemistry*, 1974, *13*, 871

Pampiglione, G, & Moynahan, EJ. The tuberous sclerosis syndrome: clinical and EEG studies in 100 children. *Journal of Neurology, Neurosurgery and Psychiatry*, 1976, *39*, 666–673

Parker, CE, Mavalwala, J, Koch, R, Hatashita, A, & Derencsenyl, A. The syndrome associated with the partial deletion of the long arms of chromosome 18 (18q-), *California Medicine*, 1972, *117*, 65–72

Pelizaeus, F. Ueber eine eigentumliche Form spasticher Läh mung mit Cerebraler-scheinungen auf hereditärer Grundlage. *Arch. Psychiatr. Nervenkr*, 1885, *16*, 698

Perry, TL, Hansen, S, Tischler, B, Bunting, R, & Berry, K. Carnosinemia. *New England Journal of Medicine*, 1967, *277*, 1219–1227

Peterson, RDA, Kelly, WD, & Good, RA. Ataxia-telangiectasisa: Its association with a defective thymus, immunologic deficiency deasease and malignancy. *Lancet*, 1964, *1*, 1189–1190

Priet, JH. *Medical Cytogenetics and Cell Culture*. (2nd ed.). Philadelphia: Lei and Febigen, 1977

Riccardi, VM, Atkins, L, & Holmes, LB. Absent patellae, mild mental retardation, skeletal and genitourinary anomalies and C group autosomal mosaicism. *Journal of Pediatrics*, 1970, *77*, 664–672

Robertson, WC, Gomez, MR, Reese, DF, & Okazaki, H. Computerized tomography in demylinating disease of the young. *Neurology*, 1977, *27*, 838–842

Rollins, HR. Personality in mongolism with special reference to the incidence of catatonic psychosis. *American Journal of Diseases of Childhood*, 1946 *48*, 764–779

Roth, JC, & Epstein, GJ. Infantile spasms and hypopigmented macules: Early manifestations of tuberous sclerosis. *Archives of Neurology*, 1971, *25*, 547–551

Schipke, R, Riege, D, & Scoville, W. Acute subdural hemorrhage at birth. *Pediatrics*, 1954, *14*, 468–474

Schaumberg, HH, Powers, JM, Reine, CS, Suzuki, K, & Richardson, EP. Adrenoleukodystrophy: A clinical and pathological study of 17 cases. *Archives of Neurology*, 1975. *32*, 577–591

Schmickel, RD, Chu, ENY, Trosko, JE, & Chang, CC. Cockayne syndrome: A cellular sensitivity to ultra violet light. *Pediatrics*, 1977, *60*, 135–139

Schneider, EL, Chaillet, JR, & Tice, RR. In vivo Bud R labelling of mammalian chromosomes. *Experimental Cell Research*, 1976, *100*, 396–399

Schreiber, MS. Acute subdural hematoma in the newborn. *Medical Journal of Australia*, 1959, *46*, 157–158

Scott-Emuakpor, A, Heffelfinger, J, & Higgins, JV. A syndrome of microcephaly and cataracts in four siblings. *American Journal of Diseases of Childhood*, 1977, *131*, 167–169

Scriver, CR, Mackenzie, J, Clow, CL, & Delvin, E. Thiamine responsive maple syrup urine disease. *Lancet*, 1971, *1*, 310–312

Sell, SH, Webb, WW, Pate, JE, & Doyne, EO. Psychologic sequalae of bacterial meningitis: Controlled studies, *Pediatrics*, 1972, *49*, 212–217

Shen, YZ. Purulent meningitis in newborns and young infants, a clinical and long term neurological follow up study in Taiwan. *Asian Medical Journal*, 1978, *25*, 364–366

Sherwin, RM, & Berthrong, M. Alexander's disease with sudanophilic leucodystrophy. *Archives of Pathology and Laboratory Medicine*, 1970, *89*, 321–328

Simell, O, Visakorpi, JK, & Donner, M. Saccharopinuri. *Archives of Diseases of Childhood*, 1972, *47*, 52–55

Sipe, JC, & O'Brien, JS. Ultrastructure of skin biopsy specimens in lysomal storage disease. *Clinical Genetics*, 1979, *15*, 118–125

Smith, DW. *Recognizable Patterns of Human Malformations* (2nd Ed.). Philadelphia: W.B. Saunders Co., 1976

Stevens, D, & Parsonage, M. Mutation in Huntington's chorea. *Journal of Neurology, Neurosurgery and Psychiatry*, 1969, *32*, 140–143

Sturge, WA. A case of partial epilepsy apparently due to a lesion of one of the vasomotor centres in the brain. *Clinical Society London Trans.*, 1879, *12*, 163

Sutherland, CR. Fragile sites on human chromosomes: demonstration of their dependence on the type of tissue culture medium. *Science*, 1977, *197*, 541–562

Syllabu, L, & Henner, K. Contribution a l'independance de l'athetase double idiopathique et congenital. *Revue Neurologique*, 1926, *1*, 541–562

Terrence, CF, Delany, JF, & Alberts, MC. Computed tomography for Huntington's disease. *Neuroradiology*, 1977, *13*, 173

Tharapal, AT, & Summit, R. A cytogenetic survey of 200 unclassifiable mentally retarded children with congenital anomalies and 200 normal subjects. *Human Genetics*, 1977, *37*, 329–335

Tijo, JH, & Levan, H. The chromosome number in man. *Heredity*, 1956, *32*, 1–6

Turner, G, Gill, R, & Daniel, A. Marker X-chromosome, mental retardation and macro-ordhidism. *New England Journal of Medicine*, 1978, *299*, 1472

Turner, G, & Turner, B. X-linked mental retardation. *Journal of Medical Genetics*, 1974, *11*, 109–113

Turner, G, Turner, B, & Collins, E. X-linked mental retardation without physical abnormality: Benpennings Syndrome. *Developmental Medicine and Child Neurology*, 1971, *13*, 71

Ullman, MD, Pyeritz, RE, Maser, HW, Wenger, DA, & Kolodny, EH. Application of "high performance" liquid chromatography to the study of sphingolipidoses. *Clinical Chemistry*, 1980, *26*, 1499–1502

Vogel, FS, & McClenahan, JL. Anomalies of major cerebral arteries associated with congenital malformations of the brain. *American Journal of Pathology*, 1942, *28*, 701–718

Von Recklinghausen, FD. *Uber die Multiplen Fibrome der Haut und Ihre Beziehung zu den Multiplen Neuromen*. Berlin: A. Hirschwald 1882

Wahrman, J, & Fried, K. The Jerusalem prospective newborn survey of mongolism. *Annals of the New York Academy Science*, 1970, *171*, 341–360

Wang, HC, Melnyk, J, McDonald, LT, Ulchida, IA, Carr, HD, & Goldberg, B. Ring chromosomes in human beings. *Nature*, 1962, *195*, 733–734

Wolf, U, Beinwein, H, Porsch, R, Schroter, R, & Baitsch, H. Defizenz an der kurzen armen eines chromosome nr. 4. *Humangenetik*, 1965, *7*, 397–404

Yakovlev, PJ. Pathoarchitectonic studies of cerebral malformations. *Journal of Neuropathology and Experimental Neurology*, 1959, *18*, 22–55

Yakovlev, QJ, & Wadsworth, RC. Schizencephalies. *Journal of Neuropathology and Experimental Neurology*, 1946, *5*, 116–169

Zellweger, H. Familial mosaicism attributable to a new gene. *Lancet*, 1965, *1*, 445–457

Zollinger, H. Das XXXY-syndrome. *Helvetica Paediatrica Acta*, 1969, *24*, 589–599

PART 5

Litigation

14

Legal Concerns

OVERVIEW

Broadly defined, assessment is the process of collecting, organizing, and synthesizing data for the purposes of decision making and monitoring changes in behavior. These data are typically used for making decisions about screening, classification, program placement, instructional and training interventions, and overall pupil and program evaluations (Salvia & Ysseldyke, 1978). In contrast, evaluation is a somewhat broader term, including a component of decision making subsequent to the initial assessment (Anderson, Ball & Murphy, 1975; White, 1980).

Assessment (and ultimately evaluation) is the sine qua non that precedes the delivery of services to mentally retarded persons. Certainly this must occur before a child receives special education services (Duffy, Salvia, Tucker, & Ysseldyke, 1981), and there are thorough substantive and procedural requirements to ensure this is done in a fair and meaningful fashion (Federal Register, 1977). Overall,

assessment identifies the individual's present developmental level; the individual's strengths, abilities, and developmental needs; the conditions that impede the individual's development; and where possible, the cause of the disability. (AC/MRDD, 1981, p. 6)

Notice the lack of emphasis on deficits in this definition.

There is a large class of mentally retarded persons who do not attend public schools and thus are given less attention for program consideration, and in the professional literature. These are people who have turned 21, the age of majority for exit from public special education programs, or the very young, more severely disabled. The needs of these people, at least the adults, receive little attention in university special education curricula, yet there is an escalating effort to provide more training, program and life management services for them *(Halderman*

437

v. Pennhurst, 1979, 1982; *Welsch v. Likins,* 1974); although not necessarily voluntarily on the part of the state.

Whether a person is a candidate for a mandated program such as public education *(PL 94-142)* or an entitlement program such as an Intermediate Care Facility *(42 Code of Federal Regulations,* 1978), appropriate assessment is necessary to determine eligibility and the subsequent nature of services to be provided (Poland, Thurlow, Ysseldyke, & Mirkin, 1982). In some instances a child or adult is an obvious candidate, as in the case of someone severely mentally retarded, and the assessment serves to identify needs. In others the assessment is necessary to identify the handicap and then to indicate needs; this occurs with most educable mentally retarded (EMR) children and the assessment process is typically controversial *(Larry P. v. Riles,* 1979; *PASE v. Hannon,* 1980).

For years assessment of the mentally retarded, at least in schools, meant measurement of intelligence, or IQ testing. Children were placed into ability "tracks," for example, by virtue of a score on a test *(Hobson v. Hansen,* 1967). Such a practice identified disproportionate numbers of "disadvantaged minorities" to be placed in classes for slow students, thus creating classification by race and/or economic status, which the court said was illegal. The *Hobson* issues, greatly influenced by *Brown v. Board of Education* (1954), appear as a catalyst for the initiation of numerous lawsuits examining classification of children, or the right to services in the public education sector.

In California, Mexican-American children were being placed in public school EMR classes with a frequency much greater than their proportionate representation in the general population *(Diana v. State Board of Education,* 1970). This situation was also the case with black children in California and they too, like plaintiffs in *Diana,* attacked the discriminatory nature of the assessment system that classified them as mentally retarded *(Larry P. v. Riles,* 1972). The same issues resulted in significantly different consideration by the courts in Illinois *(PASE v. Hannon,* 1980), and there still remains some confusion as to what is legally acceptable assessment in order to determine whether or not mental retardation is present, at least for the purpose of placement in public special education programs.

Assessment led to the exclusion of children from services, because they were "too handicapped," thus presenting an excessive burden on existing special education programs. Representatives of mentally retarded children in Pennsylvania, by attacking this discrimination, established an unqualified right to education, in part by convincing the court that all children can benefit from education and training *(Pennsylvania Association for Retarded Children v. Commonwealth of Pennsylvania,* 1972). Labels such as "mentally retarded," "emotionally disturbed," and "hyperactive" put many poor, black children on waiting lists for services in Washington, D.C., thus effectively excluding many from services indefinitely *(Mills v. Board of Education of the District of Columbia,* 1972, 1980).

The courts have been forced into the social/political arena because of the pervasive inadequacies of public institutions and have dealt extensively with

issues such as desegregation, prison and institution reform, special education services, and numerous others *(Weinberg, 1982)*. Consider Judge Peckham's analysis in *Larry P. v. Riles* (1979):

The court has necessarily been drawn into the emotionally charged debate about the nature of "intelligence" and its basis in "genes" or the "environment." This debate, which finds reknowned experts disagreeing sharply, obviously cannot be resolved by judicial decree. Despite these problems, however, court intervention has been necessary. The history of this litigation has demonstrated the failure of legislators and administrative agencies to confront problems that clearly had to be faced, and it has revealed an all too typical willingness either to do nothing or to pass on issues to the courts. (p. 932)

While assessment in public education has received the most notoriety, much attention has been paid to its influence and/or lack of presence in services for mentally retarded people beyond school age, and especially those in institution *(Halderman v. Pennhurst, 1979; Wyatt v. Stickney, 1972)*. The main issue with this population is not with the identification of mental retardation itself, because this is usually known, but rather with a determination of program needs and an identification of problems. It is generally understood that this type of client must bear a label compatible with the rules and regulations of the service system in order to be eligible for program funding (Gallagher, 1976).

Assessment, when perceived as something that occurs in public education only, or primarily, belies the significance this process has in a legal sense in all services to the mentally retarded. Some questions that must be asked in order to begin to investigate the broader significance of this issue, include:

1. What standard should be used for determining mental retardation?
2. Does assessment properly influence the placement of the client in the least restrictive alternative?
3. How does assessment relate to the release of someone from an institution?
4. What types of assessments are necessary in order to civilly commit someone for mental retardation services?
5. What assessment must occur prior to the use of psychotropic drugs, aversive interventions, or other "at risk" procedures?
6. What assessments are necessary to enroll a child in a full year public school program, as opposed to the traditional "school year"?

During the past decade the law—legislation, regulation, and litigation—has had profound impact upon assessment of the mentally retarded. There is a stated Congressional preference for the least restrictive alternative, a concept that relies upon assessment to determine needs *(Developmentally Disabled Assistance and Bill of Rights Act, 1975; Education for All Handicapped Children Act, 1975)*. Some broad legal considerations and implications of proper and appropriate assessment of school-aged and non-school-aged mentally retarded persons are examined.

Assessment of School-Aged Children

The primary issues for this population are two-fold: (1) whether or not the child is actually mentally retarded, and, (2) if mentally retarded, the nature of the total evaluation process to result in assignment to the least restrictive educational setting consistent with his or her assessed needs. The former is a social concern as much as it is educational; the latter, if there is no dispute as to the existence of mental retardation, is heavily contingent upon the "mainstreaming" philosophy and resources of the individual school district. Since there is little dispute when someone is moderately to profoundly mentally retarded, the disorder is generally controversial only when attempting to differentiate between those truly mildly retarded and those who fall within the lower end of the range of normal intelligence, or are mentally ill or learning disabled.

"Mild mental retardation typically is identified only in the public school context, which establishes demands for abstract congnitive skills" (Reschly, 1981, p. 1099). Normally the classroom teacher observes learning difficulties and subsequently refers a child for additional assessment, thus making the school the principal social agent for the identification of mild mental retardation (Mercer, 1973). Unfortunately the more traditional psychological tests used for this assessment, and especially those for measuring IQ, have been preceived as tools of discrimination, especially against minority students (Bersoff, 1981). This situation has been well established in some cases in litigation challenging the disproportionate numbers of minority pupils labeled as mildly mentally retarded (Diana v. State Board of Education, 1970; Larry P. v. Riles, 1972, 1974, 1979).

There exists no singular legal or pure definition of mental retardation, but the one promulgated by the American Association on Mental Deficiency (AAMD, 1977) has become the most pervasive. Emphasizing the interactive effects of deficits in intelligence and adaptive behavior, it has been accepted by the American Psychiatric Association (1980) as the diagnostic standard in the field of mental health as well. Most state education regulations require consideration of deficits in both areas (Patrick & Reschly, 1982); and the definition in the Regulations inplementing part B of the Education of the Handicapped Act (Federal Register, 1977) is identical, except for the unnecessary and qualifying concluding statement:

"Mentally retarded" means significantly subaverage general intellectual functioning existing concurrently with deficits in adaptive behavior and manifested during the developmental periods, which adversely affects a child's educational performance. (p. 42478)

It seems both obvious and tautological to indicated that legitimately diagnosed mental retardation would "adversely affect a child's educational performance."

Since all meaningful definitions of mental retardation, historic or current, rely on deficits in intelligence, the logical response by psychometricians and educators has been to utilize standardized tests for the measurement of IQ, which often lead to a label of mental retardation; and thus the basis for the major public school assessment controversy of the past decade. The jury (and some judges too) is still out as to whether the use of standardized IQ tests lead to excessive and inaccurate labeling of minority students as mildly mentally retarded. The courts have been drawn into this matter in part because administrators and legislators have been inept, or have ignored the issue *(Larry P. v. Riles,* 1979).

The most recent litigation of significance has not resolved the issue and, in fact, in the two most salient cases federal judges drew conclusions practically diametrically opposed *(Larry P. v. Riles,* 1979; *PASE v. Hannon,* 1980). Though these cases are complex and impossible to analyze in great detail here, the primary issue was whether or not standardized IQ tests are racially and culturally biased against black students, thus allowing for a disproportionate number to be labeled as mentally retarded and placed in special education programs. These decisions are nationally significant not only as issues of racism and handicapism, but also because they indicate "that the battle lines have been drawn around the issue of the selection of children for special education curriculums" (American Bar Association, 1980, p. 301).

In summary, Judge Peckham ruled in *Larry P.* (1979) as follows:

In violation of Title VI of the Civil Rights Act of 1964, the Rehabilitation Act of 1973, and the Education for All Handicapped Children Act of 1975, defendants have utilized standardized intelligence tests that are racially and culturally biased, have a discriminatory impact against black children, and have not been validated for the purpose of essentially permanent placements of black children into educationally dead-end, isolated, and stigmatizing classes for the so-called educable mentally retarded. Further, these federal laws have been violated by defendants' general use of placement mechanisms that, taken together, have not been validated and result in a large overrepresentation of black children in the special E.M.R. classes. (p. 933)

In specific contrast was the general ruling in *PASE* (1980) by Judge Grady:

I believe and today hold that the WISC, WISC-R and Stanford-Binet tests, when used in conjunction with the statutorily mandated "other criteria for determining an appropriate educational program for a child" (20 U.S.C. sec. 1412(2)(D)(5) [SIC], do not discriminate against black children in the Chicago public schools. Defendants are complying with that statutory mandate; (p. 883)

and,

Intelligent administration of the I.Q. tests by qualified psychologists, followed by the evaluation procedures defendants use, should rarely result in the misassessment of a child of normal intelligence as one who is mentally retarded. There is no evidence in this record that such misassessments as do occur are the result of racial bias in the test items or in any other aspect of the assessment process currently in use in the Chicago public school system. (p.883)

Further analysis of the lengthy opinions in these cases points out some substantial differences in the way the courtroom records were developed, records that would serve to guide each judge in rendering his conclusions. Judge Peckham *(Larry P.)* was proceeding with a strong indication that IQ tests had an inordinate amount of influence in determining placements in classes for the Educable Mentally Retarded (EMR). This occurred even though there was an early (1970—1971)

> The legislature hereby finds and declares that there should not be disproportionate enrollment of any socioeconomic, minority, or ethnic group pupils in classes for the mentally retarded and that the verbal portion of the intelligence tests which are utilized by some schools for such placement tends to underestimate the academic ability of such pupils. (1971 Cal. Stats ch. 78, cited in *Larry P. v. Riles,* 1979, p. 940)

as well as a mandate for measures of adaptive behavior in the diagnostic process.

Judge Grady, on the other hand, was greatly influenced by the substantive and procedural due process safeguards present in the Chicago public school system assessment procedures:

> It is important to understand that an I.Q. test is not the first level, nor is an I.Q. score the catalyst for the assessment process. The first level of investigation is the classroom. Unless the child is having difficulty with his studies in the classroom, the questions of EMH placement will never arise and there is no occasion for an I.Q. test. Individually administered I.Q. tests of the kind involved in this case have never been given routinely in the Chicago school system, and the former practice of giving group-administered general intelligence tests to all students was discontinued some years ago. *(PASE v. Hannon,* 1980, p. 879)

The judge continued by citing rather elaborate protections obviously derived from PL 94–142, and concluded generally that IQ scores are not given undue weight in the diagnostic and placement process.

The outcome of *Larry P.* was that IQ tests are culturally bviased against black children, while the *PASE* court said they were not. In a legal analysis Bersoff (1981) claims that Judge Peckham drew is conclusion based in part upon an inaccurate definition of *unbiased,* as well as devoting little discussion to the empirical support for his reasoning. Judge Grady, while legitimately complimenting Judge Peckham for the scholarly nature of his opinion, felt he initiated "little analysis of the threshold question of whether test bias in fact exists" *(PASE v. Hannon,* 1980, p. 114). In marked contrast, Judge Grady's opinion in *PASE* resulted from his subjective (and perhaps unprecedented) analysis of each item on the tests in question, a method that Bersoff (1981) calls "embarrassingly unsophisticated and ingenuous" (p. 1049). Needless to say, it appears the issue of cultural bias in IQ testing is far from resolved.

Other cases have dealt with the issue of misclassification of minority students, or have been initiated and deserve close attention. See, for example, *Diana v. State Board of Education,* 1972, settled by agreement of parties; *Hobson v. Hansen* (1967) *aff'd sub nom Smuck v. Hobson,* (1969), judicial order abolishing "tracking" system as illegal; *Johnson v. Denver Public Schools,* still in litigation at this writing; *Mattie T., et al v. Holloday,* et al (1979), very similar to *Larry P.* but settled by consent decree; *Mills v. Board of Education of the District of Columbia* (1972, 1980), still under scrutiny of the federal court for failure to comply with the original order, and defendants were recently cited for contempt; and, *NAACP v. State of Georgia* (1982), recently filed with substantive issues similar to *Larry P.* and *PASE.*

A major issue closely alligned with the IQ "influence" is the legal definition of mental retardation as adopted by state education codes. It was noted in *Larry P.* (1979), for example, that in 1970 the California legislature lowered the maximum IQ for special education placement from a range of about 75–85, to about 70 (depending upon the standard deviation of the test used); this led subsequently to massive reassessments and a tremendous decrease in the number (50 percent or more) of educable mentally retarded students (MacMillian & Borthwick, 1980).

Patrick and Reschly (1982) in an extensive study of state educational criteria for mental retardation, found reasonably significant disparity amongst the states with maximum IQ scores ranging from 69 to 85, although some states did not specify a maximum, or cutoff. They note that lack of consistency, or a standard, could cause a child labeled as mentally retarded in one state to be ineligible for special education services should he or she move to another; whether this is "good" or "bad" is a philosophical matter for further discussion elsewhere. It was encouraging to learn from their research that presently a majority of the states require the assessment of adaptive behavior in the diagnostic process, and most inlcude consideration of it in their definition of mental retardation.

The consideration of the adaptive behavior influence is especially critical for minority children (Mercer, 1975):

Assessment of adaptive behavior is important in evaluating persons from ethnic minorities and lower socioeconomic levels, backgrounds that do not conform to the model social and cultural pattern of the community. Many of them may fail intelligence tests mainly because they have not had the opportunity to learn the cognitive skills and to acquire the knowledge needed to pass such tests. Yet they demonstrate by their ability to cope with problems in other areas of life that they are not comprehensively incompetent. (p. 138)

Since the most accepted definition of mental retardation is that of the AAMD (1977) it is essential to understand the organization's definition of adaptive behavior.

Adaptive Behavior is defined as the effectiveness or degree with which an individual meets the standards of personal independence and social responsibility for age and cultural group. (p. 11)

Assessment of adaptive behavior is perhaps the most critical component in determing mild mental retardation, at least from a legal perspective, and has great utility for program development in the evalutation process for persons more severely mentally retarded. Included in the Public Education Law (Federal Register, 1977) as a component of the legal definition of mental retardation for school-aged children, it is an area of prime consideration for special education placement:

(a) In interpreting evaluation data and in making placement decisions, each public agency shall:
   (1) Draw upon information from a variety of sources, including aptitude and achievement tests, teacher recommendations, physical condition, social or cultural background, and adaptive behavior (p. 42497).

This multifactored approach to assessment is a significant step toward more appropriate identification and programming (Poland, Thurlow, Yesseldyke & Mirkin, 1982).

While IQ has become the most controversial of assessment components, other areas, and especially adaptive behavior, have come to the forefront in order to minimize the significance of standardized IQ testing. Judge Grady *(PASE)* downplayed the IQ influence, suggesting it was one of many due process considerations leading to an appropriate determination of eligibility for special education services. Judge Peckham, as part of the ordered remedy in *Larry P. v. Riles* (1979), directed the reevaluation of every black child currently identified as EMR:

Such reevaluation shall include information derived from:
   (1) diagnostic tests designed to reveal specific learning needs and to prescribe specific pedagogical approaches,
   (2) adaptive behavior observation;
   (3) the child's developmental and health histories (p. 990).

The law seems clear in its preference for multifaceted assessment of mentally retarded children, including intelligence testing that does not lead to discrimination based on cultural or socioeconomic background (Federal Register, 1977; Patrick & Reschly, 1982; Public Law 94–142, 1975). "The purposes underlying the pyschoeducational assessment are to make decisions concerning classification/placement and program planning/intervention" (Reschly, 1981, p. 1094), not to concentrate on labeling of children. It appears from the litigation to date that the less the reliance on the IQ score in assessment/evaluation, the less the possibility of identifying a disproportionate number of minority children as mildly retarded, or in improperly classifying anyone.

A controversy that has grown out of a liberal interpretation of the public education law is the issue of the extended school year, or 12 month educational program and the methods for determining eligibility (Larsen, Goodman, & Glean, 1981; Leonard, 1981; Makuch, 1981). Obviously a threat to the sanctity of the 180 day school "year," the original litigation in this area resulted in the following standard *(Armstrong v. Kline, 1979)*:

A handicapped student is entitled to an education program in excess of 180 days per year if regression caused by an interruption in educational programming, together with the student's limited recoupment capacity, renders it impossible or unlikely that the student will attain the level of self-sufficiency and independence from caretakers that the student would otherwise be expected to reach in view of his/her handicapping condition. (p. 419)

Upheld on appeal although by different legal analysis *(Battle v. Commonwealth,* 1980), the matter has been denied review or reconsideration by the U.S. Supreme Court *(Scanlon v. Battle,* 1981). See also *Georgia ARC v. McDaniel,* 1981; and *Mahoney v. Administrative School District No. 1,* 1971.

A general standard for eligibility for year-round programming promulgated by the Office for Civil Rights, Department of Health and Human Services requires a determination as to whether an extended program is essential to meet the child's individual needs, and whether such a need has been established by appropriate evaluation methods (Dept. of Health & Human Services, 1979). The *Battle* (1980) and *Armstrong* (1979) courts indicated two broad classes of handicapped children who might qualify, the severely/profoundly mentally impaired, including multihandicapped, and the severely emotionally disturbed. Larsen et al. (1981) suggest eligibility hinges on three variables:

(a) the type of handicapping condition, as stressed by the court in *Battle v. Commonwealth;*
(b) the evidence of a regression-recoupment disability; and,
(c) the goal of self sufficiency. (p. 259)

Inasmuch as we are moving toward a national standard, the degree to which a school district participates in full year educational programming will depend significantly upon definitions and sophistication of assessment processes.

It appears there is still room for error in assessment *(Hoffman v. Bd. of Education of the City of New York,* 1979), although lack of timeliness can be costly to a school district *(Allen v. McDonough,* 1979; 1980).

In *Hoffman* the New York Court of Appeals overturned a monetary award by a lower court to a man who had been misdiagnosed as mentally retarded, thus spending most of his school years in special education programs. In its decision the Court expressed a "hands-off" preference for the judiciary:

The court was convinced that allowing "educational malpractice" suits, whether based on allegations of nonfeasance (failure to act) or misfeasance (improper performance), would violate "the principle that courts ought not interfere with the professional judgment of those charged by the Constitution and by statute with the responsibility for the administration of the schools of this state." (p. 81)

In *Allen* (1979–1980) the court ordered compensatory education for 1300 children whose schooling was delayed because of tardiness in completing evaluations and annual reviews, and finally appointed a special master to force compliance with its order.

The Non-Public School Client

Unlike the IQ controversy surrounding the identification of mildly handicapped public school students, there is no one area of comparable contention concerning assessment and services received outside the public school sector; there are, however, several major issues. Among these is the broad matter of assessment itself, and how such information is used to influence decisions relating to residential placement and commitment, rights to habilitation, and the refusal of services or interventions.

A general prinicple established in the U.S. Supreme Court in *O'Conner v. Donaldson* (1975) has had tremendous impact upon the use of psychiatric/psychological assessment information:

In short, a State cannot constitutionally confine without more a nondangerous individual who is capable of surviving safely in freedom by himself or with the help of willing and responsible family members or friends. (p. 576)

One of the implications of this case is that assessment information must demonstrate a legitimate need for confinement if a person is to be civilly committed to an institution.

As an example of a standard for civil commitment based exclusively upon assessment, consider the following from a recent Federal court order:

A person shall be determined to be a mentally retarded person in need of residential placement only upon the following:

(1) The person is impaired in adaptive behavior to a significant degree and is functioning at an intellectual level two standard deviation measurements below the norm as determined by acceptable psychological testing techniques;

(2) The impairment and the resultant disability were manifested before the person's 18th birthday and are likely to continue for an indefinite period; and

(3) The person, because of his retardation presents a substantial risk of physical injury to himself or physical debilitation as demonstrated by behavior within 30 days of the petition which shows that he is unable to provide for, and is not providing for his most basic need for nourishment, personal and medical care, shelter, self-protection and safety and that provision for such needs is not available and cannot be developed or provided in his own home or in his own community without residential placement. *(Goldy v. Beal, 1976, p. 2)*

This Pennsylvania federal court case generated standards for commitment that rely primarily on assessment consistent with the definition of Mental Deficiency (1977). It is further necessary in the assessment process to demonstrate the inability of the client to reasonably survive without supervision, an indication of deficits in adaptive behavior severe enough to suggest incapacity for life management. While this is not a universal standard for commitment of a mentally retarded person to an institution it certainly suggests the minimum scrutiny that should be present in facilitating such a profound decision.

While assessment is crucial in establishing the need for confinement, it is perhaps more critical (at least from a philosophical perspective) in ensuring services in less restrictive settings (Turnbull, Ellis, Boggs, Brooks, & Biklen, 1981). There are numerous cases wherein plaintiffs argued successfully that their assessed needs could be met in alternative living arrangements. In *Dixon v. Wein-*

berger (1975), for example, the plaintiffs convinced the court that more than 40 percent of the patients of large, public mental hospital did not need the restrictiveness of an institution; the court relied on other well-known cases dealing with the principle of least restricitve *(Convington v. Harris,* 1969; *Lake v. Cameron,* 1966; *Rouse v. Cameron,* 1966).

In *Halderman, et al v. Pennhurst State School & Hospital* (1977) the federal court said initially that institutions "such as Pennhurst" are unconstitutional, and that all mentally retarded persons have a right to serivces in less restrictive settings. Upon appeal and further consideration this position was modified by the Third Circuit Court of Appeals *(Halderman v. Pennhurst,* 1979), with some allowance for assessment and professional judgment:

For some patients a transfer from Pennhurst might be too unsettling a move. Longterm patients, for example, may have suffered such degeneration in the minimum skills needed for community living that habilitation outside an institution is a practical impossibility. Indeed, the Pennhurst Parents-Staff Association, which has participated as an amicus in this appeal, contends that this is true for many patients. Moreover, there seems to be some support among practitioners for this view as well. We need not decide that issue here. All that we need recognize is that there may be some individual patients who, because of age, profound degree of retardation, special needs or some other reason, will not be able to adjust to life outside of an institution and thus will be harmed by such a change.

Thus, the residents have a qualified, not absolute, right to leave the institution, based upon professional assessment of their needs and "prognosis" in a less restrictive setting. This issue has again been recognized *(Halderman v. Pennhurst,* 1982) in another opinion by the Third Circuit in this complex and seemingly interminable litigation.

One of the reasons mentally retarded clients remain in residential institutions is the paucity of alternative services, even though assessment data and professional judgment have indicated the need for something less restrictive (Turnbull et al., 1981). Some courts *(Brewster et al. v. Dukakis et al.,* 1979; *Michigan ARC v. Smith,* 1979) have rejected the lack of alternatives as an acceptalbe rationale for denying deinstitutionalization when client needs dictate movement. The *Brewster* decree reflects the feelings of both courts:

Recommendations as to residential and nonresidential program placements will be based on an evaluation of the actual needs of the resident or client rather than on what programs are currently available. In cases where the services needed by a client are unavailable, the Individual Service Plan will recommend an interim program based on available services which meet, as nearly as possible, the actual needs of the client.

Obviously assessment implies a much broader connotation outside of the public school special education system. In recent rulings the federal courts have shown an increasing deference toward professional judgment, which suggests the necessity for particular attention to the assessment of client needs. In *Youngberg v. Romeo* (1982), for example, the U.S. Supreme Court was examining (in part) the client's right to be free from restraints imposed by the state, and whether the state's action was reasonable and necessary or whether liability may be imposed against its employees:

In determining what is "reasonable"—in this and in any case presenting a claim for training by a state—we emphasize that courts must show deference to the judgment exercised by a qualified professional. By so limiting judicial review of challenges to conditions in state institutions, interference by the federal judiciary with the internal operations of these institutions should be minimized. Moreover, there certainly is no reason to think judges or juries are better qualified than appropriate professionals in making such decisions.

The Court also seemed to be reassuring professionals of its recognition that they (the professionals) often had to make difficult program decisions, especially when presented with disruptive or difficult-to-manage behavior:

In determining whether the state has met its obligations in these respects, decisions made by the appropriate professional are entitled to a presumption of correctness. Such a presumption is necessary to enable institutions of this type—often, unfortunately, overcrowded and understaffed—to continue to function. A single professional may have to make decisions with respect to a number of residents with a widely varying needs and problems in the course of a normal day. The administrators, and particularly professonal personnel, should not be required to make each decision in the shadow of an action for damages.

The same court recognized in an earlier case that professionals, not judges and hearing officers, are the most qualified to assess the needs of children in deciding the matter of commitment for mental health services *(Parham v. J. R., 1979)*.

Whether or not mentally retarded persons can refuse treatment interventions such as psychotropic drugs or aversive interventions, a most complex issue, depends a great deal upon their assessed needs, the nature of the intervention, and their competency to understand the matter (American Bar Association, 1982; Griffith & Coval, in press). The use of drugs, perhaps the most controversial treatment issue with the retarded, may be legitimate depending upon client needs but the risks are often inordinate (Breuning, Davis, & Poling, 1982). Much of the litigation in this area, while not taking exception to the proper use of drug therapy, has pointed to little if any consideration of client needs *(Welsch v. Likins,* 1974; *Wuori v. Zitnay,* 978; *Wyatt v. Stickney,* 1972) and in one case awarded approximately $750,000 in damages for blatant misuse *(Clites v. Iowa,* 1980; 1982).

Forcing aversive or other at risk interventions may be permissible but only if one acts within the scope of authority as authorized by existing laws, regulations, and professional codes, and there is a documented demonstration that the intervention is the least restrictive alternative (Turnbull et al., 1981). Competent assessment is the critical issue here and the service provider is absolutely required to document and justify any measures that pose undue risk to clients.

The litigation cited thus far, certainly some of the most significant in the area of mental health/mental retardation law, has one recurring theme: very little was being done for mentally disabled people based upon their assessed needs (if they were assessed at all), thus indicating the lack of credence given the assessment process in the service systems involved. Another way of looking at the same problem is this: while most state service systems purport to support the concept of least restrictive, they do not have the resources or ability to provide the continuum of services necessary to serve mentally retarded people based upon their assessed needs. What incentive, therefore, exists for a service system to be truly supportive of ongoing or periodic assessment?

There is only one clear example of national legislation and regulations creating clear opportunity for services in the least restrictive setting based upon assessed needs, that being PL 94–142 (1975) and the subsequent enabling regulations (1977). The primary incentive for passage of this law was earlier litigation (see, e.g., *Pennsylvania Association for Retarded Children v. Commonwealth of Pennsylvania,* 1972) and the realization that similar suits would be successful, and with continued perseverance a school-aged handicapped child stands a reasonable probability of receiving adequate services. Thus there is one clear national mandate with enough examples to date of judicial and administrative enforcement, as well as significant federal funding, to demonstrate the law has "teeth."

Beyond educational services to school-aged persons there exists only a national perference for services based upon identified needs. The Developmentally Disabled Assistance and Bill of Rights Act (1975), for example, states in part:

The treatment, services, and habilitation for a person with developmental disabilities should be designed to maximize the developmental potential of the person and should be provided in the setting that is least restrictive of the person's liberty. (sec. 6010)

The U.S. Supreme Court in *Pennhurst v. Halderman* (1981), however, stated there was "nothing in the Act or its legislative history to suggest that Congress intended to require the States to assume the high cost of providing 'appropriate treatment' in the 'least restrictive environment' to their mentally retarded citizens" (p. 14), and concluded:

Congress in recent years has enacted several laws designed to improve the way in which this Nation treats the mentally retarded. The Developmentally Disabled Assistance and Bill of Rights Act is one such law. It establishes a national policy to provide better care and treatment to the retarded and creates funding incentives to induce the States to do so. But the Act does no more than that. We would be attributing far too much to Congress if we held that it required the States, at their own expense, to provide certain kinds of treatment. (pp. 27–28)

Other federal laws/regulations have supported the concept of available services based upon identified needs, which is another way of saying in the least restrictive setting. The regulations promulgated under section 504 of the *Rehabilitation Act of 1973* specify a strong preference for this concept *(Federal Register,*

1977). The Standards for Intermediate Care Facilities for the Mentally Retarded (ICF/MR) promulgated under Title XIX of the Social Security Act state that people should not be admitted to such programs (primarily residential institutions) unless their needs can be met (42 *Code of Federal Regulations*, 1978); because there is so much federal money behind this entitlement program there exists a powerful incentive for states to keep full all eligible institutional beds. Only recently has there been a reallocation of small amounts of ICF/MR funds to community living alternatives. Title XX of the same Act has as one goal "preventing or reducing inappropriate institutional care" (45 *Code of Federal Regulations*, 1980, p. 393), something which would require thorough and competent assessment.

Summary

The purpose of this discussion has been to raise legal concerns of great significance to professionals involved in the assessment of mentally retarded persons, for the purposes of classification and program development. Such assessment has traditionally been fraught with three major problems: (1) bias in measurement procedures; (2) lack of service options for clients resulting in services being rendered on the basis of availability, not client needs; and (3) lack of necessary assessments, as documented in institutional litigation, especially in cases of the continued misuse of procedures involving great risk.

There is a reasonable impetus in special education today to make the assessment process nondiscriminatory. One possible approach is to use data on intervention effectiveness (Magliocca & Stephens, 1980; Ysseldyke & Regan, 1980), or criterion referenced measures linked to achievement or behavioral content (Lidz, 1979). Another strategy for minimizing bias involves multifactored assessment with minimal reliance on IQ measures, and a de-emphasis of labels with the mildly retarded population (Duffy et al., 1981; Reschly, 1981); such an approach would specify educational needs, and even deficits, but would avoid pejorative labeling.

Systemic deficiencies, such as inadequate services, can rarely be controlled or influenced by individual professionals but other variables can. Thorough knowledge of state and federal codes, regulations, and case law will help formulate legally acceptable assessment strategies. In questionable or volatile situations administrators should push for second opinions; there are some data to indicate deficiencies in assessment skill and knowledge in a significant number of clinicians (Bennett, 1981). Due process mechanisms can ensure that risky procedures are used only after proper and thorough assessment (Griffith, 1982); such measures show a significant concern for client and staff rights.

Assessment, as the courts have demonstrated, need not result in the ideal program but rather must lead to adequate and reasonable services. In the first challenge to the U.S. Supreme Court of services provided under the Education for All Handicapped Children Act (1975), the Court held, in part, that Congress:

did not intend to impose upon the States any greater substantive educational standard than is necessary to make such access to public education meaningful. *(Board of Education v. Amy Rowley,* 1982, p. 4926)

Thus the school district was meeting its statutory obligations to Amy Rowley inasmuch as she was performing better than average academically and was not required to provide a sign-language interpreter, even though it was the opinion of some professionals that this would improve her academic achievement.

Today is absolutely the era of individual rights, and students and clients have numerous alternatives for bringing grievances and seeking redress. What ultimately is being tested when assessment is questioned is the quality of the service system, both its administrators and clinicians; this is an area that can be greatly influenced by quality control, adherence to professional standards, and by consideration of rights through an understanding of legal influences.

REFERENCES

Accreditation Council for Services for Mentally Retarded and Other Developmentally Disabled Persons (AC/MRDD). *Standards for services for developmentally disabled individuals.* Washington, DC: Author, 1981

Allen v. McDonough, No. 14948 (Mass., Suffolk County Super. Ct. May 25, 1979), as reported in American Bar Association, *Mental Disability Law Reporter,* 1979, *3,* 327; 1980, *4,* 404

American Association on Mental Deficiency. *Manual on terminology and classification in mental retardation.* Washington, DC: Author, 1977

American Bar Association, Commission on the Mentally Disabled. Summary and Analysis. *Mental Disability Law Reporter,* 1980, *4,* 299–303

American Psychiatric Association. *Diagnostic and statistical manual of mental disorders.* Washington DC: Author, 1980

Anderson, SB, Ball, S, & Murphy, RT. *Encyclopedia of educational evaluation.* San Francisco: Jossey-Bass, 1975

Armstrong v. Kline, 476 F. Supp. 583 (E.D. Pa. 1979), remedial order dated 9/5/79, as reported in American Bar Association, *Mental Disability Law Reporter,* 1979, *3,* 419

Battle v. Commonwealth, Nos. 79-2158, 79-2188, 79-2189, 79-2190, 79-2568, 79-2569, 79-2570 (3rd Cir. July 15, 1980)

Bennett, RE. Professional competence and the assessment of exceptional children. *Journal of Special Education,* 1981, *15,* 437–446

Bersoff, DN. Testing and the law. *American Psychologist,* 1981, *36,* 1047–1056

Board of Education v. Amy Rowley, US Supreme Court No. 80–1002, 50 *U.S. Law Week,* 4925–4937

Breuning, SE, Davis VJ, & Poling, AD. Pharmacotherapy with the mentally retarded: Implications for clinical psychologists. *Clinical Psychology Review,* 1982, *2,* 79–114

Brewster, et al. v. Dukakis, et al., C.A. No. 76-4423-F (E.D. Mass., Dec. 6, 1978) Final Consent Decree as reported in, American Bar Association, *Mental Disability Law Reporter,* 1979, *3,* 44–50

Brown v. Board of Education, 347 US 483 (1954)

Clites v. State of Iowa, Iowa District Court for Pottawattamie County, Law No. 46274, August 7, 1980. Affirmed, Court of Appeals of Iowa No. 2-65599, June 29, 1982

42 Code of Federal Regulations (CFR), Subpart 442–440, 1978. Standards for intermediate care facilities for the mentally retarded

45 Code of Federal Regulation, Subchapter K, Part 1396 – Social services programs for individuals and families: Title XX of the social security act, 1980

Covington V. Harris, 419 F. 2d 617 (D.C. Cir. 1969)

Dept. of Health & Human Services, Office for Civil Rights (OCR), Office of Standards, Policy and Research (OSPR) *Memo,* May 5, 1979

Developmentally Disabled Assistance and Bill of Rights Act, 42 U.S.C. secs. 6000 et seq., 1975

Diana v. State Board of Education, No. C-70 37 RFP (D.C.N. Cal. Feb., 1970). Cited in *Syracuse Law Review,* p. 1157, Vol. 23, No. 4, 1972

Dixon v. Weinberger, 405 F. Supp. 974 (D.D.C. 1975)

Duffy, JB, Salvia, J, Tucker, J, & Ysseldyke, J. Nonbiased assessment: A need for operationalism. *Exceptional Children,* 1981, *47,* 427–434

Education for All Handicapped Children Act, 20 U.S.C. section 1401 *et seq.,* 1975 (PL 94-142)

Federal Register. Education of handicapped children, Implementation of part B of the education of the handicapped act. August 23, 1977, 42474–42518

Federal Register. Nondiscrimination on basis of handicap (implementing section 504 of the Rehabilitation Act of 1973). May 4, 1977, 22676–22702

Gallagher, JJ. The sacred and profane use of labeling. *Mental Retardation,* 1976, *14,* 3–7

Georgia ARC v. McDaniel, 511 F. Supp. 1263 (N.D. Ga. 1981)

Goldy v. Beal, 429 F. Supp. 640 (M.D. 1976) order filed Oct. 28, 1976

Griffith, RG. The administrative issues: An ethical and legal perspective. In S. Axelrod, & J Apsche (Eds.), *The effects of punishment on human behavior.* New York: Academic Press, 1982

Griffith, RG, & Coval, TE. The mentally retarded and the right to refuse habilitation. In SE Breuning, JL Matson, & RP Barrett (Eds.). *Advances in mental retardation and developmental disabilities.* Greenwich, CT: Jai Press (in press)

Halderman, et al v. Pennhurst State School & Hospital, 446 F. Supp. 1295 (E.D. Pa. 1977)

Halderman v. Pennhurst, 612 F. 2d 84 and 131 (3d Cir. 1979)

Halderman v. Pennhurst, 673 F. 2d 647 (3d. Cir. 1982)

Hobson v. Hansen, 269 F. Supp. 401 (D.D.C. 1967), *aff'd sub non. Smuck v. Hobson,* 132 US App. D.C. 372, 408 F. 2d 175 (D.C. Cir. 1969)

Hoffman v. Board of Education of the City of New York, No. 562 (N.Y. Ct. App. Dec. 17, 1979), as reported in American Bar Association, *Mental Disability Law Reporter,* 1980, *4,* 81

Johnson v. Denver Public Schools, complaint filed with Office for Civil Rights, Dept. HEW, November 27, 1979

Lake v. Cameron, 364 F. 2d 657 (D.C. Cir. 1966)

Larry P. v. Riles, 343 F. Supp. 1306 (N.D. Cal. 1972) *aff'd* 502 F. 2d 963 (9th Cir. 1974)

Larry P. v. Riles, 495 F. Supp. 926 (N.D. Cal. 1979)

Larson, L, Goodman, L, & Glean, R. Issues in the implementation of extended school year programs for handicapped students. *Exceptional Children,* 1981, *47,* 256–263

Leonard, J. 180 day barrier: Issues and concerns. *Exceptional Children,* 1981, *47,* 246–253

Lidz, CS. Criterion referenced assessment: The new bandwagon? *Exceptional Children,* 1979, *46,* 131–132

MacMillan, DL, & Borthwick, S. The new educable mentally retarded population: Can they be mainstreamed? *Mental Retardation,* 1980, *18,* 155–158

Magliocca, LA, & Stephens, TM. Child identification or child inventory? A critique of the federal design of child identification systems implemented under P.L. 94-142. *Journal of Special Education,* 1980, *14,* 23–36

Mahoney v. Administrative School District No. 1, 601 P. 2d. 826 (Or. Ct. App. 1979), as reported in American Bar Association, *Mentally Disability Law Reporter,* 1980 *4,* 42

Makuch, GJ. Year-round special education and related services: A state director's perspective. *Exceptional Children,* 1981, *47,* 272–274

Mattie T., et al v. Holladay et al. No. DC-75-31-S (N.D. Miss., Jan. 26, 1979), as reported in *Mentally Disability Law Reporter*, 1979, *3*, 98–99

Mercer, J. *Labeling the mentally retarded.* Berkeley: University of California Press, 1973

Mercer, JR. Psychological assessment and the rights of children. In N Hobbs (Ed.), *Issues in the classification of children* (Vol. 1). San Francisco: Jossey-Bass, 1975

Michigan ARC v. Smith, 475 F. Supp. 990 (E.D. Mich. 1979)

Mills v. Board of Education of the District of Columbia, 348 F. Supp. 866 (D.D.C. 1972); also No. 1939-71 (D.D.C. June 18, 1980), as reported in *Mental Disability Law Reporter,* 1980, *4*, 267–268

NAACP v. State of Georgia, 1982. *Education of the Handicapped,* June, 30, 1982, *8*

O'Connor v. Donaldson, 442 US 563 (1975)

PASE v. Hannon, 506 F. Supp. 831 (N.D. Ill. 1980)

Patrick, J. L., & Reschly, D. J. Relationship of state educational criteria and demographic variables to school-system prevalence of mental retardation. *American Journal of Mental Deficiency,* 1982, *86*, 351–360

Parham v. J. R., 442 US 584 (1979)

Pennsylvania Association for Retarded Children v. Commonwealth of Pennsylvania, 343 F. Supp. 279 (E.D. Pa. 1972)

Pennhurst State School and Hospital et al. v. Halderman, et al., 451 US 1 (1981)

P.L. 94-142, 20 U.S.C. 1401 et. seq. (1975)

Poland, SF, Thurlow, ML, Ysseldyke, JE, & Mirkin, PK. Current psychoeducational assessment and decision-making practices as reported by directors of special education. *Journal of School Psychology,* 1982, *20*, 171–179

Reschly, DJ. Psychological testing in educational classification and placement. *American Psychologist,* 1981, 36, 1094–1102

Rouse v. Cameron, 125 US App. D.C. 366 373 F. 2d 451 (1966)

Salvia, J, & Ysseldyke, JE. *Assessment in special and remedial education.* Boston: Houghton Mifflin, 1978

Scanlon v. Battle, cert. denied, 49 U.S.L.W. 3954 (US June 22, 1981)

Turnbull, HR, Ellis, JW, Boggs, EM, Brooks, PO, & Biklen, DP. *The least restrictive alternative: Principles and practices.* Wahington, DC: American Association on Mental Deficiency, 1981

Weinberg, JK. The courts as social reformers. *Law and Human Behavior,* 1982, *6*, 97–105

Welsch v. Likins, 373 F. Supp. 487 (D. Minn. 1974)

White, OR. Child assessment. In B Wilcox, & R York (Eds.), *Quality education for the severely handicapped: The federal investment.* Washington, DC: US Department of Education, 1980

Wuori v. Zitnay, Civil Action N. 75-80 S.D. (D. Me. July 21, 1978)

Wyatt v. Stickney, 344 F. Supp. 373, 344 F. Supp. 387 (M.D. Ala. 1972)

Youngberg, Superintendent, Pennhurst State School and Hospital, et al. v. Romeo, An Incompetent, By his Mother and next Friend, Romeo. US Supreme Court, No. 80-1429, 1982

Ysseldyke, JE, Regan, RR. Nondiscriminatory assessment: A formative model. *Exceptional Children,* 1980, *46*, 465–466

Author Index

Abel, EL, 11
Achenbach, TM, 124
Adachi, M, 420
Adams, DA, 69, 399
Adams, G, 322
Adkins, JA, 185
Agran, M, 31, 273
Agras, S, 135
Aicardi, J, 402
Aiello, Jr, 312
Aita, JA, 423
Alberts, MC, 419
Albright, F, 413
Alexander, FA, 424
Alexander, GL, 422
Alexander, WS, 420, 422
Alisch, C, 318
Allen, GJ, 200, 324
Aman, MG, 146
Anastasi, A, 95, 342, 344, 391
Anderson, LD, 252
Anderson SB, 437
Andrews, DM, 252
Aninger, M, 318, 319
Appell, MJ, 251
Argyle, M, 196
Arthur, G, 99
Arasenio-Nunes, ML, 402
Argyris, C, 184
Atkins, L, 410
Autio, S, 402
Ayllon, T, 101
Azrin, NH, 30, 50, 55, 78, 194

Bach, G, 407
Bacon, A, 262

Baer, DM, 56, 169, 291, 296, 311, 340, 386
Baikie, AG, 408
Bailey, J, 311
Bailey, JS, 37, 53, 68, 303
Bain, HW, 421
Baitsch, H, 410
Baker, BL, 247
Baldessarini, RJ, 164
Baldie, B, 352
Ball, S, 437
Balla, D, 9, 317, 318
Balow, I, 349, 350
Bamberger, H, 419
Bander, KW, 200
Baratz, SB, 9
Baratz, JC, 9
Barbeau, A, 419
Barbee, JR, 195
Barber, TX, 69, 70
Barker, R, 316
Barlow, DH, 124, 135, 165, 167, 168, 171
Barnard, 350
Barnes, KR, 159
Barr, ML, 414
Barrett, RP, 4, 13, 18, 19, 20, 92, 138, 171
Barrettich, F, 124
Bates, P, 55, 183, 191, 247
Bauman, K, 322
Bauman, RJ, 44, 407
Baumeister, AA, 27, 33, 129, 248, 276, 320, 482
Bayley, N, 16
Baxley, GB, 146, 153, 174
Beck, AT, 124
Becker, WC, 333, 342, 351, 353, 360, 362, 363, 364, 365, 366, 368, 373, 374, 376, 378, 380, 390
Beckler, MS, 68

Beinwein, H, 410
Bell, CR, 274
Bellack, AS, 69, 124, 133
Bellack, M, 184, 186, 187, 193
Bellamy, GT, 247, 276
Benda, CE, 417
Bennett, GK, 162, 252
Bennett, RE, 450
Berberich, JP, 291
Bereiter, C, 342, 386
Berger, PA, 147, 150
Berger, R, 412
Berkson, G, 27, 320
Berler, ES, 187, 195
Berliner, DC, 337, 366, 367
Berman, JL, 402
Bernstein, NR, 122
Berry, D, 403
Bersoff, DN, 440, 442
Bertram, EG, 414
Bethrong, M, 420
Bettonio, J, 403
Bialer, I, 116, 163
Biemer, EG, 407
Bieri, J, 403
Bijou, SW, 87, 91, 349
Biklen, DP, 446
Billingsley, F, 53, 54
Binet, A, 88
Bird, E, 185
Birenbaum, A, 318
Birnbrauer, JS, 5
Bitter, JA, 262
Bixler, 349
Black, JL, 131
Blanchard, EB, 187
Blank, M, 386
Blanton, RL, 91
Block, JH, 373, 374
Bloom, BS, 340, 355, 366, 369, 374
Blount, WR, 183
Bodero, E, 423
Boggs, EM, 446
Bolinsky, K, 318, 319
Bolstad, OD, 68
Book, JA, 417
Bornstein, PH, 186, 191
Borthwick, S, 443
Bost, LW, 22
Bostow, DE, 37, 53
Botterbusch, KF, 260
Boyd, SB, 194
Boykin, R, 49
Braam, CA, 291, 296, 301, 303, 306
Braam, SJ, 291, 303, 306
Bracey, S, 355, 362

Bradley-Johnson, S, 291
Bradlyn, AS, 186, 187, 188, 189
Brann, AW, 424
Braukman, CJ, 187
Breaj, WR, 408
Breuning, SE, 68, 95, 101, 102, 138, 143, 145, 146,
    147, 148, 150, 151, 157, 158, 159, 160, 161,
    162, 163, 164, 165, 166, 167, 169, 172, 173,
    174, 175, 448
Brice-Gray, K, 389
Brody, GH, 183, 191, 196
Brolin, DE, 247, 260, 276, 253
Bronstein, TP, 413
Brooks, PO, 320, 446
Brown, J, 319
Brownlee, L, 319
Bruner, E, 306
Bruner, JS, 87
Bryant, B, 196
Buckhalt, JA, 383
Budd, EC, 122, 138
Budoff, M, 277, 374
Bundey, S, 422
Bunting, R, 403
Burton, RY, 14, 119
Butler, E, 320
Butler, LT, 403
Butterfield, E, 318

Cable, WF, 403, 407
Calhoun, KS, 69
Call, T, 319
Cambell, K, 251
Campbell, M, 162
Cann, H, 414
Carnine, D, 335, 338, 339, 350, 361, 364, 373, 376,
    380, 381, 383, 388, 389, 391
Carpenter, T, 319
Carr, HD, 412
Carsrud, A, 318
Carsrud, K, 318
Carter, DM, 407
Casperson, T, 408
Casterline, D, 304
Cataldo, M, 316, 320, 326
Cattell, RB, 4, 87
Centrick, C, 407
Chaillet, JR, 408
Chang, CC, 421
Charters, WW, 337
Chase, TN, 419
Cheney, TH, 200
Chennault, M, 186
Chess, S, 186
Chinsky, J, 324
Christensen, DE, 159, 161

Christoff, KA, 186, 187, 194
Chu, ENY, 421
Ciminero, AR, 158
Clark, DB, 417
Clark, GR, 115
Clark, HB, 194
Cleary, J, 68, 72, 77, 82, 161, 167, 171
Cleland, C, 34
Clements, RL, 22
Clemer, N, 402
Clingman, IM, 101, 102
Clow, CL, 400
Cobb, HV, 247
Cockayne, EA, 420
Cohen, BM, 194
Cohen, H, 318
Cohen, MM, 149, 151, 407
Cohen, R, 407
Cole, LJ, 17, 104, 269
Collart, M, 407
Collins, E, 415
Collman, RD, 409, 419
Cone, J, 34, 37, 49
Conger, AJ, 200
Conroy, J, 318
Copper, JE, 121
Corbett, JA, 152
Corbo, LM, 419
Corey, JR, 306
Cornblath, M, 404
Corte, HE, 36
Coulter, WA, 17, 108, 262
Court-Brown, WM, 408
Coval, TE, 448
Cowles, M, 79
Coyne, T, 324
Crawford, J, 312
Cresson, O, Jr, 357, 387
Crimmins, DB, 186
Cronbach, LJ, 4, 251
Croneberg, C, 304
Croughan, JL, 121
Crower, F, 423
Cruickshank, W, 320
Cullari, S, 68, 143, 164, 173
Cullinan, D, 354
Cunninghan, GC, 402
Curran, JP, 200
Curtius, HS, 403
Cutting, DS, 187
Cuvo, A, 55

Daniel, A, 415
Darbyshire, M, 185
Davenport, RK, 27

Davidson, NA, 101, 102, 158, 164
Davis, C, 79
Davis, G, 340, 365
Davis, P, 55
Davis, VJ, 68, 101, 102, 138, 145, 147, 148, 150,
    151, 159, 160, 163, 164, 172, 174, 291, 448
Dawson, J, 422
Day, RW, 402
DeGracie, V, 350
DeGrouchy, J, 408, 412
Dekaban, A, 417
Delaney, JF, 419
Delquardi, J, 321
Delvin, E, 400
Demaine, G, 319
Dentler, RA, 183
Derencsenyl, A, 413
Dettling, J, 130
Dial, JG, 255
Dikman, S, 152
Dillman, CM, 363
DiLorenzo, TM, 122, 133, 185
DiMarcia, A, 146, 148, 150
Dingman, HF, 93
Distefano, MK, 253
Dixon, B, 306
Dixon, L, 335
Dobes, RW, 68
Doctor, AC, 260, 261
Dolch, EW, 360, 361
Doll, DA, 104
Doll, EA, 17, 18, 181, 183
Domino, G, 10
Donlon, TF, 351
Donnell, G, 410
Donner, M, 403
Donohue, WL, 421
Dorry, G, 361
Dorsey, M, 322
Dotson, VA, 69
Doyne, EO, 427
Drabman, R, 158, 183, 56
Drake, LR, 194
Dressel, ME, 195
DuBois, G, 22
Duffy, JB, 437, 450
Dunn, LM, 16, 103, 349
Durkin, D, 372
Durost, W, 349
D'Zurilla, TJ, 196, 197, 198, 274, 275, 262

Eadie, MJ, 152
Earl, CJC, 117
Edelstein, BA, 187, 200
Eisler, RM, 187
Elkin, L, 253

Elliott, RM, 252
Ellis, JW, 446
Ellis, NR, 119, 253, 311
Ellison, PH, 407
Elzey, FF, 19, 262, 269, 270
Endicott, J, 121
Engelmann, S, 291, 301, 306, 335, 337, 338, 339, 342, 351, 353, 355, 360, 362, 363, 364, 366, 368, 383, 386, 388, 390, 391
Epstein, GJ, 422
Epstein, M, 354
Erickson, MT, 4, 16
Esveldt-Dawson, K, 55, 185
Etheridge, JM, 194
Etzel, 335
Evans, K, 422
Evans, IM, 14, 56
Eyman, RK, 318, 319
Eysenck, SBG, 124, 125

Falconer, MA, 422
Farmer, TW, 402, 407
Farr, RC, 350
Farrell, AD, 200
Favell, J, 311, 323
Fazekas, JF, 424
Felce, D, 318
Felsenthal, D, 247
Ferguson, DG, 68, 101, 102, 146, 158, 159, 161, 163, 164, 173, 174
Ferster, CB, 20
Feuerstein, M, 134
Feuerstein, R, 277
Figuero, R, 17, 104, 269
Fink, W, 389
Fishell, KN, 251
Fishler, K, 410
Fitch, D, 421
Fitts, H, 193
Fixsen, DF, 187
Flesch, R, 361
Flores, T, 194
Ford, FR, 417
Ford, R, 402
Forehand, R, 27, 33
Foster, R, 5, 17, 34, 49, 104, 105, 122, 181, 261, 263, 264, 360
Fowler, A, 101, 318
Fox, J, 321, 324, 325
Foxx, RM, 36, 50
Fraser, MB, 410
Frazer, D, 318
Frederick, WN, 14
Frederiker, LW, 193
Freeman, JM, 421
Freeman, R, 145, 146

Fremer, J, 354
Freuch, JL, 99
Fried, K, 409
Friedrick, WL, 14
Friman, PC, 187
Fugua, RW, 72, 146, 157, 159, 167
Furman, W, 186, 188, 195

Gallagher, JJ, 439
Garattini, S, 149
Gardner, WI, 20, 150
Gautier, M, 408
Gautieres, F, 402
Gaylord-Ross, R, 28
Geller, MI, 191, 193
German, J, 412
Gersten, R, 335, 352, 354, 362, 366
Ghadini, H, 403
Gibbs, EL, 152
Gibbs, FA, 152
Gibbs, JJ, 152
Gibson, FW, 187
Gilbert, FS, 200
Gilchrist, LD, 193
Gill, R, 415
Gilles, FH, 424
Gillis, RD, 132
Gittleman-Klein, R, 149, 162
Girardeau, G, 335
Givens, T, 181
Glaser, R, 339, 351, 354
Glass, GV, 79
Glazeski, RC, 195
Glean, R, 444
Gleason, WP, 181
Glenn, L, 317
Goddard, HH, 88
Goetz, EM, 37
Gold, AP, 421
Gold, MW, 248, 251, 253, 260, 261, 276
Goldberg, B, 412
Goldfried, MR, 196, 197, 198, 262, 274, 275
Golding, B, 324
Goldsmith, JB, 187
Goldstein, H, 88
Gomez, MR, 419, 422
Good, RA, 423
Goodman, L, 444
Goodner, DM, 415
Gordon, W, 319
Gorelick, J. 253
Goth, A, 147
Goyos, AC, 53
Graham, P, 118
Grant, G, 318, 319
Graves, KG, 186

Green, WH, 162
Greenblatt, DJ, 149
Greensberg, L, 162
Greenspar, S, 261
Greenstein, RM, 414
Greenwood, C, 321
Greer, E, 319
Griffith, RG, 448, 450
Grium, LG, 20
Gonlund, NE, 363
Groover, RV, 426
Grossman, H, 3, 8, 65, 91, 92, 104, 106, 181, 262,
    320
Gualtieri, CT, 150, 163
Guamaccia, VJ, 124, 268
Guard, K, 319
Guess, D, 290, 291, 296, 301, 386
Guilford, JP, 4, 87
Gump, P, 323, 325
Gunzburg, H, 263, 319
Guralnick, MJ, 129

Haberland, C, 410
Hagmeier, LD, 30, 271, 273
Hake, DF, 36
Hall, C, 195
Hall, G, 296, 337
Hall, JG, 423
Hall, R, 321
Halle, JW, 296
Halpern, AS, 19, 247, 248, 261, 263, 276
Halstead, WC, 87
Halverson, CF, 151
Hamad, C, 319
Hamilton, J, 277
Hamilton, M, 319
Hamilton, JL, 374
Hammer, D, 56
Hampe, E, 124
Harawalt, DA, 271
Hanley, WB, 400
Hanner, S, 364, 391
Hansen, S, 403
Hardiman, SA, 37
Haring, BG, 337, 373
Harmatz, JS, 132
Harper, RS, 247, 261, 262
Harris, DJ, 414
Harris, J, 321, 324
Harris, R, 152
Hart, B, 296
Hartmann, DP, 76, 160, 167
Hassibi, M, 11
Hatashita, A, 413
Hathaway, SK, 124

Hathorn, S, 186
Hawk, B, 150
Hawkins, RP, 21, 68, 69
Hawver, DA, 251, 253
Hayes, SC, 28, 69, 76, 167, 171
Haynes, SM, 122
Heaton-Word, A, 118
Hebb, DO, 87
Heber, R, 3, 18, 91, 104, 181
Heidbreder, E, 252
Heimberg, RG, 200
Heins, ED, 354
Heiry, A, 247, 362
Helzer, JE, 121
Henderson, D, 318
Henes, C, 319
Hendy, J, 324
Henker, B, 166
Henner, K, 423
Herbert-Jackson, E, 37
Herman, S, 200
Hermann, BP, 152, 164
Hernstein, RJ, 88
Hersen, AS, 35, 50, 54, 69, 77, 81, 82, 124, 133,
    184, 186, 187, 193
Hersen, M, 165, 167, 168
Hetherington, EM, 119
Heuset, M, 422
Hicks, SP, 417
Himadi, WG, 186
Hinwich, HE, 424
Hively, W, 365
Hobbs, N, 95
Hobbs, SA, 200
Hoffman, J, 416
Hoffman, MB, 277
Hofmeister, A, 363
Holden, RH, 16
Hollandsworth, JG, 195
Hollis, JH, 159
Holmes, EW, 407
Holmes, LB, 410
Holtman, A, 403
Homer, AL, 52, 71
Honigfeld, G, 132
Hopkins, KD, 79
Horner, RH, 247, 276
Horst, DP, 352
Hsia, DY, 402, 404
Hsu, TC, 408
Hubbell, M, 319
Hug, E, 409
Hughes, PS, 149
Huitema, BE, 71, 79, 81
Hull, J, 319
Humble, R, 407

Huntington, G, 418
Hutchinson-Ruprechts, ML, 36

Inman, DP, 247, 276
Inovye, I, 136, 404
Intagliata, J, 319
Irvin, LK, 19, 247, 261, 263, 276
Isett, R, 318, 319
Iwata, BA, 129, 322, 389

Jackson, B, 303
Jacobs, RA, 408, 414
Jacobson, JW, 118
James, FE, 117, 319
Jastak, JF, 16, 103, 251, 349
Jastak, SR, 16, 103, 251, 349
Jenkins, J, 341, 347, 349, 350
Jensen, AR, 4
Jensen, V, 185
Jervis, GA, 419
Jeune, M, 404
Johnson, CM, 101, 291
Johnson, JL, 271
Johnson, JM, 335
Johnson, SM, 68
Johnson, WG, 187
Johnston, JM, 77, 81
Johnstone, G, 53
Jones, M, 323
Jones, RJ, 194, 337
Junginger, J, 131

Kalachnik, JE, 164
Kallman, WM, 134
Kagin, E, 104, 105
Kanin, LJ, 88
Kanter, JN, 420
Kaplan, HR, 194
Kaplan, SJ, 194
Karan, OC, 248, 261, 276
Karp, L, 11
Kaskowitz, D, 367
Kauffman, JM, 337
Kaufman, AS, 15, 17, 403
Kazdin, AE, 4, 19, 20, 21, 22, 30, 49, 52, 55, 56,
    68, 69, 75, 76, 77, 82, 108, 125, 133, 160,
    165, 167, 169, 185, 270, 320
Kehoe, B, 185
Keil, EC, 195
Kelly, JA, 182, 185, 186, 187, 188, 189, 191, 192,
    193, 194, 195
Kelly, K, 101
Kelly, MB, 69, 76
Kelley, WD, 423
Kemp, JE, 363
Kent, LR, 289

Kent, R, 49
Keppel, G, 165
King, T, 319
Kirk, RE, 79, 165
Kirson, T, 146, 150
Kivitz, MS, 115
Klaus, DJ, 354
Klawans, HL, 419
Klein, D, 146, 162
Kless, CJ, 132
Klinefelter, HF, 413
Kling, JW, 377
Klukas, N, 131
Knolboch, H, 16
Knox, DL, 417
Koch, R, 16, 410
Kohn, G, 407
Kohn, J, 407
Kolb, LC, 5
Kolodny, EH, 401, 403, 407
Komrower, GM, 404
Kopel, SA, 75, 76, 167
Kramer, W, 422
Kratochwill, TR, 77
Krischell, CH, 88
Krumholz, A, 403
Kryzanowski, JA, 389
Kuder, GF, 251
Kulp, S, 44
Kupietz, S, 163
Kupke, TE, 200
Kushlick, A, 318

Laca, Z, 414
Lafourcade, J, 412
Lagos, JC, 422
LaGreca, AM, 274, 275, 276
Lambert, NM, 17, 104, 268, 269
Lambert, NM, 181
Lamparski, D, 187
Lamson, DS, 52, 270
Lamy, M, 412
Landesmann-Dwyer, S, 317, 321
Landing, BH, 426
Larson, L, 444, 445
Lasser, A, 407
Latt, SA, 408
Lawrence, PS, 187
Lawrence, W, 318
Laughlin, CS, 186, 187, 191, 195
LeBlank, JM, 37
Lee, DH, 404
Lee, M, 96
Lee, VL, 306
Lefkowitz, MM, 119, 124
Legum, C, 407

Lehmann, JP, 247
Lei, T, 319
Lejeune, J, 408, 410, 412
Leland, H, 5, 17, 104, 105, 122, 181, 261, 263, 269
Leonard, J, 444
Leuke, RR, 403
Levan, H, 408
Levine, S, 19, 262, 269, 270
Levitan, GW, 12
Levy, N, 403
Lewinshohn, PM, 184
Lewis, C, 389
Lewis, IC, 421
Lewis, JE, 17, 18, 19, 104, 105
Libet, J, 184
Liddell, A, 122
Lidz, CS, 450
Lindenberg, R, 416
Lindsley, OR, 35
Lindsten, T, 408
Linehan, MM, 12
Link, R, 19, 263
Linkenhoker, D, 262
Linsao, LS, 400
Lipinski, DP, 131, 149
Lipman, RS, 146, 148, 150, 151
Liss, L, 416
Little, LM, 200
Livni, N, 407
Lloyd, L, 354, 366
Locker, BJ, 36
Loeb, H, 402
Longhurst, TM, 186, 187
Longstaff, HP, 252
Loucks, S, 337
Louis-Bar, D, 423
Lovaas, OI, 285, 293
Lubs, HA, 414, 415
Lundbald, S, 402
Luszcz, M, 319
Lutey, C, 16
Luzzatti, L, 414
Lyerla, TA, 407
Lyon, G, 399
Lyons, M, 122
Lyons, PD, 187

Macintyre, MN, 412
Mackenzie, J, 400
Mackler, B, 183
MacMillan, OL, 443
Macrae, JW, 194
Madsen, CH, 200
Mager, RF, 355, 363
Magliocca, LA, 450
Maggs, A, 335, 352, 353, 354, 366

Mahoney, MJ, 407
Makino, S, 408
Makuch, GJ, 444
Maloney, P, 187, 190
Mansdorf, IJ, 129
Mar, DE, 271, 272
Marchetti, A, 185
Marholin, D, 146, 157, 174
Markawardt, FC, 16, 103, 349
Markesberry, WB, 407
Markovic, S, 414
Markovic, V, 414
Marks, H, 319
Mariotto, MJ, 200
Martin, B, 119
Martin, G, 185
Martin, GL, 185
Martin, JJ, 407
Martin, PW, 14, 53
Martindale, A, 44
Martinez-Diaz, JA, 200
Maser, HW, 407
Mash, ET, 23, 28
Mason, JM, 361
Matson, DD, 416
Matson, JL, 19, 30, 55, 56, 92, 116, 118, 122, 124, 125, 129, 130, 133, 138, 159, 163, 167, 175, 185, 270, 320
Mauer, GR, 29, 35
Mavissakalian, MR, 135
Mayeda, T, 319
McBride, W, 319
McCalmon, D, 271, 272
McCarron, LT, 255, 262
McCaughey, WTE, 419
McClain, R, 319
McClenahan, JL, 416
McClure, RF, 186, 187
McConahey, OL, 146
McCoy, JF, 383
McDonald, LT, 412
McDonald, WB, 421
McFall, RM, 187
McGillivary, J, 324
McGregor, TN, 408
McKinley, JC, 124
McKusik, VA, 417
McLaughlin, B, 151
McLean, JE, 303
McNabb, CE, 200
McNally, RJ, 12
Meier, MY, 306
Melnyk, J, 412
Menchetti, BM, 52, 55, 247, 270, 274
Mendelson, M, 124
Menkes, JH, 419, 426, 427

Menolascino, FJ, 122
Mercer, JR, 17, 18, 91, 95, 104, 105, 440, 443
Merrill, MH, 3, 4, 15, 96
Merzbacher, L, 420
Mesibov, G, 317
Metcalf, M, 162
Meyer, V, 122
Meyers, CE, 262, 269, 270, 319
Michael, JL, 286, 289, 291, 294, 303, 304
Millen, JW, 415
Miller, LC, 124
Miller, M, 423
Miller, OJ, 408
Miller, PM, 187, 319
Milstien, S, 403
Milunsky, A, 420
Ming, PL, 415
Mink, I, 319
Minkin, BL, 187, 188
Minkin, N, 187, 188
Minnes, P, 324
Mirkin, PK, 438, 444
Mitchell, A, 410
Mithaug, DE, 247, 261, 270, 271, 272, 273, 276
Mock, J, 124
Molloy, JT, 185
Monaghan, M, 68, 161
Montgomery, D, 200
Moody, JP, 132
Moores, B, 318, 319
Moos, RH, 158, 314
Morganstern, KP, 122
Moric-Petraic, S, 414
Morrow, HW, 17, 108, 262
Mosher, DL, 200
Mosland, RL, 90
Moynahan, EJ, 421
Mulhern, T, 129
Muma, JR, 182
Munson, R, 53
Murphy, RT, 36, 437
Murphy, SF, 424
Myers, RE, 424

Nadler, HL, 404
Naiman, JL, 425, 426
Naylor, GJ, 117, 132, 137
Neef, NA, 389
Neel, J, 423
Nelhaus, G, 417
Nelson, RO, 14, 28, 49, 131, 187
Netley, C, 400
Newman, D, 10
Newman, M, 335
Nicoll, R, 268
Niederwieser, A, 403

Nihira, K, 5, 17, 23, 104, 105, 122, 181, 261, 262, 263, 268, 269, 319
Nikkila, EA, 404
Nishimura, E, 408
Nitko, AJ, 339, 351, 354
Noble, H, 124
Norden, NE, 402
Norman, RM, 422
Novick, MR, 387
Nunes, DL, 36
Nunnally, J, 106
Nutter, D, 22

O'Brien, F, 30, 55
O'Brien, JS, 407
Okazaki, H, 419
Omenn, GS, 11
O'Neil, J, 319
Ornoy, A, 407
Osborn, J, 291, 301, 353
Oskin, FA, 425, 426

Packer, RA, 335, 338, 361, 363
Page, TJ, 389
Paine, SC, 335
Pallotta-Cornick, A, 53
Palmer, FH, 382
Pampiglione, G, 421
Panesofar, E, 247
Pany, D, 341, 347, 349, 350
Park, TS, 415
Parker, CE, 413
Parsonage, M, 418
Partington, JW, 287, 293, 294, 303
Pasanella, AL, 337, 356
Pasamanick, B, 16
Passman, RH, 36
Pate, JE, 427
Patrick, JL, 440, 443, 444
Patterson, DG, 186, 195, 252
Paulson, GW, 419
Pear, JJ, 301
Peck, CL, 129
Pegler, AM, 306
Pelizaeus, F, 420
Pennypacker, HS, 68, 77, 81
Penrose, LS, 117, 138
Penry, JK, 152
Perheentupa, J, 404
Perloff, BF, 291
Perrin, TO, 194
Perry, R, 162
Perry, TL, 403
Peterson, DR, 12, 52
Peterson, L, 71
Peterson, RDA, 423

Phillips, D, 146, 157
Phillips, EL, 186, 187, 193
Platt, JJ, 196, 197, 198
Piaget, J, 4, 87, 289
Pinto, RP, 195
Pitkanen, E, 404
Poland, SF, 438, 444
Poling, AD, 68, 72, 77, 82, 95, 101, 102, 145, 146,
    147, 158, 159, 161, 162, 166, 167, 171, 172,
    174, 448
Polsgrove, L, 368
Pomerat, CM, 408
Pook, RB, 148
Popham, WJ, 339, 351, 354
Porsch, R, 410
Portersfield, JK, 37
Powell, J, 44
Pratt, M, 319, 320
Prescott, GA, 349, 350
Priet, JH, 408
Primrose, PA, 117
Prior, M, 324
Proshansky, H, 322
Pullman, RM, 148
Pyeritz, RE, 407

Quay, HC, 124, 320

Rachavan, SS, 407
Rachman, SJ, 124
Raczynski, JM, 134
Raffeld, P, 19, 263
Rago, WV, 34
Rahmlow, 363
Rand, Y, 277
Rasmussen, PL, 311
Ratcliff, KS, 121
Ray, DA, 290, 293, 296, 301, 303
Ray, WJ, 134
Raymore, S, 303
Re, M, 318
Reating, N, 146, 150
Reed, AC, 417
Reese, DF, 419
Regan, RR, 450
Reid, DH, 22
Reid, NH, 117, 137
Reifenstein, EC, 413
Reiss, S, 12
Reizenstein, J, 319
Renzagliz, A, 39
Repp, AC, 68
Repp, CF, 68
Reschly, DJ, 440, 443, 444, 450
Rethore, MO, 412
Reater, KE, 37

Reynolds, WM, 263
Richman, G, 322
Riccardi, VM, 410
Riddle, I, 311
Riege, D, 424
Rieth, 368, 371
Riggs, 377
Rimland, B, 150
Risley, TR, 37, 169, 296, 311, 316, 320, 323, 326
Rivinus, TM, 132
Roberts, JR, 253
Roberts, DM, 68
Robertson, WC, 419
Robins, LN, 121
Robinson, HB, 87, 88, 90, 91, 93, 96, 104, 151
Robinson, NH, 87, 88, 90, 91, 93, 96, 104
Robinson, NM, 151
Robinson, RG, 152
Rodd-Marks, J, 319
Rogers-Warren, A, 31, 296, 312, 321
Rollins, HR, 410
Rosen, D, 312
Rosen, M, 115, 190, 191, 199
Rosenbaum, MS, 56
Rosenberg, S, 183
Rosenshine, BV, 337, 366, 367, 368, 369, 370, 371,
    372
Rosov, 335, 382
Ross, DM, 196
Ross, SA, 196
Ross, RT, 4, 7, 8, 16, 19, 27
Roth, JC, 422
Royer, P, 412
Rubouts, R, 419
Rucker, CN, 186
Rueber, TM, 290, 293, 303
Rusch, FR, 31, 52, 55, 247, 261, 270, 272, 273, 276
Rusch, JC, 247
Ruschworth, RG, 422
Russell, CD, 291
Russell, JE, 36
Rutherford, G, 386
Rutter, M, 118
Ryan, W, 9
Rychtarik, RG, 186

Sackett, G, 277
Sailor, WS, 291, 386
Salmon, C, 412
Salter, L, 129
Salvia, J, 95, 97, 98, 100, 344, 391, 437
Salzinger, K, 285, 304
Samels, J, 185
Samuels, JS, 356, 363
Sarason, SB, 90
Sartorious, N, 121

Sasso, G, 36
Sattler, JM, 15, 95, 96
Schaeffer, B, 291
Schalock, RL, 247, 248, 261, 262, 276
Schauls, J, 403
Scheerenberger, RC, 247
Schellhaas, M, 261, 263, 269
Schiefelbusch, RL, 337, 373
Schimiza, A, 136
Schinke, SP, 193
Schipke, R, 424
Schircks, B, 403
Schmickel, RD, 421
Schmidt, RP, 152
Schneider, EL, 408
Schoenrock, CJ, 14, 123, 138
Scholl, W, 423
Schoultz, B, 261
Schreiber, MS, 424
Schroeder, S, 163, 319
Schroter, R, 410
Schrott, HG, 11
Schull, C, 251
Schutz, RP, 31, 55, 270, 272, 273, 274
Schwartz, R, 404
Schweide, E, 16
Scoville, W, 424
Scott-Emyakpor, A, 417
Scriver, CR, 400
Scrivern, M, 342
Sedgwich, RP, 423
Sekeles, B, 407
Sekeles, E, 407
Sell, SH, 427
Sellman, AH, 16
Seltzer, G, 247
Seltzer, M, 247
Semmel, MI, 368
Senatore, V, 125, 130
Sewell, J, 148
Shahood, JM, 420
Shamow, JC, 306
Shapiro, ES, 4, 13, 18, 19, 20, 171
Sheldon-Wildgen, J, 195
Shellhaas, M, 5, 17, 104, 122, 181
Shen, YZ, 426
Sherman, JA, 195
Sherwin, RM, 420
Shibata, B, 101
Shores, RE, 183
Shure, MB, 196, 197, 198
Shut, JW, 417
Sidman, M, 35, 77, 357, 361, 387
Sigelman, CK, 14, 123, 138
Silbert, J, 339, 350, 361, 373, 380, 381, 391
Silverstein, A, 319

Simell, O, 403
Simon, T, 88
Simpson, R, 36
Sims, EV, Jr, 389
Sindelar, PT, 335
Singh, NN, 146, 148
Sinick, D, 255, 260
Sipe, JC, 407
Skillings, RE, 193
Skinner, BF, 286, 289, 294, 296, 298, 299, 301, 304
Slack, DJ, 68
Slifer, K, 322
Sloan, W, 253
Smith, AC, 16
Smith, DW, 417
Smith, J, 318
Smith, JT, 148
Smith, TE, 193
Snelbecker, G, 318
Solomon, F, 386
Soucar, E, 319
Spanhel, CC, 14, 123, 138
Spearman, C, 41, 87
Spencer, D, 319
Spielvogel, C, 420
Spitz, HH, 119
Spitzer, RL, 121
Spivack, G, 196, 197, 198
Spradlin, JE, 286, 296
Sprague, RL, 90, 145, 146, 148, 149, 150, 151, 152, 153, 155, 160, 162, 164, 166, 173, 174
Spreat, S, 318
Springbett, BM, 194
Somersalo, O, 404
Sommer, R, 322
Spradlin, J, 335
Spring, C, 162
Stafford, MW, 291, 296, 303
Stallings, J, 367
Stalonas, PM, 187
Stang, S, 303
Stangl, J, 322
Stauffer, M, 417
Steinke, GV, 200
Stelcy, D, 306
Stephens, TM, 450
Sternlick, M, 116
Stevens, D, 195, 367, 372, 418
Stewart, JE, 271, 272
Stokes, TE, 340
Stokes, TF, 56
Stokoe, WC, 304
Stoller, A, 409, 419
St. Omer, VV, 159
Stone, RA, 194
Stone, WL, 274

Stoneman, A, 183, 191, 196
Stoudenmire, J, 129
Striefel, S, 291
Strain, PS, 183
Straw, MR, 4, 20, 21, 108, 160
Strong, JA, 408
Sulzbacher, SI, 146, 147
Sturge, WA, 422
Sulzer-Azaroff, B, 29, 35, 76
Summit, R, 408
Sundberg, ML, 287, 290, 293, 294, 296, 301, 303, 304
Sutherland, CR, 415, 426
Sutter, D, 319
Swanson, PD, 416
Syllabu, L, 423

Tallon, R, 322
Tanner, BA, 36
Tarjan, G, 93
Tawney, JW, 337, 368
Taylor, CB, 135
Terrence, CF, 419
Terdal, LG, 23
Terman, LM, 3, 4, 15, 88, 96
Teulin, HE, 122
Tharapal, AT, 408
Thomas, SG, 14
Thompson, D, 312, 319
Thompson, J, 319
Thompson, T, 146, 303
Throne, JM, 4, 317
Thurlow, ML, 438, 444
Thurman, C, 186, 187
Thurston, LC, 87
Tice, RR, 408
Tiffen, J, 253
Tijo, JH, 408
Timbers, BJ, 187
Timbers, GD, 187
Timmerman, WJ, 260, 261
Tischler, B, 403
Tizard, J, 118
Tobias, J, 163, 253, 260
Tognoli, J, 319
Toman, JEP, 151
Tondeur, M, 402
Toppe, L, 162
Toppett, M, 402
Treffrey, D, 185
Troops, NA, 252
Trosko, JE, 421
Trower, P, 186, 196
Tschirgi, HD, 194
Tu, J, 148
Tucker, J, 437

Turleau, C, 408
Turnbull, HR, 446, 448
Turner, B, 415
Turner, G, 415
Turpin, R, 408
Turpin, WB, 22
Twardosz, S, 316

Ulchida, IA, 412
Ullman, MD, 407
Ullman, RK, 164
Ulman, JD, 76

Vanderveer, B, 16
VanHassett, VB, 133
VanHouten, R, 77, 270
Veit, S, 324
Vincenzo, FM, 186
Visakorpi, JK, 403
Viscontini, M, 403
Voeltz, L, 56
Vogel, FS, 416
Volkmor, CB, 337, 356
VonRecklinghausen, FD, 423
Vrey, JR, 186, 187, 188, 195
Vukelick, R, 36

Wadsworth, RC, 416
Wagner, EE, 253, 257
Wahler, R, 321, 324, 325
Wahrman, J, 409
Waldrop, M, 151
Walker, MK, 151
Wallander, JL, 200
Walls, RT, 262, 263
Walters, G, 335
Wang, HC, 412
Waranch, HR, 129
Ward, CH, 124
Ward, M, 87, 190
Warren, S, 31, 296, 312
Watson, C, 185
Webb, WW, 427
Wechsler, D, 3, 4, 15, 96
Wehman, P, 54, 247
Weinberg, JK, 439
Weisberg, P, 36, 338, 350, 361, 375, 380, 389
Weiss, RL, 124
Weissman, MM, 182
Weithers, 55
Welch, SJ, 301
Wells, K, 306
Welner, A, 121
Wenger, DA, 407
Werner, TJ, 262, 263

Werry, JS, 143, 145, 146, 148, 152, 156, 158, 159, 160, 162, 166, 173
Wessberg, HW, 200
Wetherby, B, 291
Whalen, CK, 166
White, OR, 53, 437
White, WAT, 335
Whitmore, K, 118
Wilcox, B, 247
Wilcox, MR, 181
Willems, EP, 31, 56, 312, 313, 331
Willer, B, 319
Williams, CM, 251
Wilson, CT, 335
Wilson-Morris, M, 357, 387
Windmiller, M, 17, 104, 269
Winere, JL, 14
Wing, JK, 122
Wing, L, 121, 122
Winsberg, B, 163
Wohl, MK, 129
Wolf, MM, 30, 36, 50, 77, 187, 270, 322
Wolf, U, 410
Wolfe, A, 311
Wolfe, M, 169
Wolfensberger, W, 33, 260, 261, 317
Wonderlich, SA, 71
Wong, SE, 193
Woodbury, DM, 152
Worrall, EP, 132
Wright, GN, 255

Wright, JC, 200
Wysocki, T, 72, 146, 157, 159, 167

Yakovlev, PJ, 415
Yakovlev, QJ, 416
Yanagi, G, 319
Yarrow, MR, 14
Yee, S, 319
Yellin, A, 162
Yesseldyke, JE, 95, 97, 98, 100, 344, 391, 437, 438, 444, 450
Young, RM, 101, 291
Yule, M, 118

Zane, T, 262, 263
Zeaman, B, 361
Zech, L, 408
Zegiob, L, 131
Zeiss, RA, 131
Zella, WF, 101, 291
Zellweger, H, 409
Zetlin, A, 262
Ziechner, A, 200
Zieler, M, 36
Zigler, E, 318
Zimmerman, EH, 291
Zimmerman, J, 291
Zimmerman, R, 146
Zisfein, L, 190, 191, 199
Zollinger, H, 414

Subject Index

AAMD Adaptive Behavior Scale, 17–18, 229–230, 263–269, 318–320
Academic skills, 335–392
Adaptive behavior, 3, 5, 17–18, 210–212, 213–234
Adaptive Behavior Inventory for Children, (ABIC), 18, 231–233
Allen v. McDonough, 445
Applied behavior analysis, 28, 53
Assessment strategies, 11–22, 31
   interviews, 12–14
   intelligence tests, 14–17
   behavior checklists, 17–19
   rating scales, 17–19

Balthazar Scales of Adaptive Behavior, 233–234
Baseline assessment, 50–52
Battle v. Commonwealth, 445
Behavioral assessment systems, 27
Behavioral observation, 19–21, 234–235
Between subjects designs, 71–72, 78–83
   randomized groups design, 80
   repeated measures design, 80
Brown v. Board of Education, 438

Code complexity, 44
Codic repertoire, 303–305
   assessment of, 305–306
   interpretation of, 306
Criterion-referenced tests, 339, 351, 354–360
Cultural-familial MR, 8–9

Diana v. State Board of Education, 438, 440, 442
Differential reinforcement, 52, 70–71
Direct instruction, 361–362, 365
Dominant gene disorder, 10–11
Down's Syndrome, 10

Duplic repertoire, 291
   echoic, 291–292
   imitative, 292–293

Ecobehavioral assessment strategies, 312, 313–314, 322–331
Ecological patterns, 311–331
Etiological factors, 8–9

Genetic factors, 9–11
   experimental strategies, 73

Habilitation, 311
Halderman v. Pennhurst, 437, 439, 447, 449
Hobson v. Hansen, 438, 442
Hoffman v. Board of Education of the City of New York, 445

Instructional programs, 364–366
Intelligence, 4
Interobserver reliability, 49–50, 68–69
Intraverbal repertoire, 301–302
   assessment of, 302–303
   interpretation of, 303

Johnson v. Denver Public Schools, 442

Klinefelter's Syndrome, 10

Language, 285–306
Larry R. v. Riles, 438, 440, 441, 443, 444
Learning Potential
   Assessment Device (LPAD), 227

Mand repertoire, 294–295
   assessment of, 295

Mental retardation
  prevalence rates, 5–6
  classification of, 5–8
*Mills v. Board of Education of the District of
  Columbia,* 438, 443

Norm-referenced tests, 339–347, 366
  validity of, 340
  limitations of, 342
  scores, 342–347

Observational assessment, 35, 49, 58, 66–69
  duration recording, 39–41
  frequency recording, 37–39
  interval time sample recording, 41–44, 66–68
  latency recording, 41
Observer bias, 44
Observer expectancy, 44
O'Conner v. Donaldson, 445
Operational definitions, 35

PARC v. Pennsylvania, 438, 449
Parsons Language Sample, 286–287
PASE v. Hannon, 438, 441
Phenylketonuria (PKU), 10–11
Progress Assessment Chart, 319
Prevocational assessment and Curriculum Guide,
  271–272
Public Law 94–142, 438, 439, 440, 444, 449, 450

Receptive language 289–291
  assessment of, 290–291
Recessive gene disorder, 10–11
Response cost, 71

San Francisco Vocational Competency Scale,
  269–270
Scanlon v. Battle, 445
Self-care, 209–241
  feeding, 235–237

toileting, 237
hygiene, 238
dressing, 238
Self-injurious behavior, 27, 28, 36
Self-observation, 48–49
Social skills, 181–201
  grooming, 184–185
  conversational, 185–189
  assertiveness skills, 189–193
  employment, 193–196
  dating, 199–201
Social validation, 30
Stanford-Binet Intelligence Scale, 15, 251, 352
System of multicultural Pluralistic Assessment
  (SOMPA), 18

Tact repertoire, 296
  assessment of, 297–301
Trainee Performance Sample (TPS), 277
Treatment evaluation, 65–71
Turner's Syndrome, 10

Vineland Social Matural Scale, 18–19, 230–231
Vocational Assessment and Curriculum Guide,
  272–274
Vocational Problem Behavior Inventory, 274–276
Vocation training, 247–278
  assessment of, 248
  motor measurement, 253
  work sample, 255–261
  survival skill, 270
  process assessment, 276

Wechsler Scales, 15–16, 251
Welsh v. Likins, 438
Within-subject design, 71, 72, 73–78
  A–B design, 73–75
  multiple baseline, 75–76
Wyatt v. Stickney, 439, 448